THE ILLUSTRATED

mahabharata

A DEFINITIVE GUIDE TO INDIA'S GREATEST EPIC

THE ILLUSTRATED

Mahabharata

A DEFINITIVE GUIDE TO INDIA'S GREATEST EPIC

Penguin Random House

DORLING KINDERSLEY INDIA

EDITORS
Bushra Ahmed, Rajrupa Das, Medha Gupta, Hina Jain, Seetha Natesh, Rupa Rao

US EDITOR
Karyn Gerhard

DESIGNERS
Devika Awasthi, Isha Nagar, Astha Singh, Ashish Verma

ILLUSTRATOR
Arun Pottirayil

PICTURE RESEARCHER
Surya Sankash Sarangi

DTP DESIGNERS
Nandkishor Acharya, Harish Aggarwal

JACKET TEAM
Sreshtha Bhattacharya
Suhita Dharamjit
Shefali Upadhyay

MANAGING EDITOR
Alka Ranjan

MANAGING ART EDITOR
Pallavi Narain

DESIGN CONSULTANT
Shefali Upadhyay

PICTURE RESEARCH MANAGER
Taiyaba Khatoon

PRE-PRODUCTION MANAGER
Narender Kumar

PRODUCTION MANAGER
Pankaj Sharma

CARTOGRAPHY MANAGER
Suresh Kumar

MANAGING DIRECTOR
Aparna Sharma

CONTRIBUTORS
Devdutt Pattanaik, leadership consultant and mythologist
Bibek Debroy, economist and *Mahabharata* scholar

First American Edition, 2017
Published in the United States by DK Publishing,
a division of Penguin Random House LLC
1745 Broadway, 20th Floor, New York, NY 10019

26 10 9 8
014–295511–Sep/2017

Published in Great Britain by Dorling Kindersley Limited

A catalog record for this book is available from the Library of Congress.
ISBN 978-1-4654-6291-6

DK books are available at special discounts when purchased in bulk for sales promotions, premiums, fund-raising, or educational use.
For details, contact: DK Publishing Special Markets, 1745 Broadway, 20th Floor, New York, NY 10019
SpecialSales@dk.com

Printed and bound in China

www.dk.com

MIX
Paper | Supporting responsible forestry
FSC™ C018179

This book was made with Forest Stewardship Council™ certified paper – one small step in DK's commitment to a sustainable future.
Learn more at www.dk.com/uk/information/sustainability

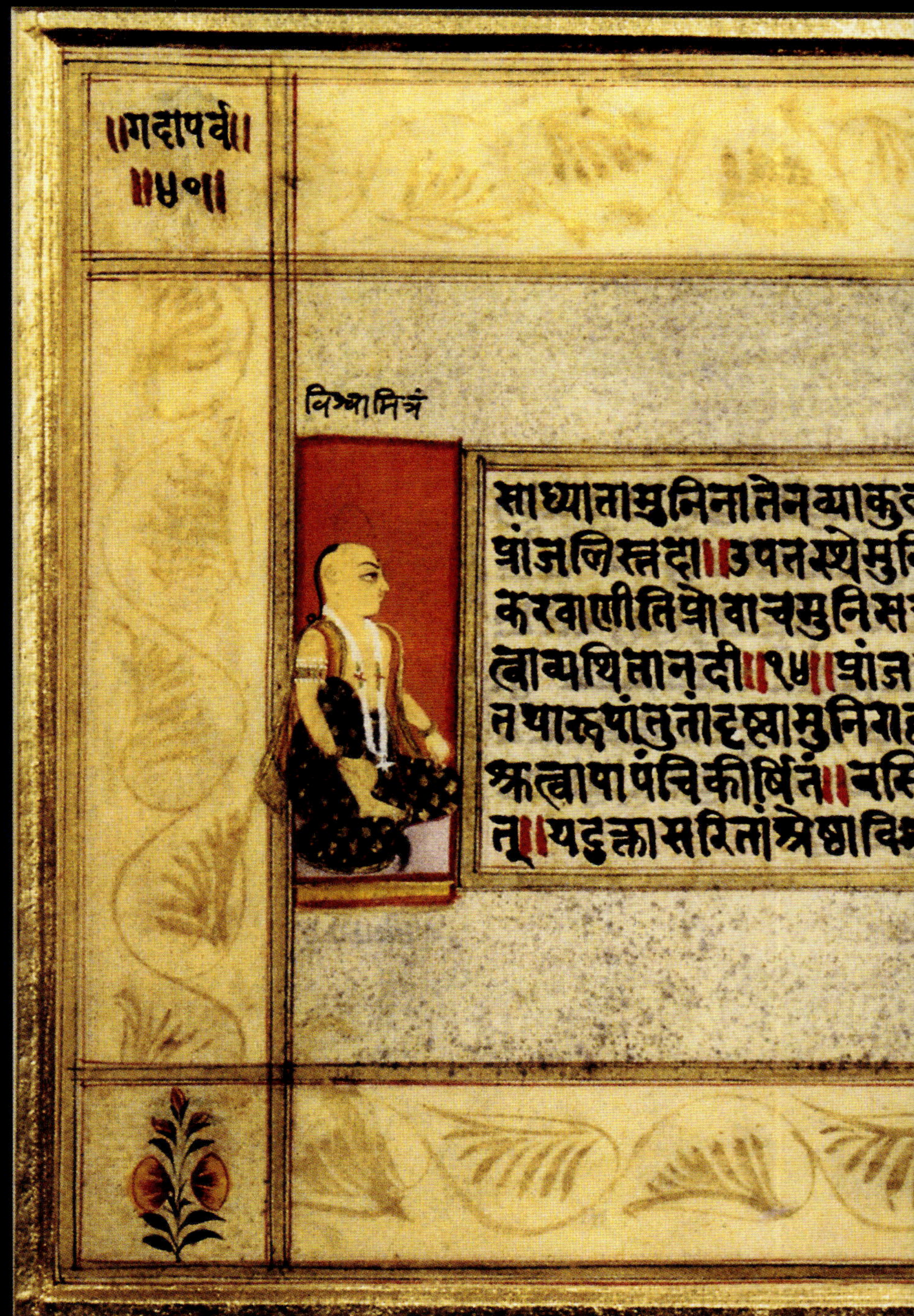

A PALM LEAF MANUSCRIPT OF *THE MAHABHARATA*

CONTENTS

16

MOUSALA PARVA: THE BOOK OF THE MACE

17

MAHAPRASTHANIKA PARVA: THE BOOK OF RENUNCIATION

18

SWARGAROHANA PARVA: THE BOOK OF THE ASCENT

HARIVAMSHA

REFERENCE

FOREWORD

The stories of the Mahabharata resonate with us even today, because the dilemmas and conflicts are perennial, even though today's context is different. That's the reason these accounts have been told and retold, not just in Sanskrit, but also in vernacular languages. There is derivative literature drawing on those stories; there are Jain versions; there are depictions in films, television serials, plays, dances, paintings, and sculpture. The tale is so engrossing that it can be told again and again.

Despite several retellings floating around, there is nothing quite like the present illustrated retelling of the epic. This one is captivating and different because it draws on all those cultural strands, past and contemporary, to enrich the story. It is not a simple textual rendering in prose, which, however well done, can be boring. The book is a visual treat because the text is laced with illustrations from manuscripts, paintings, and etchings, sometimes from unexpected places, including abroad.

It is also more than that. Appreciation of the Mahabharata requires understanding of the geography, historical timelines, social norms, rituals, beliefs, and practices. The contemporary reader, even if he or she happens to be Indian, may not be familiar with all this. Peppered with facts and minute details, this book is not just an illustrated retelling, it is also partly an illustrated explanation of what is a formidable text, in terms of size—the Critical Edition of the epic has around 80,000 shlokas (verses), and with the non-Critical versions, it nears 100,000 shlokas. Such an extent can be a deterrent. Where this retelling scores is in making the rendition attractive and interesting. Incidentally, the Harivamsha is included and there is a extended section on the Bhagavad Gita.

The Mahabharata has survived because of retelling and passing down through the ages. We now have one more welcome effort in that long legacy.

BIBEK DEBROY

An economist by profession, Bibek Debroy is currently Member, Niti Aayog, a policy think tank of the Indian government. He has written and edited several books, including the translation of the Critical Edition of the Mahabharata in ten volumes. Most of the quotes in this book have been taken from this translation of the epic.

INTRODUCTION

The **Hindu Scriptures**

The Shastras, or scriptures, codify key Hindu concepts said to have been revealed by Brahma and elaborated on by saints and seers. These texts were orally passed on from one generation to the next for many centuries before they were written down.

Traditionally, Hindu texts are divided into two categories, Shruti and Smriti. Literally meaning "that which is heard," Shruti scriptures are believed to be divine revelations, and thus, the most authoritative texts on beliefs. As authorless creations of the divine, these were passed down orally from one generation to the next without any additions or amendments.

Shruti texts include the Vedas, a collection of hymns that are among the world's most ancient extant texts. The oldest among these is the Rig Veda, which some people date back to 1500 BCE. This ancient text, along with the Sama Veda, Yajur Veda, and Atharva Veda, was composed over a period of 1,000 years. Along with the Vedas, the Brahmanas (treatises on ritual), the Aranyakas (discussions on ritual and meditation), and the Upanishads (philosophical elaborations on the Vedas) are also considered Shruti texts. All Shruti literature has been composed in Sanskrit.

Smriti texts explain and expand on the ideas in the Shruti texts, and as their derivatives, are seen as less authoritative. Unlike the Shruti texts, "Smriti," meaning "that which is remembered," are texts attributed to different authors and were traditionally written down and transmitted.

The Smriti corpus includes a vast body of texts on diverse subjects, such as the Vedangas (which are connected with the study of the Vedas), the Itihasas (the epics, the Mahabharata and Ramayana), Puranas (legends and lore, such as creation myths), Dharma Shastra, Artha Shastra, and Sutras (codices of special, technical knowledge), Bhasyas (reviews and commentaries on Shruti and non-Shruti texts), and Nibandhas (digests) on a variety of topics such as politics, ethics culture, arts and society. Though some of these texts were composed in regional languages, the majority of the Shruti texts are in Sanskrit.

ITIHASA
The Mahabharata and Ramayana are part of Itihasa literature, and narrate incidents said to have actually occurred ("itihasa" translates to "so it happened"). These epics are seen as records of contemporary history, as opposed to the Puranas, which tell tales of the remote past.

THE UPANISHADS
Literally meaning "sitting close to," "Upanishad" implies listening closely to a guru's discourses. These Shruti treatises discuss some of the principal tenets of Hinduism, such as moksha—release from the cycle of rebirth. This may be why they are known as Vedanta, "the highest purpose of the Vedas." There are more than 200 Upanishads, of which about 12 are considered to be "mukhya," or major.

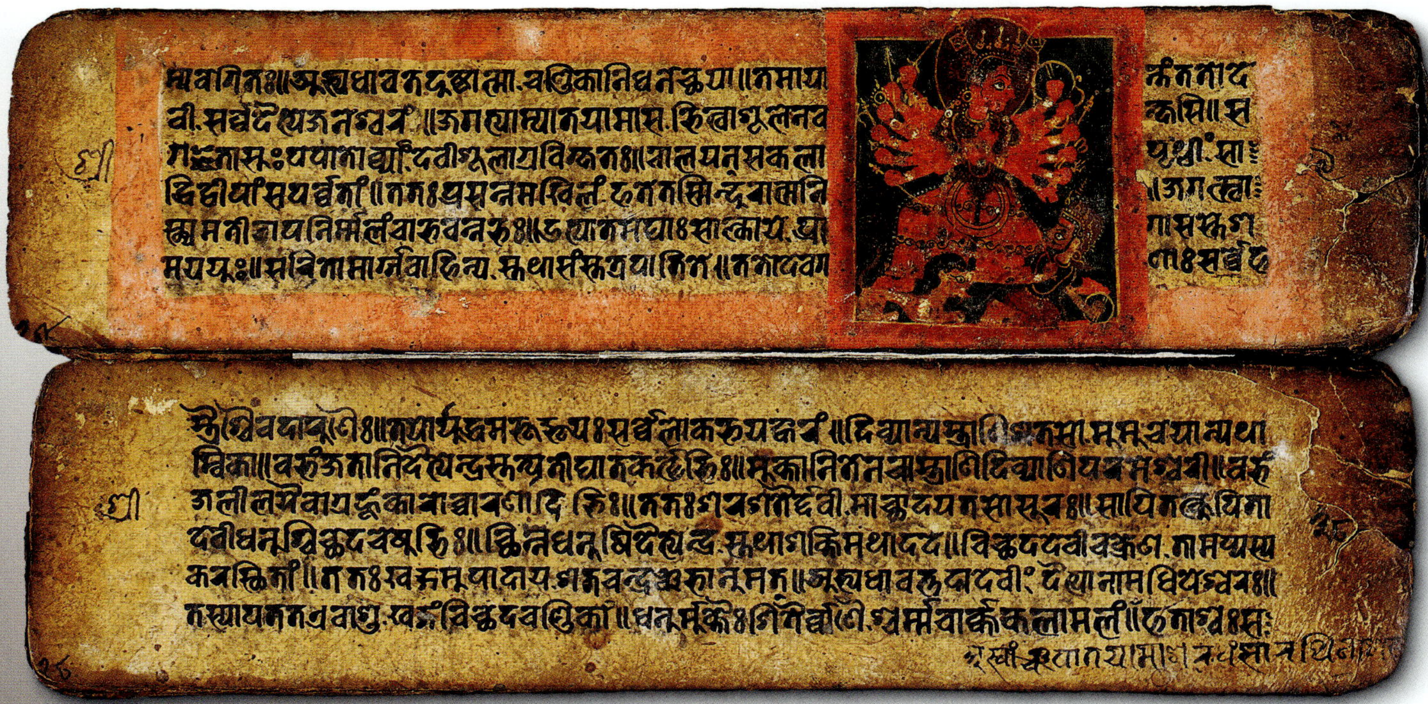

THE PURANAS

The Puranas are Smriti texts that describe events said to have occurred in the remote past (as opposed to the Itihasa, which records contemporary history). They include diverse topics such as legends of kings and discourses on philosophy, grammar, and geography. The oldest of all Puranas, the *Markandeya Purana* contains the Devi Mahatmya, the oldest treatise on the all-powerful Mother Goddess.

THE VEDAS

Foremost in Shruti literature, the Vedas are considered to be knowledge revealed by Brahma himself. The Rig Veda, the bedrock on which the other three texts are based, codifies hymns of praise. The Sama Veda is the book of liturgical melodies; the Yajur Veda lists mantras for rituals; and the Atharva Veda offers guidance on everyday life.

A **Pantheon** of **Gods**

The Mahabharata was written during a period of transition from the Vedic to the Puranic times. This transition saw the older nature gods, such as Agni and Vayu, interact with newer gods, such as Shiva and Krishna, creating a pantheon that is still revered today.

The origins of Hindu philosophy can be traced as far back as the Iron Age. From 1700 BCE, the decline of the Indus Valley Civilization coincided with the gradual increase in the power and influence of the Aryans in this region. What followed was an intermingling of beliefs and cultures from which emerged a tradition of sacrificial worship and ritual that found expression in the hymns of the Vedas. These sacrifices were offerings to important deities, such as Agni, the god of fire, Varuna, the god of sky, water, and celestial ocean, and Indra, the god of thunder, rain, and war. These Vedic gods, the embodiment of natural forces that affected daily life, were worshipped to maintain the order of the cosmos.

As the philosophy developed, the Vedic gods were joined, and in many cases superseded, by others such as Vishnu. Later Hindu literature, especially the Puranas, describes a huge range of gods and goddesses, reflecting a blending of different traditions and periods in the history of the philosophy. From among these gods there emerged a ruling triumvirate representing different aspects of existence—Brahma, the creator; Vishnu, the protector; and Shiva, the destroyer. In the Mahabharata, we witness the interaction of the old and new gods—Indra and Agni (Vedic gods) with Krishna (an avatar of Vishnu). In the earlier part of the epic, Vedic gods seem more dominant, but are later overshadowed by Vishnu. Shiva and his various aspects, including his consorts, also occupy an important position in the epic.

INDRA, THE GOD OF THUNDER
Described as the king of Devas who rules over Swarga (or heaven) in the epic, Indra fathers Arjuna, the third of the Pandava brothers.

VARUNA, THE GOD OF WATER
One of the oldest Hindu deities, once revered as the supreme god of the Vedic pantheon, Varuna sustains life on earth. His mount is the crocodile-like makara.

AGNI, THE FIRE GOD
Believed to purify everything he touches, the Vedic god Agni exists on earth as fire, in the atmosphere as lightning, and in the sky as the sun. He is invoked by mortals to carry petitions to the gods.

VAYU, THE GOD OF THE WINDS
Portrayed seated on a gazelle with a banner in his hand, Vayu, the god of the winds, is, like all Vedic nature deities, powerful and heroic. Bhima, the second of the five Pandavas, is his son.

SURYA, THE SUN GOD
One of the primary Vedic nature gods, Surya travels the sky in a chariot pulled by seven horses. Karna, the firstborn son of the Pandavas' mother, is his son.

BRAHMA - SARASWATI
Portrayed with four faces, each facing a cardinal direction, the wise Brahma is considered to be the creator of the universe. All the knowledge contained in the Vedas originates from him. Saraswati, the goddess of learning, is his consort.

VISHNU - LAKSHMI
As the force that protects and preserves the world, Vishnu takes birth as a mortal when unrighteousness upsets the balance of the world. He is often described as blue complexioned, to reflect his infinite nature. Lakshmi, the goddess of wealth, is his consort.

GANESHA, THE REMOVER OF OBSTACLES
Big-bellied, with the head of an elephant, Ganesha is worshipped as the remover of obstacles, as the god of auspicious beginnings, and for his wisdom and intellect.

SHIVA - PARVATI
Shiva is the deity who destroys the universe to allow for the birth of the new one. He is often depicted as a lone ascetic, as a fearsome warrior, and as the lord of dance. His consort is Parvati, the benign form of Shakti, the female aspect of cosmic energy.

YAMA, THE LORD OF DEATH
An early Vedic deity, Yama is the lord of death and dharma. In the Mahabharata, he fathers the eldest of the five Pandava brothers, Yudhishthira.

The **Hindu Cosmos**

Both epics, the Mahabharata and the Ramayana, have a large cast of characters from different races and worlds. Divine or semi-divine, these creatures have inspired many myths, legends, and folktales of their own.

The Hindu universe is said to be divided into fourteen levels, or worlds—seven higher worlds (heavens) and seven lower worlds (hells). The earth is the lowest of the higher worlds. Inhabiting these different realms are many varied creatures of myriad origins.

In addition to the Devas (the gods) who rule the heavens and are worshipped by mortals, there are other demigods, spirits, fantastic creatures, and celestial beings. These powerful, mythical creatures are humanlike in their emotions, and lead lives that are similar to those of mortal beings. In the Hindu cosmos, all creatures co-exist across the different worlds. During their travels, the Pandavas met many of these creatures such as Baka, the Rakshasa who threatened their lives, and Angaraparna the Gandharva, who helped the Pandava brothers during their journey. The Pandavas themselves are semi-divine—all five of them can trace their paternity to the Devas.

DIVINE ANIMALS
Animals occupy a special place in Hindu cosmology. Sometimes they serve as mounts for the gods. For instance, Garuda, an eagle-like bird, is Vishnu's mount, and Airavat, a white, seven-headed elephant, is Indra's mount. Along with their masters, these animals are worshipped, too.

DEVAS
The Devas, or Suras, inhabit Swarga. Interacting freely with mortals, they grant blessings and derive power over the earth from the prayers and veneration they command from humans.

GANDHARVAS
Part-animal, part-human male nature spirits, Gandharvas are consorts of the Apsaras and serve as musicians in the palaces of the gods. They also act as messengers between mortals and the gods.

RAKSHASAS
Fierce and often portrayed as evil, Rakshasas are great warriors, expert magicians, and highly intelligent. Primal beings who follow the law of the jungle, they feature in both the Mahabharata and the Ramayana. The ten-headed Ravana is the most famous Rakshasa.

APSARAS
Celestial damsels associated with rivers and clouds, Apsaras are consorts of the Gandharvas and dance in the court of the gods. Beautiful and youthful, they are known to seduce mortals on a whim. Urvashi, Menaka, and Rambha are some well-known Apsaras.

YAKSHAS
Nature spirits with benevolent dispositions, the Yakshas are associated with woodlands and mountains. Yakshas are guardians of treasures and temples.

ASURAS
Asuras are demigods, or superhuman lords, who inhabit the netherworld. For a long time the Asuras were at war with the Devas over the nectar of immortality that emerged from the great churning (see below).

THE GREAT CHURNING
A canonical creation myth, the churning of the ocean serves as an important point of origin of the universe. As the Devas and Asuras worked at reclaiming the nectar of immortality from the depths of the ocean, many divine treasures were thrown up. The Apsaras, the wish-fulfilling tree, Parijata, the goddess Lakshmi, and many more treasures came out of the ocean. When the nectar finally emerged, the Devas and Asuras fought over it in a war that went on for ages.

History and **Time**

Although many scholars have tried dating the Mahabharata and the events contained therein, by either scrutinizing archaeological findings or through studying the Hindu concept of time embedded in the epic itself, many theories and debates still abound.

The credibility of the Mahabharata is often the subject of speculation and discussion—are the story and its characters rooted in a historical reality or were these just a result of an author's creativity?

Both the great Indian epics, the Mahabharata and the Ramayana, are rooted in the itihasa-purana tradition; "itihasa" is loosely translated as "history" in English, Texts in this literary tradition narrate events, assumed to be historical, through epic poetry. Since the itihasa-purana tradition has three main components—historical narrative, genealogy, and myth —the origins of the Mahabharata and its historical times can perhaps best be understood through these three concepts.

Historicity of the events

Various methods, such as archaeoastronomy, historical astronomy, and archaeology, have been used by academics and historians to estimate a date for the events that are narrated in the Mahabharata. Analysis of astronomical data has led to the conclusion that the epoch within which these events occurred began with a grand planetary conjunction at the beginning of 3102 BCE. This led scholars to deduce that the Kurukshetra War took place in about 3137 BCE.

Excavations at the probable sites where the events are believed to have taken place have turned up Painted Grey Ware artifacts that point toward a date sometime between 1000 and 400 BCE.

In terms of genealogy, it is evident through the study of Vedas and other Vedic literature that Parikshit and Janamejaya, both kings of the Kuru dynasty at different times, were historical persons. Moreover, the Puranas carry genealogical lists, some of which state that there was a gap of 1,050 years between Parikshit's birth (the grandson of the Pandavas) and King Mahapadma Nanda's ascension to the throne in 382 BCE. This puts the birth of Parikshit and the Kurukshetra War at around 1400 BCE.

KEY CONCEPT

EONS IN THE EPICS

The eras in the Hindu cosmos are based on accurate, and seemingly complex, calculations of time. After the completion of 100-year cycles of Brahma, Pralaya (or doomsday) takes place.

- One year = 360 days
- One yuga = 100,000 years
- Four yugas = 1 Devayuga (Believed to be equivalent to 4 x 100,000 = 400,000 years)
- 71 Devyugas = 1 manuvantara
- 28 manuvantara = 1 day of Brahma
- 100 years of Brahma = Pralaya

Dating the epic

Putting a date to the Mahabharata, however, is a difficult task. The fact that the epic itself has been revised many times has not helped matters. Some experts have concluded that the epic was composed between the 8th and 9th centuries BCE. There are also some who suggest that the text probably reached its final form in the early Gupta period, around the 4th century CE.

The concept of time

Scholars have also analyzed the Mahabharata through the study of the yugas, or ages. In the Hindu concept of time, the Kali Age started with the death of Krishna, about thirty-five years after the Kurukshetra War.

In the eternal cosmic order, time moves differently. Unlike the Western concept of the linear movement of time, in the Hindu cosmos, time is cyclical in a more cause-and-effect way. The world moves in cycles, or yugas, and each yuga comprises millions of years. Each yuga comes and goes, and the world turns as a yuga passes. The Mahabharata is believed to have occurred between the end of the Dwapara Yuga and start of the Kali Yuga.

Understanding the cyclical nature of time not only helps to better understand the epic, but also the important recurring concepts such as dharma, karma, moksha, and rebirth. These are all are rooted in the idea that time is cyclical and, in a sense, a never-ending constant.

To further emphasize the relationship of time with the worlds that the Mahabharata portrays, it is important to note that while the time on earth, or the mortal world, moves through cycles, there is an eternal time that exists in Swarga and Vaikuntha, the heavens where the gods reside. In that sense, there are two cycles of time that run simultaneously, with the righteous and eternal order of the universe, ensuring both cycles move in synchronization.

YUGAS
A yuga, or era, is a unit of time used in the Hindu universe. There are four yugas, and the Mahabharata is believed to have taken place between the Dwapara Yuga and the Kali Yuga.

Personification of time

Vishnu, as the deity responsible for sustaining the universe, personifies the universe and time. The dark blue color of his body symbolizes infinity, and the thousand-headed serpent he rests on is believed to control time. The movement of time is dependent on the divine serpent. It is said that when the serpent, Adi-Ananta-Shesha, uncoils, time moves forward and creation takes place, and when he coils again, the universe ceases to exist.

To contextualize the epics in yugas, or eras, the Ramayana takes place in the Treta Yuga, when Rama was the incarnation of Vishnu, while most of the Mahabharata takes place in the Dwapara Yuga, when Krishna was the incarnation of Vishnu.

VISHNU RESTS ON THE ADI-SHESHA
This iconic image of Vishnu reclining on the divine snake Adi-Ananta-Shesha, from the Ranganathan temple in Tamil Nadu, India, represents the Supreme divinity and the universal movement of time.

INFORMATION

THE GREAT DISSOLUTION

The end of the universe is a familiar motif in almost all religions and cultures. In the Hindu cosmos, Pralaya is the Great Dissolution, an era when all activities in the universe come to an end. When Pralaya strikes, the lower seven worlds are destroyed to enable a new order to be created, while the seven upper worlds are preserved.

PRALAYA IS BELIEVED TO BE A DISSOLUTION OF TIME WHEN THE COSMIC WATERS ENGULF THE WORLD AND THE WORLD AS WE KNOW IT CEASES TO EXIST.

The Hindu **Cosmography**

The events of the Mahabharata take place in Bharatavarsha, the land that King Bharata ruled over. The tale of his descendants, the Kauravas and Pandavas, is spread over a large expanse of land, from Afghanistan to India to Sri Lanka.

Scholars identify Bharatavarsha, the land where the story of the Mahabharata unfolds, with the Indian subcontinent, encompassing modern-day Afghanistan, Bangladesh, India, Pakistan, Nepal, Bhutan, and Sri Lanka. The Mahabharata, however, locates Bharatavarsha in a different cosmic universe, using both cosmography and cartography to describe the mythical and material realms that make up its narrative.

One of the most detailed descriptions of the Hindu universe can be found in the *Bhagavata Purana*. This "maha," or primary Purana, is attributed to Veda Vyasa, the compiler of the Vedas and the composer of the Mahabharata. The *Bhagavata Purana* describes the material cosmos as an endless ocean located within a small part of the infinite spiritual world. Within this endless ocean are found innumerable universes, or "brahmanda," each of which consists of a series of spherical covers, and an inner inhabited part. Within this inner part of the brahmanda is the bhoomandala—the earth—a flat disc with a diameter of 500 million yojanas, or 4 billion miles (6.4 billion km).

The bhoomandala contains seven concentric continents, each of which is separated by an ocean of different liquids. Jambudvipa is the innermost of these continents, and is separated from the others by an ocean of saltwater. Each of these continents is separated by seven oceans—of molasses, wine, ghee, milk, yogurt, and freshwater.

Jambudvipa, the innermost of these continents, later came to be identified with Bharatavarsha, the land that King Bharata ruled, and where the events of the Mahabharata take place. It is said to measure 100,000 yojanas, approximately 799,910 miles (1,287,475 km) in diameter. Bharatavarsha, or Jambudvipa, is peopled by a variety of beings—human, semi-human, animal, and divine. Under the continent, in the watery world beneath, is Bhogavati, the realm of the Naga, or serpent people. High above the Himalayas, whose lofty peaks touch the skies, lies Swarga, the realm of the gods ruled by Indra. Well beyond this realm lies Vaikuntha, Vishnu's abode, and Kailash, where Shiva lives.

In the Mahabharata, as in many Hindu scriptures, the boundary between the mythic and the material is fluid—beings from different worlds interact with one another and traverse between these worlds (though this may be easier for the gods than for the humans). When the Kauravas, tired of Bhima's bullying, drugged him and threw him into a river, he reached the underground world of Bhogavati, the watery realms of the Nagas. Similarly, during the Pandavas' years of exile, Arjuna climbed the Himalayas and went up to Swarga, the realm of the gods, at Indra's invitation.

As part of Itihasa literature, which claims to narrate historical events ("itihasa" translates to "this is what happened"), the Mahabharata as well as the Ramayana are also full of physical, geographical details of locations. Between the two epics, the length and breadth of the Indian subcontinent is covered. In the Ramayana ("the tale of Rama"), Rama travels from the north to Lanka in the south (identified with Sri Lanka). In the Mahabharata, the action spans the breadth of the subcontinent, from the east to the west.

The epic also gives geographic reference points for the location of kingdoms. Based on these clues, scholars have been able to identify the approximate locations for some of these kingdoms. For instance, Kurukshetra, the battlefield where the war between the Kauravas and the Pandavas was fought, is said to be located south of the Saraswati and north of the Drishtadwati rivers, and is identified with a town by this name in the state of Haryana today. Gandhari, wife of the blind king Dhritarashtra, and the Kauravas' mother, was from Gandhara, thought to be located on the border of present-day Pakistan and Afghanistan.

JAMBUDVIPA
Of the nine varshas (regions or countries) of the Jambudvipa, eight are places of heavenly enjoyment. The ninth region, Bharatavarsha, is inhabited by people.

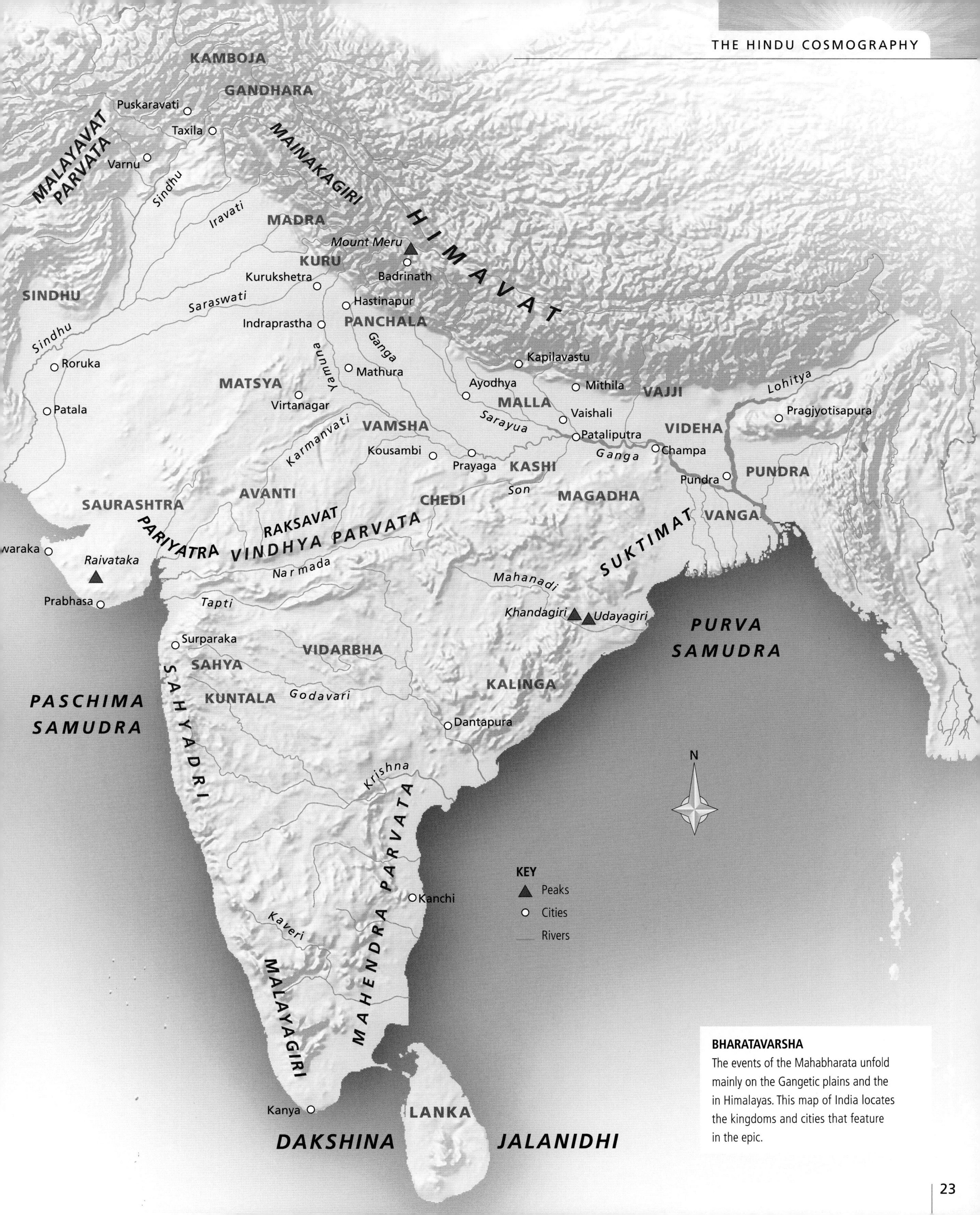

BHARATAVARSHA
The events of the Mahabharata unfold mainly on the Gangetic plains and the in Himalayas. This map of India locates the kingdoms and cities that feature in the epic.

VYASA'S CENOTAPHS
Located in Jaisalmer, Rajasthan, this 15th-century monument, better known as Vyasa Chattri, is believed to be dedicated to the author of the Mahabharata. Built in the Rajput architectural style typical of the region, each ornate pavilion forms a canopy (chattri) over the cremation ground of an important personage.

What **Ganesha Wrote**

The Mahabharata is said to have been composed by Krishna Dwaipayana, better known as Veda Vyasa for compiling the four Vedas, the books of wisdom. Keen to share the Vedic truths with the common people, Vyasa composed a tale that would resonate with the simplest of men. He enlisted Ganesha's help to write down the story.

It is believed that in the beginning was the void. There was no air, no water, neither death nor immortality was known, and day and night did not exist.

Then Brahma, the god of creation, manifested himself to dispel the vacuum. He created the waters, and placed a seed in them. In time, the seed turned into a golden egg. Then Brahma emerged from the egg, cracking it into two. He named one half of it Swarga (heaven), and the other, Prithvi (earth). He then created the gods (the Devas), and the demons (the Asuras). He created speech, and he created men and women. And he imparted to them secret knowledge that gave the world meaning and life a purpose. This knowledge relieved vedana, the yearning of the restless human soul, and became collectively known as the Veda.

The cycle of life

Those who first heard the Veda came to be known as the Rishis. Based on what they learned from the Veda, the Rishis organized humankind into a society where everyone had defined roles—the Brahmans taught the people, the Kshatriyas protected them, the Vaishyas were their providers, and the Shudras toiled for them. These roles changed with each lifetime, based on one's deeds. Thus, a Shudra in one life could be reborn a Kshatriya in another life, and a Brahman could be reborn as a Vaishya, or perhaps a plant or beast, maybe even a god or a demon, based on their actions. Thus, everything was interconnected and cyclical. The point of life in this ever-changing world was not ambition, but rather introspection.

Then came a drought—one that lasted fourteen long years; it parched the land, and squeezed dry the earth of all life. The Saraswati river dried up; subsequently the structures and strictures of society collapsed and the Veda was forgotten by humankind.

The compiler of wisdom

At long last, when the rains returned, a fisherwoman's son went on a quest to collect the scattered hymns of the Vedas. This compiler of the lost hymns was named Krishna Dwaipayana—the dark one who was born on a river island. His father was Parasara, who was the grandson of Sage Vasishtha, one of the seven Rishis who heard the Veda first. In time, Krishna Dwaipayana came to be known as Veda Vyasa, the compiler of the Vedas, the books of wisdom.

> **"Whatever is** found **here** … may be found **elsewhere**. But **whatever is not** in it, **cannot be found anywhere** else."
>
> SAGE VAISHAMPAYANA TO KING JANAMEJAYA, ADI PARVA: THE BOOK OF THE BEGINNING

Vyasa organized the hymns he collected into four books—the Rig Veda, the Yajur Veda, the Sama Veda, and the Atharva Veda. In doing this he realized that the compilations contained abstract truths that few had the wisdom to understand. So, once he completed this monumental task, Vyasa decided to write a story that would take these abstruse Vedic truths, in their purest form, to all the corners of the world. Once he had composed the story, he needed someone who could write it exactly as he narrated it. As this was no easy task, the he turned to Brahma, requesting him to identify a suitable scribe. Brahma suggested that Vyasa ask the elephant-headed Ganesha, also known as the remover of obstacles, to clear this hurdle that lay in his path.

Vyasa invoked Ganesha to enlist his help for this great task. The elephant-headed god agreed to Vyasa's request, but had a condition. He wanted the sage to narrate the story without stopping. If Vyasa paused at any time in the telling, the god would stop writing and leave. By laying down this condition, Ganesha made sure that what Vyasa dictated was free of human prejudice. »

THE CREATOR
It is said that Brahma, the god of creation, created the four Vedas, articulating one from each of his mouths. As the one who wrote the Mahabharata, which contains the wisdom of the four Vedas, Vyasa is considered by many to be the Brahma who walked the earth.

THE DIVINE SCRIBE
Veda Vyasa asked the elephant-headed god Ganesha to transcribe the Mahabharata.

THE ORAL TRADITION
Though Ganesha is believed to have written Vyasa's tale, the Mahabharata has been passed on orally, from bard to bard, to a variety of audiences.

» The sage felt himself up to the challenge. "I will," he promised Ganesha, "provided you write only that which makes sense to you." This ensured that all that was written appealed to the divine. And so Ganesha began penning Vyasa's tale.

Jaya

Vyasa told the story of the royal house of the Kurus, of the Pandavas and the Kauravas, who were his own grandchildren—a story that he had seen unfold before his very eyes. The sage called it "Jaya," meaning a tale of victory. Every so often, Vyasa would throw in some cryptic verses to slow down Ganesha and give himself time to think. Even so, he managed to keep up a steady pace. In fact, at one point Ganesha's pen broke because of the punishing speed Vyasa maintained. To keep his end of the bargain, the god broke off one of his tusks and used it as a pen to continue writing.

The story Vyasa told Ganesha took him three years to narrate and had sixty chapters. Almost all of these were lost in time. Only one part that was with Vyasa's student, Vaishampayana, was preserved. Thus, no one knows Vyasa's tale in its entirety.

Vaishampayana told Vyasa's tale to Janamejaya, the great grandson of Arjuna, who was one of the main protagonists of the story. This retelling was overheard by a Sauti, or bard, called Romaharshana, who passed it on to his son Ugrashrava. Ugrashrava in turn narrated the tale to Shonak and other sages in the Naimisha forest.

Vyasa also told his story to his son, the parrot-headed Suka, who narrated it to King Parikshit, Janamejaya's father, comforting him with its wisdom as he lay dying.

Another of Vyasa's disciples who heard his tale was Jaimini. There were a few points of the story Jaimini did not understand. As Vyasa was not around to clarify his doubts, he decided to approach Rishi Markandeya, who had been blessed with long life and had witnessed the events that had inspired Vyasa's tale. Unfortunately, by the time Jaimini found Markandeya, the sage had given up speech as part of his decision to renounce the world. Markandeya's pupils sent Jaimini to four birds who had witnessed the Kurukshetra War. The mother of these birds had been flying over the battlefield when she was struck by an arrow that ripped open her womb. The four eggs she had been carrying fell to the blood-soaked ground, which, thus softened, cushioned the fall and prevented the eggs from breaking. Then, the bell of a war elephant fell over the eggs and protected them through the battles. When they were discovered after the war, the Rishis realized that the birds had

THE TALKING BIRDS
According to the Mahabharata, the Kurukshetra War was witnessed and narrated by four birds. These are traditionally represented as parakeets, perhaps because they are able to mimic speech well.

LIST

WORD OF MOUTH

Narrators	Listeners
Vyasa	Ganesha, Jaimini, Vaishampayana, Suka
Vaishampayana	Janamejaya, Romaharshana
Romaharshana	Ugrashrava (Sauti)
Ugrashrava (Sauti)	Shonak
Suka	Parikshit
Four birds	Jaimini

heard much during the war and, as they knew more than most humans, their perspective and insights would be unique. So, the Rishis had given these birds the gift of human speech. Thus blessed, the birds were able clarify Jaimini's doubts. They also told Jaimini many stories that no one else knew.

Vijaya

As Vyasa's tale was passed on from one storyteller to another, it took on new shape. What was originally *Jaya* came to be known as *Vijaya*. Over the course of these retellings, tales of ancestors and descendants, friends and foes, teachers and students, were added, until the story transformed from a tiny sapling into a vast tree with many branches.

In time, Vyasa's tale, which had been about ideas, came to be centered on people, and was retitled *Bharata*, the story of the clan of Bharata and the land they ruled. The expansion continued with *Bharata*, which now included topics such as genealogy, history, geography, astrology, politics, economics, philosophy, and metaphysics. With all these additions, *Bharata* came to have eighteen chapters and over a hundred thousand verses. When the story of Krishna's early years, the *Harivamsha*, was added as an appendix, the *Bharata* became the *Mahabharata*, the great epic of the people of Bharata.

Retellings of the epic

Over the centuries, the Mahabharata has been retold countless times, in temples, at family gatherings and village fairs; in various languages, and in different forms; by dancers, singers, painters, wandering minstrels, and learned scholars. Wherever the epic traveled, whether Nepal, Indonesia, or Thailand, old plots were changed and new characters emerged. There was Arjuna's son, Iravan, who is worshipped by the transgenders of Tamil Nadu and Bhima's son, Barbareek, who is worshipped in Rajasthan as Khatu Shyamji. In Bengal, a tale of Draupadi leading an army of women and routing the Kauravas after the death of Abhimanyu is told. Theyyam performers of Kerala sing of how the Kauravas compelled a sorcerer to perform occult rites against the Pandavas, and how the sorcerer's wife reversed the effects.

Though these tales were not Vyasa's, they all contributed to the bard's larger objective in telling it. When he dictated the text that became the Mahabharata, Vyasa had envisioned it as embodying the teachings of the Vedas. Through the narrow lens of a family conflict, the epic offers a broad perspective on dharma (righteousness), artha (wealth), kama (desire), and moksha (transcendence)—the four goals of life—and many other ideas encoded in the Vedas. It becomes easy to understand why the Mahabharata is considered the fifth Veda—and truly the greatest story ever told. As has been said, "whatever is found here ... may be found elsewhere. But whatever is not in it, cannot be found anywhere else."

"This contains **100,000 sacred shlokas,** composed **by** Satyavati's son, **Vyasa ...** This is **equal to the Vedas.** It is sacred and **supreme.** It is the **best of all** that can be heard."

SAGE VAISHAMPAYANA TO KING JANAMEJAYA, ADI PARVA: THE BOOK OF THE BEGINNING

THE PANDAVANI

Teejan Bai, a famous exponent of the Pandavani, at a performance in 2010. Literally meaning "of or related to the Pandavas," this folk art from the northern state of Chhatisgarh tells the tales of the Pandavas, through song.

ANALYSIS

MODERN INTERPRETATION

In the 20th century, the Mahabharata cast its spell on the modern mind. Scholars wrote essays to rationalize its moral ambiguity, while novelists, painters, and filmmakers used incidents from the epic to comment on political and social issues. In many cases, the wisdom of the Mahabharata has been overshadowed by its entertainment value, its complexities oversimplified by well-meaning narrators, leading to ruptures in the traditional discourse.

THE MAHABHARATA IN 18 CHAPTERS

The Structure of the Mahabharata

Part of the epic tradition of poetry, the Mahabharata is a lengthy narrative poem constructed around the saga of a bitter quarrel between cousins over inheritance rights to a kingdom. It is the longest poem ever written, comprising more than 90,000 shlokas, or verses. In India, the epic enjoys a cultural space that bridges folk, popular, as well as classical art and literature.

The Mahabharata was written over a period of 1,000 years by multiple authors, although the original text is attributed to Sage Krishna Dwaipayana, also known as Veda Vyasa. The epic is composed as a narration by Vyasa's disciple Vaishampayana to King Janamejaya, but there are other narrations that sit within this overarching one. This complicated nesting of narratives probably reflects the existence of different historical versions of this epic. *Jaya,* which was the original story, had 8,800 shlokas, or verses. When the tale had expanded to 24,000 shlokas it came to be known as *Bharata.* By the time it had taken its present form as the *Mahabharata,* the entire telling comprised more than 90,000 shlokas. These were composed in 18 different meters, the most frequently used being the Anustubh meter, with four verses of eight syllables. Several shlokas form an adhyaya, or chapter, and several chapters together make up a parva. Depending on the version, the Mahabharata is either arranged into 100 or 18 parvas. This book follows the 18-parva version, redistributing the parvas in the 100-parva version as sub-parvas.

1 ADI PARVA: THE BOOK OF THE BEGINNING

The sub-parvas: Anukramanika; Parvasamgraha; Poushya; Pouloma; Astika; Adi-vamshavatarana; Sambhava; Jatugriha-daha; Hidimba-vadha; Baka-vadha; Chaitraratha; Draupadi-svayamvara; Vaivahika; Viduragamana; Rajya-labha; Arjuna-vanavasa; Subhadra-harana; Harana harika; and Khandava-daha

2 SABHA PARVA: THE BOOK OF THE ASSEMBLY HALL

The sub-parvas: Sabha; Mantra; Jarasandha-vadha; Digvijaya; Rajasuya; Arghabhiharana; Shishupala-vadha; Dyuta; and Anudyuta

3 VANA PARVA: THE BOOK OF THE FOREST

The sub-parvas: Aranyaka; Kirmira-vadha; Kairata; Indralokabhigamana; Tirtha-yatra; Jatasura-vadha; Yaksha-yuddha; Ajagara; Markandeya-samasya; Draupadi-Satyabhama-sambada; Ghosha-yatra; Mriga-svapna-bhaya; Vrihi-drounika; Draupadi-harana; Kundala-harana; and Araneya

4 VIRATA PARVA: THE BOOK OF VIRATA

The sub-parvas: Vairata; Kichaka-vadha; Go-grahana; and Vaivahika

5 UDYOGA PARVA: THE BOOK OF EFFORT

The sub-parvas: Udyoga; Sanjaya-yana; Prajagara; Sanatsujata; Yana-sandhi; Bhagavat-yana; Karna-upanivada; Abhiniryana; Bhishma-abhishechana; Uluka-yana; Ratha-atiratha-samkhya; and Amba-upakhyana

6 BHISHMA PARVA: THE BOOK OF BHISHMA

The sub-parvas: Jambukhanda-vinirmana; Bhumi; Bhagavad Gita; and Bhishma-vadha

7 DRONA PARVA: THE BOOK OF DRONA

The sub-parvas: Dronabhisheka; Samshaptaka-vadha; Abhimanyu-vadha; Pratijna; Jayadratha-vadha; Ghatotkacha-vadha; Drona-vadha; and Narayanastra-moksha

8 KARNA PARVA: THE BOOK OF KARNA

The sub-parva: Karna-vadha

9 SHALYA PARVA: THE BOOK OF SHALYA

The sub-parvas: Shalya-vadha; Hrada pravesha; Tirtha yatra; and Gada yuddha

10 SAUPTIKA PARVA: THE BOOK OF SLUMBER

The sub-parvas: Souptika; and Aishika

11 STREE PARVA: THE BOOK OF WOMEN

The sub-parvas: Vishoka; Stree; Shraddha; and Jala-pradanika

12 SHANTI PARVA: THE BOOK OF PEACE

The sub-parvas: Raja-dharma; Apad-dharma; and Moksha-dharma

13 ANUSHASANA PARVA: THE BOOK OF DISCIPLINE

The sub-parvas: Dana-dharma; and Bhishma-swargarohana

14 ASHWAMEDHIKA PARVA: THE BOOK OF CONQUEST

The sub-parva: Ashwamedhika

15 ASHRAMAVASIKA PARVA: THE BOOK OF HERMITAGE

The sub-parvas: Ashrama-vasa; Putra Darshana; and Naradagamana

16 MOUSALA PARVA: THE BOOK OF THE MACE

The sub-parva: Mousala

17 MAHAPRASTHANIKA PARVA: THE BOOK OF RENUNCIATION

The sub-parva: Maha-prasthanika

18 SWARGAROHANA PARVA: THE BOOK OF THE ASCENT

The sub-parva: Swargarohana

HARIVAMSHA: THE BOOK OF KRISHNA

The sub-parvas: Harivamsha; Vishnu; and Bhavishya

1
ADI PARVA: THE BOOK OF THE BEGINNING

PANDU KILLS SAGE KINDAMA
This 19th-century opaque watercolor and gold on paper is part of a larger series on the Mahabharata from the northern state of Himachal Pradesh, India. It depicts King Pandu shooting the ascetic Kindama, who had taken the form of an antelope.

Adi Parva, or the Book of the Beginning, is the first parva of the Mahabharata. As the name suggests, it gives the antecedents of the main characters, setting the context for the tale to unfold. This is the story of King Parikshit's ancestors, the Kurus, and is recounted by Sage Vaishampayana. This parva describes the birth of the Kauravas and the Pandavas, details their growing rivalry, and ends with the division of the Kuru kingdom between the cousins. One of the longest parvas in the epic, the Adi Parva has 19 sub-parvas, 225 chapters, and 7,205 shlokas, or couplets.

"The **great-souled** royal sage and lord of earth, **Janamejaya**, the **son of Parikshit**, organized a **snake-sacrifice**. There, in his presence, **Vaishampayana** recited properly the **wonderful** and sacred **stories** composed by **Krishna Dvaipayana**."

SAGE UGRASHRAVA TO THE OTHER SAGES ASSEMBLED AT THE FOREST OF NAIMISHARANYA, ADI PARVA: THE BOOK OF THE BEGINNING

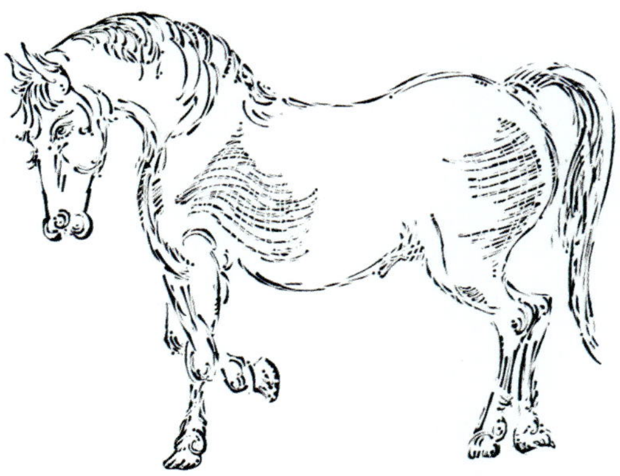

The Snake Sacrifice

Marking the beginning of the great epic, the sacrificial ritual called Sarpa Sattra sets the stage for the narration of the Mahabharata by Sage Vaishampayana—a disciple of its author, Veda Vyasa.

Parikshit, the descendant of the great Kuru clan and the king of the prosperous kingdom of Hastinapur, was consumed by a terrible dread. He was so worried that he isolated himself, not only from his subjects, but also from his wives and children, locking himself away in a tall tower. He paced back and forth in that room night and day, unable to rest, eat, or sleep. Bards were sent to tell him tales to ease his anxiety, but nothing seemed to allay his fear.

THE DAMNED FRUIT
The king of Hastinapur, Parikshit bit into a fruit, perhaps an apple, to find a worm hiding within it. The worm rapidly transformed into the serpent called Takshaka.

The cursed king

The people of Hastinapur discussed the king's condition in hushed tones. "Our king's ancestors were the great Pandavas, who emerged victorious in Kurukshetra. His father, Abhimanyu, broke the complex battle formation, Chakravyuha, all by himself. Why should one with such valiant ancestors be afraid of anything and cower so?"

Parikshit finally revealed the cause of his despair. He was cursed to die of a snakebite within seven days. This was why the illustrious king had cloistered himself, with his guards instructed to keep close watch on every window and door, and to kill any snake on sight. Any living being that entered the tower was thoroughly searched—after all, a snake could hide anywhere.

But no precaution could save the doomed king. On the seventh day, he bit into a fruit. Hiding inside the fruit was a worm that transformed itself into a frightening serpent in the blink of an eye. It was the Naga Takshaka. He sprang forward, sinking his venomous fangs into Parikshit's flesh. The king screamed for help, but it was too late—the venom spread instantly. Guards rushed to his rescue, but he was dead before they entered the room. There was no sign of the serpent—Takshaka had slithered away silently, without a trace.

PARIKSHIT'S DEATH
A 20th-century Balinese sculpture shows King Parikshit being crushed in the coils of Naga Takshaka.

The great sacrifice

The prince Janamejaya was overcome by his father's death. Enraged, he vowed to avenge Parikshit's murder, ordering the sages of the kingdom to perform a powerful yagna (sacrifice)called the Sarpa Sattra. This ritual had the power to destroy all the snakes on earth.

In keeping with the king's command, the sages prepared for the sacrifice. A massive firepit was built in the center of the city. Hundreds of priests sat around this sacrificial altar, pouring ladles of ghee on the fire stoke the flames and chanting to invoke invisible forces that drew the snakes into the firepit.

The city of Hastinapur saw innumerable squirming snakes being dragged toward the altar. The air was filled with the harrowing cries of snakes being burned alive. The people of the city watched this spectacle—some cried out against such cruelty; others supported it, calling it a fitting punishment on all Naga for killing their king. Then, from among the crowd, a young man cried out, "Stop! This is wrong."

Angered by the interruption and the blatant accusation, Janamejaya demanded to know who dared halt his yagna.

The young man was Astika, nephew of Vasuki, the king of the Nagas. "My father was the Sage Jaratkaru, a human. My mother was a Naga. I am half human and half serpent. I am you and also your enemy. I am not partial to any side. Listen to what I have to say, or none of your descendants will ever live in peace," he said. "I will explain the cause of Parikshit's death."

Astika's tale

Astika then told Janamejaya that seven days before his death, Parikshit had gone on a hunt. His pleasure interrupted by thirst, he had asked a sage sitting under a banyan tree for some water. Deep in meditation, the sage did not respond to Parikshit's request. Angry at being so ignored, the king had placed a dead snake around the sage's neck. A disciple who saw this all from afar could not take such an insult to his teacher. To teach the haughty king a lesson, he cursed him: Parikshit, king of Hastinapur, would die of a snakebite within the next seven days. His father, Astika explained to Janamejaya, was actually responsible for his own death.

Still curious, Janamejaya asked Astika what the Naga Takshaka's reasons were for killing his father.

Astika responded to the question with another tale. He told the king how Arjuna, Janamejaya's great-grandfather, had set fire to a forest called Khandavaprastha in order to clear the land on which the city of Indraprastha was built. Many serpents who lived in the forest had been killed in the fire. "Takshaka and many other Nagas like him suffered in that fire and lost everything they had. They were left homeless and orphaned."

"Takshaka vowed to

»

LEARNED SAGES

In the olden days, sages spent many years practicing austerities, meditating, and reading scriptures. True to this practice, the sage in the forest was lost in deep meditation and did not pay heed to King Parikshit's request for water.

"When the **officiating priests** began to offer oblations ... **terrible snakes** that struck fear into living creatures began to **fall into the fire**."

UGRASRAVA SAUTI, THE BARD, ADI PARVA: THE BOOK OF THE BEGINNING

KEY CONCEPT

YAGNA

One of the primary rituals in the Vedic age, the yagna, or sacrifice, was an important part of the religion. An altar was built for the yagna, into which ghee was poured by specially trained priests while they chanted hymns. Intoning these hymns, the priests would make offerings into the sacred fire to invoke cosmic forces and request blessings. If the yagna was conducted properly and was successful, the deity would grant the blessing desired.

A Sattra was a special category of yagna, which was performed at great expense and on a grand scale by hundreds of priests over a period of time.

AN OFFERING TO THE SACRED FIRE

» avenge his family's slaughter." Astika explained. "He was determined to make Arjuna or his descendants pay for the killings. Parikshit's death was his revenge —the fulfilling of his vow."

Astika pointed out that Janamejaya's indiscriminate killing of snakes would only lead to further acts of vengeance in the future. "You are repeating your ancestors' deeds and you too will suffer as they did. There will be more bloodshed, more widows will lament, and more orphans will wail, just as they did after the great war at Kurukshetra. Is that what you want?" he asked.

The question rang through the sacrificial hall, bringing the proceedings to a standstill. The priests stopped chanting. A solemn silence descended and curious eyes fell on Janamejaya, awaiting his response. Shaken but not to be moved by Astika's

THE SACRED RITUAL
This illustration from the *Razmnama*, the 16th-century Persian retelling of the Mahabharata, shows Janamejaya's grand snake sacrifice, with priests sitting around the sacrificial altar and hundreds of snakes being pulled into the firepit.

ANALYSIS

UTTANAKA'S GRUDGE

It is said that Uttanaka, the chief priest who conducted the sacrificial ritual, also had a personal reason to ensure its success.

His teacher had once asked him for the earrings of a queen as his tuition fee. After great struggle, Uttanaka managed to get the earrings, but before he could present them to his teacher, they were stolen by the Nagas. Fuming with rage, Uttanaka wanted to perform the Sarpa Sattra to annihilate the Nagas as punishment for the theft, but did not have the resources to conduct the ritual on his own.

The snake sacrifice performed by Janamejaya gave Uttanaka the perfect opportunity to avenge himself.

BURNING OF KHANDAVAPRASTHA
Khmer carving at Banteay Srei, Cambodia, shows Krishna and Arjuna outside the forest of Khandavaprastha as it burns.

explanation, Janamejaya replied with conviction, "I am doing this for the sake of justice." Astika said that Takshaka, too, had acted in the name of justice. The snake sacrifice was being conducted for the sake of justice, but it would unleash a wave of vendettas as the many who were orphaned by the sacrifice sought justice in turn.

He then raised the all-important question—who decides what is justice? "If everyone believes themselves to be right and finds their opponents at fault, how do we end this spiral of revenge?" inquired Astika, silencing the king.

Janamejaya mulled over the Naga's words. Still not convinced, he asked Astika, "Did the Pandavas not fight the battle against the Kauravas for justice?"

A war fought for dharma

Astika told him that the war was about dharma. The purpose of the war was to uphold righteousness. "Dharma is about gaining wisdom. It is not about defeating your opponents—it is about gaining victory over ourselves," he explained. Dharma results in the victory and well-being of everyone. The Kurukshetra War concluded with the Kauravas, the losing side, going to Swarga.

Janamejaya was disturbed by this revelation that the Kauravas went to paradise despite their crimes. He asked what happened to the Pandavas, his forefathers. Astika told him the went to Naraka—a place of torment, or Hell.

Shocked by this disclosure, Janamejaya exclaimed that he had not known this. "You are unaware of many things," said Astika. "Although you have inherited their kingdom, you have not gained the wisdom of the Pandavas. You do not know what is dharma—the meaning of which was revealed to Arjuna by God himself."

Now Janamejaya's curiosity knew no bounds. He had many questions for the serpent, but Astika told him to summon Sage Vaishampayana, Vyasa's disciple. "Ask him to narrate the tale his teacher composed and Ganesha wrote. Vaishampayana knows the tale of your forefathers and their life story."

> "I wish to hear that **sacred account** known as the **Mahabharata**, which spread the **fame of the Pandavas**."
>
> SAGE SHAUNAKA TO UGRASRAVA SAUTI, ADI PARVA: THE BOOK OF THE BEGINNING

The storyteller

Janamejaya sent his messengers to fetch Vaishampayana, the sage who was custodian of Vyasa's great tale. When he arrived, the sage was amazed to see thousands of serpents suspended above the sacrificial fire, and the priests, impatient to complete their ritual, sitting around the altar, awaiting instructions from their king who was now anxious to hear about his ancestors.

Vaishampayana was given a warm welcome and treated with great respect. Pleased, he agreed to narrate the great tale of the Kuru clan, and of all the kings who had ruled Bharatavarsha. This tale he narrated was known as "Jaya." Later expanded manifold it became known as the grand epic "Mahabharata."

Before he started his retelling Vaishampayana told Janamejaya to listen carefully to what was said, without being distracted by the plot or the twists and turns in the tale. "For within the complex labyrinth of the narrative lies true wisdom. That wisdom is your real inheritance," said the sage.

And then he began.

The **Story** of **Budh**

The Mahabharata tells the story of the Chandravamshis, the descendants of the moon, known for being passionate and ruled by their emotions. They are in stark contrast to the logical and upright Suryavamshis, the descendants of the sun.

The realm of Swarga (paradise) is a land of no suffering. Its residents, the Devas (gods), know it as Amravati, where all wishes come true and all dreams are fulfilled.

To sustain the pleasures of Amravati, the Devas have to defend their land from their archenemies, the Asuras, who live under the earth. Brihaspati, lord of the planet Jupiter and priest to the Devas, conducts yagnas to ensure their victory and continued well-being. For the success of these rituals, Brihaspati needs his wife Tara, the goddess of stars, by his side.

HISTORY AND CULTURE

SURYAVAMSHA

Most rulers of ancient India traced their descent from either the sun or the moon. The solar dynasty, Suryavamsha, traced its descent from Surya, the Vedic sun god. While many of the characters from the Mahabharata belong to the emotionally volatile Chandravamsha, or lunar dynasty, the protagonist of the Ramayana, Ram, and his brothers are Suryavamshis. They are known for their integrity, honor, and self-discipline.

Even today, most royal Rajput families trace their lineage to Rama, who is also worshipped as the "kuldevta," or family deity, of many Suryavamshis.

AN 18TH-CENTURY PAINTING OF RAMA, THE PRINCE OF AYODHYA

Tara's elopement

One day, Tara eloped with the moon god, Chandra. She was tired of her analytical husband who took more interest in rituals than in her. Unlike Brihaspati, who saw her merely as an essential partner in the performance of his duties, Chandra adored her. Outraged, Brihaspati threatened the Devas with his inability to conduct yagnas without his wife, and asked Indra, king of the Devas, to order her return.

This was a great dilemma for the Devas—while they were aware of Brihaspati's lack of interest in Tara, they were also wary of the consequences of not performing the yagna. They stood divided—should Tara be forced to return to a husband who did not love her, or should she be allowed to stay with her lover, who made her feel alive?

Pragmatism prevailed

After much debate, Indra made a tough decision—the yagna was more important than Tara's happiness. Without the ritual, the earth would drown in gloom and darkness. Tara would have to return to her husband even though it would make her unhappy. A reluctant Tara returned to Brihaspati. Soon after, it became obvious that she was with child. Both Chandra and Brihaspati claimed to be the father. Tara chose to remain silent, refusing to divulge the identity of the man whose child she was carrying. Then, to the astonishment of all, the unborn child cried out, "I deserve to know who my father is. Tell me, Mother, I want to know."

Lord of Buddhi

Impressed by the child's desire to know the truth, the Devas pronounced him the lord of buddhi, the intellect—that

THE MOON GOD
An 18th-century painting of Chandra, from a folio in the *Book of Dreams* from Rajasthan, India. Although Budh's biological father was Chandra, he was known as Brihaspati's son.

part of the mind that enables one to differentiate between right and wrong, and make the correct choices. He was named Budh.

Compelled by the probing question of her child, Tara had no option but to reveal the name of the father—Chandra.

Brihaspati's curse

Hearing this, the usually calm Brihaspati lost his composure and, in a fit of rage, cried, "May this illicit child of my unfaithful wife not have a gender. May he be neither male nor female," he cursed. Horrified by the harsh curse, the Devas asked Indra to intervene in his capacity as king. Indra decreed that even though the child had been cursed by Brihaspati, he would be known as his son, not Chandra's.

The law of fatherhood

"Who sowed the seed is inconsequential—the owner of the field matters more," Indra reasoned. "As Tara's husband, you, Brihaspati, will be the father of her children, whether they are yours or anyone else's."

In due course, Tara gave birth to the child, Budh, lord of the planet Mercury, a shape-shifter who was neither male nor female. A descendant of the emotional Chandra, Budh was raised in the house of the logical Brihaspati in accordance with Indra's ruling.

Following this event, this law came to define fatherhood; marriage took precedence over biological claim. It was this law that gave the five Pandavas recognition as the sons of Pandu, even though he could not father children.

Budh's anxiety

Growing up, Budh often found himself worrying about finding a life companion because of his gender ambiguity. His mother Tara reassured him, telling him that he would find a suitable partner when the time came.

Sure enough, Budh soon met a woman called Ila and fell in love with her. Ila had once been a man, a prince called Sudyumna, the son of Manu, the first king of humans.

One fateful day, Sudyumna went into a forest over which Shiva, the god of destruction, had cast a spell. He had turned all male creatures into females to please his consort, Shakti, who did not want any male to disturb her when she was in the company of her lord. Appalled at losing his manhood, Sudyumna begged Shakti to restore it. To his dismay, the goddess said she could not undo the spell, but offered to help nonetheless. "I cannot reverse the spell," she said, "but I can alter it—you will turn into a man when the moon waxes and into a woman when the moon wanes."

BRIHASPATI
This 17th-century sculpture shows Brihaspati, the lord of the planet Jupiter, as a portly, bearded priest. He holds a kalash, or pot of water, in one hand and prayer beads in the other.

Origin of the Chandravamshis

Budh, who was of neuter gender, found a perfect match in Ila, who was both man and woman. The two had many sons, who were called Ailas, the progeny of Ila. Their lineage was known as the Chandravamshis, descendants of the moon. The association with Chandra, however, did not please either Brihaspati or the Devas. It is thought that this is the reason why logical reasoning often eluded the passionate Chandravamshi kings.

MYTHOLOGY AND FOLKLORE

NAVAGRAHA

The Navagraha comprises nine celestial bodies—Surya (Sun), Chandra (Moon), Mangala (Mars), Budh (Mercury), Brihaspati (Jupiter), Shukra (Venus), Shani (Saturn), Rahu (North Lunar Node), and Ketu (South Lunar Node). All nine are regarded as deities by Hindus.

According to the Hindu science of astrology, each planet, or graha, exerts its influence on the nature and fate of a person. Each graha is associated with one quality. For instance, Brihaspati is the lord of logic and rationality, Chandra governs passion, and Surya is the god of power.

Hindu astrology places great value on the relative position of grahas. This is why the place and time of birth is so important in drawing up a horoscope. A graha can enhance the power of another graha; or they can negate each other. Sometimes the entire combination has an overall positive or negative effect.

THE NINE CELESTIAL BODIES, OR NAVAGRAHA, DEPICTED ON A STONE RELIEF

Pururava's **Obsession**

This much-celebrated love story of Pururava and Urvashi underlines the emotional nature of the Chandravamshis and hints at things to come. King Pururava fell so deeply in love with the river nymph Urvashi that he agreed to all her playful demands, leaving her with no choice but to marry him. His obsessive love for Urvashi led to his eventual ruin.

An ancestor of the Kuru clan, Pururava was a Chandravamshi, the lineage of the moon god Chandra, governed by its passionate nature. One day, Pururava saw an Apsara named Urvashi bathing in a river. A celestial being who lived with the gods, Urvashi only occasionally stepped down on earth. She was considered so beautiful that it was said that nature itself would stop to watch her. Animals gazed at her, while every tree, bush, and blade of grass wanted to touch her. Her beauty was legendary—and Pururava fell deeply in love with her. He lost no time in asking Urvashi to marry him. "Be my wife and live with me," he implored.

In teasing indulgence of his obsession, the Apsara gave a list of conditions to the king before she would agree to marry him. "I will be your queen if you promise me two things—you will take care of my pet goats, and never let anyone but me see you naked," she said. To her great surprise, Pururava instantly agreed. Left with no choice but to acquiesce, Urvashi married Pururava.

KING OF GODS
Indra, the king of the Devas, is often portrayed riding the white elephant Airavat, as in this miniature from Junagarh, Rajasthan, India. Urvashi was an Apsara in his court.

Return to heaven

King Pururava and his new queen settled into domestic bliss. It was a new, enjoyable experience for Urvashi, and she bore her human husband many sons. She may have spent a long time on earth, but it is said that the lifetime of a human is just the blink of an eye for Indra. The king of gods could not bear even a moment's separation from Urvashi, and was impatient for her return to Amravati, the home of the gods. He ordered the Gandharvas, the celestial musicians, to bring her back from earth.

The promises broken

One day, while Pururava was making love to Urvashi, the Gandharvas stole her pet goats from under their bed. Urvashi

> "Ho there, **my consort**! **Stay**, thou fierce-souled lady, and **let us reason** for a while **together**."
>
> PURURAVA TO URVASHI, RIG VEDA, URVASI-PURURAVAS

ART AND LITERATURE

A GRAND LOVE STORY

The love story of Pururava and Urvashi has been recorded in the Rig Veda, the oldest Vedic text, dated about 1500 BCE. It has also been immortalized by the Sanskrit poet Kalidasa, in his play *Vikramorvasiyam*, written in 500 CE. In this version, it is the nymph who pursues the king. The gods then allow her to stay with Pururava so long as he never sets eyes on the child the two will have together. Years later, when the father meets his son, Urvashi returns to her heavenly abode. Pururava's story is also told in another ancient Indian text *Kalpasutra*. In this telling his first son, Ayu, by Urvashi, establishes the kingdom of Kuru-panchala in the east and their second son, Amavasu, the Gandhara kingdom in the west. These two kingdoms set the stage for the eventual war at Kurukshetra.

A MODERN PRINT OF AN ANCIENT HINDU SCRIPTURE

"Pururavas, return thou to thy dwelling: I, like the wind, am difficult to capture."

URVASHI TO PURURAVA, RIG VEDA, URVASI-PURURAVAS

saw them from the corner of her eye and cried, "My goats are being stolen! Keep your promise, husband. Please bring them back to me." Pururava, in his haste to catch the thieves, jumped off the bed and ran after the Gandharvas without stopping to put on clothes. As soon as he stepped outside the palace, Indra hurled a thunderbolt—lightning flashed across the sky and exposed Pururava's nakedness to the world. The promises that had kept Urvashi on earth for so many years were broken, and the Apsara returned to Amravati. Without Urvashi, Pururava lost all reason and could no longer rule his kingdom. The sages were forced to replace him with one of his more capable sons.

Some say that Pururava still weeps in the forest and searches for Urvashi by the river banks; others believe that she turned him into a Gandharva and he follows her as a musician.

Generations later, Pururava's all-consuming passion for Urvashi would manifest in his descendant Shantanu, who would fall headlong in love not once but twice—first with Ganga and then Satyavati—with disastrous consequences.

URVASHI'S DEPARTURE
This 1896 chromolithograph by Raja Ravi Varma depicts Urvashi returning to heaven while a besotted Pururava tries to stop her.

Dushyanta and Shakuntala

At Sage Kanva's hermitage, King Dushyanta met Shakuntala, the sage's daughter. They fell in love, married according to the ancient customs of the forest, and settled into a happy life together. But Dushyanta had to go back to his kingdom, promising his bride he would return soon.

Kaushika was a Suryavamshi king, a descendant of the house of the sun who desired to become more powerful than any man or god. To achieve this ambition, he renounced all worldly ties, gave up his material possessions, and took a vow of celibacy. But no sooner had he settled down to meditate than he was distracted by an Apsara. The highly desirable Menaka had been sent by Indra for this very purpose—the king of Devas feared for his throne, if Kaushika succeeded in his meditation.

The abandoned child

Despite all efforts to keep temptation at bay, Kaushika succumbed to Menaka's charms. From this passionate union a baby girl was born. But instead of being welcomed by her parents, the child was abandoned on in the forest—for Kaushika she was proof of his failure to curb his desire; for Menaka, she merely symbolized the success of yet another conquest.

The child was found nestled under the wings of a flock of shakun birds by a sage called Kanva. He named her Shakuntala, and took her to his hermitage to raise as his own daughter. Shakuntala grew up into a beautiful woman, living in the forest among animals and trees, with little contact with the world outside.

MENAKA AND KAUSHIKA
In many versions of the tale, the Apsara Menaka is shown trying to convince King Kaushika to accept their newborn child, Shakuntala.

A love forgotten

One day, King Dushyanta, a descendant of Pururava, arrived at Kanva's hermitage during the course of a hunt. He thought to pay his respects to the sage and rest for a few days. On his arrival, he learned Kanva was away on a pilgrimage, but he met the sage's innocent young daughter. Taken by her beauty, Dushyanta fell in love with her and asked her to marry him.

A coy Shakuntala, though enamored by the personable visitor, replied "If you want to marry me, you must first ask my father's permission."

But Dushyanta persisted. "Your father is away," he said. "But there is another way allowed by our tradition. We can marry as the Gandharvas do, with the trees as a witness to our union."

Not able to refuse the handsome king, Shakuntala agreed to marry him. The ceremony was conducted with the trees as witness and the two spent many days together in the hermitage as husband and wife.

The time came for Dushyanta to return home. "I need to go and I cannot take you with me without your father's knowledge—it is not right. I will come back for you," he promised, before leaving for his kingdom. The days went by and Kanva returned home. As soon as he saw Shakuntala, he understood that his daughter was in love with someone and was carrying his child. Overjoyed, the sage celebrated with his daughter, and together they awaited Dushyanta's return.

Days turned into weeks, and weeks into months, with no sign of Dushyanta. Shakuntala gave birth to a son and named him Bharata. The boy grew up in the care of Shakuntala and

PANGS OF SEPARATION
This 19th-century chromolithograph by well-known artist Raja Ravi Varma shows Shakuntala writing a love letter to her beloved, as her friends look on.

"O **beautiful** one! Be my wife ... **Marry me** according to **gandharva rites**, because it is said that a gandharva marriage is the best."

DUSHYANTA TO SHAKUNTALA, ADI PARVA: THE BOOK OF THE BEGINNING

Kanva. They all but forgot about Dushyanta's promise, until Bharata asked about his father.

Kanva decided that it was time for his grandson to get to know his father and asked Shakuntala to take Bharata to Dushyanta.

Adorned with flowers and draped in cloth the forest had offered her as gifts, Shakuntala looked beautiful when she met her husband. But Dushyanta showed no sign of recognizing her. "Are there any witnesses to this wedding you claim took place?" he asked.

"The trees," replied Shakuntala. The assembled court laughed at her, mocking her simplicity. But Shakuntala was not to be cowed. Steadfast in her resolve, she asserted with dignity, "I have not come here to seek my husband, but to introduce my son to his father." That said, she left Bharata facing his father and turned to walk away.

At this, a voice boomed from the sky, reprimanding Dushyanta —Shakuntala was indeed his wife and Bharata his son. Dushyanta apologized for his behavior, acknowledging Shakuntala as his queen and Bharata his heir in front of the entire kingdom.

With ancestors from both the lunar and solar line, Bharata went on to become a fair and compassionate king—so much so, that the land he ruled came to be known as Bharatavarsha, or simply Bharata.

"O **evil** ascetic! I **remember nothing**. Who do you **belong** to? I do not remember having had any relation with you … **Go or stay**, as you wish. Do what you want."

DUSHYANTA TO SHAKUNTALA, ADI PARVA: THE BOOK OF THE BEGINNING

ART AND LITERATURE

KALIDASA'S PLAY

Another version of Shakuntala's story persists in popular culture, as Kalidasa's play *Abhijnana Shakuntalam*. The plot of this play, written around 500 CE in Sanskrit, differs from the one in the Mahabharata. In Kalidasa's version, Shakuntala is brought to Dushyanta as soon as her father discovers she is pregnant. Dushyanta, however, fails to recognize her because of a Rishi's curse on him. While Kalidasa's Shakuntala pursues her husband, Vyasa's Shakuntala goes to seek her son's father. Although she fears social stigma in Kalidasa's play, in the epic, Shakuntala is indifferent to it.

YAYATI ON THE THRONE
A Bikaner-style painting depicting the young Chandravamshi ruler Yayati, who ruled according to dharma and pleased all his subjects.

Yayati's Story

A tale of a father's wish for everlasting youth and a son's supreme sacrifice for his father, Yayati and Puru's story lends an insight into the Chandravamshi bloodline, from which the mighty Kauravas and Pandavas descended.

Sarmishtha, the daughter of Vishaparva, king of the Asuras, and Devayani, the daughter of Shukra, priest of the Asuras, were the best of friends.

Then one day, the two girls got into a big fight. Dressing in a hurry after a swim, Devayani put on Sarmishtha's robes by mistake. Sarmishtha took umbrage. Not content with calling Devayani a thief and her father a beggar, Sarmishtha pushed Devayani into a well and stormed off in a fit of rage.

When Devayani managed to get home, she complained to her father, making him promise to teach the Asura princess a lesson. Shukra announced his decision. "I will not perform any yagnas for the king until he apologizes on behalf of his daughter for this insult." Alarmed, Vishaparva begged him to change his mind—the yagnas were imperative to maintain the balance of power with the enemy, the Devas.

A princess punished

But Shukra would not resume the yagnas until the princess had been punished. "Make the princess serve my daughter as her maid. Only then will I return to the sacrificial hall," he proclaimed. Left with no choice, the king made his daughter serve Devayani as her lady-in-waiting. Sarmishtha's humiliation would, however, turn out to be a blessing in disguise.

Devayani had been rescued from the well by Yayati, a Chandravamshi king. While helping her out, he had held her hand. Having done so, tradition demanded that he marry her. So Devayani married Yayati and went with him to his kingdom as his wife. Eager to further humiliate Sarmishtha, Devayani asked her maid to accompany her.

One day, Yayati noticed his wife's maid. Unlike Devayani, who was a priest's daughter, Sarmishtha was a princess, and had the spirit to match. Deeply in love, the two were married in secret.

Devayani suspected nothing until one day she heard Sarmishtha's son refer to Yayati as his father. Realizing that she had been deceived by her husband and her maid, the enraged Devayani left Yayati's palace and went back to her father. At her request, Shukra cursed his son-in-law with old age and impotence. But it soon became clear that Devayani, wife to an old and weak Yayati, was the one to suffer the most.

A curse modified

Shukra could not undo his curse, but he modified it. "You can regain your youth," he said, "if one of your sons accepts the curse, and hence, old age and impotency on your behalf." Yayati immediately sent for his sons. Yadu, the older, refused outright. Dejected, Yayati then turned to Puru, his younger son. Without any hesitation, Puru accepted the curse, suffering old age while his father regained his youth and virility.

Years later, realizing the transient nature of youth, Yayati released Puru from the curse. He declared Puru his heir, even though he was the younger of his sons. Yadu, on the other hand, was cursed. "Because you did not help your father, you will never be a king, and neither will your descendants."

As Yayati's heir, Puru became patriarch of the illustrious Kuru clan. From him descended the Kauravas and Pandavas.

> "Having **received Puru's youth, Yayati** ... was delighted and indulged in **pleasures**—as **he desired**."
>
> SAGE VAISHAMPAYANA TO JANAMEJAYA, ADI PARVA: THE BOOK OF THE BEGINNING

KEY CONCEPT

THE YAYATI COMPLEX

Austrian psychoanalyst Sigmund Freud proposed the theory of the Oedipus complex. Based on the Greek mythological character Oedipus, this theory is drawn from a son's need to compete with the father for his mother's affections. Gaining precedence over the father, the son is consequently consumed by guilt. However, Indian scholars such as AK Ramanujan and Sudhir Kakkar find the Oedipus complex inadequate in the Indian context, where sons tend to submit to their fathers' demands and are revered for doing so.

The Indian scholars ascribe to the theory of the Yayati complex, in which a father demands and extracts a sacrifice from the son. Motivated by the Yayati complex, the older generation dominates society and the Indian world view. This explains the stranglehold of tradition over modernity in Indian society.

A 19TH-CENTURY PAINTING OF OEDIPUS

Madhavi's Forgiveness

Despite being unapologetically bartered by her father, Madhavi forgave him. Her tale gives valuable insight into the importance of forgiveness—a recurring theme in the Mahabharata.

An ancestor of the Kuru clan, King Yayati was approached by the sage Galava, who was seeking eight hundred white horses, each marked with one black ear. He wanted to present them as a gift to his teacher, Vishwamitra, to show his respect.

A daughter for barter

Yayati did not have the horses, but did not want to turn away the sage empty-handed, so he offered Galava his daughter, Madhavi, instead. Madhavi was destined to give birth to four kings. "Present her to four men who wish to father kings, and ask for two hundred horses in exchange," suggested Yayati.

Galava left the palace with Madhavi and offered her in exchange for two hundred horses to kings across the world. Three kings accepted his offer; they had sons by Madhavi, and gave two hundred white horses to the sage in exchange.

Unable to find the fourth king, Galava went back to Vishwamitra and presented him with six hundred horses to fulfil his wish. He then offered Madhavi to him as the equivalent for the remaining two hundred horses.

Vishwamitra accepted the horses as well as Madhavi, and fathered a son by her. Having given birth to four sons, Madhavi was returned to her father. However, when Yayati proposed that she should now marry, Madhavi refused. She chose to become an ascetic instead.

Ascent to heaven

Years later, Yayati passed on the crown to his son Puru. Renouncing his throne and worldly pleasures, Yayati went to Swarga. However, his time in paradise did not last long, and the gods cast him out.

PEOPLE

VISHWAMITRA

One of the more powerful sages, Vishwamitra's story is part of both the Ramayana and the Mahabharata. The Mahabharata speaks of his seduction at the hands of the beautiful Apsara Menaka, while in the Ramayana, he is depicted as the Chandravamsi king of the kingdom of Kanyakubja. He was known for his bad temper and as someone who used his yogic powers to curse anyone who angered him.

THE POWERFUL SAGE VISHWAMITRA

DEVOTION IN KIND
An 18th-century painting from Rajasthan, India, depicting a woman making an offering to an ascetic.

ANALYSIS

ASCETICISM

Madhavi's story is one of many tales in the Mahabharata that illustrates the idea of asceticism as a means to rid oneself of worldly ties and attachment.

Despite being traded like a commodity by her father, Madhavi was able to let go of anger and bitterness. She retired to the forest, taking up asceticism and shedding her rage over time. She forgave her father and helped him ascend to heaven.

The recurring themes of renunciation and asceticism, however, do not always translate to rising above attachments. Even after passing on the crown to their progeny and renouncing the kingdom, the Pandavas were unable to shed their hatred.

When he demanded an explanation, the gods told him that he had exhausted all his merits.

Yayati descended to earth to find himself in a forest where his daughter Madhavi was meditating. Seeing her father's sorry state, a compassionate Madhavi went to her sons, who were now great kings. She requested them to part with a quarter of their merits and give them to their grandfather.

Lesson in forgiveness

Outraged at the suggestion, Madhavi's sons refused at first. "He bartered you away and reaped the benefits in exchange. Why do you want us to give our merits to a man who treated you like a commodity?" they questioned their mother.

A serene Madhavi replied, "You should give him your merits because he is my father and you are my sons." She explained that nothing could undo the past or what her father had done to her. Her years of meditation had made her realize the futility of anger. She expounded on the power of forgiveness.

Madhavi's sons learned an important lesson and they did as their mother requested. Letting go of their rage, the kings gave a portion of their merits to their grandfather.

A bearer of merit once again, Yayati expressed his gratitude to his daughter and returned to the paradise of the gods.

Madhavi's lesson on the value of forgiveness was forgotten over the years. Neither the Kauravas nor the Pandavas remembered it. They held on to their anger and grievances, something that cost them dearly.

AN EXPENSIVE GIFT
Considered to be symbols of power and wealth, horses were often used as a means of payment in ancient times.

BEFORE

In both his lives, Shantanu, great-grandfather of the Kuru clan, suffered the consequences of a curse on him by the gods.

SHANTANU AS MAHABHISHA

In his previous birth Shantantu was the honorable Mahabhisha. For his good deeds Mahabhisha was allowed to enter Swarga, where he enjoyed the company of the Apsaras, the music of the Gandharvas, and the dance of the Devas. He was also offered Sura (wine of the gods), and he saw the enchanted cow Kamadhenu and the Chintamani, a gem which could fulfill any wish.

One day, the river goddess Ganga visited Amravati, Indra's court in the heavens. A slight breeze ruffled her garments, exposing her upper body. The gods averted their gaze out of respect, but a spellbound Mahabhisha kept staring at her. Ganga, too, enjoyed his attention. Angry at such a blatant display of lust, Indra ordered them to return to earth and told Ganga that she could return to Swarga only after breaking Mahabhisha's heart.

STUNNED BY BEAUTY
This Indonesian-style painting captures the fateful moment when Shantanu saw the beautiful Ganga on the banks of a river.

Shantanu and Ganga's Marriage

When Shantanu proposed marriage to Ganga, it was a love preordained and a pact based on a promise. The river goddess had laid down her own set of conditions before accepting the Kuru king's proposal.

When his children were mature enough to manage the kingdom, Pratipa, a descendant of Puru and the king of Hastinapur, decided to renounce the world and the throne. His eldest son, Devapi, was a noble and popular heir and first in line to the crown. But Devapi suffered from a skin disease and, according to an ancient law, any person with a physical defect could not be king. So Shantanu, the younger son, was crowned. Not wanting to live in the shadow of his brother, Devapi decided to leave the kingdom to live the life of a mendicant.

One day, while Pratipa was meditating on a river bank, Ganga approached him and sat on his right lap. "You sat on my right lap, which means that you wish to be my daughter. If you had chosen my left lap to sit on, it would have meant you wished to be my wife. What do you want from me?" he asked.

"Your son—I want to marry him," said Ganga.

"So it shall be," said Pratipa. A few days later, when Shantanu visited his father, Pratipa said to him, "One day, a lovely and alluring woman will ask you to be her husband. Make her your wife, that is my wish."

Later, as Shantanu wandered the river bank, he saw Ganga gliding by on a dolphin. Dazzled by her beauty, he fell in love with her instantly. "Be my wife," he said to her. "Yes!" said Ganga without a moment's hesitation, "but only if you promise never to question me or my actions."

Shantanu, bound by his solemn oath to his father and his deep love for Ganga, promised to never question her. Ganga followed him home, happy to find a husband who had agreed to her conditions and was intent on fulfilling her wishes.

SHIVA AND GANGA
A folio from an 18th-century manuscript shows Ganga's descent from heaven. Many consider her Shiva's wife and portray her as seated on his head.

> "O king! As long as you act in the way I have asked you to, **I will be with you**. But I will certainly **leave you** whenever you try to **stop me or speak to me harshly**."
>
> GANGA TO SHANTANU, ADI PARVA: THE BOOK OF THE BEGINNING

MYTHOLOGY AND FOLKLORE

RIVER GODDESSES

In Hindu mythology, river goddesses and nymphs personify the importance of water bodies. There are ten river goddesses mentioned in the texts: Apam Napat, Apaha, Apah, Dewi Danu, Ganga, Makara, Samundra, Varuna, Yamuna, and Tapti. The twin goddesses, Ganga and Yamuna, are often mentioned together. Ganga is visualized riding a dolphin, while Yamuna is depicted as mounted on a turtle.

River Ganga is extremely important in Hindu culture. It is believed that bathing in the Ganga can wash away sins and help people attain moksha.

THE PURA ULUN DANU BRATAN TEMPLE IN BALI DEDICATED TO THE RIVER GODDESS DEWI DANU

AFTER

The condition Ganga laid down for her marriage to Shantanu was much more complicated than a mere whim.

GANGA'S CHILDREN

Ganga was not only subjected to Indra's curse but also had to fulfill a promise she had made to the Vasus, gods who had been cursed to be reborn as mortals. A combination of these events compelled her to treat her children in a way no mother would—she had to drown all of them.

The **Eighth Child**

Devavrata was to have been drowned at birth by his mother Ganga, just as his seven brothers before him. But his father Shantanu's emotional pleas stopped her—an action that altered Devavrata's and Hastinapur's destiny forever.

BEFORE

Vashishtha, the great sage, cursed the Vasus, the eight attendant deities of Indra.

VASHISHTHA'S CURSE
One day, as the celestial Vasus roamed the earth with their wives, they found themselves in a forest. One of the wives saw Vashishtha's cow grazing and was struck by its beauty. When she insisted on taking it with them, her husband Prabhasa, with the help of his seven brothers, stole the cow. On discovering the theft, the enraged sage cursed the immortal brothers to be born as mortals.

RIVER GANGA
A river that flows through two countries in South Asia—India and Bangladesh—Ganga is considered sacred. Her waters, it is believed, can purify the human soul. In the epic, Ganga is personified as a beautiful river goddess.

Shantanu, the prince of Hastinapur, had agreed to marry the woman his father asked him to—one he would meet on the banks of the Ganga river.

As prophesied, one day, while strolling along the banks of the river, he saw Ganga riding a dolphin. In that very instant he fell in love with her. When he asked her to marry him, the ethereal Ganga replied, "I will, but you must promise to never question my actions." He agreed to her condition.

Ganga drowns her children

Soon, Ganga gave birth to their first son. But before Shantanu could celebrate, she took the child away and drowned him in the river. A horrified Shantanu could only look on silently, bound by his promise and the fear of losing his beloved wife. A year later, Ganga gave birth to a second son. She drowned him, too, and then the third as well. In this way seven sons were born and drowned as soon as they drew breath. Each time their father held back, saying nothing.

But on the birth of their eighth child, Shantanu could no longer keep silent. As Ganga took the child to the river, he cried out, "Stop, you heartless woman!"

A promise unfulfilled

Ganga stopped and smiled, "My king, you have broken your promise to me," she said. "And so, just as Urvashi once left your ancestor Pururava, it is time for me to leave you."

She went on to tell Shantanu about her own promise to the Vasus, "The children I killed were none other than the eight gods known as Vasus. Cursed to be reborn as mortals, the distraught Vasus had requested me to become their mother and make their stay on earth brief as possible. Alas, I could not save the last one. This child you have saved—the eighth Vasu—will live. But what a terrible life he shall have! For he will neither marry nor inherit your throne. He will have no family, yet will be obliged to live as a householder. And finally, he will die at the hands of a man who will actually be a woman."

Aghast, Shantanu said, "I will not let that happen!"

"Shantanu, you may be a king, but even you cannot change what is preordained," said Ganga, before disappearing with her son.

> "You may be king. But you cannot **change** the **destiny** of a human being. I shall take your son and raise him as a **perfect warrior**."
>
> GANGA TO SHANTANU, ADI PARVA: THE BOOK OF THE BEGINNING

Devavrata returns

The eighth son was named Devavrata. And as Ganga promised, he was trained by the martial sage Parashurama to be a skilled warrior. When he came of age and was ready to marry and assume the throne, Ganga sent him back to Hastinapur. The people loved Devavrata and looked forward to seeing him as king. But destiny had other plans.

MYTHOLOGY AND FOLKLORE

MEDEA

MEDEA BEFORE SHE KILLED HER CHILDREN

The motif of a mother killing her children is also seen in the Greek myth of Medea. She was a sorceress and the wife of Jason. When he left her for Glauce, the princess of Corinth, Medea punished him by killing their children. However, Ganga's motive for killing her children was more altruistic—to release them from a curse.

AFTER

Shantanu saw in his son, Devavrata, an able and beloved king in the making.

A PEACEFUL REIGN

Peace and prosperity marked Shantanu's rule, and his subjects expected this stability to continue when Devavrata, his son and heir, returned to the kingdom. But Shantanu fell in love again, and his son's decision and sense of duty would change their kingdom's future.

A Terrible **Vow**

To fulfil his father's desire, the young Devavrata did the unimaginable—he took a vow that not only gave him a new name, but also altered the future of his clan.

When Devavrata came of age, Ganga sent him back to his father, Shantanu. He was now a handsome prince, skilled in the art of warfare and matters of state.

In the years since Ganga had left with Devavrata, King Shantanu had fallen in love again—this time with a fisherwoman named Satyavati. Longing to make her his wife, Shantanu asked Satyavati to marry him.

Like Ganga before her, Satyavati, too, had a precondition to accepting Shantanu's proposal. She wanted to make sure that only her children would inherit the throne. Torn between duty and desire, Shantanu did not know how to meet this condition without being unfair to his heir, Devavrata, the crown prince of Hastinapur.

On learning the cause of his father's unhappiness, Devavrata met Satyavati to persuade her to marry his father. He promised to renounce his claim to the throne. Though impressed, Satyavati's father, chief of the fisherfolk, still had his doubts. "But what if your children fight with my daughter's children for their right to the throne?" he argued. Devavrata smiled at the chief and his daughter and made a decision that would change the course of the Kuru dynasty.

"I shall never marry. Neither will I ever be with a woman. And never shall I father a child," Devavrata declared, stunning the whole cosmos with his vow.

Impressed with the severity of this oath, the gods showered him with flowers and named him Bhishma—the one who takes the most terrible of vows.

As a repercussion of his vow, Bhishma would be doomed to live forever in the land of the dead—for he would father no child who could facilitate his rebirth. The Devas felt so sorry for him that they granted him a gift—the power to choose the time of his own death.

AN UNFLINCHING OATH
A Madhubani painting from Bihar, India, showing Devavrata taking the vow of celibacy in front of Satyavati. Impressed with his decision, the Devas shower him with flowers.

"From today, I take the **vow of bramhacharya**. Even if I die **without a son** I will attain the eternal **world of heaven**."

DEVAVRATA TO SATYAVATI'S FATHER, ADI PARVA: THE BOOK OF THE BEGINNING

THE AMBITIOUS QUEEN

Satyavati

"Having seen her **beauty** and **sweetness**, equal to that of a goddess, and inhaled her **fragrance**, King Shantanu desired the lady from the **fishermen tribe**."

SAGE VAISHAMPAYANA TO KING JANAMEJAYA, ADI PARVA: THE BOOK OF THE BEGINNING

Satyavati was the great-grandmother of the Kuru princes, and also the mother of Veda Vyasa, credited to be the author of the Mahabharata itself. Her overriding ambition to be the queen mother of a great dynasty, and her strategies to realize her dreams led to consequences that several Kuru generations had to bear.

The fisherwoman

The story of Satyavati's birth is like an elaborate fable. King Uparichara, while on a hunting expedition, thought of his wife and ejected semen. Not wanting to waste it, he wrapped it up and gave it to a parrot to carry to his wife so that she could bear him a child. On its way, the parrot dropped the packet in a river, where it was eaten by a fish. A fisherman caught this fish and found a boy and a girl inside its belly. The king later accepted the boy, but he left the girl to be raised by the chief of the fisherfolk. Although she was named Satyavati, she was teasingly called Matsyagandha, as she reeked of fish.

As she grew up, Satyavati ferried people across the Ganga river. One day, as she was taking Sage Parasara across the river, he expressed his desire to make love to her and have a child by her. Satyavati, however, was afraid of the consequences of such an act. Drawing a curtain of mist over the ferry, the sage assured Satyavati, "I will make sure that you have a child instantly and retain your virginity. You will exude a fragrance so wonderful that men will find you irresistible." Before she reached the shore, Satyavati had become a mother, regained her virginity, and turned into a sweet-smelling woman. Their child was named Krishna Dwaipayana, who eventually came to be known as Veda Vyasa.

The queen

It was Matsyagandha's new fragrance that got her the attention of King Shantanu of Hastinapuri, who fell desperately in love with her. But Satyavati laid down a condition before accepting his offer of marriage—she wanted to be sure that only her children would be his heirs. For the sake of his father's happiness, Devavrata, Shantanu's son with Ganga, renounced the throne and vowed to never have children who may challenge Satyavati's heirs. This unprecedented sacrifice earned Devavrata the name Bhishma—the one who took the most terrible of vows.

In due course, Satyavati had two sons—Chitrangada and Vichitravirya. Shantanu died soon after, leaving his wife and sons in the care of Bhishma. Satyavati wanted her sons to grow up fast and marry

SCULPTURE REPRESENTING SATYAVATI
Satyavati was known for her beauty and voluptuous body, markers of classical Indian beauty. This fiber statue of a woman tries to capture that idea of Indian beauty.

ANALYSIS

THE SPURNED DAUGHTER

Satyavati showed a single-minded dedication toward becoming a queen and the matriarch of a great dynasty. Her need for status and power could have been born out of the childhood insecurity of having been abandoned by her biological father, who gave her away to fisherfolk, preferring to keep her brother—perhaps a harsh lesson in rejection for the little girl. Satyavati's disregard for the consequences of her actions led to the ruin of many lives. To honor Satyavati's condition and help his father marry her, Shantanu's son, Devavrata, gave up his claim to the throne. Even then, Satyavati did not stop him from embracing celibacy and childlessness. This was an unthinkable sacrifice at a time when sons were considered essential for ensuring a dead man's passage to the next life. Nor did she care that the daughters-in-law she required for her unsuitable, possibly impotent, son would have to be abducted. She even made them sleep with a man, the unattractive ascetic Vyasa, against their will. All of this was done to ensure the birth of grandsons who would rule her kingdom.

so that they could produce children, for she was determined to be the mother of a great line of kings. Unfortunately, Chitrangada died in a duel, and Vichitravirya turned out to be a weakling who could not find a wife for himself. Bhishma abducted the princesses of Kashi for Vichitravirya, but he died before fathering any children.

The Kuru matriarch

Satyavati's dream of being the mother of kings was shattered. Desperate, she went to Bhishma and asked him to get her widowed daughters-in-law pregnant. But Bhishma refused to break his vow of celibacy. Then, Satyavati turned to her firstborn, Vyasa, for help. He agreed, but pointed out that he had lived as an ascetic and looked frightening with his matted hair and coarse skin. But Satyavati was impatient, and said "I cannot wait any longer. Go now, as you are. The queens will welcome you."

Vyasa fathered Dhritarashtra with Ambika and Pandu with Ambalika. By law, these two princes were considered the children of Vichitravirya. However, Satyavati's ambitions of becoming a queen mother were once again foiled—Dhritarashtra was born blind and Pandu was a pale weakling.

Satyavati lived to see dissension and falling out within the clan she had worked so hard to create. The sons of Dhritarashtra and Pandu never got along, their rivalry for the throne turning into bitter enmity. When the royal teacher Drona organized a public ceremony to present the skills of the Kuru princes, Satyavati was forced to watch the Pandavas and Kauravas feud bitterly in public. She decided she could no longer witness the decline of her family. Accompanied by her daughters-in-law Ambika and Ambalika, she retired to the forest and eventually died there.

BIOGRAPHY IN BRIEF

- **Born** to King Uparichara, Satyavati, along with her twin brother, was conceived inside the belly of a fish.
- **Brought up by** the chief of the fishermen community when her own father rejected her.
- **Growing up**, she ferried travelers across the Ganga river. She was called Matsyagandha as she smelled of fish.
- **Gave birth to Vyasa** after succumbing to Sage Parasara's desire to make love to her, with the proviso that she would have her baby instantly as well as recover her virginity.
- **Received a blessing** from Sage Parasara that she would become so fragrant that she would be alluring to all men.
- **Wooed by king Shantanu**, Satyavati said she would agree to marry him on the condition that only her children would accede to the throne. To enable this, Shantanu's firstborn Bhishma gave up his claim to the throne.
- **Married** Shantanu and gave birth to sons Chitrangada and Vichitravirya. Chitrangada died early.
- **Asked Bhishma to procure wives** for Vichitravirya. He abducted the three Kashi princesses: Amba, Ambika, and Ambalika.
- **After Vichitravirya died childless**, Satyavati made her eldest son Vyasa live with Ambika and Ambalika. Her grandsons, Dhritarashtra and Pandu were born from this union.
- **Her great-grandchildren**, the Pandavas and Kauravas, turned into bitter foes.
- **Decided to leave the palace** on witnessing a public fight between the Pandavas and Kauravas. She retreated to the forest with her daughters-in-law Ambika and Ambalika.
- **Died** in the forest.

BHISHMA'S VOW
A 1907 painting by Raja Ravi Varma shows Bhishma promising the fisherfolk chief that he would never marry or father a child.

BEFORE

Satyavati's determination to be the matriarch of a powerful line of kings led her to take desperate and sometimes brutal steps with far-reaching consequences.

SATYAVATI'S CHILDREN

Satyavati's stepson Bhishma's vow of celibacy, taken to ensure that Satyavati's progeny would inherit Shantanu's kingdom, resulted in his spurning his betrothed, the sister of the king of Kashi. Out of Satyavati's two sons from Shantanu, Chitrangada died in a duel—unmarried—and the other, Vichitravirya, was considered a weakling, possibly impotent. Bhishma, on Satyavati's insistence, took upon the task of finding Vichitravirya a wife.

HISTORY AND CULTURE

SWAYAMVARA

A SCENE FROM A RAMLILA PERFORMANCE IN MUMBAI, INDIA, SHOWS SITA CHOOSING RAMA DURING HER SWAYAMVARA.

A swayamvara was an ancient Indian marriage practice in which a woman was allowed to choose her husband from a gathering of men. In both the Mahabharata and Ramayana, Draupadi and Sita meet their future husbands in a swayamvara. The event is also mentioned in pre-Islamic Iran in the *Shahnama* of Firdausi—Kitayun, the eldest daughter of the emperor of Constantinople (present-day Istanbul), selects the Iranian Gushtasp from an assembly of able men.

The Three Princesses

The king of Kashi had organized a swayamvara so his three daughters could select a husband from among the many guests invited. No invitation was sent to Vichitravirya or Bhishma.

According to some, the king of Kashi's refusal to invite Vichitravirya to the swayamvara was because it was well known that he was unfit to be a husband. Others felt that it was a deliberate act to humiliate Bhishma who had not, while taking the vow of celibacy, taken into account the consequences it would have on the woman to whom he was engaged—the sister of the king of Kashi. Taking serious umbrage at not being invited, Bhishma decided to abduct the three princesses for Vichitravirya. He rode into Kashi and carried out his bold plan.

Amba's plight

Amba, the eldest daughter of the king of Kashi, begged that she be released as she wanted to marry King Shalva, and had planned to select him as her groom at the swayamvara. "You already have two wives. Why do you need another?" she reasoned. Both Vichitravirya and Bhishma agreed to let her go to the man she loved. Shalva, however, refused to marry her as she had already been claimed by another. "How can I accept a woman who was abducted and then returned to me as charity; especially the one who was supposed to be my queen?" he asked.

Amba returned to Vichitravirya but he was too proud to take her back. Not knowing what to do, Amba went to Bhishma. "You should take responsibility as it was you who took us on your chariot. This makes you, not your half-brother, our true husband," she insisted. Amba asked him to marry her but Bhishma dismissed her, telling her of his vow. She was furious. "You have left me helpless. Now I am nobody's wife. What gave you the right to abduct me if your vow prevented you from marrying?" she fumed.

Determined to avenge her humiliation, Amba sought a warrior who would stand up for her. All the warriors she met feared Bhishma, whose fame as a warrior was known far and wide. They refused to help Amba, saying that Bhishma was invincible. A desperate Amba approached the warrior-sage Parashurama, who was Bhishma's teacher. Deeply distressed by her story, Parashurama challenged Bhishma to a duel. But their terrible battle went on for days until, finally, Parashurama gave up. "Since Bhishma is impossible to kill, this fight has to stop. If it continues, both of us will release weapons that will destroy the world," he said.

Bhishma's nemesis

Amba then took a vow. She would not eat or sleep until the Devas told her how to kill

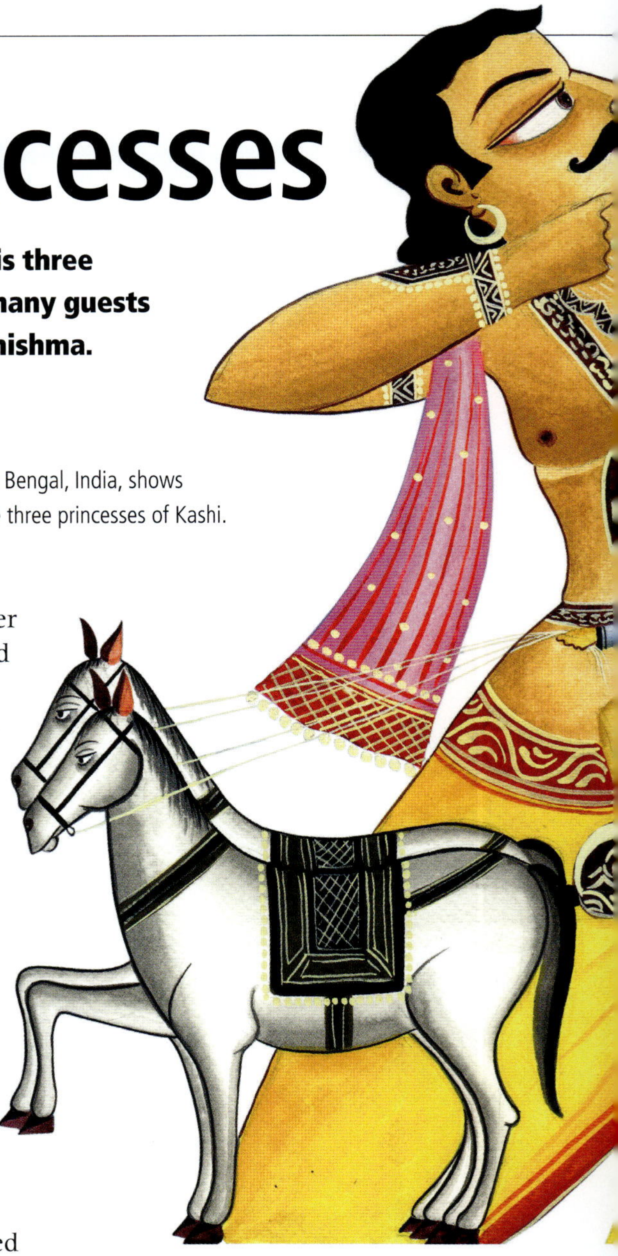

THE ABDUCTION

A Kalighat-style painting from Bengal, India, shows Bhishma drivng away with the three princesses of Kashi.

> "I have earlier **chosen** the king of Soubha as my husband … **decide** what the **course of dharma** entails."
>
> AMBA, THE PRINCESS OF KASHI TO BHISHMA, ADI PARVA: THE BOOK OF THE BEGINNING

AFTER

After Vichitravirya's death, Satyavati begged Bhishma to have children with her widowed daughters-in-law, but he refused to break his vow of celibacy.

VICHITRAVIRYA'S CHILDREN
Satyavati then called upon her son Veda Vyasa, from Sage Parasara, to impregnate Amba and Ambalika. In her hurry to set her plan in motion, she ignored Vyasa's request for time to prepare and sent the wild-looking ascetic to her daughters-in-law. Frightened by him, the princesses gave birth to afflicted children—the blind Dhritarashtra and the weakling Pandu. A third child, Vidura, was born of a maid sent by Ambika to take her place the second time.

Bhishma. She meditated for days, finally compelling Shiva to appear before her. The god told her that she would be the cause of Bhishma's death in her next life. To hasten Bhishma's downfall, Amba killed herself by jumping into a fiery pit. She was then reborn as Shikhandi in the household of Drupada, the king of Panchala. Shikhandi was born a woman but Drupada raised her to be a man. The oracles had prophesied that, later in life, she would acquire a man's body, as she was destined to be the cause of Bhishma's death.

Shikhandi's participation in the Kurukshetra War was based on his possessing a man's body. But Bhishma's belief that Shikhandi was born a woman made him lower his weapons in the battle, giving his opponents an advantage they were quick to exploit.

Satyavati's shattered dreams

Amba's sisters, Ambika and Ambalika, married Vichitravirya. Unfortunately, he died childless soon after. Despite all Satyavati's efforts, the direct bloodline of the Kuru clan came to an end.

GENDER AMBIGUITY
Hindu gods may sometimes be portrayed as transgender; Durga here is Ardhanarishvara—half-male, half-female—a composite of Shiva and Parvati. Shikhandi's half-woman, half-man persona would later result in Bhishma's death.

AN ESSENTIAL RITE OF PASSAGE

Marriage

"O beautiful one! I am **full of desire** for you and so are you. You should become my **wife** according to the **gandharva form of marriage**."

DUSHYANTA TO SHAKUNTALA, ADI PARVA: THE BOOK OF THE BEGINNING

THE SACRED KNOT
The bride and bridegroom are ritually tied together, the knot symbolic of their everlasting commitment to each other.

The Mahabharata highlights many complex issues relating to matrimonial forms and practices prevalent in ancient India. Some marriages were based on mutual love, others were alliances arranged for political benefit. A wife could be won in a contest of martial skill, or kidnapped at a contest's venue by the potential groom or his family. A woman could select a husband at a gathering of eligible hopefuls in a swayamvara, but she could also be given away by her father without any right to protest. Not all marriages gave the wife the same status, either. Non-Aryan wives, for instance, do not really feature as part of the main narrative. Even the children of such marriages are less important than their Aryan half-brothers.

MARRIAGE IN VEDIC LITERATURE

Vedic law approved of a man's marriage to women who were equal or lower in terms of social position. Marriage and married life was prescribed as one of the four stages of life. It was a duty, an obligation—the one way to have a child, a son, to facilitate the re-entry of forefathers to the land of the living. Only sons of the lawfully wedded wife could perform the rites of passage, not those born of concubines or of other unions. If a man was unable to father children, or died childless, his wife could go to other men, with the permission of her husband or his family. Children of such a union belonged to the husband. A woman was restricted to three men with whom she could live in order to conceive a son for her husband. So, including the husband, a woman could be with up to four men in her life; any more implied she was of a loose moral character.

WEDDING CEREMONY
In India, marriage rituals are still performed according to ancient Vedic rites, with the wedding solemnized after the couple have walked around the sacred fire seven times.

ALLIANCES AND SOCIAL STATUS

Marriage was also important as a strong basis for political alliances. When Krishna and Balarama evacuated the Yadavas from Mathura after the devastation wrecked upon the city by Jarasandha's army, they went west, eventually arriving at the island of Dwaraka. Balarama's marriage to the local princess, Revati, gained the Yadavas rights over the island. Krishna further secured this new island home by marrying the daughters of surrounding kingdoms' rulers. Roaming homeless after the burning of the lac palace, the Pandavas had no power until Draupadi entered their lives. It was with the powerful Drupada as their father-in-law that the Kauravas acquired the stature to negotiate. "Now you can return to Hastinapur and reveal that you are alive," Krishna told Kunti. "They will dare not harm you again, for your sons are married to the daughter of the mighty Drupada. They will go out of their way to make peace with you." The extended relationships that marriage created with the woman's family were just as important and played a prominent role in family politics at every stage of the narrative. The war at Kurukshetra, the series of events that led up to it, the skirmishes that took place and, therefore, the outcome, were all heavily influenced by relatives by marriage. For example, Shakuni, the maternal uncle of the Kauravas, and Krishna, Kunti's sister's son, was the Pandavas' maternal cousin.

KAMADEVA AND RATI
Kamadeva, the Hindu god of love, shoots flower arrows with a sugar-cane bow. Rati was his wife and constant companion.

LIST

TYPES OF UNIONS

Of the eight ways in which Vedic literature specifies a man and woman can come together, only the first five are sanctioned by the scriptures. The last three are not considered righteous.

- The way of Prajapati, the father of all creatures: When a woman is given away as charity to help a needy man.
- The way of Brahma, the Creator who is entrapped by his own creation—When a bride is accepted more for her dowry than for herself.
- The way of the Devas: When a daughter is given as a fee for services rendered to the father.
- The way of the Rishi: When a daughter is given for ritual purposes.
- The way of the Gandharvas: When a woman chooses her husband freely.
- The way of the Asuras (subterranean dwellers): When a woman is purchased.
- The way of the Rakshasas (barbarians): When a woman is abducted.
- The way of the Pisachas (vampires): When a woman is violated.

PANDAVAS AND DRAUPADI
Although each of the five Pandavas was also married to other women, Draupadi was their shared wife in the polyandrous marriage. Here, the Pandavas and Draupadi are portrayed in the Bharatnatyam dance form.

POLYGAMY AND POLYANDRY

For a man to have more than one wife appeared to have been the norm for much of the history of Hindu India. Krishna was married to many women, as was his brother Balarama. The sisters Amba, Ambika, and Ambalika were abducted by Bhishma as wives for his half-brother Vichitravirya. Kunti and Madri were both married to Pandu. Besides Draupadi, each Pandava also had other wives. Vyasa mentions Arjuna's marriages to Ulupi, Chitrangada, and Subhadra. Multiple marriages for men were not only acceptable, but expected.

On the other hand, though the epic has many instances of women exhibiting sexual freedom, it is uncomfortable with polyandry. That Draupadi had five husbands, for example, required explanation and justification. Thus, the Pandavas became incarnations of the god Indra, and Draupadi his wife, Shri—not polyandrous at all.

LOVE MATCHES

Right from the story of Pururava and the Apsara Urvashi, the Mahabharata is full of instances of marriages based on love. Both Ulupi and Chitrangada fell in love with Arjuna, the latter without ever having seen him. Ulupi proposed marriage, even quoted the scriptures to overcome resistance from Arjuna Meanwhile Chitrangada, the great warrior woman, changed herself into a coy young girl to attract Arjuna, only to find he loved—and wanted to marry—her true self. Attracted by Bhima's strength and power, Hidimbi convinced Kunti to accept her as a daughter-in-law. However, because a marriage created alliances between families, even a "love" marriage had wider political implications. Undoubtedly, Krishna was aware of this when he encouraged his sister Subhadra's runaway marriage to Arjuna and, later, that of his niece, Vatsala, with Arjuna's son Abhimanyu.

The **Birth** of Dhritarashtra and Pandu

Bhishma was the last true Kuru, and Satyavati knew that his oath of celibacy had put the continuance of the Kuru bloodline in peril. Determined to remedy this situation, the matriarch set yet another plan in motion.

BEFORE

On Satyavati's insistence, Bhishma decided to find a bride for his stepbrother, Vichitravirya.

SATYAVATI'S DAUGHTERS-IN-LAW
Bhishma abducted the three princesses of Kashi—Amba, Ambika, and Ambalika—to be Vichitravirya's wives. Amba, who was in love with another man, begged to be sent back and both Bhishma and Vichitravirya agreed to her request. However, when she was rejected by her beloved, she vowed to take revenge on Bhishma, blaming him for her pitiable condition. Vichitravirya died without siring children and Satyavati's plans came to nothing.

VEDA VYASA
Krishna Dwaipayana, or Vyasa, is the storyteller of the Mahabharata. He is also said to have fathered Dhritarashtra, Pandu, and Vidura.

An anxious Satyavati went to Bhishma to beseech him to save the Kuru lineage. "By the law of niyoga, outlined in the books of dharma, any children that my daughters-in-law bear will belong to their deceased husbands. I ask of you to do what my sons could not," Satyavati said to him.

But Bhishma remained unmoved. He said, "The law may be so, Mother. My vow shall remain. I will not break it, not even for you, for whom I took this vow."

> "The **perpetuation** of Shantanu's **dharma**, the **lineage** and **fame** of the **Kuru dynasty** … is now vested in you."
>
> SATYAVATI TO BHISHMA, ADI PARVA: THE BOOK OF THE BEGINNING

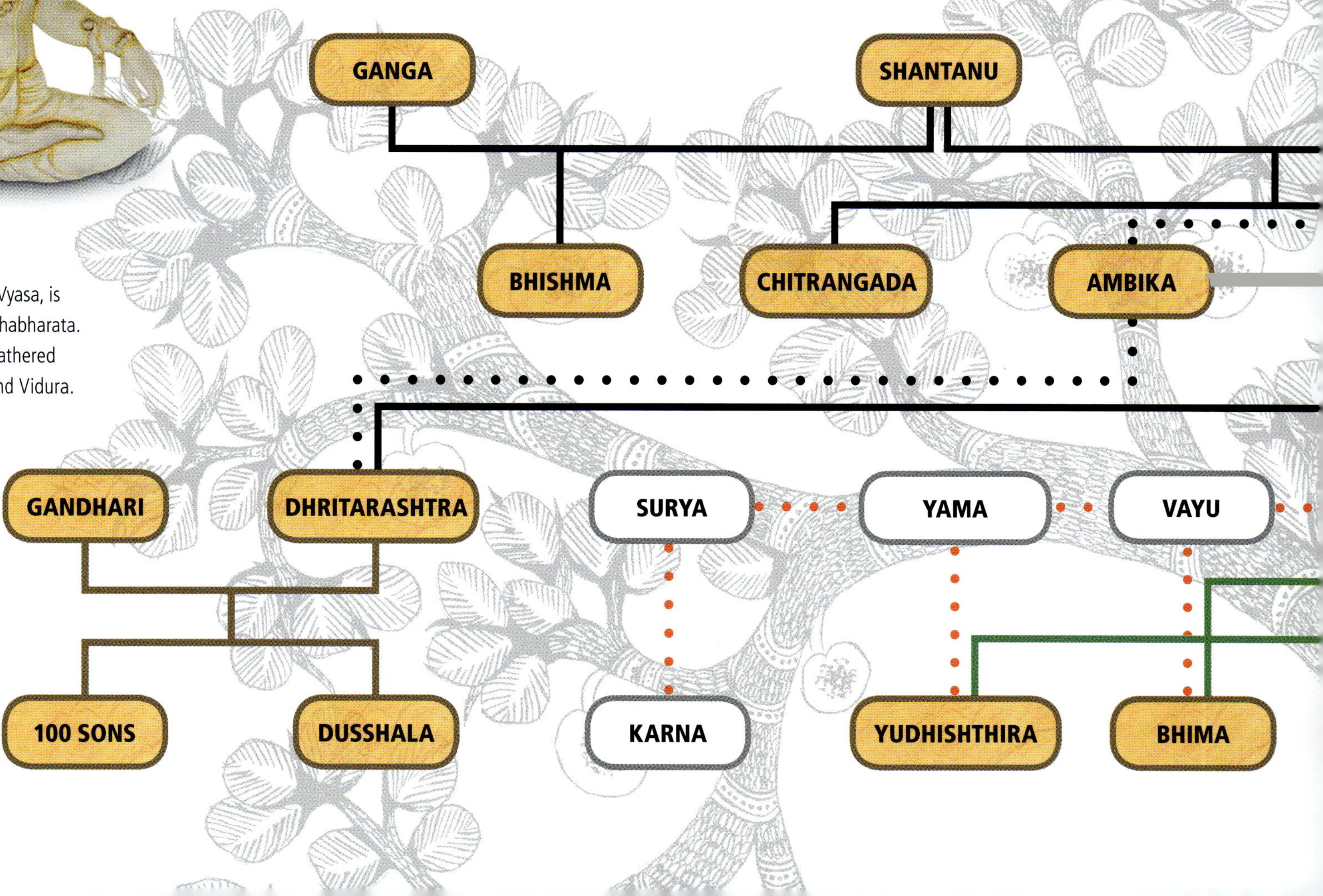

Satyavati's determination
Desperate, Satyavati thought of her first son, Krishna Dwaipayana, and sent for him. Also known as Vyasa, Dwaipayana lived with his father, Sage Parasara. "Make my son's wives pregnant," Satyavati ordered her son.

Vyasa replied, "If you wish so." But having lived a rough life in the forest, Vyasa wanted some time to make himself worthy of the royal princesses. He said, "Give me a year to prepare. I have lived in the forest as an ascetic for fourteen years. My hair is dry and matted, my skin coarse and rough, and my gaunt features will scare away the princesses."

Not one for patience, the matriarch testily commanded, "I cannot wait. Go as you are. They will welcome you."

Vyasa first went to Ambika. She was so repulsed by his looks that she shut her eyes when he touched her. The child born of this union was blind, and was named Dhritarashtra. Next, Vyasa went to Ambalika. His ghastly appearance evoked such fear in her that she turned ashen. The child conceived from this union, called Pandu, was pale and weak. Disappointed by her less than perfect heirs, Satyavati instructed Vyasa to go to Ambika again. This time, however, he met Ambika's maid on the bed, not the princess. The two made love fearlessly, thus creating a child who would be healthy and wise. This child was named Vidura. Though he was fit to be a king in every sense, his maternal lineage would never allow him to wear the crown.

VIDURA'S CURSE

Once, a group of thieves took refuge in the hermitage of Sage Mandavya. The king's guards later accused the sage of aiding the thieves, and as punishment tortured and impaled him. After his death, he asked Yama, the lord of death, the reason for his suffering, for he had hurt no living being in his life. Yama replied, "As a child, you used to impale tiny insects on a straw with delight. The suffering you faced was repayment of that karmic debt." Mandavya protested, but a dispassionate Yama said, "Such is the law of karma." Furious, Mandavya cursed Yama that he would be reborn as a human and suffer the fate of never being a king despite having all the qualities of the perfect ruler. And so Vidura was born.

AFTER

Dhritarashtra, Pandu, and Vidura were brought up and trained by their uncle Bhishma to be able leaders of the Kuru clan.

FUTURE KINGS
As the years went by, Bhishma raised the three as his own sons. Ironically, Bhishma, who had sworn never to beget a family of his own, was then entrapped by his father's family – a stepmother, two widowed sisters-in-law, their maid, and three nephews.

THE LAW OF NIYOGA
According to the ancient Hindu law of niyoga, a woman who is a widow or whose husband is incapable of siring a child, can appoint a man to help her bear one. In the epic, there were two instances of this – Satyavati asked her son Vyasa to impregnate the three princesses, and later, Pandu asked his wives, Kunti and Madri, to take the help of the gods to ensure his bloodline prevailed.

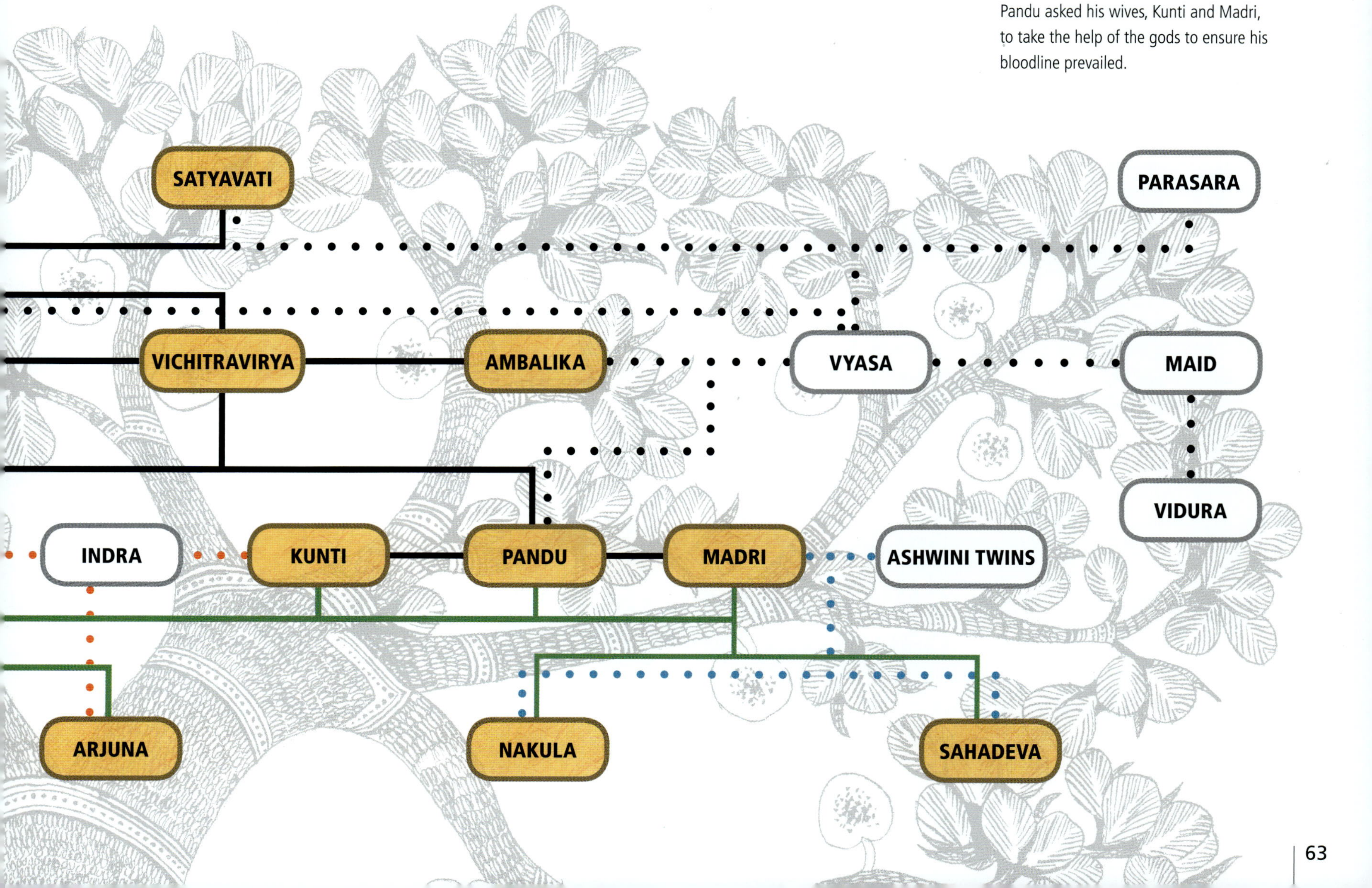

The **Wives** of **Pandu**

In time, Satyavati's grandsons grew up to become young princes and suitable wives were sought for them. Even as Kunti agreed to marry the younger prince, Pandu, a second wife was also purchased for him.

BEFORE

The prosperous city of Mathura, south of Hastinapur on the banks of the Yamuna river, was ruled by the Yadava council.

KUNTI IS ADOPTED

Surasena, a member of the Yadava council, had a beautiful daughter named Pritha. He had promised his firstborn to his father's sister's son, Kuntibhoja, who had no child of his own. Honoring his promise, Surasena gave his daughter, Pritha, to Kuntibhoja, who renamed her Kunti. She was appointed to honor and serve the guests who visited her adoptive father's house.

HISTORY AND CULTURE

THE KINGDOM OF MADRA

The kingdom of Madra was grouped with the western kingdoms. Madra's capital was Sagala, modern-day Sialkot in the Punjab province of Pakistan.

The Madra culture was different from the prevailing Vedic culture. In Madra women were given more liberty, Brahmins exercised less influence on the society, and rituals were not as rigorously practiced. For these reasons, the Kurus and Panchalas considered the people of Madra to be inferior.

IQBAL SQUARE IN SIALKOT, PAKISTAN, WHERE THE ANCIENT CITY OF SAGALA WAS SITUATED

Kuntibhoja's daughter was beautiful, virtuous, and devoted to dharma, all of which were qualities fit for a princess.

When Kunti was of marriageable age, her father arranged a swayamwara so she could choose a husband. As custom dictated, kings from across the world were invited to participate in the event.

Kunti chooses Pandu

Many kings from far and wide attended the swayamvara, but Kunti found the handsome king of Hastinapur, Pandu, a suitable match. Kuntibhoja was more than happy to approve of her choice, as this alliance with a Kuru descendant would give his kingdom great pestige and make it even more powerful.

Pandu marries again

Soon after his marriage to Kunti, Pandu went on an expedition to the kingdom of Madra with his grand-uncle, Bhishma. There he was to take another wife. Perhaps it was due to his inability to father a child with Kunti that Madri, the princess of Madra and sister of its ruler, Shalya, was purchased to be his second wife. Madri was known for her exceptional beauty.

It was a common practice for men to have more than one wife for the sake of progeny. In cases where the first wife was not able to bear a child for a period of time, a second and younger wife was often seen as a means to ensure the survival of the legacy of a royal house. It is even thought that rumors of Kunti's premarital liaison had stained her reputation, and could have been yet another reason for Pandu to look for a second wife.

AN INCOMPARABLE BEAUTY

Most representations of Madri depict her as an alluring, voluptuous woman, much like this dancer carved on a 17th-century ivory plaque from Tamil Nadu, India.

Expanding the kingdom

After his marriage to Madri, Pandu traveled to the four corners of the earth to wage wars against other kingdoms.

With every expedition, the young king tasted success, expanding his empire and spreading the fame of the Kuru clan. The vanquished kings paid tribute to the great warrior and showered him with riches. A victorious Pandu returned to Hastinapur to be welcomed with great joy and festivities.

PANDU WITH HIS FIRST WIFE

A 20th-century watercolor from Jammu and Kashmir, India, showing Pandu with his wife Kunti.

> "Blessed with unlimited good fortune, **Kuru's descendant and Kuntibhoja's daughter** were married ... Thereafter, with Devavrata Bhishma, he went to the **capital city of the Madra kingdom**."
>
> SAGE VAISHAMPAYANA TO KING JANAMEJAYA, ADI PARVA: THE BOOK OF THE BEGINNING

"Madri ... was **famous in the three worlds** and among all the kings for **her beauty**, which was **unmatched on earth**."

SAGE VAISHAMPAYANA TO KING JANAMEJAYA, ADI PARVA: THE BOOK OF THE BEGINNING

MYTHOLOGY AND FOLKLORE

BHIL BHARATA

In the Bhil Bharata narrated by the Doongri Bhils of Gujarat, India, the story of Kunti and Gandhari's birth is quite different. It refers to seven sages who sat deep in meditation. Word about the sages' intense concentration spread far and wide, eventually reaching the ears of the gods. Shiva and his consort, Shakti, were intrigued. They took the form of eagles and went to see them.

As the pair of eagles flew over the sages, they were buffeted by strong winds. Carried by the winds, the female eagle was impaled on the trident of the sages. Oblivious, they remained engrossed in their meditation. When they finally opened their eyes, the sages were overwhelmed with sorrow. They decided to use their powers to bring it back to life. From the flesh emerged Kunti, who would marry Pandu; and from its skeleton was born Gandhari, who would marry Dhritarashtra.

SHIVA AND SHAKTI TOOK THE FORM OF EAGLES TO VISIT THE SAGES

AFTER

Following his victories, Pandu's fame as the king of Hastinapur grew far and wide.

RETURN OF THE KING
On his return, Pandu's elder brother, Dhritarashtra, commanded him to offer his riches and earnings to the elders. Pandu offered his wealth to Bhishma, Satyavati, Ambika, and Ambalika.

His only regret was that he was not able to have any children. To vent his frustration, he would often go on hunts. The thought of dying childless, like his father, troubled Pandu incessantly.

BEFORE

Although Bhishma vowed not to marry, he took it upon himself to do all he could to ensure the continuity of his dynasty.

THE KURU LINEAGE
Bhishma was the last of the true Kurus. His nephews, Dhritarashtra and Pandu, were considered the sons of Vichitravirya through the law of niyoga. Because of this, they could still be the heirs to the throne of Hastinapur, ensuring that the Kuru clan continued into the next generation.

As the family elder, Bhishma took a keen interest in the upbringing of his grandnephews. So, when Dhritarashtra and Pandu came of age, Bhishma decided to find suitable wives for both of them.

PLAYING THE PART
A still from Peter Brook's 1989 film *The Mahabharata*, showing the royal couple, Dhritarashtra and Gandhari.

ANALYSIS

BLINDNESS

In the epic, blindness serves as a metaphor. Dhritarashtra's blindness is literal, caused by his mother's failure to look into Vyasa's eyes when he came to meet her. On the other hand, Gandhari chose to blind herself, to share the life her husband lived.
But both Gandhari and Dhritarashtra are metaphorically blind, as they fail to see their children's faults, especially those of Duryodhana. Gandhari refused listen to Vidura's advice, or heed any portents of doom that accompanied Duryodhana's birth. And later, despite witnessing his sons' crude and cruel behavior of inflicting atrocities, and even inciting war, Dhritarashtra chose to remain silent and made no effort to stop them.

Dhritarashtra's Marriage to Gandhari

When the young and beautiful princess of Gandhara was chosen to marry the elder prince of Hastinapur, she did not know of his blindness. But when she found out about Dhritarashtra's affliction, Gandhari decided to blindfold herself to share her husband's suffering and fate.

At about the same time that Pandu married Kunti and Madri, Bhishma decided to get his older grandnephew married as well. For Dhritarashtra, he had in mind a partner who was not just beautiful and virtuous but also from a powerful dynasty. Suvala's daughter, the princess of Gandhara, would, he felt, be a suitable match for the blind prince.

Suvala's daughter
Bhishma had heard that the princess of Gandhara was not only fair and beautiful, but had the good fortune of having been granted a blessing by Shiva himself—she would be the mother of a hundred sons. Eager to ensure the continuity of his clan, Bhishma sent word to Suvala asking for his daughter's hand in marriage for Dhritarashtra.

Suvala, the king of Gandhara, was hesitant. He knew that the older son of the Kuru household

ANALYSIS

WHO INHERITS THE THRONE?

Throughout the epic, the poet Vyasa deliberates on the rules of inheritance. While in many cases the question of who should be king was fairly simple, it could often become complicated, as the laws of the firstborn's inheritance were stringent and unforgiving.

Should the eldest son be the king or should it be the fittest son? It was Dhritarashtra's obvious physical impediment that kept him from the throne, but no one questioned Pandu's infertility. Similarly, the question of pure bloodline haunts the epic's characters. Should a child be shunned even if he had the capabilities to be a just ruler, as in the case of Vidura and Karna, or does a pure bloodline rule supreme?

"Because of the **blindness**, Suvala **hesitated**. But taking into account the **famous lineage** and the conduct and intelligence of the Kurus, **he agreed**."

SAGE VAISHAMPAYANA TO JANAMEJAYA, ADI PARVA: THE BOOK OF THE BEGINNING

was blind. But knowing how powerful and famous the Kuru dynasty was, he agreed to the match and started preparing for the impending nuptials.

Gandhari's choice

On hearing of her future husband's blindness, Gandhari came to a decision—as a devoted wife and life partner to Dhritarashtra she would not experience more than he could. She tied a piece of cloth over her eyes, blindfolding herself to share her husband's world of darkness.

For the wedding ceremony, Gandhari made her way to her marital home with the customary offerings and riches. In keeping with tradition, Shakuni, her brother, the prince of Gandhara, went along with her.

GANDHARI WOMEN
Gandhara's geographical location can be identified as northeast Afghanistan. Gandhari's beauty and physical features must have resembled that of the women native to this region.

AFTER

Gandhari became an obedient daughter-in-law and a devoted wife. It was only a matter of time before she bore the blind prince's children.

DHRITARASHTRA'S HEIR

Though the eldest son, Dhritarashtra was forbidden from sitting on the throne because of his disability. This decision deeply wounded the blind prince, but he never voiced his protest, for he was well versed in the quirks of law.

Now that he had a young wife, he knew what he needed to do to reclaim what should have been his by right. At night, in bed, the prince whispered to his new bride, "We should make a son quickly, Gandhari, before Pandu makes one, so that we can prevent him from claiming what should rightfully be mine."

THE POWERFUL KINGDOM

Gandhara

GANDHARA
The kingdom of Gandhara is believed to have been located in present-day northwest Pakistan and northeast Afghanistan.

"Shakuni, the **king of Gandhara**, followed him, surrounded in every direction by **mountainous people** from the region of Gandhara."

SANJAY TO DHRITARASHTRA, BHISHMA PARVA: THE BOOK OF BHISHMA

Two key characters in the epic hail from Gandhara—Gandhari and Shakuni. Dhritarashtra's wife and the Kauravas' mother, Gandhari was the daughter of Suvala, the king of Gandhara. Her brother Shakuni, the prince of Gandhara, lived in the court of Hastinapura as a counselor to his nephew Duryodhana. In the Kurukshetra War the Gandhara army was, naturally, allied to the Kauravas. After the war and Yudhishthira's coronation, when the Pandavas decided to perform the Ashwamedha yagna to annex territories and extend the empire, Arjuna defeated Shakuni's son to conquer Gandhara.

The region of Gandhara
Described in the epic as a hilly western region, Gandhara is said to correspond to the historical kingdom of Gandhara, located to the west of the Indus river, in present-day northwest Pakistan and northeast Afghanistan, extending across the Swat valley and Pothohar plateau regions. The main cities

TAXILA
Excavations at Sirkap, Taxila, in Pakistan, part of the UNESCO World Heritage list, have unearthed remains of an ancient civilization.

MOSAIC OF ALEXANDER THE GREAT A Roman mosaic of King Alexander the Great at the Battle of Issus in 333 BCE can be seen in Pompeii, Italy. Alexander invaded the kingdom of Gandhara in 327 BCE.

of the kingdom were the famous Takshashila (Taxila), Purushapura (modern-day Peshawar in Pakistan), and Pushkalavati (modern Charsada, northeast of Peshawar). Taxila, with one the earliest universities in the world, was a great Buddhist center of learning. Students came here from as far as Kashi (Varanasi, India) and Magadha (modern-day Bihar, India). The city also lay at the crossroads of some major trading routes between Central Asia and South Asia.

Historical references

The Rig Veda (circa 1500 BCE) mentions the Gandhari people, who are likely to have been a tribe. The earliest historical references to Gandhara date to the 6th century BCE, when the Persian king Darius I (circa 556 BCE) added it to the Achaemenid Empire. around 327 BCE, Alexander the Great invaded Gandhara as he marched toward India, leaving behind a Greek population and lasting influences.

In 305 BCE, Chandragupta Maurya of Magadha won the region from Alexander's general Seleucus Nicator. The most celebrated king of the Maurya dynasty, Ashoka (268–232 BCE), spread Buddhism in the region and established the famous Dharmarajika Monastery at Taxila. With the decline of the Mauryas, the Greeks from the Bactrian region established their control (184 BCE), followed by the Scythians (110 BCE) and Parthians (early 1st century CE).

The golden period

The Kushans established their rule with Peshawar as the seat of power. Their reign was at its peak under Emperor Kanishka (128–151 CE) who was a patron of Buddhism. The period between the 1st and 3rd centuries CE was also the high point of the Gandhara civilization, when art, culture, and architecture thrived. It was a period of superlative sculpture, stupas, and monasteries. In 500 CE, the Huns took over and Buddhism declined.

Decline and discovery

When Mahmud Ghazni invaded the kingdom repeatedly in 1001 CE, he rang its death knell. Its cities and monuments were destroyed, and the region languished in obscurity.

British orientalists rediscovered these ancient glories. In 1848, noted archaeologist Alexander Cunningham found Gandhara sculptures near Peshawar in Pakistan, and identified the site of Taxila in the 1860s. John Marshall, who started excavations at Taxila, discovered many cities and monasteries. Excavations in the area continue to this day.

HISTORY AND CULTURE

GANDHARA ART

Gandhara art flourished between the 1st and 3rd centuries CE. This region had absorbed strong Greek influences from the time of Alexander the Great as well as from the Greco-Bactrian rule and the subsequent influx of the Bactrian people.

In the 1st century CE, Parthian and Roman merchants brought the art of their lands to the region, while Buddhist missionaries contributed their ideas.

The result was a style characterized by strong influences from the Hellenistic world but exhibiting Buddhist devotion. These were some of the earliest anthropomorphic representations of the Buddha. The Buddha images, inspired by the sculptural styles of Hellenistic Greece, were realistic and sophisticated and are still highly celebrated.

A GREY SCHIST SCULPTURE OF BUDDHA FROM GANDHARA, PAKISTAN

BEFORE

Kunti had been given a mantra by sage Durvasa that would enable her to summon any god and have a child with him.

KUNTI'S BLESSING

In youthful curiosity and unmindful of the consequences, the young, unmarried Kunti had tried the mantra and invoked the sun god, Surya. She bore his child but, to save her reputation, abandoned him. Kunti's firstborn would go on to fight her other sons in the Kurukshetra War.

When Kunti was of marriageable age, a swayamvara was organized in which, from among the guests, she chose Pandu—Satyavati's grandson and the prince of Hastinapur—as her husband.

The Birth of Kunti's Children

Though he had won fame and fortune, Pandu, the king of Hastinapur, remained childless. Seeing his growing anxiety, Kunti offered her husband a solution.

Frustrated at his inability to father a child with either Kunti or Madri, Pandu wondered if he was destined to die childless. One day, while on a hunt, his arrow struck an antelope mating with a doe. On closer inspection, the pair turned out to be Sage Kindama and his wife, who had used their powers to turn themselves into animals so that they could be intimate out in the open. In the throes of death, the sage cursed Pandu, "You, who have so violently stopped me from making love to my wife, may you never know the pleasure of lovemaking! You will die the instant you touch a woman!"

Since Pandu could no longer be a proper husband to his wives, or father a child, he left his kingdom in the care of his older brother, and went off to live as a hermit. Both of his wives, Kunti and Madri, gave up the palace to go with him, because it was a wife's dharma to support her husband regardless of circumstance.

"Since I am myself **incapable of procreation**, I will ask you to obtain sons through **my equals or betters**."

PANDU TO KUNTI, ADI PARVA: THE BOOK OF THE BEGINNING

ANALYSIS

PANDU'S "WEAKNESS"

There is reasonable evidence in the Mahabharata to conclude that Pandu was impotent, or at least sterile. The name "Pandu" means pale and yellowish—a description that fits a weak man. Also, although the epic does not clarify this, it may have been that Pandu's second wife, Madri, was purchased for him because of his inability to father a child with Kunti. There is proof of his first wife's fertility—she already had a child, although born in secret. Clearly she was not the reason for their childlessness.

VAYU, THE GOD OF THE WINDS
Though Vedic gods such as Vayu feature in the Mahabharata, the text gives prominence to Puranic gods such as Shiva and Vishnu.

Pandu's grief

After a few months, the news that Dhritarashtra's wife Gandhari was pregnant reached Pandu and filled him with despair. Fate had lost Pandu his throne, and he was not destined to sire future kings. His brother's lineage now seemed firmly established. Consoling him, Kunti judged that time had come to reveal the secret of the blessing she had received, as it would enable them to have children. However, unsure of his reaction, she prepared him by laying out the groundwork of the existing paternity laws.

Kunti's solution

She started by telling Pandu how, in days gone by, women had been free to live with any man they liked. This was allowed because procreation was of prime importance, and sons were essential to facilitate the re-entry of forefathers into the land of the living. When Sage Shvetaketu saw his mother with other men, and realized how unperturbed his father Uddalaka was, he introduced the laws of monogamy and paternity, decreeing that women could only have children by their husband. This enabled all men to know their fathers. However, if a man was incapable of having children, he could allow his wife to be with other men. Children born of these unions would be considered the husband's offspring.

Pandu was convinced by Kunti's argument and, with new hope, decided to ask a sage to come to his wives. Kunti then told him of the mantra Sage Durvasa had given her. "Why call sages when I can call Devas?" she asked her husband.

Pleased with this solution, Pandu said,"Can you call Yama, the lord of dharma, who is the model for all kings?"

Kunti's children

Kunti used the mantra and had a child with Yama. This child, Pandu's firstborn, was named Yudhishthira and would grow up to be the most honest of men. Next, Pandu asked Kunti to call Vayu, the god of the winds. Vayu and Kunti's son was Bhima, the strongest of men. Kunti then invoked Indra, the king of the gods and ruler of the sky. With him she had Arjuna, who would become the best archer in the world. As she had chosen Indra of her own volition, and not because her husband had asked her to, she was particularly fond of Arjuna who was often called Partha—the son of Pritha, Kunti's given name at birth.

THE ELDEST PANDAVA
This painting in Kerala mural style from south India depicts Yudhishthira's birth. The infant Yudhishthira is in his mother Kunti's arms as his father, Yama, the god of dharma, looks on.

LORD INDRA
One of the four gods invoked by Kunti, Indra—the king of the gods—was the father of Arjuna. This copper statue of Indra from Nepal is dated from the medieval period, c. 1200. It is displayed at the Philadelphia Museum of Art.

AFTER

Keen to have more children, Pandu requested Kunti to invoke more gods, but she refused.

KUNTI'S DILEMMA
After the birth of Arjuna, Pandu asked Kunti to call another Deva so that she may have another son, but she refused. "The law of dharma doesn't allow me to do so," Kunti said. She then went on to tell him of the law that stated that a woman was allowed to be with only three men if her husband could not give her a child. If a woman slept with more than four men, her husband included, society could consider her promiscuous and call her a whore. Pandu thought the four men Kunti referred to were the three gods (Yama, Vayu, and Indra) and himself. Kunti, however, was referring to those three gods who had given her three sons after marriage, and the one god who had given her a son before marriage—a secret that she shared with no one.

BEFORE

Pandu's despair over his inability to father children made Kunti share the secret of her blessing with him.

KUNTI'S CHILDREN
Her blessing, a gift from Sage Durvasa, gave Kunti the ability to invoke gods to impregnate her. With Pandu's consent and blessings, Kunti invoked Yama, Vayu, and Indra, and gave birth to three sons: Yudhishthira, Bhima, and Arjuna. She refused to invoke more gods despite Pandu's insistence, as she did not want to be called promiscuous; someone who had consorted with more than the four men allowed by the laws of dharma.

The **Birth** of **Madri's Twins**

Thrilled to finally have three sons by Kunti, Pandu asked his first wife to use her blessing to help Madri have children of her own. This would also provide him with more heirs.

Pandu was very pleased that his wife Kunti had three sons who would grow up as heirs to the kingdom of Hastinapur. His desire for more children, however, and his urge to be fair to his second wife, Madri, who had accompanied them to the forest, led him to ask Kunti to invoke a deity for Madri. "Since the law of dharma does not allow you to go to more than four men, call a Deva for Madri. This way, she can be a mother too, and I will be the father of more sons," he said.

Kunti obeyed and asked Madri, "Whom shall I call?"

"The Ashwini twins," answered Madri.

The twins
The two gods, lords of the morning and evening star, instantly appeared and gave Madri twin sons—Nakula, who would be the most handsome of men, and Sahadeva, who would be knowledgeable in the world. Pandu was eager for Madri to bear more children. "Invoke one more Deva so that Madri can have more sons," he told Kunti.

Kunti's insecurity
Uncomfortable with the situation, Kunti refused to obey her husband. Madri had cleverly called twin gods and become the mother of two sons. Kunti feared that, given another chance, Madri

"Your co-wife **doesn't** have children either. Let the **right** offspring **also be fathered** on her."

PANDU TO KUNTI, ADI PARVA: THE BOOK OF THE BEGINNING

HISTORY AND CULTURE

DIVINE TWINS

Twins hold an interesting place in many cultures—they are either considered auspicious or ominous. In Greek and Roman mythology, Castor and Pollux, or Polydeuces, are twin brothers, together known as the Dioskouroi, similar to the Ashwini twins. The Ashwini, or Ashwini Kumaras, in Hindu mythology are two Vedic gods. In the Rig Veda, they are depicted as the divine twin horsemen, sons of Saranyu who was a goddess of the clouds and wife of Surya in his form as Vivasvant. Symbolizing the shining quality of sunrise and sunset, they appear in the sky before dawn in a golden chariot, bringing treasures to men and preventing misfortune and sickness. Depcited as humans with the heads of horses, they are the doctors of the gods and are Devas of Ayurvedic medicine.

STATUES OF CASTOR AND POLLUX, ROME, ITALY

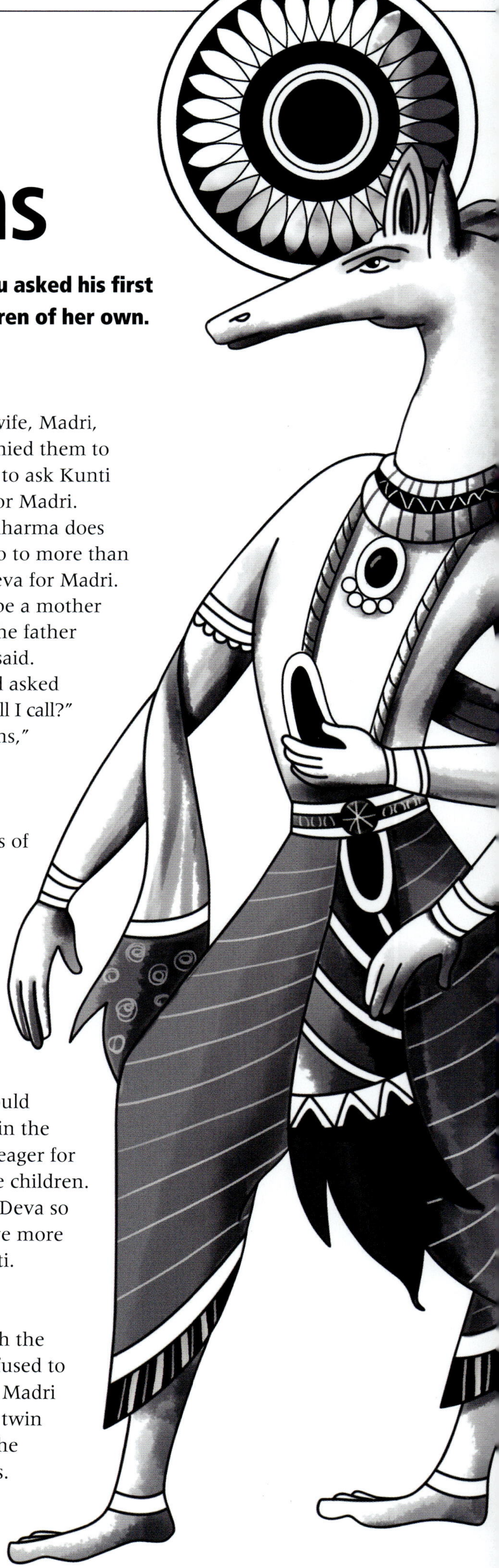

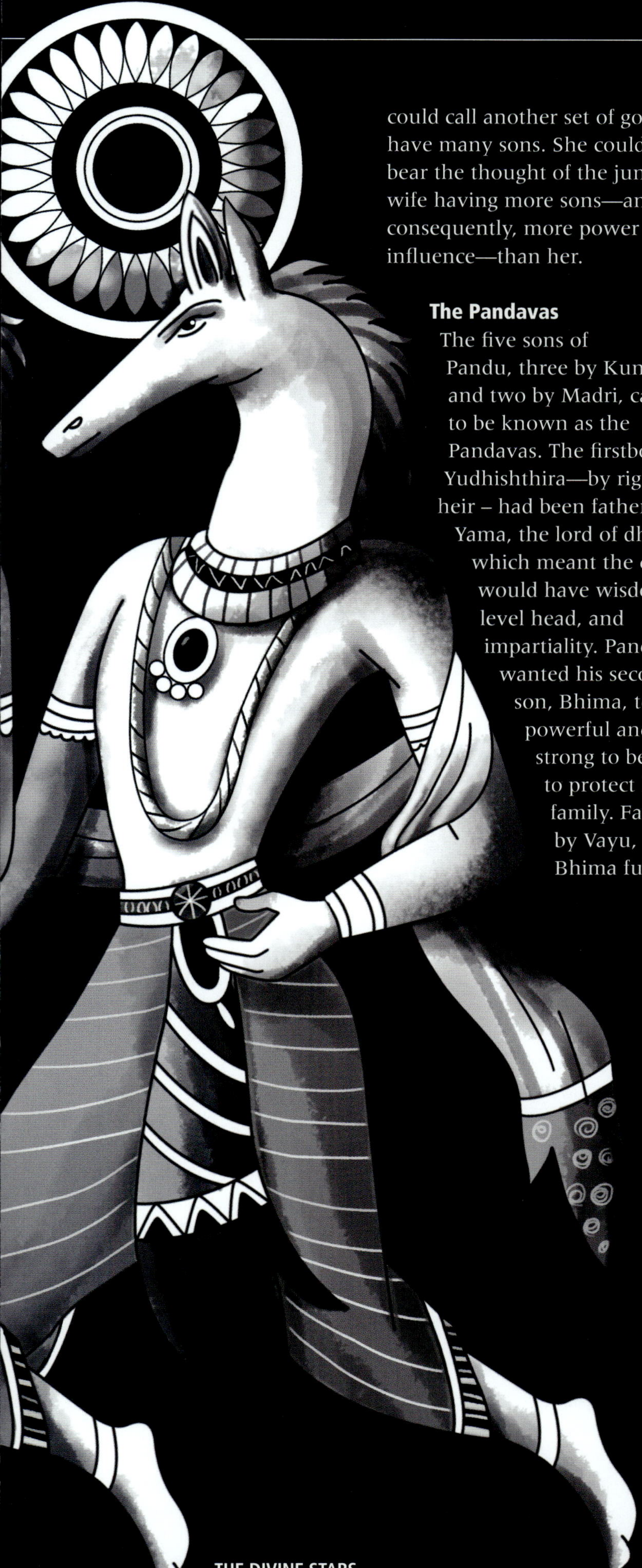

could call another set of gods and have many sons. She could not bear the thought of the junior wife having more sons—and, consequently, more power and influence—than her.

The Pandavas

The five sons of Pandu, three by Kunti, and two by Madri, came to be known as the Pandavas. The firstborn, Yudhishthira—by right his heir – had been fathered by Yama, the lord of dharma, which meant the child would have wisdom, a level head, and impartiality. Pandu wanted his second son, Bhima, to be powerful and strong to be able to protect his family. Fathered by Vayu, Bhima fulfilled all those qualities. The third child would have to be a conqueror, a great warrior of extreme valor, yet humane; one who could be as merciful as he could be harsh. Arjuna, born from Indra, the lord of heavens, was blessed with these powers.

With three elder brothers armed with all the skills to protect the kingdom, the twins, Nakula and Sahadeva, would see to the nation's prosperity. They would have healing powers, and be well versed in science, arts, economy, administration, and finance. The Ashwini twins blessed their sons with these powers.

Pandu's dreams and ambitions had been fulfilled. With Yudhishthira's honesty, Bhima's strength, Arjuna's skill, Nakula's beauty, and Sahadeva's wisdom, his five sons collectively had the qualities required of one perfect king.

NAKULA AND SAHADEVA
These statues of Nakula and Sahadeva are from the Vishnu temple, in Deogarh, Uttar Pradesh, India. Built around 500 CE, the temple showcases the ornate sculptural style of the early Gupta period.

> "Think of some **god** once and through him you will certainly **obtain a son** who will be **like him.**"
>
> KUNTI TO MADRI, ADI PARVA: THE BOOK OF THE BEGINNING

THE DIVINE STARS
The Ashwinis are divine twins who are usually represented as humans with horse heads. They are the morning and evening stars, and are believed to prevent bad luck and ill health.

AFTER

Pandu had reconciled himself to his hermitlike existence despite the presence of two beautiful wives.

LIVING A CURSE
Pandu settled into a happy life in the forest with his wives Kunti and Madri, and their five children. It was a peaceful existence in the company of many sages. Pandu was, however, a young man and missed being intimate with his two wives. Sage Kindama's curse meant that in order to survive, he had to be celibate and abstain from acting upon his desire to make love to either of his wives.

BEFORE

Kunti used Sage Durvasa's blessing and bore three sons for Pandu.

THE BIRTH OF KUNTI'S CHILDREN
After Pandu abdicated the throne, the crown was passed on to his brother Dhritarashtra, whose wife, Gandhari, conceived soon after. The news depressed Pandu, as fate had not only taken the crown from him, but Gandhari's pregnancy ensured that he would not even sire heirs to the throne. Then Kunti decided to use her blessing, which allowed her to summon any god and bear his child instantly. She had three sons by the gods and the news soon reached the palace.

The **Birth** of the **Kauravas**

Frustrated that Kunti had become a mother before her, Gandhari took matters into her own hands—she would force the child out of her womb.

Gandhari was furious when she learned that Kunti had given birth before her. Though she had conceived before her sister-in-law, her pregnancy continued for more than two years.

A desperate measure

Impatient, Gandhari decided to force the child out of her. She ordered her maids to strike her belly with an iron bar. The maids hesitated, but Gandhari was adamant. Reluctantly, they obeyed her, striking their queen on the belly repeatedly. "Hit harder," cried Gandhari after each blow. Finally, her womb trembled and heaved, expelling a ball of flesh as cold as the iron bar she had used to beat it out of her. The queen asked anxiously, "Is the baby crying? Is it a boy or a girl?" With great trepidation, the maids told her that she had delivered a lifeless form. Gandhari was beside herself and wailed inconsolably.

Vyasa's instruction

However, she soon pulled herself together and summoned Sage Vyasa. "You promised me that I would be mother of a hundred sons. All I delivered was a ball of quivering flesh. Where are my sons?" she demanded. Feeling sorry for her, Vyasa instructed Gandhari's maid to divide the ball of flesh into a hundred pieces and place each in a jar filled with ghee. He promised Gandhari that the flesh would incubate for a year and then transform into sons.

A hundred and one children

Relieved, Gandhari then asked if she could have a daughter as well. To fulfil her wish, the sage asked the maid to divide the ball of flesh into a hundred and one pieces instead. A year later, the first pot was broken and a child emerged from it. Gandhari named him Duryodhana. From each subsequent pot emerged a son, until she reached the hundred and first pot. From this was born the desired daughter, who was named Dusshala. The hundred sons would be known as the Kauravas. There was another son, Yuyutsu, born of a

THE BLIND MOTHER
In this still from the play *101 Lullabies* staged in 2012, an actor plays Gandhari, who, having taken a vow to live blindfolded, did not remove it even to see her newborn children.

ANALYSIS

A HUNDRED CHILDREN

The birth of Gandhari's children has been a topic of interest and research for many scholars. It is often speculated whether the miraculous birth of the Kauravas was the result of occult secrets known to ancient sages. They may have had the power to transform the remains of a miscarriage into live children by incubating them. Or, perhaps the birth was conceived by a poet's fertile imagination. The latter possibility rings true, as the Rishi called upon to create Gandhari's hundred children is none other than the poet of the epic, Vyasa.

EARTHEN JARS FILLED WITH GHEE WERE USED TO INCUBATE THE PIECES OF FLESH

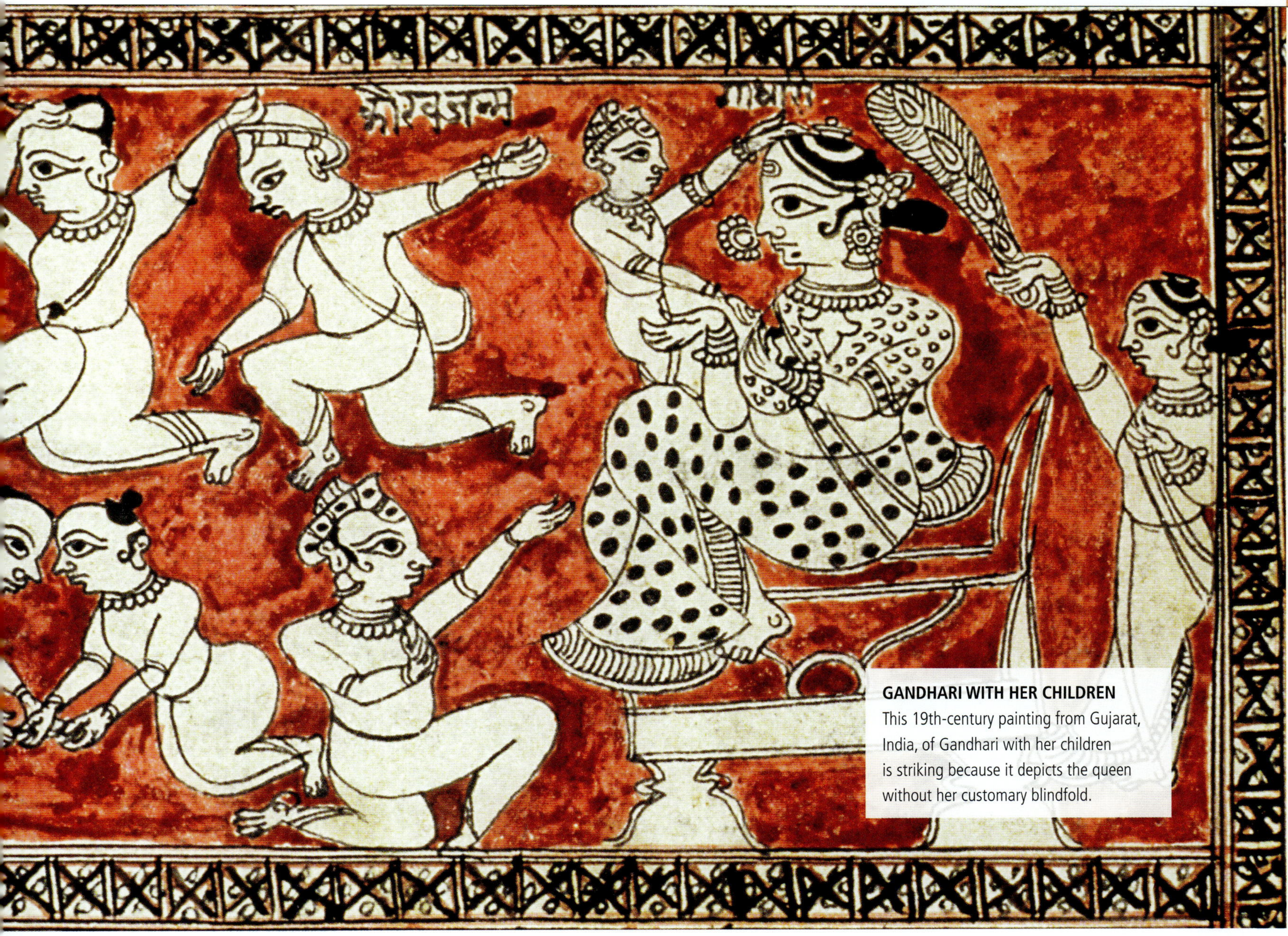

GANDHARI WITH HER CHILDREN
This 19th-century painting from Gujarat, India, of Gandhari with her children is striking because it depicts the queen without her customary blindfold.

union between Dhritarashtra and a maid during Gandhari's extended pregnancy. He was also brought up with the Kauravas.

> **"Gandhari bore the embryo for two years** without giving birth and was **overcome with grief**. Then she heard that a **son had been born to Kunti."**

SAGE VAISHAMPAYANA TO KING JANAMEJAYA, ADI PARVA: THE BOOK OF THE BEGINNING

AFTER

When Duryodhana was born, the palace resounded with the howling of dogs.

THE ELDEST KAURAVA

Vidura took note of the ominous signs, and advised his brother to get rid of the child. Gandhari, however, was not ready to let the child out of her sight. Holding the newborn close to her chest, she said firmly, "I will not allow anyone to harm my son. My firstborn is my favorite."

BEFORE

Pandu was cursed by Kindama, a sage he shot down while hunting in the forest.

KINDAMA'S CURSE

One day, while on a hunt in the forest, Pandu shot down an antelope. As he approached his kill, he realized that the antelope had been mating with a doe. To make matters worse, the antelope turned out to be the powerful sage Kindama, who had transformed both his wife and himself into animals. As he lay dying, Kindama cursed Pandu that he would never be able to enjoy the company of a woman—if he ever so much as touched a woman, he would die instantly.

SAGE KINDAMA TOOK THE FORM OF AN ANTELOPE

The **Death** of the **Cursed King**

Pandu gave up the pleasures of the palace to live as a hermit in the forest. But one day, unable to resist Madri's beauty, he gave in to passion—and Kindama's curse claimed his life.

After being cursed by Kindama, Pandu, had renounced the throne of Hastinapur and retired to the forest to live the life of a hermit. His wives, Kunti and Madri, went with him. They and their children spent their time in the company of learned men and sages leading a quiet, peaceful life.

Mindful by the curse, Pandu avoided intimacy with his wives. Then one day the sight of sunlight skin through the fabric draped around the body of his younger wife, Madri, undid his resolve. Pandu could not resist reaching out to her. Barely had his fingers grazed Madri, than Kindama's curse came into effect, killing him.

Madri was heartbroken. Leaving the twins, Nakula and Sahadeva, in Kunti's care, Madri jumped into her husband's burning pyre, committing Sati.

Pandu's secret

Before his death, Pandu had revealed a secret to his sons. He had told them that years of abstinence and meditation had given him great knowledge, which was deeply rooted in his body. He had asked them to eat some of his flesh after his death to imbibe that knowledge. "That is my legacy to you," he said.

However, after Pandu's cremation, the Pandavas could not do what their father had asked them to. But Sahadeva, the youngest, noticed ants carrying away a small piece of his father's flesh. Curious, he put that piece into his mouth.

HISTORY AND CULTURE

SATI

Sati is an ancient Hindu practice in which a widow threw herself on her husband's pyre in the hope that she would be reunited with him in the next life. In the nineteenth century, social pressure made Sati expected of widows, particularly those from royal houses.

The practice became the focus of many social reformers such as Raja Ram Mohan Roy and was abolished in 1829 by an Act passed by the then governor-general of Bengal, Lord William Bentinck.

AN 18TH-CENTURY PAINTING OF RAMABAI, WIFE OF MADHAV RAO I, FOURTH PESHWA OF THE MARATHA EMPIRE, ON HIS FUNERAL PYRE.

> "The king has gone to the **land of the dead** because of his **desire** for me. Therefore, my body should be **burned with the king's body**."
>
> MADRI TO KUNTI, ADI PARVA: THE BOOK OF THE BEGINNING

Instantly, he knew everything—things that had happened in the past and those that would happen in the future.

The all-knowing twin

Sahadeva rushed to Kunti and his brothers to tell them what had happened, but was stopped by a stranger who asked him, "Do you want the Supreme as your friend?"

"Yes," answered Sahadeva.

"Then never volunteer to reveal what you know to anyone. When asked a question, always reply with a question," instructed the stranger. Sahadeva realized that he was speaking to Vishnu's avatar, Krishna. He had no choice but to follow these instructions. From then on, though he knew everything, he would never be able reveal this knowledge or do anything to change the course of events.

All his life, Sahadeva waited for people to ask him the right question. He was asked many, but never the right one. In time, he came to realize that the future could be deciphered through careful observation of nature. Armed with this knowledge, he created various sciences to predict the future.

> "**Pandu**, the descendant of the **Kuru lineage** … succumbed to the law of time when **united with his wife.**"
>
> SAGE VAISHAMPAYANA TO KING JANAMEJAYA, ADI PARVA: THE BOOK OF THE BEGINNING

PASSIONATE EMBRACE
A 10th-century sculpture from Khajuraho, Madhya Pradhesh, India, of a couple locked in erotic play. Such sculptures were often inspired by stories from the ancient epics.

AFTER

Following the death of their father, the young Pandavas went to Hastinapur.

KUNTI'S RETURN TO THE PALACE
After the death of Pandu and Madri, the sages escorted Kunti and her children back to Hastinapur, where the Pandavas would be raised as princes of the royal household of the Kurus.

THE KURU CAPITAL

Hastinapur

HASTINAPUR
The ancient town of Hastinapur is located about 55 miles (90 km) northeast of Delhi, in the Meerut district of Uttar Pradesh, India.

> "Shantanu lived in Hastinapura, the **beautiful capital** of the **Kurus**."
>
> SAGE VAISHAMPAYANA TO JANAMEJAYA, ADI PARVA: THE BOOK OF THE BEGINNING

Hastinapur was the capital of the Kuru kingdom. The key events in the Mahabharata either took place in the city or were triggered by the power struggle for its throne. The name "Hastinapur" may have come from Hastin, a little-known ancestor of the Pandavas. Some say that Hastin was another name for Puru. Scholars also speculate that the word "Hastinapur," which means "the city of elephants," suggests that in the time of the Mahabharata, herds of elephants roamed in and around what is now Punjab and Haryana.

In the Mahabharata

Hastinapur is first mentioned in the Mahabharata by King Pratipa, a descendant of King Puru (See pp. 50–51). Beginning with Pratipa's children, Hastinapur was faced with a recurrening question—who would be the next king? Would his claim be based on ability or bloodline? It was the dispute over Hastinapur that was the main reason behind the Kurukshetra War.

In mythology and history

In Jain chronicles, Hastinapur is described as an ancient city built by the gods themselves. Three of the twenty-four great Tirthankaras, or the gods of Jainism—Shantinath,

BALARAMA'S ANGER
This 17th-century watercolor captures an episode from the epic where Balarama, angry with Duryodhana for imprisoning Krishna's son Samba (See pp. 182–83), hooked his plow to the foundation of Hastinapur and pulled it toward the sea.

Kunthunath, and Aranath—were born in this city, giving it the status of a pilgrimage spot.

However, there is no historical record of continuous occupation of Hastinapur. Situated on an old bed of the Ganga river called Budhi Ganga, in Uttar Pradesh, this small town was mentioned in the ancient scriptures as the capital of the ancestor of the Pandavas and the Kauravas, Emperor Bharata, after whom India's official name—Bharat—is derived. Present-day Hastinapur is a sacred place for both Hindus and Jains, with several Jain temples found there. On the banks of the Budhi Ganga stand the Draupadi Ghat and Karna Ghat, both named after prominent characters of the Mahabharata. The biggest pilgrim attraction is the Digambar Jain Bada Mandir, the core of which was built by Raja Harsukh Rai in 1801. It is dedicated to the sixteenth Jain Tirthankara, Shantinath. In the 1950s, Hastinapur gained prominence when excavations by the noted archaeologist B.B. Lal studied the presence of ancient pottery remains called Painted Grey Ware (PGW). He dated the PGW settlement at Hastinapur to 1100–800 BCE, coinciding with the time of the epic. However, the history of Hastinapur could not be entirely studied as the site was inhabited and excavation could only be carried out on a limited scale.

HISTORY AND CULTURE

PAINTED GREY WARE

In the early 1950s, archaeologist B.B. Lal conducted excavations in some sites mentioned in the Mahabharata. Grey pottery embellished with designs in black paint was found in all the sites and came to be called Painted Grey Ware (PGW). Lal associated these sites—Hastinapur, Kurukshetra, and Ahichhatra among them—as locations of the Mahabharata period, lending historcial fact to the tale.

Based on his findings, it was revealed that the PGW culture was centered on villages and proto-urban settlements. People cultivated rice, wheat, and barley, domesticated cattle, sheep, pigs, and horses, and lived in houses made of wattle-and-daub, mud, or bricks. There was evidence of paved streets and water channels, as well as evidence of ornaments of gold, ivory, copper, and semi-precious stones being traded in the area.

THE PAINTED GREY WARE CULTURE IS CHARACTERIZED BY FINE GREY POTTERY

DIGAMBAR JAIN TEMPLE
Built in 1801 under the auspices of Raja Harsukh Rai, the Ashtapad Jain temple at Hastinapur draws thousands of pilgrims every year.

DEFINING RELATIONSHIPS, RIGHTS, AND OBLIGATIONS

Parents, Children, and Inheritance Rights

"O Sage! A **son saves** a **father** from the **hell** known as put."

THE GODS TO SAGE MANDAPALA, ADI PARVA: THE BOOK OF THE BEGINNING

SUCCESSION
Sons were important, as it was through the male line that the lineage continued. Daughters, when they married, became part of the husband's family.

THE SEAT OF POWER
A recurring theme in the epic is the question of who is more deserving of the throne—the son of a king or someone more worthy.

It is very easy to see the Mahabharata just as a family feud over inheritance. The narrative becomes an epic only when the complexity of events and issues that culminate in the war at Kurukshetra is explored. On another level, it is the tale of what happens when the older generation sacrifices the happiness of the younger for its own pleasure; of what happens when parents choose to remain blind to the faults of their children; of the passing of karma—merits and demerits—through generations.

On yet another level, the entire telling of the Mahabharata is about inheritance—the story of his ancestors was received by Janamejaya, great-grandson of the Pandavas, as a lesson on how to live life in accordance with the rules of dharma.

FILIAL DUTY

Dharma dictates that children should honor and obey their parents. The Mahabharata is replete with instances of unquestioning obedience to parents. Puru became an infirm, impotent old man when he accepted a curse on behalf of his father, Yayati. Madhavi's sons gave up a quarter of their merits at their mother's request to help her father return to Swarga. Devavrata renounced conjugal life so that his father could remarry. The five Pandavas and Draupadi accepted Kunti's decree that her sons share what Arjuna won at the archery competition, while Arjuna's son Iravan sacrificed his life for his father, as did Ghatotkacha, Bhima's son. Such exemplary filial piety begs the question Yayati's older son, Yadu, dared to ask: "Is it not adharma to try and prevent the natural impact of time? Is it right for a father to expect his son to accept old age and senility on his behalf?" But Yadu's audacity got him disinherited and earned him a curse on his descendants.

NIYOGA, VARNA, AND INHERITANCE

The law of niyoga states that a woman's children belong to her husband regardless of biological fatherhood. This means that a man who is impotent, even one who dies childless, can still be a father. Thus, Dhritarashtra, Pandu, and Vidura became the "sons" of Vichitravirya, even though it was Vyasa who made their mothers pregnant.

However, only children of the lawfully wedded wife could be "true" sons and inheritors. Vidura, despite being more worthy, could not be king because his mother was a maid.

At the same time, according to varna dharma, a son should follow his father's vocation. The Pandavas were warriors because their niyoga father was Pandu, a Kshatriya. Since Karna did not know who his birth-mother was, he did not know who her husband was and so, could not know what vocation he should follow. All he knew was his inner calling to be a warrior. Drona, a Brahman, motivated by the love of power and wealth, picked up weapons and became a warrior, inculcating this ambition in his son, Ashwatthama, as well. Such ambition was adharma, unsuitable for Brahmans whose duty it was to teach, counsel, and protect human life.

There are other sons featured in the epic who appear to be, in some ways, of lesser importance. They did not become part of their father's family at all. These were children born of liaisons with non-Aryan women—they remained with their mothers' families, and their lives were deemed expendable. For instance, Iravan, Arjuna's son from the Naga woman Ulupi, was asked by his father to sacrifice his life to ensure victory for the Pandavas at Kurukshetra. In contrast to this demand was Arjuna's blind fury on the battlefield following the death of Abhimanyu, his son with Subhadra.

HONORING PARENTS
To honor his parents and ancestors is regarded as the foremost duty of a son—one that earns him extensive merit.

THE RIGHTFUL INHERITORS

What makes a king? Is being born into the royal family enough qualification? Should the eldest son inherit the throne or the most capable? Vyasa ponders this point throughout the epic. For Bharata, the noblest of kings, ruler of the continent of Jambudvipa, which came to be known as Bharatavarsha, the criteria for kingship rested in worthiness, not bloodlines. Later kings did not follow in Bharata's footsteps. Yayati made his younger son Puru, his successor "because he suffered for me." Dhritarashtra preferred his son Duryodhana, over his nephew Yudhishthira, even though the eldest Pandava was clearly more worthy. His own jealousy of Pandu (who became king because Dhritarashtra himself was blind) made him fan his sons' hatred of their Pandava cousins. He refused to listen to the advice of elders such as Bhishma or well-wishers such as Vidura who cautioned and advised him again and again to cede to the Pandavas' request and give them their rightful share of the kingdom.

DURYODHANA
As the eldest son of the reigning ruler, Duryodhana considered himself next in line to the throne.

YUDHISHTHIRA
From Yudhishthira's point of view, he was the heir of Pandu, the consecrated king, whereas Dhritarashtra was merely a regent.

Bhima **Poisoned**

The Kauravas did not take kindly to the idea of sharing either their heirs-apparent status or their home with the Pandavas. Bhima's constant bullying brought matters to a head, and they decided to take extreme steps.

BEFORE

After Pandu and Madri's death, the sages in the forest escorted Kunti and the Pandavas to the Kuru capital, Hastinapur.

KUNTI'S RETURN TO HASTINAPUR
Life at the palace was difficult for a widow and her children. Even though Kunti and the Pandavas were under Bhishma and Dhritarashtra's protection, cracks in the family facade started showing early. The Kauravas were worried that they would have to share their inheritance with the Pandavas. Meanwhile, the Pandavas felt that they did not have any real power in the court, and lived in the shadow of the blind king and his wife.

PEOPLE

NAGAS

IVORY STATUE OF A SNAKE WITH INLAY WORK

The Naga people of Indian lore were believed to be hooded serpents who lived in rivers and under the earth, in the realm called Rasa-tala. Said to be highly venomous, they were the guardians of gems that fulfilled wishes, cured ailments, restored fertility, granted children and good fortune—some could even resurrect the dead.

Anthropologists think that the Nagas referred to in the Mahabharata were actually agricultural communities who worshipped serpents. To this day, serpents are worshipped in many parts of India, and milk is offered to them, often symbolically, on special occasions, especially by couples who want to have children.

The seeds of rivalry between the Kauravas and the Pandavas were sown long ago when, because of Dhritarashtra's blindness, his younger brother was crowned king. The Kauravas believed their father had been wronged and that the throne of Hastinapur was rightfully theirs. The Pandavas, however, felt that their uncle was only a regent, looking after the kingdom in the absence of their father, the coronated king.

Even if one disregarded the past, the question remained: should the oldest Kuru prince, Yudhishthira, be considered the heir to the throne, or should it be Duryodhana, the eldest son of the older brother, Dhritarashtra? As both parties believed they were equally entitled to the throne, an uneasy truce was established. But soon, this gave way to overt rivalry and outright hatred.

Bhima, the bully

As the king's dependants, the Pandavas felt very insecure. The young Bhima turned to his extraordinary physical strength and prowess to establish his supremacy. He did not have the restraint and wisdom of Yudhishthira or Arjuna, and would often bully his Kaurava cousins, picking them up and throwing them on the ground, or shaking trees they had climbed till they fell down and hurt themselves.

Eventually, tired of this bullying, the angry Kauravas decided to avenge their humiliations. Well aware of Bhima's love for food, they waited for an opportune moment to offer him sweets laced with poison. The unsuspecting Bhima ate the sweets and fell

THE KING OF THE NAGAS
In some versions of the Mahabharata, Vasuki, the king of the Nagas, is said to have bestowed on Bhima the strength of a thousand elephants.

A PLATTER OF SWEETS
The Kauravas took advantage of Bhima's weakness for food and offered him poisoned sweets.

unconscious. The Kauravas tied him up with ropes and threw him into a river.

Rescue by the Nagas

Unconscious and bound, Bhima would have drowned. Fortunately, the Nagas who lived in the river came to his aid. Their leader Aryaka rescued Bhima and asked the Nagas to draw the poison out of him. Aryaka then took Bhima to the Naga capital of Bhogawati to present him to their king, Vasuki, who gave his guest a warm welcome.

"Your mother's ancestor, Yadu, was married to the daughter of the great Naga Dhumravarna," he told Bhima. "You have the blood of Nagas running in your veins."

The Nagas celebrated Bhima's visit to their realm and treated him to a great banquet. They also gave him a potion that made him immune to all kinds of poison.

Revived from this ordeal and restored to health, Bhima returned home stronger and better protected than before. Kunti and his brothers, who had lost all hope, were relieved to see him. The Kauravas, however, were crushed, and grew more and more resentful.

"I must find some trick so as to kill him. Then I will overpower … Yudhishthira. I will … reign as the sovereign of the earth."

DURYODHANA, ADI PARVA: THE BOOK OF THE BEGINNING

MYTHOLOGY AND FOLKLORE

AVIYAL

According to a folk tale from Tamil Nadu, the entire Kuru clan had assumed that Bhima had drowned in the river. After a fortnight of his "death," they ritually mourned him and organized a funeral feast. This was the day that Bhima returned. So that the vegetables and spices prepared for the feast would not go to waste, Bhima offered to make a special meal. He mixed these with coconut milk, creating the popular Tamil dish "aviyal." which translates to "mixture."

AVIYAL IS A VEGETABLE CURRY COOKED WITH COCONUT, TURMERIC, AND CUMIN

AFTER

The rift in the Kuru household widened as the rivalry between the cousins intensified.

A HOUSE DIVIDED

This incident made it all the more difficult for enmities to be suspended. The Kuru clan was now clearly split into the Pandava and Kaurava factions. The smallest issues blew out of proportion and turned into major fights. Despite Gandhari and Kunti's admonitions, the young princes continued to clash.

THE ELDEST KAURAVA

Duryodhana

"I am an evil man ... I am miserable on seeing the blazing prosperity of Kunti's son."

DURYODHANA TO VIDURA, SABHA PARVA: THE BOOK OF THE ASSEMBLY HALL

The Kaurava princes were born under mysterious circumstances. Dhritarashtra's wife Gandhari had delivered a lump of cold flesh which, on the advice of Sage Vyasa, was broken into pieces and incubated in jars of ghee. After one year, the flesh transformed into a hundred and one Kaurava children, the eldest of whom was Duryodhana.

A jealous prince

Duryodhana and his brothers grew up worried that they would have to share their inheritance with their cousins, the Pandavas. Duryodhana argued for his claim to the throne, asserting that the Pandavas were fathered by males who were not from the royal bloodline (See pp. 70–71). Also, his father Dhritarashtra, as the eldest son, had a greater right to ascend the throne. But Vidura reminded him that Pandu had been crowned king first, and that Yudhishthira was the oldest of the cousins. Although Vidura's explanation silenced Duryodhana, it did not stop him from hating his cousins, especially Bhima, who was his competitor in mace warfare.

When the Pandavas transformed the forest of Khandavaprastha into the beautiful city of Indraprastha, Duryodhana felt intensely jealous. At Yudhishthira's coronation, Duryodhana went around the great city and saw the grandeur of the palaces. He realized that his cousins had created something magnificent out of nothing while he had never created anything in his life. As he walked along the corridors of the Pandavas' palace, he slipped and fell into a pond. Draupadi, who happened to be present, laughed and mockingly said, "The blind son of blind parents." Duryodhana then swore that one day he would take pleasure in Draupadi's humiliation and mock her in the same way.

A loyal friend

Duryodhana felt weaker than the Pandavas, even though he had ninety-nine brothers. He was aware that Yudhishthira had an archer in Arjuna, a man of strength in Bhima, and an adviser

THE ELDEST KAURAVA
The chief antagonist of the epic, Duryodhana was known to be a great warrior and a loyal friend to Karna. This 10th-century statue of the eldest Kaurava originally stood at the Koh Ker temple in Cambodia.

in Sahadeva, whereas he only had Dusshasana. The situation changed when Karna became his friend—Karna was as great an archer as Arjuna.

Duryodhana first met Karna at a gathering of Kshatriyas, where Karna was insulted by the Pandavas for his lowly birth. Duryodhana came to his rescue, saying Karna was a Kshatriya by merit. He took Karna as a friend, and also got him appointed as the king of Anga. With Karna by his side, Duryodhana felt as powerful as Yudhishthira.

When Karna died on the seventeenth day of the Kurukshetra War, Duryodhana was inconsolable. He, who had not wept at the fall of Bhishma, broke down when he heard that his dear friend was gone.

A relentless adversary

Duryodhana had come back from Indraprastha jealous of his cousins' newfound prosperity. As someone who had always turned to his maternal uncle for advice, he eagerly fell in with Shakuni's plan to cheat the Pandavas at a game of dice. As expected, Yudhishthira gambled and lost all that he had, even his family and wife Draupadi. To insult the Pandavas further, Duryodhana made his brother Dusshasana drag Draupadi to the court. He even asked Dusshasana to strip her naked. Although she was saved by divine intervention, Bhima swore to break Duryodhana's thigh to avenge her humiliation. The Pandavas suffered thirteen years of exile due to Duryodhana's schemes. After the exile was over, they sent emissaries to ask for their share of land. But Duryodhana refused to part with even the tiniest bit of the territory. He even foolishly tried to imprison Krishna.

A short-sighted warrior

Before the war began, both Arjuna and Duryodhana had gone to Krishna for help. Duryodhana, however, was imprudent enough to wish for Krishna's battalion over Krishna himself. He thought that with eleven armies fighting for him against the Pandavas' seven, victory was his for sure.

Duryodhana had lost most of his allies in the first seventeen days of the war. Eventually, when all the Kauravas were dead, Gandhari instructed Duryodhana to appear before her naked as the piety in her gaze would render him invincible from attacks. Duryodhana agreed and removed his clothes, bathed, and then walked naked toward his mother's chambers. But when Krishna mocked him, he tied a banana leaf around his waist, covering his thighs and genitals, leaving these parts vulnerable.

Graceful in death

On the last day of the war, Duryodhana came face to face with Bhima. Both were equally strong, and Bhima could not subdue his opponent. Aware of his weak spot, Krishna signaled Bhima to strike Duryodhana on his thigh. Following the cue, Bhima fatally injured Duryodhana.

Breathing his last, Duryodhana said to the Pandavas, "I have lived a life fitting for a prince in the palace, and today, I am dying the death of a warrior. You, on the contrary, have spent your life in the forest, and now you shall rule on a throne made of corpses."

As Duryodhana lay dying, Ashwatthama, Drona's son, came to inform him that he had killed Draupadi's five sons, mistaking them for the Pandavas. The eldest Kaurava lamented, "Have we stooped to killing children? I may have lost the battle, but nobody has emerged victorious here."

Duryodhana and his brothers died the death of warriors, purifying themselves of their sins and earning the right to enter heaven.

HISTORY AND CULTURE

PATUKALAM FESTIVAL

In the Patukalam festival celebrated at Sevelimedu in Kanchipuram, Tamil Nadu, India, the Mahabharata war is re-enacted on a ground symbolic of Kurukshetra.

A giant image of Duryodhana is made of mud and laid on the ground. On its right thigh, a pot full of red fluid is placed, which is smashed at the end of the performance by the actor playing Bhima, who goes into a frenzied trance. After this ritual, the crowd takes fistfuls of the mud used to make Duryodhana's image. This mud is preserved by people as it is supposed to protect granaries.

A DURYODHANA IDOL MADE OF MUD, TURMERIC, AND KUMKUM AT THE PATUKALAM FESTIVAL

BIOGRAPHY IN BRIEF

- **Born** to Dhritarashtra and Gandhari as a lump of flesh, which was incubated in a pot of ghee.
- **Instructed** by the royal teacher Drona, along with his ninety-nine brothers and five Pandava cousins. He also learned mace warfare under Balarama.
- **Conspired** with his brothers to poison and drown his rival Bhima, but Bhima was saved by the water-dwelling Nagas.
- **Married** Bhanumati, the princess of the kingdom of Pragjyotisha, and remained loyal to her, never coveting other women.
- **Befriended** Karna, son of a charioteer and a commoner, after he demonstrated better prowess than Arjuna and was publicly humiliated by Pandavas for his low birth.
- **Was humiliated** when he fell into a pond in the Pandavas' new palace, and Draupadi laughed at him, calling him the "blind son of blind parents." He swore revenge.
- **Organized a gambling match** at the suggestion of his maternal uncle Shakuni, a master at dice. He invited the Pandavas to gamble and Yudhishthira lost everything, including his family.
- **Humiliated Draupadi** by dragging her to the assembly hall, asking her to sit on his lap, and ordering Dusshasana to disrobe her. Draupadi was saved by divine intervention.
- **Banished the Pandavas** to the forest for thirteen years after defeating them in a dice game.
- **Refused to share the kingdom** even after the Pandavas came back from exile. He even spurned Krishna's peace negotiations, knowing that it would lead to war.
- **Opted for Narayani army** when asked to choose between Krishna's army and Krishna himself.
- **Appointed powerful commanders** such as Bhishma, Drona, Karna, and Shalva, in the war. Within eighteen days of fighting he lost all his commanders, as well as his ninety-nine brothers.
- **Asked** to appear naked before Gandhari to make his body invulnerable. Tricked by Krishna, he covered his loins, leaving them vulnerable to attack.
- **Fought with Bhima** and was defeated after a fatal blow to his thigh.
- **Died** on the battlefield. His death brought the war to an end.
- **Went to heaven** after his death, reaping the merit of having died in the hallowed land of Kurukshetra.

BEFORE

The five sons of Pandu and the hundred sons of Dhritarashtra were under the care of Bhishma, who had the onerous task of keeping the Kuru clan in order.

IN LOCO PARENTIS

As king, Dhritarashtra was far too busy to attend to the daily affairs of the princes, so the responsibility of their education fell to Bhishma. The Pandavas turned to Bhishma for advice and guidance as he was the only father they knew.

KEY CONCEPT

GURU–SHISHYA TRADITION

India is the home of the guru–shishya tradition where pupils stay in the house of the teacher. The teacher is supposed to treat his students as his own sons. This tradition is prevalent even today, especially in the fields of music and dance. At times, teachers are blinded by their love for their children and give them priority over their students at the cost of true talent. Vyasa may have experienced this in his lifetime, too. Arjuna also experienced this—had it not been for his dogged determination and talent, Drona would have kept the most significant of his teachings for his own son, Ashwatthama.

A STUDENT RECEIVES HIS GURU'S BLESSINGS

The **Royal Tutor**

Educating the princes of the Kuru clan was no easy task. Bhishma decided to appoint the finest teacher he could find for the Kauravas and the Pandavas. In time, their mentor, Drona, would become much more than just a teacher to them.

> "**Bhishma** ... **asked** around for a **preceptor** who would be **learned** in archery and would be **valorous**."
>
> SAGE VAISHAMPAYANA TO KING JANAMEJAYA, ADI PARVA: THE BOOK OF THE BEGINNING

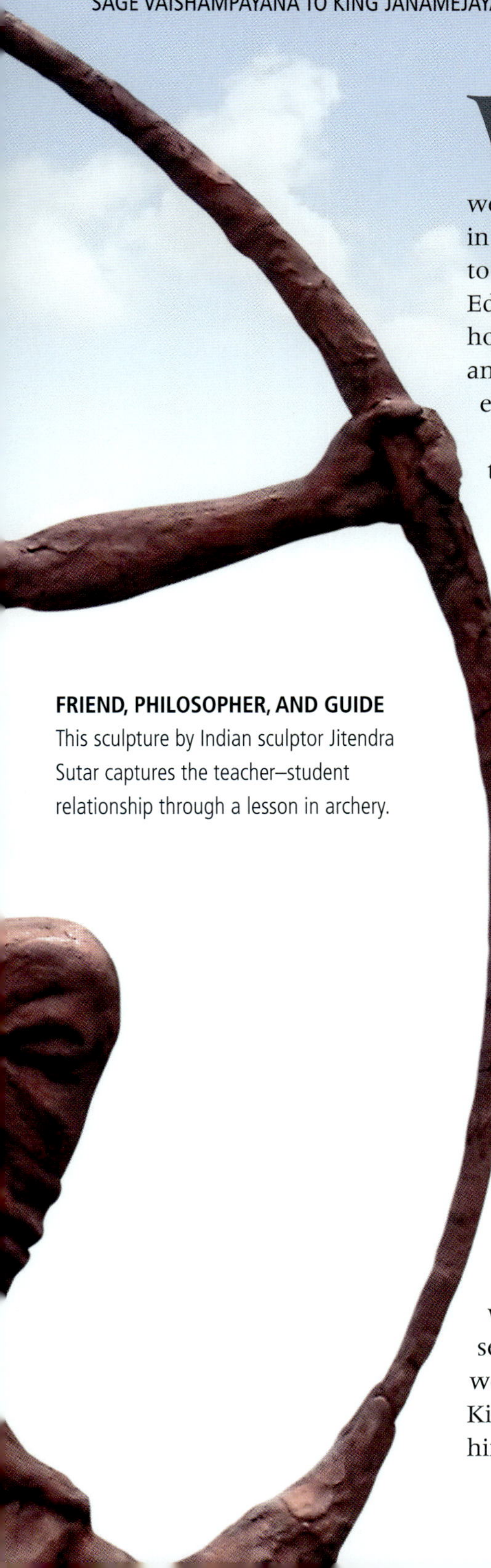

FRIEND, PHILOSOPHER, AND GUIDE
This sculpture by Indian sculptor Jitendra Sutar captures the teacher–student relationship through a lesson in archery.

When Bhishma felt that the Kauravas and the Pandavas were old enough to be schooled in princely duties, he decided to appoint tutors for them. Educating the heirs apparent, however, was a big responsibility, and not a job that he could entrust to just anyone.

The first teacher, or guru, that Bhishma appointed for the young princes was Kripa. Years ago, Bhishma's father, King Shantanu, had found a boy and a girl abandoned in the forest. A trident and pot by their side indicated that they were the children of a sage. Shantanu named them Kripa and Kripi and raised them in the palace.

Kripa became a teacher; Kripi married Drona, the son of Sage Bharadwaj. Drona and Kripi had a son, whom they named Ashwatthama.

The prince and the pauper

Drona was extremely poor, so much so that his son, Ashwatthama, never knew the taste of milk and could not distinguish it from rice water. Finally, not wanting to see his family starve, Drona went to his childhood friend, King Drupada of Panchala, to ask him for a cow, reminding him of a promise made in his youth to share his wealth with his friend. The king, however, laughed it off. "Only those of equal stature can be friends. We were friends once; now I am a rich king and you are a poor priest. Ask for alms and I shall gladly give you a cow in charity. But do not stand before me to claim cows in the name of friendship," he retorted.

Burning with humiliation, Drona swore to become Drupada's equal someday. He went to Parashurama to learn the art of warfare. The warrior-ascetic agreed to teach him on the condition that this knowledge never be shared with any Kshatriya. But the minute he mastered these skills, Drona forgot his promise and headed for Hastinapur, bent on becoming the princes' teacher and using them to take revenge on Drupada.

Drona's prowess

When Drona reached Hastinapur, he found the princes trying to retrieve a ball from a well. He threw a blade of grass at the ball with such force that it pierced it. He then threw another blade of grass, which pinned itself to the free end of the one lodged in the ball. Soon he had a chain of grass that could be used to pull the ball up. Next, Drona threw his ring into the water. He then shot an arrow that ricocheted back with the ring. The awed princes ran to Bhishma to tell him of the stranger's astonishing prowess. Bhishma decided that Drona would make an excellent teacher and, after consulting Kripa, made him the royal tutor. But Drona had a condition—he would teach the princes only if they captured Drupada alive as his fee. "So be it," agreed the Kuru princes, and their education began.

AFTER

Arjuna's immense dedication and focus helped him become a master archer.

SHOOTING IN THE DARK
One night, while Arjuna was eating, a strong gust of wind blew out the lamps. But he noticed that even in the darkness, his fingers could find their way to his mouth. "If I can do this, surely, with practice, my arrows can hit their target even in the dark,"he thought. He began to practice archery blindfolded and soon became adept at it, earning the name "Gudakesha", one who has conquered sleep. He also learned to shoot arrows with either hand, and thus came to be called Sabyasachi. His immense focus also made him stand out from the others. In a test where the princes were required to shoot a stuffed parrot, Arjuna was the only one to hit the target, the eye of the parrot.

BEFORE

When Drona started training the Kuru princes, Arjuna noticed that his teacher was reluctant to share certain skills.

DRONA'S PROMISE

The priest wished to share the depth of his knowledge solely with his son, Ashwatthama, but as Arjuna followed them everywhere, these lessons soon extended to him as well.

One day, when Drona was bathing in the river, a crocodile caught his foot. Arjuna, following his teacher as usual, immediately shot an arrow at the crocodile and rescued Drona. Impressed by the persistence of his student, Drona promised Arjuna that he would make him the greatest archer in the world—not out of gratitude, but because Arjuna deserved it for his hard work, determination, and focus.

The **Greatest Archer**

Drona had promised to make Arjuna the greatest archer in the world. When he saw that a forest dweller called Ekalavya outshone the young Pandava, Drona needed to ensure that he could keep his promise.

Drona's fame as a teacher began to spread and soon reached the ears of a Nishada, or forest dweller, called Ekalavya. The young boy was eager to learn archery and approached Drona. But Drona, a Brahman and teacher of princes, did not want to have anything to do with a lowly forest boy. So he turned Ekalavya away, saying that he was far too busy to accept any more students.

"Then how do I learn?" asked the crestfallen boy.

"As a **consequence** of his **exceptional faith and** supreme devotion, he **acquired great dexterity** in fixing an arrow ... **aiming and releasing it.**"

SAGE VAISHAMPAYANA TO KING JANAMEJAYA, ADI PARVA: THE BOOK OF THE BEGINNING

HISTORY AND CULTURE

SANS THE RIGHT THUMB

To most people who read the Mahabharata, Drona and Arjuna are heroes. But the Bheels from Madhya Pradesh, India, who trace their ancestry to Ekalavya, see them more in the light of villains.

The Bheels worship Ekalavya, and learn the art of archery from a very young age. As a mark of respect for their ancestor—and a symbolic protest against Drona, who violated the sacred guru–shishya relationship—they do not use their thumbs when practicing archery. This is a custom that has been passed down through the generations.

The name "Bheel" is said to be derived from the Dravidian term "bil," which means bow. Even today, the bow and arrow, locally called "teer-kamthi," are symbols of prestige and good fortune.

"If you have faith in me, you can teach yourself," replied Drona, without giving much thought to his advice. But Ekalavya took the teacher's words seriously.

Ekalavya's devotion

The Nishada withdrew to a clearing in a forest near Hastinapur and made a likeness of Drona. Paying it respect, Ekalavya began to practice archery under its watchful gaze with single-minded devotion.

One day, while practicing, Ekalavya was disturbed by a barking dog. Annoyed by this interruption, he shot seven arrows at the dog.

The arrows entered the dog's mouth without harming it in any way but kept its jaws open, making it impossible for the dog to bark. Silenced, the dog, which belonged to the Kuru princes, rushed back to them. When the princes, who had come to the forest on a hunting expedition, saw this extraordinary display of archery, they were full of admiration.

Arjuna's jealousy

An envious Arjuna immediately realized that this was the work of a great archer. He went to Drona with a complaint, "You said you would make me the greatest archer in the world, but whoever is capable of this feat must surely be far greater."

Drona's "fees"

A surprised Drona went off to investigate. He found Ekalavya practicing in the woods. On seeing his teacher, the young Nishadha fell at Drona's feet.

"Who taught you to shoot like this?" asked Drona.

"You did," responded the young Nishada, thrilled to see his "tutor" again. "Not in person, of course," he hastily added. "But you blessed me and inspired me to teach myself."

Drona thought of the promise he had made to Arjuna—the mantle of the greatest archer belonged to his student. "If I am your tutor, where's my fee?" he asked Ekalavya.

"Whatever you wish," replied Ekalavya humbly.

"The thumb of your right hand," demanded Drona, cold and unfeeling. A price such as this would ensure that Ekalavya would never use the bow and arrow with such skill again.

Without a moment's hesitation, Ekalavya took a knife, cut off his right thumb, and laid it at Drona's feet.

> "Since he was the **son of a nishada**, Drona ... thought about it and **refused** to accept him as a **student** of archery."
>
> SAGE VAISHAMPAYANA TO KING JANAMEJAYA, ADI PARVA: THE BOOK OF THE BEGINNING

THE TRADITION CONTINUES
Many tribal communities in India still use traditional weapons such as the bow and arrow for hunting. In this image, a man from the Kamar tribe in Chhattisgarh, a state in central India, wields an indigenously made bow and arrow.

AFTER

Though Arjuna had been jealous of Ekalavya, he was shaken by Drona's ruthlessness.

ARJUNA'S REACTION
Drona's fee seemed extremely cruel to Arjuna, who could not think of a worse fate than to never wield a bow and arrow. Drona explained to Arjuna, "Not everyone can be allowed to become archers. What I did was necessary for the sake of social stability. But I also ensured that there will be no one greater than you in archery." Arjuna was far too stunned to comment.

SOCIAL GROUPING BASED ON OCCUPATION

Caste

> "For the **three varnas, three pursuits** have been indicated in the **sacred texts** ... When these are followed, the **world's welfare is ensured**."

HANUMAN TO BHIMA, VANA PARVA: THE BOOK OF THE FOREST

Social organization in the age of the epics was based on the chaturvarna, a broad, four-part division of society on the basis of occupation. It is likely that this was initially an open, fluid grouping that became increasingly rigid over time.

Traditionally traced to the Purusha Sukta hymn of the Rig Veda, chaturvarna looks at society as an organism with its head, hands, thighs, and feet formed by those involved in ritual, administration, trade, and service activities. These make up the four varnas—Brahman, Kshatriya, Vaishya, and Shudra. In the Bhagavad Gita, Krishna explains the origin and function of the caste system to Arjuna, telling him, "This fourfold order was established by me on the basis of the divisions of quality and work. But though I have created it, understand that I am incapable of action or change." Therefore, division of society into varnas assumed divine origin and sanction.

VARNA AND CASTE

To use the term "caste" for varna is not strictly accurate, for each varna is further divided into smaller groups—jaatis—whose rules of membership more closely match the Western definition of caste. However, in common usage, caste is used interchangeably for both varna and jaati. It broadly refers to an endogamous group, its position in the social order is defined by occupation, and entry into it is defined by birth.

The Mahabharata does not refer to the classical four-tiered Vedic society of Brahman, Kshatriya, Vaishya, and Shudra. Instead, it refers to a three-tiered society where Rajanyas or Kshatriyas (warriors-kings-rulers) provided for Rishis or Brahmans (priests-teachers) and ruled over commoners—cowherds, farmers, fisherfolk, charioteers, potters, carpenters, among others. This could be because the main characters of the epic are mostly all Kshatriyas and Brahmans. The other two castes play a relatively minor role; a greater role is played by those outside society, the forest dwellers, such as the Nishadhas, Nagas, Rakshasas, and Gandharvas.

THE HIERARCHY

In such a system based on the division of labor, hierarchy could well be ambiguous. Brahmans would lead in the ritual and spiritual sphere; Kshatriyas, the political; and Vaishyas in the economic. The Shudra, as the service provider to these three, would be placed below them in status. In actual fact, the Brahman was venerated as the repository of knowledge and wisdom and placed at the top of the hierarchy—a request for alms could not be denied; an insult, even unintended, required penance. Killing a Brahman was the worst sin in all of Aryavarta. There was no place in society for one who committed such a sin. When faced with their guru, Drona, on the battlefield of Kurukshetra, the Pandavas were at a loss. How could they possibly kill their teacher, a Brahman? Eventually, Krishna intervened, pointing out that Drona was merely the son of a Brahman. By choosing to live for wealth and power as a Kshatriya, he had gone against dharma—therefore, it was fitting that he be killed on the battlefield.

DISCRIMINATION

Author of the Mahabharata and compiler of the Vedas, Veda Vyasa, was born to the Rishi Parashara and Satyavati, the adopted daughter of fisherman-chief Dusharaj. She was referred to as "Matsyagandha," she who smells of fish. In a later age, as the son of a fisherwoman, Vyasa would be considered as belonging to a lower caste and unfit to even touch or recite the Vedas. Though it is not mentioned in the chaturvarna caste division, over time untouchability came to be an integral aspect of caste in India. The efforts of social reformers such as Jyotirao Phule, Mahatma Gandhi, and B.R. Ambedkar, culminated in the Constitution of the newly independent India abolishing the practice of untouchability or any form of caste-based discrimination in 1947. However, it is clear that such deeply entrenched patterns of social behavior are very difficult to change. Untouchability and other forms of caste-based discrimination are still practiced in many parts of the country.

VARNA DHARMA

Social stability in this system depended on varna dharma—a man's duty to follow his father's vocation—and taking another path could lead to severe consequences. Though he was a Brahman and tutor of the Kuru princes, Drona, driven by ambition, wanted his own son, Ashwatthama, to be the better warrior. Under his guidance, Aswatthama's ambition grew to know no bounds. He wanted to become the most powerful warrior in the world. At the end of the war at Kurukshetra, unable to bear defeat and carried away by the desire for revenge, Ashwatthama vowed to the dying Duryodhana that he would destroy the Pandavas. He attempted to keep his vow by directing the deadly Brahmaastra toward the wombs of the Pandava women. As Brahman-born, it was his duty to live as a priest, to use his knowledge of hymns and incantations to preserve life, not to destroy it. Much worse was that, by killing unborn children, he denied ancestors a chance to be reborn. These were the reasons why Krishna showed no mercy when he cursed him.

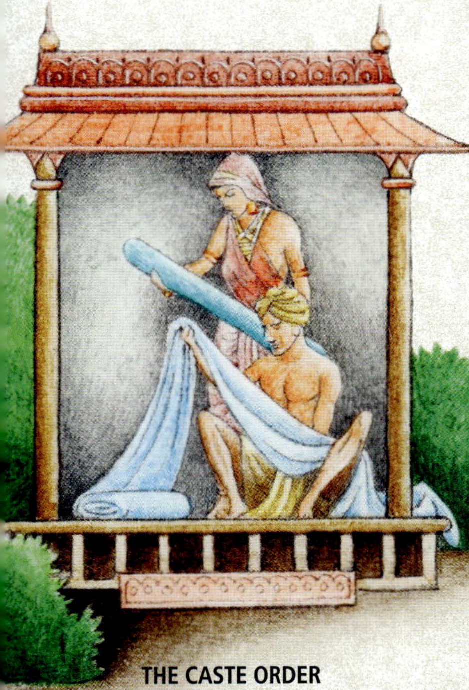

THE CASTE ORDER
The varna (caste system) categorized people into four hierarchical groups based on the division of labor.

CREATION OF THE VARNAS
The Rig Veda describes the varnas as created from the body parts of the primeval man (Purusha) who was sacrificed by the gods.

Even though they were fathered by the Brahman sage Vyasa, Dhritarashtra and Pandu were accepted as Kuru princes, sons of Vichitravirya. Society accepted a woman's husband as the father of a child regardless of biological fatherhood. Their brother, Vidura, despite his learning and high moral character, was not acceptable as either a Kshatriya or a Brahman, because his mother was a servant, a Shudra.

Similarly, as sons of Pandu, the Pandavas are warriors and kings, but Karna, though of the same parentage, is not. Abandoned by an unwed Kunti who was fearful of her reputation, he had been found and brought up by a charioteer. As a charioteer's son, he was unacceptable to Draupadi as a potential husband and, despite displaying all the skills of a warrior, was prevented from participating in her swayamvara. Nor did the elders of the Kuru household ever accept him. Though he was Duryodhana's friend and unfailingly loyal, they always saw him as the son of a low-caste charioteer.

BEFORE

In time, Drona, the royal tutor, felt confident that the Kuru princes had mastered the use of arms and were ready to display their skills in a tournament.

THE TOURNAMENT

The tutor went to Dhritarashtra and asked him to permit a public display of his pupils' skills. The blind king was happy to hear that the princes had completed their education. He agreed to the idea, regretting the fact that he would not be able to see the ceremony. Once the decision was made, Bhishma, Kripa, and other elders chose a propitious time and place, and settled on the rules and other details, asking Vidura to look after all the arrangements.

A **Show** of **Skill**

The graduation ceremony of the Kuru princes was meant to be a celebration of their talent and skill in front of the kingdom. Events, however, took a dramatic turn, with the rivalry between the Kauravas and the Pandavas taking center stage.

Once the auspicious day was fixed, arrangements for the tournament were in full swing. Drona had a large arena built with a grand viewing platform for the king; another platform was set up for the royal womenfolk, and yet another for the general public. The richer citizens got their own platforms made so that they could get a good view of the spectacle. The people of Hastinapur were curious, and there was speculation about which prince would emerge the winner.

On the day of the tournament, the king, accompanied by Sage Kripa and Bhishma, took his seat. Vidura sat next to the king to describe the proceedings to him, while Kunti did the same for the queen. Satyavati was also in attendance, along with her daughers-in-law. The ceremony began with auspicious music and prayers, and weapons were placed in the arena.

The tournament

Led by Yudhishthira, the princes entered the arena in the order of their age, and began to show off their skills in warfare, from archery, swords, and shields, to fighting atop chariots, horses, and elephants. The crowd was impressed with the princes' proficiency in these arts and cheered them on enthusiastically.

Then a mace combat between Duryodhana and Bhima began. The fight was fierce and the audience was deeply divided into camps supporting the two. When the roars of the crowd became fervent, Drona called a halt to the combat, fearing that things would get out of control. He then introduced Arjuna to the crowd,

DRONA TRAINS THE KURU PRINCES
In this scene from Peter Brook's film *The Mahabharata* (1989), the Pandavas and Kauravas train hard to best one another.

PEOPLE

THE TUTOR'S TEACHER

Drona, the royal tutor, was taught by Parashurama, the sixth avatar of Vishnu, who came to restore balance on earth when it was overrun by the cruelty of the Kshatriyas.

A devotee of Shiva, Parashurama learned the scriptures and the martial art of Kalaripayattu from the deity himself, and also received from him many celestial weapons and the power of invincibility. Parashurama is considered to be immortal, or "chiranjeevi," and is among the foremost Rishis in the Kali Yuga. He is also described as the martial instructor of Vishnu's tenth avatar, Kalki, who is destined to bring about the destruction of this world.

PARASHURAMA

> "On **witnessing** the **strength** of the **princes** in the use of bows and arrows, **they** [the crowd] were **amazed** and thought they were in a **city of the gandharvas**."

SAGE VAISAMPAYANA TO JANAMEJAYA, ADI PARVA: THE BOOK OF THE BEGINNING

which greeted his arrival with great excitement. Hearing the people praise her son, Kunti's heart filled with pride. Arjuna shot at various targets; created fire, water, wind, and rain; pierced the earth; created a mountain; and made objects invisible. Drona's favorite disciple dazzled everyone with his skills, not only with the bow and arrow, but with the sword, the club, and other weapons.

The unexpected challenger

Then a stranger entered the arena. He sported a brilliant suit of armor and his ears shone with radiant jewels. Introducing himself as Karna, he declared, "I can do all that Arjuna can and much more."

»

SWORD FIGHTING
Nakula and Sahadeva were said to be skilled at sword fighting, a martial art that continued to be popular well into the late 19th century.

THE TRIAL OF THE PRINCES
This lithograph by Nandalal Bose is featured in the book *Myths of Hindus and Buddhists*, co-authored by Sister Nivedita and Anand K Coomaraswamy, in 1913. Bose was one of the pioneers of modern Indian art.

» Duryodhana, who had been unhappy with the people's appreciation of Arjuna, was delighted when Drona asked Karna to prove his claims. Karna proceeded to match and surpass all of Arjuna's feats earning praise from the crowd, which soon began to exclaim that he was better than Arjuna.

The charioteer's son

Suddenly, to the astonishment of all, Adiratha, the chief of the royal stables, ran into the arena and hugged Karna warmly. "You have done me proud, my son," he declared.

Bhima realized that Karna was not a Kshatriya. "What! The son of a mere charioteer challenging Kshatriyas in an archery tournament! How dare he!" he yelled.

A humiliated Karna had no response, but help came from an unexpected source. Duryodhana stood up to declare, "Merit matters far more than birth. Karna is a Kshatriya by merit, and we should treat him as one." "No," countered Yudhishthira. "According to dharma, a man should follow in his father's footsteps. Karna's father is a charioteer. So he cannot be a Kshatriya." Karna wanted to say that he had only been brought up by a charioteer, not born into his family, but that would raise questions about his parentage to which he did not have answers. He only knew that he had been found floating on the river in a basket, and so he stayed silent.

A friendship forged

Duryodhana did not give up. "Kshatriya or not, this man is a great archer. I will not let him be insulted. From now on, he is closer to my heart than my brothers. Those who insult him insult me," he announced. The Kaurava prince then asked his father to declare Karna a warlord. Dhritarashtra, who always indulged his sons, crowned Karna the king of Anga. Karna was overwhelmed—in all his life, no one had ever defended him with such passion. He decided that he would be a friend to the Kauravas till the day he died.

Though the Pandavas protested Karna's coronation, the Kauravas were vehement—they felt that with Karna on their side, they could be as powerful as the Pandavas, if not more. Watching the cousins come to blows, Bhishma was worried that the family feud would turn into a public spectacle.

Suddenly, they heard a cry from the women's pavilion. Kunti, recognizing Karna as the son she had abandoned, had fainted. As people rushed to her side, Bhishma decided to declare the tournament closed and asked the princes to return to the palace.

THE FACE-OFF
This bas-relief from Odisha, India, circa 13th century CE, shows Arjuna and Karna at the tournament.

"**Altercations** are nothing but **the resort of the weak ... Speak with arrows** until my arrow **carries off your head** in your preceptor's presence."

KARNA TO ARJUNA, ADI PARVA: THE BOOK OF THE BEGINNING

HISTORY AND CULTURE

KARNA'S CASTE

The Mahabharata uses the word "suta" to describe Karna's caste. According to the *Manu Smriti*, an ancient text on Hinduism, sutas were the children of a Kshatriya man and a Brahman woman. People of the Suta caste were either charioteers or storytellers. As storytellers, Sutas also narrated and preserved the stories of the royal clans and their genealogies. Another function of Sutas was to report events and carry messages. Sanjay, Dhritarashtra's charioteer who narrated the events of the Mahabharata war to his master, was also a Suta.

DHRITARASHTRA LISTENING TO SANJAY NARRATING THE EVENTS OF THE WAR

AFTER »

Satyavati decided to treat the distressing fight between the Kauravas and the Pandavas as a sign to retire from family life.

SATYAVATI'S RETREAT
Watching her great-grandsons lash out at each other, Satyavati was distraught. The tension between the Kauravas and the Pandavas was unbearable. The family she had worked so hard to create would soon destroy itself, and she could not bear to see this. It was time for her to leave. Accompanied by her daughters-in-law Ambika and Ambalika, Satyavati decided to go to the forest.

THE ROYAL MATRIARCH

Kunti

> **"Kuntibhoja's daughter** was beautiful and possessed all the **qualities**."

SAGE VAISHAMPAYANA TO KING JANAMEJAYA, ADI PARVA: THE BOOK OF THE BEGINNING

INDONESIAN RETELLING
Wayang kulit, or shadow play using puppets, is a Javanese form of theatrical performance. The leather puppets are often used to narrate stories from Hindu epics, such as the Ramayana or the Mahabharata. Depicted here is the shadow puppet of Kunti.

Surasena, a member of the Yadava council ruling the prosperous city of Mathura, had a daughter named Pritha. He gave up his daughter for adoption to his childless cousin and friend, Kuntibhoja, who renamed her Kunti.

An unwed mother

As a young princess, Kunti was given the duty of serving Sage Durvasa by her adoptive father. Kunti pleased him and, in return, he gave her a special mantra by which she could invoke any Deva and have a child by him. Curious, she invoked Surya, the sun god, and had a son by him. Fearing social contempt, Kunti put the child in a basket and set it afloat it in a river. The child was found and brought up by the charioteer Adiratha and his wife, Radha, who named him Karna.

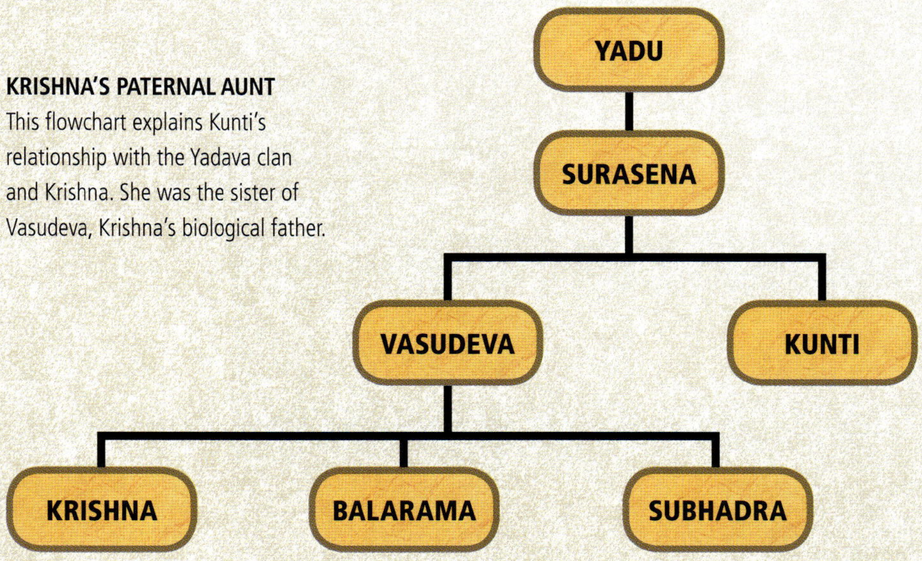

KRISHNA'S PATERNAL AUNT
This flowchart explains Kunti's relationship with the Yadava clan and Krishna. She was the sister of Vasudeva, Krishna's biological father.

Loving wife and mother

When Kunti came of age she chose Pandu, the king of Hastinapur, to be her husband.

After some years, when Pandu retired to a forest to lead the life of a hermit, Kunti, along with Pandu's second wife, Madri, dutifully followed her husband to the forest. They were living peacefully in the forest when they heard of Gandhari's pregnancy. The news depressed Pandu, who was worried that he would die childless. Kunti then told him about Sage Durvasa and his special mantra.

Encouraged by her husband, Kunti invoked the gods Yama, Vayu, and Indra to give birth to Yudhishthira, Bhima, and Arjuna. She also invoked the Ashwini twins for Madri, who begat Nakula and Sahadeva from the twin gods. However, she did not let Madri bear more children as she did not want the junior wife to have more children and be more influential than herself.

A dependent widow

After Pandu and Madri's death, Kunti went back to Hastinapur with her five sons to live with Dhritarashtra's family. She was a dependent widow in the palace, and her sons suffered the hostility of their cousins, the Kauravas, who even poisoned and tried to drown Bhima. Once, when she performed a ritual using mud elephant figurines, Gandhari did the same with gold elephants, to assert her superiority. Kunti took a lot of pride in her sons' achievements, for they were her only source of joy. Arjuna stood out as the star pupil during the graduation ceremony organized by Drona. Just as Kunti watched her youngest son with pride, there entered a lad who not only challenged Arjuna but outshone him. Although Kunti recognized the golden armor and earrings of her firstborn, she did not have the courage to reveal Karna's true identity.

Years of trial

When Kunti's sons grew up, the Kauravas gifted them a palace made of combustible lac, with the intention of burning them down with the house. With help from her brother-in-law Vidura, Kunti and her children escaped at night and spent a year in anonymity. The Pandavas then surfaced at Draupadi's swayamvara, where Arjuna won Draupadi's hand. When he went to his mother and exclaimed, "Look what I won!" Kunti, without even looking back, asked him to share the prize equally with his brothers.

Kunti realized how beautiful Draupadi was and how her sons appreciated this. To keep her sons united, she decreed that Draupadi be shared by all the five Pandavas as a common wife.

When the Kauravas deceitfully defeated Yudhishthira at a game of dice and sent the Pandavas into exile, Kunti had to remain in the palace without her family for thirteen years. After the exile was over, she watched as war between her sons and the Kauravas became imminent. She was distraught that her firstborn, Karna, established in the Kaurava camp as Duryodhana's closest friend, was an enemy of her sons and a bitter rival of Arjuna.

Kunti's secret

After a lifetime of guilt, Kunti met Karna the day before he was to enter the battlefield. She told him the truth of his birth and begged him to return to her and his brothers. Bound by his ethics and loyalty to his friend Duryodhana, Karna refused. But he promised that he would only kill Arjuna and spare her other sons. She would always have five sons, including one great archer: either Karna or Arjuna. After the death of Karna, Kunti finally revealed the truth about him to her shocked and remorseful sons.

In her last years, Kunti saw peace and prosperity, as Yudhishthira ruled over Hastinapur. She eventually retreated to the forest with the other elders of the clan, where they all died in a forest fire.

THE ARCHER ARJUNA
This statue of Arjuna stands tall at Bali, Indonesia. It is believed that Arjuna was Kunti's favorite because she invoked Indra, his father, of her own volition and not at Pandu's request.

BIOGRAPHY IN BRIEF

- **Born** in the Yadava clan to Surasena, but was adopted by his cousin Kuntibhoja.
- **Pleased Sage Durvasa** and received a mantra to invoke any god and have a child by him.
- **Invoked the sun god** out of curiosity, and gave birth to Karna. Abandoned the child to escape the shame of being an unwed mother.
- **Married** Pandu, the prince of Hastinapur.
- **Followed Pandu to the forest** when he decided to abdicate, following a curse that he would die if he indulged in sexual relations.
- **Invoked** gods Yama, Vayu, and Indra, and had sons Yudhishthira, Bhima, and Arjuna. Shared the mantra with Madri who gave birth to her stepsons Nakula and Sahadeva.
- **Returned to the palace** with the five princes after Pandu's death.
- **Brought up her fatherless sons** who faced the Kauravas' hostility.
- **Escaped the fire** at the house of lac with her sons.
- **Asked her sons** to share Draupadi as a common wife.
- **Stayed in Hastinapur** after her sons were exiled.
- **Asked Krishna** to tell her sons to fight for what was right in the Kurukshetra War.
- **Revealed to Karna** the truth of his birth and asked him to come over to his brothers' side.
- **Mourned for Karna** after his death.
- **Saw her sons** win the war and take the throne of Hastinapur.
- **Retired to the forest** with other elders and died in a forest fire.

ANALYSIS

LOVE TRYST OR SEXUAL HOSPITALITY?

Some scholars believe that the tale of Kunti's premarital tryst with Surya is an attempt to hide the truth, and that she was asked by her father Kuntibhoja to satisfy all the needs of Sage Durvasa in keeping with the laws of hospitality. The Mahabharata alludes more than once to sexual hospitality, wherein a guest was allowed access to the host's wife or daughter for pleasure. This practice, glorified in the past, came to be frowned upon with the passage of time.

There are also speculations that Karna was a love-child, born out of a premarital liaison with a Suryavamshi (See Glossary), hence the reference to the sun god. This story is often told as a cautionary tale against the dangers of submitting to passion before marriage.

BEFORE

The Pandavas and the Kauravas were jealous of each other and often fought. Sometimes, even their mothers fell prey to petty one-upmanship.

A HOUSE DIVIDED

Kunti decided to perform a ritual for the well-being of her sons and ordered for clay elephants to be made. Gandhari, too, decided to perform the ceremony, but ordered gold elephants to upstage Kunti. To console his mother, Arjuna told Kunti that he would get her an elephant from heaven. He then bridged the earth and sky with arrows so that Airavat, Indra's celestial elephant, could descend to earth. Yet again, the world marveled at the skill of Kunti's sons.

A SCULPTURE OF INDRA ON HIS MOUNT, THE THREE-HEADED ELEPHANT, AIRAVAT

A **House** of **Lac**

Living together in Hastinapur, the cousins squabbled over the smallest of things. To put a stop to this, Dhritarashtra ordered a separate palace for the Pandavas. But behind this seemingly kind gesture was a sinister motive, as Kunti and her sons would soon discover.

"When those warriors and their mother have been **burned to death**, today my unparalleled brother, **Pandu,** is truly **dead**."

DHRITARASHTRA TO HIS RELATIVES, ADI PARVA: THE BOOK OF THE BEGINNING

When Kunti and her sons returned to Hastinapur after Pandu and Madri's death, a fierce rivalry broke out between the Pandavas and Kauravas as each believed that they were the rightful heirs to the throne.

Vidura explained to Duryodhana that Pandu was crowned king before his father.

"Since my father is the older of the two, it makes me the rightful inheritor of the throne," argued Duryodhana.

"Going by your logic," replied Vidura, "Yudhishthira should be king as he is the oldest grandchild of Vichitravirya, your grandfather." Duryodhana chose not to argue but harbored a deep hatred for his cousins, who reciprocated the feeling. So the Kuru household stood divided into two rival camps—the Pandavas on the one side, and the Kauravas on the other.

The people of the kingdom were, however, undecided. Yudhishthira was honest and ably supported by four brothers – one strong, one skilled, one beautiful, and one wise. But these five princes had treated Karna roughly, whereas Duryodhana had been more than kind to him. Moreover, he was the son of blind parents, and people felt sorry for him.

Vidura, who had observed the ill will between the cousins and seen how the kingdom was divided in its opinion over the two camps, advised Dhritarashtra to build a separate house for the Pandavas. "The household will be divided further once they all get married and women from other lands join in. I can foresee a time when matters will get worse," he said.

A FAILED ASSASSINATION ATTEMPT
Had Vidura not forewarned the Pandavas about their new house made of combustible material and made provisions for their escape, this attempt on their lives would have been successful.

> "From **the smell of fat** and **ghee** mixed with **lac**, it is clear that **this house** is made of **inflammable materials**."
>
> YUDHISHTHIRA TO BHIMA, ADI PARVA: THE BOOK OF THE BEGINNING

A house for the Pandavas

Dhritarashtra liked this idea. He ordered a magnificent palace to be built for his sister-in-law and nephews at Varanavata, away from the public eye and close to a forest.

Kunti and the Pandavas, who had been living at the palace, were overjoyed at this display of affection and were thrilled at the prospect of having their own home. However, when Vidura visited the palace, he was shocked to discover that it was made of lac and other highly flammable material.

He rushed to warn Kunti. "I am certain that my brother wishes to kill you and your children. He plans to gift you a house you cannot refuse and intends to burn it down after you move in. But I will ensure your safety. I have had a tunnel built below the house that will lead you to the forest. Accept the gift of the house graciously, but use the tunnel to escape. When you return, you will be on high moral ground. This will secure your children's rightful inheritance," he said.

The great escape

On the very night that Kunti and her children moved into the palace, it was set on fire. Though the palace was engulfed in flames, the Pandavas and their mother escaped through the tunnel. So that it would appear that the conspiracy had succeeded, and to foil further attempts on the Pandavas' lives, Vidura also arranged for five men and one woman to be drugged and had them placed in the burning palace.

BHIMA, THE SAVIOR
This Jaipur-style painting depicts Bhima carrying his mother and brothers after their escape from the blazing palace through a secret tunnel.

When the fire died down, six charred bodies were discovered. Everyone assumed that these bodies were Kunti and her sons. The entire Kuru kingdom mourned their deaths.

Though the Pandavas had escaped unscathed, they were shaken by this attempt on their lives. With this incident, their petty family feud had taken a truly ugly turn.

ANALYSIS

VIDURA, YAMA, AND YUDHISHTHIRA

YAMA, THE GOD OF DHARMA AND DEATH

Rationalists and scholars have analyzed Vidura's relationship with Kunti and the Pandavas in various ways. To some, Vidura is Yama born as a mortal because of a curse. Yudhishthira, being the son of Yama, finds a father figure in Vidura.

Other scholars such as Iravati Karve believe that perhaps Pandu invited his younger brother Vidura to make Kunti pregnant. This would explain his soft spot for Kunti and her sons, and his readiness to help them in their hour of need.

AFTER

The world was shocked at the death of Kunti and the Pandavas. Bhishma and Drona were inconsolable in their grief.

A STATE OF MOURNING
Gandhari and Dhritarashtra shed tears over the death of their sister-in-law and nephews. Even Duryodhana and Dusshasana cried for their cousins. However, Vidura, who knew the truth, kept a careful watch. Whose grief was genuine, and who among these mourners shed crocodile tears?

Bhima Slays Demons

Fearing for their lives, the Pandavas decided to wander through the kingdom. They took refuge in a forest, but danger lurked there as well. Bhima came to the rescue, and also won himself a wife in the bargain.

BEFORE

It had become impossible for the Kauravas and the Pandavas to live peacefully under the same roof.

PANDAVAS EVADE A DEATH TRAP
On Vidura's advice, the king had announced that he would build the Pandavas a palace. But the Pandavas and Kunti discovered that the house they had been gifted was really a death trap. They managed to escape the burning house, though they let everyone believe that they had died in the inferno.

After their escape from the house of lac, Kunti and the Pandavas wandered from place to place disguised as impoverished Brahmans. They had decided not to return to Hastinapur, where there were many people who wished them ill and who would find it easy to make another attempt on their lives. "Let us remain in hiding till we have allies of our own," suggested Kunti, and her sons agreed.

The bane of Ekachakra

When they got tired of foraging in the forest, Kunti and her sons would go to villages, relying on the villagers for food and shelter. One night they were in the village of Ekachakra when Kunti overheard their hosts, a Brahman couple, talking in hushed tones. "Please do not go to feed the demon," she heard the woman pleading. "If he eats you, what will become of me and our daughter?"

In reply to Kunti's concerned question they told her about the fearsome Rakshasa named Baka, who had made life difficult for the villagers, destroying property and killing anyone who crossed his path whenever he was hungry. In an attempt to keep this carnage in check, the villagers had promised to send the Rakshasa a cartload of food every two weeks. Baka not only ate the food, but also devoured the bulls and the person who delivered it. The families in the village took turns providing the food, and this time, it was the turn of the Pandavas' hosts.

Hearing this tale, Kunti told her hosts, "You have given us shelter; the least we could do is help. I have five sons; one of them can go in your place."

> "**Great distress** has befallen me. I do not know **how to escape**. I am cursed. **What path** will I and my relatives **follow**? It is better that I should die with all of them. **I cannot live**."
>
> THE BRAHMAN TO HIS WIFE, ADI PARVA: THE BOOK OF THE BEGINNING

HISTORY AND CULTURE

HIDIMBI TEMPLE

In the north Indian state of Himachal Pradesh, in the hill station of Manali, is a temple dedicated to a goddess called Hidimbi. The temple, located in a cedar forest, is said to be built around the cave where Hidimbi lived with her brother, Hidimba.

Built over a huge rock that is worshipped as the goddess, the temple has a 79-foot-high, four-tiered pagodalike roof and beautiful, intricately carved wooden doors.

HIDIMBI TEMPLE, MANALI, HIMACHAL PRADESH, INDIA

FOOD FOR THE DEMON
Every two weeks, a cart full of food was sent to the demon Baka, who ate the food, the bulls, and the driver.

She then told Bhima to deliver the cartload of food to the Rakshasa. The resourceful Kunti had not only arranged plenty of food for the ever-hungry Bhima, but also ensured that the village was rid the demon, Baka.

Baka meets his death

It had been a long time since Bhima had eaten his fill. All the way to the forest, he was tantalized by the aroma of the food in the cart. He could barely wait till he entered the forest to begin feasting. When Baka saw Bhima eating the food meant for him, he was furious and charged at the insolent cart driver.

Bhima held the Rakshasa pinned to the cart with one hand and proceeded to finish his meal before giving him his attention. The earth shook in fear as the two fought like wild dogs, baying for each other's blood, thrashing around on the ground until, finally, Bhima broke Baka's neck.

The next day, the cart was found in the village, Baka's body draped over it. Strangely, the Brahman's guests were nowhere to be seen. The thankful villagers guessed that these guests were warriors. "Is it not the dharma of Kshatriyas to protect the helpless without expecting a reward in return?" they asked one another.

Marriage to a Rakshasa

The Pandavas and their mother had retreated into the forest and set up camp in a clearing. A few days later, they were attacked by Baka's brother, Hidimba, who wanted to avenge Baka's death. A fierce duel ensued, but eventually Bhima managed to kill Hidimba.

Watching her brother bested, Hidimba's sister, Hidimbi, was drawn to Bhima's strength and decided to marry him. She came to Kunti and her sons offering food, clothing, and shelter. Impressed, Kunti accepted Hidimbi as her daughter-in-law.

Time passed, and Hidimbi bore Bhima a son whom they named Ghatotkacha. It was a good life, but Kunti was getting worried.

RAKSHASA STANDING SENTINEL
Temples in India are adorned with an assortment of sculpted gods and demons. This statue of a Rakshasa guards the tower of the Arunachaleswar temple in Tamil Nadu, India.

"I see a **means** through which you can **escape** from the **rakshasa** … I have **five sons**. One of them **will go.**"

KUNTI TO THE BRAHMAN, ADI PARVA: THE BOOK OF THE BEGINNING

AFTER

Living in the forest with the Rakshasas, Bhima felt a growing attachment to Hidimbi and their son, Ghatotkacha.

HIDIMBI AND GHATOTKACHA

Kunti observed Bhima's affection for his wife and child with growing disquiet. She feared that it might distance Bhima from his brothers, a relationship that she held above all others. With this on her mind, she called him one day to point out, "It is time to move on and leave this place. Our destiny does not lie with the Rakshasas." Reminding Bhima that they must move onward to fulfil their destiny, she asked her sons to break camp and continue their journey.

BEFORE

Traveling on with his mother and brother, a heavyhearted Bhima left his wife Hidimbi and son, Ghatotkacha.

A SORROWFUL PARTING

As Bhima was leaving, Ghatotkacha made him a promise. If there ever came a time when he needed help, Bhima only had to think of Ghatotkacha and he would come. With one last look at his Rakshasa wife and child, Bhima walked away in sorrow.

"**Know me** to be the **gandharva** named **Angaraparna** ... This is **my** ... **forest** on the banks of the Ganga."

ANGARAPARNA TO THE PANDAVAS, ADI PARVA: THE BOOK OF THE BEGINNING

GANDHARVAS

Sophisticated forest dwellers whose statues adorn many Hindu temples, Gandharvas also serve as celestial musicians. They are said to travel in flying chariots and are excellent marksmen with a bow and arrow.

A Gandharva's Gift

As the Pandavas went deeper into the forest, a chance encounter with a Gandharva not only taught them an important lesson, but gave their journey a different direction.

Bidding farewell to his wife and child, Bhima left the Rakshasa settlement with his brothers and mother and continued traveling through the forest.

A Gandharva called Angaraparna

One day, as the Pandavas were collecting water from a lake, they were attacked by a Gandharva called Angaraparna, who claimed to be the master of the lake. A fierce fight broke out between Angaraparna and the Pandavas, during which Arjuna was forced to use a powerful arrow. Charged with the power of Agni, the fire god, the arrow set aflame the Gandharva's chariot. Though skilled, Angaraparna was no match for the Pandavas' prowess, and was taken captive by Arjuna.

On hearing what had occurred, Angaraparna's wife came to the Pandavas to beg for her husband's life. Yudhishthira relented and asked Arjuna to let the Gandharva go free. In gratitude, Angaraparna gifted a hundred horses to each of the Pandavas. However, sensing in them a great deal of rage, he thought he would draw their attention to the importance of forgiveness by telling them about Shaktri, Sage Vashishtha's son.

A story of forgiveness

Once, Shaktri was crossing a narrow bridge, when his path was blocked by a king named Kalmashpada. Neither would back down; in his arrogance Shaktri cursed the king, turning him into a Rakshasa. But the curse backfired. The demon Kalmashpada had an appetite for human flesh and devoured Shaktri.

On learning of his son Shaktri's death, Sage Vashishtha was overwhelmed by grief. He tried to kill himself by jumping into a fire, off a cliff, and into a river. All his attempts failed—none of the elements were willing to harm the sage. "If for nothing else," they begged, "live for the sake of your unborn grandchild."

Spiral of vengeance

In due course, Vashishtha's widowed daughter-in-law gave birth to a son called Parasara. When Parasara grew up, he wanted to avenge his father's death by performing a yagna that would destroy all man-eating Rakshasas, including his father's killer, Kalmashpada. Vashishtha dissuaded him, advising Parasara to let go of his anger and forgive, reminding him that his father had died as a consequence of his own curse. "An act of vengeance," he went on, "only creates a spiral of vendetta." Parasara realized this truth and agreed to abandon the ritual meant to destroy the Rakshasas. "Parasara learned to let go of his anger and forgive his enemies. May you find peace, just as he did," Angaraparna said, blessing the Pandavas.

Realizing that Angaraparna sensed the bitterness and resentment in their hearts, the Pandavas revealed their true identity and shared their life story.

Angaraparna asked them to make the best use of the horses. He urged them to get a priest, and find themselves wives and land, to establish their own kingdom and become rulers. "Overcome your rage," he advised. "Make your own fortune."

A HUNDRED HORSES

Set free by Arjuna despite losing the fight, Angaraparna gave to each of the Pandavas a hundred powerful horses as an expression of his gratitude.

"O best of men! I wish to give each of you **100 horses** … These … can assume **any speed** at will and can **go anywhere** at will."

ANGARAPARNA TO THE PANDAVAS, ADI PARVA: THE BOOK OF THE BEGINNING

HISTORY AND CULTURE

HORSES

Although horses appear in Paleolithic cave art as early as 30,000 BCE, they were wild and often hunted for meat. Horses began to be domesticated only around 4000 BCE, in Central Asia.

Horses are not native to the Indian subcontinent. The gifting of horses by the Gandharva suggests that the Pandavas may have taken refuge in the north-west, where traders brought horses from central Asia and Arabia to trade in the subcontinent.

AFTER

Accepting Angaraparna's advice, the Pandavas journeyed in search of a priest, a wife, and land to establish a kingdom.

THE PANDAVAS GO TO PANCHALA

In a forest outside the kingdom of Panchala, the Pandavas and Kunti met Sage Dhaumya, who agreed to become their priest. His first observation was that Kunti's household was incomplete without a daughter-in-law. He directed the Pandavas to participate in the archery contest being held by the king of Panchala for his daughter's swayamvara.

ENGULFED IN FLAMES
This miniature in the Bikaner-style from Rajasthan, India, shows Drupada's twins, Draupadi and Dhrishtadyumna, emerging from the fire pit.

BEFORE

The relationship between Drona and Drupada soured when the king laughed at Drona, refuting childhood friendship on the basis of present difference in status.

SOURED FRIENDSHIP
To avenge his humiliation, Drona went to the great warrior-priest Parashurama and learned the art of warfare. He then became the teacher of the Kuru princes, and taught them the art of war. When ready, he asked his students to launch an attack on Panchala. Keeping half of the conquered kingdom himself, he gave Drupada the southern half to rule.

"I am **inflamed with enmity** for Drona. **Pacify** my heart."

KING DRUPADA TO SAGE YAJA, ADI PARVA: THE BOOK OF THE BEGINNING

The **Twins** Born of **Fire**

Convinced that no mere mortal could help him avenge his defeat by Drona, Drupada, king of Panchala, sought divine intervention, turning to the deity of destruction himself.

Drona asked the Kuru princes to conquer Panchala for him as his tuition fee. Keeping half the kingdom for himself, he then returned half to Drupada. "I am now master of one half of Panchala, and you, ruler of the other half. This makes us equal. Can we be friends now?" the royal tutor asked King Drupada.

"A youth who **resembled a god** arose from the flames … Then a **young maiden** arose from the **centre of the altar**."

BRAHMANS DESCRIBING DHRISHTADYUMNA AND DRAUPADI TO THE PANDAVAS, ADI PARVA: THE BOOK OF THE BEGINNING

Invoking Shiva

Although Drupada agreed that they could, his heart burned with a desire for revenge. He sought a way to destroy Drona as well as his patrons, the Kuru princes. He organized a yagna to invoke Shiva. "A son to kill Bhishma, another to kill Drona, and a daughter who would marry into the Kuru household to divide it," were the blessings Drupada asked of the deity.

In due course, his wife gave birth to a daughter. At her birth, the oracles foretold that she would, in time, acquire the body of a man and be responsible for Bhishma's death. Drupada's firstborn, whom he named Shikhandi, was none other than Amba, reborn in Panchala to avenge her humiliation by Bhishma.

Yaja and Upayaja

Not satisfied with just a daughter, Drupada sent for the sages Yaja and Upayaja. These sages had the profound knowledge to brew a potion that could bless women with children.

The sages arrived, performed a great yagna, and concocted the potion. But when Yaja and Upayaja went to deliver the brew to the queen, she was in her bathing chamber.

Impatient, the sages refused to wait for the queen, and, to Drupada's horror, threw the concoction into the fire pit of the yagna.

The birth of the twins

As soon as the sages threw the potion into the fire pit, two children who would fulfil Drupada's desire for vengeance emerged. The boy, Dhrishtadyumna, would go on to kill Drona; the girl, Draupadi, would one day divide the Kuru clan. Drupada was now blessed with three children who would each have a big hand to play in the history of the Kurus.

MYTHOLOGY AND FOLKLORE

SHIVA

Believed to grant power to devotees who please him with their prayers and austerities, Shiva is invoked by several people in the epic. Before the war, Krishna asks Arjuna to seek his blessings and procure the Pashupatastra. Gandhari appeals to him for a blessing that would get her recognition as a woman of unblemished virtue. Amba turns to him when seeking vengeance against Bhishma. Jayadratha, the Kauravas' brother-in-law, prays for his help to fight the Pandavas for a day.

SHIVA, THE DEITY OF DESTRUCTION

AFTER

Drupada raised his children with single-minded focus of the annihilation of the Kuru clan.

DRUPADA'S WISH
In keeping with his aim of destroying the Kuru household, Drupada wanted Draupadi marry Arjuna, the greatest archer in the world and one who had defeated him at war. Even though Arjuna was his enemy, he was greatly impressed with the young prince's archery skills. However, everyone believed that the Pandava brothers had been killed in the palace fire. Drupada was left with no choice but to organize a contest that would reveal another archer deserving of his daughter.

BEFORE

Fearing for their lives, the Pandavas remained hidden in the forest, letting everyone believe that they had all perished in the fire.

A GANDHARVA'S ADVICE

The Pandavas had lived in the forests around the Kuru kingdom since their escape from the house of lac. There they had encountered a Gandharva named Angaraparna, who, on learning of their identity, advised them to let go of their anger and make their own way in the world. He suggested that they get married, acquire powerful allies, and add a priest to their entourage. He told them to seek out Sage Dhaumya, who would help them in all this.

Draupadi's **Swayamvara**

Following Sage Dhaumya's advice, the Pandavas made their way to Panchala, where a swayamvara was being held. Dressed as a Brahman, Arjuna managed to win Draupadi in the contest and, in turn, form an alliance with a mighty dynasty.

As directed by the Gandharva Angaraparna, the Pandavas arrived at Sage Dhaumya's hermitage in Utkochaka and requested him to act as their chief priest. Dhaumya agreed, and also told them about the swayamvara the king of Panchala was holding for his daughter. He urged them to participate in it." Attend the princess Draupadi's swayamvara, disguised as priests. If she is meant to be Arjuna's bride, nothing in the world can stop that from happening."

Drupada plans the swayamvara

Drupada, the king of Panchala, had been disheartened when he heard the rumor that the Pandavas and their mother, Kunti, had been killed in a palace fire. He had wanted Arjuna, considered the best archer in the world, to marry his daughter. The king then decided to hold an archery contest to find the next best archer for his daughter. To this end, he had a special bow and a target built and had them placed in a great hall.

The target, which was golden and shaped like a fish, would rotate on a wheel suspended from the roof. Those who aspired to win Draupadi's hand would have to string the bow and shoot the eye of the rotating fish, while looking at its reflection in a vat of oil placed directly below it. Once all was ready, Drupada invited

THE GATHERING
People from all kingdoms came to visit Panchala to witness the swayamvara. Celebrations were held to honor the guests, as seen in this 18th-century watercolor folio.

kings and princes from far and near. "He who strings this bow and shoots the target will win my daughter," he said. Eager suitors came from faraway lands to compete for Draupadi's hand.

The grand swayamvara

The Pandavas followed Dhaumya's advice and headed to Panchala. Disguised as priests, they sat in the designated pavilion meant for Rishis, Tapasvins, and Brahmans.

The king of Panchala had built a spectacular arena for the visiting warriors and priests. A large platform had been constructed in the northeast corner of the city. The congregation hall was enclosed by a wall, surrounded by a moat on all sides. The air resounded with music and was filled with the sweet scent of agaru, a fragrant tree. There were large white palaces for the suitors, each with 100 doors, beautiful seats and couches, and plush, expensive beds. Every day more and more people joined the assembly; jewels were distributed, and dancers and actors entertained the guests.

The contest begins

On the sixteenth day of the celebrations, the beautiful princess Draupadi entered the arena with a golden prize in her hands for the winner.

Draupadi's brother, Dhrishtadyumna, stood in the center and addressed the gathering,"O assembled kings! Hear that this is the bow, that is the target, and these are the arrows. With these five arrows, shoot the target through the hole in the center of the machine. I truly say that the handsome and strong one born in a noble family who accomplishes this great feat today will obtain my sister as his wife."

Kings from all parts of Bharatavarsha tried their luck, but none of them succeeded in making the target, for hitting the eye of the fish suspended on a rotating wheel was indeed a difficult task and required excellent marksmanship. Some could not even string the bow. Some fell into the vat of oil while trying to spot the reflection of the fish. The rest shot arrows that hit everything except the eye of the fish.

Karna's rejection

Duryodhana did not participate, as he was already married to Bhanumati, the princess of Kalinga. The oldest Kaurava had promised Bhanumati that he would take no other wife, so he had sent his dear friend Karna to the swayamvara in his place.

As Karna stepped into the arena, Draupadi stood up and stopped him. "The son of a charioteer cannot compete for my hand," she announced. A humiliated Karna was forced to withdraw from the challenge—his low birth had once again been established in public.

Arjuna enters the arena

When all the Kshatriyas failed the test, Draupadi's father, Drupada, invited the Brahmans to take part in the contest. Taken aback by the announcement, the kings grumbled and muttered amongst themselves. Thus, when the "Brahman" Arjuna rose to pick up the bow, he became the focus of the kings' displeasure. "If Kshatriyas like Karna and Shalya, famous all over the world for their great »

> "The handsome and brave one… who **accomplishes** this **great feat**, will **obtain** as his **wife** my sister **Krishnaa** (Draupadi)."
>
> DHRISHTADYUMNA, ADI PARVA: THE BOOK OF THE BEGINNING

PEOPLE

SAGE DHAUMYA

Dhaumya was the chief priest of the Pandavas, and was held in great esteem by all the five brothers. In those days, head priests such as Dhaumya were an important part of the household. They not only performed important rituals of worship, but also fulfilled the role of a teacher or guide.

Priests often had a close teacher-disciple relationship with their protégés. Dhaumya himself is known to have had three disciples, who went to great lengths to please him. The first, Aruni, used his own body to block a breach in a canal that watered his teacher's farm. The second, Upamanyu, who took Dhaumya's cattle to graze, but was barred from drinking milk of the cows, ended up eating poisonous leaves that blinded him temporarily. The third, Veda, stayed so long with his guide that one day he realized he was an old man with grey hair.

In the Mahabharata, Dhaumya had divined that before the war, all of dharma had rested with the Pandavas—a quarter with every brother. But with the dawn of the Kali Yuga, this would not be so. Arjuna would submit to conceit, Bhima to gluttony, Nakula to pleasure, and Sahadeva to arrogance. Only Yudhishthira's tenacity to uphold dharma would sustain the world through the final quarter of the Kali Yuga.

PRIESTS PERFORMED SACRED RITUALS AND ALSO EDUCATED YOUNG PRINCES IN MATTERS OF GOVERNANCE AND LIFE.

» strength and who are well versed in the skill of archery could not string the bow, how can this Brahman, with no knowledge of weapons, succeed?" they asked.

Concentrating solely on the target, Arjuna stepped into the arena and stood still. He picked up the bow, looked at the reflection of the eye of the rotating fish, and released the arrow. The arrow hit the mark and the audience cheered—Arjuna had won Draupadi. Everyone assembled in the hall was struck by his strength and precision. People could not believe that a Brahman had done what a Kshatriya could not.

An uproar in the hall

While the Brahmans praised the priest who had won the hand of the Panchala princess, the kings were incensed.

Moreover, on hearing that the king was ready to give away his daughter to the winner, the assembled kings and princes objected. "We have all gathered here and he passes us over like a straw. He wishes to give Draupadi to a Brahman! In this assembly of kings, which is like a conclave of the gods, can he not find a single king who is his equal?" They stood in Arjuna's path and tried to stop him.

Leading the group of royals, Karna attacked Arjuna. The two were soon locked in a long duel

"Let us **find out** who they are and then we will happily fight with them again ... This **lady** has been **won according to dharma**."

KRISHNA TO THE ASSEMBLED KINGS, ADI PARVA: THE BOOK OF THE BEGINNING

PEOPLE

THE ATTENDEES OF THE PANCHALA SWAYAMVARA

Historically, during a swayamvara the woman would chose a husband from among the assembled men. Later, this tradition changed—it became an archery contest and the bride was reduced to a winner's trophy. However, the woman still had the right to disqualify a man.

According to tradition, the brother of the bride-to-be would introduce all the assembled suitors to his sister, so that she could form an opinion about the participants. Dhrishtadyumna, Draupadi's twin brother, introduced all the kings in the gathering to Draupadi before the contest started.

- Duryodhana, son of Dhritarashtra
- Vikarna, son of Dhritarashtra
- Karna, king of Anga
- Shakuni, son of Subala, king of Gandhara
- Ashwatthama and Bhoja, skilled warriors
- Jayadratha, king of Sindhu
- Virata, king of Magadha
- Sankha and Uttara, sons of Virata
- Chandrasena, son of Samudrasena
- Tamralipta, king of Pattana
- Shalya, king of Madra
- Drona
- Rukmagandha and Rukmaratha, sons of Shalya
- King Kaitava
- Subhangada, king of Vatsa
- King Senabindu
- Samba, son of Rukmini
- King Brihanta
- King Manimana
- King Dandadhara
- King Sahadeva
- King Jayatsena
- King Abhibhu
- Sudamna and Suvarchasa, sons of Abhibhu
- King Jalasamdha
- Bhuri, Bhurishrava and Shala, sons of Somadatta
- Shibi, son of Ushinara
- Kritavarma, son of Hridika

"O **fortunate** one! ... These **brave** ones will try to shoot the excellent target **for your hand** ... you will **choose** the **one** who **hits it**"

DHRISHTADYUMNA, DRAUPADI'S TWIN BROTHER, ADI PARVA: THE BOOK OF THE BEGINNING

in which they equaled each other. Karna then realized that his opponent was no ordinary Brahman, but a warrior skilled in the martial arts.

On the other side of the arena, King Shalya and Bhima were attacking each other ferociously.

ARJUNA HITS THE TARGET
Originating as Kalighat temple souvenirs in 19th-century Bengal, the Kalighat style of painting dealt with religious themes. The painting here shows Arjuna, dressed as a priest, shooting at the target, as Draupadi looks on.

To put an end to the fight, Bhima picked up Shalya in his arms and threw him to the ground. The move had the intended effect—both Shalya and Karna became convinced that these Brahmans were invincible and that Arjuna had support in the assembly. By this time, the other Pandava brothers—Yudhishthira, Bhima, Nakula, and Sahadeva—had come to stand by Arjuna's side. Krishna, a Yadava chieftain who was watching all this from a distance, requested the kings to exercise restraint and gently reminded them all, "This lady has been won according to dharma." Hearing Krishna invoke the law of dharma, the supreme code of conduct, everyone backed down and accepted Arjuna as the winner.

Arjuna takes his bride

The king of Panchala was pleased that his daughter had found a worthy match. He happily gave away his daughter to Arjuna, and the Pandavas made their way back to their mother, Kunti, who had been waiting anxiously for their return.

AFTER

Following Dhaumya's instructions, the Pandavas had not only won a beautiful woman as their wife, but had also forged a powerful alliance with a mighty kingdom.

KUNTI MEETS DRAUPADI
After Arjuna won Draupadi, the Pandavas marched back home. Before leaving, they had told their mother that they would go begging for alms. Thus, Kunti had expected them to return much sooner—and had no idea what a surprise her sons had in store for her.

THE PANDAVA ARCHER

Arjuna

"He is born in the **lineage of Bharata** ... In all the worlds ... I do not see anyone who can **vanquish Partha** [Arjuna] with **valor**."

SAGE VAISHAMPAYANA TO KING JANAMEJAYA, ADI PARVA: THE BOOK OF THE BEGINNING

Arjuna was the third son of Kunti and Pandu, the king of Hastinapur. Using a divine mantra, Kunti called upon Indra, the king of the Devas, and begat Arjuna. Since she had invoked Indra of her own volition and not at Pandu's behest, Arjuna, became her favorite child.

The great archer

Arjuna is considered the greatest archer in the Indian epics, second only to Rama, the hero of the Ramayana. He and his brothers were taught by the royal teacher Drona. Arjuna possessed all the qualities of a good student—persistence, determination, the ability to work hard, and focus.

Arjuna practiced archery blindfolded at night, which earned him the name "Gudakesha," or "he who has conquered sleep." He could also shoot using both his hands, and hence, came to be known as Sabyasachi. Once, in an archery test, Drona asked his students to point their arrows at the eye of a stuffed parrot placed high on the wall. "What do you see?" he asked them. They all tried to impress their teacher with how much they could see, but a focused Arjuna saw only an eye.

Arjuna emerged as the star pupil at the graduation ceremony that Drona organized. He used his bow to shoot multiple arrows, never missing a target, making the Kauravas envious of him. But Karna, Kunti's son with Surya the sun god, performed all of Arjuna's feats, surpassing him in each one of them; this would begin a rivalry that would last for life.

Arjuna's wives

The Pandavas lived under constant threat from their cousins, the Kauravas. To secure their lives, they tried to make powerful allies. They went to Draupadi's swayamvara in disguise, where Arjuna, using his archery skills, won the princess's hand. He took his bride to his mother, who asked him to share the "prize" equally with his brothers. Draupadi thus became the Pandavas' common wife. To prevent discord, the brothers decided that Draupadi would be exclusive to each of them for a year. Arjuna once entered Draupadi's chambers during the year she was with Yudhishthira and as punishment had to go into exile for a year. During this

ANALYSIS

ARJUNA'S INSECURITY

Vyasa portrays Arjuna as a highly insecure and competitive man. His prowess as an archer went hand in hand with his pride in being a great warrior and insecurity about others overshadowing him. As a student, he was so upset by Ekalavya's skill that his teacher Drona had to ask the young tribal to cut off his thumb. When Karna's skill threatened Arjuna, he resorted to laughing at his rival's low caste. Arjuna had to be taught a lesson in humility by Shiva, since he was too arrogant to stomach being challenged by a forest dweller. His insecurity made him resort to bravado: in Vyasa's tale he repeatedly swears to kill himself if he was unable to fulfil an oath, such as saving the dying children of a Brahman, or killing Jayadratha before sunset (see pp. 308–09).

THE SKILLED ARCHER
This statue of Arjuna wielding his bow is in the south Indian city of Chennai, Tamil Nadu. The youngest son of Kunti, Arjuna is recognized as the greatest archer in the Mahabharata.

period, he fell in love with and married many women. Vyasa refers to three of these women—Ulupi, Chitrangada, and Subhadra.

The years of exile

When the Pandavas were exiled for thirteen years by the Kauravas, Arjuna became convinced that a war would follow. He felt there was more merit in preparing for that battle than brooding over his fate. He prayed to Shiva and obtained the powerful Pashupatastra, which could decimate humanity.

Arjuna also lived with his father Indra in Amravati, the land of the gods, and helped the Devas fight demons. He was cursed by an Apsara to turn into a eunuch. He used this curse during the last year of exile to disguise himself as Brihannala, the eunuch.

God for a friend

Arjuna shared a special bond with Krishna, who taught him invaluable lessons and assumed the role of his charioteer in the war. He showed Arjuna that the two of them were Nara and Narayana, two inseparable warrior-ascetics who were created to restore dharma on earth. The relationship of Arjuna and Krishna was that of man and God—inseparable. Before the war, Krishna asked Arjuna to choose between his Narayani army and himself, unarmed. Arjuna chose his friend, Krishna, without a moment's hesitation.

At war

In Kurukshetra, Arjuna was the greatest warrior on the Pandavas' side. On the day of the war, he looked at the armies around him and saw brothers, uncles, and nephews, ready to fight and kill one another. "I cannot do this," he said. "This cannot be dharma!" To the surprise of everyone, he lowered his bow. It was then that Krishna explained the true nature of the world to Arjuna. This was the Bhagavad Gita, the song of God. Krishna showed Arjuna his true divine form. Krishna's song changed Arjuna's perspective of the battlefield. This was not Kurukshetra, where war was about property or vengeance. This was Dharmakshetra, an arena where Arjuna would triumph over his fear, guilt, and rage. When his son Abhimanyu was killed unethically by the Kauravas, Arjuna was filled with ire. His death made the war more personal for him.

On the seventeenth day, at long last, Arjuna came face to face with Karna, his archnemesis. After a fierce duel, Karna's chariot wheel got stuck in the ground. He had to get down from his chariot to replace the wheel. Prompted by Krishna, Arjuna killed his unarmed rival.

The final lesson

When the Yadava clan was destroyed, Arjuna went to Dwaraka to rescue the women and children. On their way back, they were attacked by barbarians. Arjuna raised his bow to defend them, but realized that he was no more the archer he used to be. Arjuna finally understood the message given to him by God. Life would continue, with joys and sorrows, triumphs and tragedies. It was up to him to respond wisely, and to enjoy simple pleasures, unshaken by the endless turmoil of the world.

When Yudhishthira decided to renounce the world and ascend to heaven in his mortal body, Arjuna, along with his brothers and Draupadi, followed him. On their way, all but the eldest Pandava lost their lives.

BIOGRAPHY IN BRIEF

- **Born** to Kunti and fathered by the king of gods, Indra, with the help of a divine mantra. The law of niyoga allowed Arjuna to be accepted as Pandu's son.
- **Taught** by Drona, he excelled at archery.
- **Grew jealous** of the tribal Ekalavya's archery skills. To establish Arjuna's superiority, Drona tricked Ekalavya into chopping off his thumb.
- **Emerged as the star pupil** at the graduation ceremony organized by Drona, but Karna got the better of him.
- **Married** Draupadi after winning her hand in her swayamvara, but shared his wife with his brothers. He also married Ulupi, Chitrangada, and Subhadra.
- **Received Gandiva**, the divine bow, from Agni the fire god, after burning Khandavaprastha.
- **Exiled** with his brothers after Yudhishthira lost his kingdom in a gambling match to the Kauravas.
- **Obtained the Pashupatastra** after praying to Shiva, the god of destruction.
- **Cursed** by Urvashi to become a eunuch for a year. Disguised as Brihannala during his year in exile and taught dance to the princess of Matsya.
- **Chose Krishna** over his Narayani army, before the Kurukshetra War. Krishna became his charioteer.
- **Heard the Gita** from Krishna after losing his nerve in the battlefield, unable to kill clansmen and teachers.
- **Killed Bhishma** by hiding behind Shikhandi, who was destined to cause Bhishma's death.
- **Lost Abhimanyu**, his son with Subhadra, and swore to avenge his death.
- **Attacked an unarmed Karna** and killed him while Karna was releasing the wheel of his chariot from mud.
- **Renounced** the material world with his brothers and wife.
- **Died** on his way to heaven, while climbing a mountain. Yudhishthira saw him being punished for arrogance and insecurity in hell.

BRONZE STATUE OF INDRA, ARJUNA'S FATHER

BEFORE

When all the Kshatriyas gathered for Draupadi's swayamvara failed to make a mark, Drupada invited the Brahmans to participate.

ARJUNA WINS DRAUPADI

Disguised as a Brahman, Arjuna rose to take aim at the reflection of the rotating fish. The spectators were surprised to see that a priest could do what the Kshatriyas could not.

Some of the assembled warriors expressed their displeasure and tried to stop Arjuna from claiming Draupadi as his wife. They relented when they found out that the bow-wielding priest had the protection of his four strong brothers.

A MINIATURE PAINTING ON IVORY SHOWING ARJUNA AT DRAUPADI'S SWAYAMVARA

The **Common** Wife

After the swayamvara, Arjuna returned to his mother Kunti with his new bride, Draupadi. A preoccupied Kunti asked him to share the day's winnings equally with his brothers, sealing Draupadi's fate as the wife of all the Pandava brothers.

The day was drawing to a close, but there was no sign of the five Pandavas. Kunti was worried; apprehension filled her mind. Were they safe? Had they been recognized and killed by the Kauravas? Had an evil demon caught them unawares? Her deep love for her sons gave rise to misgivings she was unable to set aside.

It was late by the time the Pandavas and Draupadi arrived at the potter's house where they had taken refuge. Kunti had her back to the door and had not noticed them arriving. Eager to share his news and unable to restrain his excitement, Arjuna burst out, "Mother! Look what I won."

DRAUPADI AND HER HUSBANDS
A dance performance from Chennai, India, depicting Draupadi with her five husbands.

"Those maharathas ... **sons of a king among men**, took the hand of that **supreme among women**, in succession, one day after another."

SAGE VAISHAMPAYANA TO KING JANAMEJAYA, ADI PARVA: THE BOOK OF THE BEGINNING

Kunti's decision

Needing a moment to compose herself, Kunti did not turn around. "Make sure you share the prize equally with your brothers," she said.

When she saw Draupadi standing next to Arjuna, she was taken aback. Torn by her own words, she grappled with her unintended error.

She did not want to commit adharma by going back on her words and was quick to notice that all her sons were captivated by Draupadi's beauty. She knew that jealousy could rip apart the solidarity that was key to their power and invincibility. She repeated her words again, emphasizing that, dharma permitting, she expected her sons to abide by that decision. Yudhishthira confirmed that dharma did allow such a union, and cited the story of Vidula, who had married the ten Prachetas brothers.

So it was that Draupadi became the common wife of the five brothers, who married her on consecutive days.

A previous life

In their earlier lives, the Pandavas had lived as Indras, or lords, of the celestial city of Amravati. With their might, they had successfully defended the honor of their wife Sachi. Unfortunately, in their current life as the sons of Pandu, they would fail to protect their wife Draupadi from the shame and humiliation to which she would later be subjected.

HISTORY AND CULTURE

POLYANDRY

There are tribes in India that historically practiced fraternal polyandry—where a woman marries all the brothers in a household—like Draupadi did. And in the Kinnaur region in the northern state of Himachal Pradhesh, locals claim the custom has been followed since the times of the Pandavas.

In south India, the Todas of the Nilgiri plateau region also practice fraternal polyandry. It is speculated that this custom was followed to avoid division of property in the family, and where a skewed gender ratio resulted in a greater number of men as compared to women.

A TODA MARRIAGE BEING SOLEMNIZED

"Fearing that **conflict** might arise **between the brothers**, the king said, 'This **fortunate Draupadi** will be a **wife for all of us**.'"

YUDHISHTHIRA TO HIS BROTHERS, ADI PARVA: THE BOOK OF THE BEGINNING

AFTER

The five brothers loved Draupadi equally. So, to avoid any conflict among themselves they devised a plan.

SHARING OF DRAUPADI

It was decided that each brother would spend one year with Draupadi. She would be exclusively his wife, with all the rules of monogamy applicable for that time. It was only when the year was over that she would go to another.

Draupadi did not object to her husbands marrying other women; her only condition was that none of these wives were to reside in Indraprastha.

BEFORE

Soon after Draupadi married the Pandavas, a stranger came to their house.

KRISHNA'S ENTRY

The visitor introduced himself as Krishna, Kunti's nephew—her brother Vasudeva's son. Immediately included as part of the family, Krishna advised Kunti to return to Hastinapur. He was sure that the Kauravas would be more amenable now that the Pandavas had married the daughter of the mighty Panchala king, Drupada. Kunti asked Krishna if he thought that Dhritarashtra would give her sons the kingdom. "I don't think so," replied Krishna, "But there is another way."

So the Pandavas returned to Hastinapur with their mother and their new bride, hoping for the best.

HISTORY AND CULTURE

JHOOM CULTIVATION

Jhoom cultivation is the practice of slash-and-burn, where the forest cover is cleared, dried, and then burned so the land can be used for purposes of agriculture. Popular in the northeastern part of India, this practice is followed after the crop is harvested, after which the land is left to regenerate. The slash-and-burn mode of cultivation is an ancient one, believed to have been in use since the Neolithic age. Today, the heavy ecological damage this method of cultivation causes earns it severe criticism.

THE SLASH-AND-BURN PRACTICE BELIEVED TO BE PREVALENT SINCE THE NEOLITHIC AGE

Khandavaprastha

The Pandavas were received with great joy and fanfare on their return to Hastinapur, but whispers of foul play persisted. To put these to rest, Dhritarashtra, the king of Hastinapur, gave them the forest of Khandavaprastha.

The city celebrated the Pandavas' return and rejoiced that they were alive and well. At court, they were greeted with affection. Looking at those familiar faces, the brothers could not help but wonder who had planned their deaths.

Vidura advised Dhritarashtra to put all talk of conspiracies and foul play to rest by giving up the throne in favor of Yudhishthira. But the king was unwilling—his sons would not serve the sons of Pandu. Krishna, who had accompanied his cousins to Hastinapur, counseled Vidura to divide the kingdom. Acting on this advice, in a public ceremony Dhritarashtra gave the Pandavas a part of the kingdom known as Khandavaprastha.

The forest inferno

Khandavaprastha was forested land, home to many birds, beasts, Nagas, and Rakshasas. It had to be destroyed—how else could a kingdom be established?

Agni, the god of fire, approached the Pandavas, and volunteered to burn the forest for them. "I have lost my luster from all the ghee that has been poured into me. Burning something will help me recover," he said.

The Pandavas accepted Agni's offer, and soon the forest was engulfed in flames. The trees, the shrubs, down to the very last blade of grass began to burn, and the forest resounded with the calls of birds and beasts.

"Kill them all," advised Krishna. "Ensure that no one else can claim this land. This is the price of ownership; the burden of civilization. However, take care not to fall prey to greed: stop when your needs have been met."

THE RAZING OF THE FOREST
This relief from the Banteay Srei temple in Cambodia depicts animals fleeing the Khandava forest while Arjuna and Krishna look on.

A great slaughter ensued. Deer, lions, monkeys, serpents, turtles, pigeons, parrots, bees, ants—not even the Nagas or the Rakshasas were spared. Caught in the blazing flames, the Nagas turned to their friend Indra for help.

A parasol of arrows

Indra came to the Nagas' aid, hurling thunder and rain over the forest. Seeing this, Krishna asked Arjuna to make a parasol of arrows to ensure that the rain could not affect the fire. Under this great umbrella of arrows the forest burned for days, until Agni regained his luster. Pleased and satiated, the fire god gifted Arjuna the Gandiva—the bow created by Brahma himself—and Krishna, the infallible Sudarshana Chakra, to help them establish and maintain dharma. Agni then returned to his celestial abode.

A city for a life

With Agni's help, the Pandavas had stripped the forest of all life. But one being—the Asura Maya—had managed to escape. Emerging from the flames, he had begged the Pandavas to spare him. "I am the architect of the Asuras. In exchange for my life I will build you a great city" he offered.

So, on the land that had once been the great forest of Khandavaprastha, the Pandavas built a great city designed by Maya. They decided to name it Indraprastha, meaning "City of Indra," and resolved to make it heaven on earth. In return for sparing his life, Maya gave Arjuna a conch-shell trumpet called Devadutta.

Under Yudhishthira's rule Indraprastha soon grew to be a prosperous city and the envy of all Bharatavarsha.

DEVADUTTA, THE NAME OF ARJUNA'S CONCH SHELL, MEANS "GIFTED BY THE GODS"

"O lord! **Blaze as you wish** and encircle this great forest. We are **capable of helping you**."

ARJUNA AND KRISHNA TO AGNI, THE GOD OF FIRE, ADI PARVA: THE BOOK OF THE BEGINNING

HISTORY AND CULTURE

DIVINE ARCHITECTS

The Devas and the Asuras had architects who built great cities based on the principles of Vastu shastra, the Hindu system of architecture. Vishwakarma, who served the Devas, and Maya, who served the Asuras, were known throughout the world for their skills. In Sanskrit, "maya" means illusion. Indraprastha was an extraordinary place, full of many wondrous sights and sounds.

VASTU PURUSHA MANDALA, USED FOR GENERATING DESIGNS IN VASTU SHASTRA

AFTER

Before long, Indraprastha grew into a bustling city attracting people from all Bharatavarsha.

A FLOURISHING CAPITAL
Men of all ranks made this city their new home. Yudhishthira instituted and maintained the code of dharma there. All men were supposed to carry out their duties determined by their father's role in society and by their stage in life. All women were supposed to take care of their fathers, brothers, husbands, and sons and help them fulfil their duty.

THE CITY OF THE PANDAVAS

Indraprastha

INDRAPRASTHA
It is believed that the area of the ancient city of Indraprastha coincides with the location of present-day Delhi, India.

> **"**Reflecting the **image of heaven**, it came to be known as **Indraprastha**.**"**
>
> SAGE VAISHAMPAYANA TO JANAMEJAYA, ADI PARVA: THE BOOK OF THE BEGINNING

Indraprastha, meaning "City of Indra," was the home of the Pandavas in the Mahabharata. As the story goes, Dhritarashtra gave the Pandavas the forest of Khandavaprastha to build their kingdom. It was burned down by the brothers on the advice of Krishna to build their new city. Nothing survived the great conflagration except Maya, the architect of the demons. In return for his life being spared, Maya built a great city for the Pandavas, who named it Indraprastha.
(see pp. 114–15)

Indraprastha in the Mahabharata

Soon after the Pandavas established Indraprastha, the prosperous city became the envy of all Bharatavarsha. It was known for its fields, orchards, river ports, and markets, and people from different occupations made the city their new home. Yudhishthira, as the newly crowned king of Indraprastha, instituted and maintained the code of dharma in the city. When the eldest Kaurava, Duryodhana, visited Indraprastha to attend

Yudhishthira's coronation ceremony, he was intensely jealous of his cousins' newfound prosperity. So engrossed was he in gazing at the new palace that he slipped and fell into a pond. Draupadi, standing nearby, mocked Duryodhana, calling him the blind son of blind parents. A humiliated Duryodhana went away filled with the desire to take revenge.

EMPEROR ASHOKA WITH HIS ARMY
A mural shows Emperor Ashoka and his troops marching forward. Rock edicts of the emperor found in Delhi have led to the supposition that the city may have been of great importance during the Mauryan period.

Indraprastha in history

Some historians believe that the site of the ancient city of Indraprastha is the same as modern-day Delhi—specifically, the place where the Purana Qila, or the Old Fort, now stands. This theory has not been substantiated and is still open to debate. But if true, it would make Indraprastha the first city of Delhi, of the many that have existed in the vicinity of the Indian capital.

The earliest credible records that led to the belief that Purana Qila in Delhi was the site of Indraprastha are from the 14th century. Two 14th-century inscriptions found in Delhi refer to the word "Indraprastha." It finds mention again in the British-era *Delhi Gazetteer*, which states that Yudhishthira built the city of Indraprastha on the banks of the Yamuna river, between the "more modern Kotila of Firoz Shah and Humayun's Tomb, about 2 miles (3.2 km) south of the present site of Delhi." At that time the Yamuna flowed next to Indraprastha, but later its course shifted away from that site. The source claims, "the Nigambodh Ghat, near the old Calcutta Gate of the present city, is believed to have formed part of the ancient capital, but with this exception not a stone of it remains standing. Its name however is preserved as that of Indrapat." Another fact that supports this hypothesis is that until 1913, there was a village named Indrapat inside the Old Fort.

A rock edict of Emperor Ashoka, found in Srinivasapuri in Delhi, has led some scholars to infer that the city may have been of great importance during the period of the Mauryan empire.

Archaeological records

The site was explored by noted British archaeologist Alexander Cunningham in the 19th century and has witnessed many excavations since then. In the excavations of 1950s, conducted by archaeologist B.B. Lal of the Archaeological Survey of India, Northern Black Polished Ware and Painted Grey Ware were found, suggesting habitation around the 10th century and during 700–500 BCE. Later excavations have confirmed remains from eight periods: Maurya (4th–3rd century BCE); Sunga (2nd–1st century BCE); Saka–Kushan (1st–3rd century CE); Gupta (4th–6th century CE); post-Gupta (7th–9th century CE); Rajput (10th–12th century CE); Delhi Sultanate (13th–15th century CE); and Mughal (16th–19th century CE). However, the question of whether people from the Mahabharata lived here is still a matter of speculation.

The site continues to be of interest to the Archaeological Survey of India, and they have carried out excavations until very recently.

THE MOSQUE AT PURANA QILA
The Qila-i-Kuna Mosque, built by Sher Shah Suri, founder of the Sur dynasty, in 1541 inside the Purana Qila, is said to be the site of the city of Indraprastha.

HISTORY AND CULTURE

BHAIRAVA TEMPLE

The temple of Kilkari Bhairava outside Purana Qila is believed to have been established by the Pandavas at the entrance of the city of Indraprastha. While some stories identify Bhairava as a demon, others recognize him as a tantric. It is believed that Bhairava approached the mother goddess with lust and she, incensed, beheaded him. The head apologized to her and sang songs in her praise. Appeased, she declared that Bhairava's head would be worshipped. For devotees, Bhairava is a form of Shiva, who rides a dog and is offered bottles of alcohol.

It is said that Bhima brought the image of Bhairava to this shrine from the hills. Bhairava's condition was that once he was picked up, he should not be placed on the ground. But Bhima stopped to eat at the gates, so the shrine came to be located there.

BEFORE

To avoid conflict between the brothers, it was decided that each Pandava would spend a year at a time with Draupadi. This way, each brother would get to spend time with her without any interference.

ARJUNA'S EXILE

One day, a few cowherds came rushing to Arjuna for help, as thieves were stealing the Pandavas' cows. Arjuna rushed to the palace to collect his bow. He looked everywhere but to no avail. Not knowing where else to look, he decided to search Draupadi's chamber. As soon as he entered the room, he found her in the company of Yudhishthira.

By entering the room out of turn and interrupting the couple, Arjuna had broken the rule, and he had to spend a year in exile as punishment. He left Indraprastha and went on a pilgrimage to holy shrines across the land.

ARJUNA AND ULUPI

An Indonesian-style painting by British illustrator Warwick Goble depicts Arjuna and Ulupi. This painting is featured in the book *Indian Myth and Legend* by Donald A Mackenzie, published in 1913.

Arjuna's Other Wives

Having broken the pact the brothers made about sharing Draupadi, Arjuna had to leave Indraprastha for a year. During this period, he went on a pilgrimage, had many adventures and strange encounters, and also married many women.

Arjuna visited many places of worship. On one of his visits to a shrine near a lake, he was attacked by five crocodiles. He managed to wrestle and kill them. To his surprise, the crocodiles transformed into nymphs. They said to him, "Once, when we disturbed a Rishi's meditation, he cursed us and turned us into crocodiles. We were told that a warrior would liberate us."

Another time, while he was near a river, a Naga woman named Ulupi dragged Arjuna under the water. She beseeched him to marry her. "Make me yours," she said.

Arjuna refused, to which Ulupi retorted, "To reject a woman who comes to you willingly and full of desire is an act against dharma."

Arjuna had no choice but to spend the night with her. He left her the next day and soon forgot all about the woman in the river, not knowing that she would have his child, a son named Iravan, who would play a crucial role in the great war at Kurukshetra.

The warrior princess

Arjuna then reached the kingdom of Manipur. He had heard wonderful tales about the warrior princess of Manipur, Chitrangada, who would dress as a man and live like a prince in her kingdom.

Chitrangada, too, had heard wonderful stories about Arjuna and had fallen in love with him without even laying eyes on him. Anxious that Arjuna not be repelled by her masculine form, she prayed to Lord Shiva to turn her into a coy, young girl. But when she approached Arjuna, he hardly paid any attention to her as he had seen many other feminine women. »

MYTHOLOGY AND FOLKLORE

AYLI

One of Arjuna's many consorts was an Amazon queen named Ayli. According to Tamil folklore she was a warrior princess from the temple town of Madurai in south India.

She was renowned for her strength and it was known that no man could defeat her. Arjuna wanted to make her his wife and asked his friend Krishna to help him.

At first, Krishna asked him to forget about making the formidable princess his wife, but Arjuna persisted. Krishna then transformed Arjuna into a serpent and disguised himself as a snake charmer. Then, he took Arjuna with him through the gates of the city.

Fascinated by the beautiful snake, Ayli asked the snake charmer to leave the snake in her bed chamber – and later that night, Arjuna seduced the princess.

ARJUNA IS SAID TO HAVE TAKEN THE FORM OF A SNAKE TO SEDUCE THE TAMIL PRINCESS, AYLI

"**O Kounteya! I saw you** descend into the water to have a bath **and was robbed of my senses** ... The god of love is churning me. **I am yet a maiden. Please me** today by giving yourself to me."

ULUPI TO ARJUNA, ADI PARVA: THE BOOK OF THE BEGINNING

ARJUNA AND CHITRANGADA
Fearing that her masculine appearance would repel Arjuna, Chitrangada invoked Lord Shiva and asked him to transform her into a demure, young girl.

> "O Pandava, you can take her, **as long as you agree** to this condition … **The son,** the perpetuator of this lineage **will be the bride price**."
>
> THE KING OF MANIPUR TO ARJUNA, ADI PARVA: THE BOOK OF THE BEGINNING

Instead, Arjuna's eyes searched for the warrior woman about whom he had heard so much. When Chitrangada realized this, she begged Shiva to turn her back into her original form—a warrior princess with a masculine personality. As soon as Arjuna saw her regal form, he fell in love with her. He asked the king of Manipur for his daughter's hand in marriage. The king replied, "Yes, but only if you allow me to adopt the son she bears with you." Arjuna agreed to this condition and married Chitrangada.

Later, the princess gave birth to a son named Babruvahana. This son would play a big role in Arjuna's life in the years after the great war.

Krishna's sister Subhadra

Arjuna also visited Dwaraka, the port city on the west coast where the Yadavas had settled. Krishna's sister Subhadra lived there. Though their older brother Balarama had promised her to Duryodhana, Krishna knew that she was in love with Arjuna. He had therefore encouraged Arjuna to elope with her and told him enter the city disguised as a beggar.

As soon as Subhadra realized that the beggar was none other than Arjuna, she left the city with him. To show the world that her love for Arjuna was true and that she was leaving with him on her own volition, Subhadra held the reins of the chariot for the whole city to see. Balarama was none too pleased

ART AND LITERATURE

TAGORE'S CHITRANGADA

Rabindranath Tagore took the story of Chitrangada and transformed it into *Chitra*, a dance drama. It tells the story of the princess of Manipur who met Arjuna and fell in love with him. In the play, Tagore portrays her as the heir to the throne who dressed like a man and was a great warrior. With a blessing from Kamadeva, the god of love and desire, she is transformed into a beautiful, feminine woman—but Arjuna is more impressed by her warrior persona than her beauty.

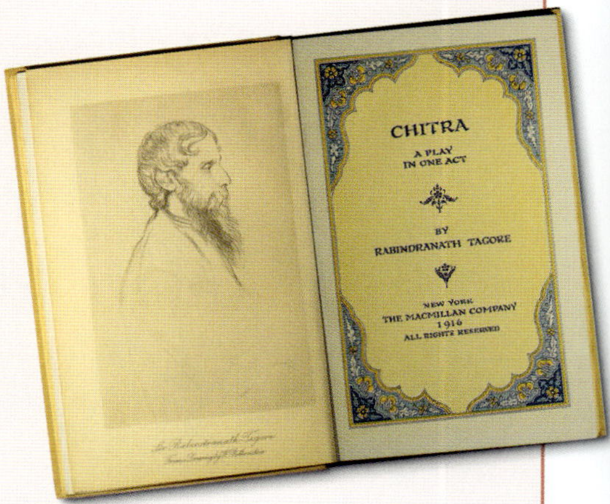

RABINDRANATH TAGORE WROTE THIS DANCE DRAMA IN 1892.

to have his sister disobey his wishes. He grew angrier on learning that the man she had eloped with was none other than Arjuna. He wanted to chase them and get his sister back. But Krishna stopped him, saying, "She is in love with Arjuna. See how happy she is. She went with him on her own."

Balarama finally understood that his sister was in love, and let the couple live in peace.

MYTHOLOGY AND FOLKLORE

SUMBADRA AND SRIKANDI

In Indonesian folklore Arjuna is said to have married seven women other than Draupadi. Among them were Sumbadra, Krishna's sister who was gentle and self-effacing, and Draupadi's sister Srikandi, a saucy and skilled archer. Srikandi later participated in the battle at Kurukshetra and was responsible for Bhishma's death. It is believed that Srikandi is the Indonesian interpretation of the gender-neutral character of Shikhandi in the Mahabharata.

Bhanumati, the woman who later became Duryodhana's wife, was also in love with Arjuna. But the warrior found it inappropriate to marry a woman who has already been promised to his cousin. However, in the Sanskrit Mahabharata, Arjuna gloats over the fact that Duryodhana's wife loved him.

"This **alliance** is appropriate. **Subhadra** is **illustrious**, **Partha** is **equally so.**"

KRISHNA TO BALARAMA, ADI PARVA: THE BOOK OF THE BEGINNING

AFTER

Arjuna now had to grapple with a conundrum, for the brothers had promised Draupadi that they would not bring any wife back to Indraprastha.

DRAUPADI AND SUBHADRA

Arjuna knew that he could not take Subhadra home as Draupadi had made a rule that no other Pandava wife would be allowed inside the city. Krishna advised Subhadra to enter Draupadi's chamber as a milkmaid and ask for shelter for herself and her husband. Taking pity on her plight, Draupadi agreed to help her and accepted Subhadra as her sister. That is when Subhadra disclosed her true identity. Draupadi realized she had been tricked but she forgave Subhadra and allowed her to live in the palace.

THREE DEITIES

This varnished watercolor on canvas depicts the three siblings—Krishna (as Jagannath), Subhadra, and Balarama (as Balabhadra)—as deities. They are often worshipped in Odisha, India.

BATTLE OF WILLS

A 19th-century Mughal-style painting depicts Krishna and the archer Arjuna, two strong-willed warriors.

BEFORE

A Gandharva named Gaya was flying over Dwaraka one day when he spat on the ground.

AN INFURIATED KRISHNA
Gaya's spit fell on Krishna's head. Furious at his insolence, Krishna took an oath to behead the creature who showed him such disrespect. He then picked up his weapons, including the dreaded Sudarshana Chakra, mounted his chariot, and set out in pursuit of Gaya.

Gaya **Beheaded**

Quite unintentionally, the Gandharva Gaya not only put his own life at stake, but caused a confrontation between Krishna and Arjuna. With neither ready to compromise, the gods had to intervene to prevent massive destruction.

Terrified of Krishna, Gaya ran to Indraprastha and fell at the feet of Subhadra, Arjuna's wife.

"O noble lady! Save me from a mad warrior who is after my life and threatens to kill me for a crime committed accidentally," he wailed.

Feeling sorry for the poor creature, Subhadra promised to help. "Do not be scared. My husband, Arjuna, is the mightiest archer on earth. He will offer you protection," she reassured him. Gaya smiled in relief.

Subhadra's predicament

Shortly thereafter, fuming with rage, Krishna came to the gates of the city and ordered Gaya, who he had seen entering the gates, to step out.

On seeing Krishna, Subhadra realized that the mad warrior that Gaya had been referring to was none other than her own brother. Having already promised to help the Gandharva, she could not go back on her word. She told Krishna that Arjuna had sworn to protect Gaya and, therefore, Krishna could not harm him.

Reiterating his oath to behead Gaya, Krishna told Subhadra that nothing would stop him from killing the offender.

Krishna against Arjuna

Soon, Krishna and Arjuna stood facing each other. Arjuna held the mighty bow, Gandiva, in his hand, while Krishna's Sudarshana Chakra whirred around his finger. Gaya lay quivering at Subhadra's feet. Men of their word, neither of the two warriors was ready to step back.

"The fundamental principle of dharma instructs one to honor one's word," said Arjuna.

A duel between the two would have been catastrophic. If Arjuna struck Krishna, the world would come to an end, and if Krishna struck Arjuna, it would mean the defeat of the Pandavas, and ultimately, the end of all hope for the world.

Intervention by the gods

The Devas, who saw all this unfold from Swarga, were alarmed. Fearing the worst, they begged Brahma, the creator of the world, and Shiva, the destroyer of the world, to intervene and avert the unimaginable. The creator and destroyer reached the spot to stop the battling warriors.

"Stop," they said. "The earth trembles as you draw your weapons against each other."

To resolve the conflict, Brahma asked Arjuna to let Krishna fulfil his oath and behead Gaya. He promised Arjuna that he would restore Gaya to life, making sure that he was not dishonored either.

"Both of you will be able to keep your word and fulfil your oath," said Brahma.

Realizing the gravity of the situation, Arjuna lowered his bow and let Krishna behead Gaya. As promised, Brahma then resurrected the Gandharva.

MYTHOLOGY AND FOLKLORE

YAKSHAGANA

The story of Gaya, who creates conflict between Arjuna and Krishna, is not part of the classical Sanskrit narrative, but features in many regional retellings. Written by Halemakki Rama in the 17th century, the play *Gayacharitre* tells the story of Gaya, and is performed by Yakshagana artists. Staged primarily in the coastal districts of Karnataka, India, the Yakshagana theater style combines literature, music, dance, and painting. It is traditionally performed from dusk to dawn.

A YAKSHAGANA PERFORMER

THE CREATOR
A 9th-century sculpture of Brahma, the deity of creation, made of volcanic stone, from Central Java, Indonesia.

AFTER

Brought back to life by Brahma, the creator, Gaya thanked Arjuna for saving him.

GAYA'S APOLOGY
Gaya begged Krishna to forgive him for spitting on him and causing such cosmic disruption.

The story of Gaya explains how even good intentions can disrupt the bonds of friendship. It is also a lesson on how people can exploit friendship to their own advantage.

BEFORE

Having broken the agreement on their marriage to Draupadi, Arjuna had to undertake a year's penance. He chose a pilgrimage.

ARJUNA'S PRIDE

One day, Arjuna thought about the bridge of stones that Rama had built to Lanka to rescue his wife, Sita, whom the Rakshasa king Ravana had abducted. He wondered why the king had not been able to build a bridge of arrows instead. "If I could build a bridge of arrows from heaven to earth, could it be that Rama was not as good an archer as I?" he wondered aloud.

THIS PAINTING FROM ODISHA, INDIA, SHOWS RAMA'S ARMY OF MONKEYS BUILDING A BRIDGE TO LANKA

Arjuna's True Destiny

A chance encounter with the monkey god Hanuman put a check on Arjuna's vanity and made him realize the purpose of his existence.

THE CHILDREN OF THE GODS
An antique medallion showing Arjuna and Hanuman; detail of the same medallion (right).

Hanuman, the monkey god and a great devotee of Rama, could not bear to hear Arjuna doubt Rama's prowess. Assuming the form of a frail, ordinary monkey he leaped down from a nearby tree. "A bridge of arrows could have hardly supported the weight of all the monkeys. That's why Rama had to build a bridge of stones. Why don't you build a bridge of arrows across this river and see if it can take the weight of even one monkey?" he challenged.

Arjuna confidently accepted the dare. Shooting one arrow after another, he created a bridge across the river and invited the monkey to try it. But the minute Hanuman placed a paw on the bridge, it gave way. Laughing, Hanuman asked Arjuna, "Are you sure you built a bridge that brought Airavat down from heaven to earth?"

Meeting Hanuman

The taunt pierced Arjuna deeply, humiliating him so much that he even contemplated killing himself. Fortunately, a sage who had watched the whole drama advised Arjuna to build a bridge of arrows once again. "This time, however, chant 'Rama-Krishna-Hari' with every arrow you shoot," he said.

Arjuna followed the sage's advice and found that this time the bridge held firm under the monkey's weight. Then Hanuman revealed his true, powerful form and began to jump and dance on the bridge—it still stood firm. He then began to increase in size, growing taller and taller, until he was as large as a mountain. Despite the enormous pressure on it, the bridge did not as much buckle. The sage explained the miracle to a dumbfounded Arjuna. "The name of Rama ensured that the bridge of stones to Lanka did not sink under the monkeys' weight. Chanting Krishna's name ensures that this bridge of arrows withstands Hanuman's weight. Strength alone is not enough in this world; you need divine grace as well. Krishna is Rama, and both are Hari, or Vishnu. Always remember, without Krishna, you are nothing. You are Nara and he is Narayana."

A chastened Arjuna bowed to the sage and fell at Hanuman's feet, begging for forgiveness. But he was also puzzled.

"What did you mean – I am Nara and Krishna is Narayana?" he asked.

"You will soon learn the meaning," replied Hanuman, before taking leave of Arjuna.

MYTHOLOGY AND FOLKLORE

HANUMAN, THE MONKEY GOD

Hanuman is an important figure in the story of Rama, an incarnation of Vishnu, and is revered for being Rama's greatest devotee.

When Rama's wife, Sita, was abducted by the Rakshasa king Ravana, Hanuman gathered an army of monkeys for Rama and led them in the battle that ensued.

The son of the wind god Vayu and endowed with superhuman strength, Hanuman is one of the "chiranjivis" (those who will live until the end of the current age, the Kali Yuga). He is also mentioned in several texts such as the Mahabharata, the Puranas, and Jain scriptures.

THE MONKEY GOD WITH HIS FAVORITE WEAPON, THE GADA, OR MACE

"Hanuman ... was as **gigantic** as Indra's flagpole ... He was yellow, like lightning. He looked like a **flash of lightning**. He was as **swift** as lightning."

SAGE VAISHAMPAYANA TO JANAMEJAYA, VANA PARVA: THE BOOK OF THE FOREST

"You are mine and I am yours. All that is mine is yours too ... You are **Nara and I am Hari Narayana** ... O Partha! You are no other than I. **I am no other than you."**

KRISHNA TO ARJUNA, ADI PARVA: THE BOOK OF THE BEGINNING

THE ETERNAL VISHNU
This 17th-century painting from Rajasthan, India, shows Vishnu with his consort Lakshmi, resting between the destruction of the world and the creation of a new universe. He is lying on the serpent Adi-Ananta-Shesha who represents eternity.

A Brahman's request

A few days later, an anxious Brahman approached Arjuna and appealed to him for help.

The Brahman and his wife were suffering from a strange affliction. Each time the woman gave birth, their baby would vanish without a trace. Now his wife was pregnant again and due to deliver soon. The Brahman feared that this child too would meet the same fate. The worried father-to-be wanted Arjuna's help to protect his baby.

Arjuna's promise

The archer promised to save the Brahman's children. He assured him that with his mighty bow, Gandiva, he would fight Yama, the god of death himself, if the need arose. "If I fail," Arjuna declared, "I will burn myself alive." Krishna said he would join Arjuna in this endeavor.

On the day the Brahman's wife went into labor, Arjuna built a tight barricade of arrows around their house and stood guard at the door. "Now let me see who can take the child away," he thought, satisfied with how he had safeguarded the house. A few minutes later, he heard the shrill cry of a baby. Then the silence that followed was broken by a heartbroken wail. "My baby has disappeared!" The distraught Brahman cried out. "Oh Arjuna, you failed!"

Unable to face the Brahman's reproaches and wracked by guilt, Arjuna was seriously

KEY CONCEPT

THE NOTION OF AN ALL-POWERFUL GOD

A PAINTING FROM THAILAND SHOWING GANESHA, SHIVA, AND VISHNU

The notion of an all-powerful God with whom one could have a deeply personal devotional relationship entered quite late in the evolution of Hindu philosophy. The earliest scriptures, the Vedas, comprise hymns to appease the cosmic forces such as the sun, or nature deities such as Indra the god of thunder, but there is no mention of "one" God. Later scriptures such as the Upanishads described a universal Atman, or supreme soul, that humans must realize within themselves.

The idea of God as propagated by the Bhagavata ("devotee") cult—viewing him as a father figure and an intimate friend—was immensely comforting. The devotee could worship him directly without bothering with arcane rituals, and turn to him in a crisis, with the belief that God would see him through difficulties. The Mahabharata is one of the earliest texts to endorse this idea in the person of Krishna, an incarnation of Vishnu. Krishna's presence makes the epic a sacred scripture and supports the idea of a more personal god.

contemplating ending his life when Krishna intervened. "Come with me. Let me show you something first," he said leading Arjuna toward his chariot.

It was a long journey and after a while, Arjuna noticed that the chariot was no longer touching the earth—they were navigating the inky sky; their path lit by Krishna's Sudarshana Chakra, which was whirring in front of them. The chariot flew over oceans of salt water; an ocean of fresh water replete with fantastic creatures; an ocean of fire full of reptiles; then an ocean of treacle; and finally arrived at a sea of milk.

A divine vision

At the center of the sea of milk, Vishnu, the god of preservation, reclined on the coils of the thousand-hooded serpent, Adi-Ananta-Sesha. In his four arms he held a conch shell, a mace, a discus, and a lotus. Lakshmi, the goddess of wealth, sat at his feet, while Saraswati, the goddess of learning, sat on his tongue. Awestruck, Arjuna fell at Vishnu's feet. When he stood up, he saw the deity holding the missing babies.

"I brought them here to tell you the true purpose of your existence," he told Arjuna, who looked toward Krishna for an explanation.

"Long ago, you were Nara and I was Narayana," Vishnu began. "Together we defeated many demons and established peace across the land. Now we are Arjuna and Krishna, born to restore dharma on earth."

"Krishna is wisdom. You are action," he continued. "One without the other is meaningless. You will win your battles only when you are together."

MYTHOLOGY AND FOLKLORE

NARA AND NARAYANA, THE WARRIOR-ASCETICS

Nara and Narayana were two sages who lived under a badari (berry) tree in the Himalayas. Their names feature repeatedly in the Mahabharata as previous incarnations of Arjuna and Krishna. Regarded as warrior-ascetics, they are believed to be among the earliest worshippers of Vishnu.

In Sanskrit, "nara" means human while "narayana" is the supreme deity, reflecting the relationship of Arjuna and Krishna (man and God) as inseparable. By associating Arjuna and Krishna with Nara and Narayana, Vyasa makes them creatures of destiny. Their birth is not random; they are born for a reason.

AFTER

Arjuna's year of wandering drew to a close and he made his way back to his family.

PLANS FOR THE RAJASUYA

While Arjuna was away, Yudhishthira was planning a Rajasuya yagna—a ceremony through which he could declare his independence from the Kuru household and establish himself as a powerful king.

The eldest Pandava had only been waiting for his brother's return to perform the ceremony. Once Arjuna was reunited with his family, preparations for the eldest Pandava's coronation began in earnest.

2

SABHA PARVA: THE BOOK OF THE ASSEMBLY HALL

THE GAMBLE
Kathakali, an ancient dance form from the southern state of Kerala, India, often enacts episodes from the Mahabharata, such as this scene of the gambling match. The game of dice between the Pandavas and the Kauravas was a turning point in the epic.

Sabha Parva, or the Book of the Assembly Hall, is the second parva in the Mahabharata. The word "sabha" means assembly hall or council. The parva begins with an account of the assembly hall built for the Pandavas by Maya, the Asura architect. Yudhishthira's coronation also takes place at this same hall. The parva describes Duryodhana's envy of the Pandavas' newfound prosperity, and the game of dice between the Pandavas and the Kauravas, which had dire consequences. The parva ends with the Pandavas' exile. The Sabha Parva has 9 sub-parvas, 72 chapters, and 2,387 shlokas, or couplets.

"The asura built a **matchless sabha.** It was beautiful … encrusted with jewels, and famous in the three worlds. The **supreme assembly hall** … had golden pillars. Its radiance was divine … Brahma's palace was **no match**."

SAGE VAISHAMPAYANA TO KING JANAMEJAYA, SABHA PARVA: THE BOOK OF THE ASSEMBLY HALL

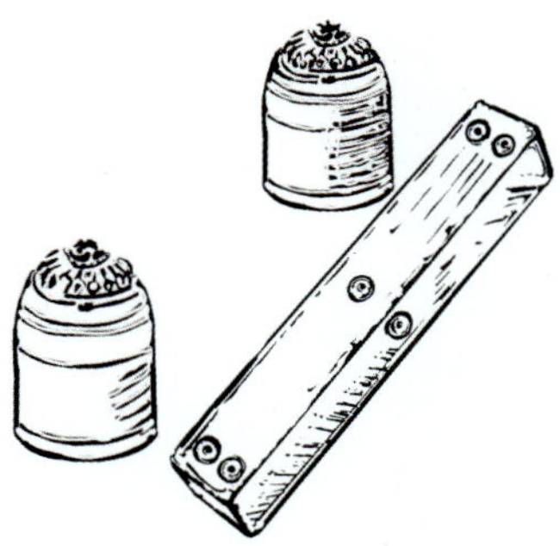

BEFORE

The Pandavas transformed the forest of Khandavaprastha into a prosperous city.

INDRAPRASTHA

They named this city Indraprastha, determined to make it a paradise on earth. With fields, markets, and ports, Indraprastha began to flourish. Priests, warriors, farmers, herdsmen, and artisans from all over flocked to make it their new home.

Since his kingdom was doing well, Yudhishthira was keen to proclaim his independence from the Kuru kingdom.

The **Rajasuya** Ceremony

Now that he had a kingdom, Yudhishthira wanted to perform the Rajasuya yagna. This ceremony would establish Indraprastha as a kingdom in its own right and ensure that the participating rulers accepted his sovereignty.

With his brothers by his side and allies such as Drupada to support him, Yudhishthira felt it was time to perform the Rajasuya yagna. This was a ceremony in which kingdoms announced their sovereignty. Before performing this ceremony, a ruler of a kingdom had to prove his military might, ensuring that other kings of the land accepted him as an equal.

By performing the Rajasuya ceremony, Yudhishthira would also formally break all ties with his uncle and announce to the world that his kingdom was autonomous. He consulted his priests and advisors on whether this would be the correct action to take. "Do not reflect any more and set your mind on the Rajasuya," they advised. Though everyone supported the idea, Yudhishthira was concerned that he was being selfish. So, he sought Krishna's advice, assuring him that the final decision would be shaped by his opinion.

Krishna's advice

For a Rajasuya ceremony to be a success, Yudhishthira would need the participation of the other kings of the land. Knowing that this could pose a problem, Krishna made a suggestion. "You have to first prove that you are worthy of the crown. The best way to do so is to overpower Jarasandha. This way you will demonstrate your power and your claim to kingship will remain uncontested."

"Are you talking about the king of Magadha, destroyer of Mathura!" exclaimed Yudhishthira, taken aback, as Jarasandha was a powerful ruler who was said to have imprisoned a hundred kings. It was also rumored that he was planning to conduct a human sacrifice. As an ally of Kansa—the man who had imprisoned Krishna's parents and done his best to kill Krishna —Jarasandha was Krishna's enemy. In fact, it was because of the fear of Jarasandha that Krishna and the Yadavas had left Mathura and had retreated to Dwaraka.

Battling Jarasandha

In theory, Krishna's idea was a sound one. With this one move, the Yadavas would be rid of the man who had destroyed Mathura and also establish the Pandavas' supremacy beyond doubt. But Yudhishthira was not convinced. Jarasandha's armies inspired fear throughout Bharatavarsha and the eldest Pandava was concerned that Magadha's battle-hardened soldiers would crush his forces in

> "O king! You are learned in the ways of dharma. You are worthy of performing the great sacrifice of rajasuya."
>
> SAGES TO YUDHISHTHIRA, SABHA PARVA: THE BOOK OF THE ASSEMBLY HALL

MYTHOLOGY AND FOLKLORE

PURUSHA-MRIGA

Half-human, half-beasts, purusha-mrigas are a part of the south Indian temple tradition. Images of men and women with the feet of a lion, tiger, or deer adorn the walls of many temples of Shiva and Vishnu in the southern states of Tamil Nadu and Andhra Pradesh. These creatures serve as mounts who carry the idols of the gods and goddesses in grand processions during festivals. According to a Tamil folk story, Yudhishthira needed a purusha-mriga to bless the Rajasuya ceremony, and sent Bhima to invite one for the grand yagna.

PURUSHA-MRIGAS WERE DEVOTEES OF SHIVA, THE GOD OF DESTRUCTION

no time. Accepting Yudhishthira's fears, Krishna came up with a plan to nullify the enemy's strengths and give the Pandavas a chance at victory.

The solution, said Krishna, was to avoid a battle altogether. He proposed that the Pandavas trick Jarasandha into fighting them individually. In hand-to-hand combat, Bhima was a good match for Jarasandha; and, given his immense arrogance and pride, there was no doubt the king of Magadha would accept Bhima's challenge.

"**Yudhishthira sighed** and thinking about performing **rajasuya**, could find **no peace** … after reflecting a great deal, [he] **made up his mind** to perform the **rajasuya**."

SAGE VAISHAMPAYANA TO KING JANAMEJAYA, SABHA PARVA: THE BOOK OF THE ASSEMBLY HALL

AFTER

To quell his doubts, Krishna assured Yudhishthira that a nimble brain could outdo physical might.

DISGUISED AS PRIESTS
Krishna asked Bhima and Arjuna to go to Magadha disguised as priests. In keeping with the laws of hospitality, Jarasandha would offer his guests anything they desired. They could then challenge him to a hand-to-hand duel unto death.

GRAND YAGNAS
Yagnas are still an important part of Hindu culture. In 2015, a grand yagna was organized for the coronation of the twenty-seventh heir to the throne of the Wadiyar dynasty of the former princely state of Mysore, India.

BEFORE

Preparations for the Rajasuya ceremony—the Vedic sacrifice performed by a king to mark his coronation and declare autonomous rule—were in full swing.

A DECLARATION OF POWER
The Rajasuya yagna was held to confer sovereignty on a kingdom. It was essential for Yudhishthira to carry out this ritual, for not only did he want to declare his supremacy as a ruler, but also signal to the other kings that he was breaking all ties with his uncle, Dhritarashtra.

The **Death** of **Jarasandha**

Krishna had not forgotten his defeat at the hands of the fierce and powerful Jarasandha, king of Magadha, at Mathura. Yudhishthira's coronation gave him the perfect opportunity to avenge his humiliation.

Jarasandha's death would be a triumph for the Pandavas, and Krishna had a plan to bring about his end.

Krishna proposed that the eldest Pandava should fight King Jarasandha to make sure his claim to sovereignty was uncontested. Yudhishthira was hesitant, for Jarasandha's strength was well known. But then Krishna said, "Physical strength is no match for a nimble brain. We will go to Jarasandha's city disguised as priests."

And so Krishna, Arjuna, and Bhima went to Magadha dressed as priests, confident that the king would agree to any request they made. According to the laws of hospitality, a king could not refuse a priest. Their plan worked. Jarasandha welcomed them and said, "Ask for anything!"

"We wish to duel with you unto death," they replied. Jarasandha realized that such a request could only come from Kshatriyas, but he accepted the challenge and, dismissing Krishna and Arjuna as weak opponents, chose to fight Bhima.

> "He [Bhima] **whirled** him around **one hundred** times. Trampling him [Jarasandha] … **he roared aloud**."
>
> SAGE VAISHAMPAYANA TO KING JANAMEJAYA, SABHA PARVA: THE BOOK OF THE ASSEMBLY HALL

A CONTEST TO WATCH
Kings from all over the land and even the gods came to witness this battle between the mighty warriors Bhima and Jarasandha.

An equal contest

As Bhima was about to enter the wrestling arena, Krishna picked up a leaf and tore it along the spine. "This is the only way to kill Jarasandha. His father had divided a potion between his two wives, so each of them gave birth to half a baby. It was the demoness Jara who fused the two halves and gave the king his heir. Jarasandha can be killed only if he is split into two," Krishna said.

The fight began; Bhima fought fiercely, but he could not overpower Jarasandha. They fought for hours, charging at each other like wild elephants. Bhima pinned the king to the ground, caught his legs, and with all his might, tore his body into two.

A cheer rose from the crowd. But then everyone fell silent as the left half of the body moved and fused with the right half, becoming whole again—and Jarasandha stood up unhurt. When Bhima looked at Krishna for an answer, he picked up another leaf, split it into two along the spine—but threw the left half of the leaf to the right, and the right half to the left. Bhima understood what had to be done.

A fight to the death

The duel resumed more fiercely than before. The pillars of the wrestling hall trembled, and even the Devas appeared on the horizon to cheer Bhima. Finally, flinging Jarasandha to the ground, Bhima ripped him into two again. This time, he threw the two halves in opposite directions. The king of Magadha had been killed at last.

TORN IN TWO
A folio from the *Razmnama* showing the end of the ferocious match between Jarasandha, the king of Magadha, and Bhima. Krishna and Arjuna are shown dressed as priests.

HISTORY AND CULTURE

MAGADHA

Magadha was one of the sixteen "mahajanapadas," or great states, of ancient India that existed from the 6th century BCE to the 4th century BCE. A prosperous kingdom, Magadha was located along the main trade routes of the time. It was also the seat of power of the Maurya and the Gupta dynasties, under whom there were huge advances in the fields of science, mathematics, astronomy, and philosophy.

"O **Bhima**! I will **fight you**. It is **better** to be **vanquished** by a **superior** one."

JARASANDHA TO BHIMA, SABHA PARVA: THE BOOK OF THE ASSEMBLY HALL

AFTER

Thanks to Krishna's orchestration and clever planning, Jarasandha was defeated.

A DOUBLE-EDGED VICTORY
The savagely fought wrestling match had ended in a lethal finale with the death of the king of Magadha. Now, Krishna and the Yadavas could rejoice—the man who had destroyed their city was dead—and Yudhishthira could hold the Rajasuya yagna and declare himself uncontested king of Bharatavarsha.

BEFORE

In order to be recognized as the king of Indraprastha, Yudhishthira had to perform the Rajasuya yagna to establish his uncontested kingship.

INVALUABLE ADVICE

When Krishna heard Yudhishthira express his desire to be crowned king, he told Yudhishthira that he would first need to prove he was worthy of the independence the Rajasuya yagna would bring. Together they planned and executed the defeat of Jarasandha, the king of Magadha and an old foe of Krishna's. They eliminated any opposition they might have had to Indraprastha becoming a sovereign state. The Pandavas then began preparing for Yudhishthira's coronation.

Duryodhana's **Envy**

Duryodhana was invited to Yudhishthira's coronation as the king of Indraprastha. Confident that the new kingdom of the Pandavas could be no match for Hastinapur, the Kaurava prince was surprised and envious to see the magnificent new palace and kingdom.

With Jarasandha's death, Yudhishthira had eliminated all challenges that could come in the way of Indraprastha becoming a sovereign kingdom. All that remained was the coronation of Yudhishthira. Kings from across the land were invited to participate in the ceremony as symbolic acknowledgement of Indraprastha's independence. Among others, the sovereigns of the Rakshasas, Devas, Asuras, Yakshas, Nagas, and Gandharvas were invited to participate in the celebrations. Among the guests were also Duryodhana and Shishupala, the king of Chedi.

With the help of Maya, the great architect of the Asuras, the Pandavas built a city that was as magnificent as it was beautiful. What had once been the forest of Khandavaprastha had been transformed into a city full of marvels.

Architectural wonder

Maya had chosen a tract of land and toiled over it for fourteen months. On it, he had built an assembly hall of breathtaking architectural beauty.

Walking around, Duryodhana took note that the hall measured ten thousand cubits and was supported by golden pillars. Decorated with various gems, the vast hall also had a pond full of lotuses that permeated the air with their unique fragrance. As

MAGNIFICENT EDIFICE
While the grandeur and opulence of the Pandavas' palace in Indraprastha cannot be duplicated, this image of the interiors of the Shah-e-Cheragh mosque in Shiraz, Iran, with its mirrored inner domes, gives some idea of what the vision of Maya, the architect of the Asuras, could have been.

> **"**On seeing the blazing **prosperity** of the **Pandavas,** I am **afflicted** with **jealousy** and **am burning,** though I am not made that way.**"**
>
> DURYODHANA TO SHAKUNI, SABHA PARVA: THE BOOK OF THE ASSEMBLY HALL

these lotuses had leaves of lapis lazuli and stalks made of gems, many were deceived into thinking that the pool was not real. Around the hall were giant trees that shaded it from the harsh sun and whose flowers perfumed the air. Thousands of Rakshasas guarded this hall of wonders, the grandeur of which rivaled that of Indra's court.

The main palace was built in such a way that the breeze passed through all its corridors and sunlight bounced off all its walls. The other palaces of Indraprastha were also large, the streets wide and clean, the gardens full of blossoms, and the orchards laden with fruit. Poets equated the great palace of the Pandavas to the sabha of Indra, the city of Amravati, and the kingdom to heaven. Duryodhana was filled with envy. He was especially disturbed by the realization that his rivals had created something splendid out of nothing while he had never built anything in his life. His feelings of inferiority and his jealousy of his cousins grew as the time of Yudhishthira's coronation drew closer.

Duryodhana's vow

Duryodhana's disbelief at the majesty of the Pandavas' new city disoriented him. Walking across the corridors of the assembly hall, he was so busy looking up at the ornate ceiling that he lost his footing and fell into the pond. Draupadi, who was passing by, saw this and laughed at him. "This had to happen to the blind son of blind parents," she said. Her mockery of his parents' disability incensed Duryodhana. Already consumed by jealousy, he was deeply angered by Draupadi's remark. He swore that he would avenge this insult by publicly humiliating her.

STUNG BY MOCKERY
Draupadi's insensitive remarks added fuel to the fire, inciting Duryodhana's ire.

ANALYSIS

THE FALLOUT

Draupadi's insensitive remark aggravated Duryodhana's already heightened sense of being wronged by the Pandavas. All his life he had felt that they were usurpers who had taken away the titles that rightfully belonged to the Kauravas. Their newfound wealth and prosperity had increased his bitterness and the remark about his parents added insult to injury.

His visit to Indraprastha would be seared in his memory, setting off a chain of events that would have dire repercussions for the entire Kuru clan.

AFTER

Upon his return to Hastinapur, Duryodhana brooded over his humiliation and the Pandavas' new-found prosperity.

SHAKUNI'S PLAN
Duryodhana shared his feelings of envy and inferiority with his maternal uncle Shakuni, who devised a plan: he asked Duryodhana to invite Yudhishthira to a game of dice. "Though he is a terrible gambler, he will come, for he cannot refuse a game," he said.

Shakuni then suggested that he play on Duryodhana's behalf. Shakuni was so skilled at the game that there was no doubt he would win all the possessions of which the Pandavas were proud.

BEFORE

At the time of his birth, oracles had foretold that Shishupala would die at Krishna's hands.

THE PROMISE

Shishupala's heartbroken mother had begged Krishna, her nephew, to spare her son's life. In the face of a mother's pleas, Krishna promised his aunt that he would ignore a hundred insults from Shishupala, but no more. He would not forgive the hundred and first insult, even if it meant death.

Shishupala Beheaded

At Yudhishthira's coronation, the ruler of Chedi was outraged that the Pandavas preferred a cowherd over a court full of kings. In attempting to avenge his pride, he overstepped the limit with Krishna and committed his final offense.

It was time for the coronation. Yudhishthira sat in the assembly hall surrounded by his brothers, and with Draupadi at his side. Brahmins, chanting prayers, poured milk and honey over him and declared him king. While guests like Bhishma and Drupada rejoiced, others such as Duryodhana and Karna could barely contain their outrage. The priests then asked the king to select a guest of honor. Although the assembly hall was full of great warriors, statesmen, and philosophers, it was still an easy choice for Yudhishthira, who chose Krishna without hesitation. He knew that the Pandavas could not have achieved all that they had without Krishna's help.

Shishupala's insolence

As the brothers began to offer Krishna gifts, Shishupala, the king of Chedi, leaped up from his seat. "A hundred kings are gathered in this assembly hall, and yet the Pandavas choose to honor Krishna, who is nothing but a cowherd! They honor the man who killed his own uncle, and who allowed his city, Mathura, to be burned down before he ran away to take shelter elsewhere!"

Enraged at this insult to Krishna, the Pandavas raised

KRISHNA

MYTHOLOGY AND FOLKLORE

VISHNU'S DOORKEEPERS

According to the *Bhagavata Purana*, Shishupala and his friend Dantavakra were Jaya and Vijaya, the demigod doorkeepers of Vishnu. The two had stopped four sages from entering Vishnu's abode when he was resting. The sages cursed them—they would have to endure three lifetimes away from Vishnu. Thus, they were first born as the Asuras Hiranayaksha and Hiranyakashipu. The second time they were born as Ravana and Kumbhakarna, and finally as Shishupala and Dantavakra. In all three lifetimes, their actions had forced Vishnu himself to descend to earth, taking the form of a boar, a man-lion, and then as Rama and Krishna, to get rid of them.

"This is ... **an insult** ... **O Janardana**! ... Though **undeserving**, you **set great store on this homage** ... You are **not a king** and this royal **homage to you** is **like a wife to the impotent**."

SHISHUPALA TO KRISHNA, SABHA PARVA: THE BOOK OF THE ASSEMBLY HALL

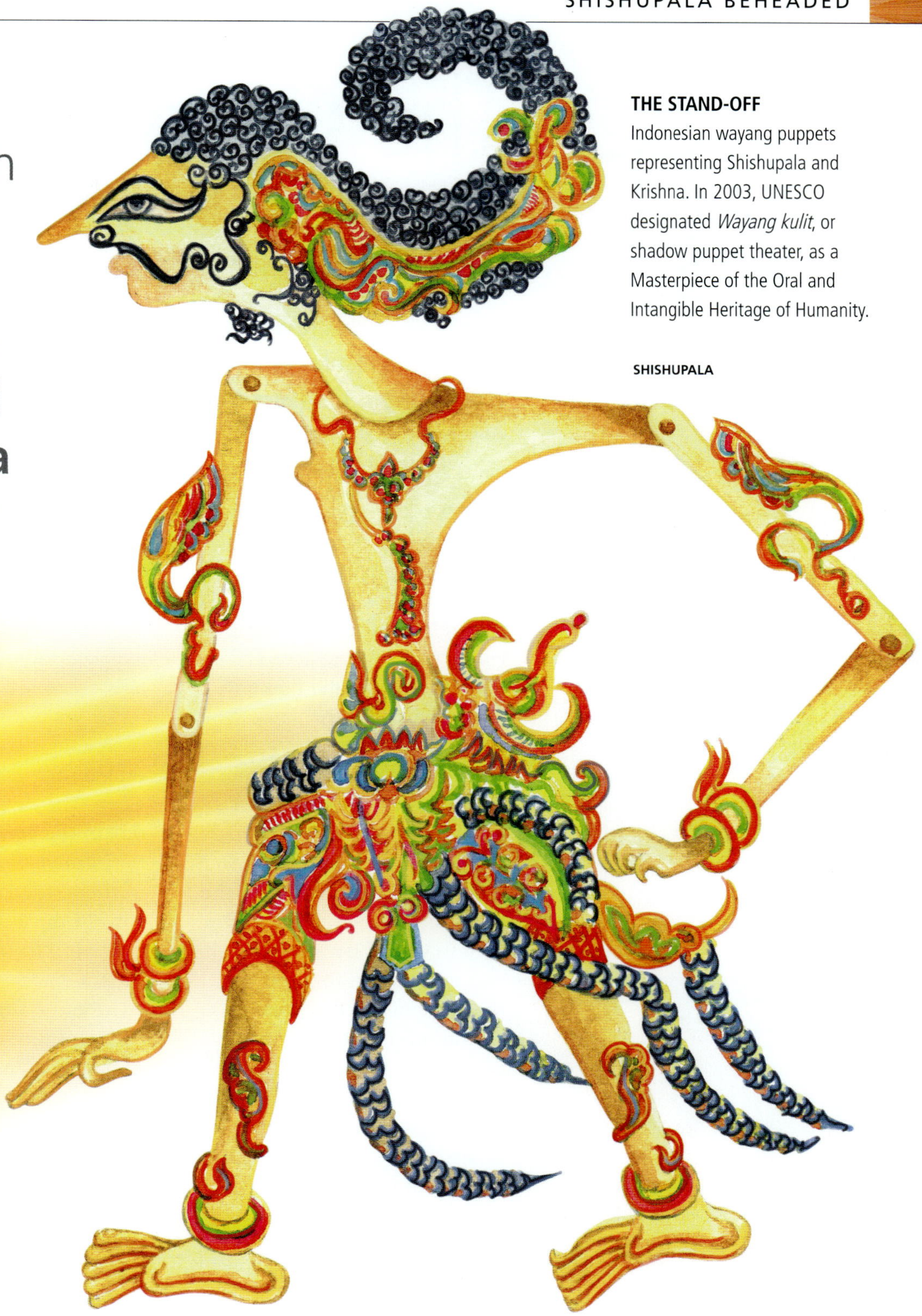

THE STAND-OFF
Indonesian wayang puppets representing Shishupala and Krishna. In 2003, UNESCO designated *Wayang kulit*, or shadow puppet theater, as a Masterpiece of the Oral and Intangible Heritage of Humanity.

SHISHUPALA

their weapons. Seeing this, a number of other rulers who felt that he had spoken the truth stood up to defend Shishupala. The royal hall was about to turn into a battlefield.

Krishna rose from his seat and addressed the assembly. "This is between Shishupala and me. Let him say his piece," he said.

Like fuel to fire, this calm speech fanned Shishupala's anger. He hurled abuse after abuse at Krishna, who heard it all without reacting. At the hundredth insult, Krishna raised his hand and reminded Shishupala of the promise he had made his mother, "Enough, cousin. If you insult me again, I will kill you."

The final straw

Heedless in his hatred, Shishupala laughed and launched the hundred and first insult. In the blink of an eye Krishna hurled his discus, the Sudarshan Chakra, at Shishupala and beheaded him. A deathly silence enveloped the hall as he toppled over. The shell-shocked kings moved away. They could not believe that a common cowherd had killed a king while the Pandavas did nothing. Pointing at the Pandavas, they asked, "Is this how you treat your guests?" Many left immediately. The great coronation ceremony had ended on an extremely inauspicious note.

AFTER

Among the kings who stormed out were Shalva and Dantavakra, two of Shishupala's friends. They decided to teach Krishna a lesson.

ATTACK ON DWARAKA
The two kings raised their armies and launched an attack on Dwaraka. This forced Krishna to leave Indraprastha to defend his own kingdom.

BEFORE

Duryodhana came back from Indraprastha a broken man consumed by envy. Unable to see his nephew in such a state, his uncle Shakuni came up with a devious plan.

AN OLD INJURY

Hearing his nephew lamenting the Pandavas' prosperity, Shakuni, Gandhari's brother, proposed a gambling match, knowing well that Yudhishthira loved gambling but was bad at the game. Shakuni told his nephew that he would play in his place and win, as he could make the dice fall any way he wanted. With each victory they would take away more and more of the Pandavas' possessions; by the end, Duryodhana would be the lord of Indraprastha and the Pandavas nothing but beggars.

Duryodhana was very pleased with this plan. But little did he know that his uncle was exacting revenge on the Kuru household for an incident in the past.

HISTORY AND CULTURE

THE GAME OF DICE

India is the home of several board games. Some, such as snakes and ladders, are totally dependent on luck, while others, such as the dice game, or pachisi, involve a mixture of luck and skill. There are also games such as chess which are based totally on skill.

In Vedic times, gambling with dice was considered sacred. A king could not ignore a challenge to a duel, nor could he turn down an invitation to a gambling match. Gambling was seen as a way to show that the player was blessed by the gods. In the Mahabharata, Krishna symbolizes intelligence and Draupadi luck—the Pandavas enter the gambling hall without either.

PACHISI COURT AT FATEHPUR SIKRI, AGRA

The **Gambling Match**

Aware of Yudhishthira's weakness for gambling, Duryodhana invited the Pandavas for a game of dice. But this invitation was for more than just a gambling match—it was a ploy to destroy the Pandavas.

The Pandavas were invited by their cousins, the Kauravas, to play a game of dice at Hastinapur. As a refusal would be considered rude, Yudhishthira accepted the invitation. Little did he know that his love for the game would turn catastrophic.

Krishna was not with them at the time. After the death of Shishupala of Chedi at Yudhishthira's coronation, Shalva and Dantavakra, friends of the slain king, had attacked the Yadava city of Dwaraka. Krishna was away fighting them, and unaware of the Kauravas' invitation or of the Pandavas' decision to accept.

Draupadi, too, was unaware of this development. She was menstruating and, as was the custom in those days, she had isolated herself in the women's quarters.

Her husbands had spent the evening before the game observing rituals, eating the best food, and listening to the sweet voices of bards. They had ended their day with a restful sleep. The next morning, as the day of the game dawned, having performed all the rites expected of them, the Pandavas proceeded toward the assembly hall without any word from either Krishna or Draupadi.

The game was based on the throw of dice and the movement of pawns on a game board. A player needed both luck and skill to defeat his opponent. As the game pitted two players against each other, it was decided that Yudhishthira would play for all five Pandava brothers. The Kauravas agreed that their uncle Shakuni would play for them, as had been planned. The stakes would be decided at the start of each game. »

THE ROYAL CONTEST

This painting from the Shekhawati region in the western state of Rajasthan, India, depicts a gambling match. It fits the description of the gambling hall at Hastinapur, where many kings had gathered to witness the historic game.

> "Then Shakuni, who knew **the heart of the dice**, grasped the dice. And Shakuni told Yudhishthira, **I have won**."
>
> SAGE VAISHAMPAYANA TO KING JANAMEJAYA, SABHA PARVA: THE BOOK OF THE ASSEMBLY HALL

The game begins

Initially, the stakes were small ones, such as an umbrella or a necklace. The dice rolled and Shakuni declared after each round, "Behold, I have won."

A true gambler, Yudhishthira got increasingly restless with every defeat, and visibly desperate to win everything back. But each time, Shakuni would roll his dice and nnounce, "Behold, I have won."

Yudhishthira staked his chariots of gold. Shakuni rolled the dice and said, "Behold, I have won!"

Next, the Pandava staked all the jewels in his palace. Shakuni rolled the dice again and said, "Behold, I have won!"

The servant girls were staked, and Shakuni rolled the dice and said, "Behold, I have won!"

Yudhishthira staked all his servant boys. Shakuni rolled the dice and said, "I have won!"

A desperate Yudhishthira then staked his elephants, his cows, his horses, then his sheep and goats. Each time, Shakuni rolled the dice and said, "Behold, I have won!"

Yudhishthira kept losing, and though his brothers suspected that the dice was loaded, they could do nothing to prove it.

YUDHISHTHIRA'S FALL
An actor portrays Yudhishthira as dharmaraja, a king who strives to walk the righteous path but errs like a common man.

As the game progressed the Pandavas were gradually stripped of all their possessions: gold and grain, livestock and land, and even the jewels on their body. Horrified, the watching elders begged Yudhishthira to end the game. "There is no shame if you withdraw. This game has poisoned your mind!" they cried. But Yudhishthira could not be moved.

Every time the dice rolled, he was convinced he would win back all that he had lost. The Kauravas, seeing their plan working so well, did everything they could to encourage this belief, mocking him all the while.

A game of high stakes

Bhishma, Vidura, Drona, and Kripa watched the game in silence. "Perhaps it is time we stopped this madness," Vidura ventured. But Dhritarashtra remained quiet. He would not stop his sons who were on a winning streak, and he could not stop Yudhishthira in a public forum, for he was a king.

By the eleventh game, Yudhishthira had lost all his wealth. Everyone agreed that it was time he stopped, but the eldest Pandava was oblivious to anything but the game. He began staking his brothers. First, the beautiful Nakula, then the learned Sahadeva, followed by the mighty Bhima, and finally, Arjuna. And he lost them all. After his brothers, Yudhishthira staked himself—and lost.

HIGH STAKES
Yudhishthira staked all his possessions one by one; his jewelery, his crown, all the treasure his kingdom held, and all that he treasured.

> "Her eyes are **red with love** and I will play with you for her ... O king! O Soubala! I will make the **beautiful Draupadi of Panchala**, slender of waist, **my stake**. Let us play."
>
> YUDHISHTHIRA, SABHA PARVA: THE BOOK OF THE ASSEMBLY HALL

The last wager

Then, the unthinkable happened. "I stake my wife,"announced Yudhishthira. Those watching gasped. Vidura dropped his head in his hands in dismay.

But Duryodhana smiled and accepted the wager. Shakuni, the skilled dice player, rolled the dice for the seventeenth time, and smiled. "Behold, I have won."

AFTER

Yudhishthira had done the unimaginable—he had staked his wife like a common pawn.

DRAUPADI SUMMONED
Despite their shock and utter disbelief that a princess was actually being wagered in a game, everyone in the hall remained quiet. The spectacle continued, delighting Duryodhana and his uncle, who saw their plan working far better than expected. Once Shakuni declared he had won this round as well, Duryodhana insisted on summoning Draupadi to the hall. Dusshasana went to drag Draupadi from her chamber to the gambling hall as the triumphant Kauravas waited to claim their prize.

A PAIR OF DICE

DUSSHASANA DRAGS DRAUPADI
When Draupadi objected to being staked in a game of dice, an impatient Dusshasana went to her chambers and dragged her to the gambling hall. This 20th-century representation of the scene is from the Hulton Archive.

The **Disrobing** of **Draupadi**

With nothing else left to wager, Draupadi became the last pawn in the game of dice. As a triumphant Dusshasana dragged the queen in front of the people gathered in the assembly hall, only divine intervention could save the last vestiges of her honor.

The news from the gambling hall reached Draupadi. Pratikami, her doorkeeper, informed her that Yudhishthira had lost her in a game of dice, and that she was being summoned to the hall.

"Ask my gambler husband if he put himself at stake first, or me. If he lost himself first, how can he have any right over me," Draupadi fumed.

Incensed at her arrogant reply to his summons, Duryodhana sent his younger brother to bring her to the hall by force. Dusshasana stormed into the women's quarters to find Draupadi sitting with her hair untied, draped only in a sari stained with blood. Uncaring, he grabbed her hair and dragged her to the assembly hall. Draupadi resisted, trying to hold on to pillars for support, but she was no match for him. Her pleas for help were met with silence.

"For shame, stop!" she cried out, "I am Drupada's daughter, I am your sister-in-law, daughter-in-law of the house."

But Duryodhana laughed, crudely inviting Draupadi to sit in his lap by slapping his thigh.

Karna further insulted her, "Ancient law bars a woman from having five husbands. This makes you a loose woman who can be treated as your masters deem fit."

Duryodhana then ordered the Pandavas to remove their clothes. "Let us see the quality of slaves we have acquired," he said. "Her too," he went on, gesturing toward Draupadi. The assembly was stunned, but not a voice of protest was heard. As Dusshasana grabbed hold of her sari, Draupadi raised her hands to implore, "Save me, my God, for only you can!"

The skies rumbled and darkened, even the sun seemed to hide in shame. The assembly hall seemed frozen in petrified silence. Each pull at Draupadi's sari only revealed more cloth—Dusshasana kept pulling and unravelling, but Draupadi's body remained draped and covered. Draupadi's God had answered her prayer and thwarted her humiliation.

> **"**O **Yajnaseni**! … you have been **won** at the **game** and are now **a slave**. One can sport with a slave **as one desires**.**"**
>
> DUSSHASANA TO DRAUPADI, SABHA PARVA: THE BOOK OF THE ASSEMBLY HALL

DRAUPADI'S HUMILIATION
When Dusshasana tried to disrobe Draupadi, Krishna ensured that her sari remained draped over her body, to protect her from public humiliation.

BEFORE

Draupadi's honor remained untouched despite Dusshasana's attempt to humiliate her. Everyone assembled in the hall had witnessed the divine intervention against the atrocity the committed by the Kauravas.

DIVINE INTERVENTION

The Pandavas' wife had been dragged into the assembly hall. On Duryodhana's instruction Dusshasana had attempted to strip her. But Draupadi's direct appeal to the divine had caused a miracle—and jolted the elders out of their stupor.

PACHISI

A cross-and-circle board game that was popular in ancient India, Pachisi is played on a cross-shaped board with six or seven pawns and a set of dice. The name comes from the Hindi word for twenty-five—"pachis"—which is also the largest possible score in one throw.

The **Final Game**

A hush fell over the gambling hall as the gathering realized that the consequences of the Kauravas' behavior would engulf the two royal houses. Just when it seemed the crisis was averted, Yudhishthira accepted an offer to play a final game.

Draupadi drew herself up, her eyes flashing in righteous anger. "I shall not forget what the Kauravas have done here. I vow that only after I have washed my hair in Dusshasana's blood will I ever tie it again."

Enraged by the way his wife had been insulted, the mighty Bhima could not hold back any longer. "Hear the oath I take today: I will kill the Kauravas, one by one, drink Dusshasana's blood, and break the thigh that Duryodhana patted while insulting my wife." Even the dice seemed to tremble before the anger in his voice.

Outside, dogs began to howl, donkeys brayed, birds screeched, and cats whimpered. Vidura interpreted these omens of disaster and rushed toward Dhritarashtra. "Brother, stop this madness before it gets out of hand. Even the gods look down on you and your sons."

The blind king felt his heart freeze. Fearing for his family he shouted, "Stop! Draupadi! Say no more!" He went up to his daughter-in-law and apologized for letting the game go too far and for the insult she suffered. He offered her three blessings.

The three blessings

Draupadi accepted."First, I want freedom for all my husbands. Then I want everything that they lost restored to them." Having said that she was silent.

Dhritrashtra tried to coax her. "The third blessing, something for yourself, oh Queen?"

"I want nothing for myself," was Draupadi's stoic response. "Greed is unbecoming of a Kshatriya's wife."

Dhritrashtra granted Draupadi the blessings and asked his sons to let the Pandavas leave.

A last game

The brothers had picked up their weapons and were leaving the hall with their wife when they heard Karna chuckle. "Just look at the brave Pandava warriors now. Saved by a woman! Have they no shame? They meekly accept in charity what they lost, instead of attempting to win it back with honor."

"O **Pandavas**! Ignore cattle, treasuries, and gold ... There is a **single stake** of **exile** in the **forest** ... this is the stake with which **we play**."

SHAKUNI TO THE PANDAVAS, SABHA PARVA: THE BOOK OF THE ASSEMBLY HALL

"Come back and play one final game, Yudhishthira. The one game to win back all you have lost," tempted the Kauravas.

His brothers were dismayed to see Yudhisthira hesitate and ask, "What if I lose?"

"This time let us make the wager final—twelve years of exile in the forest for the one who loses. The losers will leave with no more than the clothes they wear. If you lose, you will have no claim on Indraprastha for that period, and you will have to spend the thirteenth year in hiding. Should you be discovered during this final year, you will go back into exile for another twelve years."

His brothers could see the gleam return to Yudhishthira's eyes at the prospect of gambling again. Even as they protested, he accepted the terms of the game and made his way to the gambling table. Draupadi added her pleas but Yudhishthira refused to listen. "I will surely win this last game," he said.

Once again the dice were rolled. They came to a stop and Shakuni's exultant voice was heard. "Behold. I have won again!"

The Pandavas had lost the final game. They had no alternative but to accept the terms of the wager.

Yudhishthira bowed to the king and to all the assembly. He left the hall accompanied by his wife and brothers. They had nothing more than the clothes they were wearing and their weapons.

The walk to the forest

The Pandavas made their way out of the city. Still uneasy, the blind Dhritarashtra asked his charioteer, Sanjay, to relate every detail to him. Sanjay described how, while leaving the palace, Yudhishthira covered his face with a cloth to prevent the anger that simmered in his gaze from destroying the city. Bhima strode impatiently, flexing his strong arms, as if imagining breaking the bones of each and every Kaurava. Arjuna walked behind him, trailing from his hands a fistful of sand indicative of the shower of arrows he would shoot at his enemies. The beautiful Nakula had covered himself with mud so that no woman's heart would break on seeing him walk into the forest. Wise Sahadeva had painted his face black, the darkness expressive of his shame. Draupadi walked proudly, her dark unbound hair a billowing banner behind her—a foreboding of the terror to come.

A mother's sorrow

Unable to bear the parting, Kunti ran after them in tears. Yudhishthira caught her in his arms. Explaining that her sons did not want her to suffer the hardships ahead of them, he asked her to return to the palace and wait for their return. With a heavy heart, Kunti remained beside Vidura and watched her sons and their wife leave.

At the gates, the whole city had gathered in sorrow. Passing through, the exiles bid farewell to their people. They bathed in the Ganga and, crossing the river, went toward the forest that would now be their home.

AFTER

Their defeat in the final game had sealed the Pandavas' fate.

PREPARING FOR EXILE

It is said there was a solar eclipse the day the Pandavas left for their thirteen-year exile. They dressed in deerskins for their journey and left the city carrying only their weapons with them.

The whole city was moved by their plight. Seeing her family leave, Kunti could barely contain her sorrow. For the thirteen years they were away, she lived with Vidura in his palace.

THE PANDAVAS HEAD TOWARDS THE FOREST FOR THEIR TIME AS EXILES

KAURAVAS' MATERNAL UNCLE

Shakuni

"I will **rob** ... Yudhishthira of the **prosperity** ... which has been **burning you** ... Know that the bow and arrows are **my dice**. The heart of the dice is the **string of my bow**."

SHAKUNI TO DURYODHANA, SABHA PARVA: THE BOOK OF THE ASSEMBLY HALL

Shakuni was the son of Gandhara's King Suvala and the brother of Gandhari. He was Duryodhana's maternal uncle and, along with Karna, his chief adviser. It is believed that it was Shakuni's wicked ideas that stoked Duryodhana's feelings of envy and revenge against the Pandavas, and gave them concrete shape.

The making of a villain

Many folk traditions narrate the story of Shakuni and his family, explaining his hatred for the Kuru household.

When Shakuni's sister Gandhari was born, astrologers had foretold that her first husband would have a short life. Her father, therefore, got her married to a goat, which was sacrificed soon after. Technically, this made Gandhari a widow.

Bhishma, the Kuru patriarch, was furious when his spies found out this secret about Gandhari—a widow had entered his noble household! An enraged Bhishma locked Suvala and his sons in a dungeon to punish them, feeding them a fistful of rice each day. As the rice was not enough for everyone, they were bound to starve and die. Suvala then came up with an idea, "Let only the most intelligent one among us eat. Let him live and avenge the great wrong done to his family." Shakuni, the youngest, was the chosen one. He was fed, while the rest of the family

THE CUNNING UNCLE
This Kathakali performer wears a predominantly black costume, called "Kari," which is worn to depict evil characters, both male and female.

HISTORY AND CULTURE

WORSHIPPING SHAKUNI

Shakuni is worshipped in the Mayamkottu Malancharuvu Malanada temple run by the Kuravar community, in Kollam district of Kerala, India. According to popular lore, Shakuni traveled across the country with his nephews, the Kauravas, and chose this place to divide the weapons among themselves. The place came to be known as Pakutheswaram, which has since become Pavithreswaram. The Kuravars believe that Shakuni returned here after the war, worshipped Shiva, and with his blessings, attained salvation. As one who reached the state of moksha, Shakuni commands reverence among the locals who believe that a large stone in the shrine is the seat where Shakuni performed his penance. Shakuni is also believed to be a personification of the Dwapara Yuga, one of the four cyclical yugas, or eras, of the Hindu calendar (see p. 21).

starved to death. Before dying, Suvala hit Shakuni's foot with his stick, cracking his ankle, so he would remember this great crime against his family every time he limped.

After his family's death, Shakuni went to live in Hastinapur with the Kauravas. He pretended to be their friend, but plotted their downfall all along.

Several accounts say that Shakuni was very close to his sister Gandhari and was furious that she was married to a blind man. He never came around to Gandhari blindfolding herself after marriage. In some variants of Shakuni's story, Duryodhana, not Bhishma, is held responsible for killing Shakuni's father and brothers. In other versions, Suvala and his sons are put in prison by Dhritarashtra for refusing to let Gandhari marry a blind man. The story of Gandhari marrying the goat comes from the Jain retellings of the Mahabharata.

Shakuni's tale is a reminder to everyone not to judge people without knowing their story. Even the worst of villains have a story that might explain their actions, without condoning them.

An ace gambler

According to one legend, Suvala had noticed his son's fondness for the game of dice. He told his son to turn his finger bones to dice after his death. He told Shakuni, "They will be fueled by my anger and will roll in your favor." This gave Shakuni an unparalleled edge at dice.

When Duryodhana returned from Yudhishthira's coronation at Indraprastha, he was burning with envy. Shakuni came up with a plan to use Yudhishthira's weakness for gambling against him. The Kauravas wanted to use Shakuni's skill at the game to make Yudhishthira lose all that he possessed.

"By the end of the game, you would have won the Pandava kingdom, Indraprastha, and they would be reduced to beggars," asserted Shakuni. Duryodhana was overjoyed at the prospect of Pandavas' downfall.

As expected, Yudhishthira readily accepted their invitation for the game. The Pandavas lost everything, including themselves and their wife, in successive games. After winning the final round, the Kauravas sent their cousins into exile for thirteen years.

Shakuni in the war

The forces of Gandhara fought on the Kauravas' side in the Kurukshetra War. On the eleventh day, Shakuni led his armies against Arjuna, but lost to the latter's prowess with the bow and arrow.

After the death of Shalya, Kauravas' last commander, Shakuni realized that Bhima, Arjuna, and Yudhishthira were all leading the army, and the rear flanks were unprotected. He rallied his soldiers from Gandhara and ambushed the Pandava army from behind.

Yudhishthira asked Nakula and Sahadeva, who were stationed closer to the rear end of the army, to tackle Shakuni. A great fight followed. In the end, Sahadeva, the youngest and most silent of the Pandava brothers, managed to strike down and kill Shakuni.

BIOGRAPHY IN BRIEF

- **Born** to King Suvala (or Subala) of the Gandhara kingdom. As Suvala's son, he was also called Saubala.
- **His sister** was Gandhari. Shakuni was against Gandhari being married to the blind Dhritarashtra and to her blindfolding herself after marriage.
- **His two sons** were called Uluka and Vrikasur.
- **Shakuni and his family** were imprisoned by Bhishma, who felt they had cheated the Kuru family by hiding facts about Gandhari.
- **Shakuni survived** as the family fed all their rations to him, choosing him as the intelligent one who should survive and avenge them.
- **Suvala hit Shakuni's foot** so that each time he limped he would remember the crimes against his family and feel inspired to take revenge.
- **At Suvala's instruction**, Shakuni took the finger bones from his father's body and turned them into dice. Filled with Suvala's anger, the dice would turn whichever way Shakuni desired.
- **After his family's death**, Shakuni went to live with Gandhari's in-laws in Hastinapur. He instigated his nephew Duryodhana against the Pandavas.
- **Advised Duryodhana** to invite Yudhishthira to a dice game, knowing that he would play on the Kauravas' behalf and win with the aid of his special dice.
- **At the gambling match**, Shakuni played against Yudhishthira and won every round. In successive games, Yudhishthira lost his property, his kingdom, his brothers, himself, and his wife, Draupadi.
- **Accompanied Duryodhana to the forest** where the Pandavas lived in exile, to aggravate their humiliation. However, the two were attacked by the Gandharvas and rescued by the Pandavas.
- **In the war**, Shakuni, fighting for Duryodhana, led the forces of Gandhara.
- **During the war**, he lost a duel against Arjuna on the eleventh day.
- **Unethically attacked** the Pandava forces from behind, on the eighteenth day of the war, recognizing that the end of the war and the Kauravas' defeat was close.
- **Died** at the hands of Sahadeva, who countered Shakuni's attacks with his twin, Nakula.

THE THROW OF DICE
Made of carved bone, these 11th-century dice are from Syria. It is believed that Shakuni's dice were made of his father's finger bones.

3

VANA PARVA: THE BOOK OF THE FOREST

A FOREST HOME
Having lost the gambling match, the Pandavas were exiled for thirteen years. They spent much of this time in the Kamyaka forest, located to the west of the Kuru kingdom. It is said that the forest was situated along the banks of the now extinct Saraswati river.

Vana Parva, or the Book of the Forest, the third parva in the Mahabharata, is also called Aranyaka Parva. Both "vana" and "aranyaka" mean forest. This section covers the experiences and adventures of the Pandavas during the first twelve years of their exile, which they spent in the forests. The parva also comprises stories told by various sages in an effort to impart wisdom and help the Pandavas come to terms with their plight. The Vana Parva has 16 sub-parvas, 299 chapters, and 10,239 shlokas, or couplets.

"How did the Parthas **spend their time** in the forest? How did they **conduct themselves?** How did **twelve years pass** in the **forest** for those great-souled ones who were destroyers of enemies? … O brahmana! Tell me, because my curiosity is great."

KING JANAMEJAYA TO SAGE VAISHAMPAYANA, VANA PARVA: THE BOOK OF THE FOREST

BEFORE

Having lost their wealth and kingdom to the Kauravas, the Pandavas left Indraprastha.

LEAVING INDRAPRASTHA

Not wanting their mother to suffer thirteen years of hardship, they asked Kunti to remain in Hastinapur. However, some of their priests, retainers, and supporters insisted on going with them. The small party bathed in the Ganga, crossed over, and bid the watching citizens goodbye.

The **Exile** Begins

The loss of their kingdom and wealth, and most of all, dignity, weighed heavily on the Pandavas. Angry, they were ready to turn back and reclaim by force what they had themselves wagered away—until wiser counsel prevailed.

During the gambling match in Hastinapur, Krishna was in Dwaraka, fending off an attack by Shishupala's friends who were eager to avenge his death. By the time he returned, the Pandavas had lost everything.

Krishna found the Pandavas and Draupadi in the Kamyaka forest, lamenting their fate. The wilderness had brought home the immensity of their loss. Royalty until a few days ago, they had been reduced to being paupers.

The Pandavas' rage

On seeing Krishna, Draupadi, who had not shed a tear until then, broke down. The Pandavas were filled with hope. With Krishna beside them, the situation looked less bleak. "Let us march to Hastinapur and destroy the Kauravas," said an angry Bhima.

"Did you not promise to spend thirteen years in exile if you lost the match?" reminded Krishna.

"Yes," replied Yudhishthira, dejectedly.

"Then you must keep your word," said Krishna.

But Bhima and Arjuna were certain that the Kauravas had cheated in the gambling match. Moreover, it was Yudhishthira who had gambled away the kingdom, not them. Now that

> "We have been **robbed** of **everything** … In our **sorrow**, we will now go to the **forest** and **live** on fruits, roots, and meat."
>
> YUDHISHTHIRA TO THE BRAHMANS, VANA PARVA: THE BOOK OF THE FOREST

HISTORY AND CULTURE

KAMYAKA FOREST

The Kamyaka forest, situated along the banks of the now-extinct Saraswati river and teeming with wildlife, was a favorite retreat for ascetics. It took three days for the Pandavas to reach Kamyaka on their chariots. They then camped near a lake and spent many years of their exile there.

Based on the fact that Kurukshetra is located in the state of Haryana, scholars estimate that the forest was spread over present-day Haryana and Rajasthan, in northwest India.

Duryodhana had got his hands on Indraprastha, they were sure that he would never return it to them.

Krishna's wisdom

"This should be a matter of concern for you only at the end of your thirteen years in exile," said Krishna, his calm a counterpoint to the Pandavas' fury. Nodding at Bhima, he continued, "You allowed Yudhishthira to play on your behalf. You are as much to be blamed for this situation as him. No one forced you to play the game of dice and wager your wife. It was your pride that prevented you from withdrawing. Abandoning all good sense, you continued to play and lost in the game. All you brothers must keep your word and suffer the exile. According to dharma, one must keep their word."

Hearing this, Draupadi spoke up. "Surely, I am not responsible for my ignominy."

"You are responsible for rejecting Karna for his low caste," said Krishna. "Being a great warrior, he would never have gambled you. Instead, you chose a priest, who turned out to be a prince and shared you with his four brothers. Since he could not protect you, here you are—helpless, humiliated, and alone, in a situation you inadvertently helped create. You must also take responsibility for it." But seeing Draupadi weep, Krishna said, "Those who have tormented you had the option of not doing so. Those around you could have intervened but they chose to abuse you. Each of these wrongdoers as well as silent witnesses will pay a price. I assure you that their widows shall weep the way you weep now."

PANDAVAS LEAVE FOR EXILE
Shadow puppet shows, or Wayang, are an important part of Javanese culture. Epics such as the Ramayana and the Mahabharata are popular stories told through these puppets.

A FOREST HOME
The Pandavas spent many years of their exile in the Kamyaka forest. This is where they would have many encounters with Rakshasas and Gandharvas.

AFTER

Krishna's promise went a long way in consoling Draupadi. In the years to come, she would take comfort from it when her spirits were low.

DRAUPADI'S CONCERN
Her mind turned to fresh worries—how would her children live in the forest with all of its dangers and the threat of enemies? Divining this, Krishna promised to take care of Draupadi's sons, who were known as the Upapandavas. He took them to Dwaraka along with Subhadra, Arjuna's wife and his sister, and her son Abhimanyu, and promised to raise them as his own.

DWARAKA, GUJARAT, INDIA

LEARNING FROM THE WILDERNESS

Forest, Field, and Settlement

"O King! When age is right, one must hand over possessions to the son and go to the forest."

DHRITARASHTRA TO YUDHISHTHIRA, ASHRAMAVASIKA PARVA: THE BOOK OF HERMITAGE

The Mahabharata presents the forest as a physical reality as well as a metaphor for the unknown, untamed realms of the mind. The rishis were the first explorers of these spaces, creating trails that linked caves and water bodies for later travelers. Warriors often accompanied or followed them, protecting them from beasts and demons. As civilization reached the unexplored realms of the world, the forests were tamed and gave way to fields, farms, and settlements. They became safe places where even the weak could thrive. Politically, this could be a retelling of the so-called Aryan invasion; of how the followers of the Vedas established their authority in India. Metaphysically, it could be interpreted as tales of the gradual domestication of the mind.

THE FOREST AS TEACHER AND GUIDE

The Pandavas were born in the forest. The forest gave them refuge after the burning of the lac palace, and it was to the forest that they were exiled after losing the game of dice. The Vana Parva deals explicitly with this period of exile and elaborates on the many lessons the Pandavas learned in the wilderness, not only from the sages and rishis they met but also from nature and the many forest dwellers that they encountered. Nagas were mentioned frequently, as were barbaric forest tribes referred to as Rakshasas, one of

whom Bhima married and had a son. Others encountered in the forest were Gandharvas, who seemed to be more sophisticated —their encounter with

A PLACE OF LEARNING

The Dharmashastras divide life into four parts. The first is brahmacharya, life as a student. Education involved not just the study of Vedic hymns, rituals, and philosophy, but also the study of the Upavedas, which included knowledge of warfare, medicine, fine arts, time, space, and polity. Students established a symbiotic relationship with a sage or rishi. They lived with him at a gurukul, a seat of learning based around his residence in the forest, for the entire period of learning. When it ended, they were expected to pay a transaction fee, guru dakshina, to nullify all obligations before leaving the gurukul. Marriage marked the beginning of grihastha, the second stage of life, to be lived as a householder with an active involvement in worldly affairs. The birth of grandchildren initiated the third stage, that of vanaprastha or retirement from the world. The householder was advised to pass on wealth to his children and all knowledge to the grandchildren. He then had to seek seclusion and a degree of detachment, and even make the physical move to the forest, where he could spend his time looking inward and contemplating. This led to the fourth, final stage, sannyasa: the renunciation of all worldly pursuits in favor of the spiritual. The elders in the Mahabharata, from Pratipa to Dhritarashtra, all retired from society and renounced the world after finishing their worldly duties. They wandered in the forests in their quest to find rishis to understand the meaning of life.

A PLACE FOR INTROSPECTION
The move away from civilization tested the individual's innate strength and values as well as his ability to adhere to dharma without external rules and regulations.

BANYAN TREE
The shade of the vast canopy of the banyan was an ideal place for a discourse. Which is why it is also known as the tree of learning,

Angaraparna helped them understand the generosity that is the essence of dharma and the stubbornness that is the essence of adharma; the Yakshas, guardian resident spirits in all of nature, made them question their understanding of the meaning of life. In the forest, Yudhishthira and Arjuna encountered Yama and Indra, the gods who had fathered them. Bhima met his brother Hanuman, the other son of Vayu, god of the wind. Arjuna also met Shiva, the god of destruction. Each meeting was a lesson that left them humbled and enlightened.

For the Pandavas, their sojourns in the forest were great learning experiences, which transformed them into better human beings and better kings. What is repeatedly underlined, however, is that this happened because they were willing to change. The Kauravas, in contrast, clung to their kingdom, refusing to listen, learn, or change in any way at all. Wilderness is the default state of nature. Within it no authority or regulation exists other than what would come to be called "matsya nyaya" or the law of the fish, the Vedic equivalent of the law of the jungle wherein the weak are eaten by the strong, which is a state of adharma. Duryodhana brought matsya nyaya into the Kaurava court while the Pandavas, even when in the forest, lived in accordance with dharma.

MYTHOLOGY AND FOLKLORE

SACRED TREES AND PLANTS

The belief in the sanctity of nature as a whole, and of individual trees and plants, is common to both Vedic and non-Vedic traditions in India. Sacred groves associated with individual deities abound, while some trees and plants are regarded as holy in themselves. For instance, *Ocimum tenuiflorum*, popularly known as the holy basil, is highly revered as Tulsi, named after a goddess and considered a devotee of Vishnu. Its leaves are integral to rituals associated with the worship of the god in all his forms. In addition to its religious significance, the plant has valuable medicinal properties and is a key ingredient in many Ayurvedic remedies.

TULSI

THE PRICE OF DESTRUCTION

The burning of the forest of Khandavaprastha to establish the settlement of Indraprastha is symbolic of the destruction of the state of nature and the establishment of dharma, civilization, and law. The forest was the home of the Nagas and Rakshasas as well as a number of birds and beasts. Destroying it meant death to them all. Is it at all possible for anyone to establish a field, an orchard, a garden, or a city without destroying a forest? Krishna deliberately asks the Pandavas to acknowledge this price and the burden that civilization brought about. Asked when the killing should stop, he replied, "At the point when needs have been met, before greed takes over. A good king is one who recognizes that fine line." But the act of destruction is a bad cause. It makes an enemy out of Takshaka Naga, the king of the forest, and starts a cycle of revenge and counter-revenge that haunts the Pandavas and their descendants right up to their great-grandson, Janamejaya.

FOREST FIRES
Civilization advances by destroying nature. The importance of knowing when to stop this destruction and establish a balance between forest and settlement was acknowledged even in the era of the great epics.

KEY CONCEPT

GLOBAL WARMING

Over the years, there has been a gradual increase in the temperature of the surface of the earth, including the oceans and the atmosphere, as the direct consequence of thoughtless human activity and consumerism because people are unable to draw a the line between "need" and "greed." As certain gases, such as water vapor and carbon dioxide, have the ability to absorb and re-radiate infrared radiation, an increase in the level of these gases in the atmosphere creates a greenhouse effect. While water vapor condenses or evaporates depending on local conditions, carbon dioxide remains in the atmosphere for hundreds of years, having a significant impact on the environment and life forms. Deforestation and the burning of fossil fuel are the two major causes for the increase of carbon dioxide levels in the atmosphere—the "price of civilization," as Krishna put it so many years ago.

LAND RAVAGED BY DROUGHT

BEFORE

Having lost the gambling match, the Pandavas and Draupadi were exiled to the forest of Kamyaka.

KRISHNA'S ADVICE

When Krishna met the Pandavas he found them angry and resentful, accusing the Kauravas of treachery and deceit. He pointed out that they had brought the situation upon themselves, and they should suffer the exile with patience.

The **Divine Vessel**

Stripped of their wealth, all the Pandavas were left with was their pride. When they were unable to feed a group of sages sent by Duryodhana, Krishna came to their rescue yet again.

When the Pandavas left Hastinapur, hundreds of sages chose to accompany them to conduct yagnas and pray for their well-being.

FEEDING HOLY MEN

As a point of honor, it is tradition that guests must always be fed, regardless of the size of the gathering.

As the Brahmans assembled for their prayers, a distraught Draupadi was filled with despair. Deprived of her riches, the young queen did not have anything to offer to the sages.

"How will I feed them all?" she wondered.

Krishna, however, took notice of the fact that a number of the sages had accompanied the Pandavas on Duryodhana's instructions to humiliate them. He divined that the sages had been asked to make the Pandavas aware of their inadequacies, in order to win the Kauravas' favor.

Eager to serve the sages well, the brothers looked for food, but to no avail. They could only get berries from the forest, which made them even more anxious.

A divine intervention

With a trick up his sleeve to rid the Pandavas of their misery, Krishna approached Draupadi and asked her to feed him.

"Feed me, Draupadi. You are known far and wide for your hospitality," he said.

Embarrassed by Krishna's request, Draupadi felt that he was mocking her misery. This was the proverbial last straw for Draupadi, who could no longer hold back her tears. Yet, Krishna prodded her. "There must surely be something you could feed me," he said.

Understanding that her friend was up to something, Draupadi wiped her tears and offered him the only thing she had. "All I have with me is this half-eaten berry. I had eaten the other half by the time you came."

Krishna took the berry and ate it with relish. To Draupadi's amusement, he even burped with satisfaction after consuming it.

As soon as Krishna ate the berry, the Brahmans felt as if they had eaten a huge meal. Feeling full and satisfied they stood up, wondering how their stomachs felt so full without so much as having had a single bite. They realized that divine powers were at play, and concluded that the gods were with the Pandavas, ensuring that even though they had no food, no

BOWL OF BOUNTY

This 8th-century bronze vessel from the ancient civilization of Phoenicia fits the description of Draupadi's vessel. Bronze was commonly in use in India when the Mahabharata was composed.

HISTORY AND CULTURE

PURNA KALASHA

In Hinduism and Jainism, the idea of abundance is symbolized by the "purna kalasha," or "full vessel." This metal pot is filled with water, then mango leaves are placed on the rim, with a coconut covering the mouth. The purna kalasha is said to hold amrita, the elixir of immortality. It is regarded as a symbol of auspiciousness, abundance, and wisdom, and is used in ceremonies that celebrate new beginnings such as housewarming or name ceremony, in Hindu and Jain households.

A PURNA KALASHA

A GIFT OF ABUNDANCE
This 1931 lithographed collector's card by the British company Liebeg shows the sun god, Surya, blessing Yudhishthira and Draupadi with the divine vessel of food.

one left their doors hungry. Satisfied with the hospitality, the sages blessed the Pandavas and Draupadi before leaving.

Invoking Surya

Krishna then advised Yudhishthira to pray to Surya, the sun god, to save them from such embarrassment in the future. When Yudhishthira invoked Surya, he appeared with a divine vessel and handed it to Draupadi. The god assured her that the vessel would always have food for guests, so no one would have to be turned away. Delighted to receive the blessed vessel, Draupadi expressed her gratitude to the sun god, Surya, and Krishna for their help.

MYTHOLOGY AND FOLKLORE

CORNUCOPIA

Greek mythology relates the cornucopia, known as the "horn of plenty," to several gods, especially those associated with harvests, prosperity, and abundance, such as the goddess of luck, Fortuna, and Plutus, the god of riches. A symbol of abundance and nourishment, a cornucopia is usually a large horn-

A CORNUCOPIA FILLED WITH FRESH PRODUCE

shaped container overflowing with fruits, vegetables, or nuts. Draupadi's vessel is often compared to the Greek cornucopia, and refers to a kitchen overflowing with food for guests.

AFTER

When his plan to put the Pandavas to shame failed, Duryodhana decided to hunt for them in the forest.

A PLOY TO KILL
Insecurity got the better of Duryodhana; he knew that the Pandavas would return after their exile to claim the throne. To secure his claim to the throne, he wanted to make sure that his cousins were hunted down in the forest and killed.

KATASRAJ TEMPLE
The Katasraj temple, in the Punjab province of Pakistan, is believed to have been the refuge of the Pandavas for four years during their exile. According to another legend, the lake is believed to be filled with Shiva's tears and is considered to be a pilgrimage site.

THE PANDAVA QUEEN

Draupadi

"How is it that the **chaste wife** of the Pandus ... has been **brought into** this assembly of kings? ... Tell me whether **I am a slave** or not a slave, and I will **act accordingly**."

DRAUPADI, SABHA PARVA: THE BOOK OF THE ASSEMBLY HALL

MYTHOLOGY AND FOLKLORE

OTHER DEPICTIONS

Draupadi is portrayed as helpless in Vyasa's Mahabharata. But in regional lore, she is presented as different heroines who are anything but passive. She is Bela in the Hindi epic *Alha Khand,* who commits sati; a goddess in the Bhil Mahabharata; and Virashakti in *Vira Panchali,* the lore of north Tamil Nadu, in which she fights demons. In south India, in festivals that last up to eighteen days, the Mahabharata is re-enacted, at the end of which men walk on fire. This is believed to represent an act of collective expiation by the men for letting down the goddess. In Bangalore, during the Karaga festival, a man dresses up as a woman and travels through the city. Representing Yudhishthira, undergoing ritual humiliation, he asks his wife, the goddess, to forgive him.

THE PANCHALA PRINCESS
This Bikaner-style illustration of Draupadi shows her with her hair untied. Following her humiliation by the Kauravas, she swore not to tie her hair till she washed it with Dusshasana's blood.

Draupadi, the wife of the five Pandavas, was born out of a desire for vengeance. Her father, King Drupada of Panchala, was consumed by the desire to take revenge on his foe Drona and his patrons, the Kuru clan. He invoked Lord Shiva and asked him for a son to kill Bhishma, the Kuru patriarch, and for a daughter who would marry into the Kuru household and divide it. Draupadi was that daughter, born from a fire built to appease Shiva.

She is depicted as a beautiful and sensuous woman, and her effect on men is a recurring theme in the Mahabharata.

The shared wife

At Draupadi's swayamvara, many archers tried their luck and failed. When Karna was about to try, Draupadi stopped him saying, "A son of a charioteer cannot contend for my hand." Arjuna won the archery contest and, thus, her hand. But Kunti, fearing that Draupadi's beauty would create discord among her sons, asked all of them to share her equally. The Pandavas had no power until Draupadi came into their lives. With the powerful Drupada as their father-in-law, they were in a position to negotiate. But her entry marked the division of the Kuru land. Her presence brought fortune but also broke a household.

All the Pandava brothers loved Draupadi equally, and they agreed to have exclusive access to her chamber by turn.

Dignified in humiliation

At the dice game organized by the Kauravas, Yudhishthira staked and lost Draupadi. When Duryodhana sent a doorkeeper to fetch her, she refused to go, questioning Yudhishthira's right to gamble her away after losing himself.

Dusshasana then grabbed her by her hair and dragged her through the palace into the gambling hall. The gathering was stunned to see Draupadi, the queen of Indraprastha, barely covered, hair unbound, lying in a heap at Duryodhana's feet. Her husbands hung their heads in shame.

No one came to her rescue, even when Duryodhana asked Dusshasana to strip her naked. As Dusshasana grabbed her robe, Draupadi raised her arms toward the heavens and cried to God. Her honor was eventually saved by divine intervention.

Draupadi swore never to forgive the Kauravas and not to tie her hair until she had washed it in Dusshasana's blood. The elders came to their senses and ended the episode. In reply to Dhritarashtra's apology, Draupadi asked for her husbands' freedom and property to be restored to them. Throughout her ordeal, she maintained a dignified calm.

A queen in exile

But when Krishna visited the Pandavas in exile, Draupadi could not hold back her tears. Krishna, however, tried to reason with her and blamed her squarely for some of her suffering. He reminded her how she had committed adharma by rejecting Karna because of his low caste. Draupadi's miseries followed her wherever she went. During the Pandavas' exile, she was harassed by men such as Jayadratha and Kichaka, who desired her and made inappropriate advances at her.

A short-lived vengeance

In the Kurukshetra War, Bhima killed Dusshasana and invited Draupadi to wash her hair with his blood, helping her fulfil the oath she had made years ago.

But on the last night of the war, Ashwatthama killed Draupadi's brothers and her five sons, mistaking them for the five Pandavas. Burning with rage, she wanted the head of the murderer—but Krishna intervened, putting an end to the cycle of violence.

The final journey

At the end of their rule, when it was finally time for the Pandavas to retire, Draupadi followed her husbands north to the great snow-clad mountain whose peak touched Swarga. But Draupadi slipped and fell to her death. Yudhishthira knew why she had not survived—though she was supposed to love all her five husbands equally, she had preferred Arjuna, desired Karna, and manipulated Bhima.

DRAUPADI'S SWAYAMWARA
A terracotta panel at the Navaratna Chototaraf temple, Bankura, West Bengal, India, shows Arjuna aiming at the eye of a fish at Draupadi's swayamvara.

BIOGRAPHY IN BRIEF

- **Daughter of** King Drupada of Panchala, she and her twin brother Dhrishtadyumna were born out of a sacred fire.
- **Rejected Karna at her swayamvara** by not letting him participate because of his low caste. Arjuna won her hand.
- **Became the common wife** after an unaware Kunti asked Arjuna to share whatever he had won in the archery contest with his brothers.
- **Had five sons with the five Pandavas:** Prativindhya from Yudhishthira; Satsoma from Bhima; Shrutakirti from Arjuna; Shatanika from Nakula; and Shrutasena from Sahadeva, collectively known as the Upapandavas.
- **Mocked Duryodhana** at Yudhishthira's coronation when he fell into a pool. He swore revenge.
- **Humiliated by Duryodhana** after Yudhishthira lost her in the gambling match. Duryodhana demanded she be stripped naked in public.
- **Went into exile** for thirteen years with her husbands, including a year in hiding in the Matsya kingdom.
- **Loved Karna secretly**, thinking of him as someone who would not have gambled her away.
- **Fulfilled her oath** of washing her hair with Dusshasana's blood after Bhima killed him in war.
- **Lost her sons** to Drona's son Ashwatthama's rage. The Kaurava survivor killed her five children, mistaking them to be the Pandavas.
- **Became the queen** after her victorious husbands came to the throne.
- **Died** after falling on her way to heaven.

ANALYSIS

DRAUPADI AND KRISHNA

Draupadi shared a special bond with Krishna. In certain traditions, it is believed that Yashoda's daughter, who had been sacrificed to save Krishna, was reborn through the fire in King Drupada's palace, making Draupadi Krishna's sister.

According to a folk narrative, when Krishna was bathing in a river, his lower garment got swept away by the water current. To save his honor and without a second thought, Draupadi gave him her upper garment to cover himself. Krishna repaid that act of generosity by saving her honor when the Kauravas tried to disrobe her.

BEFORE

The eldest Kaurava was not content with banishing his cousins to the forest. Duryodhana continued to plot, and missed no opportunity to harass them.

DURYODHANA'S PLOTS

Looking to compound their discomfort, Duryodhana instructed many priests and sages to accompany the Pandavas and participate in the yagna. Their inability to feed all the sages would embarrass the proud Kshatriyas. What he had not accounted for, however, was Krishna's active role in the Pandavas' lives.

The **Grand Expedition**

Duryodhana planned an expedition that would pass by the woods in which the Pandavas were living. Although the reason he gave for this was to count all the cows in his land, Duryodhana's true objective was to gloat over his cousins.

Duryodhana was constantly scheming and planning his cousins' downfall. The game of dice had slaked his thirst for revenge against the Pandavas but his insecurities soon resurfaced. He began to agonize over the fact that they would eventually come back to claim their share of the kingdom.

Duryodhana's stratagems

His solution was simple. "The Pandavas have gone into the forest but they will come back. Let us hunt them down in the forest instead. Then my position will be secure forever," proposed Duryodhana. Veda Vyasa, who happened to hear of this plan, was horrified. He admonished the blind Dhritarashtra and his blindfolded wife, Gandhari, and advised them to stop their sons. Vidura counseled his brother to salvage the situation by calling the Pandavas back and punishing his sons.

Tired of being criticized by his half-brother, Dhritarashtra snapped at Vidura. "Why don't you leave Hastinapur and join the Pandavas if you are so concerned for them?" Deeply hurt, Vidura left the palace to join Pandu's sons in the forest. Dhritarashtra, who was very fond of him, almost immediately regretted his words and sent a servant to convince him to return.

Yudhishthira knew how much the two brothers loved each other. He advised his uncle to go back to Hastinapur, emphasizing how much his voice of reason was needed at the palace.

Rishi Maitreya accompanied Vidura back, and cautioned the Kauravas against the new, ill-advised move they were planning. He mentioned the Pandavas' encounter with the Rakshasa Kirmira, describing how Bhima had killed the monster and earned glory and the blessings of sages living in the forest."Let them live in peace," was Maitreya's advice.

On hearing this, Duryodhana decided to give up his plan to kill the Pandavas. Karna then came up with another idea.

HISTORY AND CULTURE

DANCE ENACTMENTS IN KERALA

Kerala, like other parts of India, has its own regional versions of the Mahabharata. Episodes from the epic are enacted in dances such as Kathakali and Theyyam. In one such enactment, Theyyam dancers tell of how the Kauravas use black magic against the Pandavas but they fail each time, either due to Krishna's grace or Draupadi's power.

A THEYYAM DANCER

Karna's scheme

"Now that you are the master of all that the Pandavas once possessed, you can make them feel small. Why don't you travel across your vast kingdom to count all the cows you have? Karna suggested. On the way, you can meet the Pandavas to see how they are faring and sympathize with them. This way, you can humiliate them and keep your promise to not hunt them down." The idea of being able to laugh at Draupadi the way she had laughed at him and to sit with the Pandavas while they were living in poverty appealed to Duryodhana.

The grand expedition

So, a counting of the cows, or a ghoshayatra, was organized. This grand procession would go around Indraprastha and Hastinapur and count all the cows that now belonged to the Kauravas. Since its primary objective was to taunt the Pandavas, at twilight the expedition set up camp in the vicinity of their home in the forest. Tents were set up, food was cooked, and musicians entertained the revellers.

Bhima, sent to investigate all the commotion, recognized the deliberate attempt to make fun of their situation.

"They have intentionally camped upwind of us and are cooking my favorite dishes in open pots so that I can smell the food," he fumed. "They are doing everything they can to mock our misfortunes." Arjuna, who could see Karna stringing his bow, was of the opinion that the Kauravas planned to hunt them down. Yudhishthira cautioned his brothers to control themselves and not be dragged into any more traps laid by their cousins.

Kauravas attacked

Suddenly the Kaurava camp was attacked by Gandharvas. Taken by surprise, the Kauravas, Karna, Shakuni and other warriors were soon captured and bound.

When he heard what had happened, Yudhishthira felt it his duty to go to their rescue. It was the path of dharma to help the helpless, he told his brothers and Draupadi.

Bhima and Arjuna reluctantly gathered their weapons and made their way to the Kaurava camp. After a small clash with the Gandharvas, they were able to free the captives. The Kauravas were now indebted to them. The expedition had misfired.

"There were eight thousand chariots, thirty thousand elephants … carriages, shopping carts … traders, bards, and men … in hundreds and thousands."

SAGE VAISHAMPAYANA TO KING JANAMEJAYA, VANA PARVA: THE BOOK OF THE FOREST

TRAVELING IN STYLE
This mural from the walls of the Bodinayakanur Palace in Tamil Nadu, India, shows a large procession including palanquins, soldiers, and womenfolk. Duryodhana's procession, planned with the intention of taunting his cousins, was probably on a much grander scale.

AFTER

Shamed by the Pandavas' magnanimity, the Kauravas returned to Hastinapur.

DURYODHANA'S DECISION
The embarrassment of being attacked and taken hostage by the Gandharvas, only to be rescued by the Pandavas, filled the Kauravas with shame. Karna was even more humiliated when he saw Arjuna defeat the very Gandharvas who had captured him. After this incident Duryodhana decided that he would leave the Pandavas alone till the thirteenth year of their exile. "I will find them then and force them to return to the forest," he thought. He would not meet the Pandavas again for more than a decade.

BEFORE

Jayadratha, the king of Sindhu, was married to Dusshala, the only daughter of Gandhari and Dhritarashtra—the only daughter in the large Kuru clan.

THE KING OF SINDHU
Jayadratha, the son of Vriddhakshatra, was passing through the Kamyaka forest on his way to the kingdom of Salwa. According to tradition, he was accompanied by a retinue of several princes and a small army.

"... the **powerful Bhimasena** ... chased the one who was running away. He **angrily grabbed** him by the hair on his head."

SAGE VAISHAMPAYANA TO KING JANAMEJAYA, VANA PARVA: THE BOOK OF THE FOREST

Jayadratha's Proposition

During the Pandavas' forced sojourn in exile, Jayadratha, the brother-in-law of the Kauravas, was traveling through the forest. The king found Draupadi all alone, an easy prey to be taken advantage of—or so he thought.

King Jayadratha was going through the forest of Kamyaka where the Pandavas were living out their forced exile. As fate would have it, his entourage passed by the cave where the Pandavas had made their temporary home. On seeing the beautiful Draupadi, Jayadratha sent an emissary to find out who she was.

When he learned that she was the wife of the exiled Pandavas and alone at the moment, Jayadratha decided to approach her, breaking all social protocol.

Since Jayadratha was married to Dusshala, and hence related to the Pandavas as well, Draupadi was glad to see a kinsman. At the same time, she wondered why he had come to visit her. Could it be that he wanted to show solidarity and express his disapproval of the Kauravas' actions—or had he come all the way from Sindhu, his kingdom, just to gloat?

"The sons of Pandu are **without** fortune ... Be my **wife**. Abandon them and obtain **happiness**."

JAYADRATHA TO DRAUPADI, VANA PARVA: THE BOOK OF THE FOREST

An improper offer

As she served him fruit and water, Draupadi assured him that her husbands, who had gone to gather food, would be back soon. But lecherous Jayadratha replied, "I hope not. I came only to see you." He put a box in front of her and opened it to reveal an exquisite collection of fabrics, jewels, and cosmetics. "There's much more if you come with me to Sindhu."

Draupadi was revolted and afraid. Bristling with anger at Jayadratha's audacity, she reminded him that she was the wife of the great Pandavas and asked him if he had forgotten their powers.

But the king refused to cower. "You are nothing but a beggar now; a whore of five brothers, disrobed in public by the Kauravas. Be my concubine and come with me to my palace. I will give you a much better life," said Jayadratha insolently as he dragged her to his chariot.

Draupadi resisted and screamed for help. Dhaumya, the Pandavas' priest, tried to plead with the king, but to no avail.

On their return, the Pandavas heard of Draupadi's abduction and immediately rushed after Jayadratha to avenge their wife's honor. A battle ensued, and the Pandavas easily defeated Jayadratha's infantry. Arjuna's arrows broke Jayadratha's carriage wheels and incapacitated his horses, while Bhima pounced on the king and beat him senseless. Bhima would have pummeled Jayadratha to death had it not been for Yudhishthira, who intervened just in time.

An act of pity

Yudhishthira explained that, as the husband of Dusshala, their first cousin Jayadratha should be shown mercy. Though his brothers were furious at Jayadratha—and Draupadi even more so—they gave in to Yudhishthira's dispassionate reasoning. They let the king go, but not before Bhima had pulled out Jayadratha's hair, leaving behind only five tufts on his head to serve as a reminder of his transgressions.

ANALYSIS

STATUS OF WOMEN

Draupadi in the Mahabharata, and Sita in the Ramayana, are portrayed as highly desirable women. Both women have to fend off unwelcome advances from men. Yet, unlike the Ramayana, where Sita had to prove her chastity, the Mahabharata portrays Draupadi as a loyal and chaste wife who goes through many trials. In the epic, Vyasa ponders on what makes a woman a wife. In a civilized society, the laws of marital fidelity make a woman a wife. But in the forest, where rules seem to get suspended, does this still hold true?

AN ACTOR PLAYING DRAUPADI

AFTER

Tired of the constant trouble created by the Kauravas, the Pandavas went deeper into the forest.

In the Dwaitavana, the Pandavas met Rishi Markandeya who told Yudhishthira the story of Rama, prince of Ayodhya.

INDECENT PROPOSAL
The man's lustful eyes and the woman's anxious expression in this painting by Dhiren Sasmal, in a way, evokes the dramatic encounter between Draupadi and Jayadratha.

The **Story** of **Rama**

The tale of an obedient son who is exiled for many years, the Ramayana is a poignant reminder to the Pandavas that their misfortunes were not unique nor exclusive. Just as Rama survived and triumphed over his suffering, so would the Pandavas.

The Pandavas were exhausted and bitter—their cousins and other relatives continued to create trouble for them, for instance Jayadratha, the king of Sindhu, had attempted to abduct Draupadi. They decided that it would be best to leave Kamyaka go deeper into the forest, and set up camp in denser jungle known as the Dwaitavana.

The days went by; the Pandavas did not have much to fill their days except conversation. The idea of spending the long years of exile in this way made them impatient, but Yudhishthira, although troubled on behalf of his brothers and wife, kept his calm. But when Bhima angrily asked him, "Are you not angry and humiliated? Don't you feel aggrieved at fate, annoyed with the Kauravas?" the eldest Pandava could not keep quiet. "Is there another man who has suffered as much as me?" he wondered aloud.

Sage Markandeya heard him and said, "There was once a king called Rama, who suffered

"The valorous Rama, with dharma in his soul, went to the forest."

SAGE MARKANDEYA TO YUDHISHTHIRA, VANA PARVA: THE BOOK OF THE FOREST

as much, if not more. He was exiled for fourteen years. While you have brought this misery upon yourself, Rama led a life of suffering because of his adherence to dharma." Looking toward Draupadi and Bhima, he said, "Your brothers followed you into exile because they had no choice, but Rama's brother, Lakshman, followed him because of deep love and affection for his elder brother."

The sage then proceeded to narrate the Ramopakhyan, the story of Rama, to the Pandavas.

THE KHON

A traditional Thai dance drama, Khon was usually performed in the royal court. Most stories are from the Ramayana, focusing on the characters of Rama and Hanuman.

The prince of Ayodhya

Dasharatha, the king of Ayodhya, had three wives and four sons. Rama—Koushalya's son, and the eldest—grew up to be a handsome prince and brave warrior who lived by the rules of dharma. There came a time when Dasharatha wanted to hold a ceremony to establish Rama as his heir apparent. As the eve of Rama's coronation approached, Kaikeyi, Dasharatha's second queen, was unable to contain her jealousy that her son, Bharata, would never be king.

Kaikeyi set out to meet the king, decked in jewels and clad in beautiful clothes. She reminded him of a blessing he had offered her long ago. Dasharatha, unaware of her intentions, offered to fulfil his promise. Kaikeyi then said to Dasharatha, "Let my son, Bharata, be made the king of Ayodhya. And send Rama to the forest for fourteen years."

Dasharatha had no choice but to ask Rama to leave Ayodhya and anoint Bharata as king. A dutiful son, Rama fulfilled his father's wishes without protest. Leaving his royal robes in the palace, he made his way to the forest in clothes of bark, armed only with his bow for protection in the wild. His wife, Sita, and brother, Lakshman, chose to accompany him.

But despite all Kaikeyi's efforts, her son, Bharata, refused to take the throne. He did not want to wear a crown that was tainted by deceit. He decided to serve as a regent instead, and wait for the return of Rama.

RAMA IN EXILE

This opaque watercolor-and-ink folio from an 18th-century Ramayana from Gujarat, India, shows Rama, along with his brother Lakshman and wife Sita, in the Panchavati forest while he was in exile.

The fourteen-year exile

The long years in the forest were full of hardships for Rama, his wife, and brother. They traveled through different lands battling demons, taking shelter in caves when needed, and often meeting sages whose tales would fill them with hope and wisdom. In the final year of exile, the three encountered a Rakshasa woman called Surpanakha.

»

PEOPLE

RAVANA

The son of a Rishi and a Rakshasa, Ravana was the learned king of Lanka, and is still revered in parts of southern India. According to a theory, Rama was a white Aryan invader and Ravana represents the leader of the dark-skinned southern tribes. While many writers speak of Rama as the upholder of civilization who drove out the threat presented by the south Indian Rakshasas, some Tamil writers argue that Rama was the invader, and Ravana was the local defender.

RAVANA, THE TEN-HEADED KING

RAVANA ABDUCTS SITA
Many scenes from the Ramayana, like this one depicting Ravana abducting Sita, can be seen at the Banteay Srei temple, Cambodia.

ART AND LITERATURE

VALMIKI'S RAMAYANA

The Ramayana is an epic poem written by Sage Valmiki. The "Ramopakhyan" version of the tale, found in the Mahabharata, recounts Rama's tale in brief. The two versions have quite a few similarities, and many passages between Valmiki's and Vyasa's tales correspond closely. However, there are also quite a few deviations, not least of which is the fact that in Vyasa's version, Sita is King Janaka's biological daughter, while in Valmiki's Ramayana, she is a foundling that the king discovers in a field while tilling the soil.

» On seeing the two brothers, a smitten Surpanakha approached them repeatedly. But Rama and Lakshman refused to respond to her advances. Angry and jealous, she tried to kill Sita. Rama and Lakshman stopped her in time; but, to teach her a lesson, they cut off her nose and lips and chased her away.

Sita's abduction

A mutilated Surpanakha ran to her brother Ravana, king of the Rakshasas, and demanded that he avenge her humiliation. Seeing his sister hurt, Ravana was enraged. He set off to the forest in search of his sister's attackers. Rama and Lakshman had left their hut in chase of golden deer, leaving Sita alone. Ravana went to Sita in the guise of an ascetic. As Sita offered him food and drink, the king grabbed her, tossed her over his shoulders, and took her to his home—the island kingdom of Lanka.

On their return, Rama and Lakshman heard about the abduction and took a vow to destroy the king who had dared to kidnap Sita.

Army of monkeys

Rama knew he needed to raise an army and forge new allies, in order to rescue his wife. As fate would have it, he met the monkey Hanuman. On hearing of Rama's search for an able ally, Hanuman took the brothers to meet his leader, Sugriva, who was engaged in a dispute over the throne of the kingdom of Kishkinda with his brother, Vali. Sugriva was happy to lend his support in this righteous battle, but he had a condition—he wanted Rama's help to defeat Vali.

Rama killed Vali with a single arrow, and Sugriva started gathering an army. Soon, he had put together a great army of monkeys, bears, and vultures. Making their way toward Lanka, the army was blocked by the sea. The brave monkeys and bears constructed a bridge of stones to facilitate the crossing. Meanwhile, Ravana's spies had carried news of Rama's army to him, including details about the bridge that they had built.

Reaching Lanka

As Rama and his army crossed over to Lanka, Ravana took up his mighty bow and shot two missiles, breaking the bridge. As Rama's army stormed the city, Ravana saw his city crawling with monkeys and bears.

"**Ravana**, the **lord** of the **rakshasas** and skilled in **maya**, resorted to maya. **Hundreds** … of **rakshasas** were seen to **emerge** from his **body**. They **held** arrows, **lances** and **swords**."

SAGE MARKANDEYA TO YUDHISHTHIRA, VANA PARVA: THE BOOK OF THE FOREST

A fierce battle ensued: the Rakshasas fought ferociously to defend their king and city, and the monkeys and bears fought valiantly to rescue Sita.

The war lasted for days and the city was laid waste. Ravana's brother, Kumbhakarna, and his friend Mahiravana, who were legendary warriors, were also defeated in the battle.

At long last, Ravana and Rama met on the battlefield. The clash would have lasted forever, but Vibhishana, Ravana's younger brother who had defected to the other side, revealed Ravana's secret—a pot of nectar of immortality hidden in his navel, a gift from his grandfather, Brahma the creator. Rama aimed at Ravana's navel, killing him, and the war came to an end.

Return to Ayodhya

The kingdom mourned their fallen king. Vibhishana was crowned the king of Lanka. The exile ended, and Rama returned to Ayodhya, where he was made king, with Sita as his queen.

HANUMAN'S VISIT TO LANKA
Dating between the 16th and 19th century, this painting belonging to the Deccani school of art captures Hanuman's visit to Lanka to meet Sita.

THE BATTLE
This 17th-century ink-and-color by the famous painter Sahibdin, from the Mewar school of art, depicts the battle between Rama's monkey army and Ravana's demons.

ANALYSIS

TEST OF VIRTUE

After Rama returned to Ayodhya, he was crowned king. But his subjects were unable to accept Sita as his queen—they suspected her of having been unfaithful to their king, as she had spent considerable time in captivity with Ravana, the king of Lanka.

Since the onus lay on the woman to prove her innocence, Sita had to walk through fire to prove her fidelity to Rama. Despite successfully doing this, doubt prevailed, and Sita was banished to the forest. Later, she was asked prove her chastity again before being allowed to return to Ayodhya. Unable to bear the insult, Sita prayed to the earth goddess, and as final proof of her purity, urged the goddess to open up and accept her.

ARJUNA'S PENANCE
This open-air bas-relief stands in Mahabalipuram, India, a UNESCO World Heritage Site. The emaciated figure performing austerities is believed to be Arjuna, praying to Shiva for the Pashupatastra.

Shiva Humbles Arjuna

Certain that a war with his cousins was inevitable, Arjuna decided to leave his brothers and use this time to pray and perform austerities to Shiva, the deity of destruction. He wanted Shiva's blessing and divine weapons to use in the war.

BEFORE

Tired of being troubled by the Kauravas, the Pandavas withdrew from the Kamyaka forest and went deeper into the wilderness of the Dwaita forest.

ARJUNA'S DECISION

Though time went by, the sting of their humiliation still stayed fresh. With little to do but mull over past events, Draupadi's bitterness and Bhima's rage simmered unabated. Yudhishthira, not one to give in to anger, was burdened by guilt. While the others brooded over the past and raged at their situation, Arjuna concluded that there was far more merit in taking action. He decided to prepare for the war that was sure to come.

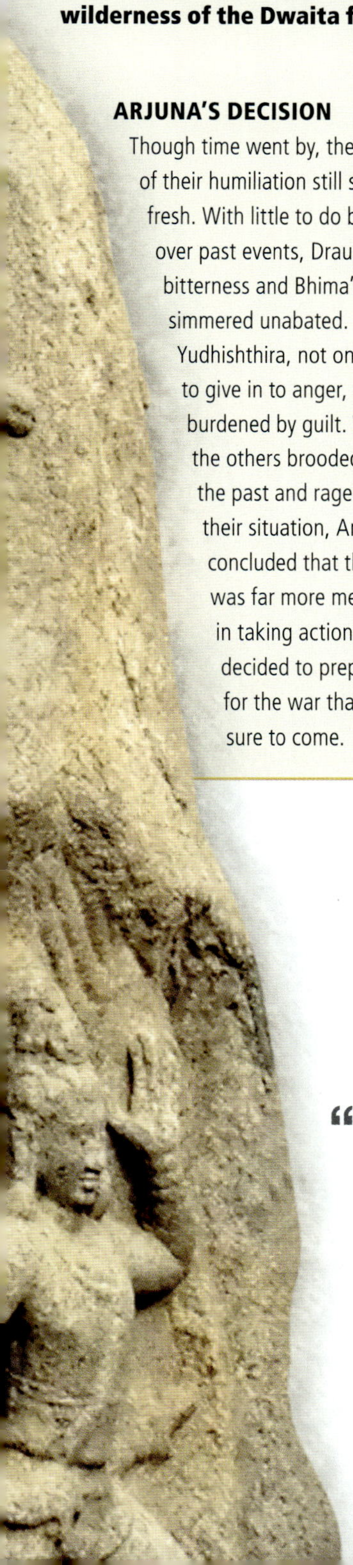

Arjuna left his brothers and wife and traveled north toward the high Himalayas. He wanted to invoke the deity of destruction, Shiva, and obtain the divine Pashupatastra, a weapon that contained the strength of all the birds and beasts.

Coming to a forest of pine, Arjuna chose a smooth, oval stone from the river bed for a linga, the symbol of Shiva, and planted it in a clearing. Having made an offering of flowers to the linga, he sat down in front of it to meditate. Emptying his mind of all distractions, suspending his senses and withholding his breath, he focused on Shiva. Several days went by as Arjuna remained motionless.

One day, a wild boar charged at the seated figure. Instinctively, Arjuna picked up his bow and shot an arrow. However, when he approached it, he saw that the boar had been hit by two arrows. A Kirat (hunter) and his wife were claiming the kill. Beaming with pride, the wife told Arjuna, "My husband killed the boar." "No, it was my arrow that killed it," Arjuna retorted. But the couple disagreed.

"Do you know who I am?" demanded Arjuna, unused to being challenged.

"A spoiled boy who always has his way," mocked the hunter.

"I am Arjuna, the mightiest archer the world has seen," said the Pandava.

"Really? By which yardstick?" the hunter asked. His wife added fuel to fire. "You may be a prince in the city but your name has no weight here. In the forest, you are just a common dog who must make way for the lion."

Incensed by these insults, Arjuna challenged the hunter to a fight. "The winner will be the superior warrior, and surely the hunter of the boar."

The hunter accepted with a mocking air and calmly proceeded to strike down every arrow that Arjuna shot. Running out of arrows, Arjuna had to concede that the Kirat was a skilled archer. He then picked up his sword, but it broke under the hunter's onslaught. He began hand-to-hand combat, only to be bested once again.

With his spirits crushed and his confidence broken, a desperate Arjuna went to Shiva's shrine to cover it with flowers again. When he opened his eyes, he saw the hunter sitting in front of him, covered with the same flowers. It was Shiva himself.

Arjuna realized that the hunter's wife was the goddess Shakti and the boar was Nandi, the bull, Shiva's sacred mount. "I wanted to test your strength of purpose," said Shiva. "I see that you don't give up."

Overwhelmed, Arjuna fell at Shiva's feet. Blessing him, Shiva gave him the Pashupatastra, and advised him to use it wisely.

HISTORY AND CULTURE

KALIA LOHAR

In the Garhwal region of the Himalayas, a dance drama of the Mahabharata, the "Pandava leela," is performed every autumn. Depicted in it is the legend of Kalia Lohar ("lohar" is the Hindi word for blacksmith), who forged weapons for the Pandavas during their exile. The locals believe that Kalia was Shiva himself, and worship him in this form. To this day, blacksmiths in the Garhwal region set aside five pieces of coal, representing the five Pandavas, before they begin work.

> "O Mahadeva! Pardon my crime… Out of ignorance… I fought with you."
>
> ARJUNA TO KIRATA, THE HUNTER, VANA PARVA: THE BOOK OF THE FOREST

AFTER

Blessed with the divine weapon, Arjuna also had a vision of Shiva and Shakti's true forms.

A DIVINE VISION

Arjuna saw Shiva—his hair was matted; his body smeared with ash and covered with the skin of a lion and tiger. He held a trident and a rattle drum, and a begging bowl formed from a skull. Around his neck was a string of rudraksha beads and a hooded snake. Shiva sat on Nandi, the bull, with his wife Shakti, who was dressed in the sixteen love charms of marriage. Before the vision ended, the couple, who embodied the soul and the flesh, blessed Arjuna.

Arjuna in Paradise

From honing his battle skills by fighting with the Asuras to learning the art of music and dance from the Gandharvas, Arjuna's time in Swarga, or heaven, proved to be delightful. But there is always trouble in paradise.

When Indra saw his son climbing up the snow-clad mountains, he greeted him with dark rain-filled clouds. As flashes of thunder and lightning split the sky, Arjuna saw Indra's golden chariot descend from the skies toward him.

Matali, Indra's charioteer, had come down to invite Arjuna to Swarga on behalf of his father.

"Why does my father call for me?" asked Arjuna.

"Indra needs your help. He is troubled by the Asuras. Using the Pashupatastra, you can defeat them more easily than the Devas can," Matali explained.

Delighted to be sought out for his skills by the gods themselves, Arjuna promised to do his best. Together, he and the Devas defeated many fearsome Asuras.

BEFORE

Arjuna had moved north of the Kamyaka forest, near the base of the mountains, to pray to Shiva.

SHIVA'S GIFTS

Impressed with the severity of Arjuna's penance, Shiva gave him the Pashupatastra. Shiva and his consort, Shakti, also blessed Arjuna, revealing their true forms to him.

Leaving the clearing at the foothills of the mountains, Arjuna then traveled further north to climb the high Himalayas.

BAS-RELIEF OF A DANCING SHIVA, PO KLONG GARAI TEMPLE, PHAN RANG, VIETNAM

"The **gods,** gandharvas, siddhas and **supreme rishis** happily welcomed **Partha** [Arjuna] … He was blessed and **praised**, **accompanied** by the sounds of divine **instruments**."

SAGE VAISHAMPAYANA TO KING JANAMEJAYA, VANA PARVA: THE BOOK OF THE FOREST

ARJUNA DANCING WITH GANDHARVAS
This Kalighat-style painting from Bengal, India, shows Arjuna dancing with the Gandharvas, while his father, Indra, king of Swarga, looks on.

A divine invitation

Pleased with Arjuna's success, Indra welcomed him to Swarga. Arjuna spent many days indulging in the joys of paradise. He took a special interest in dancing, learning it from the Gandharvas, the celestial beings adept in music and dance.

Arjuna's warrior's body was made for dancing, and he soon mastered the art. As the Apsaras watched him move in time to the music, they were entranced. Even Urvashi, foremost among the Apsaras, was smitten. "Be mine," she asked Arjuna. This was not possible for Arjuna, who looked at her as family. "You were the wife of my ancestor, Pururava. I cannot think of you that way," replied Arjuna, uncomfortable.

"The rules of mortals do not apply to immortals," Urvashi said, dismissing Arjuna's logic.

"But they apply to me." said Arjuna.

The bitter fruit

Urvashi could not believe that she, who was considered irresistible, had been spurned. "You reject me?" she asked, incensed, and spat out a curse. "Only a eunuch refuses a willing woman! May you lose your manhood instantly!"

Arjuna went to Indra, hoping that his father would reverse the curse. But Indra could only modify it. "You will lose your manhood, but only for a year. Turn it to your advantage," he advised. "Use it in the last year of your exile, when you have to live in disguise, without being recognized." And so, in the thirteenth year of exile, Arjuna used this curse to evade discovery by the Kauravas.

ANALYSIS

URVASHI AND ARJUNA

Urvashi's values are different from Arjuna's. She is part of nature, where desire is not contained by man-made rules and ethics. Arjuna, however, is part of human society, where desire is defined by morality and ethics.

Because of this, what Urvashi considers to be mere passion is tantamount to incest for Arjuna. This episode shows how confrontation can happen when two different value systems come into conflict.

SANDSTONE CARVING OF AN APSARA, THAILAND

AFTER

Although he enjoyed being in heaven, Arjuna dearly missed his brothers and Draupadi.

THE PILGRIMS' PROGRESS

To fulfil Arjuna's wish, Indra asked Sage Lomasha to take the other Pandavas to the hermitage of Nara and Narayana. Arjuna would meet them there after spending some more time with Indra. When Lomasha met the exiles, he found that they missed Arjuna with a similar intensity. He told them tales of Arjuna's adventures and gave them a message from Indra. "Spend your time traveling, learning new skills, and gaining wisdom. You will be better rulers for it," he said.

A **Journey** Full of **Tales**

While Arjuna was away in Amravati, the other brothers and Draupadi spent their time in the company of sages and learned men. As they made their way through the forest, their passage was filled with stories, discussions, and life lessons.

Arjuna's time at Indra's home was spent amid the comforts and marvels of Amravati, but thoughts of Draupadi and his brothers kept bothering him: Were they safe and well? Did they have enough to eat? Were the Kauravas still troubling them? Seeing Arjuna anxious, Indra requested Rishi Lomasha to keep the Pandavas company until Arjuna's return. He also asked the Rishi to bring the brothers to the hermitage of Nara and Narayana, located on top of the snow-clad peaks of the Himalayas, where Arjuna would join them in time. When Lomasha met the Pandavas, he found that they were equally concerned about their brother and sorely missed him. Learning that the sage had arrived from Amravati, they plied him with questions about their brother.

ARJUNA AND THE CELESTIALS
This 19th-century folio from *Kiratarjuniya*, a short lyrical narrative of Arjuna's encounter with Shiva disguised as a hunter, shows Arjuna in paradise. While Arjuna was enjoying himself in Amravati, his siblings and wife were leading a life of learning in the forest.

SAGE NARADA
An 18th-century miniature of Sage Narada. A recurring figure in the Hindu epics, Narada is a traveling musician and storyteller.

Sensing their anxiety, Lomasha reassured them. "Arjuna is in good health and enjoying himself in Amravati. He will be there for a little longer and will meet you at the hermitage of Nara and Narayana. I also bring you advice from Indra. He has suggested that you use these years of exile wisely; travel across the rose-apple continent of Jambudvipa; see new places, learn new skills, and spend time with sages and other learned folk. All this will help you gain wisdom. On your return to Indraprastha, you will be the better rulers for it."

Long years of exile loomed in front of the Pandavas, and they knew it was wiser to use the time constructively, to gain knowledge, than to remain idle, cursing their fate.

Stories of the wise

So began the great pilgrimage of the Pandavas. A procession of sages, including chief priest Dhaumya, Narada, Parvata, and Lomasha, accompanied them as they went south, then to the east, and then west. They observed many rituals, bathed in the holy rivers, took dips in lakes guarded by ancient deities, and meditated in caves.

During this journey, they also met many great Rishis such as Vrihadashwa and Arshitsena, who told them stories and discussed philosophy.

On family

They narrated the story of Rishi Agastya who had constant bad dreams about his ancestors. In every nightmare, they appeared hung upside down over a bottomless pit, crying that they would never be able to escape this miserable state unless they were reborn. For this, they told Agastya they needed him, their descendant, to marry and produce children. Heeding their advice, Agastya married the princess Lopamudra and had children. By marrying, Agastya repaid his debt to his ancestors and helped them be reborn.

From marriage, the sages moved on to the importance of sons to a parent. They told the Pandavas about a man called Kahoda. When his unborn son corrected his understanding of the Vedas, Kahoda was incensed. He cursed the child to suffer from eight physical defects. This was how his son came to be called Ashtavakra—the one with eight deformities. Later, Ashtavakra defeated a scholar named Bandi in a debate. An old foe of Kahoda, Bandi had defeated him in a public gathering of learned men. So the son, who had been cursed by his father, ended up avenging his father's insult.

The tale of Kaushika illustrated the importance of handling worldly responsibilities instead of running away from them. Kaushika had abandoned his parents to become a hermit. Though he gained many great powers, he was unable to have any peace of mind. He then learned, from a housewife and then a butcher, that peace of mind does not come from renouncing worldly life; it comes from a true understanding of the soul and the world around. Kaushika realized that one must accept that life is the result of past karmas and that »

HISTORY AND CULTURE

ORAL TRADITIONS

Oral retellings are a big part of Indian culture, just like the parables in other cultures. Stories are seen as profound truths that shape a person's understanding of the world. A story may seem non-religious, but is rooted in religious values. For instance, the notion of rebirth is absent in cultures that believe in one life. Buddhism values rebirth, which is reflected in the *Jataka* folk tales that narrate the stories of Buddha's past life. That European fairy tales always speak of "happily ever after" implies an influence of the notion of heaven found in the Bible.

THE BIBLE, TOO, WAS INITIALLY A SET OF STORIES TRANSMITTED ORALLY

"They were **attired in** tough **bark** and deerskin. ... With **swords tied** and with quivers and arrows, the **brave Pandavas** set out, their faces **toward the east**."

SAGE VAISHAMPAYANA TO JANAMEJAYA, VANA PARVA: THE BOOK OF THE FOREST

one has the power to choose one's response to every situation. As soon as he realized that the truth resides not in the forest but in one's heart, Kaushika returned home and took care of his parents. More than any powers, this insight into the workings of the world brought Kaushika peace of mind.

On abstinence

Then there was a tale about Sage Vibhandaka, who so strongly believed in a life of abstinence that he refused to teach his son, Rishyashringa, anything about women. Thus, the region where Rishyashringa lived suffered a long spell of drought. It was only when Shanta, the king's daughter, succeeded in teaching Rishyashringa how to keep the company of women that the rains blessed the land once more. This story taught the Pandavas the importance of balancing spirituality with sexual desires, equating extreme monasticism with sterility.

On greed

The Rishis spoke of the importance of keeping one's word through the story of King Sala, who had borrowed some swift horses from Rishi Vamadeva for one month, but then refused to return them. Full of wrath, Vamadeva killed Sala. But Sala's brother, Dala, also refused to part with the horses. He tried killing Vamadeva by striking him with an arrow, but it ended up killing his own son. Seeing all this, Dala's queen begged Vamadeva to forgive her husband and forced Dala to return the horses that belonged to the sage.

On forgiveness

Once a Rishi called Raibhya found his daughter-in-law in the arms of a young man named Yavakri. Enraged at her indiscretion, he killed Yavakri. Yavakri's father, Bharadvaja, cursed Raibhya that he would die at the hands of his own son, Paravasu. The curse came true a few days later when Paravasu, mistaking his father for a wild animal, killed him. To save himself, Paravasu accused his brother Aravasu of the crime. Although Aravasu protested his innocence, no one believed him. Angry and disillusioned, Aravasu retreated to the forest where he performed severe austerities to gain occult powers so that he could clear his reputation and teach his brother a lesson. But as the days passed, Aravasu's mind reached a stage of wisdom where he felt all his desire for vengeance melt away. His mind

FORCE OF NATURE
Many Hindu tales use natural phenomena as metaphors for human conditions, such as drought for abstinence and rain for fertility.

at peace at last, he realized that there was far greater joy in forgiving than in revenge.

On legacy

The sages illustrated the importance of legacy through the tale of King Indradyumna. After spending many centuries in Swarga, Indradyumna was cast out and told that he could return only if people on earth still recalled his good deeds. The king first went to Sage Markandeya, who had lived longer than most humans. Markandeya, however, did not remember him and asked him to meet an owl who had lived longer than him. The owl did not remember Indradyumna, and neither did the stork that he visited next. The king then went to the turtle Akupara, who had outlived most animals. The turtle remembered Indradyumna as the king who had built the lake in which he lived. But Indradyumna did not remember ever building a lake. The turtle explained that though he had not had the lake built, it existed as a result of his generosity. During his reign, the king had given away many cows. These cows had kicked up so much dust while leaving their sheds that they had created a depression that turned into a lake following the rains. That lake later became home to many fishes and turtles and serpents and birds. Thus, Indradyumna could never be forgotten—there were many on earth who had benefitted from his actions. This old, forgotten deed allowed Indradyumna to regain his place in paradise and live among the gods once again.

"Right **till the end**, any **man** on earth should be engaged in **good deeds**. He should **avoid evil** conduct and **seek** refuge in **dharma**."

GODS TO INDRADYUMNA, VANA PARVA: THE BOOK OF THE FOREST

About ancestors

The Rishis also told Yudhishthira about his ancestor Kuru, after whom Kurukshetra, the land near Hastinapur, was named. Kuru had tilled the earth using his flesh as seed and blood as water until an exasperated Indra asked him what he sought. Kuru wanted nothing for himself, but asked for paradise for those who died in Kurukshetra. Indra agreed but had one condition, saying it was not enough for a person to die on Kurukshetra; the manner of their death should matter, too. Only those who voluntarily rejected this world or died in war would ascend to heaven. Kurukshetra would see more blood spilled lifetimes later.

Thus, the period of exile became a time of learning for the Pandavas and their wife.

ANALYSIS

THE EXILE

In the twelve years of exile, the Pandavas and their wife were never alone. They were always accompanied by their family priest Dhaumya and many other Rishis who took them to holy spots and told them stories. In Hindu culture, traveling to holy spots and listening to sacred stories are believed to reduce the burden of karmic debts and increase the load of karmic equity. The Pandavas used their long period of exile to free themselves from the debts of destiny.

PASSING ON KNOWLEDGE

In pre-colonial India, sages would mentor kings; this 18th-century Rajasthani watercolor from India depicts a king and his retinue listening to a sage. The Pandavas, too, had an entourage of priests teaching them through their exile.

REVELATION AND REALIZATION THROUGH JOURNEYS

Pilgrimage

> **"**This is the **supreme** mystery of the rishis, the **pure merit** from visiting **tirthas**, superior even to sacrifices.**"**

PULASTYA TO BHISHMA, VANA PARVA: THE BOOK OF THE FOREST

As a journey undertaken for spiritual purposes, usually to a shrine or a holy place, a pilgrimage is an important part of Hindu spiritual practice. Travel, realized the sages, not only broadens the outlook of sedentary, inward-looking communities, but also leads to inner peace. Myths, legends, and sacred texts mention holy places all over the Indian subcontinent, or Bharatavarsha, as it was called. They narrate stories connected with these sites and elaborate on the blessings to be obtained by visiting them. These narrations fired the imagination and aspirations of communities, inspiring them to undertake at least once in their lifetime a journey which, though long and exceedingly arduous, could be spiritually satisfying.

KEDARNATH
Shiva showed himself to the Pandavas in the form of a bull in this Himalayan temple. He did so when they sought atonement for their sins after the Kurukshetra War.

THE TIRTH-YATRA PARVA

The Vana Parva, which is a narration of the time the Pandavas spent exiled in the forests, has a section titled Tirtha-yatra Parva. The sacred places the Pandavas are directed to visit reveal a great deal about the prevailing sense of geography in that era. While Jambudvipa extended all the way to the southern tip of the peninsula, the degree of detail in the descriptions of regions shows a much greater familiarity with the topography of the north than that of southern India.

MAKING THE SACRED FAMILIAR
Even today, the oral tradition is integral to the passing down of myths and rituals associated with religious practice.

TRAVELS AND TALES

Aware that a conflict with the Kauravas was inevitable, Arjuna left his brothers to travel north in search of divine weapons. His travels took him to his father Indra in Swarga, with whom he spent some time. Realizing that Arjuna was concerned about his brothers, Indra sent Sage Lomasha to advise the other Pandavas to make the best use of their days in exile and to visit the numerous sacred locations scattered across the land known as Jampudvipa, or the rose-apple continent. By spending time with learned men and sages, they would gain new skills and imbibe wisdom. Indra believed that their experiences and lessons learned over this period would help them rule better when their time came. Accompanied by many sages, including Lomasha and Dhaumya, their family priest, Yudhishthira, Bhima, Nakula, Sahadeva and their wife

Draupadi journeyed south, then east, after which they went west. They bathed in the confluence of holy rivers and in lakes guarded by ancient deities. On the way, they also meditated in caves. They had dialogues and discussed philosophies with learned rishis, who told them stories to illustrate the profound truths of life, elaborate on the duties and obligations of individuals, and shape their understanding of the world. Yudhishthira and his brothers heard of Sage Agastya who was tormented by dreams of his ancestors suffering in the land of the dead until he married, had children, and so facilitated their rebirth. They learned the value of keeping one's word from the story of King Sala; the importance of worldly responsibilities from the tale of the hermit Kaushika; the virtue of forgiveness; the harm greed causes; and why a man should be generous and build a legacy through good deeds. In addition, they heard many other stories that taught them the importance of making the right choices. By the end of the journey, they had gained a new perspective on life.

PLACES OF PILGRIMAGE

A tirtha is a place of spiritual crossing, where the individual experiences a direct connection with the gods and moves from one state of existence to another. These can be geographical sites, such as rivers, mountains, or lakes, as well as temples or even towns associated with various gods. In addition, there are tirthas of the heart such as truth, charity, celibacy, self-control, and wisdom, that one should practice for the purification of both mind and body. A tirtha-yatra is a journey, usually to a tirtha, in search of answers. The Pandavas visit many tirthas—from Kanya Tirtha (probably Kanyakumari) in the extreme south to Badari Vishala or Badrinath in the high Himalayas in the extreme north; Ganga Sagar in the east to Pushkar in the west. Many of these are still popular with pilgrims, as are those that have been established because of their association with the Pandavas.

KEY CONCEPT

PILGRIMAGE AND KATHA

In Hindu tradition, the katha (story) provides a context to the beliefs and values of an individual and forms the bedrock of beliefs and practices that ultimately led to the Hindu canon.

Together with pilgrimage, participation in the narration of the katha, even as an audience, is believed to reduce the burden of karmic debts and increase the load of karmic equity. Even today, a number of rivers, passes, mountain peaks, and caves in the Himalayas are associated with events and characters mentioned in the Mahabharata. In Garhwal, there is a temple dedicated to Hidimba, Bhima's Rakshasa wife, and the Pandava leela, a recounting of the Pandavas' heroic deeds, is integral to the region's culture.

SACRED PLACES

The Mahabharata mentions pilgrimage centers across the subcontinent, indicating the vast expanses of land that had been traversed and explored by that era.

BEFORE

The Pandavas spent eleven years of their exile visiting various holy sites.

SNOW-CLAD PEAKS OF THE HIMALAYAS

TOWARD THE HIMALAYAS

As the twelfth year of their exile began, the Pandava brothers and Draupadi decided to travel north. They planned to make their way toward the snow-clad Himalayas, in the direction of the Pole Star. This was where Sage Lomasha had said Arjuna would meet them upon his descent from Amravati.

"We showed you **honor** and you **lived happily**. O one who is **not wise**! Having partaken of our food, how can you **abduct us**?"

YUDHISHTHIRA TO JATA, VANA PARVA: THE BOOK OF THE FOREST

A **Demon** in **Disguise**

On their journey to reunite with Arjuna, the Pandavas were waylaid by a Rakshasa called Jata. Once again, it was Bhima's outstanding strength that rescued them.

On their journey to the Himalayas, the Pandavas were accompanied by many wise men. Among them, disguised as a sage and pretending to be well versed in weaponry, was a Rakshasa called Jata. He lived and traveled with the Pandavas' entourage, all the time coveting their weapons, and waiting for a chance to attack them.

Jata's true form

One day, Bhima was away on a hunt. His brothers and Draupadi were resting and the sages busy collecting herbs and flowers. Jata saw his opportunity. Picking up the weapons he had been eyeing, he assumed his true, giant form. Then he swept up Yudhishthira, Nakula, Sahadeva, and Draupadi in his arms and fled into the woods. He intended to eat the brothers and ravish their wife.

The youngest of the brothers, Sahadeva, cried out for help, alerting Bhima, who turned around and ran in the direction of the sound.

Caught in the demon's arms, Yudhishthira admonished Jata, "You fool! Abducting us will earn you no merit!"

“**By myself**, with my brothers, by the **dharma** that I have observed well and by my oblations, I **swear** that I will **finish off this Rakshasa.**”

BHIMA TO NAKULA AND SAHADEVA, VANA PARVA: THE BOOK OF THE FOREST

The eldest Pandava told him that unless a man has caused a Rakshasa injury he should not be harmed. There was no reason to turn against a trustworthy human. He reminded Jata that the Pandavas had offered him food and shelter. If this was the manner in which he returned their hospitality, Jata deserved a painful death. “Whatever hope you have of being reborn as a human or even a god is lost because of the demerit earned by killing us and ravishing our wife,” said Yudhishthira. He explained to Jata that because his actions were so devoid of dharma, they would be the cause for him to be born as an animal, vegetable, or even an insect in his next life.

Yudhishthira’s words had the desired effect and set Jata thinking. Lost in thought, he slowed down, making it easy for Bhima to catch up with him.

The mighty Bhima rebuked Jata. He said he had noticed Jata eyeing their weapons, but had not taken any action against him. Now Jata had abducted his brothers and Draupadi; this would bring about his death.

A fierce battle

Frightened by Bhima’s anger, Jata let go of the brothers and Draupadi, whom he had been carrying till now, and prepared himself for Bhima’s attack. Burning with rage, Bhima pounced on the Rakshasa.

A terrible battle followed. Both warriors were strong and skilled. They wrestled, punched each other, used their weapons, and uprooted large trees and hurled them at each other.

The battle went on for hours. Finally, Bhima managed to strike Jata with his powerful mace. Jata fell to the ground, dead.

MYTHOLOGY AND FOLKLORE

BHAIRAVA

Bhima is worshipped as Bhairava by the Newar community of Nepal, where his devotees offer him blood sacrifices. Bhairava is a fierce, violent form of Shiva. He is regarded as the companion of Shiva’s consort, Shakti.

The name Bhairava is derived from the word “bhaya,” or terror. Embodying the emotion of terror, Bhairava makes one aware of death, and hence life. He is also worshipped by sorcerers, who associate him with wisdom.

NEPALI DEVOTEES PULL A CHARIOT CARRYING BHIMA AS BHAIRAVA

CHHAU DANCER AS A DEMON
A semi-classical dance form from Jharkhand, India, the Saraikela version of Chhau features masked dancers who portray various mythological characters. Rakshasas, Asuras, and Devas all play an important role in telling the story of the Mahabharata.

AFTER

After their encounter with Jata, the Pandavas continued on their journey to the Himalayas.

A DIFFICULT EXPEDITION

While the beautiful slopes and snow-capped peaks were breathtaking, the steep and dangerous climb was also very challenging. The brothers and Draupadi faced many difficulties as they climbed higher into the mountains. Often the biting cold wind made it difficult for them to move, forcing them to take refuge in a cave. Yudhishthira found himself breathless. Unable to bear the strain of the difficult journey any longer, Draupadi fainted. The twins, Nakula and Sahadeva, rushed to her side, calming her with soothing words.

But despite the hardships, they pressed on, driven by the promise that they would soon meet Arjuna.

BEFORE

In Arjuna's absence, the other exiles had embarked on a long pilgrimage across Jambudvipa.

REUNION WITH ARJUNA
When Rishi Lomasha informed the Pandavas and Draupadi that Arjuna would meet them in the Himalayas, the party set off heading north. Scaling the rugged Himalayas was, however, no easy task, and with each step that brought them closer to their destination, it became that much more difficult to reach.

FORBIDDING HEIGHTS
Rivers, passes, mountain peaks, and caves are associated with various crucial events in the epic and play an important role in the lives of the characters. Most of this part of the journey took place in the Himalayas.

Scaling the Mountains

It had been years since his brothers and Draupadi had seen Arjuna. When they heard that he would meet them in the Himalayas, they set out to climb the high mountains.

Though climbing the mountains made for an arduous journey, the Pandavas had to persevere. After five years of separation from their brother, they were eager to see him and also to learn about the weapons he had acquired. After a while, though, it became clear that even one more step would be too much for Draupadi. Bhima decided it was time to summon help. He thought of his Rakshasa son Ghatotkacha, whom he had left behind in the forest with his wife Hidimbi. Ghatotkacha had made Bhima a promise. "Think of me when you need my help, and I will be there."

As soon as Bhima thought of Ghatotkacha, the young Rakshasa, who possessed the power of flight, arrived. He had brought with him several other Rakshasas. Seating the Pandavas and Draupadi on their shoulders, they carried them beyond the high peaks to Alakapuri, the city of the Yakshas.

Adventures in the Himalayas
Alakapuri is located close to Mount Kailash, the home of Shiva. Here the Pandavas and Draupadi were welcomed by Kubera, the king of Yakshas and treasurer of the gods.

Related to the Rakshasas through Pulastya's son, Vaishrava, who was a common ancestor, the Yakshas were guardians of the mountains and lakes and of the treasures hidden there. They were also extremely fond of riddles.

The Pandavas also visited Badari, the cave where the warrior-ascetics Nara and Narayana had once meditated. While they were there the sages

Lomasha and Dhaumya told them it was whispered that Nara and Narayana were destined to walk the earth once more as Arjuna and Krishna.

A joyful reunion

Soon Arjuna arrived on a flying chariot. It was a joyful reunion—Draupadi ran to greet him, his brothers hugged him, and the sages welcomed him with garlands. Then Arjuna's brothers wanted him to show them the divine weapons he had acquired.

Arjuna unwrapped the weapons. No sooner had he done that than the earth began to tremble, the winds ceased, and the sun dimmed. From all four directions voices called out a warning, "Beware! These weapons are capable of destroying all life. Do not treat them with such little respect." Realizing the danger that he had courted, Arjuna covered the weapons in their celestial cloth again, so that no mortal could lay eyes on them.

MASROOR ROCK CUT TEMPLES
Dedicated to Vishnu, this complex of monolithic temples in the Kangra Valley, Himachal Pradesh, is said to have been built by the Pandavas during their exile.

MYTHOLOGY AND FOLKLORE

HIMALAYAN FOLK TALES

Folk tales about the Pandavas abound in the Himalayan region. One such story tells of a herd of grazing cattle among whom the Pandavas spotted Shiva, who had taken the form of a most ferocious bull. Bhima tried to catch the bull but it vanished into the earth. All that remained above the ground was its hump. Till today, this is worshipped as Kedarnath.

Another tale tells of Arjuna's defeat by a warrior who turned out to be his son Nagarjuna, born of a local Naga princess. This tale is similar to that of Babruvahana, found later in the Sanskrit telling.

KEDARNATH TEMPLE, GARHWAL, HIMALAYAS

> "**Son!** Your unvanquished mother is **exhausted** ... You are **strong. Carry her** on your shoulders."

BHIMA TO GHATOTKACHA, VANA PARVA: THE BOOK OF THE FOREST

AFTER

Once the five brothers were reunited, Ghatotkacha and the other Rakshasas returned home.

NEWS ABOUT THE KAURAVAS
Before he left, Ghatotkacha gave the Pandavas news from Hastinapur and Dwaraka. He told them about their children as well as the Kauravas and the Yadavas.

BEFORE

To reunite with Arjuna, his brothers and Draupadi had to scale the Himalayas.

THE PANDAVAS' CHILDREN
When they found the ascent too arduous, Bhima summoned Ghatotkacha for his help. Once they reached their destination, Ghatotkacha spoke to the Pandavas about their children.

It had been quite some time since the Pandavas had seen their children, and they listened eagerly to his news. Ghatotkacha told the Pandavas that the Upapandavas, their children with Draupadi, had grown into fine young men, and that Subhadra's son, Abhimanyu, had become an accomplished warrior.

News of Home

Before leaving for home, Ghatotkacha regaled the Pandavas with his tales from Dwaraka and Hastinapur. Though a welcome break from their hardships, these light-hearted stories made them see their close friends in a new light.

Ghatotkacha told the Pandavas and their entourage about Arjuna's son Abhimanyu's elopement with Balarama's daughter Vatsala. Though Balarama had arranged Vatsala's marriage with Duryodhana's son, Lakshman, the girl was in love with her childhood playmate, Abhimanyu. As the wedding day neared, Vatsala sought out Krishna and asked him to help her. Krishna had then sent for Ghatotkacha. "He told me to carry Vatsala on my shoulders and take her to the hills outside Dwaraka, where he would arrange for Abhimanyu to marry her according to the rites of the Gandharvas, with the trees as witnesses," he recounted.

Krishna's deception

After he united Vatsala with her beloved, Ghatotkacha had gone back to the wedding disguised as Vatsala. "I pretended to be the

GHATOTKACHA AS VATSALA
This 19th-century opaque watercolor painting in the Chitrakathi style is part of a larger series, made in Paithan, in the state of Maharashtra. It shows Ghatotkacha disguised as Vatsala in Balarama's house, before "her" wedding ceremony with Duryodhana's son, Lakshman.

HISTORY AND CULTURE

VATSALA'S WEDDING

This story about Vatsala, also known as Shashirekha, is not part of the original Mahabharata, but a folk tale from Andhra Pradesh. Called "*Shashirekha Parinayam*" (meaning "Shashirekha's Marriage"), this story has been depicted across a variety of mediums.

Illustrations of this tale, in the Chitrakathi style, have been found in 19th-century manuscripts in the central state of Maharashtra, and the story has been performed in folk art such as "*Tholu Bommalata*," a shadow puppet theater. The story has also been the inspiration for many Telugu films, such as *Sasirekha Parinayam* (1936) and *Mayabazar* (1957).

bride, and during the ceremony I squeezed Lakshman's hand so hard that he fainted. When I revealed my identity, there was chaos in Dwaraka. The Kauravas accused the Yadavas of duping them," he recalled.

Bhima, whose grudge with Duryodhana was well known, laughed. "Duryodhana must have been furious," he said. "He wanted to marry Balarama's sister Subhadra, but she eloped with Arjuna. He arranged for his son Laxman to marry Balarama's daughter, Vatsala, but she ran away with Arjuna's son."

ART AND LITERATURE

BHAGAVATA PURANA

THIS 17TH-CENTURY ILLUSTRATION SHOWS KRISHNA TRANSFORMING A HUNCHBACKED WOMAN INTO A BEAUTIFUL MAIDEN

The story of the wedding of Krishna's son Samba with Duryodhana's daughter Lakshmani is found in the Bhagavata Purana. Considered to be one of the "Mahapuranas" or great Puranas, this Sanskrit text depicts Krishna as an incarnation of Vishnu, equating him with the Vedas and asserting that he was born to establish dharma on earth.

Many of the well-known stories of Krishna's childhood can be traced to the Bhagavata Purana, as well as legends about the origin of Hindu festivals such as Holi and Diwali.

Samba's imprisonment

Ghatotkacha told the Pandavas that Duryodhana was incensed at this deception and decided to teach the Yadavas a lesson. Then and there, he canceled the wedding of his daughter Lakshmani to Krishna's son, Samba.

"Naturally, Samba was upset when he heard that Duryodhana had called off his wedding. He decided to sneak into Hastinapur and abduct Lakshmani. Unluckily for him, he was caught in the act, and unceremoniously thrown into prison," he continued.

"When he heard that Samba had been imprisoned, Balarama immediately set off for Hastinapur to rescue his nephew. There, he demanded that Duryodhana, his former pupil, should not only release Samba but also allow him to return to Dwaraka along with Lakshmani, the woman he loved," chuckled Bhima's son.

"Duryodhana not only refused, he also hurled insults at the Yadavas, who he said had gained a reputation for never keeping their word. He mocked their ancestor Yadu, whose refusal to suffer for his father had cost him and his descendants the throne," said Ghatotkacha.

Balarama's rage

"Balarama was angered by Duryodhana's tirade," continued Ghatotkacha to a riveted audience. "As his anger grew, so did his size, until he was a giant whose head reached the skies. Balarama took his plough and hooked it to the foundations of Hastinapur with one mighty swing. He then proceeded to drag the great city of the Kurus towards the sea. That is when Duryodhana realized that Balarama was no ordinary human. The man who had been a teacher and friend to him was much more than just a Yadava whose skills in mace warfare were unparalleled.

Balarama, unlike Krishna, had always treated Duryodhana with extra affection. Now, when he had angered Balarama, Duryodhana saw a side of him that could not be imagined. Humbled, he fell at Balarama's feet and begged forgiveness. Though Balarama is quick to anger, he is also easily pacified. He forgave the Kauravas and returned to Dwaraka with Samba and his new wife," recounted Ghatotkacha, ending his tale.

As they saw Ghatotkacha off, the Pandavas kept wondering about Balarama's true identity. It was then that the sages in their party made a grand revelation. Krishna' older brother, they said, was actually Adisesha, one of the primordial beings, on whose serpentine coils rested Vishnu, and who regulated time and creation itself.

AFTER

The Pandavas were shaken by Ghatotkacha's story and the sages' revelations.

BALARAMA'S TRUE FORM

Though the Pandavas had always suspected that Balarama and Krishna were not quite what they appeared to be, such tales pointed to a truth far more staggering than they could imagine.

A 2ND-CENTURY SANDSTONE STATUE OF BALARAMA, UTTAR PRADESH, INDIA

BEFORE

One day, as Draupadi was sitting in the forest, spending time in exile, a gust of wind carried an extraordinary flower toward her.

DRAUPADI'S REQUEST

It was a lotus, one with a thousand petals and a heavenly fragrance. An excited Draupadi immediately wanted more. She went to Bhima, asking him to get her some more. Draupadi's face was suffused with pleasure and anticipation. Long used to seeing her brooding on the wrongs done to her, Bhima saw a Draupadi he had not seen in a long time. Unable to refuse, he immediately set out in search of the fragrant flower.

Bhima Learns a Lesson

Ardent love for his wife Draupadi made Bhima go to great lengths to please her, especially during the years of exile. But this time, in his eagerness to make her happy, Bhima learned a lesson in humility.

Wandering through the forest pursuing the elusive, evocative fragrance, Bhima's thoughts kept going back to Draupadi's happy face. Features that had become drawn over the years of hardship had suddenly softened in delight, reminding him of her as a new bride. Come what may, I have to find that flower, he resolved.

A man on a mission

Bhima's strides were long and forceful, impatient to chart the quickest route to end his search for the lotus. He walked straight, taking no turns, smashing through whatever what in his path—whether trees, boulders, or trees. Animals and birds flew off in fear as they saw him approach. He walked on in this manner until he came upon a plantain grove so thick that sunlight could not reach the ground.

The tale of a tail

Moving through, he noticed an old, frail monkey blocking his way forward. "Move aside," growled Bhima.

"I am far too weak to do that at my age. But do feel free to move my tail aside and carry on," said the monkey in a feeble voice.

Bhima nudged the tail casually with his foot, expecting to sweep it aside, but the tail did not budge. Surprised, he tried again, with the same result. However hard he tried, he could not kick it aside. His mind now focused, Bhima put down his mace and tried with all his might to lift the tail. Once again, despite his best efforts, the tail wouldn't move.

No ordinary monkey

It then dawned on Bhima that no ordinary monkey could be this strong. Who could this be but Hanuman, the monkey god who had helped Lord Rama in his fight against the demon king Ravana and had helped to rescue his wife, Sita! As the son of Vayu, the god of the winds, he was also Bhima's brother.

"Yes, I am Hanuman, your brother," smiled the monkey god.

Bhima realized that through Hanuman, he had been taught a valuable lesson in humility. Suitably chastened, he paid his respects and went on his way, his steps a little less haughty.

> "O **tiger among monkeys**! Please ... **pardon** my **harsh words ...** please tell me who you are. I am **asking you** and I wish to know."
>
> BHIMA TO HANUMAN, VANA PARVA: THE BOOK OF THE FOREST

THE SCENTED LOTUS
The flower that caught Draupadi's imagination is called "saugandhika" in Sanskrit, which means "fragrant" or "perfumed."

AFTER

After meeting Hanuman, Bhima resumed his quest for the flower that had so captivated Draupadi.

AN ATTACK BY GANDHARVAS

Bhima followed the fragrance of the flowers until he reached a pool that seemed to have hundreds of those large, sweet-smelling, golden lotuses. Bhima's heart swelled with happiness at the sight.

He began to pluck them, imagining Draupadi's happiness at receiving the flowers, when suddenly he was attacked by Gandharvas, forest creatures who guarded the lake. Bhima swatted them aside with ease before gathering a huge bouquet that he carried back to present to a delighted Draupadi.

HISTORY AND CULTURE

POIKKAL KUTHIRAI ATTAM

A FEMALE DANCER WEARING A DUMMY HORSE

The city of Thanjavur in the southern Indian state of Tamil Nadu is known for its horse dances. The dancers wear highly decorated dummy horses at the waist to appear as if astride a horse. The dummy horsemen, presented as a king and queen pair, represent Bhima and Draupadi's legendary romance. In the performance, known as Poikal Kudurai Attam, the horse figures dance to a variety of drums and percussion instruments.

THE PLANTAIN GROVE
This painting in the Kerala mural style depicts Hanuman in the plantain grove that Bhima passes through in his quest for the strongly scented lotus.

BEFORE

The period of exile in the forest had given Draupadi time to reflect on the past and accept that she was the only one responsible for her fate.

DRAUPADI'S FATE

When Draupadi questioned Krishna about the cause of her miseries, he told her that her rejection of Karna at her swayamvara was her undoing.

Krishna explained that a great warrior like Karna would never have gambled her away. Instead of choosing a man on the basis of his own merit, Draupadi chose a priest over a charioteer, and in doing so, sealed her fate. The priest turned out to be a prince who shared her with his brothers, let her be staked, and failed to protect her.

Draupadi's **Secret**

The innocent act of plucking a fruit triggered a dramatic chain of events—Draupadi voiced a secret she had long held and the Pandavas learned of her true identity.

One day, while Draupadi was wandering in the forest in search of food, she chanced upon a rose-apple, or jambu, tree. A low-hanging fruit on the tree made her mouth water. Tempted by the luscious fruit, she plucked it.

As soon as she picked the fruit, the tree spoke out, "O noble lady! What have you done? This fruit had been hanging on this tree for many years."

An unintended lapse

The tree informed her that, in its shade on the other side, a sage had been sitting in meditation for twelve long years. He was to end his meditation that evening and the fruit was to be his first meal in all that time. Now Draupadi had contaminated the tree with her touch, making its fruit unfit for the sage.

"You have plucked a fruit marked for the sage. He will remain hungry now. The demerit of making a sage go hungry will be yours," said the tree.

A test of character

Terrified, Draupadi called out to her husbands and beseeched them to attach the fruit to the tree again. Despite their desire to help their wife, it was beyond the Pandavas to do as she asked.

The tree spoke again, "If you were truly faithful, you could have attached the fruit with the power of your chastity."

Alarmed by the allegation, Draupadi defended herself. "Even though I am married to five men, I am always faithful to the one who comes to my bed for a year."

The tree instructed her to be honest and admit to loving someone else. Draupadi was flustered by this public discussion of her most intimate thoughts, but she thought for a moment and admitted to loving Krishna —as a friend.

The revelation

The tree was not satisfied. It accused her of being dishonest and asked her to reveal the truth. Draupadi broke down and admitted her love for Karna. Though she was chaste at heart, Draupadi confessed that she regretted refusing Karna because he was low-born. She cried that she would have avoided public humiliation and shame if she had married the great archer Karna.

The Pandavas found themselves in a dilemma—unsure whether they should be angry with their wife, or feel guilty for failing her. Not only had they been unable to save her honor, they were also responsible for her repeated humiliation in public.

The revelation cleansed Draupadi. Now clear and pure of conscience, she was able to attach the fruit to the jambu tree again. That evening, the sage opened his eyes after twelve years of meditation. He took a bath in a nearby river, ate the fruit as his first meal, and blessed the Pandavas and their wife.

The Pandavas—Bhima and Arjuna in particular—found it hard to come to terms with Draupadi's revelation. One night, upon seeing Yudhishthira touching Draupadi's feet they demanded an explanation. Their brother asked them to sit up with him that night. He showed them a million deities invoking a goddess under a vermilion-colored banyan tree. They seated her on a throne and showered her with flowers. Bhima and Arjuna could not believe their eyes: the goddess was none other than Draupadi.

MYTHOLOGY AND FOLKLORE

JAMBU FRUIT

Folk narratives are more nuanced, in contrast to their classical Sanskrit counterparts, and celebrate the imperfections of human nature.

The tale of the jambu tree is taken from a folk play called *Jambul-akhyan*, from Maharashtra, India. It is a popular belief that the fruit stains the tongue as a reminder of the secrets that one keeps from the world. The jambu fruit indicated that Draupadi had kept a secret from her husbands.

THE ROSE-APPLE OR JAMBU

MYTHOLOGY AND FOLKLORE

DRAUPADI AS A GODDESS

In parts of south India and countries with a large Tamil population such as Sri Lanka, Singapore, and South Africa, Draupadi is worshipped as a form of the mother goddess Mariamman. The cult of Draupadi has its own set of rituals, such as the Thimithi festival. During the celebrations, episodes from the Mahabharata are enacted, and the festival culminates with the devotees walking over hot coals to receive the blessings of the goddess.

A DEVOTEE CARRYING AN IDOL OF DRAUPADI DURING THE THIMITHI FESTIVAL

AFTER

The night's revelation had made Bhima and Arjuna see their wife in a new light.

A GODDESS IN DISGUISE

Taken aback, perhaps even offended, at their elder brother's show of respect for their wife, who had admitted her love for another, Bhima and Arjuna were chastened. They had not only failed to protect Draupadi, but also dared to judge the character of one who was a goddess.

AN ACT OF INNOCENCE
This painting in the Madhubani-style shows Draupadi plucking the fruit off the jambu tree. As a repercussion to this action, Draupadi was forced to reveal her love for Karna.

Savitri and Satyavan

The Pandavas and Draupadi met many sages during their exile. These learned men shared their wisdom and knowledge through stories of great men and women who overcame trying circumstances. One such story was that of Savitri and Satyavan.

A WOMAN WHO KNEW HER MIND
When Yama claimed her husband, Savitri outwitted the god of death and brought Satyavan back. For this feat Savitri is worshipped across India, as in the famous Kalighat temple in Kolkata, West Bengal, India.

One day, a tired and dispirited Draupadi asked the sages if it was possible to change one's fate. In reponse to her plaintive question, they told her the story of Savitri, who outwitted destiny and death through her deep love for Satyavan and her steadfast determination to get him back.

Savitri was the only child of King Ashwapati. She had fallen in love with a poor woodcutter called Satyavan and wanted to marry him. She knew he was the son of a man who had lost everything and was doomed to die in one year. Ashwapati was not happy, but gave his consent. Without hesitation Savitri gave up all the palace comforts to live as Satyavan's wife.

SATI SAVITRI
This poster of a 1927 movie, made by filmmaker Baburao Painter, is based on the story of Savitri and Satyavan.

"O Savitri! Go choose another husband. The illustrious Narada ... has told me that his life is short. He will give up his body within a year."

ASHWAPATI TO HIS DAUGHTER, SAVITRI, VANA PARVA: THE BOOK OF THE FOREST

MYTHOLOGY AND FOLKLORE

ORPHEUS

Love that transcends worlds is an idea that permeates stories across all cultures. Savitri's love for her husband has a parallel in the Greek legend of Orpheus.

According to Greek mythology, Eurydice, the wife of poet and musician Orpheus, was set upon by a satyr on their wedding. As she tried to escape, she fell into a nest of vipers and died. Orpheus was so overcome with grief that he ventured into the underworld to bring her back. Hades, god of the underworld, agreed to let her go, but on one condition—Orpheus would not turn and look at his wife until both of them reached the world of the living. Orpheus kept to this pact through the journey. But, just as he stepped into the land of the living, he could not resist looking back. Since Eurydice still hadn't stepped out of the underworld, his promise was broken and Eurydice was left behind forever.

A STATUE OF ORPHEUS IN VIENNA

Savitri's pursuit

As had been foretold, Satyavan died a year later. Savitri saw Yama, the god of death, come and take her husband's life, leaving behind the empty shell that was his body. But Savitri did not stay to cremate Satyavan's body; instead, she left her husband's corpse lying where it was and followed Yama.

As Yama made his way to the land of the dead, he became aware that Savitri was following him. But it was a long and arduous journey and Yama was sure she would soon grow weary. But each time he looked, there she was, following him doggedly and showing no signs of exhaustion, resolute in following her husband's life.

"Your husband's life is mine now. Accept your fate. Go back and cremate his body," he ordered. But Savitri cared more for her husband's life than the lifeless corpse lying on the forest floor.

Yama's blessings

Tired of this relentless pursuit, Yama thought he would bribe her into giving up. "I will grant you three blessings," he said. "You can ask me for anything but your husband's life. Then you must go."

Savitri bowed respectfully. With the first blessing she asked that her father-in-law regain his kingdom. With the second, she asked that her father be blessed with a son. The final blessing she reserved for herself, and asked that she be the mother of Satyavan's sons. Relieved that his ruse had worked, Yama granted her wishes and walked on. But when he reached the banks of the Vaitarini river, which separates the land of the living from that of the dead, he found Savitri still trailing him. "I granted your wishes! Why are you still here?" he asked her.

Savitri bowed her head in respect again and replied, "The first two blessings were granted, that is true. What I wanted to know was how the third is to be fulfilled. How can I bear my husband's children when he is lying dead on the forest floor?"

Yama realized that Savitri had outwitted him—he had to bring back her husband to life. So it was that Savitri managed to change her destiny.

PRAYERS AND RITUALS

Hindu women tie sacred threads around a banyan tree as a prayer for their husbands' long life. Satyavan is believed to have died under a banyan tree, and Yama appeared under it to grant Savitri the blessings.

"O Savitri! ... The life of Satyavan, your husband has run out. I will bind him and take him. That is my intention.

YAMA, THE LORD OF DEATH, TO SAVITRI, VANA PARVA: THE BOOK OF THE FOREST

BEFORE

The Pandavas had spent four years of their exile living in the same part of the forest.

A NEW HOME

Uneasy with this settled life, where anyone who wished to find the Pandavas could easily do so, Bhima suggested that they move elsewhere. The brothers all agreed, and so they moved on.

For some time after this they stayed on the move, visiting many pilgrimage sites, mountain groves, caves, and lakes. They traveled through many Himalayan kingdoms and reached a great forest as magnificent as Chaitraratha, the pleasure garden of Kubera, treasurer of the gods. The Pandavas decided to settle down here for a while.

Nahusha's Question

Caught in Nahusha's coils, Bhima could only be saved if Yudhishthira answered his question satisfactorily. On the eldest Pandava's answer depended the release of a long-standing curse as well as his brother's life.

The forest that the exiles had settled in teemed with wildlife. The trees were loaded with flowers and fruit, and offered plenty of shade. Geese and ducks swam the forest streams, while boars and deer roamed freely.

"Bhima ... was ... unable to move ... the brave one tried ... to extricate himself. But he did not succeed."

SAGE VAISHAMPAYANA TO JANAMEJAYA, VANA PARVA: THE BOOK OF THE FOREST

In the python's grasp

One day, while hunting in the forest, Bhima came upon a giant serpent. His yellow coils, speckled with black, were piled high. He looked at Bhima with copper eyes and flicked his tongue. The serpent lunged at Bhima and caught him around the chest. So strong was the serpent's grip that Bhima, who had the strength of a thousand elephants, was unable to move a muscle. Realizing that this was no ordinary python, Bhima asked, "O best of serpents! Who are you?"

"O mighty-armed one!," replied the serpent, "I have been hungry for a long time and it is fortunate that the gods and destiny have sent me food. I will certainly tell you the story of how it was that I became a serpent. It was the anger of the learned ones that turned me into this. You must have heard of Nahusha. He was a descendant of Pururava. I am he."

ANALYSIS

TEST OF WORTH

Sachi, Indra's consort, is said to be a form of Lakshmi the goddess of fortune. Sachi is faithful to the position of Indra as king of Devas, not to Indra himself. (It is said that one can become an Indra by earning more merits than the previous Indra.) Though not yet an Indra, Nahusha wanted Sachi, and paid for it. Thus this tale is less about the consequences of coveting another's wife, and more about being worthy of a position.

THE QUEEN OF INDRA, SACHI, IS ALSO KNOWN AS INDRANI

A MIGHTY GRIP

This Mughal miniature from the *Razmnama* shows Yudhishthira speaking with the serpent that has Bhima in its coils.

THE SAPTA RISHI
Known as the Big Dipper or Plough, this famous seven-star asterism is shaped like a ladle, and that gives it its name. In India, however, it is recognized as "Sapta Rishi" (literally meaning "seven sages"); each of its stars is identified with a famous Hindu sage.

Nahusha's story

The python then told Bhima his story. "I was such a great king that the Devas made me temporary ruler of Amravati while their king, Indra, had gone to cleanse himself of a crime he had committed. In Amravati, I sat on Indra's elephant and wielded his thunderbolt. This newfound power went to my head. I began to feel that I was entitled to have access to Indra's queen, Sachi, as well. The queen, naturally, was not pleased by my proposition."

"Deciding to teach me a lesson, she told me she would allow me in her bed, but only if the Sapta Rishis, the seven celestial guardians of the Vedas, agreed to carry me in a palanquin to her palace. Lost to lust, I foolishly forced the venerable sages to serve as my palanquin bearers."

"So great was my haste to reach Sachi that I kicked Rishi Agastya in the head because he was walking too slowly. Enraged by my disrespect and my behavior, so unbecoming of the position bestowed upon me by the Devas, Agastya cursed me. I would fall from Swarga to the earth, not as a human but as a python, forever crawling on my stomach. When I pleaded with him, the sage relented, saying that I would be freed from this wretched body only after Yudhishthira, my descendant, teaches me the true meaning of Brahman."

Yudhishthira's wisdom

Bhima tried to tell Nahusha that Yudhishthira was his elder brother, but the python did not believe him. As Nahusha opened his mouth to swallow him, a desperate Bhima began to shout for help, hoping that his brothers would come to his aid.

Hearing Bhima's cries, the other Pandavas rushed to look for their brother, and found him in the clutches of the giant serpent. "Eat me instead," offered Yudhishthira, attempting to free his brother. "I am the firstborn son of Pandu, Bhima's older brother."

"I will not free him. Nor do I desire any other food. But if you answer the questions I ask you, I will free your brother," promised the snake. Loosening his grip on Bhima, Nahusha continued, "If you really are who you claim to be, then your answer will release not just your brother from my coils, it will also free me from this terrible situation. So tell me, who is a Brahman? "

The meaning of Brahman

After years of discussions with Rishis, Yudhishthira had realized that the answer to this question was not as straightforward as it seemed. He answered Nahusha, "Most people believe that a Brahman is one who is the son of a Brahman. That is not correct. A Brahman is one who, by mastering his senses and disciplining his mind, has attained the knowledge of the eternal, infinite, and boundless soul. This makes him content, gentle, and generous, for he is one with the truth."

Seeing that his answer satisfied Nahusha, Yudhishthira, in turn, asked the serpent questions about living a righteous life. Finally, impressed by his answers, Yudhishthira requested Nahusha to explain how, despite his intelligence, delusion had overcome him.

The serpent responded, "I was blinded by my prosperity. Though I was enlightened, I lost sight of the truth and behaved badly. Since then I have been paying for it. With your answer, you have freed me from a grievous curse and have done me great service," he said, releasing Bhima from his coils unhurt.

> "O Indra among serpents! It is said that a **Brahman is one in whom truthfulness**, charity, **forgiveness**, good conduct, **lack of cruelty**, self-control and **compassion** can be seen."
>
> YUDHISHTHIRA TO NAHUSHA, VANA PARVA: THE BOOK OF THE FOREST

MYTHOLOGY

THE SEVEN SAGES

The Sapta Rishis, or seven sages, are said to be the patriarchs of Vedic Hinduism. According to the Sama Veda, one of the oldest Hindu scriptures, these sages are Agastya, Atri, Bharadvaja, Gautam, Jamadagni, Vashishtha, and Vishwamitra.

This list, however, keeps changing with each "manuvantara," a period of time that marks the reign of an Indra, the king of gods. A new Indra is appointed for each manuvantara, along with a new set of Sapta Rishis.

In some parts of India, however, people consider the seven stars of the Big Dipper as the Sapta Rishis and identify them as the sages Vashishtha, Marichi, Pulastya, Pulaha, Atri, Angiras, and Kratu.

AFTER

With the meaning of Brahman revealed to him, Nahusha was released from his curse.

ASCENT TO HEAVEN

Filled with happiness, Nahusha gave up his physical body. Assuming a celestial form, he blessed his descendants before going back to his heavenly abode.

Relieved that Bhima's life had been spared, the Pandavas returned to their home in the woods and recounted the tale of Bhima's escape to Draupadi, Dhaumya, and the other sages.

BEFORE

One night, the eldest Pandava had a dream. A deer came to him and, weeping copiously, begged him to leave the forest.

THE SPOTTED DEER IS NATIVE TO INDIA

A CRY FOR HELP

In his dream, the deer told Yudhishthira that in the time he and his brothers had been in Dwaitavana, the number of deer had dwindled drastically as the Pandavas had hunted down so many. The deer begged Yudhishthira to leave this forest along with his brothers. Moved by the deer's plea, the Pandavas decided to leave Dwaitavana and went back to the Kamyaka woods.

Yudhishthira's **Test**

An encounter with a Yaksha, the guardian deity of a lake, turned into a challenge for the eldest Pandava. The Yaksha's questions would test Yudhishthira's knowledge, patience, and courage—the lives of his brothers hung in the balance.

While they were staying in the Kamyaka forest, the Pandavas were approached by a sage who sought their help. He told them that the sticks he used to produce fire for his prayers and rituals had been hanging on the branch of a tree, when they became entangled in the horns of a passing antelope. He asked the Pandavas to help him get them back, directing them to a lake where the antelope went to drink water every evening.

Yudhishthira thought it a simple task, and sent Nakula to hunt down the animal and retrieve the fire sticks. At the lake, Nakula spotted the antelope, but it ran away before he could shoot it down. Nakula was setting off in pursuit when, consumed by an overwhelming thirst, he paused and bent down to drink from the lake.

The Yaksha's warning

Just as Nakula was about to take a sip of the crystal clear waters, he heard a voice echoed through the forest.

"I am the lord of this lake," said the Yaksha. "Do not touch the water. You may drink only after you have answered my questions."

Nakula looked around. Seeing no one, he dismissed the voice as the imagination of his fatigued body and mind. Paying no heed to the warning, he drank. As soon as the water touched his lips, he dropped dead.

> "I have taken your **younger brothers** to the **land of the dead**. O prince! If you do not **answer my questions**, you will be the fifth."
>
> YAKSHA, THE LORD OF THE LAKE, TO YUDHISHTHIRA, VANA PARVA: THE BOOK OF THE FOREST

Wondering what was taking his brother so long, Yudhishthira sent Sahadeva to check if all was well with Nakula. When Sahadeva did not return, Arjuna went to look for the twins; then Bhima went searching for all three.

With no sign of any of his bothers, an anxious Yudhishthira ran to the lake, only to find all of them dead on its banks. Utterly devastated, he looked around, trying frantically to fathom what could possibly have happened, but could see nothing.

Suddenly, he felt an extreme thirst. As he bent down to drink from the lake, heard a voice reverberate around him. Immediately understanding that this was no ordinary creature, the wise Yudhishthira asked, "Are you the one who hurt my brothers?"

"Yes. I warned them, but they did not listen to me, and so they are dead. This pool is mine, and unless you answer my questions, you cannot drink its water," came the reply.

The Yaksha's questions

When Yudhishthira agreed to answer his questions, the Yaksha appeared in the form of a heron. "Who causes the sun to rise? Who makes the sun set in the horizon?" asked the Yaksha.

"The Supreme makes the sun to rise and it is the sun's duty to set," Yudhishthira replied.

"Wherein lies the truth?"

"It is captured in the Veda."

"What, when renounced, makes a man appealing?"

"Renouncing pride."

"What, when renounced makes a man happy and wealthy?"

"Renouncing avarice makes a man happy and renouncing desire makes one wealthy."

"What is faster than the wind?"

"The mind."

"What is the most fascinating thing about the world?"

"The fact that every day creatures die, yet everyone lives life as if immortal."

"What is the only thing man can conquer?"

"Only his own mind."

Yaksha continued to ask Yudhishthira questions, probing deeply into his understanding of the nature of the world,

GUARDIAN SPIRITS

In Buddhist lore, the Yakshas are considered to be guardians of the gates. In Thai temple art, they feature as an important architectural element from the 14th century on.

society, and the soul. Finally satisfied, and with no more questions, the Yaksha said, "I shall let one of your brothers live. Choose!"

"Nakula," said Yudhishthira, without hesitation.

This puzzled Yaksha. "Why him?" he asked. "He shares none of your blood."

"Kunti and Madri are my father's two wives. I, a son born of Kunti, am alive; one born of Madri should be too."

Impressed by Yudhishthira's wisdom and sense of justice, the Yaksha revealed his true form—Yama, the god of dharma and justice and Yudhishthira's father. Restoring the younger Pandavas to life, he blessed them all.

THE POISONED LAKE
This 20th-century illustration captures the Pandavas at the lake where the Yaksha challenged them.

MYTHOLOGY AND FOLKLORE

HERONS

In Hindu mythology, herons are associated with Saraswati, goddess of knowledge. In this episode of the Mahabharata, the Yaksha takes the form of a heron as it represents the capacity of the mind to reason. Just as the mythical heron can separate milk from water, so can the discriminating mind separate the truth from lies.

IN HINDU MYTHOLOGY, HERONS ARE ASSOCIATED WITH KNOWLEDGE

AFTER

With the thirteenth year of exile approaching, the Pandavas prepared for the year in hiding.

DEPARTING FROM THE FOREST

After spending twelve years of great hardship in the forest, the brothers and their wife prepared for the final year of exile.

They approached Dhaumya and the other sages to seek blessings and reassurance for the year to come.

They were now ready to begin their last year of exile—disguised so that no one could recognize them.

THE ELDEST PANDAVA

Yudhishthira

> **"**Yudhishthira, with **dharma in his soul**, will **conquer** the earth and **protect** it.**"**

MATALI, INDRA'S CHARIOTEER, TO ARJUNA, VANA PARVA: THE BOOK OF THE FOREST

Encouraged by her husband Pandu, who could not sire any children, Kunti invoked Yama, the lord of dharma, by using a divine mantra and bore a child by him. This eldest Pandava was named Yudhishthira, who came to be known as the most honest of men.

Yudhishthira grew up in Hastinapur with his four brothers and Kaurava cousins. Unable to see eye to eye with each other, the cousins divided the Kuru household into two rival camps, each claiming to be the rightful heir to the throne. Yudhishthira's claim lay in being the eldest son of the consecrated king of Hastinapur, Pandu.

The king of Indraprastha

Their rivalry grew to such an extent that once the Kauravas tried to kill the sons of Pandu by putting them in a house of lac and setting it on fire (see pp. 114–15). The Pandavas took refuge in a forest for a year, at the end of which they married Draupadi, the princess of Panchala.

By marrying Draupadi, the Pandavas had also won for themselves a powerful ally in Drupada, her father. Emboldened, they went back to Hastinapur to claim their share of the kingdom. Dhritarashtra gave them the forest of Khandavaprastha instead. Happy with what they got, the Pandavas built the city of Indraprastha and crowned Yudhishthira as the king.

The gambling match

But fate had other plans. Duryodhana, the eldest Kaurava who was invited to Yudhishthira's coronation ceremony, was consumed by envy on seeing his cousins' prosperity. Shakuni, his uncle, came up with a plan to invite the eldest Pandava to a game of dice, fully aware of his weakness for the game. As expected, Yudhishthira accepted the invitation. Shakuni won each game, and the eldest Pandava lost everything—his wealth, his brothers, himself, and even his wife Draupadi, who was publicly humiliated.

After losing the game, the Pandavas were forced to go into exile in the forest for thirteen years, the last year in anonymity.

Embodiment of dharma

Known for his upright character, Yudhishthira is sometimes referred to as Dharmaraja. The Mahabharata recounts many instances of his integrity and refined sense of ethics. Throughout his period in exile, Yudhishthira remained calm, urging his brothers to be patient. Yet, their fury filled him with great shame and guilt. During those years, he met many sages and heard discourses on wisdom, which enriched him. His encounter with a Yaksha, the lord of a lake, was actually a test to judge his sense of fairness, put forth by his father, Yama, the god of dharma (see pp. 192–93).

ART AND LITERATURE

YUDHISHTHIRA AND DRAUPADI

Author Pavan K. Varma adapted a key incident from the Mahabharata in a book, *Yudhishtar and Draupadi* (1996). Written in verse, the book describes Yudhishthira's infatuation for Draupadi, his shame at not being her choice, his guilt, and ego. It also recounts Draupadi's anger at being made a common wife without her consent and her fury at being gambled away. In the book, when Yudhishthira's brothers lay dead by the Yaksha's lake, Yudhishthira and Draupadi were alone together for the first time ever and Draupadi forgave the eldest Pandava. The book has been translated into Hindi by poet-writer Gulzar and has been dramatized as well.

VARMA'S BOOK IS ABOUT YUDHISHTHIRA'S LOVE FOR DRAUPADI

The only lie

The Kurukshetra War was another test of Yudhishthira's character. When Drona took charge of the Kaurava army, Krishna suggested that the only way to defeat the royal teacher was to convince him that his son, Ashwatthama, was dead. The Pandavas spread the rumor of his son's death. Drona turned to Yudhishthira, known for his honesty, and asked, "Is it true? Is Ashwatthama dead?" With a heavy heart, Yudhishthira spoke his first lie. "Yes, Ashwatthama is dead," he said, and murmured, "But I don't know if it was an elephant or a man."

Unable to hear the murmur in the din of the battle, the devastated father lost the will to live and was instantly killed.

The king of Hastinapur

The Pandavas won the war, and Yudhishthira was crowned the king of Hastinapur. After a successful kingship, he renounced the worldly life. The arduous journey to heaven culminated in his whole family dying, but a stoic Yudhishthira continued to his destination. At the gate of Swarga, he was asked to leave behind the dog that had followed him. But Yudhishthira refused to enter heaven without the dog.

Yudhishthira was shocked to find the Kauravas in heaven, and his family suffering in hell. The Devas then showed him how he was still full of anger. He realized he was not the great man he thought he was. Enlightened, he forgave the Kauravas and ascended to a heaven higher than Swarga, the celestial abode of Vishnu.

BIOGRAPHY IN BRIEF

- **Born** to Kunti and Yama, the god of dharma, Yudhishthira was the eldest son of Pandu.
- **Grew up** in Hastinapur with his four brothers and Kaurava cousins.
- **Mastered the skill of spear fighting** under the guidance of the royal tutor, Drona.
- **Shared Draupadi** with his brothers after Arjuna won her hand at her swayamvara. Also married the tribal princess Devika and had sons Prativindhya and Yaudheya from them.
- **Made Indraprastha his capital** and performed the Rajasuya yagna.
- **Played a game of dice** with the Kauravas and lost his kingdom, his brothers, and himself. He gambled away his wife, Draupadi, after which she was humiliated in public.
- **Served exile** for a period of thirteen years, the last year incognito.
- **Answered the Yaksha's questions** during exile, saving his brothers from death.
- **Took the guise of Kanka**, an adviser to the king of Matsya, during their last year in exile that was spent in hiding.
- **Fought the Kurukshetra War** with his brothers and many kings by his side.
- **Lied to Drona** that his son Ashwatthama had died, causing Drona's death.
- **Killed Shalya**, his stepmother Madri's brother, by fighting without rancor.
- **Was crowned** the king of Hastinapur after the war and ruled peacefully for thirty-six years.
- **Renounced the kingdom** and ascended the mountain that led to heaven.
- **Entered heaven** to find the Kauravas there and later saw the Pandavas suffering in hell. Was made to realize that he was still enslaved by anger. Forgave his enemies and attained enlightenment.

YUDHISHTHIRA'S EFFIGY
A huge, colouful figure of Yudhishthira made of wood and fiberglass is placed at the Padmanabhaswamy temple during the Panguni festival in Kerala, India.

THE FIVE BROTHERS
Wayang puppets from Java, Indonesia, depict actions of the five Pandava brothers. Yudhishthira is at the front.

Nala and **Damayanti**

Twelve years into their exile, and the Pandavas still lamented their lot. Sage Vrihadashwa told them the tale of Nala and Damayanti's trials to put an end to this wallowing in self-pity.

As the Pandavas' final year of exile approached, Yudhishthira asked Sage Vrihadashwa to teach him the art of playing dice. At one of these lessons, watching the dice roll, the deposed king's mind wandered to that fateful game that had brought him and his family to their present situation. "We have to spend our last year of exile in hiding. And if we are discovered, we will have to stay in the forest for yet another twelve years. What a miserable fate—and all because of that game of dice! Is there anyone who has suffered like me?" he cried.

Trying to comfort the king, the sage responded, "You have said you think that there is no man more unfortunate than you are. That's not true. I can narrate an account, if you wish to hear it. This is the story of a king who was more miserable than you."

THE SWAN EMISSARY
In some versions of the tale, Damayanti falls in love with Nala when a swan that he had sent to profess his love praises the Nishada king profusely.

> "Such **a beautiful one** had not been seen or heard of before ... The beautiful lady **disturbed** the minds of the **gods themselves**."
>
> SAGE VRIHADASHWA TO THE PANDAVAS, VANA PARVA: THE BOOK OF THE FOREST

A prince and a princess

The sage began his story about a king of the Nishada tribe. Nala was learned in the scriptures, skilled in strategy, good with horses, and loved by women. Damayanti was the princess of Vidarbha, daughter of King Bhima. She was said to be so full of beauty and grace that the gods themselves desired her. The two had heard of each other and had fallen in love without having seen each other.

One day, Nala caught a swan in his palace garden. Fearing for its life, the swan offered to sing praises of the king to Damayanti, so that she would think of no other man but him. Nala released the swan, and the bird flew to Vidarbha. There it performed its task so well that Damayanti grew thin and wan longing for her distant lover. This worried King Bhima so much that he decided to arrange for her to get married.

When news of Damayanti's swayamvara reached heaven, the gods decided to attend as suitors. They met Nala there and, thinking that his aura and beauty would help them with their suit, they asked him to encourage the princess to take one of them as her husband. When Nala heard what the gods wanted of him, he asked them to choose another messenger. The gods, however, would not be swayed.

Damayanti's decision

With a heavy heart, the Nishada went to meet Damayanti on behalf of the gods. When the princess realized that Nala was asking her to marry one of the gods, she told him of her love for him. Nala was overjoyed but concerned that this would greatly displease the gods. Damayanti had a solution; she suggested that he attend the swayamvara along with them—sure of who it was she desired, she would choose Nala as her groom. Since his arguments against this plan would not dissuade her, Nala returned to the gods and reported all that had transpired.

When her wedding day arrived, Damayanti was faced with five men who looked exactly like Nala. Unsure of what to do, the princess prayed to the gods, requesting them to help her choose the man she loved. Pleased by her devotion, the gods gave Damayanti the key to identifying the real Nala—he was the one who was perspiring, whose feet touched the ground, the one who threw a shadow, and whose garland was wilted. Damayanti lightly touched Nala's garment and garlanded him. The gods were delighted and granted the happy groom many blessings.

Kali's vow

On their way back to heaven, the gods met the demon Kali, who was vice itself, and Dwapara, who embodied the yuga, or age, when the corruption of humanity began. They were on their way to Damayanti's swayamvara, in which Kali, who was in love with Damayanti, wanted to participate. When he heard that Damayanti had chosen Nala over the gods in attendance, he was very angry.

The gods assured him that they were happy with Damayanti's choice. "It is with our blessing that Damayanti chose Nala. He knows all about dharma and observes all the vows. The values of truth, perseverance, purity, generosity, austerity, self-control, and a love for peace can all be found in him," they observed.

But Kali's anger was not appeased. He vowed revenge and kept a careful watch on Nala's actions, for the smallest act of sin on the king's part would give Kali the chance to destroy his life. »

KEY CONCEPT

KALI AS MISFORTUNE

The gruesome harbinger of bad luck, Kali strikes those who practice bad hygiene or touch polluted and inauspicious things. The demon Kali is, however, quite distinct from the goddess Kali, who destroys evil.

The sages explained Nala's trials and tribulations through the idea of Kali, the herald of misfortune. They helped Yudhishthira cope with his immense shame and guilt about losing his good sense and his fortune, and becoming the cause of his family's destitution and sorrow by blaming Kali for his bad choices in that fateful game of dice.

DAMAYANTI'S DILEMMA
This painting by the illustrator Warwick Goble shows Damayanti at her wedding, confronted by five men who all look like Nala.

Nala's defeat

Twelve years passed as Nala, Damayanti, and the two children born to them lived happily. Then one day, Nala performed the evening prayer ritual without first bathing. Kali saw his chance. He went to Nala's brother, Pushkara, with the insidious suggestion that he win the kingdom from Nala in a game of dice.

Pushara liked the idea and, though he was not keen, Nala could not bring himself to refuse his brother's repeated invitations. The game between the two lasted for months, and under Kali's influence, Nala lost his silver, his gold, and finally, his kingdom. When he had nothing else left to wager, Pushkara asked him to stake his last valuable possession—Damayanti. It was only then that the king came to his senses. Getting up from the game, he and his wife left the palace for the forest with nothing but the clothes they wore, leaving their children in the care of the king of Vidarbha, Damayanti's father. Looking at his wife walking beside him, Nala was ashamed for having let down the woman who insisted on sharing this life of misery with him.

The forest was a cruel place. Nala could not hunt without weapons, and Damayanti did not know how to forage for food. Desperately hungry, Nala tried to use the cloth he was wearing to catch some birds. But the birds flew away with the cloth, leaving Nala naked. As he saw the birds flying off, Nala was completely crushed "I have lost everything," he sighed.

"You still have me," reminded Damayanti. "I will always be by your side," she told him, ripping her own cloth in half and sharing it with her husband.

Damayanti abandoned

Together they wandered in the forest; he wracked by guilt, and she determined to stand by him. Finally, unable to see her suffer any more, Nala left Damayanti while she was sleeping. He hoped that, on finding herself alone, she would return to her father. But Damayanti could not bring herself to abandon her husband. She wandered in the forest looking for him.

One day, a venomous snake lay in her path. Fortunately, a passing hunter came to her rescue. Damayanti thanked him, but soon realized that the hunter was more interested in her body than in her gratitude. Damayanti was, however, chaste; as soon as the hunter touched her, he burst into flames.

She then came upon a caravan of traders who asked her to join them. But a herd of elephants attacked them that very night. Believing that Damayanti had brought them ill luck, the traders drove her away.

Abandoned and alone once again, Damayanti walked toward the city of Chedi. As she approached the gates of the city, children began to pelt her with stones, shouting that she was a madwoman.

The queen of Chedi noticed this cruelty and kindly took Damayanti into her service. Here she was recognized by a priest as the princess of Vidarbha. The queen learned who she was and persuaded Damayanti to return to her father's house.

The search for Nala

In Vidarbha, Damayanti asked her father to help her search for Nala. Her father appointed the priest Parnada to do the job.

NALA ABANDONING DAMAYANTI
Raja Ravi Varma paintings were greatly inspired by Hindu mythology. Here he captures the moment when Nala, burdened by shame, steals away from Damayanti.

THE RIDE TO VIDARBHA
To reach the southern kingdom of Vidarbha overnight from Ayodhya in the north, King Rituparna needed swift horses and a very skilled horseman.

"How will I recognize him?" Parnada wanted to know. So Damayanti taught the priest a song about a king who lost his kingdom and his wife in a game of dice. "Only Nala will respond to it," she said.

Parnada traveled across many kingdoms without receiving a response to his song. Then, in Ayodhya, an ugly dwarf named Bahuka sang back to the priest, "I might be unlucky but I still care for you." Parnada rushed to inform Damayanti.

"But the man is ugly and serves as a cook," he warned. The dwarf's response, however, had convinced Damayanti that it was Nala, and she devised a plan to get him to Vidarbha.

She sent a priest to deliver a message to King Rituparna of Ayodhya. "Tell him that because Nala cannot be found, the king of Vidarbha has decided to get Damayanti remarried. He has invited all the kings of the land for the swayamvara, so that she can choose a husband from among them. Let him know that the ceremony will be held on the day that follows your arrival."

"The very next day! How can Rituparna reach Vidarbha in one day?" exclaimed the priest.

"Nala is the world's fastest charioteer," explained the queen. "If Nala is in Ayodhya, he will bring the king here. You see, Rituparna will want to come at any cost—he was one of my suitors before I married Nala, and he still desires me."

The overnight journey

Though unconvinced, the priest did as she asked. Sure enough, Rituparna offered a handsome reward to anyone who could get him to Vidarbha overnight. "I can take you there," claimed his cook, Bahuka. "But you have to teach me the secret of rolling dice,"

"So it shall be," promised Rituparna, eager to reach Vidarbha in time. Through the night, the king shared his knowledge of dice with Bahuka. By dawn, when they reached Vidarbha, Bahuka had become an expert at the game.

Just inside the gates of the city, Bahuka noticed two children playing. Stopping the chariot he hugged them and wept. Damayanti knew that only her husband would do that.

> "**O loved one**! You are the one who **sliced off** half my garment. **Where are you**?"
>
> DAMAYANTI'S SONG TO NALA, VANA PARVA: THE BOOK OF THE FOREST

"That man is Nala," she said, elated. Everyone around her told her that such an ugly dwarf could not be her husband, but Damayanti was adamant. "I may not recognize the body but I do recognize that heart. Follow him and take note. He may not look like my husband, but he will certainly act like him. You'll notice that the world will treat him royally, for he has the soul of a king,"

Sure enough, Bahuka had such regal bearing that when he passed through gates, he did not bend—the gates rose to let him enter with his head held up. When he entered the kitchen, meals began to cook on their own.

When Damayanti was told about this, she ran to him, crying "Nala, Nala!" with joy.

The reunion

"Yes, I am Nala," said Bahuka. He had been transformed into a dwarf by the venomous breath of a dreaded Naga called Karkotaka, as punishment for his errors. Karkotaka had also advised Nala to learn the secret of the dice from Rituparna. "My ugliness and servitude were punishments for my mistakes," he explained. I have paid the price and can now go back to being myself.

Reunited with his wife and children and armed with the knowledge of dice, Nala went to his kingdom and challenged Pushkara to another game of dice. "If I lose, you can have my wife," he baited his brother, knowing that it would prompt him to take up the challenge as nothing else would.

In the game that ensued, Nala won all that he had once lost—family and fortune.

"So shall it be with you, Yudhishthira," said Sage Vrihadashwa, blessing the eldest Pandava.

ANALYSIS

LEARNING LESSONS

Throughout the exile, the sages in the Pandavas' retinue used stories to teach the brothers lessons and helped them come to terms with their reality.

The story of Nala and Damayanti has clear parallels with the Pandavas' current situation, and tells them not to let self-pity get the better of them. Though Nala faced severe trials, he never swerved from the path of righteousness and, over time, was able to prevail over Kali's influence and regain his kingdom.

The story also gives them clues about how they could spend their final year of exile in hiding. For instance, Bhima became a cook and Nakula became a stable hand, while, Draupadi, like Damayanti, became a queen's maid.

4
VIRATA PARVA: THE BOOK OF VIRATA

THE INVASION OF MATSYA
This Pichwai painting from Rajasthan in western India evokes a scene from the Virata Parva. Susarma, the ruler of Trigarta, invades the Matsya kingdom and steals King Virata's cows.

Virata Parva, or the Book of Virata, is the fourth parva of the Mahabharata. It is named after the king of Matsya in whose court the Pandavas spent the thirteenth year of exile. After living in the forest for twelve years, the Pandavas spend the final year of exile disguised as servants in Virata's kingdom, Matsya. During this time they learn to empathize with those who serve the ruling class and appreciate their contribution to society. At the end of the year, the Pandavas expect Duryodhana to honor the terms of the gambling match and return their kingdom. The parva consists of 4 sub-parvas, 67 chapters, and 1,376 shlokas, or couplets.

"O **emperor!** Know that **I am a brahmana** who has **lost everything** and has come **in search of livelihood** ... O lord! **I wish to live here** with you, following **your instructions."**

YUDHISHTHIRA, DISGUISED AS A PRIEST, TO KING VIRATA, VIRATA PARVA: THE BOOK OF VIRATA

Living in Disguise

To fulfil the terms of the wager, the Pandavas and Draupadi had to spend the thirteenth year of their exile undiscovered, mingling with people but never revealing their own identities. They decided to spend this year in the kingdom of Matsya.

Each of the Pandavas went to the court of Virata, the ruler of the Matsya kingdom, to seek employment. Yudhishthira went as Kanka, a Brahman skilled in the administration of a kingdom. Bhima called himself Ballava, and promised Virata he was the greatest cook in the world.

"I have been trained in dance by the Apsaras themselves," declared Arjuna, presenting himself dressed in women's clothes as a eunuch named Brihannala. Virata appointed him to teach his daughter, Uttari, the art of dancing. Nakula and Sahadeva, as Damagranthi

> "Thus did the Pandavas ... **dwell in Matsya**, following the **pledges** that they had given. They lived a **careful life of concealment**."
>
> SAGE VAISHAMPAYANA TO KING JANAMEJAYA, VIRATA PARVA: THE BOOK OF VIRATA

BEFORE

Twelve years had passed since the gambling match in which the Pandavas had lost everything.

CONCEALING THE WEAPONS

The Pandavas had to pass the thirteenth year of their exile in disguise. To avoid being recognized, they decided to hide all those possessions that could give their identity away. They concealed their weapons in a bundle of cloth shaped like a corpse and tied it to the branch of a sami tree. They then proceeded to begin their year of living incognito in the kingdom of Matsya.

SAMI TREE, NATIVE TO ARID REGIONS OF INDIA

SAIRANDHRI WITH THE QUEEN

Queen Sudeshna meeting Draupadi, disguised as Sairandhri. This 17th-century watercolor is part of a folio of the Mahabharata made in the south Indian town of Seringapatam, Karnataka.

"In accordance with the **promise** that they had made, they entered the **great city**, to live in disguise in that kingdom for the **thirteenth** year.**"**

SAGE VAISHAMPAYANA TO KING JANAMEJAYA, VIRATA PARVA: THE BOOK OF VIRATA

and Tantipala, were employed to take care of Virata's horses and cows. Draupadi came to Virata's court as a beautician called Sairandhri, and was employed to attend to Queen Sudeshna, Virata's wife. The six "servants" were good at their jobs, but stood out because of their dignity and self-confidence: they each made clear demands before they accepted employment; one being that they would not eat leftovers.

Princely servants

In this year, the Pandavas learned how it felt to serve others. They could not even meet and take comfort from each other, as it was crucial to keep their identities secret. So, Yudhishthira played dice with Virata and advised the king on dharma; Bhima cooked delicious meals, but could not eat the food himself; Arjuna, who could not bear to be parted from his bow, had exchanged it for dancing bells; Nakula cleaned stables; Sahadeva looked after cows; and Draupadi, unused to receiving commands, had to do Sudeshna's bidding. Despite many trials, they played their parts so well that no one guessed that the six additions to Virata's court were the Pandavas and their queen, Draupadi.

BRIHANNALA WITH UTTARI

Arjuna, disguised as the eunuch Brihannala, teaches dance to the king's daughter. The dance drama, "Virata Parvam," is performed in the classical Indian ballet form of Bharatnatayam by the Bharathanjali Trust.

HISTORY AND CULTURE

THE KINGDOM OF MATSYA

The Indonesian rendering of the Mahabharata suggests that Virata was a descendant of Satyavati's twin brother. This is based on the fact that "matsya," the name of Virata's kingdom, means "fish," suggesting a strong association with the fisherfolk.

Virata's kingdom was to the south of the Kuru kingdom and west of the Yamuna river, which separated it from Panchala. It roughly corresponded to the former princely state of Jaipur in Rajasthan, India. The capital of Matsya was Viratanagar (present-day Bairat, Rajasthan), which is said to have been named after its founder king, Virata.

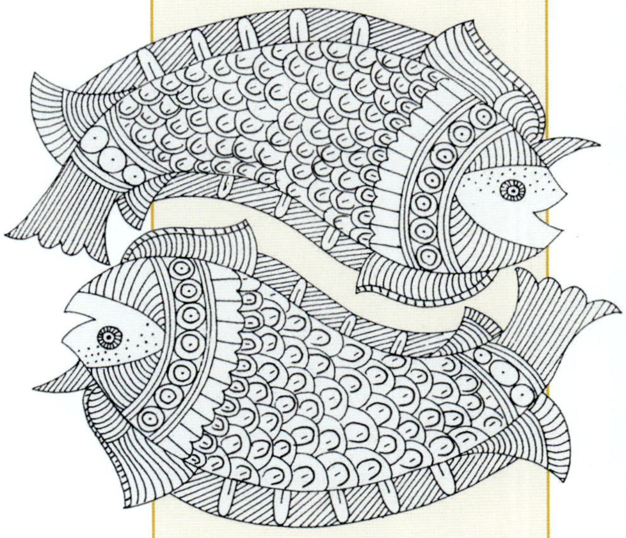

FISH DRAWN IN THE MADHUBANI STYLE

AFTER

The thirteenth year of the Pandavas' exile was as crucial for Duryodhana as it was for the Pandavas themselves.

DURYODHANA'S SEARCH

According to the terms of the wager, if the Pandavas could be identified during this year, they would have to remain in exile for another twelve years. Keen to discover their whereabouts, Duryodhana sent his spies far and wide in search of his cousins.

BEFORE

The Pandava brothers and their wife, Draupadi, spent their thirteenth year in the kingdom of Matsya.

IN HIDING

As Duryodhana's spies searched for the Pandavas, the Matsya king and queen, Virata and Sudeshna, were not aware that their new servants were actually the five brothers and their wife. The king did notice that these servants were self-assured and dignified—each of them had clear demands before they accepted employment, unlike all his other servants, and went about their work without speaking to one another. Nobody, not even the king, had the slightest suspicion that they were related to each other.

The **Killing** of **Kichaka**

During her year spent as Sairandhri in Matsya, Draupadi had to fend off the unwarranted attention of Kichaka, the brother-in-law of King Virata. This triggered off a set of events that threatened the Pandavas' anonymity in exile.

The Pandavas spent many months living in disguise at Virata's court, carrying out their onerous duties day after day without any incident. Unfortunately for them, Draupadi's beauty could not remain hidden for long.

Kichaka's lust

Draupadi served the queen as a beautician and had taken the name Sairandhri. She caught the fancy of Kichaka, the queen's brother, who was also the commander of the royal armies of Matsya. Even though Draupadi rejected his advances, he leered at her shamelessly, making his intentions quite clear. Kichaka's lascivious gestures made her so uncomfortable that she went so far as to complain to the queen. But blinded by her love for her brother, Sudeshna refused to believe any ill of him.

Eventually, overcome with lust, Kichaka asked his sister to send her maid to his chambers. Despite being aware of his intentions, Sudeshna ordered Draupadi to carry a jar of wine to him.

Draupadi's cry for help

Aware of Kichaka's amorous intentions, Draupadi tried to avoid the chore, but the queen insisted. Draupadi turned to Yudhishthira for help, but her husband refused to intervene. "We cannot risk discovery until the end of the year. We are helpless and will have to endure this humiliation."

Aware that Arjuna and the twins would not go against their eldest brother's wishes, Draupadi went to Bhima, who was employed as the cook of the court Ballava. Learning of her predicament, the quick-tempered Bhima flew into a rage.

Bhima to the rescue

That evening, Kichaka entered his chamber to find a lady he thought to be Sairandhri sitting on his bed. As soon as he put his arms around her, he realized that this was not a woman at all. But by then it was too late—Kichaka was being crushed in a very strong embrace. In his inebriated state he could do little to escape. The "woman" was none other than Bhima, who broke Kichaka's bones and smashed his skull.

> "This beautiful one's form **intoxicates** me … your beautiful serving **maid** possesses **extreme beauty**."
>
> KICHAKA TO QUEEN SUDESHNA, VIRATA PARVA: THE BOOK OF VIRATA

A DEADLY EMBRACE
This Chitrakathi painting shows Bhima approaching Kichaka to kill him as Draupadi looks on.

ART AND LITERATURE

POLITICAL ALLEGORY

Kichaka-Vadha (1907) is a play based on the episode of the killing of Kichaka. Written by Krushnaji Prabhakar Khadilkar, a Marathi writer, and staged by the Maharashtra Natak Mandali in 1910, the play was an allegorical attack on British rule in India. Kichaka was a metaphor for the British Raj, while India was represented by Draupadi. Yudhishthira was shown as a leader but it was Bhima's extremist views, including violence against tyranny, which caught the attention of the revolutionaries and national leaders who attended the play. It was banned by the authorities at that time.

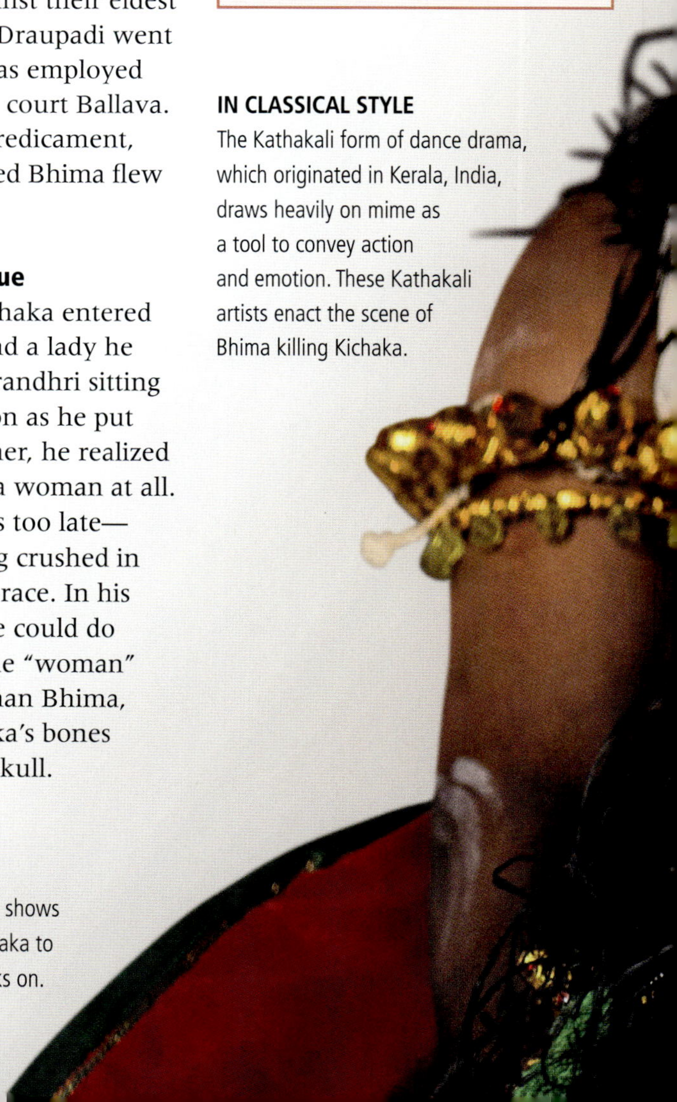

IN CLASSICAL STYLE
The Kathakali form of dance drama, which originated in Kerala, India, draws heavily on mime as a tool to convey action and emotion. These Kathakali artists enact the scene of Bhima killing Kichaka.

Suspecting that Sairandhri had a hand in Kichaka's death, Sudeshna plotted with her other brothers to burn her alive on Kichaka's funeral pyre. They managed to capture her, but Bhima, alert now that he realized how vulnerable his wife's position was, heard her calling for help. Uprooting a tree, he lashed out with it. Before anyone caught sight of Bhima or even realized what was going on, the men holding Sairandhri lay dead and she was standing free.

The news spread like wildfire. Everyone wondered who could have killed the queen's brothers and, in particular, such a powerful warrior as Kichaka.

> "Kill the **evil one** who molests me! **Destroy him** like an **earthen pot against stone**."
>
> DRAUPADI TO BHIMA, VIRATA PARVA: THE BOOK OF VIRATA

AFTER

When Kichaka and his brothers were killed, all eyes turned on Sairandhri.

SAIRANDHRI SPINS A TALE

Knowing that the death of Sudeshna's brothers could risk the Pandavas' discovery, Draupadi fabricated a story. She declared that she was the wife of Gandharvas who could appear out of thin air to protect her from any harm. Mourning the death of her brothers, Sudeshna ordered Sairandhri to leave the kingdom. But King Virata was afraid of angering the Gandharvas and allowed her to stay in the palace.

VIRATA'S CATTLE
In this folio of the *Razmnama*, a Persian retelling of the Mahabharata commissioned by Emperor Akbar, King Susarma of Trigarta can be seen herding away King Virata's cattle as the women of Matsya's kingdom look on.

The **Attack** on the Matsya Kingdom

It was an attack by the Kauravas on King Virata's kingdom that finally revealed the Pandavas' true identity and brought their long exile to a close. The episode ended well for them, with a victory in battle and new alliances.

BEFORE

The killing of Kichaka and his brothers made the Kauravas suspect Bhima was in Matsya.

THE KAURAVAS' SUSPICION

"Only someone as mighty as Bhima, who had killed Baka, Hidimba, Kirmira, and Jatasura, would have been able to kill the formidable brothers of the queen of the Matsya," thought Duryodhana. Now that he knew where the Pandavas were hiding, he was excited at the prospect of catching them before the end of the thirteenth year and banishing them to the forest for another twelve years.

A STATUE OF BHIMA, HAMPI, KARNATAKA, INDIA

Certain that the Pandavas were hiding in the kingdom of Matsya, Duryodhana asked King Susarma of Trigarta to attack Matsya and steal Virata's cows. He knew that with Kichaka and his brothers dead, Virata did not have the warriors to ward off such an attack and guard the kingdom.

Matsya's warriors

The king of Matsya, however, found help from unexpected quarters. Kanka, his advisor, stepped forward to say he was well versed in fighting with the spear; Ballava, the cook, said that he was adept at using the mace; and Damagranthi and Tantipala, who looked after his horses and cattle, claimed they were proficient with the sword.

Virata was concerned that if all of them left in pursuit of the cattle thieves, the women would be left defenseless. Reassured by his youngest son, Uttara, who, boasting of his own expertise at archery, offered to stay back and guard the city, the king rode off in pursuit of his stolen cattle.

ART AND LITERATURE

PANCHARATRA

Bhasa, a renowned Sanskrit playwright, lived around the 2nd century CE, much before the legendary poet Kalidasa. In his play, *Pancharatra*—The Five Nights—dated 100 CE, Duryodhana urges his teacher, Drona, to expose the exiled Pandavas within five days. If he can't, Duryodhana will have to part with the Pandavas' share. Drona fails in his mission and the kingdom is divided. Peace follows between the Pandavas and Kauravas.

As soon as the capital was left unguarded the Kaurava army attacked the kingdom.

"They will storm the palace and drag the women away as slaves," cried a terrified queen.

Uttara assured the queen he would drive the invaders away single-handedly—but then realized that he did not have a charioteer. His sister's dance teacher, the eunuch Brihannala, volunteered his services and offered to drive the young prince. Uttara had no choice but to accept his services.

The eunuch and the boy

The Kauravas saw a chariot approach from Virata's kingdom. The charioteer was a eunuch and the warrior was a boy. They laughed in disdain and blew their conch shells to terrifying effect. One look at the great warriors in front of him on elephants, horses, and chariots, holding awe-inspiring weapons, and Uttara lose his nerve.

Terrified, he got down from the chariot and started running away. His charioteer ran after him and carried him back to the chariot. Consoling the teary-eyed prince, Brihannala drove the chariot away from the battlefield toward the forest, finally stopping under a sami tree.

Looking up, Uttara saw what seemed to be corpses wrapped in shrouds and tied to the branches. "Dead bodies cannot harm you," said Brihannala, asking the scared and mystified Uttara to bring them down. Uttara did as he was told, drawing confidence from the fact that his eunuch-charioteer suddenly seemed to have turned manly and self-assured.

»

HISTORY AND CULTURE

VEDIC WARS

The episode of the Kauravas' attack on Matsya is named the "Go-harana" Parva in the Mahabharata. Go-harana, or seizing cattle, was the most common reason to start a fight in Vedic times when owning livestock was the primary marker of the prosperity of the state. According to the epic, the war was fought over thousands of cows and involved hundreds of chariots, elephants, and foot soldiers from Matsya, Hastinapur, and Trigarta.

ROYAL CHARIOTS WERE OFTEN GILDED, AS IN THIS INSTALLATION AT MURUDESHWAR, KARNATAKA, INDIA

"Let us **attack** Virata's kingdom ... **grab his cattle** and his **many other riches**."

KARNA TO DURYODHANA, VIRATA PARVA: THE BOOK OF VIRATA

BHIMA HELPS VIRATA

An artist's interpretation of the story in the *Razmnama* shows Virata as a prisoner (left, in green), and Bhima with his mace, rushing to rescue him from the Kauravas.

» Uttara brought down the corpses from the trees and uncovered them. To his utter astonishment, he saw they were actually glorious weapons—spears, bows and arrows, maces, and swords.

The revelation

"These are the Pandavas' weapons," explained Brihannala. A bewildered Uttara asked how she knew that.

"Because I am Arjuna, the son of Kunti and the third Pandava," said Brihannala.

Uttara fell at the Pandava prince's feet at this revelation. He returned to the battlefield with renewed confidence. This time when their chariot approached the Kauravas, the roles had reversed; the young boy was the charioteer while the eunuch was the warrior. Once again, the Kauravas laughed in disdain as they blew their conch shell trumpets. But this time, the "eunuch" lifted his bow and efficiently brought down the flags of Duryodhana, Bhishma, Karna, and Drona, with his arrows.

Karna exclaimed in recognition, "That appears to be a eunuch, but the bow in his hands looks very much like the Gandiva, and his flag flies a monkey emblem. Undoubtedly, that is Arjuna."

Duryodhana smiled with satisfaction. They had forced the Pandavas to reveal themselves before the one year of their time as unknown exiles was over. His cousins would now have to return to the forest for another twelve years. The very thought filled Duryodhana with joy.

GATHERING WEAPONS

This detail of a frieze from the Chennakeshava temple, in Belur, India, is an artistic depiction of the Pandavas' weapons being taken down from the sami tree.

> **"**From the **roar of the chariot**, the **blast of the conch shell** and the **trembling of the earth**, it can be no one other than **Savyasachi** … Let us stand here … in battle formations.**"**

DRONA TO HIS ARMY, VIRATA PARVA: THE BOOK OF VIRATA

ANALYSIS

BLIND PARENTAL LOVE

On hearing Virata's boast of Uttara's "bravery," Kanka's honest response was that with Brihannala by the prince's side, his victory was inevitable. This deeply offended the king and in his anger, he flung a dice at Kanka's face so hard that Kanka's nose began to bleed. This story, perhaps, draws a parallel between Virata's blind love for Uttara and the inability of Duryodhana's parents to see their son's behavioral excesses. Vyasa wondered if parents are naturally blind, like King Dhritarashtra was, to the shortcomings of their children, or if they choose to be blind like his wife Gandhari did.

The voice of reason

Bhishma,however, introduced a cautionary note. The Pandavas were not such fools that they would reveal themselves before the end of the thirteenth year. "How is a year calculated?" Bhishma asked Duryodhana. "It is calculated either by the movement of the sun through the twelve solar houses of the zodiac, or by the time taken for the moon to be full across the twenty-seven lunar houses, or by the calendar given by astrologers. All three are different. The astrologers add two extra months every fifth year, so that their man-made calendar corresponds to the natural cycle of the sun and the moon. Going by that calculation, more than five months have passed since the thirteenth year of the Pandava exile." Bhishma said, pointing out that the Pandavas could have revealed themselves five months earlier, but not wanting to invite objections on technical grounds, they had waited this long to disclose their location. They had successfully fulfilled the conditions of their exile. Drona saw the logic in what Bhishma said and agreed with him.

Duryodhana was adamant. He insisted that by his calculations, the Pandavas' thirteen years of exile were not yet complete and they must suffer another twelve years of exile. He ordered Karna and Dusshasana to attack, to kill Arjuna and destroy the kingdom of Matsya.

Arjuna pays his respects

Before any from the Kauravas side could attack, Arjuna released three arrows. The first two landed at Bhishma and Drona's feet, indicating Arjuna's reverence for the two elders. His third arrow put the entire Kaurava army to sleep. Arjuna then asked Uttara to go and collect the upper garments of the four leaders of the Kaurava army—Duryodhana, Bhishma, Drona, and Karna.

"When they wake up, they will know that I spared their lives. This way, they will go away, humiliated," he said, adding that this disgrace would be a far bigger defeat for the Kauravas.

HISTORY AND CULTURE

MEASURING TIME

People in ancient India were conversant with the complexities involved in measuring time. They gave due attention to the movements of the sun and the moon across the twelve solar constellations and twenty-seven lunar constellations, or Nakshatras, while preparing a calendar. There is some time difference between a calendar based on the movement of the moon around the earth, and the one based on the earth's revolution around the sun. In order to align the twelve months of the lunar calendar with the six seasons and the movements of the sun and the moon, the notion of an extra month, or "adhik-maas," was created to be used from time to time. This was not too different from the contemporary method of adding an extra day in the leap year, every fourth year. Later calendars, such as the one shown here, were adapted to suit different regions of the country.

THIS FABRIC ALMANAC CORRESPONDS TO THE WESTERN YEARS 1871–72. THE COLUMNS ON BOTH SIDES SHOW THE TWELVE SIGNS OF THE ZODIAC.

AFTER

After both Susurma and the Kaurava army had been defeated, the Pandavas revealed their true identities to King Virata of Matsya.

ABHIMANYU DEPICTED IN A FOLK PAINTING FROM PAITHAN, MAHARASHTRA, INDIA

UTTARI'S MARRIAGE

The day after the attack was foiled, Virata came to his throne to find his advisor Kanka sitting on it with the maid Sairandhri. Gathered around him were Ballava, the cook, the eunuch Brihannala, the horse keeper Damagranthi, and Tantipala, the cowherd. Brihannala introduced Yudhishthira and his brothers to a bewildered Virata. Virata and Sudeshna apologized profusely to the Pandavas for having treated them as servants. As a gesture of goodwill, Virata offered his daughter Uttari to Arjuna in marriage. But Arjuna had taught Uttari for a year; she was like a daughter to him. He accepted her as his daughter-in-law, for his son Abhimanyu.

5
UDYOGA PARVA: THE BOOK OF EFFORT

PEACE NEGOTIATIONS
"Krishna Counsels the Pandava Leaders" is a 19th-century opaque watercolor-on-paper series on the Mahabharata. Krishna addresses various kings to broker peace between the Pandavas and Kauravas.

Udyoga Parva, or the Book of Effort, is the fifth parva in the Mahabharata. The word "udyoga" means effort, or perseverance. The parva recounts the Pandavas' return from exile. Indraprastha has been taken over by the Kauravas. The brothers start afresh and renew their efforts to recover their kingdom. They enlist Krishna's help to advocate on their behalf, but the Kauravas' refusal to share even the tiniest bit of land with their cousins makes war inevitable. More negotiations follow as the elders try to avert war. This section ends with the failure of all efforts at maintaining peace and describes the preparations for the war. The parva has 12 sub-parvas, 197 chapters, and 6,001 shlokas, or couplets.

"Think what is **best** for the **Kurus** and the **Pandavas**, what is in **accordance with dharma**, is appropriate, and also ensures **glory**. Let the messenger try to persuade them [Kurus] that **half** of the **kingdom** should **be returned** to Yudhishthira."

KRISHNA TO THE ASSEMBLY OF KINGS, UDYOGA PARVA: THE BOOK OF EFFORT

BEFORE

The end of the Pandavas' exile was marked by a battle with the Kauravas, who attacked kingdom of Matsya.

END OF EXILE

Duryodhana was convinced that the Pandavas had revealed themselves before the end of the thirteenth year. Since the last year had to be lived in complete anonymity, this meant that the Pandavas would have to go back into exile yet again. The Pandavas' victory over the Kauravas in the Matsya kingdom had ended with Abhimanyu's wedding to Virata's daughter, Uttari. The Pandavas took this opportunity to reconnect with their allies and plan the next steps toward regaining their share of the kingdom from the Kauravas.

Emissaries

The exile served, the Pandavas sent several messengers to Hastinapur to negotiate on their behalf. Duryodhana, firm in his belief that the Pandavas had failed to fulfill all the terms of anonymity, refused to share the kingdom with his cousins.

Once the celebration of Abhimanyu's marriage to the Matsya princess was over, the Pandavas met with their allies to discuss how best to try and regain Indraprastha. Among those present were their host, King Virata of Matsya; Draupadi's father, Drupada; Krishna; Balarama; and Satyaki, Krishna's friend and Arjuna's student.

Hailing the Pandavas' claim to their kingdom as just and truthful, Krishna suggested sending an emissary to Hastinapur to convey to the Kauravas that the Pandavas had completed their exile as stipulated and to persuade them to return Indraprastha to the Pandavas. The emissary, while there, could also gauge Duryodhana's intentions on which they could then base any further planning.

Krishna feared the worst; he was convinced that Duryodhana would never agree to return the Pandavas' share without a fight. To prepare themselves for any possible outcome, he suggested that, while the emissary was in Hastinapur, the Pandavas should reach out to their allies and other kings across the land, and so pre-empt the Kauravas.

The Pandavas' messenger

The Pandavas chose King Drupada's learned priest to state their case in Hastinapur. Briefing the Brahman on the negotiations, Drupada asked him to speak to the elders of the Kuru household about dharma and emphasize its importance. This would not only disengage the elders from Duryodhana's plans, but also keep him from influencing them.

MYTHOLOGY AND FOLKLORE

A LESSON IN HUMILITY

On learning that war was imminent, the sages Sanat and Kanva attempted to convince the Kauravas to share the kingdom with their cousins, and so avert the tragedy. Their pleas fell on deaf ears. The sages then narrated this story of Indra and Garuda to Duryodhana and his brothers, hoping they would take note of its moral teaching against arrogance.

Matali, Indra's charioteer, could not find a suitable groom for his beautiful daughter, Gunakeshi, until he met the serpent Sumukha. Unfortunately, Garuda, the king of birds, had already decided to eat Sumukha. The charioteer begged and pleaded, to no avail. Garuda simply ignored him. In desperation, Matali asked Indra to intervene. Summoned by Indra, Garuda displayed his prowess arrogantly. To teach him a lesson, Indra placed one hand on the king of birds. Garuda found that Indra's hand was so heavy that he could not bear the weight. Humbled, he agreed to let the young Sumukha live.

INDRA RIDING GARUDA
AS SCULPTED ON A THAI TEMPLE FACADE

Drupada advised his priest to speak of the hardships the Pandavas had suffered during their exile to the compassionate among the clan to gain their sympathy. He stressed that the presence of the priest in Hastinapur as an emissary of Pandavas would distract the Kauravas and keep them from preparing for war.

> "I am **as ready for peace as I am for war**. For the sake of dharma and artha, I can be mild. But **I can also be terrible**."
>
> YUDHISHTHIRA TO SANJAY, UDYOGA PARVA: THE BOOK OF EFFORT

The Kauravas' response

Duryodhana met the Pandavas' emissary but sent him back instantly. He maintained that even though the Pandavas had completed thirteen years of exile by the lunar calendar, they had shown themselves before the year ended on the solar calendar. According to the agreement of the wager, this meant their exile was to be extended by another twelve years.

He then sent the charioteer, Sanjay, to the Pandavas, to tell them not to return as they were not welcome in Indraprastha any longer—its citizens had long forgotten the brothers who had built the city but lightheartedly gambled it away.

Sanjay returned to Hastinapur with the Pandavas' response. He specifically relayed Arjuna's message, which said that though Ajuna was prepared for battle, he would be willing to lay down his weapons and forgive the Kauravas if the kingdom of Indraprastha was returned to its rightful ruler.

KAURAVAS' ASSEMBLY
Duryodhana had refused the Pandavas' request for a part of the kingdom. This illustration depicts Sanjay, the charioteer, relating the scene as it unfolded to Dhritarashtra.

The sages negotiate

Following Sanjay's return, sages such as Sanat and Kanva came to Hastinapur to explain to Dhritarashtra why the Kauravas' stand against their cousins' claims was unethical. They spoke of the might of Arjuna and Krishna, who were no ordinary men, and Nara and Narayana, born to establish dharma on earth. Moreover, Krishna was Vishnu—which mortal could defeat him?

They spoke of Garuda, the divine king of birds who was humbled by Indra, to caution Duryodhana against arrogance. But the eldest Kaurava's disdain and Dhritarashtra's silence led them to leave Hastinapur in despair, convinced that they could do nothing to save the Kuru household from the path of self-destruction.

AFTER

When Duryodhana refused to give the Pandavas their land, Krishna decided to go to Hastinapur himself.

THE FINAL NEGOTIATION
The emissaries' failure to get Duryodhana to return the Pandavas their kingdom resulted in a stalemate. A war seemed inevitable. Krishna then decided he would go to Hastinapur and use all the skills at his disposal to negotiate a deal so as to avoid war. But all his arguments to convince Duryodhana to part with the Pandavas' kingdom proved futile as well.

BEFORE

The Pandavas and Kauravas exchanged emissaries to negotiate the return of the Pandava kingdom, but Duryodhana, the eldest Kaurava, remained adamant in his refusal to part with Indraprastha.

DURYODHANA'S REFUSAL
Following the completion of their exile, the Pandavas sent a messenger to Hastinapur, asking for their land. In response, Duryodhana sent Sanjay, his father's charioteer, to tell the Pandavas not to return, as they were no longer welcome in Indraprastha.

"Let the **Kouravas survive** ... Let this lineage **not be destroyed**. O lord of men! May you **not be called** a **destroyer** of the **lineage**."

KRISHNA TO DURYODHANA,
UDYOGA PARVA: THE BOOK OF EFFORT

GUARDS SURROUNDING KRISHNA
This painting by Raja Ravi Varma shows Krishna in Hastinapur, negotiating on behalf of the Pandavas before the war. The Yadava warrior Satyaki has drawn his sword in response to Duryodhana's order to his guards to arrest Krishna.

Krishna's Negotiations with the **Kauravas**

As all emissaries came back empty-handed, Krishna decided to make one last attempt to negotiate a compromise between the two feuding parties and make the Kauravas see reason.

Krishna traveled to Hastinapur to negotiate a settlement with the Kauravas before the situation deteriorated any further. He noticed that Duryodhana had made special arrangements to ensure his comfort on the way. Tents had been set up along the highway and there were men holding pots of water and baskets of food on both sides of the street. But Krishna refused all hospitality. On reaching Hastinapur, he chose to stay in Vidura's house instead of the Kauravas' palace. "Only if my meeting with the Kauravas is successful will I break bread with them," he stated.

Vidura's autonomy

The impartial conduct of Dhritarashtra's younger brother was well known. Vidura never ate in the king's palace. This decision to be independent was deliberate, taken to maintain his autonomy and to express his displeasure at the way Dhritarashtra and his sons had treated the Pandavas.

The negotiations

At the palace, Krishna's meeting with Dhritarashtra and his sons did not go well. All Krishna's arguments fell on deaf ears.

"Why would I return a kingdom that I rule well? One whose citizens do not want to see the gamblers who squandered it away on the throne again?" Duryodhana questioned.

Krishna countered this argument by reminding Duryodhana that he had promised to return the kingdom to the Pandavas after their exile. And if he did not honor his word now, it would go against the principles of dharma. "You gave your word. The question is not whether you rule well, or if the citizens of Indraprastha are happy with your rule. According to the terms of the gambling match, the Pandavas could only claim Indraprastha if they endured thirteen years of exile. They have kept their word. Now it is your turn," he advised. Duryodhana refused.

Krishna then made a final plea and asked if, for the sake of peace, Duryodhana would part with the villages of Paniprastha, Tilprastha, Sonaprastha, Vrikshprastha, and Indraprastha, so that the Pandavas could live with some dignity.

"Not even the smallest bit of territory will I cede to the Pandavas," Duryodhana said, rejecting Krishna's proposal in no uncertain terms. Dhritarashtra, who had listened to all of Krishna's entreaties, did not say a word, supporting his sons with his silence. There was no room at all for Krishna to negotiate any further. »

ANALYSIS

THE ART OF NEGOTIATION

The *Arthashastra*, the treatise on statecraft, enumerates four methods to make people do one's bidding: Saam, Daam, Dand, and Bhed—Negotiation, Bribe, Punishment, and Dissension. Krishna used all four when he visited Hastinapur to negotiate a deal between the two sides. Using both logic and emotion, he first tried to convince the Kauravas to do the right thing according to dharma when he asked them to keep their promise. When that did not work, he was willing to settle for five villages for the Pandavas, and ultimately brought down his demand to five houses in one village. As a last resort, Krishna narrated tales of the Pandavas' prowess to instill fear in the Kauravas. When none of these worked, he decided to divide and conquer the Kauravas.

KRISHNA IN CULTURE
In this 1998 Kathakali performance at the Guruvayur temple, Kerala, India, Kalamandalam Gopi plays Krishna. A friend of the Pandavas, Krishna did his best to avert war and bring peace.

"**Make peace** with the Pandavas. They are **wise and brave**. They have great enterprise, and are **self-controlled** and **extremely learned**."

KRISHNA TO DURYODHANA, UDYOGA PARVA: THE BOOK OF EFFORT

Krishna's premonition

Duryodhana's stark refusal reminded Krishna of an incident when, following a solar eclipse, kings from all over Bharatavarsha had gathered in Kurukshetra to purify themselves by bathing in the five lakes there. He had been captivated by the pomp and glory of the assembled royalty, but had been overcome by a foreboding that the next time these kings would gather in Kurukshetra, it would be to meet death. With Duryodhana's refusal to budge from his stance, war appeared imminent, and Krishna's fears seemed to be coming true.

"By dishonoring your word," Krishna said to Duryodhana, "you have destroyed the very foundation of dharma. By refusing to compromise for the sake of peace, you have shown yourself ill-suited to rule. You must, therefore, be vanquished."

Krishna stood up and spoke. "Let there be war on the plains of Kurukshetra between those who uphold dharma and those who follow the law of the jungle. Let the earth drink the blood of those who do not deserve her bounty," he proclaimed to the assembly.

Duryodhana was deeply angered. "How dare an upstart cowherd threaten me!" he exclaimed, and ordered his guards to seize Krishna.

With their spears pointing at Krishna, Duryodhana's guards filled the court. The assembled court looked on, shocked by these orders—arresting Krishna was unthinkable.

The divine form of Krishna

"Are you sure you want to do this? You think of me as a single person and wish to capture me," Krishna said to Duryodhana and started laughing.

What then manifest was a vision that terrified all present; Krishna appeared not as an ordinary mortal but as a being with a thousand heads, grinding entire worlds between his teeth. He towered over the gathered assembly, his head reaching beyond the skies and his feet beyond the seas.

The pantheon of gods were visible in him. Brahma, the god of creation, appeared on his forehead and Rudra, a form of Shiva, on his chest. The four guardians of the world were on his arms. The forms of Yakshas, Gandharvas, and Rakshasas were also visible.

Balarama and Arjuna could be seen on his arms. Yudhishthira, Bhima, Nakula, and Sahadeva were on his back. His weapons—the disc called Sudarshan; the mace, Kaumodaki; the bow, Saranga; the sword called Nandaka; and the conch shell Panchajanya—were all visible.

Fire and smoke erupted from his eyes, nose, and ears. Rays like the sun's emanated from his body. Terrified by the vision, the kings assembled in the court closed their eyes.

Dhritarashtra's wish

Unable to see, but perturbed by the tense, charged atmosphere, the blind king Dhritarashtra cried out, "What is it? What is it that all of you see?" But none present could summon the words or the courage to reply.

When he got no answer, the king turned to Krishna and asked that he be granted the power of sight. Krishna obliged: for the first time in his life, the blind king could see. The vision brought tears to his eyes, and the realization that, having seen the Supreme, he did not want to see anything else. Instantly, the vision was eclipsed. When light returned, Krishna was gone.

Kunti's wisdom

Before leaving, Krishna met Kunti to tell her all that had transpired. He asked his aunt if she had any advice for her sons, now that war was inevitable. She responded by asking him to remind the Pandavas of dharma and the righteousness of always fighting for their rights.

After Krishna's visit, the Kauravas sent their final emissary to formally declare war against the Pandavas.

HISTORY AND CULTURE

THE MENACING FOURSOME

Duryodhana's blatant disregard of the Pandavas' claim was ably abetted by his brother Dusshasana, maternal uncle Shakuni, and best friend, Karna. His confidence in these three was strong enough for him to ignore the advice of the elders. This idea of the menacing foursome has found its way into the Hindi language as "Chandal Chaukadi"—loosely translated as "villainous quartet." Shakuni's schemes had a larger endgame—unknown to Duryodhana, his uncle was hellbent on the ruin of the entire Kuru clan, determined to avenge the humiliation suffered by him and his family at Bhishma's hands.

Karna, on the other hand, considered Duryodhana his friend for life, and would stand by Duryodhana as steadfastly as he believed Duryodhana had stood by him.

"**Beneficial words** were spoken by me ... but he did not accept them ... all of them are under **Duryodhana's control**."

KRISHNA TO KUNTI, UDYOGA PARVA: THE BOOK OF EFFORT

DURYODHANA'S ARROGANCE
Duryodhana (centre) strikes an arrogant pose in this Chauu performance of the Mahabharata. The dance form originates in the eastern states of India.

"**I do not see** the **slightest bit of wrong** that I have committed. All of you ... blame only me ... The **Pandavas happily agreed** to the gambling match ... How was this **my crime**?"

DURYODHANA TO KRISHNA, UDYOGA PARVA: THE BOOK OF EFFORT

AFTER

After his attempts to broker peace with the Kauravas failed, Krishna decided to pay a visit to Duryodhana's friend, Karna.

IMPORTANT MEETING
Krishna knew a war between the Kauravas and Pandavas would be bloody and bring about the destruction of the Kuru clan. He hoped he could convince Karna to switch sides; after all, he knew something about Karna that would swing his decision in the Pandavas' favor.

VISHNU IN HIS DIVINE FORM
Vishnu as the Cosmic Man (Vishvarupa) is portrayed here in his destructive form, with four arms, each holding one of his attributes: a conch shell, a lotus flower, a mace, and the weapon called Sudarshana Chakra (meaning "beautiful disc"). The figures that cover his body refer to his role as the Universal Man who encompasses all of creation: the Vishvarupa (literally "all forms").

Karna's Test of Character

The son of Kunti and Surya the sun god, Karna was an acclaimed warrior and Arjuna's equal. Knowing that the battle would tilt in favor of the Pandavas if he persuaded Karna to defect to their side, Krishna revealed a secret that put Karna in a dilemma.

BEFORE

The Pandavas had sent many emissaries to the Kauravas to negotiate a compromise.

WAR DECLARED

All their efforts had, however, come to naught. Duryodhana had remained adamant in his decision, refusing to part with even a the tiniest piece of land. Krishna, who had been the Pandavas' last hope, had no choice but declare war on the Kauravas. Even as both parties scrambled to gather allies, Krishna made a last-ditch effort to avert war by deciding to speak to Karna, whose support in the war would be critical to Kauravas' victory. On his way, he met Kunti and told her of his meeting with the Kauravas.

"O Janardana! **I cannot be false** to **Dhritarashtra's** intelligent **son because** of death, bondage, **fear,** or **greed**."

KARNA TO KRISHNA, UDYOGA PARVA: THE BOOK OF EFFORT

ART AND LITERATURE

RASHMIRATHI

Written by the Hindi poet Ramdhari Singh "Dinkar," *Rashmirathi* is a retelling of the Mahabharata from the perspective of Karna and was first published in 1954. The title is a composite of the words "rashmi" and "rathi," which means the radiant one who rides a chariot. It alludes to Karna's origins as the son of the sun god. The poem portrays Karna as an unsung hero and deliberates on the injustice meted out to him. It also discusses his relationship with Kunti and the Pandavas, the rivalry between him and Arjuna, and his loyalty to Duryodhana.

After his meeting with Kunti, Krishna went to visit to Karna. "Why do you fight alongside the Kauravas even when you know that Duryodhana is in the wrong? Why support him when you know that going back on the agreement, refusing to part with even a small piece of land, is unrighteous?" Krishna asked the king. "If even now you say that you will not fight for this unjust cause, it may make Duryodhana rethink his stand and bring about peace."

"What you're asking for is impossible," Karna replied. "I cannot abandon the man who befriended me, who stood by me when the world laughed at me for being a charioteer's son. I will never do that."

Krishna pointed out that blind loyalty to one who had gone back on his word was against dharma. But Karna was unmoved. He felt he owed Duryodhana everything.

A secret revealed

Seeing Karna firm in his decision to stand by his friend, Krishna revealed a secret that Karna had for long yearned to know—the secret of his birth. "You are Kunti's firstborn, from her union with Surya, the sun god. This makes Pandu, Kunti's husband, your father in the eyes of the law. The Pandavas, whom you are preparing to fight, are your own brothers. Indeed, you are the eldest Pandava."

Krishna then described Karna's future—if he joined hands with the Pandavas. Karna, as the eldest of Kunti's sons, would be the one to ascend the throne of Indraprastha. His mother and brothers would embrace him with open arms. The Pandavas would love and serve him faithfully. And as Kunti had decreed that Draupadi would be shared by the brothers, she would be his queen as well.

"Come with me and you will **become a king** … Are you not tempted by the offer of a kingdom? **Do you not desire to rule the earth** that I will give to you?"

KRISHNA TO KARNA, UDYOGA PARVA: THE BOOK OF EFFORT

Steadfast Karna

As he heard these words, Karna knew that Krishna spoke the truth, and a lifetime of alienation washed away. He was no longer the boy of unknown origins, abandoned at birth.

After the rejection he had faced all his life, the idea of going into the Pandava fold was tantalizing. It held the promise of identity, respect, love, and status. Yet Karna declined. Whatever respect and love he had received so far had been from Duryodhana, not the Pandavas. Closing the door on the temptation Krishna dangled, Karna declared, "Your bribes and blandishments do not move me—I stand true to my word. Righteous or not, my loyalty lies with Duryodhana. I'm prepared to die for him, and even fight my own brothers."

AFTER

Despite his friendship with Duryodhana, the elders of the Kuru clan did not like Karna.

KARNA'S DECISION

To Bhishma, Karna was an ambitious upstart who encouraged Duryodhana's foolish ways. On the eve of the war, when Karna declared that he would single-handedly defeat the Pandavas for his friend, Bhishma laughed, reminding Karna that the Pandavas were superior warriors. "You seem to have forgotten that Arjuna alone defended Virata from the Kauravas. And it was Arjuna who saved Duryodhana from the Gandharvas while you looked on helplessly! You are a fool to think you are his equal!"

An enraged Karna declared that he would not set foot on the battlefield while Bhishma commanded the Kaurava armies. Duryodhana was alarmed. These two men were his two best hopes to win the war, but he could not get them to reconcile. Eventually, Duryodhana let Karna go—if Bhishma did not fight, neither would Drona nor the rest of the Kauravas. Besides, Karna could rest while the others fought, and be ready when he was really needed.

KARNA'S CONUNDRUM
This Bikaner-style painting from Rajasthan, India, depicts Krishna persuading Karna not to support the Kauravas but claim his birthright as the eldest Pandava.

BEFORE

Despite Krishna's best efforts to mediate peace, war became a reality for both sides.

PREPARATIONS BEGIN

The Kauravas had sent a formal declaration of war to the Pandavas through the emissary Uluka. With this final call, both sides began to prepare for war. Krishna had, in his effort to undermine and shake the Kauravas' confidence, attempted to sway Karna's loyalty. But Karna remained steadfast—he would not let down a friend who had stood up for him when the world looked down upon him as a lowly charioteer's son.

Choosing **Sides**

With war declared, the time had come for all the kings of Aryavarta to decide their allegiance. As the Pandavas and Kauravas tried to win support, the burning question remained—which side would the kings choose?

The kings of Aryavarta were torn between the two factions, for many on both sides were friends, and in some cases even related by blood or marriage.

Shalya deceived

Shalya, the king of Madra, was the maternal uncle of the Pandava twins Nakula and Sahadeva. It was understood that he would join the Pandavas. On hearing of the war, Shalya started out for Kurukshetra with his armies. As he made his way to the battlefield, he came across organized rest camps with food and drink, fodder for the animals, and entertainment.

Shalya assumed that it was the Pandavas who were responsible for these provisions. By the time he was told these arrangements had made by the Kauravas it was too late. He had partaken of the Kauravas' hospitality, and felt obliged to fight on their side against his own nephews.

Shalya was dismayed at the prospect of fighting against his nephews, but Krishna pointed out the advantages of the situation. "We can use this as an opportunity to undermine the Kauravas. I am certain that they will ask you to serve as Karna's charioteer to humiliate the Pandavas and boost Karna's ego. When you ride out into the battlefield, try and make Karna insecure by repeatedly praising Arjuna. Insecure men make terrible warriors."

Balarama's choice

After Arjuna managed to get Krishna's support in the war, it was time for both sides to approach Balarama, Krishna's elder brother.

Both Duryodhana and Bhima went personally to Balarama to ask for his support.

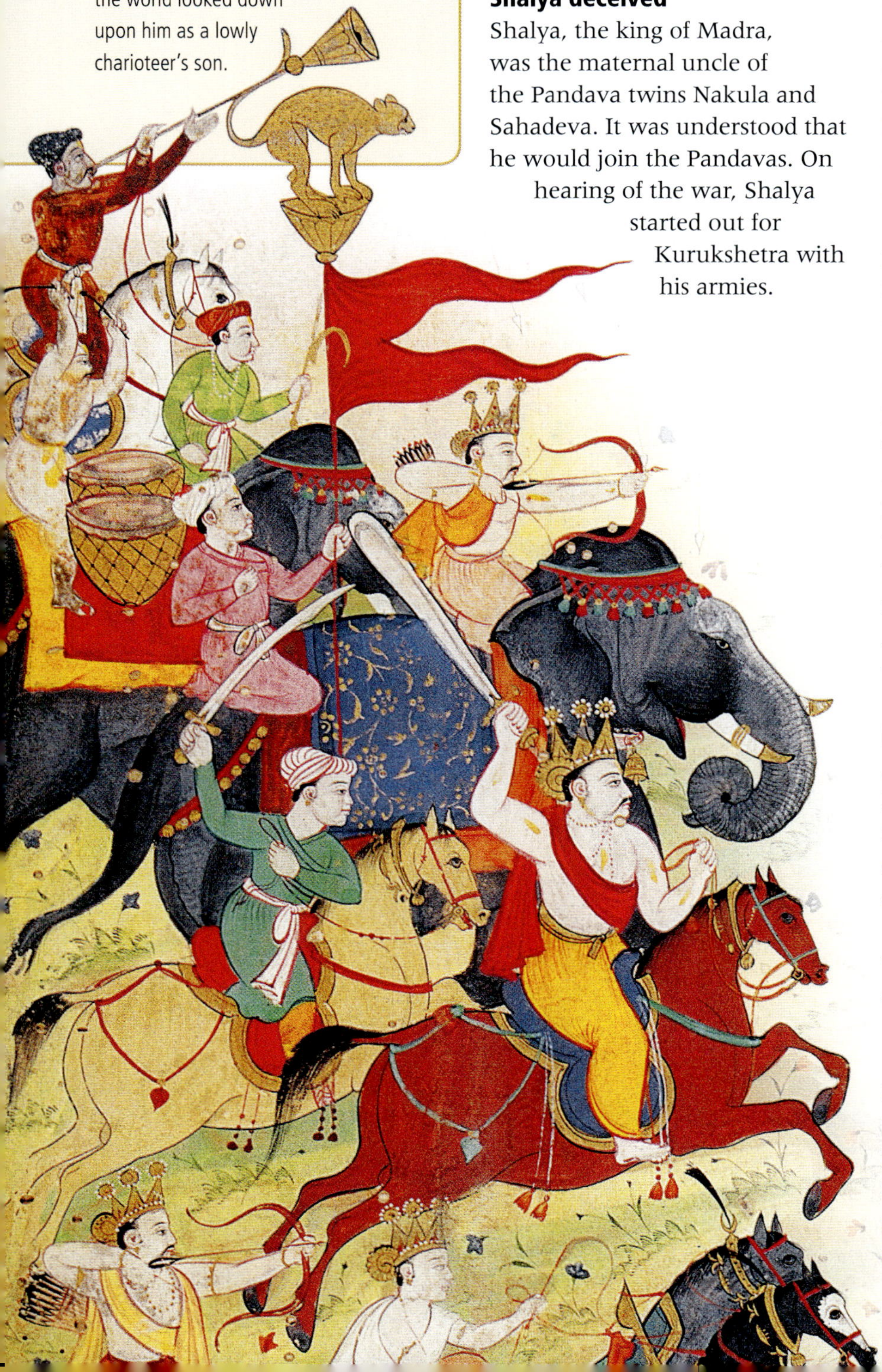

FIERCE FACE-OFF
This illustration of the two warring sides is from the *Razmnama* ,or "Book of War." This Persian translation of the epic talks about the many military strategies and formations.

A DIFFICULT CHOICE
An 18th-century representation from south India of Krishna's elder brother Balarama, who chose to distance himself from the war.

It was a difficult choice for the Yadava, as both of them were his cousins. They were also his students—he had taught them the art of mace-fighting.

The elder Yadava could not help but make one last entreaty to the warring cousins. He begged them to forgive each other, and not destroy their families and peers over a mere piece of land. Seeing that his words were falling on deaf ears, Balarama made his decision—he would not fight the war at all, but go on a pilgrimage instead. Leaving his students Balarama counseled them, "If you insist on fighting, do it honorably, uphold the rules of warfare. Never strike anyone who is unarmed or helpless. Never strike below the waist or on the back."

LIST

THE PANDAVA SIDE

- Dhrishtadyumna, Draupadi's brother
- Drupada, king of Panchala
- Virata, king of Matsya
- Sahadeva, king of Magadha
- Satyaki, a Yadava chief
- Dhristaketu, king of Chedi
- Vrihatkshatra, king of Kekaya

On neither side

Another king who chose to remain neutral in the war was the king of Udupi, who took on the responsibility of feeding both the Pandava and Kaurava armies. Folklore has it that each day the king managed to serve the exact amount of food required for the soldiers. When asked how he did this, the king answered, "Each night I serve Krishna boiled peanuts, which he likes to eat. I count the number he has eaten and multiply it by a thousand. If he eats ten peanuts, I know ten thousand people will die in battle the next day. That is how I always cook the right amount."

A rejected king

As Arjuna was leaving Dwaraka, Rukmi, Krishna's brother-in-law, went to him. "There's no need to fear the Kauravas," he said, "I have a great bow that the gods have given to me. With me by your side, victory is sure to be yours." Arjuna, bristling at Rukmi's implication that he feared the Kauravas, pointedly refused Rukmi's help. A humiliated Rukmi went to the Kauravas to offer support. But Duryodhana too rejected him; it would be beneath his dignity to accept one whom his enemy had rejected. In this way, an eager warrior did not get to participate in the war at all.

LIST

THE KAURAVA SIDE

- Drona, of the Bharadvaja clan of priests
- Ashwatthama, Drona's son, king of north Panchala
- Kripa, of the Gautama clan of priests
- Shakuni, king of Gandhara
- Karna, king of Anga
- Jayadratha, king of Sindhu
- Shalya, king of Madra
- Kritavarma, a Yadava chief
- Bhurishrava, king of Bahlika
- Sudakshina, king of Trigarta
- Srutayudha, king of Kalinga

"On learning that **a great force** was being gathered for the sons of Pandu, Dhritarashtra's son also **assembled many lords of the earth**."

SAGE VAISHAMPAYANA TO JANAMEJAYA, UDYOGA PARVA: THE BOOK OF EFFORT

AFTER

The rivalry with their cousins and a greed for power united all the Kauravas. But there were two who stood out as exceptions.

VIKARNA AND YUYUTSU

Duryodhana's brothers Vikarna and Yuyutsu did not approve of his deeds. Both of them had argued against Draupadi being staked in the game and disrobed in public. Yet when it came to an actual war, Vikarna chose to remain faithful to his immediate family, choosing blood over dharma. Yuyutsu, the son of Dhritarashtra by a maid, put justice first and crossed over to the Pandava side.

KRISHNA'S OLDER BROTHER

Balarama

"I will come to the aid of neither Partha, nor Duryodhana … this is the decision I have arrived at. Go and fight in accordance with dharma."

BALARAMA TO DURYODHANA, UDYOGA PARVA: THE BOOK OF EFFORT

BALARAMA
Usually depicted as fair-skinned and wearing blue clothes, with a garland of flowers around his neck, Balarama is shown carrying either a plow or a mace on his left shoulder.

Krishna's elder brother Balarama is believed to be an incarnation of Adi-Ananta-Sesha, the thousand-hooded serpent in whose coils Vishnu rested. Balarama's refusal to fight in the Mahabharata war has made many see him as a form of Shiva, the ascetic.

In Jain tradition, he is considered superior to Krishna because he refused to participate in the Kurukshetra War. In the next world cycle, according to Jain scriptures, Balarama will be reborn as a Tirthankara ahead of Krishna because of his adherence to ahimsa, or non-violence.

A divine child

Balarama's birth was prophetic. Kansa, the king of Mathura, had heard that his sister Devaki's eighth child would be his nemesis. The king imprisoned his sister and brother-in-law and killed each of their newborn children. The sages told the couple that their seventh child would be the herald of Vishnu and the eighth would be Vishnu himself. When Devaki conceived the seventh child, a goddess called Yogamaya moved the unborn child into the womb of Vasudeva's first wife, Rohini, and Kansa was told that Devaki had a miscarriage. This incident earned Balarama an alternative name, Sankarshan, which means "the one who was transferred between two wombs," or "the one who joins two families."

In another legend, it is believed that Vishnu himself placed two strands of his hair, one white and one black, in Devaki's womb. The white strand became Balarama, Devaki's seventh child. He was named "Rama" for his divine qualities and "Bala" for his extraordinary strength. The dark strand of hair was later born as the dark-skinned Krishna.

Early years

Balarama grew up as a cowherd in Gokul, close to present-day Mathura. After Jarasandha's repeated attacks on Mathura, Krishna and Balarama traveled to Dwaraka, ruled by King Revata. The princess, Revati, had grown into a giantess, and no human agreed to marry her. Balarama married her and in return, the pleased king gave him Dwaraka.

Rage and forgiveness

Balarama taught the art of mace warfare to both Duryodhana and Bhima, but reserved a soft spot for the former. It has been speculated that Balarama is a form of Shiva, guileless in nature and unable to see the flaws of the Kauravas. When Duryodhana declared that his daughter Lakshmani would not marry Krishna's son Samba as planned, Samba tried to abduct Lakshmani but he was caught and put in prison. Balarama went to Hastinapur and demanded that Samba be released. Duryodhana refused and started insulting the Yadavas. In a rage, Balarama assumed a giant form, his head reaching the sky. He swung his plough and hooked it on the foundations of Hastinapur and dragged the great city toward the sea. Duryodhana, realizing that he was no ordinary human, fell at Balarama's feet and begged forgiveness. Balarama was quick to anger but also easily pacified; he forgave the Kauravas and returned to Dwaraka.

Opting out of war

Before the war, both Duryodhana and Bhima tried to persuade their teacher to join them. Balarama's effort to convince the two not to go to war went in vain; neither was willing to give up their hatred. Balarama made the decision to opt out of the war and go on a pilgrimage instead. As he left, he advised his students to fight fairly and by the rules.

The end

After the war, the Yadava clan came to an horrific end when the men started fighting each other. There was mass slaughter and the entire race was destroyed. Watching his family die, Balarama lost his will to live. It is believed he died while meditating where the Somnath temple stands in present-day Gujarat.

HISTORY AND CULTURE

BALARAMA PURNIMA

Balarama Purnima is celebrated to mark Balarama's birth anniversary, which falls on the full moon day of the Hindu month of Shravan. The deity is given a ritual bath, dressed in new clothes and ornaments, and fed special sweetmeats.

Balarama is worshipped as Balabhadra, along with his siblings Krishna (as Jagannath) and Subhadra, in the Jagannath temple at Puri, Odisha. Millions of people line up to see the annual pilgrimage in which the deities are ritually brought out in a procession. The siblings are also worshipped in the Baladeview temple Kendrapara, and the Ananta Vasudeva temple Bhubaneswar, both in Odisha. Most temples dedicated to Krishna also include an idol of Balarama; the brothers are often worshipped jointly as Krishna–Balarama.

BIOGRAPHY IN BRIEF

- **Conceived** by Devaki, Balarama was divinely transferred to the womb of his stepmother Rohini.
- **Named** "Rama" for one who brings good, with the prefix "Bala" added for his strength.
- **Grew up** with foster parents Nanda and Yashoda to escape the wrath of the cruel King Kansa, who had vowed to kill all the children of his sister Devaki.
- **At a wrestling competition** organized by Kansa at Mathura, the king instructed formidable wrestlers Chanura and Mushtika to kill Krishna and Balarama, but Mushtika was easily killed by Balarama.
- **Under the tutelage of Sage Sandipani**, Balarama was educated in ways suitable for a Kshatriya.
- **After fleeing Mathura,** Balarama married Revati, daughter of the king of Dwaraka, earning the city of Dwaraka for the Yadavas.

LATE 19TH-CENTURY RAJASTHANI WATERCOLOR ON PAPER DEPICTING BALARAMA AND REVATI.

- **Taught Bhima and Duryodhana** the art of wrestling and fighting with a mace.
- **Refused to join either side** in the Kurukshetra War, and instead went on a pilgrimage.
- **Chose to die** after being traumatized by the infighting and destruction within his clan.

ADI-ANANTA-SESHA REINCARNATE

Balarama is often seen as an incarnation of Adi-Ananta-Sesha, or the thousand-hooded serpent, who in turn is considered a manifestation of Vishnu. This sculpture shows Brahma and Shiva praying to Vishnu as he rests on the divine serpent, while his consort Lakshmi massages his feet.

BEFORE

With peace negotiations having failed, both sides scrambled to prepare for war. The Kauravas had ten armies on their side, while the Pandavas had seven.

SIDES TAKEN

Karna, despite having been told about the reality of his birth, decided to stand by his friend Duryodhana and not go to his brothers, the Pandavas. Shalya, the king of Madra, Nakula and Sahadeva's maternal uncle, had been deceived by circumstances to fight on the side of the Kauravas. Krishna, with his Yadava followers, had not yet announced his allegiance. He had a powerful army and both the Kauravas and Pandavas were keen to meet him and get his support.

Krishna and His Narayani Army

Now that war was imminent, both the Kauravas and the Pandavas were gathering as many allies as they could. What neither side knew as yet was which side Krishna would choose. Both Duryodhana and Arjuna went to Dwaraka to ask for Krishna's allegiance.

Duryodhana set off for Dwaraka to seek an audience with Krishna around the same time as Arjuna. On entering Krishna's chambers, Duryodhana found him taking a nap. Deciding to wait until Krishna woke up, he sat down at the head of the bed. A little later, Arjuna entered the room, and took his place at the foot of the bed.

Both cousins were confident of Krishna's support for different reasons. Duryodhana was sure of Krishna's patronage because his daughter, Lakshmani, was married to Krishna's son, Samba. The Pandavas were Krishna's maternal cousins, and Arjuna had married Krishna's sister, Subhadra. This led him to believe that Krishna would give his pleas some consideration.

On waking, Krishna greeted Arjuna and Duryodhana, then looked at his cousin. "What brings you here?" he asked Arjuna.

Nervous that Krishna would grant Arjuna what he himself wanted to claim, Duryodhana interrupted, "I came in before Arjuna. Surely my request gets precedence over his."

ARJUNA'S CHOICE

This 18th-century watercolor from Himachal Pradesh, India, titled "Arjuna Chooses Lord Krishna As His Charioteer."

Arjuna's choice

Unmoved by Duryodhana's outburst, Krishna replied, "You may have arrived before him, but I saw Arjuna before I saw you. So I shall ask him first." Turning to Arjuna, he asked, "Which do you choose—my army or me unarmed?"

Duryodhana's breath caught in his throat. If he chose the army, Arjuna could amass one hundred million Yadava soldiers, tilting the scales in the Pandavas' favor. These soldiers, known as the Narayani army, were said to be equal to Krishna in strength and skill and were unassailable warriors famed for their valor. How could Krishna weigh against all this, especially now that he had decided neither to bear arms nor fight in the battle?

To Duryodhana's deep amazement, Arjuna chose without a moment's hesitation. "You. I want you by my side when I fight the Kauravas, not your army," he declared.

"Today, **I have come to you first**. From ancient times, the virtuous serve those who arrive first … You always deserve honor. **You always follow virtuous conduct.**"

DURYODHANA TO KRISHNA, UDYOGA PARVA: THE BOOK OF EFFORT

ANALYSIS

THE KAURAVAS' CHOICES

Though the Kauravas lived in wealth, their life was filled with envy and bitterness. In contrast, though they lived in poverty, in forests, in exile, as dependants in the house of their uncle, the Pandavas' life was rich in learning. This shows that the presence of Lakshmi, goddess of wealth, does not guarantee wisdom. On the other hand, Saraswati, goddess of knowledge, brings wisdom as well as prosperity wherever she goes.

THE WAIT

This terracotta panel on the Gopinath temple in Dasghara in West Bengal, India, shows Arjuna (left) sitting by Krishna's feet as he sleeps, while Duryodhana (right) sits near his head.

Duryodhana's delight
The Kaurava prince, who had been concerned that Arjuna would choose Krishna's army, was overjoyed. Not only would the Narayani army be his, but Krishna, a noted warrior, would not fight in the battle.

Duryodhana heaved a sigh of relief at this development. With the Narayani, he had a total of eleven armies fighting for the Kauravas, while the Pandavas had only seven: victory would surely be his.

Arjuna was pleased, as he valued the power of strategy more than the might of arms. To him, Krishna was more than all the armies of the Pandavas and Kauravas put together.

The Yadava chieftain had offered Arjuna a choice between what he was and what he had. Arjuna had chosen the former, while Duryodhana prized the latter. This had revealed the difference between the cousins. One sought the soul, where the other was satisfied with matter.

AFTER

The day of the war saw all armies assembled in Kurukshetra. King Dhritarashtra's charioteer, Sanjay, blessed with divine sight, would describe each battle to the king and queen.

THE FACE-OFF
The rules of war were announced. The commanders of both armies invited warriors to change sides or drop out if they wished to do so. Yudhishthira went up to Bhishma and Drona and took their blessings. Arjuna entered the battlefield and saw the lineup of all his near and dear ones prepared to fight to the death. The sudden realization that all this blood would be shed for a quarrel over a piece of land shook him. It made him doubt himself, and he lowered his bow. Krishna, acting as his charioteer, chose then to speak to him about his duty and the path to righteousness.

6

BHISHMA PARVA: THE BOOK OF BHISHMA

THE KAURAVA COMMANDER-IN-CHIEF
This 17th-century Mughal-style painting depicts various scenes from the Bhishma Parva. Bhishma's last moments, as he lay on a bed of arrows for eight days before his death, are captured. The great warrior was fatally wounded by Arjuna on the tenth day of the war.

Bhishma Parva, or the Book of Bhishma, is the sixth parva in the Mahabharata. It is titled after Bhishma, the Kuru patriarch, commander-in-chief of the Kaurava army for the first ten days of the Kurukshetra War. The parva includes the Bhagavad Gita, the discourse between Krishna and Arjuna just before the battle begins. Sanjay, Dhritarashtra's charioteer, who is blessed with divine sight, describes the battles being fought in detail. The armies clash, and both sides are well matched in strength and valor. The parva has 4 sub-parvas, 117 chapters, and contains 5,381 shlokas, or couplets.

"On seeing him ready for battle … the **Pandavas trembled in fear,** like a herd of cattle on seeing a lion. He **protected your army** … Every day he **killed ten thousand warriors** … Like **a tree struck by the wind, he has been killed.**"

SANJAY TO DHRITARASHTRA, BHISHMA PARVA: THE BOOK OF BHISHMA

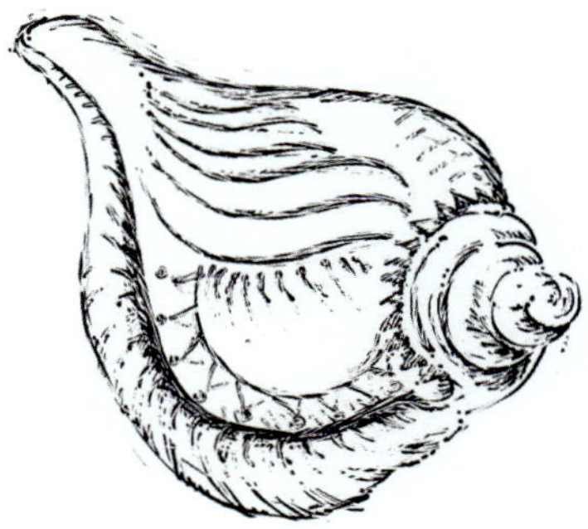

THE SACRED LAND

Kurukshetra

"Let this entire circle of **kshatriyas** meet their death … in Kurukshetra, the most **sacred spot** in the three worlds.**"**

KRISHNA, UDYOGA PARVA: THE BOOK OF EFFORT

A CENTER OF WORSHIP
Reportedly Duryodhana's hiding place during the war, the Brahma Sarovar at Kurukshetra annually draws thousands of worshippers who come to take a holy bath during a solar eclipse.

MAPPING KURUKSHETRA
A city in the Indian state of Haryana, Kurukshetra is located 100 miles (160 km) north of Delhi, the capital city of India.

Named after King Kuru, the Kauravas' ancestor, Kurukshetra is best known as the barren stretch of land where the battle of Mahabharata was fought. Specifically, Kurukshetra is where Krishna delivered the divine sermon—the Bhagavad Gita—to Arjuna. After failing to negotiate for peace with the Kauravas, Krishna declared, "Let there be war at Kurukshetra between those who uphold dharma and those who follow the law of the jungle."

The present-day city and district of Kurukshetra came into being after independence. Historically, the old town in this area was Thanesar, which contained an area called Kulchetar that tradition identified with the "Kurukshetra" of the Mahabharata.

In holy books

According to the Mahabharata, Kurukshetra was not restricted to the present-day city but to a much larger area of more than 62 miles (100 km). It had a number of tanks, temples, and other holy places connected with ancient traditions. Kurukshetra is mentioned in the Atharva Veda, the Brahmanas, and, of course, the Mahabharata. It is said that Kurukshetra was also visited by Gautam Buddha, who may have given discourses here.

In history

According to archaeologists, the Thanesar–Kurukshetra area was first explored in the 1870s by Alexander Cunningham. He revealed that Chinese pilgrim Hieun Tsang (602–664 CE) had also visited the site. Historians believe that this land reached the height of its progress during the reign of King Harshavardhana (590–647 CE) of the Pushyabhuti dynasty. Since then, several excavations have taken place in Kurukshetra and the area around it. The earliest archeological remains found were the ruins of Dudakheri, near Thanesar, where iron shards, late Harappan pottery, and Painted Grey Ware were discovered. Noted archaeologist B.B. Lal identified Painted Grey Ware culture sites dating to the time of the Mahabharata. Finds here included a bull-shaped pendant, terracotta beads, semi-precious stones, pottery, and models of intact graves.

Archaeologists have also found evidence of Kushana (1st–3rd century), Gupta (4th–6th century), and Rajput (8th–12th century) periods here. It is a known fact that Guru Nanak, the Sikh Guru, visited Kurukshetra in 1504 during a solar eclipse. All Sikh Gurus, except the second one, are said to have been here. The area was also a Sufi center, and the tomb of the Sufi saint Sheikh Chilli, a spiritual teacher of Mughal prince Dara Shikoh (1615–1659 CE), lies here.

In the eighteenth century, Kurukshetra changed hands between the Mughals and the Sikhs. It came under British rule in 1805. Post independence, many refugees from Pakistan settled here. When the state of Haryana was formed in 1968, the new government decided to revive the traditional importance of Kurukshetra by naming the city and district after it. The city is now recognized as an important Hindu pilgrimage center. During eclipses, hundred of thousands of pilgrims take a dip in the Brahma Sarovar and Sannihit Sarovar ponds in Kurukshetra. Jyotisar, 3 miles (5 km) away, is another sacred town, believed to be the spot where the Bhagavad Gita was spoken.

ART AND LITERATURE

AN EPIC POEM

Kurukshetra is an epic poem written by the famous Hindi poet Ramdhari Singh "Dinkar" in 1946.

The highly celebrated narrative poem is in a dialogue form between Bhima and Yudhishthira, based on the Shanti Parva of the Mahabharata. In the poem, Dinkar accepts that war is destructive but argues that it is necessary for the protection of freedom. The poem was written at a time when the memories of World War II were fresh in the mind of the poet.

BEFORE

As the war drew closer, members of the Kuru clan had to decide on which side their allegiance lay. Nobody knew, however, whom Krishna would support.

TALLYING THE NUMBERS
Both the Kauravas and the Pandavas wanted Krishna on their side. Krishna offered the warring cousins a choice between him, alone and unarmed, and his entire Narayani army. Arjuna chose Krishna without his army; Duryodhana was pleased to have the Narayani army on his side.

Krishna's elder brother Balarama refused to lend his support to either side as he was opposed to the idea of war. Krishna's brother-in-law Rukmi could not fight as he was rejected by both sides.

ANALYSIS

FINAL ALLEGIANCES

Loyalty and allegiance are recurring themes in Indian epics. The composition of the two warring sides in the Mahabharata war remained fluid until the very last minute when the leaders of both armies permitted the assembled warriors to switch sides or even opt out of the war completely, if that was what they wanted to do.

Duryodhana's brother Vikarna, who had openly voiced his protest against Draupadi's humiliation at the dice game, could not abandon his brothers and joined the war on the Kauravas' side. His half-brother Yuyutsu, however, went over to the Pandavas' side, to fight for what he understood was right.

ASSEMBLING ON THE BATTLEFIELD
This painting shows the armies of the Pandavas and Kauravas confronting each other. The actual battle has yet to begin.

The **Meeting** of the **Armies**

The Pandavas spent the night before the battle praying to Durga, the goddess of war. As the day dawned, both armies took their places, confronting each other on the battlefield in Kurukshetra.

The beginning of the war warranted manifold preparations. Both sides set up camps for all the kings and their armies. From conducting myriad rituals to propitiate the gods and taking care of the material needs of soldiers, to working out war strategies and planning every possible move against the enemy forces, the commanders on both side left no stone unturned.

In the palace at Hastinapur, Dhritarashtra's charioteer Sanjay, given the gift of divine sight to enable him to witness the events on the battlefield, prepared to narrate every detail to the blind king and his blindfolded queen.

> "When the **two armies** were **equally arranged** ... they were **equally cheerful** ... as resplendent as forests ... **large and terrible** in form."
>
> SANJAY TO DHRITARASHTRA, BHISHMA PARVA: THE BOOK OF BHISHMA

Taking command

Duryodhana hand-picked his trusted allies to lead the eleven divisions of his army—Kripa and Drona, the royal tutors; Shalya, king of Madra; Jayadratha, king of Sindhu, Sudakshina of Trigarta; Kritavarma, a Yadava chieftain; Ashwatthama, Drona's son; Karna, king of Anga; Bhurishrava, from Bahlika; Shakuni, king of Gandhara; and King Srutayudha of Kalinga.

He then requested Bhishma to be the commander-in-chief of his armies. Bhishma agreed but made it clear that he would not kill the Pandavas. He did however, promise to slay ten thousand warriors every day.

Following the prescribed rituals, Duryodhana then consecrated Bhishma to the chanting of hymns by Brahmans, rousing drumrolls, and blowing of conch shells. Yudhishthira had appointed commanders for his seven army divisions as well. He had decided on Arjuna; Draupadi's father Drupada; Virata, king of Matsya; Satyaki, Krishna's trusted ally and Yadava chieftain; Dhrishtaketu, king of Chedi; the king of Kekaya, Vrihatkshatra; and Sahadeva, king of Magadha. Yudhishthira then anointed Dhrishtadyumna, Draupadi's brother, as the commander-in-chief.

Armies at the ready

These chosen commanders were all Maharathis, skilled warriors who could take on many warriors by themselves. Each Maharathi had a banner by which he could be identified and a signature conch-shell trumpet. Blowing on the conch shell demonstrated his strength and stamina, while the sound was meant to inspire his followers and strike fear in the hearts of his enemies. Each one carried his favorite weapons: sword, spear, mace, or bow and arrows.

The battlefield was dotted with the paraphernalia of war: different kinds of axles, quivers, javelins, assault poles, flags, ropes, nooses, missiles, axes, and spades were just a few of the variety that could be seen.

The Pandava armies stood facing east. When the sun rose, they shone like gold.

The elders' blessings

Yudhishthira walked up to the Kaurava army and fell at the feet of his preceptors, Bhishma and Drona.

"I have come to seek your blessings," he said, "so that I fight as a true warrior should. And I come to ask your forgiveness, for from this moment on, I will see you not as my family but as my enemy and do my utmost to strike you down."

Bhishma and Drona hugged Pandu's firstborn, and mourned the terrible situation they found themselves in. In the war to follow, the blood of the warriors would turn the earth red. All ties and bonds would be forgotten. Father would fight sons, brother would fight brother, uncle would fight nephew, and the best of friends would turn into great foes. This war would mark the end not just of one household but of an entire civilization.

HISTORY AND CULTURE

VENERATING ELDERS

In India, the elderly are revered and their blessing is considered equivalent to being blessed by god. When Bhishma sacrificed his throne and conjugal life for his father Shantanu, he was celebrated as an ideal son.

The god-like status of elders is reinforced when the younger generation seeks the blessings of the elders by touching their feet. Thus, there was no paradox in Yudhishthira seeking his granduncle Bhishma's and his teacher Drona's blessings, even when they supported the Kauravas and their unjust cause.

INDIAN TRADITION AND CUSTOMS GIVE GREAT RESPECT TO ELDERS.

AFTER

When Arjuna looked at his relatives on the other side of the enemy line, he was wracked by guilt and self-doubt, and lowered his weapons.

KRISHNA'S TEACHINGS

On seeing Arjuna in such a state of mind, Krishna reminded him of the hardships he had suffered at the hands of his enemies. He reminded him of his duty to fight for justice and not be fearful of the outcome.

Akshouhini

As in any war, strength lay in numbers. Both the Pandavas and Kauravas attempted to amass as many military divisions, or akshouhinis, as they could. How well they deployed these divisions would decide the outcome of the war.

When the sun rose on the first day of war, it saw the pennants of all the akshouhinis fluttering in the wind. Between the Kauravas' eleven akshouhinis and the Pandavas' seven, there were nearly 4 million soldiers. Each of these military units had 21,870 chariots, 21,870 elephants, 65,610 horses, and 109,350 foot soldiers.

Every akshouhini was further divided into smaller units, the smallest of which was a "patti." A patti had the same ratio of the different units of the akshouhini, just in smaller numbers: each patti had one elephant, or gaja; one chariot, or ratha; three horses, or ashwas; and five foot soldiers, or padhatas. Three pattis made a "sena-mukha;" three sena-mukha formed a "gulma;" three gulma formed a "gana;" three gana, a "vahini;" three vahini a "pruthana;" three pruthana, a "chamu;" and three chamu made an "anikini." Ten anikini formed one akshouhini. Each akshouhini was led by a "maharatha," who could take on 10,000 warriors and was skilled in all weapons. The armies also had "atiratha," who could fight 60,000 soldiers on his own, as well as "rathi," who could fight 5,000 soldiers by himself. Bhishma, Karna, Arjuna, and Abhimanyu were considered equal to two maharathas, in terms of their skills in the art of warfare.

RATHA
Chariots were used in India as far back as the 2nd millennium BCE, and are mentioned in the Rig Veda. They allowed easy mobility for the warrior, as well as a place to engage in a combat.

INFANTRY
The largest unit of an akshouhini, foot soldiers engaged with the enemy in close combat. As a consequence, they were also the largest casualties of war.

ELEPHANTRY
An important part of an akshouhini, elephants were highly valued: they could crush the enemy by their sheer size, and offered a stable shooting platform for archers.

VYUHA
Though the warriors engaged in direct combat (see far left), they grouped themselves into battle formations or "vyuhas" to engage with the enemy. Most vyuhas were named for the shapes they formed, such as krauncha heron), kurma (turtle), and so on. The chakravyuha or wheel formation (see left) was used by the Kauravas under Drona's command to trap Abhimanyu.

CAVALRY
Horses were widely used in battle and were highly prized. The Mahabharata describes the efforts the armies took to breed and train horses for warfare.

THE EIGHTH INCARNATION OF LORD VISHNU

Krishna

> "Narada has said that where there is **Krishna, victory is there**. Victory is Krishna's **quality**."
>
> SANJAY, BHISHMA PARVA: THE BOOK OF BHISHMA

Krishna is integral to the Mahabharata. As an incarnation of Vishnu, his actions—wise or strategic—do not generate either demerit or merit. Full of awareness and detachment, his actions are a part of "leela," the divine performance. Krishna teaches the Pandavas to learn, change, and outgrow the beast within them.

HISTORY AND CULTURE

JANMASHTAMI

Janmashtami—the day of Krishna's birth—is celebrated on the eighth day of the waning moon, in the Hindu month of Shravan, which falls in August or September. The celebrations are particularly joyous in Mathura and Vrindavan, cities associated with Krishna's birth and youth. Tableaux of an infant Krishna on a swing or eating butter are consecrated at homes and at temples. Sacred performances of his dance with the milkmaids are enacted. In Maharashtra, in a ceremony called "dahi-handi," young men build human pyramids to reach pots of buttermilk hanging high above in imitation of the child-god. It is also a day of fasting, devotional singing, and recitations of the sacred legends of Krishna's life.

The god-child

Krishna was the son of the Yadava chief Vasudeva and his wife Devaki. Oracles had foretold that the eighth child of Vasudeva and Devaki would be the killer of Kansa, Devaki's brother and dictator of Mathura. Krishna was that eighth child, who grew up to fulfil the prophecy, and was hailed as the liberator of the Yadavas.

Friend of the Pandavas

Krishna was related to the Pandavas—Kunti, mother of the Pandavas, was his father's sister.

To escape repeated attacks on Mathura by Jarasandha, Kansa's father-in-law, to avenge Kansa's death, Krishna moved to Dwaraka. To strengthen his new kingdom, Krishna married several women from the surrounding states. It was this desire to forge political alliances through marriage that brought him to the court of Drupada, where he met

THE BLUE GOD
A bright yellow dhoti, a garland of fragrant forest flowers round his neck, and a peacock feather stuck in the topknot on his head are important parts of Krishna's iconography. This painting in Padmanabhapuram Palace, Tamil Nadu, India, depicts Krishna wielding all his weapons and the flute.

the Pandavas for the first time during Draupadi's swayamvara. He advised the Pandavas, who had fled Hastinapur after an attempt on their lives by the Kauravas, to return to the kingdom and make a claim to the throne. Krishna also suggested the division of the Kuru kingdom between the Pandavas and Kauravas. The brothers sought Krishna's advice not only on political matters, but also on issues of personal interest. It was he who advised the Pandavas that Draupadi should remain exclusive to one Pandava brother for a year at a time.

Draupadi's savior

Krishna came repeatedly to help, give solace to, and guide Draupadi. Her own husband had staked and lost her in a gambling match, and the Pandavas had stood paralyzed as she was humiliated in the hall. When Dusshasana tried to disrobe her, she had only Krishna to turn to. And he did intervene miraculously. Every time Dusshasana pulled away her sari, he found her covered with more and more fabric.

The song of God

When the Kurukshetra War was declared, Arjuna chose an unarmed Krishna over his Narayani army. Facing his brothers, uncles, and nephews across the battlefield, Arjuna's heart sank, and he put down his weapons. Krishna then recited the Bhagavad Gita, the song of God. He explained the temporary nature of things and the importance of performing one's duty without being attached to the outcome.

Krishna's song changed Arjuna's perspective of the battlefield. He understood that the war was about triumph over his fear, guilt, and rage.

The master strategist

The first task of the war for the Pandavas was to vanquish the great Bhishma. Krishna showed the way. He proposed placing Shikhandi, a woman in her past life, against Bhishma, knowing that he would not raise weapons against a woman, this strategy eventually led to his death.

After the death of his son Abhimanyu, Arjuna vowed to kill Jayadratha before sunset the next day. Krishna created conditions that led everyone in the battlefield to believe the sun had set, helping Arjuna to shoot Jayadratha. Krishna was also instrumental in bringing about Karna's death. When Arjuna hesitated to shoot an unarmed Karna, Krishna urged him to slay his enemy.

He was also the reason Bhima could kill Duryodhana. The two were evenly matched in their fight, but Krishna signaled to Bhima that he should hit Duryodhana close to the genitals. This was against the rules, but Bhima never questioned Krishna. Having wounded Duryodhana, Bhima exulted, but Krishna admonished him, teaching him to be gracious in victory.

Death

After his brother Balarama died, Krishna realized it was time for him to end his mortal life, too. He sat under a banyan tree, shaking his leg, reminiscing over his human life. Just then, a poisoned arrow shot by a hunter struck his left foot. The poison took effect and Krishna's life slowly slipped away. After death, Krishna went to Vaikuntha, the higher heaven.

BIOGRAPHY IN BRIEF

- **Born** to Devaki and Vasudeva as their eighth child. Oracles had foretold that he would be the killer of his maternal uncle Kansa, the dictator of Mathura.
- **Was exchanged** by Vasudeva at his birth with Yashoda's daughter.
- **Grew up** among cowherds and milkmaids of Gokul, a municipality in present-day Mathura.
- **Disrupted Kansa's yagna**, angering Indra, the rain god, who caused torrential rains. Picked up the Govardhan mountain, turning it into a giant parasol, to protect the village.
- **Shared a special bond** with the milkmaids, who danced around him as he played the flute.
- **Killed Kansa** as prophesied by the oracles.
- **Moved to Dwaraka** with the entire Yadava clan after Kansa's father-in-law and the king of Magadha, Jarasandha's repeated attacks on Mathura.
- **Met the Pandavas** at Panchala king Drupada's court, and became their friend and adviser.
- **Killed Shishupala** and showed Bhima the way to kill Jarasandha.
- **Defended Dwaraka** from an attack by Kings Shalva and Dantavakra, friends of Shishupala.

KRISHNA PLAYS THE FLUTE, AS THE MILKMAIDS SURROUND HIM

- **Rescued Draupadi** from being disrobed by the Kauravas during a game of dice.
- **Made several attempts** to resolve the feud between the Kauravas and the Pandavas, but failed.
- **Recited the Bhagavad Gita** to Arjuna, encouraging him to fight the Kurukshetra War and explaining to him the true nature of reality.
- **Became an integral part of the Pandava camp** during the war as Arjuna's charioteer. He devised strategies, gave advice, and protected the Pandavas from fatal weapons.
- **Was cursed** by a mourning Gandhari that he would lose his children and grandchildren, and that he would die at the hands of a common hunter.
- **Died** after being shot by a hunter named Jara, who mistook his foot to be the ear of a deer.

THE SONG OF GOD

The **Bhagavad Gita**

The Gita, as it is commonly known, is a long dialogue between Arjuna and Krishna that takes place on the battlefield of Kurukshetra. It is one of the most widely read Hindu scriptures, and has gained a worldwide audience today.

On the day the Kurukshetra War began, Arjuna looked at his opponents lined up on the far side of the battlefield and realized that they were his own family and friends. Convinced that killing his near and dear ones to gain control of a kingdom was against dharma, he cast down his bow and wished to withdraw from the battle. When Krishna—his friend, mentor, and charioteer—saw Arjuna full of self-doubt and ready to give up the fight, he reminded the warrior of his duties, telling him that he would not incur bad karma from participating in the war. In this dialogue between the two, Krishna is identified as God.

The Gita is said to contain the essence of Vedic wisdom. Historians date the text in its current form to 300 CE and, barring the first chapter, it is considered to be a later addition to the Mahabharata. At the crux of the Gita are questions about living a spiritually wealthy life without giving up one's duties. This is perhaps one of the reasons for its appeal, and may also help explain why it has been translated into a number of languages. In addition to the discourse that has become popular as the Bhagavad Gita, there are several other discussions on similar concepts, such as the Anu Gita, where Krishna summarizes the teachings of the Bhagavad Gita to Arjuna, and the Kama Gita, in which Krishna speaks to Yudhishthira about the importance of understanding desire as the force behind all action.

The text of the Bhagavad Gita was first translated into English in 1785 by the Orientalist Charles Wilkins, under the patronage of the then governor general of India, Warren Hastings. It then reached Europe and was translated into many other European languages.

In India, the Gita reached a wide audience through its publications in regional languages. One of its earliest translations is the *Dnyaneshwari*, written in the 13th century by the poet-saint Dnyaneshwar in Marathi. Many others have ensured that the wisdom of the Gita reached the common man through song and stories. In fact, until the 19th century, few except the educated elite had read it in the original Sanskrit text.

Like much of the Mahabharata, the Gita is presented as a tale within a tale, with Dhritarashtra's charioteer, Sanjay, narrating the action on the battlefield to the blind king. It is contained in the Bhishma Parva, where the Kurukshetra War begins. For the most part, it is composed in the Anustubh meter, with four lines of eight syllables; in places, it changes to the Trishtubh meter, which has four lines of eleven syllables.

The Gita has 18 chapters, each of which is qualified by the word "yoga, meaning "union" or "path"—in this context, with the Supreme Spirit. It has 700 shlokas, or couplets, a sampling of which is presented in this section.

1. ARJUNAVISHADA YOGA

Arjuna's **Dejection**

The first chapter of the Gita is titled "Arjunavishada Yoga" and has 47 shlokas, or couplets. It begins with Dhritarashtra asking Sanjay to narrate the incidents on the battlefield. The chapter describes Arjuna's despondent state of mind on seeing his friends and family lined up on either side of the battlefield, and his subsequent refusal to take up arms against his own kith and kin.

धृतराष्ट्र उवाच –
धर्मक्षेत्रे कुरुक्षेत्रे समवेता युयुत्सवः ।
मामकाः पाण्डवाश्चैव किमकुर्वत संजय ॥१॥

Dhritarashtra said, "O Sanjaya! Having gathered on the holy plains of Kurukshetra, wanting to fight, what did my sons and the sons of Pandu do?" (1)

अथ व्यवस्थितान्दृष्ट्वा धार्तराष्ट्रान् कपिध्वजः ।
प्रवृत्ते शस्त्रसंपाते धनुरुद्यम्य पाण्डवः ॥२०॥

Then, the son of Pandu, with the monkey on his banner, saw the friends of Dhritarashtra thus arranged in battle formation and got ready to use his weapons. O ruler of the earth, he raised his bow. (20)

हृषीकेशं तदा वाक्यमिदमाह महीपते ।
अर्जुन उवाच –
सेनयोरुभयोर्मध्ये रथं स्थापय मेऽच्युत ॥२१॥

And told Hrishikesha the following words. "O Achyuta! Place my chariot in between the two armies." (21)

यावदेतान्निरीक्षेऽहं योद्धुकामानवस्थितान् ।
कैर्मया सह योद्धव्यमस्मिन् रणसमुद्यमे ॥२२॥

"While I look at those who are desirous of battle and are assembled here. Let me see with whom I will have to fight in this war-related business." (22)

निहत्य धार्तराष्ट्रान्नः का प्रीतिः स्याज्जनार्दन ।
पापमेवाश्रयेदस्मान् हत्वैतानाततायिनः ॥३६॥

"O Janardana! What pleasure will we derive from killing the sons of Dhritarashtra? Although they are criminals, sin alone will be our lot if we kill them." (36)

तस्मान्नार्हा वयं हन्तुं धार्तराष्ट्रान् स्वबान्धवान् ।
स्वजनं हि कथं हत्वा सुखिनः स्याम माधव ॥३७॥

"Therefore, we cannot kill the sons of Dhritarashtra, with their friends. O Madhava! How can we be happy after killing our relatives?" (37)

अहो बत महत्पापं कर्तुं व्यवसिता वयम् ।
यद्राज्यसुखलोभेन हन्तुं स्वजनमुद्यताः ॥४५॥

"Alas! Because of our greed for the kingdom and for happiness, we have got ready to kill our relatives. We were certain to commit a great sin." (45)

यदि मामप्रतीकारमशस्त्रं शस्त्रपाणयः ।
धार्तराष्ट्रा रणे हन्युस्तन्मे क्षेमतरं भवेत् ॥४६॥

"With me unarmed and unresisting, if the sons of Dhritarashtra, with weapons in their hands, should kill me in battle, that will be better for me." (46)

2. SANKHYA YOGA

The **Knowledge** of the **Self**

This chapter of the Gita is titled "Sankhya Yoga" and has 72 shlokas, or couplets. This is where Krishna initiates his discussion with Arjuna. The chapter acts as a summary of the Gita, and discusses all three paths to salvation—that of knowledge (jnana yoga); action (karma yoga); and devotion (bhakti yoga), although it dwells very little on the last.

श्रीभगवानुवाच –
अशोच्यानन्वशोचस्त्वं प्रज्ञावादांश्च भाषसे ।
गतासूनगतासूंश्च नानुशोचन्ति पण्डिताः ॥११॥

"You speak as if you are wise, but you are grieving over those that one should not sorrow over. The wise don't sorrow over those who are dead or those who are alive." (11)

न त्वेवाहं जातु नासं न त्वं नेमे जनाधिपाः ।
न चैव न भविष्यामः सर्वे वयमतः परम् ॥१२॥

"It is not that I, or you, or these kings, did not exist before this. Nor is it that we won't exist in the future, all of us will be there." (12)

नासतो विद्यते भावो नाभावो विद्यते सतः ।
उभयोरपि दृष्टोऽन्तस्त्वनयोस्तत्त्वदर्शिभिः ॥१६॥

"That which is untrue does not have an existence. That which is true cannot be destroyed. But those who know the truth realize the ends of both these." (16)

वासांसि जीर्णानि यथा विहाय नवानि
गृह्णाति नरोऽपराणि ।
तथा शरीराणि विहाय जीर्णान्यन्यानि
संयाति नवानि देही ॥२२॥

"Like a person discards worn-out clothes and accepts others that are new, like that, the soul discards worn-out bodies and attains others that are new." (22)

जातस्य हि ध्रुवो मृत्युर्ध्रुवं जन्म मृतस्य च ।
तस्मादपरिहार्येऽर्थे न त्वं शोचितुमर्हसि ॥२७॥

"Death is inevitable for one who is born and birth is inevitable for one who dies. Therefore, because this is inevitable, you should not grieve." (27)

देही नित्यमवध्योऽयं देहे सर्वस्य भारत ।
तस्मात् सर्वाणि भूतानि न त्वं शोचितुमर्हसि ॥३०॥

"O descendant of Bharata! In everyone's body, the atman is indestructible. Therefore, you should not mourn about any being." (30)

यामिमां पुष्पितां वाचं प्रवदन्त्यविपश्चितः ।
वेदवादरताः पार्थ नान्यदस्तीतिवादिनः ॥४२॥

"O Partha! Those who are ignorant say these flowery words, praising the Vedas and claiming there is nothing else." (42)

भोगैश्वर्यप्रसक्तानां तयापहृतचेतसाम् ।
व्यवसायात्मिका बुद्धिः समाधौ न विधीयते ॥४४॥

"They are addicted to pleasure and wealth and, because of those words, their minds are deluded. They cannot focus on one object—they do not have the intellect that allows one to discriminate." (44)

3. KARMA YOGA

The **Path** of **Action**

This chapter of the Gita is titled "Karma Yoga," and has 43 shlokas, or couplets. It discusses the merits of the path of knowledge and that of action. Based on the discussion so far, Arjuna infers that the path of knowledge is superior to that of action. Krishna explains that Arjuna is mistaken—one should not eschew action, but be detached from the outcome of the actions themselves.

न कर्मणामनारम्भान्नैष्कर्म्यं पुरुषोऽश्नुते ।
न च संन्यसनादेव सिद्धिं समधिगच्छति ॥४॥

"Without performing action, man is not freed from the bondage of action. And resorting to sannyasa does not result in liberation." (4)

नियतं कुरु कर्म त्वं कर्म ज्यायो ह्यकर्मणः ।
शरीरयात्रापि च ते न प्रसिद्ध्येदकर्मणः ॥८॥

"Therefore, do the prescribed action. Because action is superior to not performing action. And without action, even survival of the body is not possible." (8)

सक्ताः कर्मण्यविद्वांसो यथा कुर्वन्ति भारत ।
कुर्याद्विद्वांस्तथासक्तश्चिकीर्षुर्लोकसंग्रहम् ॥२५॥

"O descendant of Bharata! Ignorant people perform action by being attached to that action. But the wise perform similar action unattached, for the welfare and preservation of the worlds." (25)

श्रेयान् स्वधर्मो विगुणः परधर्मात् स्वनुष्ठितात् ।
स्वधर्मे निधनं श्रेयः परधर्मो भयावहः ॥३५॥

"One's own dharma, even if followed imperfectly, is superior to someone else's dharma, even if followed perfectly. It is better to be slain while following one's own dharma. Someone else's dharma is tinged with fear." (35)

4. JNANA-KARMA-SANNYASA YOGA

The Path of **Knowledge**, **Action**, and **Renunciation**

This chapter of the Gita is titled "Jnana-karma-sannyasa Yoga" and has 42 shlokas, or couplets. In it, Krishna tells Arjuna that the knowledge being revealed to him has been disclosed to many people since ancient times, and discusses the reasons for his own birth. He also elaborates on jnana yoga and karma yoga, explaining that at the intersection of the two lies true wisdom.

यदा यदा हि धर्मस्य ग्लानिर्भवति भारत ।
अभ्युत्थानमधर्मस्य तदात्मानं सृजाम्यहम् ॥७॥

"O descendant of Bharata! Whenever dharma goes into a decline and adharma is on the ascendance, then I create myself." (7)

परित्राणाय साधूनां विनाशाय च दुष्कृताम् ।
धर्मसंस्थापनार्थाय संभवामि युगे युगे ॥८॥

"To protect the righteous and to destroy the sinners and to establish dharma, I manifest myself from yuga to yuga." (8)

जन्म कर्म च मे दिव्यमेवं यो वेत्ति तत्त्वतः ।
त्यक्त्वा देहं पुनर्जन्म नैति मामेति सोऽर्जुन ॥९॥

"O Arjuna! He who thus knows the nature of my divine birth and action, he is not born again when he dies, but attains me." (9)

वीतरागभयक्रोधा मन्मया मामुपाश्रिताः ।
बहवो ज्ञानतपसा पूता मद्भावमागताः ॥१०॥

"Many, purified through the meditation of knowledge, have immersed themselves in me and sought refuge in me, discarding attachment, fear and anger." (10)

न मां कर्माणि लिम्पन्ति न मे कर्मफले स्पृहा ।
इति मां योऽभिजानाति कर्मभिर्न स बध्यते ॥१४॥

"Actions do not touch me, nor do I desire the fruits of action. He who knows me in this fashion is not tied down by action." (14)

त्यक्त्वा कर्मफलासङ्ग नित्यतृप्तो निराश्रयः ।
कर्मण्यभिप्रवृत्तोऽति नैव किञ्चित् करोति सः ॥२०॥

"He who has given up attachment to action and its fruit is always content and without refuge. Even when he is immersed in action, he does nothing." (20)

श्रद्धावाँल्लभते ज्ञानं तत्परः संयतेन्द्रियः ।
ज्ञानं लब्ध्वा परां शान्तिमचिरेणाधिगच्छति ॥३९॥

"Knowledge is attained by the faithful, the unwavering and those who control their senses. Having attained knowledge, they quickly achieve supreme peace." (39)

तस्मादज्ञानसंभूतं हृत्स्थं ज्ञानासिनात्मनः ।
छित्त्वैनं संशयं योगमातिष्ठोत्तिष्ठ भारत ॥४२॥

"O descendant of Bharata! Therefore, use the sword of knowledge to slice away this doubt in your heart, resulting from your own ignorance. Follow yoga! Arise!" (42)

5. KARMA-SANNYASA YOGA

The Path of **Renunciation**

Titled "Sannyasa Yoga," this chapter is also known as "Karma-Sannyasa Yoga," or the path of action and renunciation. It has 29 shlokas, or couplets. The chapter discusses the merits of sannyasa (inaction) and karma (action), stating that it is important to take action, but without getting attached to the outcome.

ज्ञेयः स नित्यसंन्यासी यो न द्वेष्टि न काङ्क्षति ।
निर्द्वन्द्वो हि महाबाहो सुखं बन्धात् प्रमुच्यते ॥३॥

"O mighty-armed! He who does not desire and he who does not hate, know him to be a perpetual sannyasi. Freed from opposites, he is happily freed from bondage." (3)

साङ्ख्ययोगौ पृथग्बालाः प्रवदन्ति न पण्डिताः ।
एकमप्यास्थितः सम्यगुभयोर्विन्दते फलम् ॥४॥

"The ignorant, not the wise, speak of renunciation and action as distinct. If one of these is followed properly, the fruits of both result."(4)

योऽन्तःसुखोऽन्तरारामस्तथान्तर्ज्योतिरेव यः ।
स योगी ब्रह्मनिर्वाणं ब्रह्मभूतोऽधिगच्छति ॥२४॥

"He whose happiness is inside, he whose pleasure is inside and he whose light is inside, that yogi alone has realized the brahman and obtains liberation in the brahman." (24)

कामक्रोधवियुक्तानां यतीनां यतचेतसाम् ।
अभितो ब्रह्मनिर्वाणं वर्तते विदितात्मनाम् ॥२६॥

"Freed from desire and anger, controlled in mind and knowing the atman, such sages attain liberation in the brahman all around them." (26)

6. DHYANA YOGA

The Path of **Meditation**

Titled "Dhyana Yoga" in Sanskrit, this chapter has 47 shlokas, or couplets. It takes the previously introduced discussion on dhyana (meditation) forward.

उद्धरेदात्मनात्मानं नात्मानमवसादयेत् ।
आत्मैव ह्यात्मनो बन्धुरात्मैव रिपुरात्मनः ॥५॥

"Use the atman to raise the atman. Do not lower the atman. The atman is the atman's friend and the atman is the atman's enemy." (5)

बन्धुरात्मात्मनस्तस्य येनात्मैवात्मना जितः ।
अनात्मनस्तु शत्रुत्वे वर्तेतात्मैव शत्रुवत् ॥६॥

"The atman, which has been used to conquer the atman, is the atman's friend. For someone who has failed to control the atman, the atman harms like an enemy." (6)

प्राप्य पुण्यकृतां लोकानुषित्वा शाश्वतीः समाः ।
शुचीनां श्रीमतां गेहे योगभ्रष्टोऽभिजायते ॥४१॥

"He who has deviated from the path of yoga attains the worlds of the righteous and dwells there for many years. Thereafter, he is born in a righteous and wealthy household." (41)

प्रयत्नाद्यतमानस्तु योगी संशुध्दकिल्बिषः ।
अनेकजन्मसंसिध्दस्ततो याति पराङ्गतिम् ॥४५॥

"Striving harder than on that earlier occasion, pure in heart, the yogi obtains liberation after many lives and, later, achieves the supreme objective." (45)

7. JNANAVIJNANA YOGA

The Path of **Knowledge**

This chapter is called "Jnanavijnana Yoga," and contains 30 shlokas, or couplets. While the first six chapters discussed jnana yoga and bhakti yoga, the emphasis was clearly on karma yoga. With this chapter, the focus shifts to bhakti yoga, and the two paths to it, through jnana (guidance) and vijnana (self-discovery).

त्रिभिर्गुणमयैर्भावैरेभिः सर्वमिदं जगत् ।
मोहितं नाभिजानाति मामेभ्यः परमव्ययम् ॥१३॥

"This entire universe is deluded by these three gunas and the resultant conditions. And is not able to know me, who is above these and without change." (13)

न मां दुष्कृतिनो मूढाः प्रपद्यन्ते नराधमाः ।
माययापहृतज्ञाना आसुरं भावमाश्रिताः ॥१५॥

"The evil-doers, ignorant and worst among men, lose their knowledge because of maya and resort to demonic states. They do not worship me." (15)

बहूनां जन्मनामन्ते ज्ञानवान् मां प्रपद्यते ।
वासुदेवः सर्वमिति स महात्मा सुदुर्लभः ॥१९॥

"After many births are over, he attains the knowledge that Vasudeva is everything and attains me. Such great souls are extremely rare." (19)

जरामरणमोक्षाय मामाश्रित्य यतन्ति ये ।
ते ब्रह्म तद्विदुः कृत्स्नमध्यात्मं कर्म चाखिलम् ॥२९॥

"Those who want to free themselves from decay and death and seek refuge in me, they know about the brahman, about the individual atman and about action in its entirety." (29)

8. AKSHARA BRAHMA YOGA

The Path to the **Supreme Spirit**

In this chapter of 28 shlokas, or couplets, titled "Akshara Brahma Yoga," Krishna answers Arjuna's questions on the nature of the supreme God. The chapter dwells on the ways to merge with the divine.

आब्रह्मभुवनाल्लोकाः पुनरावर्तिनोऽर्जुन ।
मामुपेत्य तु कौन्तेय पुनर्जन्म न विद्यते ॥१६॥

"O Arjuna! From all the worlds up to brahmaloka, beings have to return. But O son of Kunti! There is no rebirth for those who have attained me." (16)

अव्यक्तोऽक्षर इत्युक्तस्तमाहुः परमां गतिम् ।
यं प्राप्य न निवर्तन्ते तद्धाम परमं मम ॥२१॥

"What is spoken of as the unmanifest and indestructible, what is said to be the supreme liberation, attaining which beings do not have to return, that is my supreme abode." (21)

शुक्लकृष्णे गती ह्येते जगतः शाश्वते मते ।
एकया यात्यनावृत्तिमन्ययाऽवर्तते पुनः ॥२६॥

"In this world, these two paths of light and darkness are said to be eternal. One leads to non-return and the other leads to return." (26)

नैते सृती पार्थ जानन् योगी मुह्यति कश्चन ।
तस्मात् सर्वेषु कालेषु योगयुक्तो भवार्जुन ॥२७॥

"O son of Pritha! Knowing these two paths, a yogi is never deluded. O Arjuna! Therefore, at all times, resort to yoga." (27)

9. RAJAVIDYA RAJAGUHYA YOGA

The Path of **Royal Knowledge and Royal Secrets**

This chapter, titled "Rajavidya Rajaguhya Yoga," has 34 shlokas, or couplets. This chapter continues with the discussion in the previous chapter, arguing that the path of bhakti yoga is available for everyone and is easier to follow than that of jnana yoga.

मया ततमिदं सर्वं जगदव्यक्तमूर्तिना ।
मत्स्थानि सर्वभूतानि न चाहं तेष्ववस्थितः ॥४॥

"This entire universe is pervaded by me in my unmanifest form. All beings are established in me. But I am not established in them." (4)

ज्ञानयज्ञेन चाप्यन्ये यजन्तो मामुपासते ।
एकत्वेन पृथक्त्वेन बहुधा विश्वतो मुखम् ॥१५॥

"Some worship me through the yajna that is the path of knowledge. Some worship me as one, others as separate. I, who pervade the universe, am worshipped in many forms." (15)

अहं क्रतुरहं यज्ञः स्वधाहमहमौषधम् ।
मन्त्रोऽहमहमेवाज्यमहमग्निरहं हुतम् ॥१६॥

"I am kratu, I am yajna, I am svadha, I am the herbs, I am the mantra, I indeed am the clarified butter, I am the fire, I am the offering." (16)

येऽप्यन्यदेवताभक्ता यजन्ते श्रद्धयान्विताः ।
तेऽपि मामेव कौन्तेय यजन्त्यविधिपूर्वकम् ॥२३॥

"O son of Kunti! Those with devotion who faithfully worship other gods, they too, worship me alone. But not in the indicated way." (23)

अहं हि सर्वयज्ञानां भोक्ता च प्रभुरेव च ।
न तु मामभिजानन्ति तत्त्वेनातश्च्यवन्ति ते ॥२४॥

"Because I alone am the receiver of offerings and the granter of fruits at all yajnas. But they do not know my true nature and, therefore, are cast down." (24)

अपि चेत् सुदुराचारो भजते मामनन्यभाक् ।
साधुरेव स मन्तव्यः सम्यग्व्यवसितो हि सः ॥३०॥

"Even if the most evil of persons worships me single-mindedly, he should be thought of as a righteous person. Because his resolve is correct." (30)

मां हि पार्थ व्यपाश्रित्य येऽपि स्युः पापयोनयः।
स्त्रियो वैश्यास्तथा शूद्रास्तेऽपि यान्ति परां गतिम् ॥३२॥

"O son of Pritha! Even those who are of evil birth, women, vaishyas and shudras, having sought refuge in me, they will certainly attain supreme liberation." (32)

मन्मना भव मद्भक्तो मद्याजी मां नमस्कुरु।
मामेवैष्यसि युक्त्वैवमात्मनं मत्परायणः ॥३४॥

"With mind immersed in me, become my devotee, my worshipper and one who offers obeisance to me. In this way, with your atman united in me as the refuge, you will attain me alone." (34)

10. VIBHUTI YOGA

The **Divine Glory**

This chapter of 42 shlokas, or couplets, is titled "Vibhuti Yoga." Continuing with the themes addressed in chapters 7, 8, and 9, it describes the nature of paramatman (Supreme Spirit), and its vibhuti (strength or divinity).

बुद्धिर्ज्ञानमसम्मोहः क्षमा सत्यं दमः शमः ।
सुखं दुःखं भवोऽभावो भयं चाभयमेव च ॥४॥

"Intellect, knowledge, freedom from delusion, forgiveness, truthfulness, control over thoughts, happiness, unhappiness, creation, destruction, fear and freedom from fear ... " (4)

अहिंसा समता तुष्टिस्तपो दानं यशोऽयशः ।
भवन्ति भावा भूतानां मत्त एव पृथग्विधाः ॥५॥

" ... Non-violence, equality, satisfaction, austerity, donations, fame and lack of fame: all these states of beings indeed owe their origin to me." (5)

अहं सर्वस्य प्रभवो मत्तः सर्वं प्रवर्तते ।
इति मत्वा भजन्ते मां बुधा भावसमन्विताः ॥८॥

"I am the origin of everything. From me everything is instituted. Knowing this, the wise, immersed in devotion, worship me." (8)

अहमात्मा गुडाकेश सर्वभूताशयस्थितः ।
अहमादिश्च मध्यं च भूतानामन्त एव च ॥२०॥

"O Gudakesha! I am the atman established in the heart of all beings. It is I who am the origin, the middle and also the end of all beings." (20)

11. VISHVARUPADARSHANA YOGA

Vision of the **Universal Form**

This chapter, titled "Vishvarupadarshana Yoga," has 55 shlokas, or couplets. On hearing of the divinity of God in the previous chapter, Arjuna expresses a desire to see it himself. This chapter describes the vision of this universal form granted to Arjuna.

श्रीभगवानुवाच ।

पश्य में पार्थ रूपाणि शतशोऽथ सहस्रशः ।

नानाविधानि दिव्यानि नानावर्णाकृतीनि च ॥५॥

Bhagavan said, "O son of Pritha! Behold my divine multi-dimensioned, multi-hued, multi-shaped hundreds and thousands of forms." (5)

इहैकस्थं जगत्कृत्स्नं पश्याद्य सचराचरम् ।

मम देहे गुडाकेश यच्चान्यद्द्रष्टुमिच्छसि ॥७॥

"O Gudakesha! In my body, in one place, see the entire universe, with all that is moveable and immoveable. Also see today, whatever else you want to see." (7)

12. BHAKTI YOGA

The Path of **Devotion**

Titled "Bhakti Yoga," this chapter of 20 shlokas, or couplets, discusses whether bhakti yoga, which worships the saguna (manifest) form of God, is superior to jnana yoga, which worships the nirguna (formless) aspect of God. This chapter concludes the discussion on bhakti yoga.

क्लेशोऽधिकतरस्तेषामव्यक्तासक्तचेतसाम् ।
अव्यक्ता हि गतिर्दुःखं देहवद्भिरवाप्यते ॥५॥

"Those who wish to immerse their minds in the unmanifest find it more difficult. Because those who possess bodies attain the goal of the unmanifest with great perseverance." (5)

श्रेयो हि ज्ञानमभ्यासाज्ज्ञानाद्ध्यानं विशिष्यते ।
ध्यानात् कर्मफलत्यागस्त्यागाच्छान्तिरनन्तरम् ॥१२॥

"Knowledge is superior to practice. Meditation is superior to knowledge. Giving up attachment to the fruits of action is superior to meditation. After renunciation, tranquillity is attained." (12)

अद्वेष्टा सर्वभूतानां मैत्रः करुण एव च ।
निर्ममो निरहङ्कारः समदुःखसुखः क्षमी ॥१३॥

"He who has no hatred for all beings, is friendly and also displays compassion, is without sense of ego, without pride, regards happiness and unhappiness in the same way and is forgiving ... " (13)

संतुष्टः सततं योगी यतात्मा दृढनिश्चयः ।
मय्यर्पितमनोबुद्धिर्यो मद्भक्तः स मे प्रियः ॥१४॥

" ... Is always satisfied, a yogi and controlled in mind, firm in resolution and with mind and intellect immersed in me, such a devotee of mine is dear to me." (14)

13. KSHETRAKSHETRAJNAVIBHAGA YOGA

Discrimination Between **Nature** and **Self**

This chapter of 34 shlokas, or couplets, is titled "Kshetrakshetrajnavibhaga Yoga." From this chapter onward, the discussion turns to jnana yoga, a path more difficult than that of bhakti.

अध्यात्मज्ञाननित्यत्वं तत्त्वज्ञानार्थदर्शनम् ।
एतज्ज्ञानमिति प्रोक्तमज्ञानं यदतोऽन्यथा ॥११॥

" ... Devotion to knowledge about atman and search for true knowledge—these are known as knowledge. Anything opposed is ignorance." (11)

ज्योतिषामपि तज्ज्योतिस्तमसः परमुच्यते ।
ज्ञानं ज्ञेयं ज्ञानगम्यं हृदि सर्वस्य विष्ठितम् ॥१७॥

"That is the light of all bright bodies. Said to be beyond darkness. Knowledge, that which is to be known and attainable through knowledge, is established in the heart of everything." (17)

य एवं वेत्ति पुरुषं प्रकृतिं च गुणैः सह ।
सर्वथा वर्तमानोऽपि न स भूयोऽभिजायते ॥२३॥

"He who knows the nature of purusha, and of prakriti, with the qualities, whatever be the position he is in, will not be reborn." (23)

अनादित्वान्निर्गुणत्वात् परमात्मायमव्ययः ।
शरीरस्थोऽपि कौन्तेय न करोति न लिप्यते ॥३१॥

"O son of Kunti! Because it is without origin and without qualities, this paramatman is unchanging and although based in the body, does nothing. Is not attached." (31)

14. GUNATRAYAVIBHAGA YOGA

Separation Between the **Three Gunas**

Titled "Gunatrayavibhaga Yoga," this chapter has 27 shlokas, or couplets. In the previous chapter, there was a reference to three gunas (inherent qualities)—sattva, rajas, and tamas—to which all organisms are subject. This chapter discusses them, and also offers a means to conquer them.

सत्त्वं रजस्तम इति गुणाः प्रकृतिर्संभवाः ।
निबध्नन्ति महाबाहो देहे देहिनमव्ययम् ॥५॥

"O mighty-armed! The qualities sattva, rajas and tamas, generated from nature, bind the indestructible atman in the body." (5)

तत्र सत्त्वं निर्मलत्वात् प्रकाशकमनामयम् ।
सखसङ्गेन बध्नाति ज्ञानसङ्गेन चानघ ॥६॥

"O sinless one! Among these, sattva is shining because it is pure and is without sin, but ties down the atman because of attachment to happiness and knowledge." (6)

रजो रागात्मकं विद्धि तृष्णासङ्गसमुद्भवम् ।
तन्निबध्नाति कौन्तेय कर्मसङ्गेन देहिनम् ॥७॥

"O son of Kunti! Know rajas to be based on desire and the origin of thirst and attachment. That binds the atman firmly because of attachment to action." (7)

सत्त्वं सुखे संजयति रजः कर्मणि भारत ।
ज्ञानमावृत्य तु तमः प्रमादे संजयत्युत ॥९॥

"O descendant of Bharata! Sattva attaches to happiness and rajas attaches to action. Tamas veils knowledge and attaches to errors." (9)

ऊर्ध्वं गच्छन्ति सत्त्वस्था मध्ये तिष्ठन्ति राजसाः ।
जघन्यगुणवृत्तिस्था अधो गच्छन्ति तामसाः ॥१८॥

"Those with a preponderance of sattva ascend above. Those with rajas stay in the middle. Those with despicable tamas qualities descend below." (18)

गुणानेतानतीत्य त्रीन् देही देहसमुद्भवान् ।
जन्ममृत्युजरादुःखैर्विमुक्तोऽमृतमश्नुते ॥२०॥

"When the being transcends the three qualities that are the origin of the body, he attains immortality, free from birth, death, old age and unhappiness." (20)

समदुःखसुखः स्वस्थः समलोष्टाश्मकांचनः ।
तुल्यप्रियाप्रियो धीरस्तुल्यनिन्दात्मसंस्तुतिः ॥२४॥

"Equal between happiness and unhappiness, established in himself, equal between earth, stone and gold, similar in treatment of the loved and the hated, tranquil, similar between praise and censure." (24)

मानापमानयोस्तुल्यस्तुल्यो मित्रारिपक्षयोः ।
सर्वारम्भपरित्यागी गुणातीतः स उच्यते ॥२५॥

"He who treats respect and insult alike, friend and enemy alike and discards all beginnings of action, he is said to have transcended the qualities." (25)

15. PURUSHOTTAMA YOGA

Union with the **Supreme Being**

This chapter, titled "Purushottama Yoga," contains 20 shlokas, or couplets. While the previous chapter dealt with the three qualities that one needs to master to become one with divinity, this section of the Gita describes the very nature of the Supreme Spirit, the cause and creator of everything.

निर्मानमोहा जितसङ्गदोषा
अध्यात्मनित्या विनिवृत्तकामाः ।
द्वन्द्वैर्विमुक्ताः सुखदुःखसंज्ञै
गच्छन्त्यमूढाः पदमव्ययं तत् ॥५॥

"Without pride and delusion, having conquered the fault of attachment, constant in the knowledge of the atman, having restrained desire, freed from the opposites of happiness and unhappiness, the wise go to that indestructible goal." (5)

यदादित्यगतं तेजो जगद्भासयतेऽखिलम् ।
यच्चन्द्रमसि यच्चाग्नौ तत्तेजो विद्धि मामकम् ॥१२॥

"The energy in the sun that lights up the entire world, that in the moon and that too in the fire, know that energy to be mine." (12)

सर्वस्य चाहं हृदि सन्निविष्टो
मत्तः स्मृतिर्ज्ञानमपोहनं च ।
वेदैश्च सर्वैरहमेव वेद्यो
वेदान्तकृद्वेदविदेव चाहम् ॥१५॥

"I am established in the hearts of all beings. I result in memory and knowledge and their lack. Indeed, it is I who am the knowledge of the Vedas and the origin of Vedanta. And I am the knower of the Vedas." (15)

यस्मात् क्षरमतीतोऽहमक्षरादपि चोत्तमः ।
अतोऽस्मि लोके वेदे च प्रथितः पुरुषोत्तमः ॥१८॥

"Because I am beyond destruction and superior even to the indestructible, therefore, I am known as the Supreme Being in this world and in the Vedas." (18)

16. DAIVASURASAMPADDVIBHAGA YOGA

Distinction Between **the Divine** and **the Demonic**

Called "Daivasurasampaddvibhaga Yoga," this chapter has 24 shlokas, or couplets. In previous chapters, there are references to two categories of people—the divine (those who can merge with the Supreme Being), and the demonic (those incapable of this union). This chapter elaborates on the qualities and traits that define these categories.

द्वौ भूतसर्गौ लोकेऽस्मिन् दैव आसुर एव च
दैवो विस्तरशः प्रोक्त आसुरं पार्थ मे शृणु ॥६॥

"O son of Pritha! In this world, two types of beings are created, divine and demonic. The divine has been stated in detail. Hear from me about the demonic." (6)

प्रवृत्तिं च निवृत्तिं च जना न विदुरासुराः ।
न शौचं नापि चाचारो न सत्यं तेषु विद्यते ॥७॥

"Demonic people do not know about inclination and disinclination. In them, there is no purity nor righteousness, nor even truthfulness." (7)

त्रिविधं नरकस्येदं द्वारं नाशनमात्मनः ।
कामः क्रोधस्तथा लोभस्तस्मादेतत्त्रयं त्यजेत् ॥२१॥

"Desire, anger, and avarice—these are the three types of doors to hell and destroyers of the atman. Give up these three." (21)

एतैर्विमुक्तः कौन्तेय तमोद्वारैस्त्रिभिर्नरः ।
आचरत्यात्मनः श्रेयस्ततो याति परां गतिम् ॥२२॥

"O son of Kunti! The man who is freed from these three dark doors and follows that which is good for the atman, thereafter attains the supreme goal." (22)

17. SHRADDHATRAYAVIBHAGA YOGA

Distinction Between the Three Types of Faith

The chapter titled "Shraddhatrayavibhaga Yoga" argues, in 28 shlokas, or couplets, that there are three types of faith, each of which is defined by a guna—sattva, rajas, or tamas. The chapter also describes the ceremonies and sacrifices pertaining to each of these faiths.

यजन्ते सात्त्विका देवान् यक्षरक्षांसि राजसाः ।
प्रेतान् भूतगणांश्चान्ये यजन्ते तामसा जनाः ॥४॥

"Those of the sattva-type worship the gods. Those of the rajas-type, yakshas and rakshas. The others, of the tamas-type, worship ghosts and devils." (4)

आहारस्त्वपि सर्वस्य त्रिविधो भवति प्रियः ।
यज्ञस्तपस्तथा दानं तेषां भेदमिमं शृणु ॥७॥

"The favored food of all is of three types and so too, sacrifices, meditation, and donations. Listen to the distinction between these." (7)

दातव्यमिति यद्दानं दीयतेऽनुपकारिणे ।
देशे काले च पात्रे च तद्दानं सात्त्विकं स्मृतम् ॥२०॥

"Alms donated for the sake of donation, to those who have not benefited the donor, and based on place, time and subject—are said to be of the sattva-type." (20)

अदेशकाले यद्दानमपात्रेभ्यश्च दीयते ।
असत्कृतमवज्ञातं तत्तामसमुदाहृतम् ॥२२॥

"Donations in the wrong place, at the wrong time and to the wrong subject, given without respect and disdainfully—are said to be of the tamas-type." (22)

18. MOKSHASANNYASA YOGA

The Path of Liberation and Renunciation

Called "Mokshasannyasa Yoga,", this is the longest chapter of the Gita, with 78 shlokas, or couplets. This chapter sums up the teachings in the Gita, and recommends detached action rather than inaction. It also briefly discusses bhakti yoga, and ends with a section that highlights the virtues of the Gita.

श्रीभगवानुवाच ।
काम्यानां कर्मणां न्यासं संन्यासं कवयो विदुः ।
सर्वकर्मफलत्यागं प्राहुस्त्यागं विचक्षणाः ॥२॥

Bhagavan said, "The wise know the relinquishing of action that satisfies desires as sannyasa. The discriminating call the relinquishing of the fruits of all action tyaga." (2)

श्रेयान् स्वधर्मो विगुणः परधर्मात् स्वनुष्ठितात् ।
स्वभावनियतं कर्म कुर्वन्नाप्नोति किल्बिषम् ॥४७॥

"Even when performed imperfectly, svadharma is superior to someone else's dharma, performed well. Sin does not result if one's natural action is undertaken." (47)

सहजं कर्म कौन्तेय सदोषमपि न त्यजेत् ।
सर्वारम्भा हि दोषेण धूमेनाग्निरिवावृताः ॥४८॥

"O son of Kunti! Natural action should not be discarded, even if it is tainted. Because all action is tainted, just as fire is shrouded by smoke." (48)

यदहङ्कारमाश्रित्य न योत्स्य इति मन्यसे ।
मिथ्यैष व्यवसायस्ते प्रकृतिस्त्वां नियोक्ष्यति ॥५९॥

"Through a sense of ego, you are thinking that you will not fight. But this resolution is false. Nature will compel you." (59)

स्वभावजेन कौन्तेय निबद्धः स्वेन कर्मणा ।
कर्तुं नेच्छसि यन्मोहात् करिष्यस्यवशोऽपि तत् ॥६०॥

"O son of Kunti! Whatever you don't wish to do because of delusion, you will have to undertake in spite of that, because you are tied down by your natural duty." (60)

ईश्वरः सर्वभूतानां हृद्देशेऽर्जुन तिष्ठति ।
भ्रामयन् सर्वभूतानि यन्त्रारूढानि मायया ॥६१॥

"O Arjuna! God is established in the hearts of all beings and, through maya, makes all beings whirl, as if they are mounted on machines." (61)

मन्मना भव मद्भक्तो मद्याजी मां नमस्कुरु ।
मामेवैष्यसि सत्यं ते प्रतिजाने प्रियोऽसि मे ॥६५॥

"Immerse your mind only on me, be devoted to me, worship me, bow in obeisance before me. I am pledging that you will attain me, because you are my beloved." (65)

राजन् संस्मृत्य संस्मृत्य संवादमिममद्भुतम् ।
केशवार्जुनयोः पुण्यं हृष्यामि च मुहुर्मुहुः ॥७६॥

"O King! Remembering again and again this sacred and wonderful dialogue between Keshava and Arjuna, I have repeatedly been exhilarated." (76)

BEFORE

When Arjuna entered the battlefield with Krishna and saw his opponents were his own family, he could not bring himself to pick up his bow.

KRISHNA'S SERMON

Seeing Arjuna despondent, Krishna told the Pandava that the war was not about fighting for petty reasons such as staking claim over land, or avenging past insults, but to uphold dharma. As a Kshatriya, reminded Krishna, it was Arjuna's duty to uphold the principles of righteousness. Having been recalled to his duty, Arjuna prepared for battle.

The **Heralds** of **War**

The battlefield at Kurukshetra would see destruction on a scale never imagined. As the flag of each king fluttered in the wind, the rules of war were announced, reminding all present that, in the end, dharma stood supreme.

The Pandava and Kaurava armies stood facing each other on the plains of Kurukshetra, ready for the battle to begin. As a gust of wind set the banners of the commanders aflutter, the rules of war were announced.

The rules of war

The rules stated that both sides would be amicable with each other after the war. Fighting would only begin at sunrise and end at sunset. Those who withdrew from the battle could not be killed. Only two equally matched warriors, with the same weapon and mount, could fight each other. Multiple warriors could not fight a lone man. An unarmed or unconscious warrior could not be attacked. No one could interfere when two warriors were locked in a duel. No one could be attacked from behind, or be taken by surprise. No one could strike another below the belt. The rules also forbade a woman from entering the battlefield. If circumstances led to a woman entering the field, no weapon could be raised against her. Lastly, no one could attack a person who was not participating in the war.

As the two sides prepared to fight, one man had already foreseen the outcome. Sahadeva,

the most learned of men, knew that though the armies swore to uphold dharma, they would flout every last rule in a bid to gain the upper hand.

Inauspicious beginnings

The impulse to outsmart each other could be seen even before the armies assembled. Sahadeva recalled the day Duryodhana approached him to determine a muhurat—an auspicious time—for the war that would be favorable for the Kauravas. When he learned of this, Krishna had attempted to tilt the scales in the Pandavas' favor. He had tried to bring about an eclipse, an omen of doom. Appalled at Krishna's decision, both the Sun and the Moon came to him to explain that an eclipse would create a terrible imbalance in the universe.

Shutting his ears to their reasoning, Krishna pointed out that as the Earth, the Sun, and the Moon were in one place at that time, it could be regarded as an eclipse. Barely had the words left his mouth than the sky was filled with omens foretelling doom. But Sahadeva felt that even a layman could tell that nothing good could come of a war where a teacher would fight his students, brother would fight brother, or an uncle his nephews.

> "The war is not for you, Arjuna, but for **civilized human conduct** … it is to **establish dharma** and in doing so **discover the soul**."
>
> KRISHNA TO ARJUNA, BHISHMA PARVA: THE BOOK OF BHISHMA

MYTHOLOGY AND FOLKLORE

KURUKSHETRA

Located north of Delhi, India, Kurukshetra was once marked by five lakes known as the Samanta Panchaka. These were dug by Parashurama, an avatar of Vishnu, and filled with the blood of Kshatriyas he had killed to avenge the death of his father.

A popular folktale in Haryana tells of how the land where the war was fought came to be selected. On Krishna's instructions to find a land beyond redemption, Bhima identified a barren stretch where a farmer had died. Rather than cremating his son, the father continued to till the dry land, while the widow did not mourn but enjoyed her husband's share of food. Such a land, Bhima concluded, was beyond redemption and the most suitable battlefield for fighting the war of wars.

INSIGNIA
In the Kurukshetra War, each commander had his own banner that fluttered above his chariot, marked with a symbol. Each of these warriors was identified by the mark that his banner had. On Arjuna's banner sat Hanuman, the monkey god, making him invincible in battle.

AFTER

Once the rules of war had been declared, Krishna and Arjuna moved toward enemy lines.

CALL TO ARMS

As the chariot moved toward the Kauravas, Arjuna's banner, with the image of the monkey god Hanuman, seemed to issue a challenge to the enemy. The rousing call of Devadutta, Arjuna's conch shell, along with Krishna's Panchajanya pierced the air—war had begun.

BEFORE

The final formalities of the war were over—rules had been declared, and the warriors had been given a chance to change their loyalties.

KRISHNA'S SERMON

On seeing his kith and kin lined up as his opponents, Arjuna had been assailed with doubts about the righteousness of the war. Krishna counseled Arjuna that the war was not about a kingdom or vengeance. The war was for dharma, a battlefield for the preservation of transcendental values on which he would fight his own fear, guilt, and rage.

The **War Begins**

Krishna's sermon on war and duty had renewed Arjuna's sense of purpose. As he picked up his bow and Krishna maneuvered the chariot toward the enemy lines; the sound of conch shells swelled through the battlefield—the Kurukshetra War had begun.

Kurukshetra War began with the rush of thousands of warriors toward each other. Elephants, horses, chariots, and foot soldiers clashed in a fierce encounter. Sanjay, the charioteer, describing the war to King Dhritarashtra and Gandhari in Hastinapur, called it as fearsome as one between the Devas (deities) and the Asuras (demons).

Fighting it out

Sanjay described to the king and queen how the sound of the charging elephants recalled the roll of thunderous clouds in the monsoons. Rampaging, they drove soldiers away from the battlefield and upturned and destroyed chariots, forcing their occupants to run for cover. Well-trained chariot-riders, with their shafts, killed large sections of the cavalry and foot soldiers who urged and protected the elephants. He noted how skilled horsemen rushed on to the field, surrounded the chariot-warriors, slaying them with spears, darts, and swords. Some combatants, armed with bows, surrounded individual charioteers and put them to death. As the sun reached its zenith, the warriors began to slay each other in great

LIST

CONCH SHELLS

- Krishna's Panchajanya
- Yudhishthira's Anantavijaya
- Bhima's Poundrya
- Arjuna's Devadutta
- Nakula's Sughosha
- Sahadeva's Manipushpaka

numbers. Throngs of chariots, large bodies of horses, and teeming divisions of infantry and elephants mingled in battle. Sanjay described, "Maces, spiked bludgeons, lances, short arrows, and rockets were hurled at one another in dreadful engagement. Arrow showers coursed like flights of locusts. And in the melee, elephants, horses, chariots, and soldiers began to crush and grind one another. It was hard to tell which warrior belonged to the Kauravas and which to the Pandavas."

The battlefield

At sunset, when the soldiers retreated to their camps, Sanjay gave an evocative and horrifying description of the battlefield. "Drenched in blood, the earth looked like a vast plain soaked in the rainy season, covered with red flowers. Like a beautiful young maiden, the earth was attired in white robes dyed with a deep red. The field of battle, with flesh and crimson blood, indented with the hooves of steeds, dotted with severed heads, looked as if adorned with golden lotuses. Horses with garlands of gold, their necks adorned with golden ornaments, had been killed in thousands and lay all around, as did broken chariots. The earth looked delightful, like the full moon in the sky, with a garland strewn with gold-tufted arrows. Adorned with earrings made with the heads of dead warriors, the earth dazzled," Sanjay described.

Despite the loss of blood and men, neither side was able to decisively dominate the other. On the first day, the Pandavas suffered as a combative Bhishma attacked with great success and they lost warriors such as Virata's son, Uttara, who was killed by Shalya's lance that pierced his armor. By the end of the day, Yudhishthira felt dejected, especially because he could see that Arjuna was not fighting at his best while Bhishma was at his most destructive. Krishna tried his best to encourage and inspire all the warriors with his words of wisdom and courage.

Rallying the Pandava army

On the second day, an infuriated Arjuna took on Bhishma and the other great Kaurava warriors »

CALL OF WAR

This oil on canvas, titled "First Day in Kurukshetra," shows Krishna blowing his conch shell—the Panchajanya—at the beginning of the war as the Pandavas look on.

NIGHT BEFORE THE BATTLE

The Pandavas and Krishna can be seen conferring in their tent in this 18th-century watercolor-and-gold on paper from Himachal Pradesh, India.

"O king! Your son Duryodhana advanced with his brothers, placing **Bhishma at the forefront** of the army … so did the Pandavas, with **Bhimasena at the forefront**."

SANJAY TO DHRITARASHTRA, BHISHMA PARVA: THE BOOK OF BHISHMA

» such as Kripa, Drona, and Shalya. Bhishma and Arjuna fought a mighty battle with arrows. Both were perfectly matched in power, courage, and skill, as they created nets of arrows and attacked from different positions in new ways. Drona and Dhrishtadyumna fought a fierce battle. Drona managed to kill Dhrishtadyumna's charioteer and horses and destroy his chariot. Bhima came to the aid of his still-fighting commander and took him on his own chariot. Sanjay described Bhima on this day as a Yama incarnate who had successfully battled the entire army of Kalinga.

"**You should not sorrow** ... O king! **I am engaged** in **ensuring your welfare** and so are maharatha Satyaki, the aged Virata, and Drupada."

KRISHNA TO YUDHISHTHIRA, BHISHMA PARVA: THE BOOK OF BHISHMA

KRISHNA ATTACKS BHISHMA
Seeing Arjuna's reluctance to engage with Bhishma, Krishna was driven to attack Bhishma himself, with a wheel of a chariot. The scene unfolds in this 18th-century miniature from Himachal Pradesh, India.

"Whirling his mace, Bhima could be seen intoxicated with his valor. Destroying chariots and killing elephants, the mighty Bhima was slaughtering soldiers." Even Bhishma could not stop him.

Seeing the Pandavas' success on the battlefield, Bhishma advised Duryodhana to stop fighting for the day.

Heroic efforts

On the third day, Arjuna's son, Abhimanyu, and Satyaki delivered a resounding defeat to the Gandhara forces, while Yudhishthira, Nakula, and Sahadeva fought Drona's army. Meanwhile, Bhima and Ghatotkacha created mayhem among the Kauravas. Unable to make headway, Duryodhana complained bitterly to Bhishma that he was favoring the Pandavas. Provoked, Bhishma vowed, "With all the worlds as a witness, I alone will repulse the sons of Pandu, together with their soldiers and relatives."

Krishna's rage

Although Arjuna released many arrows at Bhishma, none posed any real threat. Krishna realized that Arjuna was holding back out of respect for his granduncle, even though Bhishma was on a rampage. Frustrated, Krishna rushed toward Bhishma with a chariot wheel.

Seeing Krishna approach like that, Bhishma lay down his weapons and prepared to die at his hands. Arjuna ran after Krishna, reminding him of his vow to not wield a weapon in the war. He swore that he would now do his best. The war raged on but the first nine days led to no conclusion and a decisive victory eluded both sides.

The see-saw war

The two sides seemed evenly matched. For every attack there was a counter-attack. Every weapon was matched with another equally powerful weapon. On a specific occasion, an individual warrior like Bhishma, Arjuna, or Bhima would be inspired or provoked to superhuman feats, but overall the balance would not change. Despite Arjuna's promise to Krishna, he could kill neither Bhishma nor Drona. It became clear that this war would not end soon.

HISTORY AND CULTURE

VEDIC WARS

Vyasa's descriptions make the war seem like an earth-shaking event of cosmic proportions, with the heroic, the superhuman, and the celestial intermingled. In all probability, Vedic wars involved a confrontation where the warriors of two opposing sides clashed with each other. Accompanied by elephants, horses, and foot soldiers, these warriors were mounted on chariots. Playing the role of cheerleaders, the foot soldiers were mainly present to demonstrate power and mock the opponent.

TWO CROSSED SWORDS ARE OFTEN SEEN AS A KSHATRIYA SYMBOL OF VALOUR

AFTER

With each passing day it became clear that the two sides were equally matched, and neither side would taste victory.

THE SACRIFICE
Krishna suggested a human sacrifice to please Kali, the goddess of the battlefield. Iravan, Arjuna's son with the Naga princess Ulupi, was chosen for this ritual. He agreed to the sacrifice but wished to die a married man so that he would have a wife to lament his loss. The Pandavas had a hard time finding a wife for the doomed Iravan until Krishna came up with a solution to fulfil Iravan's wish.

CAPTURED IN STONE
The world-famous temple of Angkor Wat in Cambodia has extensive stonework depicting scenes from the Mahabharata. This Khmer battle frieze shows the Pandavas fighting the Kauravas.

A **Human** Sacrifice

When the war remained evenly poised even after nine days, the Pandavas were worried. Their small army could not go on for much longer. To turn the tide in their favor, they decided to sacrifice a warrior. Who would it be?

Nine days of fighting had gone by, but there seemed to be no clear winner. The two sides appeared to be equally matched. Though much younger than Bhishma, Dhrishtadyumna seemed able to match the war-hardy Kaurava commander in skills. Frustration was high and morale low in the Pandava camp.

Sacrifice to goddess Kali

To break the impasse and turn the battle in the Pandavas' favor, Krishna proposed that they sacrifice a worthy warrior to Kali, the goddess of war. "Perhaps this will please the goddess. She may then reveal how we could win the war," he said.

The oracles were consulted. "It can't be just any warrior," they declared. "He should be worthy, and have the thirty-two sacred marks on his body."

Only three men in the Pandava camp had these marks—Arjuna, Krishna, and a young warrior called Iravan. The Pandavas could not sacrifice their brother or their friend, so they turned to this youth. "Who are you?" they asked him. "I am Iravan, Arjuna's son with Ulupi, the Naga princess," he replied. Filled with a young man's enthusiasm for war, Iravan had come to Kurukshetra despite his mother's protests. Though he barely remembered Ulupi, Arjuna welcomed the son he had never set eyes on, but who had still joined the war to help him. He asked Iravan if he would sacrifice himself. Iravan could not refuse—but he had one last wish.

A wife for Iravan

He did not want to die a virgin. "Give me a wife who will mourn my death," Iravan pleaded.

The wishes of the sacrificial victim had to be honored; the Pandavas had no choice but to agree. But no woman was willing to marry a man who was to die the very next day. The Pandavas were unable to find Iravan a wife but Krishna had a solution—he transformed into a beautiful maiden named Mohini, and married Iravan.

Iravan's wedding night, spent in Mohini's arms, brought him great delight. When the sun rose the next day, Arjuna's son was ritually beheaded. Iravan's wish was fulfilled—Mohini wept for him like no widow ever had.

« BEFORE

With every sunrise that dawned on Kurukshetra, brother killed brother, friend killed friend.

AN IMPASSE

Blood had flown like water, turning the brown earth of the battlefield red. Yet there seemed to be no clear outcome. Each passing day, soldiers threw themselves into the fray, intoxicated by the beat of the war drums and the songs of the bards, doing the bidding of their generals. With every sunset, fewer and fewer soldiers returned to camp. Yet there was no victory in sight.

A 20TH-CENTURY LITHOGRAPH OF THE KURUKSHETRA WAR

HISTORY AND CULTURE

FESTIVAL OF THE ALIS

Iravan's story is not part of the Sanskrit Mahabharata, but comes from the oral traditions of the southern Indian state of Tamil Nadu. Iravan, or Aravan, is the patron god of the transgender communities here, and is worshipped as Kuthandavar, a form of Shiva. Every year, the village of Koovagam in Tamil Nadu, in the Tamil month of Chittirai (April–May), celebrates an eighteen-day festival where Kuthandavar's sacrifice is ritually enacted. Transgenders, known as "Ali" or "Aravani," celebrate this festival, and marry Kuthandavar en masse. On the last day of the festival, dressed as widows, they break their bangles to mourn his death.

TRANSGENDERS MOURNING THE DEATH OF KUTHANDAVAR IN KOOVAGAM, TAMIL NADU, INDIA

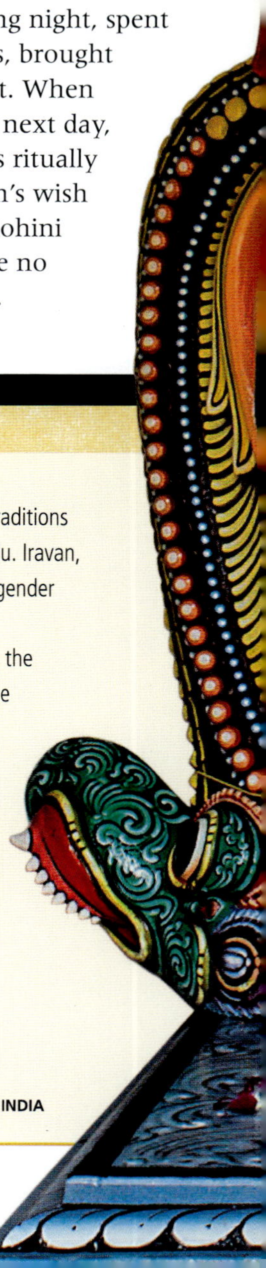

IRAVAN STATUE AT THE SRI MARIAMMAN TEMPLE, SINGAPORE
Singapore's oldest Hindu temple, the Sri Mariamman temple was built in 1827, a few years after the East India Company set up a trading settlement. Its history and cultural significance makes it a popular tourist attraction.

MYTHOLOGY AND FOLKLORE

MOHINI

In Hindu mythology, Mohini is the only female incarnation associated with Vishnu who, along with Brahma and Shiva, forms the Hindu trinity. It is said that Vishnu took the form of Mohini to help Shiva. The demon Bhasmasura had received a blessing from Shiva that allowed him to burn anyone to ashes by merely placing his hand on the person's head. One day Bhasmasura decided to test his newly acquired powers on Shiva himself. Shiva then looked to Vishnu for help. Vishnu turned himself into a beguiling beauty called Mohini to seduce the demon. Overcome, the Asura begged Mohini to marry him. "Only if you can match my dancing skills, move for move," said she. Bhasmasura, blinded by desire, exactly reflected Mohini's movements and placed a hand on his own head—and was instantly turned to ashes.

12TH-CENTURY STONE STATUE OF MOHINI

AFTER

Though they had performed the sacrifice, the Pandavas could not be sure of winning the war as long as Bhishma was alive.

THE PANDAVAS' PLAN

The Pandavas were reluctant to hurt Bhishma, since he was like a father to them. It was no wonder, then, that though Arjuna had attacked his granduncle many times over these nine days, they had all been half-hearted attempts, none that posed any real threat. Even if they wanted to, the Pandavas could not possibly kill a man who had been granted the freedom to choose the hour of his own death by the gods. But, as Krishna pointed out, though he could not be killed, Bhishma could definitely be defeated. The Pandava camp mulled over this and came up with a plan.

On a **Bed of Arrows**

With Bhishma standing by the Kauravas, victory eluded either side. Krishna devised a ploy that would lead to the downfall of the Kaurava commander, and would give the Pandavas a commanding position in the war.

BEFORE

The Pandavas knew that as long as Bhishma was alive, they could not win. But they were reluctant to hurt him; after all, he was the only father they knew. All their attempts had been half-hearted so far.

KRISHNA'S RAGE

Irked at the lack of effort by the Pandavas, Krishna jumped off the chariot on the battlefield, picked up a loose chariot wheel, and ran toward Bhishma to kill him. Arjuna realized that to bring the war to a conclusion, Krishna was willing to break the vow he had taken not to raise a weapon in the war. Arjuna reminded Krishna of his vow and begged him to stop. He also promised that he would kill Bhishma.

Although Arjuna had promised to kill Bhishma, the question that bothered the Pandava camp was how to kill someone who had been granted the ability to decide when he would die.

Aware of the conundrum, Krishna thought of a possible way out. "We may not be able to kill him, but we can certainly try and render him incapable of fighting by immobilizing him," he suggested.

A woman on the battlefield

On the tenth day of the war, the Pandavas, unable to withstand the power of Bhishma's arrows, decided to face Bhishma with Shikhandi. Mounted on Arjuna's chariot, Shikhandi challenged Bhishma to a duel. The Kaurava commander realized his end was near: he would not fight Shikhandi, whom he believed was a woman because, though she now had the body of a man, she had been born a woman.

> "I will now **fight behind you** and **destroy the enemy** with my **arrows**. Ignited with rage, **attack Bhishma**, whose valor is **terrible**."
>
> ARJUNA TO SHIKHANDI, BHISHMA PARVA: THE BOOK OF BHISHMA

Aware of Bhishma's near immunity to death, Krishna slyly suggested bringing a woman to the battlefield to face him. He knew Bhishma's honor would never allow him to raise his bow against a woman.

When Arjuna expressed doubts about the ethics of bringing a woman to the battlefield, Krishna reassured him. If he believed Shikhandi, Draupadi's elder brother, was a man, there was no reason why Arjuna could not take him into the battlefield on his chariot. But, if Bhishma believed Shikhandi was a woman, he would lower his bow, giving Arjuna the opportunity to overpower him.

Bhishma lowered his bow. Arjuna, who had positioned himself strategically behind Shikhandi to protect himself from Bhishma's attack, now aimed his arrows at the weak points in Bhishma's armor. His arrows rained down on Bhishma without any hindrance or resistance.

Blow to the Kaurava army

Duryodhana watched in disbelief as Arjuna's arrows ripped through Bhishma's body. Everyone on the field was horrified to see the great leader fall from his chariot. The arrows Arjuna had shot at him were so closely placed that when he fell, a bed of arrows supported him above the ground. The arrows pierced every inch of Bhishma's flesh, suspending him between the sky and the earth.

As a mark of respect to the patriarch, both sides stopped fighting. Arjuna went up to Bhishma and, finding that his head fell back unsupported, stuck three arrows in the ground, creating a headrest for his granduncle.

News of the Kaurava commander's fall spread across the battlefield like wildfire. Everyone grieved over the fall of Bhishma. Every soldier lowered his weapons in respect. Bhishma was the great patriarch of the Kuru clan and was respected by all.

The tenth day of the battle ended with the Kaurava army losing its great leader.

ANALYSIS

A HERO WITH FLAWS

Arjuna's bed of arrows suspended Bhishma above the ground, between the earth and sky, because in death he was rejected by both. Through this, Vyasa draws attention to the terrible consequences of what may appear to be a noble sacrifice. Neither a householder nor a hermit, Bhishma carried the burden of letting his family bloodline die because of his promise to his father. He did not fulfil his social obligations: he did not marry, did not beget children, and did not inherit his father's kingdom.

AFTER

While an ordinary man would have succumbed to the injuries, Bhishma, given a blessing that allowed him to choose the time of his death, lay on the bed of arrows until the end of war.

DEATH OF A HERO

Bhishma chose to die on the auspicious day of Uttarayan, after the winter solstice, when the sun moves closer to the Pole Star—the bright half of the lunar month, when the moon is waxing. During this time, he witnessed the war and the eventual victory of the Pandavas, and so fulfilling his vow of ensuring the throne was in safe hands in the future.

FALL OF BHISHMA

A bas-relief stone carving of episodes from the Mahabharata in Angkor Wat, Cambodia, captures Bhishma lying on a bed of arrows in the battlefield, while the Kauravas and Pandavas fight each other for supremacy.

BHISHMA'S NEMESIS

Shikhandi

"A **daughter** named **Shikhandi** was born to King Drupada. … for some reason, he has given her his **marks of a man**."

THE YAKSHAS TO STHUNA, LORD OF THE YAKSHAS,
UDYOGA PARVA: THE BOOK OF EFFORT

The tale of Shikhandi and his ambiguous gender can be understood in the context of the vengeful Amba. Shikhandi was Amba in his previous incarnation. The Amba–Shikhandi persona haunted the life story of Kuru patriarch Bhishma and ended it as well, marking a watershed moment in the Kurukshetra War.

As Amba

The king of Kashi had three daughters. He invited many kings for their swayamvara but did not extend the invitation to Hastinapur's prince Vichitravirya, Bhishma's half-brother. Bhishma took the absence of an invitation as an insult to the dignity of his household. He abducted the three princesses and gave them to his younger brother.

Amba, the eldest, was in love with a person called Shalva and begged to be allowed to go to him. But Shalva refused to take Amba back, as she had been abducted by another man and had spent some time in his company. A mortified Amba returned to Vichitravirya only to be told that what is once given away is never taken back.

Amba then demanded that Bhishma should take her as his wife, since he was the cause of her predicament. Besides, she argued, by taking her on his chariot, it was Bhishma, and not his half-brother, who had become her true husband. Bhishma dismissed her, citing his vow of celibacy.

"You have ruined my life!" cried Amba. "You had no right to abduct me if your vow did not allow you to marry. Now I am nobody's wife."

Furious, Amba prayed to Kartikeya, the god of war, who gave her a garland of lotuses, saying that anyone who took this would kill Bhishma, but no one accepted it. She went around the world seeking a warrior who would avenge her, but all Kshatriyas feared Bhishma. When the powerful king of Panchala, Drupada, refused to help her, she flung the garland in his palace.

Eventually, she turned to

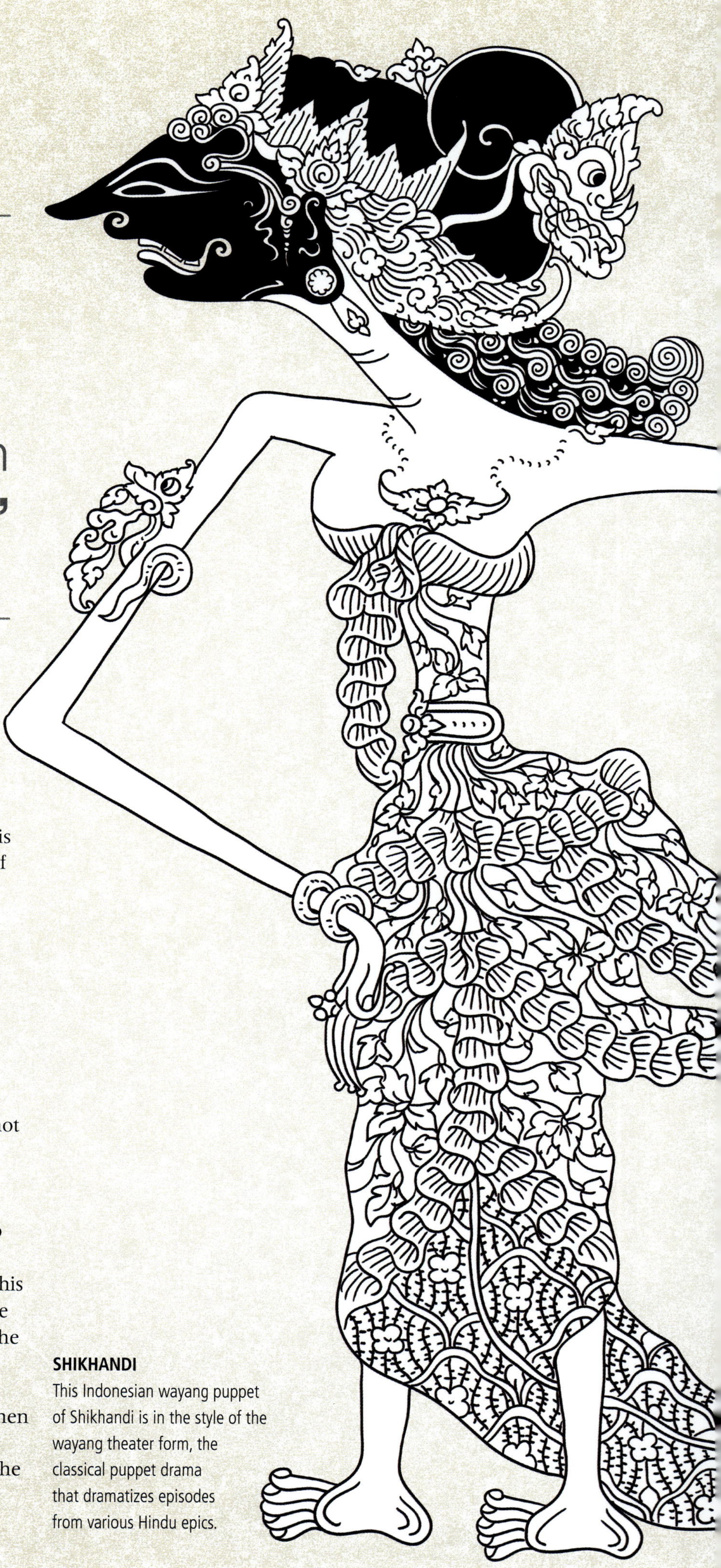

SHIKHANDI
This Indonesian wayang puppet of Shikhandi is in the style of the wayang theater form, the classical puppet drama that dramatizes episodes from various Hindu epics.

SHIKHANDI AGAINST BHISHMA
A frieze from the 17th-century terracotta temples of Bishnupur, West Bengal, India, depicts Shikhandi taking on Bhishma on the battlefield.

Parashurama, the martial-ascetic and Bhishma's teacher. Parashurama was so shocked to hear Amba's story that he challenged Bhishma to a duel. A terrible fight followed, but ended without a conclusion. In despair, Amba prayed to Shiva, the god of destruction. "You will be the cause of Bhishma's death in your next life," said Shiva. Determined to bring about Bhishma's death sooner rather than later, Amba leaped into a pit of fire to kill herself.

A daughter for Drupada

Meanwhile, King Drupada of Panchala burned with humiliation after his defeat by the students of Drona, the Kuru teacher. He wanted to destroy not only Drona but also his patrons—Bhishma and the Kuru clan. He invoked Shiva, who granted him the blessing to have a son who would kill Bhishma. Drupada's wife gave birth to a daughter Shikhandi. The oracles foretold that she would acquire a male body in due course. Drupada raised his daughter as a man. She was taught the art of warfare and statecraft. She was even given a wife. But on the wedding night, her wife ran screaming to her father, Hiranyavarna, king of Dasharna, complaining that her "husband" had a woman's body.

In anger, Hiranyavarna laid siege to Panchala. To save the kingdom from war, Shikhandi decided to kill herself. She ran to the forest where she encountered a Yaksha called Sthuna, who offered her his manhood for a night.

Shikhandi took the Yaksha's manhood and proved his manhood to his wife, forcing his father-in-law to retreat. When she went back to the forest to return her manhood, the situation had changed. Kubera, the lord of the Yakshas, displeased at Sthuna's act, cursed him that his manhood would only return at the end of Shikhandi's life. Shikhandi was overjoyed. She had now become a man and would stay so until the day he died. He returned home and told Drupada of this news. In a moment of playfulness, Shikhandi wore that garland of lotuses that Amba had flung in the palace. Drupada realized that Shikhandi would be responsible for Bhishma's death.

Revenge at last

After nine indecisive days of the Kurukshetra War, it had become necessary for the Pandavas to kill Bhishma. Krishna decided to bring Shikhandi on the battlefield.

When Arjuna expressed his doubt, Krishna said, "If you believe Shikhandi is a man, you will take him into the battlefield with you. But if Bhishma believes Shikhandi to be a woman, he will lower his bow, giving you an opportunity to overpower him."

So, on the tenth day of the war, Shikhandi mounted Arjuna's chariot and challenged Bhishma to a duel, but he refused to fight. "Born a woman you're always a woman," he said, and roared at Krishna that bringing a woman into the battlefield was adharma.

Krishna retorted, "You see her as a woman because she was born as a female. But I see her as a man because that is how her father raised her. I see her as a man because she has a Yaksha's manhood. Whose point of view is right? That Shikhandi is an unworthy opponent is your view, not Shikhandi's, who wishes to fight you."

Arjuna stood behind Shikhandi and shot hundreds of arrows at Bhishma. He fell from his chariot, and was suspended on a bed of arrows. With Bhishma's fall, Shikhandi fulfilled his destiny.

Death

On the last day of the war, Ashwatthama, Drona's son, attacked the sleeping Pandavas. He raised his sword and hacked Draupadi's brothers, Shikhandi and Dhrishtadyumna, to death.

BIOGRAPHY IN BRIEF

- **Born** as Amba to the king of Kashi. Her sisters were Ambika and Ambalika.
- **Betrothed to Shalva**, whom she intended to choose as her husband at the swayamvara organized by her father.
- **Abducted**, along with her sisters, by Bhishma, for his half-brother Vichitravirya.
- **Rejected** by Shalva after being sent back to him by Vichitravirya. Rejected by Vichitravirya and Bhishma on return.
- **Held Bhishma responsible** for her miseries.
- **Received a lotus garland** from Kartikeya, the god of war. Anyone who accepted the garland would kill Bhishma, but no one did. Threw it in Drupada's palace when he refused to take it.
- **Helped by Parashurama** when he agreed to fight Bhishma to avenge her. The fight, however, remained inconclusive.
- **Received a blessing** by Shiva to be the cause of Bhishma's death in her next life.
- **Died** after leaping into fire.
- **Reborn** as king of Panchala, Drupada's daughter, Shikhandi. Oracles prophesied that she would turn into a man later in life.
- **Raised** like a son by Drupada.
- **Married to a woman**, but her wife complained to her father, who laid siege to Panchala.
- **Borrowed manhood** for a day from a Yaksha called Sthuna and proved that she was a man.
- **Challenged Bhishma** to a duel in the Kurukshetra War. Bhishma refused to fight and Arjuna took advantage of that, pinning Bhishma to the ground with his arrows.
- **Died** at the hands of an angry Ashwatthama, Drona's son, who killed him while he was asleep in the Pandava camp.

ANALYSIS

A QUEER HISTORY

Bhishma, who was invincible on the battlefield, refused to fight Shikhandi, whom he saw as a woman. Though Shikhandi's intervention changed the course of the battle, the warrior's contribution has been given little importance. This has parallels in today's world, where the LGBTQ (Lesbian, Gay, Bisexual, Transgender, and Queer) community is fighting hard for the recognition of their rights.

7
DRONA PARVA: THE BOOK OF DRONA

DRONA'S CHARIOT FIGHT
After Bhishma's fall, Drona was appointed commander-in-chief of the Kaurava army. This 16th-century gouache on paper illustrates a skirmish between Drona (extreme left-hand corner), and Bhima and Arjuna, two of the Pandavas.

Drona Parva, or the Book of Drona, is the seventh parva of the Mahabharata. It is named after the Kuru teacher who assumes command of the Kaurava army after the fall of Bhishma. This section continues with the account of the war narrated by Sanjay, charioteer to Dhritarashtra, the ruler of the Kuru kingdom. The parva describes the fierce fight between the two armies as well as the tragic deaths of the great warriors Abhimanyu, Jayadratha, Ghatotkacha, and Drona. This parva has 8 sub-parvas, 173 chapters, and 8,069 shlokas, or couplets.

"O supreme among brahmanas! With you as our **leader,** we wish to **vanquish** the enemy. ... Let these eleven akshouhinis follow your instructions. ... **Advance** in front of us. ... We will **follow** you."

DURYODHANA TO DRONA, DRONA PARVA: THE BOOK OF DRONA

BEFORE

The realization that they would not win the war while Bhishma was alive compelled the Pandavas to eliminate the only father figure they had ever known.

THE WINNING STRATEGY
Krishna discussed with Arjuna ways to get Bhishma to lower his weapons in the battlefield so that he could be attacked and killed. They used Draupadi's elder brother Shikhandi, whose gender was undefined, to face Bhishma in battle. Refusing to fight one he believed to be a woman, Bhishma lowered his defenses and was wounded by Arjuna's arrows. The Kauravas selected Drona to be the commander-in-chief of their army.

The **Kaurava Onslaught**

With Bhishma gone, Drona was made the leader of the Kaurava army. Unlike Bhishma's strategy of exercising restraint, Drona aimed at causing maximum damage, resolving to isolate and kill Yudhishthira by systematically distracting the other Pandavas.

Drona dispatched a vast legion of elephants led by Bhagadatta, king of Pragjyotisha, against Bhima, and the dreaded charioteers of Trigarta called the Samsaptakas against Arjuna. "With Arjuna and Bhima distracted, I will be able to concentrate all efforts to kill Yudhishthira," said Drona. Even as Bhima tried his best to push back Bhagadatta's elephants, they were more than a match for him. An unnerved Bhima decided to step back. Seeing his chariot retreat, the Pandavas' army felt demoralized and was filled with despair.

ARJUNA TO THE RESCUE
Recognizing that his elder brother Bhima is surrounded, Arjuna rides towards him to help.

Arjuna's hesitation

Seeing Bhima leave, Arjuna decided to step up and attack Bhagadatta and his legion of elephants before turning toward the Samsaptaka charioteers. Hit by a sudden indecisiveness, he changed his mind. He asked Krishna to go back. "First Samsaptaka and then Bhagadatta," he said. Then, Arjuna changed his mind again. "Maybe first Bhagadatta and then Samsaptaka." Krishna saw his hesitation and rising stress and smiled. "I have full faith that you are capable of defeating both. One at a time or simultaneously," he said. Taking comfort in these words, Arjuna made up his mind and decided to tackle the Samsaptaka army. He showered arrows on them, striking the horses and elephants, smashing chariots, and killing thousands of riders. As the broken chariots piled up, there was complete confusion among the Samsaptakas' formations, which scattered in total disarray.

The divine weapon

Krishna then took Arjuna toward Bhagadatta. As the chariot moved toward him, Bhagadatta stood on top of his elephant and released a dreaded weapon—the Vaishnavastra. Arjuna shot an arrow to defend himself but Krishna stood between the missile and Arjuna, taking the impact on himself. As soon as it touched Krishna, the arrow turned into a garland of flowers. "You did not need to take the weapon upon yourself, Krishna. I could have destroyed it myself," said Arjuna. Krishna replied that the weapon had come to Bhagadatta through Krishna himself in his earlier incarnation as a boar, and only he could have taken its impact. Apologizing for his high-handedness, Arjuna shot an arrow at Bhagadatta's elephant that split its head in two. Arjuna's next arrow pierced Bhagadatta's chest and killed him. Bhima, in the meantime, had rallied around his eldest brother, foiling Drona's plan of killing Yudhishthira.

Shakuni's attack

Next, the forces of the Gandhara army, led by Shakuni, attacked Arjuna. Shakuni chanted and conjured torrential rains and darkness to accompany his arrows. Arjuna retaliated and released missiles of his own that destroyed the darkness with light and the rains with dryness. When he saw that his powers had failed, Shakuni decided to leave the battlefield.

Shrutayudha's mace

Having tried his best to defeat Arjuna and failing each time, a warrior named Shrutayudha hurled his mace at Krishna in frustration. The weapon, which had been given to him by the sea god Varuna, could not be used against an unarmed warrior. The mace rebounded off Krishna's chest and struck Shrutayudha instead, killing him on the spot.

> "Let **Partha [Arjuna] be removed** from the field of battle, **by whatever means** … and **Dharmaraja** will be **vanquished**."
>
> DRONA TO DURYODHANA, DRONA PARVA: THE BOOK OF DRONA

"That great army was **agitated** and **shattered** by Drona. The Panchalas were **destroyed**, like a mountain **by a storm**."

SANJAY TO DHRITARASHTRA, DRONA PARVA: THE BOOK OF DRONA

MYTHOLOGY AND FOLKLORE

DESTRUCTIVE WEAPONS

The Kauravas and the Pandavas fought with astras—weapons that were strengthened by incantations and hymns and contained the power of the divine. The Brahmaastra, the Vishnuastra, and the Pashupatastra were weapons belonging to Brahma, Vishnu, and Shiva. The Agniastra, the Vayuastra, and the Indraastra were powered with fire, wind, and rain. The epic describes the effects of these weapons, which have led to speculations that the ancients were familiar with nuclear technology.

THE EXPLOSIVE POWER OF NUCLEAR FISSION

BROTHERS IN ARMS
This painting from *Razmnama* shows Bhagadatta, king of Pragjyotisha, on his elephant and Duryodhana on his chariot, ready to attack Bhima.

AFTER

Drona's anger at not being able to kill any of the Pandavas made him plan a different strategy.

ABHIMANYU CORNERED
The Kauravas' commander-in-chief planned a battle strategy that would keep Arjuna away and would ensnare one of the Pandavas in a deadly trap.

Yudhishthira was caught in the enemy's battle formation. Arjuna's son Abhimanyu came to his aid and died in his place.

The Death of Abhimanyu

The son of Subhadra and Arjuna was a great warrior, famous for his sense of fair play. Attacked by his Kaurava uncles and cousins, Abhimanyu died as he lived, with courage and honor.

On the thirteenth day of the war, Drona was frustrated by his failure to harm even a single Pandava. He knew that Krishna would keep Arjuna at a safe distance from Karna, who was keeping Indra's spear to kill Arjuna, and now used this knowledge to his own advantage. Keeping Karna by his side, Drona organized his soldiers in the Chakravyuha formation designed to entrap the enemy. The plan worked—Krishna and Arjuna, the only ones who knew how to breach the moving circular maze, stayed away from Karna. Drona was able to trap the eldest Pandava.

Finding himself caught in the Chakravyuha, Yudhishthira cried out for help. Krishna drowned the sound by blowing his conch and Arjuna, unaware of his brother's plight, soldiered on.

Meanwhile, Abhimanyu, newly married and barely sixteen, was also trapped. He went to Yudhishthira, offering to help him escape—but how could a young boy rupture a formation that rendered most seasoned warriors helpless? Abhimanyu had heard Arjuna describe the Chakravyuha to his mother when he was still in her womb. But though he knew how to help others escape, he did not know how get out himself. Yudhishthira promised to come back for him and Abhimanyu set about freeing his uncle, as everyone, including Drona, watched amazed. But when Yudhishthira turned back to assist Abhimanyu, he found his path blocked by Jayadratha and his army.

Abhimanyu found himself surrounded by his uncles and cousins, including Duryodhana, Karna, and Drona. When he reminded them of the rules of war, they said that the Pandavas had played foul first by bringing a woman to the battlefield.

Abhimanyu fought back bravely—they broke his bow, sword, and spear. He then took up a chariot wheel to defend himself and killed Duryodhana's son. Then Dusshasana's son stunned him with a mace. Before he could recover his senses, the Kauravas jumped on him and cut him to pieces. Blocked by Jayadratha, Yudhishthira could only watch helplessly from the other side.

"I know only **how to break** the formation … I **don't know how to escape."**

ABHIMANYU TO YUDHISHTHIRA, DRONA PARVA: THE BOOK OF DRONA

AN INTRICATE WEB
Abhimanyu pierced all the seven rings of the Chakravyuha, the deadly battle formation, to rescue Yudhishthira.

BEFORE

The Kaurava commander, Drona, was successful in killing the first member of the Pandava family.

JAYADRATHA'S ROLE

Abhimanyu, surrounded by his uncles and cousins in the Chakravyuha formation, fought valiantly but was besieged by the Kauravas who flouted all the rules of war and attacked the lone warrior simultaneously. Yudhishthira tried to help his nephew but his path was blocked by Jayadratha and his army. He could do nothing but hear Abhimanyu's cries as he was brutally murdered.

When Yudhishthira informed Arjuna of Jayadratha's part in Abhimanyu's death, Arjuna's grief turned to deep rage against the Kauravas' brother-in-law. He made a vow to kill Jayadratha before sunset the next day or else burn himself alive.

Jayadratha's Last Laugh

The news of Arjuna's vow to kill Jayadratha by sunset the next day or set himself on fire reached Drona. Pleased, he came up with a strategy to keep Jayadratha hidden till sundown the next day, which meant that Arjuna would die.

EPIC CONFRONTATION

This facade of the Udupi Sri Krishna temple in Karnataka, India, captures the epic confrontation between Arjuna and Jayadratha. The eclipse during the confrontation is often cited by Krishna's devotees as an example of his miraculous powers.

ANALYSIS

ARJUNA'S LEARNING

The death of Abhimanyu made the war personal to Arjuna. Until then, the Bhagavad Gita had motivated him only to enter the battlefield. As the war progressed, the wisdom Krishna expounded could not sustain him. Arjuna consistently gave in to his fears and attachments, exasperating even Krishna. When Abhimanyu died, Arjuna blamed not only Yudhishthira for not protecting his son but also Krishna for taking his chariot to the far side of the battlefield. Krishna said nothing in response, as he recognized that Arjuna had finally got the message—that on the battlefield, Drona was not his teacher but an adversary to be defeated.

On the fourteenth day of the battle, Drona put the entire Kaurava army between Arjuna and Jayadratha, the king of Sindhu, whom the Pandava held responsible for his son's death and had vowed to kill before the end of that day. Despite his best efforts, Arjuna could not find Jayadratha. By now, Arjuna's anguish at his young son's death had turned into a raging fury directed at the Kauravas. He fought fiercely, releasing hundreds of arrows that shattered the chariots and weapons of the Kaurava army that stood between him and Jayadratha and blocked his way to his quarry.

The exhausted stallions

Arjuna was relentless in pursuit; even his horses eventually tired and were unable pull his chariot any further. Krishna, his charioteer, realized this and he unyoked the horses while Arjuna kept the enemy at bay. When told that the horses needed water, Arjuna turned away from the surrounding army and shot an arrow in the ground, causing a fountain to erupt. He then continued to fight as his horses quenched their thirst and readied themselves for battle again.

Rules of war

Abhimanyu's death had given Arjuna a dogged desire for revenge that made him forget the rules of warfare. He saw Bhurishrava, who fought for the Kauravas, pinning the Yadava warrior Satyaki to the ground and striking him with a sword. Ignoring the code of war to never interfere when two warriors were in a duel, Arjuna sent an arrow flying, severing Bhurishrava's sword-arm.

While Bhurishrava was expressing his outrage to Arjuna, Satyaki came to his senses. Without realizing that his enemy was in conversation with Arjuna, Satyaki swung his sword to behead the distracted Bhurishrava—an act that drew deep condemnation from the assembled warriors.

The sunset

Arjuna's search for Jayadratha continued as the sun raced westward across the sky. With the red glow of dusk, a cheer erupted from all the Kaurava warriors. They had succeeded in their mission—Jayadratha was safe. Surprised and disappointed, Arjuna said, "Oh Krishna, I have failed to find him before dusk. I shall now burn myself alive."

Krishna's ploy

Krishna whispered in Arjuna's ear, "The sun has yet to set. I have just covered it with my hand so that everyone believes it has. If you concentrate, you can find Jayadratha by his laughter. Only you can shoot him in the darkness. As soon as you kill him, I will reveal the sun." Buoyed by this disclosure, Arjuna strained his ears to hear through the jubilation that had erupted in the Kaurava camp. At last, in the dark, he heard the unmistakable peal of Jayadratha's laughter. Arjuna took aim and released an arrow that severed Jayadratha's head. Before Drona could cry that it was against the code of war to fight after sunset, Krishna uncovered the sun.

Jayadratha's father, Vriddhakshatra, had been granted a blessing to protect his son—whomever caused Jayadratha's head to fall on the ground would have their own head split into thousand pieces. To prevent this, Krishna had Arjuna's arrow carry Jayadratha's severed head through the sky and drop it in Vriddhakshatra's lap. As the father jumped up in alarm, his son's head rolled to the ground. Vriddhakshatra's head exploded into a thousand pieces as his own blessing to protect his son turned against him.

"**Tomorrow**, you will see the earth **strewn with the heads** of kings, **severed** by forceful arrows that I release."

ARJUNA TO KRISHNA, DRONA PARVA: THE BOOK OF DRONA

AFTER

Both the Kauravas and Pandavas indiscriminately disregarded the rules of the war.

DRONA'S RESPONSE

Drona was livid that despite his desperate measures, Jayadratha had been killed. He ordered his troops to continue fighting against the Pandavas after the sun had set, even though it was against the code of war ethics. The Kauravas continued to fight in the dark with some soldiers holding lamps instead of weapons.

The Pandavas retaliated in kind but had to eventually resort to an action that no one could have imagined.

BEFORE

Abhimanyu's death had shaken Arjuna. Filled with rage, he vowed to kill Jayadratha before sunset, or burn himself alive.

DRONA'S ANGER

Drona made sure to keep Jayadratha away from Arjuna. A frustrated Arjuna had all but given up hope of finding his brother-in-law, when Krishna caused a momentary eclipse, giving Arjuna an opportunity to kill Jayadratha.

KRISHNA CAUSED A SOLAR ECLIPSE

The **Battle** after **Sunset**

Krishna's trickery had resulted in Jayadratha's death. This made the Kaurava side furious, especially Drona, who refused to stop the fighting even after dusk. All rules of war were suspended as he and Arjuna clashed into the night.

After the death of Jayadratha, king of the Sindhu and brother-in-law of the Kauravas, on the fourteenth day of battle, Drona was filled with rage. He refused to stop fighting, and ordered his troops to continue on even after the sun had set.

Rules of war broken

Duryodhana and Karna looked on in alarm and reminded Drona that this was against the code of war. According to the ancient rules of war, no fighting could take place before dawn and after dusk. But Drona replied, "If Krishna can dupe us into believing day is night, why can't we make night into day?"

On the orders of their commander-in-chief, the Kauravas did not lower their weapons even as the sun went down and the battlefield was covered in a blanket of darkness.

In the dark

To help the warriors see in the dark, Duryodhana ordered some soldiers to carry lamps instead of weapons. Soon, there were lamps along the length of the Kaurava army. The commanders, bathed in the flickering lights, were resplendent as their golden armor and weapons glistened. Looking like magnificent stars that had descended on earth, they moved menacingly toward the Pandavas, determined to destroy them. The continued attack alarmed the exhausted Pandava army. Taken by surprise, they suffered many casualties.

Arjuna saw the scene unfolding and took charge. He organized his army to carry lamps as well so that they, too, could see in the darkness and fight back. He ordered seven lamps to be placed on each elephant, two on each horse, and ten on each chariot. Their path lit, the Pandavas fought back, and the darkness daunted them no more.

PEOPLE

GHATOTKACHA

Ghatotkacha, Bhima's son with his Rakshasa wife Hidimbi, was Kunti's first grandchild. Despite being the eldest scion of the Pandavas, he was never on an equal footing with his siblings, perhaps because of his Rakshasa heritage. But he was always ready to come to his father's aid, and in the war his extraordinary powers, amplified at night, helped destroy many from the Kauravas' side.

"**Darkness** covered the earth and **nothing** could be seen. ... **Men**, horses, and elephants were **immersed** in **blood**."

SANJAY TO DHRITARASHTRA, DRONA PARVA: THE BOOK OF DRONA

Ghatotkacha summoned

It was on this long night that Drona slew his sworn enemy, Drupada, the father-in-law of the Pandavas. He also killed Virata, the king of Matsya, who had given shelter to the Pandavas in their final year of exile. Watching Drona, Krishna turned to Bhima and said, "Summon Ghatotkacha, your son born of the Rakshasa queen, Hidimbi. The Pandava army is exhausted and the darkness of the night does not help. But a Rakshasa is invincible at night." Bhima summoned his son and asked him to fight in the battle. Ghatotkacha, half-human and half-Rakshasa, looked tall and ferocious in the dark of the night. With his long, sharp, teeth and claws, he had the Kaurava forces running for cover in no time. The shrewd Drona, who had anticipated this move by the Pandavas, summoned the Rakshasa Alamvusha to fight for the Kauravas. The Rakshasa, tall as a mountain, challenged Ghatotkacha. They rushed at each other with such force that sparks flew as they clashed. In the end, Ghatotkacha managed to choke Alamvusha to death.

Seeing victory slipping away, Duryodhana asked Karna to use the spear Indra gave him on the Rakshasa. Karna had planned to use the spear against Arjuna but, compelled by Duryodhana, he hurled it at Ghatotkacha. The Rakshasa screamed as the spear ripped open his chest. Blind with pain, he tottered toward Bhima, not wanting to die before he had one last look at his father.

Collateral damage

Krishna shouted out,"Don't come here—don't fall on the Pandava side. Increase your size and fall on their side. Crush as many Kauravas as you can. Be a good son, and help your father till your very last breath." Ghatotkacha nodded. He stretched himself till his head touched the sky, and threw himself on the Kaurava side, crushing hundreds of soldiers. Bhima howled in pain as he saw his eldest son die.

Duryodhana smiled as he heard Bhima cry, but his happiness was short-lived as he was told of the vast number of Kaurava soldiers Ghatotkacha had claimed in death.

End of a long day

Krishna, despite seeing Bhima in pain, was happy. His plan had worked—now that Indra's spear was gone, Karna could not harm Arjuna. In addition, Ghatotkacha's death would send Bhima into a rage, which would serve the Pandavas well in this battle.

The battle continued through the night. The troops on both sides were tired to the bone, but stopped only when both Arjuna and Drona decided to leave the battlefield for the night.

THE DEADLY WEAPON
The Patung Satria Gatotkaca statue in Bali, Indonesia, shows Ghatotkacha's final battle with Karna.

AFTER

With the death of his son, the battle now became personal for Bhima. Karna, too, had lost the one weapon that could have killed his arch-enemy, Arjuna.

RUTHLESS KILLINGS

The rules of battle had been broken and chaos, propelled by anger, resulted in many deaths and unwise decisions.

The Pandavas busied themselves with plotting the downfall of Drona.

THE SPEAR WAS A POPULAR WEAPON IN ANCIENT INDIA

BEFORE

The war had been escalating—honor had been forgotten, the rules had broken, and the course of dharma had been abandoned.

THE NIGHT BATTLE

The sun set, but the warriors still did not stop fighting. Drona, the Kaurava commander-in-chief, in his battle trance, kept pushing his soldiers to continue. This meant Arjuna had to ask his soldiers to continue fighting. It was much later in the night that Arjuna realized his soldiers were tired and weary of fighting. He then fought harder and drove Drona away from the battlefield. The soldiers returned to their camps, and tried to get some rest before the battle the next day.

Drona **Beheaded**

The mighty leader of the Kaurava army, Drona proved to be a great challenge—his well-thought-out strategies inflicted tremendous damage. The Pandavas wondered what it would take to defeat such a great warrior.

Charged with his success in killing Drupada, the father-in-law of the Pandavas, and Virata, the king of Matsya, Drona continued to attack the Pandava army even after dark. Though this was against the rules of war, both sides took advantage of this transgression. The Pandavas did not know how to stop their teacher, who had become invincible on the battleground.

"How does one defeat him?" wondered the Pandavas, driven to the edge of helplessness.

Krishna told them, "All his drive and impetus stems from his love for his son, Ashwatthama. If news reaches him of his son's death in the battlefield, he will surely lose the will to fight." And so started the great deception.

A deceitful strategy

The Pandavas circled Drona, and declared that Ashwatthama was dead. At first, Drona refused to believe them, but as the whispers continued, he turned to Yudhishthira, the most honest man in the world, and asked, "Is this true?"

Yudhishthira looked at Krishna. Krishna smiled, empathizing with the eldest Pandava. He could sense his mental agony—was truth above everything? What if a lie could bring this wretched war to an end?

With a heavy heart, Yudhishthira said, "Yes, Ashwatthama is dead!" Drona went numb upon hearing his son's name. He could not hear the rest as Yudhishthira murmured softly, "Perhaps it was an elephant by that name or, perhaps, a man."

In truth, there really was an elephant called Ashwatthama that Bhima had killed. But that was not for Drona to know. The Pandavas' plan worked like a charm.

A father's grief

Drona, badly shaken, lost his will to fight. He stopped his chariot right in the middle of the battlefield, stepped out, put down his weapons and sat down to meditate, prepared to die.

"Kill him!" Krishna shouted. But no one stepped forward. Drona was a teacher, a Brahman. To kill him would be the worst of crimes. Krishna shouted, "He was the son of a Brahman, but he lived like a Kshatriya, seeking

DRONA'S MISTAKE

A 19th-century opaque watercolor-and-gold on paper titled "Arjuna and Krishna Advance Against the Kauravas" depicts a scene from the fifteenth day of the battle.

ANALYSIS

KILLING A PRIEST

Brahmans hold an exalted position in the Hindu social order. The idea of "Bramha-hatya-paap," or killing a Brahman, is a crime like no other. A person who does so loses the right to be a member of civilized society.

By killing Drona, a Brahman by birth, Dhrishtadyumna commits Brahma-hatya-paap. Only Shiva the destroyer is allowed to perform such an act. Often, this event is understood to be mere decapitation of a lifeless body—Drona's soul had left his body, even before the sword had struck it.

BRAHMAN PRIEST IN PRAYER AND MEDITATION

wealth, power, and vengeance. Let him die like a warrior."

Hearing this, Dhrishtadyumna, son of Drupada and now commander of the Pandava forces, moved forward. In one slash of his sword beheaded Drona. Dhristadyumna had avenged his father's death.

Ashwatthama's rage

Ashwatthama saw the cruel killing of his unarmed father. He released the Narayanastra, a dreadful missile that spat fire and filled the sky with dark serpents with giant fangs.

"It will destroy us!" said Yudhishthira. But Krishna said, "It will not, throw your weapons away and step out of your chariots. The missile will not harm an unarmed person."

Everyone did as told and stood still in the battlefield. But Bhima, in his fury, rushed toward Ashwatthama, hurling abuses and threatening to turn him into pulp with his whirling mace. The Narayanastra enveloped him in a cloud of fire and poisonous serpents. Bhima would have met his end that day in battle, had not Arjuna and Krishna rushed to him, dragged him from his chariot, and disarmed him. The missile died out without hurting anyone.

Ashwatthama was outraged that his weapon had failed. "Shoot it again," said Duryodhana. "Avenge your father's death!"

"I cannot," said Ashwatthama, "the Narayanastra can be used only once. If I try again, it will turn against me."

PEOPLE

ASHWATTHAMA—THE IMMORTAL WARRIOR

The son of Drona and Kripi, Ashwatthama has dramatic origins. He is a result of a blessing given by Shiva in answer to Drona's severe penance for a child.

Ashwatthama, Drona's only child, was born with a gem on his forehead which protected him from all living beings that were not human. Afraid of nothing, he grew up to be brash and arrogant.

A survivor of the Kurukshetra War, Ashwatthama is known as one of the seven chiranjeevis, or immortals, who roam the earth. He has been cursed by Krishna to live until the end of time, or Kali Yuga, searching for death. It was his immense jealousy of Arjuna that forged his friendship with Duryodhana, the two united in their hatred for the Pandavas.

A STONE SCULPTURE IN HALEBIDU, KARNATAKA, INDIA, SHOWS THE MIGHTY BHIMA KILLING THE ELEPHANT NAMED ASHWATTHAMA

"My **father** was brought down by inferior ones after he had **cast aside** his **weapons**. A **wicked act** has been committed. ... **Dharma's son** has **acted** ignobly and **cruelly.**"

ASHWATTHAMA TO DURYODHANA , DRONA PARVA: THE BOOK OF DRONA

AFTER

On the fifteenth day of the war, the news of Drona's death shocked everyone.

WHO WILL LEAD THE KAURAVAS?

The death of Drona, a beloved teacher, was mourned by both the Kauravas and the Pandavas. Now that their commander was dead, the Kauravas needed to decide who would lead their side. Drona had been an able leader and had killed many a great warrior from the Pandava camp.

To continue their winning streak, the Kauravas needed to replace him with an equally able leader. It was decided that the only one who could take on the mantle was Duryodhana's best friend, Karna, the king of Anga, who had kept himself away from the war until then.

8

KARNA PARVA: THE BOOK OF KARNA

THE GREAT RIVALRY
This bas-relief from West Bengal, India, portrays the epic battle clash between Arjuna and Karna which ended in Karna's death.

Karna Parva, or the Book of Karna, is the eighth parva in the Mahabharata. It is named after Karna, the king of Anga, who takes command of the Kaurava army for the sixteenth and seventeenth days of the war following Drona's death. Karna and Arjuna have a particular enmity and the two finally face each other in a bloody clash on the battlefield. Dhritarashtra, the blind ruler of the Kuru kingdom, hears a detailed account of these events from his charioteer, Sanjay. This parva is a small one, with only 1 sub-parva, 69 chapters, and 3,870 shlokas, or couplets.

> "Be like the **rising sun,** the **destroyer of darkness** through its fierce rays. May they … **not** be able to look at **your arrows**. … May the Parthas and the Panchalas **not** be able to **stand before you**!"

BARDS AND BRAHMANS TO KARNA, KARNA PARVA: THE BOOK OF KARNA

A Mother's Plea

Distraught that her sons would face each other on the battlefield, Kunti appealed to her firstborn. Karna promised her that he would spare all his brothers, except Arjuna.

Upon Drona's death, the mantle of commander-in-chief of the Kaurava army fell to Karna. Kunti overheard this news and could not bear the idea that the Pandavas would face their elder brother in battle. She decided to meet Karna and put a stop to this. She hoped that he was wiser, and perhaps kinder, than her other sons, who would not understand her plea.

Kunti left the palace at Hastinapur and arrived at the battlefield just before dawn. She saw her son meditating in preparation for the upcoming battle. His golden earrings and armor—unique adornments that were part of his identity since birth—had been stripped away. His chest was raw and his ears still bled. Her heart filled with love, Kunti addressed her son for the first time. Karna looked up and recognized his mother. A lifetime of unspoken emotions rushed through his heart.

Karna bowed. "Accept the salute of the charioteer's son, Mother of the Pandavas," he said. The sarcasm in his voice pierced Kunti's heart. With tears in her eyes, she asked for his forgiveness. Ashamed of his own pettiness, Karna apologized to his mother. She had, after all, been scarcely more than a child herself when she had given birth to him.

"How can I help you? It is almost daybreak and I grant the wish made to me at this hour of the day," he said.

The purpose of her visit dawned on him. "You have not come here to give love to your wronged firstborn, but to collect charity from me," Karna said.

Mortified at his accurate assessment, Kunti told him that she did not want the brothers to fight each other. "Take your rightful place as the eldest brother, and let there be peace," she pleaded.

Karna refused to abandon Duryodhana, his friend who had stood by him when no one else had. "Ask for anything else but that," he said.

"I don't want my sons to die," Kunti cried. Karna asked if she referred to her sons born before or after her marriage. He then said, "You are known as the mother of five sons. At the end of the war, I promise that you will still have five sons, including one great archer, either Arjuna or me." Not wanting to show his pain, he turned away from her. It was time for war.

"You will either be **without Arjuna and with Karna, or if I am killed**, you will be with Arjuna."

KARNA TO KUNTI, KARNA PARVA: THE BOOK OF KARNA

A MOTHER AND SON
Kunti's meeting with her son Karna interpreted in a traditional Indonesian dance.

THE LOYAL FRIEND

Karna

> "Karna was **revered** by all those who **wielded the bow** and **desired victory**."
>
> SANJAY, DRONA PARVA: THE BOOK OF DRONA

An unacknowledged son, a fierce friend, a bitter foe, a man on the side of the wrongdoers but a model of loyalty and generosity, Karna is a figure through whom Vyasa presents the conflicts of life—friendship or family, personal ambition or universal good, loyalty or opportunity. Described as handsome and radiant, he is the tragic figure of the Mahabharata.

The abandoned child

A young, unmarried Kunti had received a divine mantra from Sage Durvasa, by which she could call upon any Deva and have a child by him. Curious, she invoked Surya, the sun god, and bore his son. But the girl got scared and set the child adrift in the river. It was later found by Adhiratha, a charioteer. He and his wife Radha raised the foundling as their own.

A skilled archer

Karna wanted to be a great fighter. He approached Drona, the Kuru teacher, who dismissed him, telling him to learn his father's trade. Karna then went to Parashurama, disguised as a Brahman because the warrior-priest had vowed only to teach the Brahmans the use of weapons. He soon became Parashurama's favorite disciple, well versed in all the martial arts. But one day, Parashurama found out about his true identity as a Kshatriya. Angry at being duped, he cursed Karna that he would forget all that he had learned at a time when he would need it the most.

At the Kuru princes' graduation ceremony, Arjuna was the star performer. But Karna surpassed him in all of his feats, earning the adulation of the crowds. When his identity as a charioteer's son was revealed, the Pandavas were outraged and questioned Karna's eligibility to participate. Duryodhana then came to his rescue, declaring him a Kshatriya by merit, and anointing him as the king of a small kingdom Anga.

A public humiliation

Karna participated in Draupadi's swayamvara at Duryodhana's request. Just as Karna was to try his hand at the contest, Draupadi said, "A charioteer's son cannot take part in my swayamvara."

Humiliated, Karna withdrew. He had his revenge later at the dice game where he called Draupadi a whore. Citing the ancient law that allowed a woman to go to four men, Karna said that since Draupadi had been with five, she was a woman of loose morals.

A test of loyalty

Before the war, Krishna visited Karna and revealed the secret of his birth, urging him to unite with his family. But Karna was firm in his resolve to stand by Duryodhana and die for him.

On the eve of the war, when Karna suggested he would defeat the Pandavas single-handed, Bhishma scoffed at him, calling him a fool for thinking he was better than Arjuna. Karna vowed not to fight in the battle so long as Bhishma was in command.

When it was time for Karna to enter the battlefield, Indra, Arjuna's father, disguised as an old man, came begging for his earrings and armor that were impermeable to any weapon. Karna instantly gave them away. Impressed by his selflessness, Indra gave him a celestial spear that never missed its target, but could be used only once.

After Drona's death, Karna became the commander of the Kaurava armies. Kunti pleaded with Karna, her firstborn, to abandon the Kauravas. But he

A DETERMINED WARRIOR Under Parashurama's tutelage, Karna became well versed in archery and martial arts. This copper sculpture by Jitendra Sutar, titled "Vedh," shows a focused Karna aiming his bow at his enemy.

refused. Instead, he promised her that he would spare all her sons except Arjuna, his archenemy.

The fatal curse

Karna and Arjuna at last came face to face. Their duel continued all day until Karna's chariot wheel got stuck in the ground. This was certain death, as he would have to get down from his chariot, lower his weapons, and turn his back. He tried hard to remember the mantra that would help him release the wheel from the ground, but was unable to. He knew his end was near. As soon as his back was turned, Krishna urged Arjuna to shoot an unarmed Karna. Goaded by Krishna, Arjuna released his arrow, killing him instantly.

ART AND LITERATURE

MRITYUNJAYA

Mrityunjaya (1967) by Shivaji Sawant is a retelling of Karna's story through various voices, including his own. The Marathi novel has been translated into many languages such as Hindi, English, Gujarati, and Malayalam. In this book, Karna speaks in first person, telling his story in a long soliloquy. Interspersed with his narrative are the voices of Kunti, Duryodhana, and his wife Vrushali. Uniquely, Sawant plays with the idea of a mystical connection between Krishna and Karna. The novel received many awards and Sawant was the first Marathi writer to be awarded with the prestigious Moortidevi Award for literature in 1994.

THE MARATHI NOVEL *MRITYUNJAYA* RETELLS THE STORY OF KARNA

BIOGRAPHY IN BRIEF

- **Born** to an adolescent Kunti and the sun god, Surya, using a divine formula. Fearing social contempt, Kunti abandoned him.
- **Raised** by the charioteer Adhiratha and his wife Radha.
- **Lied** to Parashurama that he was a Brahman to learn the art of warfare from him. Parashurama cursed him that his knowledge would fail him when he needed it the most.
- **Found a friend** in Duryodhana, who saved him from humiliation, at a public tournament.
- **Humiliated by Draupadi** at her swayamvara when she refused to let him compete because he belonged to a low caste.
- **Insulted Draupadi** by calling her a whore and the Kauravas' slave.
- **Found out the secret of his birth** from Krishna, but still refused to join the Pandavas, remaining loyal to Duryodhana.
- **Refused to fight** under Bhishma, who had mocked him; entered the war only after his death.
- **Took over as commander-in-chief** of the Kaurava armies after Drona's death.
- **Lost his divine armor** after Arjuna's father, Indra, asked him for it. Impressed, Indra gave him a celestial spear to be used just once.
- **Killed Ghatotkacha** using Indra's divine spear, which he had reserved for Arjuna, at Duryodhana's request.
- **Spared the lives of four Pandavas** in accordance with his promise to Kunti.
- **Died** while fighting an indecisive duel with Arjuna when he stepped off his chariot.

BEFORE

With both Bhishma and Drona dead, the Kaurava army was again in need of a commander-in-chief.

KARNA'S OBLIGATIONS

Karna's acrimonious relationship with Bhishma had meant that he had kept away from the battle while Bhishma was in charge. With Bhishma's successor Drona's death in the battle, the obvious choice to lead the Kauravas was Karna. As eager as he was to fight for his friend Duryodhana, he had promised Kunti, his birth mother, that he would not kill any of her sons, other than Arjuna. This promise would shape his battle strategies as the commander-in-chief of the Kaurava army.

ARJUNA CONFRONTS KARNA
A 19th-century opaque watercolor on cloth shows Karna (right) and Arjuna (left) confronting each other on the battlefield. The blue-skinned Krishna can be seen as Arjuna's charioteer.

ANALYSIS

THE NUMBERS GAME

Many scholars have noted that there are certain numeral motifs throughout the Mahabharata. For instance, the number 18 keeps recurring throughout the epic.

Structurally, there are 18 parvas in the epic, excluding the Harivamsha. Similarly, the Gita has 18 chapters. Thematically, the war is fought over 18 days, with a total of 18 armies. When the Pandavas lose their possessions to the Kauravas, it is over 18 games of dice. When the Pandavas win the war, they rule the Kuru kingdom for 36 years (two times 18).

In addition, in the Kurukshetra War, each successive commander of the Kaurava army fought for half the number of days as his predecessor. Bhishma fought for 10 days, Drona for 5, Karna for 2 days, and Shalya for the final day.

Karna Assumes Command

Having lost his commander-in-chief Drona in battle, Duryodhana's obvious choice to lead the Kaurava army was Karna. He declared his friend would be the next commander-in-chief and that Shalya, the king of Madra, would be his charioteer.

Amid much fanfare and cheering, Duryodhana made Karna the commander of the Kaurava army. His appointment was a shot in the arm for an army that had lost both Bhishma and Drona in quick succession. To mark the occasion, Duryodhana appointed Shalya as Karna's charioteer and told his friend, "All your life, you were called a charioteer who is supposed to serve warriors and kings. Now, enter the battle as a warrior with a king serving you as a charioteer."

Shalya's strategy

Karna was initially pleased with this development as it boosted his ego to have a king driving his chariot. But he soon realized that having Shalya as his charioteer was not a wise decision. Shalya had mistakenly partaken of the Kauravas' hospitality when he had arrived to join the war. Left with no choice but to honor his commitment to fight on behalf of the Kauravas, he had turned to Krishna for advice, who told him to use this situation as an opportunity. The king of Madra now used psychological warfare against Karna, continuously praising Arjuna in order to make Karna insecure.

Karna's promise

The Kaurava commander saw that Krishna steered Arjuna's chariot away from his own in order to avoid a confrontation with him. Biding his time for the encounter that was surely coming, he decided to focus his energy on the other four Pandava brothers. He defeated Nakula and Sahadeva in a duel. He then defeated Bhima and,

finally, Yudhishthira the same way. He could have killed each one of them, but to keep his vow to Kunti, he let them live. Restraining himself, he merely said, "I will let you live and give you your life in charity." Wholly unaware of their true relationship, his brothers were angry and agitated at the thought of owing their lives to the one they considered nothing more than an ambitious servant.

Yudhishthira shattered

The eldest Pandava was so distraught with his encounter with Karna that he lost his will to fight. Arjuna saw him being carried off the battlefield and, fearing that Yudhishthira was hurt, he asked Krishna to take their chariot back to the battle camp. Krishna demurred, "No, we must keep our focus on Karna. This is the time to take him on as he must be tired after fighting your four brothers. Look at your brother Bhima who is still fighting the enemy. You must also do your duty." Arjuna, however, was adamant. On seeing Arjuna back in the camp before sunset, Yudhishthira assumed that he had returned only after slaying Karna.

The Pandavas fight

Upon hearing Arjuna's reasons for returning, Yudhishthira lost his temper and called Arjuna a coward. "Shame on you. You should give your bow, Gandiva, to someone more worthy who can kill Karna."

This insult to his bow was intolerable to Arjuna. So intense was his anger that he picked up a sword and rushed toward Yudhishthira, intent on striking him. Everyone in the camp was stunned to witness the Pandava brothers fight so bitterly.

Krishna's intervention

Seeing this, Krishna intervened and narrated parables to illustrate that actions that seem right could actually be wrong, just as actions that appear wrong could sometimes be right. Arjuna should not think that words spoken under duress were real. His brother was just angry and did not mean to insult him or his bow. One must have faith and not let harsh words spoken by friends or family break the bond of trust. The brothers saw sense and apologized to each other. They then strengthened their resolve to go back and face the real enemy—Karna—instead of fighting each other. This ended Karna's first day as commander, with stress taking a toll on the warriors of both sides.

"You will be like a rising sun that **scorches with its energy** and **dispels the terrible darkness** ... you will drive away our enemy."

DURYODHANA TO KARNA, KARNA PARVA: THE BOOK OF KARNA

AFTER

The Pandavas' determination to kill Karna resulted in many bloody battles, with the latter losing his sons before he came face to face with Arjuna.

KARNA'S NEMESIS

Arjuna and Karna's final duel was fierce. More than a match for Arjuna, Karna rejected help from another mortal enemy of Arjuna's—Ashwasena the Naga, who had an old score to settle with the Pandava since his family had been burned in the cleaning of Khandavaprastha. At sundown, when Karna's chariot wheel got stuck, Karna knew his time to die had come. Shalya, his charioteer, refused to move the wheel, stating that as the king, such a chore was beneath him. Karna jumped down to extract it himself; seeing him unarmed, Krishna urged Arjuna to kill him. Despite reservations, the Pandava took his shot and killed his eldest brother. Kunti wept quietly for her firstborn when she heard the news.

BEFORE

Karna had a difficult day in the battlefield as the commander of the Kauravas, but he kept the warrior code and the promise to his mother Kunti.

THE BATTLE CONTINUES

By now, the Pandavas were desperate for Karna's blood. They knew how strong a warrior he was, and that only Arjuna could defeat him in battle. Both of them harbored an intense hatred toward each other. While Arjuna wanted to avenge the death of his son Abhimanyu, Karna wanted to avenge the death of his son Vrishasena, who had been killed by Arjuna's arrow. Despite all his sons having been killed by the Pandavas, Karna did not pause to mourn his loss, but continued fighting in the battlefield.

The Fall of **Karna**

The seventeenth day of the war had come, and both Arjuna and Karna were locked in a fight to the death. Then Karna's chariot got stuck, and he was reminded of an old curse, which told him that the time for him to die had come.

Arjuna and Karna finally faced each other on the seventeenth day of the battle. Arjuna used his arrows to push Karna's chariot a hundred yards away. Karna retaliated, but he could barely manage to push Arjuna's chariot back by ten yards. Yet, each time Karna tried, Krishna praised him.

Arjuna was upset. "Why are you showering him with praises? I pushed his chariot back a hundred yards, but he could push mine barely ten yards!"

Krishna smiled and said, "Look carefully, Arjuna. Karna's chariot has only two men in it. Your chariot carries the weight of both Nara and Narayana and has Hanuman on its banner. Surely it is more difficult a task for him than it is for you?"

The battle waged on. As Karna shot arrow after arrow at Arjuna, a serpent crawled in his quiver. This was Naga Ashwasena, who wanted to avenge the death of his mother whom Arjuna had killed when he had set Khandavaprastha ablaze to clear land for Indraprastha. Ashwasena coiled himself around an arrow Karna aimed at Arjuna. Realizing this was no ordinary arrow that sped toward them, Krishna pressed his feet against the floor of the chariot, causing it to sink lower into the ground. The arrow missed Arjuna but split his crown into two.

Arjuna was shaken by this narrow escape—his confidence was shattered. But Krishna assured him that he was the better archer.

Ashwasena returned to Karna to try and kill Arjuna with another arrow but Karna refused to mount him on his bow again. "I do not need the help of a Naga to kill Arjuna," he said. Ashwasena then charged toward Arjuna, but he was no match for the skilled archer. Arjuna killed him with a single dart.

An old curse

The duel between Karna and Arjuna raged on. The two were well matched in strength, skill, and stamina. Then, just as the sun began to set, Karna's chariot

PEOPLE

ASHWASENA

Ashwasena was the son of Takshaka, the king of Nagas, who lived in the Khandava forest. The forest had been razed with the help of Agni, the god of fire, so the city of Indraprastha could be built on that land. Burning the forest had been a death sentence to all who lived in it. Though Indra, the rain god, had answered the Nagas' call for help, Arjuna had protected Agni with a canopy of arrows. In desperation, Ashwasena's mother swallowed her son to help him escape, but she died when Arjuna beheaded her. Ashwasena then vowed to kill Arjuna to avenge her death.

KARNA FIGHTS ARJUNA

This watercolor-on-paper folio from the early 18th-century Mughal text *Razmnama* shows Karna and Arjuna fighting against each other on the seventeenth day of the war.

"O Arjuna! … **Let me extricate** the wheel from the ground. … Remember the instructions of dharma and **wait for a short while.**"

KARNA, KARNA PARVA: THE BOOK OF KARNA

TURN OF FATE
When a wheel of his chariot got stuck in the mud, Karna knew his fate had been sealed. As much as he tried, he couldn't remember the mantra that would release the wheel.

wheel sank into the ground. At that fateful moment, Karna knew his time had come. Long ago, he had come across a little girl who was crying because she dropped her glass of milk on the ground. To pacify the crying child, Karna squeezed the milk back into the container by pressing the soil between his palms. This pleased the child but infuriated the goddess of the earth, Bhoodevi, who had cursed Karna: One day she would clutch and crush him with the same power and he would surely die. Karna knew that Bhoodevi herself had pulled his chariot wheel into the ground. He tried to remember the formula his guru Parashurama had taught him to extricate a chariot stuck in mire, but could only recall another curse. When Parashurama had discovered that his student was not a Brahman but of the warrior caste, he had cursed Karna and told him, "You will forget everything I taught you the day you most need it."

A rule of war broken

Karna asked his charioteer Shalya, the king of Madra, to step out and release the chariot wheel from the ground. Shalya refused, saying as a king it was not his job to be a charioteer. Karna had no choice but to get down and free the wheel himself. To do this he would have to lower his arms and turn his back to the enemy. "It is against the rule of war to attack an unarmed warrior in battle," Karna reminded Aruna. But as soon as his back was turned, Krishna cried, "Shoot him, Arjuna! This is the perfect opportunity." Arjuna hesitated. How could he shoot an unarmed, helpless man? Krishna urged him on. "Karna is not as helpless as Draupadi was that day when the Kauravas disrobed her in public." Spurred by the memory of that fateful day, Arjuna released an arrow that ripped through Karna's heart.

That day the sun set faster as Surya mourned for his son. Kunti wept for the son she could never publicly acknowledge. And Duryodhana, who had never cried for his own brothers, sobbed when heard his dear friend was dead.

MYTHOLOGY AND FOLKLORE

KARNA'S GENEROSITY

One day, Indra, disguised as a priest, approached Karna for alms and asked for his golden armor and earrings. As Arjuna's father, he feared his son's death, and wanted to take away the armor and earrings that made Karna invincible—without that armor Arjuna would be able to kill him. Surya the sun god and Karna's father had warned him of this trick. But Karna did not hesitate. He immediately cut the armor and earrings off his body and gave them to Indra. Pleased by his selflessness, Indra gave Karna a spear that, though it could only be used once, would not miss its target.

A 9TH-CENTURY COPPER ALLOY SCULPTURE OF SURYA, THE SUN GOD AND KARNA'S FATHER, FROM INDONESIA

AFTER

Duryodhana was inconsolable in his grief over the death of Karna, who was dearer to him than his own brothers.

DURYODHANA GRIEVES
Karna and Duryodhana were not just united in their hatred of the Pandavas, they also shared a deep friendship. Karna respected Duryodhana for upholding his honor when he was shunned for his lowly birth, and Duryodhana considered Karna his best friend and cared for him more than he cared for his own brothers. Karna's death had a deep impact on Duryodhana's own will to continue with the battle.

Dusshasana's Death

In the first sixteen days of the war, Bhima had single-handedly killed ninety-eight of the Kauravas. But his thirst for blood would not be sated until Dusshasana, who had most deeply offended Draupadi's honor, was dead.

BEFORE

On the day that Dusshasana dragged Draupadi into court and attempted to disrobe her, Bhima took a terrible vow.

BHIMA'S VOW

Seeing his wife dragged into the hall by her hair, her body barely covered, made Bhima's blood boil. He swore to kill all the Kauravas, break Duryodhana's thigh, and drink Dusshasana's blood for insulting Draupadi.

To allow Bhima to fulfil his vow, the other Pandavas stayed away from the Kauravas in the battles. Every day, Bhima killed Dhritarashtra's sons with a ferocity that struck terror in the hearts of all who watched. Eventually the Kauravas took to hiding away from Bhima, behind chariots and elephants. But Bhima sought them out and, ignoring their cries for mercy, smashed their heads with his powerful mace. By the sixteenth day, only two of the hundred Kauravas remained alive—the two that Bhima held most responsible for Draupadi's humiliation—Dusshasana and Duryodhana.

A wrong avenged

Bhima then turned his sights on Dusshasana. After a fierce exchange of arrows, he hit Dusshasana with such force that the latter was flung far away. On seeing Dusshasana prone and helpless, Bhima remembered all the past cruelties inflicted by the Kauravas. He remembered the house of lac that the Kauravas had given his family and set on fire. He recalled with vivid clarity the gambling match that had divested the Pandavas of their honor and dignity, giving in return the hardship and suffering of their years of exile. Most of all, he recalled Dusshasana humiliating Draupadi, and his own burning fury and helplessness at that deep insult.

In a frenzy of rage, Bhima pinned Dusshasana to the ground, ripped him apart with his bare hands, and drank his blood, fulfilling his vow.

A vow fulfilled

Bhima then invited Draupadi to fulfill her own vow. Ever since the day Dusshasana had grabbed her by the hair, dragged her into the gambling hall, and tried to disrobe her, Draupadi had left her hair untied, vowing to tie it up again only after bathing it in his blood.

Watching Bhima wash his wife's hair in Dusshasana's blood, tying it with his entrails and decorating it with his heart, many concluded that Bhima was to Draupadi what Bhairava was to Shakti—the guardian who destroys all who look upon the earth with lustful eyes.

So, on the seventeenth day of the war, both Bhima and Draupadi fulfilled their oaths.

PEOPLE

VIKARNA'S KINDNESS

When Dusshasana had dragged Draupadi into court and humiliated her, the sole dissenting voice had been Vikarna's. This act of unexpected righteousness from a Kaurava, when even elders such as Bhishma and Dhritarashtra had been silent, had won the Pandavas' heart. When war was declared, Vikarna chose to fight alongside his brothers despite being opposed to their cause. Even as he killed Vikarna, Bhima was reminded of his honor and kind-heartedness.

A LONG WAIT
Kathakali—a classical Indian dance form with elaborate costumes, vivid make-up, and vigorous movements—is well equipped to capture the drama of Dusshasana's death at Bhima's hands.

> "This [blood] is **superior** to **mother's milk**, honey, **the blood** of my enemies **is tastier** than all of these."
>
> BHIMA, KARNA PARVA: THE BOOK OF KARNA

AFTER

By the seventeenth day of the war, Bhima had killed ninety-nine of Gandhari's hundred sons.

GANDHARI'S ANXIETY

Throughout her life, Gandhari had tried to follow dharma. When Duryodhana had come to her for her blessings before the war, she had wished for the better side to win. Yet, as one by one she heard the deaths of her sons recounted by Sanjay as she sat with Dhritarashtra, her famed sense of fair play wavered.

When the Kuru queen heard of Dusshasana's death and realized that only the first-born of her hundred sons remained alive, her heart was filled with fear. Knowing that there was little chance Bhima would spare Duryodhana, Gandhari resolved to do whatever she could to protect him.

9

SHALYA PARVA: THE BOOK OF SHALYA

RIVALS TILL THE END
The bitter rivalry and intense animosity between Bhima and Duryodhana ends in a fierce duel. This early 17th-century Bikaner-style miniature by artist Ustad Abhuji illustrates the fight between the two on the eighteenth day of the war.

Shalya Parva, or the Book of Shalya, is the ninth parva in the Mahabharata. It is named after Shalya, maternal uncle to the youngest Pandavas Nakula and Sahadeva. After Karna's death, Shalya is appointed commander-in-chief of the Kaurava army. With ninety-nine of her hundred sons killed by Bhima, Gandhari attempts to protect her only surviving son from his wrath. But in the ferocious battle that ensues, Duryodhana meets his end. This parva outlines the eighteenth—and final—day of the Kurukshetra War. It is narrated to Dhritarashtra, the blind leader of the Kuru clan, by Sanjay, his charioteer bestowed with divine vision. This parva has 4 sub-parvas, 64 chapters, and contains 3,315 shlokas, or couplets.

"He is brave and **immensely energetic**. ... The king of Madra is like a lion and an elephant in valor. He will **roam around fearlessly,** like a wrathful **destroyer** among beings, when the **time for destruction** has arrived."

KRISHNA TO YUDHISTHIRA, SHALYA PARVA: THE BOOK OF SHALYA

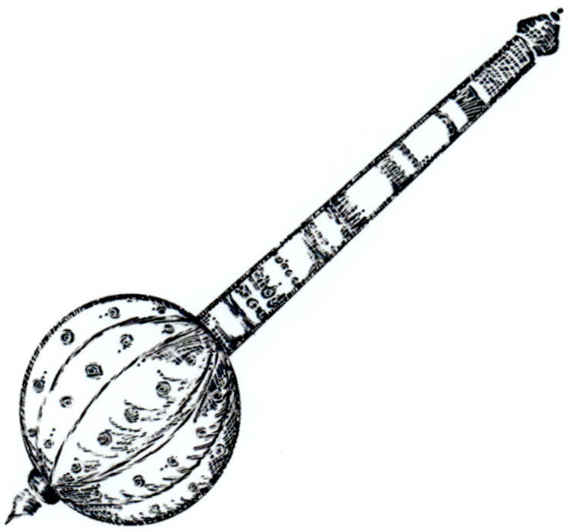

Gandhari's **Blessing**

Gandhari was shattered at the loss of her ninety-nine sons. No longer able to contain her emotions, she decided to save her eldest son Duryodhana from the ruthless death awaiting him.

Every day before marching into the battlefield, Duryodhana would go to his mother and ask for her blessings. Gandhari would bless him saying, "May the righteous side win." Duryodhana, who knew his mother's words always came true, would beg her to bless him with victory, but Gandhari steadfastly refused.

But as the war progressed, Gandhari's maternal instincts warred with impartiality. Duryodhana, her oldest, had always been her favorite. So, when Dhritarashtra reminded her that—righteous or not—Duryodhana was their son, Gandhari decided to grant him a blessing that would keep him safe in battle.

She instructed her firstborn to bathe before dawn and come to her without wearing any clothes. "I wore this blindfold when I married your father, and in all these years, never once have I taken it off. My fidelity and piety have filled my eyes, shut for all these years, with great power. Tomorrow, to protect you, I will remove my blindfold and look at you. Every part of your body my gaze touches will become impervious to weapons."

The following day, as he made his way toward his mother's chambers, Duryodhana heard a mirthful laugh. Turning around, he saw Krishna emerge from the darkness. "Have some shame," Krishna mocked. "At least cover your private parts before your mother!"

Duryodhana was mortified. Thus, when Gandhari took off her blindfold to look upon her son, her happiness turned to heartbreak. Despite her instructions, Duryodhana had taken a banana leaf and tied it around his waist. Her gaze would not touch his thighs and genitals, leaving them vulnerable. Realizing what this meant, and knowing her son's death had been decided, Gandhari wept.

"Oh **my son**. That **part of** your **body** that you have **covered** will remain **vulnerable**. And that will be **your death.**"

GANDHARI TO DURYODHANA, SHALYA PARVA: THE BOOK OF SHALYA

A MOTHER'S PROTECTION
This painting, in the Madhubani folk art tradition, shows Gandhari armoring her firstborn with her protective gaze, as Krishna looks on.

BEFORE

After Karna's death, the Kaurava army needed a new commander to lead their forces.

SHALYA TRICKED

Duryodhana had tricked Shalya, brother of Madri and maternal uncle of Nakula and Sahadeva, into joining the Kaurava side. He was further humiliated by being forced to serve as Karna's charioteer. But after Karna's death, on the eighteenth day of the battle, Shalya was given command of the Kaurava forces, and prepared to lead his forces against his own nephews.

The **Death** of **Shalya** and **Shakuni**

The eighteenth day of the battle saw the death of two leaders from the Kaurava side. But these deaths were also deeply personal, with both sides losing their uncles on the same day.

Shalya, the king of Madra and maternal uncle of the Pandavas Nakula and Sahadeva, was fooled into fighting on the Kaurava side. Not only did he have to fight against his own family, but he had to also face the indignity of being Karna's charioteer. The irony was not lost on Shalya; he, a king, had to serve as charioteer to a "king" who was actually a charioteer's son. But, as part of the Kaurava army, Shalya followed orders without protest, earning great respect from both the Pandavas and Kauravas.

On the eighteenth day, after the death of Karna, Shalya was asked to lead the Kaurava forces.

With a heavy heart he accepted the responsibility, resolving that his personal feelings would not come in the way of his duty.

Krishna saw that the king of Madra was at the helm of the Kaurava army and told Arjuna that Yudhishthira was best suited to fight Shalya, but did not elaborate when Arjuna asked him to explain why.

> "In that battle, those **two brave ones**, the king of Madra and Yudhishthira, were seen **covered with blood**, because of arrows shafted with the feathers of herons.... Those **great souls blazed**."
>
> SANJAY TO DHRITARASHTRA, SHALYA PARVA: THE BOOK OF SHALYA

Shalya's demon

What Krishna did not reveal was that within Shalya there lived a demon who fed on bitterness, animosity, hate, and violence. The more aggression the demon was faced with, the more its power increased.

Yudhishthira was not naturally aggressive at all and when faced by his uncle, he found it difficult to summon up even the smallest feeling of animosity. Even on the battlefield, his heart was filled with peace and love for his uncle, rather than hate and violence.

SHALYA'S DEATH ON THE BATTLEFIELD
This folio from the *Razmnama*, the Mughal book on the Mahabharata, shows Yudhishthira killing his own uncle, Shalya, on the battlefield of Kurukshetra.

Confronted with such love, Shalya's demon lost its power. Yudhishthira's gentle demeanor overwhelmed the demon, and its power kept dwindling instead of multiplying. Finally, the demon ceased to exist—and Shalya and Yudhishthira faced each other alone on the battlefield.

Yudhishthira picked up his spear and hurled it at his uncle with not a shred of anger or hatred. Shalya was killed on the spot. With this, the Pandavas had killed the last great leader of the Kaurava army. Victory, which had so long eluded them, now seemed certain.

Shakuni's plan

Recognizing that defeat was imminent, Shakuni came up with one last plan. While Bhima, Arjuna, and Yudhishthira were leading the army from the front, the rear was left unprotected.

Seeing the opening, Shakuni rallied his soldiers from Gandhara and ambushed the Pandava army from behind.

On hearing the commotion, the older Pandavas looked back. Though they saw Shakuni's strategy, there was little they could do. From so far in the front, they could not reach the rear ranks in time.

Yudhishthira then shouted out to his youngest brothers, the twins Nakula and Sahadeva, who were closer to the rear. "My brothers! I know you feel Shalya's loss deeply, but now is not the moment to mourn him. Now is the time to take action. Wipe your tears and bring down Shakuni, who attacks us from behind like a cowardly fox! Else all that we have gained will be lost."

Roused by their brother's speech, Nakula and Sahadeva rallied to action. Turning their painful loss into pointed fury, Madri's sons attacked Shakuni with unmatched aggression. A fierce fight followed and, in the end, it was Sahadeva's sword that made the fatal thrust.

Shakuni's death was a great loss not just to the Kaurava army but also to Duryodhana. He had seen all his siblings die in battle, but learning that he had also lost his maternal uncle—who had also been his mentor and guide—nearly undid him.

For the Pandavas, however, this was a great victory, for it was Shakuni's dice that had started their downfall.

PEOPLE

BHANUMATI

Although she does not feature prominently in the Mahabharata, Bhanumati, the princess of Kalinga, is the wife of Duryodhana. She loves him fiercely and, in turn, commands her husband's unwavering loyalty. Duryodhana was the only king who did not participate in Draupadi's swayamvara as he had promised his wife that he would not do so. In the Indonesian version, however, Bhanumati is the daughter of Shalya, and is in love with Arjuna. But Arjuna asked her to marry Duryodhana—the man she was promised to by her father.

BHANUMATI REPRESENTED IN A KATHAKALI PERFORMANCE

ANALYSIS

DOWNWARD SPIRAL

Bhishma commanded the Kaurava army for ten days. Drona led it for half of that, five days. Karna commanded it for half of Drona's duration, two days, and Shalya for one day, half of Karna's time. This downward spiral for the Kauravas is evident quite mathematically.

With the war's progress, there is a deterioration of morality and values in the epic. To defeat the Kauravas, the Pandavas have to fight Bhishma, a father-like figure; Drona, their teacher, Karna, a brother; and Shalya, an uncle. To kill them, the Pandavas had to learn how to break free from all attachments that bound them.

AFTER

This day of war saw the death of two kings and two uncles. The Pandavas lost Shalya, Madri's brother, and the Kauravas lost Shakuni, Gandhari's brother.

THE DEATH OF TWO KINGS
Sahadeva was a satisfied man at the end of the day, despite his uncle's death, for he had also killed his opponent's uncle. But while Shalya was innocent, Shakuni had orchestrated the whole gambling match which had led to the war.

Shalya and his son died in the war, which left the kingdom of Madra without a ruler. In keeping with Shalya's wishes, the kingdom went to his nephews Nakula and Sahadeva, who would become the rulers of Madra.

THE SECOND PANDAVA BROTHER

Bhima

> "With **his club**, Bhima **brought down** all those **rathas and charioteers**, with their flags, standards and weapons, like **Vishnu against the asuras**."
>
> SANJAY TO DHRITARASHTRA, KARNA PARVA: THE BOOK OF KARNA

After the birth of Yudhishthira, Pandu asked Kunti to invoke Vayu, the god of the wind, and have a son by him. The child conceived was named Bhima and was known for his extraordinary strength. He is often described as a passionate simpleton who could be provoked easily, had a gargantuan appetite, enjoyed fighting demons, and loved Draupadi passionately.

In the rural hinterland of India, the mace-wielding Bhima is the most popular Pandava. He is the great warrior who defeated many demons and made the world a safer place. Among the many tribes of India, such as the Konds in Odisha and Madhya Pradesh, Bhima is seen as the one who brought civilization to earth.

Growing-up years

Like other Kuru princes, Bhima, too, was trained under the royal tutor Drona, and learned the skill of mace warfare under Balarama. The young Bhima often bullied the Kauravas. One day, the Kauravas offered him sweets laced with poison and threw him into a river. However, the river-dwelling Nagas rescued him and made him drink a potion that would protect him from any poison in the world, making him even stronger.

Always protective about his brothers and mother, Bhima once helped the Pandavas escape an combustible house of lac that the Kauravas had made for them and set on fire, carrying his family in his arms to safety.

The family took shelter in a village that was being terrorized by the Rakshasa Baka. Bhima killed the demon and his brother Hidimba. Hidimba's sister Hidimbi was drawn by Bhima's strength and decided to make him her husband. They later had a son called Ghatotkacha.

WIELDER OF THE MACE
A stone carving of Bhima holding his mace stands at one of the gates of the temple town of Hampi in Karnataka, India. Born on the same day as his archenemy Duryodhana, Bhima eventually killed the antihero of the Mahabharata as he had sworn to.

Love for Draupadi

Bhima married Draupadi, just like his other brothers, because his mother said so. However, the romance of Bhima and Draupadi is the stuff of many folk legends. Draupadi knew that more than the others, Bhima would never refuse her anything. When Duryodhana and Dusshasana humiliated and tried to disrobe Draupadi in public, it was Bhima who could not keep quiet any more. "I will kill each and every Kaurava, drink Dusshasana's blood, and break Duryodhana's thigh with which he insulted my wife," Bhima promised. Unlike his other brothers, Bhima consistently protested against letting the Kauravas get away with their treatment of Draupadi.

Years in exile

While in the Kamyaka woods, Bhima killed many demons who troubled and harassed his family. Once on his way to get golden lotuses for Draupadi, he came across an old monkey blocking his path. But he could neither kick it away nor lift the tail. It dawned on him that the monkey was none other than the god Hanuman, his half-brother, who had come to teach him humility.

The Pandavas spent their last year of exile in disguise in the kingdom of Matsya. Bhima presented himself as a cook called Ballava. Kichaka, the queen's brother, connived to get Draupadi to his room at night, but Bhima came to Draupadi's rescue and swore to teach Kichaka a lesson. He went to his room instead of Draupadi and crushed him to death.

KILLING OF DUSSHASANA
This scene from a Kathakali performance shows Bhima drinking Dusshasana's blood and Draupadi washing her hair with it.

The Kauravas' nemesis

During the Kurukshetra War, Bhima fulfilled his vow to kill the Kauravas. Each day, he killed a few of the hundred brothers. Killing Dusshasana, who had tried to publicly disrobe Draupadi, gave him the most pleasure, and he later invited Draupadi to wash her hair with Dusshasana's blood.

On the last day of the war, only Duryodhana was left. Even after a fierce duel, Bhima could not subdue him. Krishna then indicated that Bhima should hit Duryodhana on his thigh. Although against the rules of war, Bhima swung his mace and broke Duryodhana's thighs.

Ruled by passion

Even after the war, Bhima was unable to forgive the Kauravas and took great pleasure in reminding Dhritarashtra and Gandhari how he had killed each of their sons.

On their way to Swarga all the Pandavas, save Yudhishthira, fell one by one. Bhima, too, fell. Yudhishthira knew that Bhima had been a glutton all his life, eating without bothering to serve others. He had always allowed his passions to rule him, and therefore did not merit a place in Swarga.

BIOGRAPHY IN BRIEF

- **Born** to Kunti and Vayu, the god of wind, by a divine mantra given to Kunti by Sage Durvasa.
- **Taught** by the royal tutor, Drona. Also learned the art of mace warfare from Balarama.
- **Was thrown** into a pond by his cousins the Kauravas, but survived with the help of river-dwelling Nagas.
- **Saved his family** by carrying them to safety through a tunnel during the fire at the inflammable house of lac.
- **Killed the demons** Baka and his brother Hidimba.
- **Married** Draupadi after Arjuna won her hand. Had a son, Satsoma, with her.
- **Killed Jarasandha**, the king of Magadha, before Yudhishthira's coronation, with Krishna's help.
- **Swore to kill** Dusshasana and break Duryodhana's thigh after the brothers tried to disrobe Draupadi.
- **Learned a lesson** in humility after an encounter with the monkey god, Hanuman, during the years in exile.
- **Took the guise** of a cook, Ballava, during the last year of exile spent in hiding.
- **Killed Kichaka** when he tried to force himself on Draupadi.
- **Killed all the Kaurava brothers** during the Kurukshetra War, and thus fulfilled his oath.
- **Placed an iron image** of himself before Dhritarashtra, who, thinking it was Bhima, crushed it.
- **Died** on his way to heaven with his brothers and Draupadi.

ART AND LITERATURE

RANDAMOOZHAM

The much feted Malayalam novel *Randamoozham* (1984), meaning the "second turn," by Kerala's renowned novelist MT Vasudevan Nair, not only retells the epic from Bhima's perspective, but also removes divine interventions and mythical aspects from the story. Bhima is seen as the one who never got his due, compared to the saintly Yudhishthira and the heroic Arjuna. Even his killing of all the Kauravas, not to mention so many demons earlier, did not win him the raves Arjuna got. Nair captures the angst of one who is always used but overlooked, and is seen only as a strong but brainless man, and whose wife loves another husband, Arjuna, more. The novel has been translated into English as *Bhima: The Lone Warrior*.

BEFORE

As the battle continued, the war claimed many more victims.

A PERSONAL LOSS

With the death of Shalya and Shakuni, the Kauravas had lost two able leaders. Yet the Pandavas knew that as long as Duryodhana, the eldest of his clan, lived, the war would go on.

For Nakula and Sahadeva, the eighteenth day had been bittersweet. On one hand, they had to deal with the death of their beloved uncle, Shalya, yet they knew that by killing Shakuni, they had virtually swung the battle in the Pandavas' favor.

Bhima Fights **Duryodhana**

Witnessing the humiliation of his wife, Bhima had vowed to kill every single Kaurava. He fulfilled his vow with a ferocity that shook even the gods and demons who witnessed the war on the battlefield of Kurukshetra.

A HARD BLOW

Bearing 118 spikes, a mace, such as this one, was used by the Marathas against the British. Called Vrigodharam, Bhima's mace is said to have delivered a devastating blow to his opponents.

Each day, Bhima strode into the battlefield and killed more of the Kaurava brothers. As their numbers dwindled, the sons of Gandhari did their best to avoid Bhima, but like a relentless predator, he found them and pounced on them. Ignoring their piteous pleas for mercy, he smashed their heads with his mighty mace.

As the other Pandavas knew of Bhima's pledge, they resisted the urge to strike down any Kaurava who crossed their path, saving them all for Bhima's devastating mace. Even when presented with the perfect opportunity, they would let the Kauravas go to ensure Bhima fulfilled his terrible vow. Each day of the war, Gandhari and Dhritarashtra would weep when they heard from Sanjay the growing list of their dead sons.

Killed one by one

Bhima killed the Kauravas in a blind rage, with neither grief nor sorrow. All except Vikarna, who alone had publicly opposed his brothers in the gambling hall and censured their behavior. In the war, however, Vikarna stood with his brothers out of loyalty, and so had to be killed. Greatly saddened by this death, all the Pandavas wept. Krishna was the only one unmoved. For him, dharma was to be prized over everything, even family.

By the time he fought Dusshasana, Bhima had killed all the Kauravas, except for him and his elder brother. Killing Dusshasana had given Bhima great pleasure—pinning him to the ground, Bhima had ripped out Dusshasana's bowels with his bare hands, inviting Draupadi to wash her hair with Dusshasana's blood so that she could bind her hair, left loose since that long-ago day in court. »

"They were **angry like tigers** and **roared** like monsoon clouds. The great-souled and immensely **strong ones blazed**. Duryodhana and [Bhima] **bellowed like bulls**."

SANJAY TO DHRITARASHTRA, SHALYA PARVA: THE BOOK OF SHALYA

MYTHOLOGY AND FOLKLORE

A MOTHER'S GIFT

The story of Gandhari's failed attempt to make her son invulnerable to weapons is reminiscent of another famous tale—that of the Greek hero Achilles.

In Greek mythology, Achilles was a great hero of the Trojan War and the central character of the war epic *Illiad* by Homer. In the epic poem *Achilleid*, written by Statius in the 1st century, his mother Thetis tried to make him invincible and immortal by dipping him in the river Styx. The only part that remained mortal was his heel, by which she held him. This would later be the reason for Achilles' death; he would be killed by an arrow shot at his heel by Paris, the prince of Troy.

THETIS DIPPING ACHILLES INTO THE STYX RIVER BY ANTOINE BOREL ROGAT

LIST

THE HUNDRED KAURAVAS

- Duryodhana
- Dusshasana
- Dussaha
- Jalagandha
- Sama
- Saha
- Vindha
- Anuvinda
- Durdharsha
- Subahu
- Dushpradarshan
- Durmarshan
- Durmukha
- Dushkarn
- Vivikarn
- Vikarna
- Salan
- Sathwa
- Sulochan
- Chithra
- Upachithra
- Chitraksha
- Charuchithra
- Sarasana
- Durmada
- Durviga
- Vivitsu
- Viktana
- Urnanabha
- Sunabha
- Nanda
- Upananda
- Chitrabana
- Chitravarma
- Suvarma
- Durvimochan
- Ayobahu
- Mahabahu
- Chitranga
- Chitrakundala
- Bhimvega
- Bhimba
- Balaki
- Balvardhan
- Ugrayudha
- Sushena
- Kundhadhara
- Mahodara
- Chithrayudha
- Nishangi
- Pashi
- Vridaraka
- Dridhavarma
- Dridhakshatra
- Somakirti
- Anudara
- Dridasandha
- Jarasangha
- Sathyasandha
- Sadas
- Suvak
- Ugrasrava
- Ugrasen
- Senani
- Dushparajai
- Aparajit
- Kundasai
- Vishalaksh
- Duradhara
- Dridhahastha
- Suhastha
- Vatvega
- Suvarcha
- Aadiyaketu
- Bahvasi
- Nagaadat
- Agrayayi
- Kavachi
- Kradhan
- Kundi
- Kundadhara
- Dhanurdhara
- Bhimaratha
- Virabahu
- Alolupa
- Abhaya
- Raudrakarma
- Dhridarathasraya
- Anaaghrushya
- Kundhabhedi
- Viravi
- Chitrakundala
- Dirghlochan
- Pramathi
- Veeryavan
- Dirgharoma
- Dirghabhu
- Mahabahu
- Kundashi
- Virjasa

THE FINAL SHOWDOWN
This dramatic bas-relief in Angkor, Cambodia, shows the two mighty warriors, Bhima and Duryodhana, ferociously fighting their last battle.

The last fight

Finally, there was only one Kaurava left to kill—Duryodhana. Duryodhana knew that Bhima would come after him. Though Gandhari had tried to make him invincible, Duryodhana's thighs remained vulnerable to attack.

Fearing for his life, Duryodhana ran and hid in a lake on the far side of the battlefield. After they killed Shalya and Shakuni, the Pandavas spent most of the eighteenth day searching for Duryodhana, knowing that they needed to kill the Kaurava king if the battle was to end. When they eventually found him in the lake, Bhima bellowed, "Come out, coward, and fight!"

Mustering his courage, Duryodhana replied, "I am no coward! I've been just resting my tired limbs so that I can kill you without much effort."

Rising from the lake, Duryodhana eyed Bhima, and soon the two were circling each other on the battlefield. This was going to be a battle that would shake the earth. The opponents, equal in strength and skill, and bitter enemies for too long, fought like wild elephants in heat.

The duel went on, with neither of them able to gain any ground at all, until they were both slick with sweat. Eventually, Bhima realized that, try as he might, he would not be able to subdue Duryodhana. The eldest Kaurava was far too skilled with a mace. Each time Bhima attacked, Duryodhana defended himself deftly. As the maces boomed and thundered, Bhima turned to Krishna in despair.

THE POWERFUL PANDAVA
Native to Tamil Nadu, India, Terukkuttu is a form of street theater and dance that portrays stories from the Mahabharata. The dancer here plays the mighty Bhima armed with his favorite weapon, a mace.

ART AND LITERATURE

DURYODHANA'S TALE—BHASA'S *URUBHANGAM*

Urubhanga, or *Urubhangam*, is a play written by Bhasa dating back to around 100 CE. It is based on Vyasa's Mahabharata, but dwells more on Duryodhana's character during and after his fatal fight with Bhima. It also introduces a character not known in the epic—Duryodhana's young son, Durjaya.

Bhasa's play portrays Duryodhana as a tragic hero who accepts his end with courage and fortitude. Full of remorse, Duryodhana forgives Bhima but blames Krishna for his fate. Just before Duryodhana dies, Ashwatthama names Durjaya as the king.

THE *URUBHANGAM*, ENACTED BY STUDENTS OF SHINSHU UNIVERSITY, JAPAN, 2009

Below the belt

Krishna looked straight at Bhima and then slapped himself high on the thigh. He knew that, because of Gandhari's protection, Duryodhana was invulnerable to injury—almost everywhere.

Bhima realized that what Krishna was suggesting—hitting Duryodhana below the belt—was tantamount to breaking the rules of war. Moreover, their teacher, Balarama, had demanded that they fight honorably. But Bhima did not question Krishna. Putting all his might behind it, he swung his mace and smashed it where Duryodhana least expected it—below the waist—breaking his thighs and crushing his genitals. Duryodhana fell to the ground, crying in pain and surprise, "This is foul play!"

An enraged teacher

Duryodhana called out to Balarama, "Goaded by Krishna, this student of yours has broken the code of war to kill me! Adharma! Adharma!"

Hearing Duryodhana's cry, Balarama appeared on the battlefield and saw his smashed thighs. Enraged at this blatant flouting of the rules, he raised his plow to kill Bhima, only to be stopped by Krishna, who said, "Only those who live a life of honor can expect to meet an honorable end." Balarama saw the dispassionate truth of the statement and lowered his plow.

> "In this **encounter** with clubs, I have been **brought down** by **adharma** … **you** have **used** many **crooked means**."
>
> DURYODHANA TO KRISHNA, SHALYA PARVA: THE BOOK OF SHALYA

Bhima's shame

As Duryodhana lay on the ground, bleeding to death, surrounded by the victorious Pandavas, he mourned his tragic end. But the Pandavas celebrated and jeered their fallen cousin. Swept away in the jubilation of the Pandavas' victory, Bhima jumped on Duryodhana's head and began to dance.

Furious, Krishna yelled, "Stop! How dare you humiliate him so? That man has been punished enough. Can you not be gracious in victory?"

Lowering their heads in shame, the Pandavas, chastened, proceeded to their camp.

AFTER

As the sun set on the eighteenth day of the epic battle, the victorious Pandavas returned to the battle camp.

AN EMPTY VICTORY?
At the Pandava camp, Draupadi was busy making preparations to celebrate the day's win.

But the Pandavas knew their triumph was one of shame. They had killed many men, a sizeable number of whom were their own blood relatives. As the Pandavas left the battlefield, they heard a dying Duryodhana call out, "I ruled a prosperous kingdom, and today I meet a warrior's death. I have been most fortunate. Would you say the same for yourselves; you who have been left behind to rule over a world filled with death and grief?"

HOLY TRIUMVIRATE
The three all-powerful deities—Brahma, Vishnu, and Shiva—are the source of all energy in the universe, both creative and destructive.

UNLEASHING DEATH AND DESTRUCTION

Weapons

> "O **fire**! When the **powerful** Varshneya releases the **chakra** in battle, there is nothing in the three worlds that Janardana cannot **vanquish**."
>
> ARJUNA TO AGNI, ADI PARVA: THE BOOK OF THE BEGINNING

There are essentially two categories of weapons that protagonists in the Mahabharata favored. The first was powered only by the user's strength and skill; the second was obtained as a special favor from a particular god, usually after severe trials and penance. Imbued with the added power of the divine, these weapons were capable of destruction at a much greater scale. This divine power could be innate in a weapon given by the gods, or invoked through secret incantations revealed by a teacher to his student. Weapons were the domain of the warrior caste, the Kshatriya, whose children were trained to use them with skill and expertise. The 105 princes of the Kuru clan learned the art of warfare from Drona, who had studied under the great warrior-priest Parashurama. Though he learned how to use all weapons, each warrior naturally gravitated to one that he preferred the most. Yudhishthira favored the spear, while Arjuna's skill with the bow was legendary; Bhima, Duryodhana, and Dusshasana fought with a mace, Nakula and Sahadeva with the sword.

TYPES OF WEAPONS
Various kinds of astras and shastras are mentioned in the Mahabharata. Capable of causing severe injuries on their own, they became destructive on a much larger scale when imbued with divine power.

DIVINE WEAPONS

It was the weapons that held the power of the divine—astras—that played a decisive role in the battles of the Kurukshetra War. Astras are missiles, an arrow for example, released at the enemy, as opposed to shastras such as a sword, which are gripped and used in close combat. Both could wield divine power though there are many more instances of astras being used in this manner.

The Sudarshana Chakra is the powerful spinning discus of Lord Vishnu. In the Mahabharata, it was given to Krishna by Agni, the god of fire, in gratitude after the burning of Khandavaprastha. Ashwatthama, the warrior-priest, knew it was the most powerful weapon in the world and asked Krishna for it, something not even Arjuna or Krishna's son Pradyumna, had ever dared to do. It was Ashwatthama's ambition to become the most feared warrior of all; he thought he could achieve this by using the Sudarshana Chakra against Krishna himself. As he was a Brahman, Ashwatthama's demand could not be denied.

Krishna was obliged to give him the chakra—but Ashwatthama could not so much as lift it.

At Khandavaprastha, Agni had also presented Arjuna an indestructible bow with a hundred bowstrings that hummed with thunderous fury when drawn. Called Gandiva, the bow had been created by Brahma, the Creator of the universe and was worshipped by the Devas and Gandharvas. No ordinary mortal could wield the bow and Arjuna had used it to devastating effect from the moment he received it. When Gandiva was unable to help him protect the women and children of Dwaraka after Krishna's death, Arjuna realized that his purpose on earth and that of the Gandiva had been served and their powers were ebbing away. Arjuna also successfully invoked the deity Shiva to obtain the Pashupat, an infallible weapon that assimilated the power of all birds and beasts. With it, he went to Swarga to help his father Indra fight the Asuras. When he finally rejoined his brothers and wife, Arjuna had the Pashupat with him, as well as several powerful weapons given to him by his father that were capable of destroying all life.

THE GADA
Both Bhima and Duryodhana were experts at wielding this club-like weapon and fought an epic battle against each other at Kurukshetra.

After Bhishma's death, when Karna was ready to enter the battlefield, the god Indra, out of love for his son Arjuna, went to Karna as an old man and asked him for the armor that covered his torso like skin, as alms. With no hesitation at all Karna cut it from his body and handed it over. Touched by such selflessness, Indra gave him the celestial spear Vasavi Shakti, known never to miss its mark, though it could only be used once. Karna had intended to save it to use against Arjuna but was forced to hurl it at Bhima's son Ghatotkacha.When invoked, the Narayanaastra manifested itself as a disastrous whirl of fire and heat. Its destructive capacity increased in the face of resistance. Used by Ashwatthama following the death of his father, Drona, the devastation it wrought ended only when the Pandava army responded to Krishna's call to lay down their arms and passively submit.

The Brahmaastra was another weapon that never missed its mark and had the capacity to annihilate entire armies. It was also said to have devastating side effects, including causing infertility in men, women, and the land where it was used. Four times more intense was the Brahmashirshaastra, which could be invoked from any object, even from a small blade of grass as Ashwatthama did. The Brahmaastra, which manifested all five heads of Brahma and could destroy the entire solar system, was the most powerful of all. It was also one of the most difficult astras to obtain. Only Parashurama, Bhishma, Drona, and Karna had the knowledge to invoke it.

SUDARSHANA CHAKRA
One of the most powerful weapons in Hindu mythology, the Sudarshana Chakra is said to have been created by Vishwakarma, architect of the gods, by using dust from the sun.

HISTORY AND CULTURE

THE WEAPON OF POISE

In Vedic civilization, the bow was considered the highest of weapons. It was the preferred weapon of the gods, symbolic of grace, poise, and balance. With the clear, single-minded focus on the target needed for success, it also represented desire, aspiration, and ambition, which was why when a king was crowned, he held a bow in his hand. Archery contests were highly prestigious and, as in Draupadi's swayamvara, the prize could be a daughter of the host king in marriage.

ANALYSIS

ASTRAS

On the battlefield of Kurukshetra, both sides use divine weapons charged with the power of natural elements. Since they were capable of destroying all life, the Vedas refer to them as weapons used only as a last resort. Descriptions of what happened when these weapons were fired, such as "turbulent winds raged, darkness stretched across the horizon and the earth shuddered under the scorching heat," lead to speculations that the ancients were probably familiar with nuclear technology and that astras were really nuclear warheads.

The **Talking** Head

In the midst of celebrating their victory, the Pandavas began to discuss the all-important question—who was the warrior who gave the Pandavas the upper hand? The talking head had the most interesting perspective.

After the war was over, there were festivities in the Pandava camp. The soldiers feasted on food and wine, sang and danced, and went over the events of the past eighteen days. Looking back at those turning points of the war that swayed the odds in their favor, they kept coming back to the same questions: who among the Pandavas was the greatest warrior? Which of the five had won them the war? The debate went on, until Krishna intervened, "Why don't you ask the talking head this question? He has seen more of the war than anyone else."

The "talking head" was Barbareek, son of Naga princess Ahilawati. He claimed to be Bhima's son. Others thought he was the son of Ghatotkacha, Bhima's son with Hidimbi, the Rakshasi. Barbareek, or the "talking head," had come to Kurukshetra armed with three arrows.

"With one arrow, I can destroy the Pandavas, with the second, I can take out all the Kauravas, and with the third, Krishna," he boasted.

As a test of his skill, Krishna asked Barbareek to shoot all the leaves of a banyan tree. He shot a single arrow that pierced all the leaves on the tree and then even hovered over Krishna's foot to get at the fallen leaf under it.

"On which side do you want to fight?" asked Krishna.

"The losing side," replied Barbareek. "Only that would prove me invincible."

This troubled Krishna, as Barbareek would keep switching sides, and the battle would never end. So he came up with a solution. He asked Barbareek to bring him the head of a warrior who threatened the world. "Tell me who it is, and I will destroy him," promised Barbareek.

Krishna then showed Barbareek a mirror—and demanded his head. Although he was tricked, Barbareek could not refuse. The only regret he expressed was that he would not witness the war. So, Krishna breathed life into his head and placed it on the ground. But each time he

BEFORE

The war had come to an end. The victorious Pandavas returned to the battle camp to be greeted by a very happy Draupadi.

ARJUNA'S LESSON IN HUMILITY

Traditionally, charioteers stepped out of their vehicles before the warriors, but when Krishna showed no signs of moving, an annoyed Arjuna got out of the chariot first. Krishna followed suit immediately. As soon as he did, the chariot burst into flames.

Krishna then told a stunned Arjuna that Drona had destroyed the chariot long ago, but Krishna had kept it intact. Arjuna realized that Krishna's "disrespect" had kept him safe—and another valuable lesson in humility was learned.

MYTHOLOGY AND FOLKLORE

KHATU SHYAMJI

The tale of Barbareek is not part of the Sanskrit text and comes from the oral tradition in the states of Kerala and Andhra Pradesh in south India.

In Rajasthan and Haryana in the north, Barbareek is worshipped as Khatu Shyamji, the one who always fights for the loser. The name "Khatu" is a nod to the Rajasthani village where he is worshipped, while "Shyamji" refers to a blessing that Barbareek requested from Krishna—that he be known by Krishna's name, Shyam.

THE ARROWS THAT HE HAD BROUGHT INTO THE BATTLEFIELD, NOCKED AGAINST A BOW, HAVE COME TO SYMBOLIZE KHATU SHYAMJI

was amused, the force of his laughter displaced chariots. So the head was moved to the top of a nearby hill from where he could watch the battle.

The soldiers asked Barbareek who the mightiest warrior was. Was it Arjuna, who had killed Bhishma and Karna? Or Bhima, who had single-handedly killed the hundred Kauravas? "Bhima? Arjuna?" Barbareek was puzzled. "All I saw was Vishnu's Sudarshana Chakra whizzing past and cutting the heads of evil kings. And the earth, in the shape of Kali's tongue, consumed all the blood."

Prithu's promise

Puzzled by Barbareek's reply, the Pandavas asked him to explain. Long ago, he said, Vishnu, as the king Prithu, made a promise to the earth. He vowed to be as careful with the earth as a cowherd is with his cows. The earth, pleased with the establishment of dharma, took the form of Gauri, the mother who nourishes life. But as the years passed, the kings forgot that they were custodians of the earth, not its plunderers. Tired of their depredations, the anguished earth took the form of a cow and went to Vishnu to remind him of his promise. On seeing the cow's sore udders and broken back, a furious Vishnu decided to purge the earth of the unrighteous. He took the avatar of Parashurama, Rama, and Krishna to restore order and asked Gauri to take the form of Kali, quenching her thirst with the blood of her plunderers.

A DIFFERENT VIEW
To Barbareek, the war that everyone else saw as a dispute between cousins gave Krishna an opportunity to rid the earth of the unrighteous and undeserving.

ON THE BATTLEFIELD
This 18th-century painting from south India shows the Kaurava and Pandava forces clashing on the battlefield.

AFTER

The Pandavas realized this war was not about them, but about creating balance in the cosmos. Barbareek could see this from a larger perspective.

With the war over, the Pandava camp rejoiced. But their encounter with the talking head had shown them the other side of their victory—in the end it was only about victory of the righteous.

As the celebrations resumed, they remembered the immense devastation that surrounded them. Silent amid all the grief, pain, and death, the Pandavas realized that they had not won because they were the better warriors; they had won because theirs was the righteous side.

10 SAUPTIKA PARVA: THE BOOK OF SLUMBER

THE SLEEPING WARRIORS
This 18th-century painting from Himachal Pradesh in northern India shows the warriors of the Kurukshetra War asleep after the day's fighting.

Sauptika Parva, or the Book of Slumber, is the tenth parva in the Mahabharata. Derived from the Sanskrit word "supta," meaning sleep, the parva illustrates the shameful events that take place in the dead of the night when the warriors are asleep. These events take place on the night that the Kurukshetra War ends and the Pandvas emerge victorious. Ashwatthama, the son of Drona, plays a pivotal role in this section of the Mahabharata. This parva has 2 sub-parvas, 18 chapters, and 771 shlokas, or couplets.

"The forces of **the enemy** must be struck, whether they are exhausted … **sleeping** in the middle of the night … whether their **warriors have been slain** and whether the forces are hesitant or not, one must **act in the same way**."

ASHWATTHAMA, SAUPTIKA PARVA: THE BOOK OF SLUMBER

BEFORE

The eighteen-day war had come to an end, with only three survivors from the Kaurava army.

THE LAST MEN STANDING
Over one billion, two hundred and twenty million people were killed. Out of less than twenty-four thousand survivors of the Pandava onslaught, only three were from the Kaurava army—Ashwatthama, son of Drona; Kripa, teacher of the Kuru princes; and Kritavarma, the Yadava. They moved toward a forest near the Pandava camp.

Ashwatthama's **Rage**

The war had come to an end, and the Pandavas had emerged victorious. But the three surviving Kauravas were not done yet. Nursing an intense hatred for the victors, Ashwatthama pledged to avenge their loss, even if it meant going against dharma.

Ashwatthama, Kripa, and Kritavarma sat near the lake where Duryodhana lay dying. They could hear the victors of the war, the Pandava soldiers, rejoicing. Sounds of revelry and merrymaking emanated from their camp, reminding the three Kaurava supporters of their loss. Unable to bear the sounds of laughter and joy, Drona's son Ashwatthama, said, "We might have lost, but the Pandavas have not yet won."

The spirited warrior

The eldest Kaurava marveled at Ashwatthama's display of rage and lauded his warrior spirit. "Though born a priest, you show greater spirit than a warrior. You are indeed an able leader of the army," commended Duryodhana.

Ashwatthama acknowledged the appreciation by bowing his head to his leader. He asked Duryodhana to make him the commander of the remaining Kaurava army, swearing to destroy the Pandavas at the cost of his life.

Delighted by Ashwatthama's display of loyalty and valor and surprised at the anger that burned in his heart despite death staring him in the face, Duryodhana urged Ashwatthama to do his best.

Encouraged by this, a happy Ashwatthama struck the earth with his sword, determined to seek revenge. "How will you destroy the enemy?" enquired Kripa, aware that they were only three

A SAVAGE ACT
The sight of an owl killing a hundred crows as they slept led Ashwatthama to devise a vicious plot to kill the Pandavas.

against the many Pandavas. Standing firm on his resolve, Ashwatthama confessed that, though unsure of the course of action to be followed, he was intent on avenging their loss and humiliation.

A sinister plan

As the sun set on the last day of war, the three survivors saw a large tree with a hundred crows sleeping on its many branches. Suddenly, a large owl, terrible in appearance, swooped silently toward the tree. It descended on the branches, killing the sleeping crows by severing their heads and tearing away their wings.

Witnessing the brutal act so swiftly concluded by the owl, Ashwatthama arrived at a conclusion. He had found a way to kill his enemies.

Realizing his inability to slay the powerful Pandavas in battle, he decided to attack them while they were asleep in their camps.

Sensing Ashwatthama's murderous intention, Kripa reminded him that it was unlawful to attack a sleeping warrior.

"That is not right. It is against dharma," said Kripa.

Infuriated, Ashwatthama reminded Kripa that the Pandavas had also resorted to unlawful ways during the war.

"Was it not unlawful to kill the eldest Kaurava by striking him below the waist?" questioned Ashwatthama.

He then went on to cite the many instances when the Pandavas broke the rules of the war—they let Shikhandi, a woman, enter the battlefield; they had killed his father, even though he had put down his weapons; they attacked Karna after he had alighted from his chariot.

"The Pandavas disregarded dharma. Why should we care for it?" asked Ashwatthama, blocking all their objections and silencing Kripa and Kritavarma.

"If I fight through **fair means**, there is no doubt that I will **lose my life** ... there will be **success through deceit** and great **destruction** of the enemy."

ASHWATTHAMA, SAUPTIKA PARVA: THE BOOK OF SLUMBER

ANALYSIS

ASHWATTHAMA'S JEALOUSY

It is believed that Ashwatthama was envious of Arjuna, the favorite pupil of his father, Drona.

Initially, the Kuru teacher was a little reluctant to impart all skills and give his disciples—the Kauravas and Pandavas—the benefit of his vast knowledge. He wanted to reserve it for his son Ashwatthama, whom he wanted to make the greatest and most powerful warrior in the world. But Arjuna impressed his teacher with his dogged determination and prowess in archery and gained the position as his favorite. Drona grew fond of Arjuna and became partial to him. Ashwatthama felt that Arjuna was usurping his place in Drona's heart. His jealousy grew over the years, pushing him closer to Duryodhana and into the Kaurava camp.

AFTER

Having devised a plan to avenge the Kauravas' loss, Ashwatthama convinced the other two survivors that it could work.

MARCH TO THE ENEMY CAMP

Ashwatthama's arguments made a strong case against the Pandavas. After their initial hesitation, Kripa and Kritavarma deliberated and agreed to his proposal to attack the sleeping warriors. The three men then walked toward the Pandava camp. Kripa and Kritavarma kept watch as Ashwatthama entered the camp, determined to kill the five brothers.

BEFORE

Ashwatthama was disgusted by the celebrations in the Pandava camp. Eager to exact his revenge, he asked Duryodhana to make him the commander of the remaining Kaurava army.

DEVIOUS PLAN

Ashwatthama knew he would have to come up with a clever plan to eliminate his rivals, even if it went against the rules of war. Aware of the Pandavas' strength, he decided to kill them in their sleep.

LIST

RULES OF WAR BROKEN

- **No woman shall fight in the battlefield**; broken by Arjuna, which lead to the downfall of Bhishma
- **No single warrior shall be attacked by many**; broken by Drona, when he killed Abhimanyu
- **No fighting after sunset**; broken by Arjuna to kill Jayadratha
- **No one shall interfere in a duel**; broken by Satyaki to slay Bhurishrava
- **No killing of animals**; broken by Bhima to spread misinformation that led to the death of Drona
- **No one shall strike below the waist**; broken by Bhima when he struck Duryodhana on his thigh
- **No killing of people who have laid down arms**; broken by Dhrishtadyumna as he struck a meditating Drona
- **No archer should fight one who has lowered his bow**; broken by Arjuna to slay Karna
- **No attacking people who are asleep**; broken by Ashwatthama when he raided the Pandava camp while they were asleep

The **Final Blow**

Now, more than ever, the Kaurava survivors were firm in their resolve to annihilate the Pandavas once and for all. In their determination, they ended up committing a wrong so grievous, it placed them beyond redemption.

THE DEAD WARRIORS
An engraving of the five people killed by Ashwatthama whom he thought were the Pandavas, from a 17th-century terracotta temple in Bishnupur, West Bengal, India.

Consumed by the single-minded pursuit of vengeance, the three warriors, Ashwatthama, Kripa, and Kritavarma, charged toward the Pandava camp. Blinded by rage, they spared not a single thought for dharma.

Soon, they found themselves in the enemy camp. While Kripa and Kritavarma decided to keep watch, Ashwatthama entered the section where the warriors from Panchala slept, his sword unsheathed.

The fierce form of god

At the entrance of the camp, Ashwatthama found Shiva, the deity of destruction, blocking his entry. Shiva had assumed the fearsome form of Bhairava. He was covered in blood and had a garland of heads around his neck. He was accompanied by his consort, goddess Parvati, in her most ferocious form, Kali. An ardent devotee of Shiva, Ashwatthama bowed down before the God, seeking his blessings. With Bhairava's consent, Drona's son entered the Pandava enclosure and found the brothers of Draupadi, Shikhandi and Dhrishtadyumna, sleeping.

A mindless massacre

First, he approached Draupadi's twin, Dhrishtadyumna, the commander of the Pandava army, and woke him up. Furious at the sight of his father's killer, Ashwatthama strangled the half-awake Dhrishtadyumna to death, even as the young prince begged him to be allowed to die respectably, with a sword in his hand.

FEARSOME BHAIRAVA
This Mahakala, the fierce diety propitiated by both Hindus and Buddhists, at Tashilhunpo Monastery in Tibet is believed to be Bhairava, a fearsome manifestation of Shiva. The deity is called Gönpo by Tibetans.

After avenging his father's death, Ashwatthama proceeded to kill Shikhandi, the one who brought about the downfall of Bhishma. Taken by complete surprise, Shikhandi had no chance to defend himself against the fatal attack. Pleased with the killings, Ashwatthama raised his sword and exclaimed, "There! I have avenged the death of Bhishma and Drona."

The five murders

Still burning with rage and intent on slaying the Pandavas, Ashwatthama went to the part of the camp where the five brothers slept. With violent strikes of his sword, he beheaded five warriors whom he assumed to be the Pandavas.

"I have fulfilled my vow to take revenge on the Pandavas," he declared. In an effort to destroy all his enemies, Ashwatthama then set the Pandava camp on fire. Those who tried to escape were caught and killed at the camp's entrance by Kripa and Kritavarma.

> "**Blessed** by **Shiva**, I have managed to **behead** the five **Pandava brothers**."
>
> ASHWATTHAMA, SAUPTIKA PARVA: THE BOOK OF SLUMBER

A DISPLAY OF CRUELTY
This miniature from the *Razmnama* shows the Kaurava survivors displaying the severed heads of the Pandava children to Duryodhana.

AFTER

After destroying the enemy camp, Ashwatthama rejoiced at his achievement.

A TRIBUTE TO DURYODHANA
The three warriors were delighted with their feat. They rushed back to the lake where Duryodhana lay dying, with the severed heads of the five warriors they thought were the Pandavas. They wanted to present the proof of their success to the dying Kaurava.

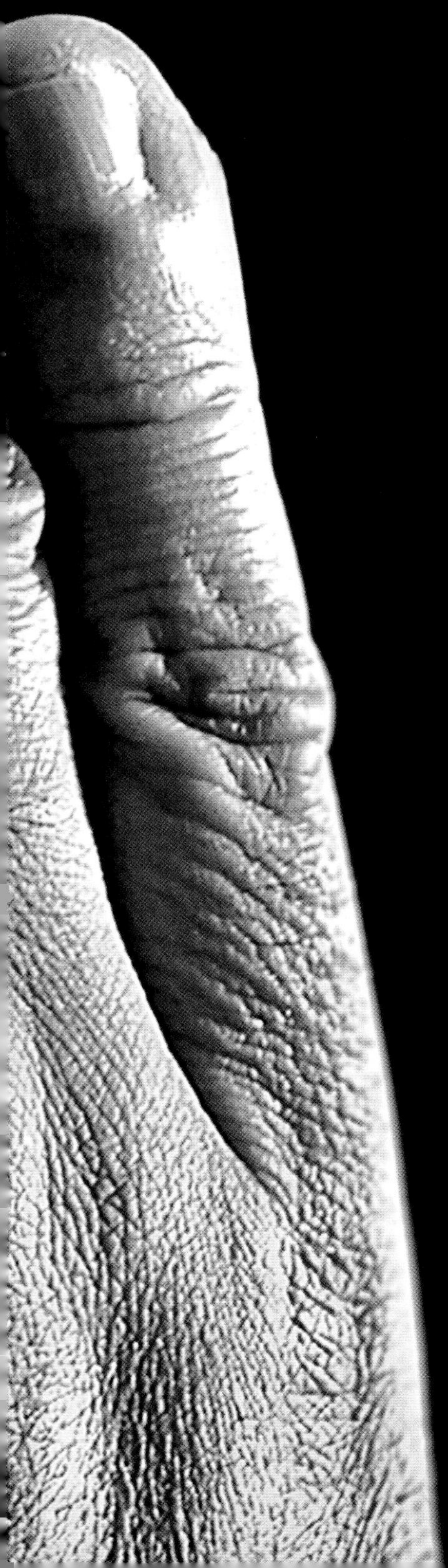

OVERCOME WITH GUILT
The thought that innocent children had been murdered filled Duryodhana with guilt and remorse. He spent his last moments meditating on the futility of violence.

SAUPTIKA PARVA: THE BOOK OF SLUMBER

Duryodhana's **Lamentation**

Blinded with rage, Duryodhana had given in to Ashwatthama's devious plan to eliminate the Pandavas. Vengeance had motivated them to commit a dastardly act.

Impatient to break the news of the Pandavas' death to Duryodhana, Ashwatthama, Kripa, and Kritavarma rushed to the banks of the lake where the eldest Kaurava lay dying. Ashwatthama had in his hands the severed heads that he assumed to be of the Pandavas, to please the dying Duryodhana.

They reached the lake to find Duryodhana eagerly awaiting them. Delighted, Ashwatthama presented the heads to Duryodhana and exclaimed, "Blessed by Shiva, I have killed the five Pandava brothers."

Finding it hard to believe, Duryodhana asked Ashwatthama for proof. "Show me Bhima's head," he ordered.

Ashwatthama readily presented the head that he thought to be Bhima's. An incensed Duryodhana held the head between his palms and crushed it like a coconut, reducing it to pulp. No sooner had he mangled the head, than he realized that something was wrong. "No! This is too weak to be the head of mighty Bhima. Whom have you killed, Ashwatthama?" Duryodhana asked.

Kripa looked at the heads closely and came to a terrible realization. "These are not the Pandava brothers. They are, in fact, children. Oh Ashwatthama, in your mad fit of fury, you have killed Draupadi's five sons," Kripa cried. Drona's son was stunned by the revelation and did not know what to say.

Overcome with guilt and disgusted with the savage act, Duryodhana let out a cry, "Have we now stooped so low as to kill children?" The spiral of vengeance seemed to have surpassed all rules of dharma and humanity.

In his last moments, the eldest Kaurava was filled with remorse. He also declared that the Pandavas would rule over a city of corpses because violence and revenge seemed to know no end. "I may have been defeated in battle, but nobody has actually won." With those despairing words, the eldest Kaurava breathed his last.

"When will this **stop**? When we are **all dead**? This is **madness**."

DURYODHANA TO ASHWATTHAMA, SAUPTIKA PARVA: THE BOOK OF SLUMBER

BEFORE

The sun rose to the terrible sight of the charred bodies of the Pandava army and Draupadi's headless brothers and sons.

DRAUPADI'S GRIEF

Draupadi screamed as she saw the remains of her family. Beside herself with grief, she cried, "My children! Oh, terrible is the price of tying my hair." The war had destroyed her family, brutally killing her innocent children.

Grief soon turned to rage. The demon of vengeance reared its evil head. Upon being informed that Ashwatthama had slaughtered her family, she angrily demanded his head.

Ashwatthama Cursed

Even after killing Draupadi's innocent children, Ashwatthama remained unrepentant. Ruthless, he went on to commit yet another heinous crime, inviting Krishna's wrath that resulted in a terrible curse.

As the Pandavas prepared to hunt down Drona's son, Ashwatthama, Krishna stepped in before the spiral of vengeance could lead to more violence and claim more lives.

He then revealed that Ashwatthama once had gone to Dwaraka and asked Krishna for his weapon, the Sudarshana Chakra. Since Ashwatthama was a Brahman, Krishna was obliged to give in to his wish and handed him the discus. Delighted, Drona's son tried to lift Krishna's discus with his left hand, and then with his right. Unsuccessful both times, he started to weep. Krishna then asked him why he wanted the Sudarshana, a weapon that no one dared ask from him—neither his friend, Arjuna, nor his son, Pradyumna.

Ashwatthama replied that he wanted the discus because he knew it was the most powerful weapon in the world. He wanted to use it against Krishna and become the greatest warrior in the world, feared by all. By narrating the incident, Krishna wanted to explain that such was Ashwatthama's nature. "Despite being born in a family of priests, Drona's upbringing transformed Ashwatthama into an ambitious monster," said Krishna. Ashwatthama craved power, but did not how to wield it. Krishna explained that Ashwatthama was neither a Brahman nor a Kshatriya; killing him would lead to no good. They should instead hunt for him and bring him back alive as a prisoner.

Scouts were sent to look for Ashwatthama. When he found out that the Pandavas were looking for him, a frenzied Ashwatthama raised his bow and shot the deadly missile known as Brahmaastra. Seeing the approach of Ashwatthama's missile, Arjuna released another Brahmaastra to neutralize the first one.

As the powerful weapons moved toward each other, the sky turned gray. A violent thunderstorm took over the earth, showering dust and gravel everywhere. Animals ran around in a state of nervous hysteria.

The earth shook, responding to the terrible heat of the missiles, each with the power of large-scale destruction.

Fearing the consequences, Krishna appealed to both warriors to recall their missiles. "Your weapons will burn the earth and destroy all form of life," he cried.

Other learned men including Vyasa who saw the fiery missiles hurtling toward each other begged the two to listen to Krishna and withdraw their weapons.

Realizing the gravity of the situation, Arjuna put his arrow back in his quiver. Ashwatthama, however, did not know how to call back his missile. Still burning with the need for revenge, he redirected his Bramhaastra to the wombs of the Pandava women instead, hoping to kill even the unborn

"On seeing that his **sons**, brothers, and friends had been **slain** in the **encounter**, his soul was **immersed** in great **grief**."

SAGE VAISHAMPAYANA TO KING JANAMEJAYA, SAUPTIKA PARVA: THE BOOK OF SLUMBER

PLUNGED INTO GRIEF
This section of a painting from the *Razmnama* shows the Pandava brothers immersed in grief, weeping for their sons, mercilessly slain by Ashwatthama.

ANALYSIS

ASHWATTHAMA'S SIN

The character of Drona's son, Ashwatthama, may also be interpreted as a lesson in what happens to those who do not adhere to dharma. Born into a family of priests, Ashwatthama should have followed his father's vocation. He defied the law by choosing to become a warrior instead. The choice was not to protect the weak, but to exploit the power that came with being a warrior. His lust for power is the reason why he is not shown any mercy by Krishna. Ashwatthama mirrors the fall of civilization, and personifies the pinnacle of human rage and greed.

HUNTING ASHWATTHAMA
An illustration depicting one of the Pandavas chasing Ashwatthama to bring him back to their camp as a captive.

> "The **weapon** that has been **invoked by me** will **descend** on the **womb of** Virata's daughter, the one that you **wish to protect**."
>
> ASHWATTHAMA TO KRISHNA, SAUPTIKA PARVA: THE BOOK OF SLUMBER

descendants of the Pandavas and annihilate the entire race of those who killed his father and friend.

This act was so terrible that a livid Krishna jumped to his feet to stand before Abhimanyu's pregnant widow, Uttari. He took the impact of Ashwatthama's missile, preventing it from harming the unborn child, the last of the Pandava's descendants.

Krishna then turned to Ashwatthama and uttered a terrible curse, the only one to ever leave his lips. "Ashwatthama, so atrocious has been your act that as as punishment, even death will shun you for the next three thousand years." In those years, Drona's son would be subjected to immense suffering. Krishna cursed him that his wounds will fester with pus and that his skin will be covered with boils, forcing him to contemplate on the nature of his crime. He would wish for death, but death would evade him. The curse would make him think of all the sins he committed and repent for them.

THE GEM THAT BROUGHT LUCK
This illustration from the *Razmnama* shows Draupadi wearing the jewel taken from Ashwatthama, who stands before her with his hands tied.

AFTER

Cursed by Krishna, Drona's son was driven away from civilization and deemed unwelcome by all of mankind.

A RARE JEWEL
Ashwatthama had a jewel in his forehead that brought him great luck. Before he was shunned from civilization, the gem was forcefully taken away from him and given to Draupadi, who handed it to Yudhishthira.

ASHWATTHAMA WAS BORN WITH A RARE GEM ON HIS FOREHEAD

THE HEROES RETURN
This early 19th-century painting by Warwick Goble shows the Pancavas returning after the Kurukshetra War. The triumphant warriors first take a dip in the Ganga river, as a cleansing ritual, before entering the city.

11 STREE PARVA: THE BOOK OF WOMEN

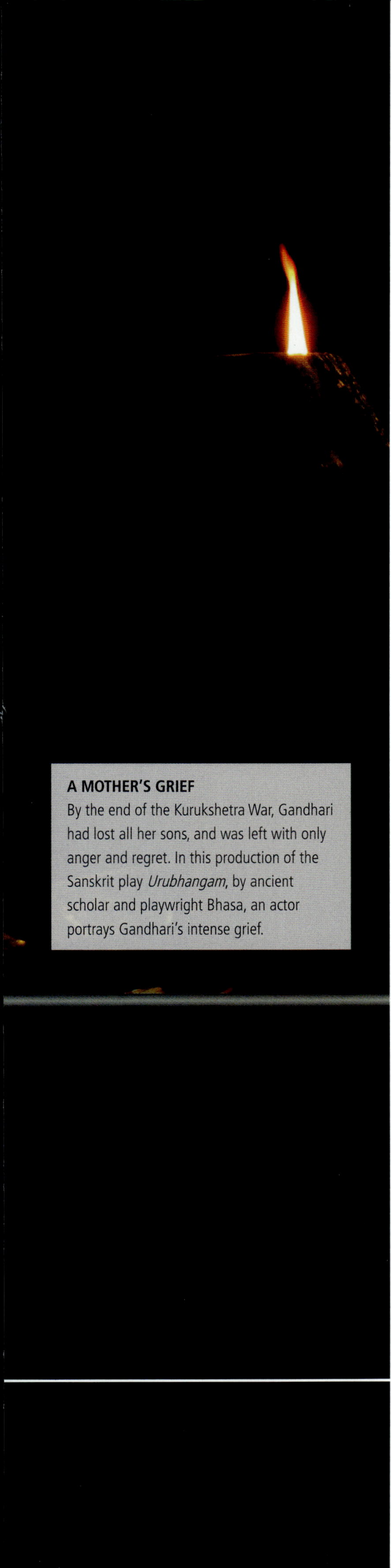

A MOTHER'S GRIEF
By the end of the Kurukshetra War, Gandhari had lost all her sons, and was left with only anger and regret. In this production of the Sanskrit play *Urubhangam*, by ancient scholar and playwright Bhasa, an actor portrays Gandhari's intense grief.

Stree Parva, or the Book of Women, is the eleventh parva in the Mahabharata. "Stree" means woman, and the parva is named for the sorrowing women who lost their families in the bloody battles. Now that the war had ended, the time to mourn the dead had arrived. This parva tells of Dhritarashtra and Gandhari's bereavement for losing all their sons in the war. Stree Parva has 4 sub-parvas, 17 chapters, and 713 shlokas, or couplets.

"Large numbers of **women** emerged … They held onto each others' arms and **wept, lamenting** their sons, brothers and fathers … They were seen there, as if the **world was** being **destroyed** at the end of a yuga."

SAGE VAISHAMPAYANA TO JANAMEJAYA, STREE PARVA: THE BOOK OF WOMEN

BEFORE

The eighteen-day war had left a trail of death and destruction in its wake.

FUTILITY OF WAR
The battlefield was strewn with dead bodies of great warriors and archers. Gandhari and Dhritarashtra had lost all their hundred sons. Draupadi had witnessed the terrible sight of the headless bodies of her brothers and sons and the charred bodies of the Pandava army. The women had only each other to share their sorrow.

The **Lamenting** Women

With their men killed in the battle of Kurukshetra, the women were left to face the aftermath of war. Looking for their husbands, all they found were headless torsos, cut hands, and crushed legs. Among these lamenting women was a distressed Kunti, grieving for her firstborn.

The air echoed with the cries of orphans as they wandered in desperation looking for the remains of their fathers. The distressed women who visited the battlefield witnessed gory scenes of dogs chewing on the tongues of the dead warriors and rats nibbling on the fingers of slain archers. The whole place reeked of rotting flesh.

Kunti's revelation

Amid the gloom that had engulfed the battlefield, the Pandavas saw Kunti wandering among the dead. "Who are you looking for?" Yudhishthira asked his mother.

"Karna," replied Kunti. Puzzled by Kunti's reply, Arjuna asked, "You mean that charioteer's son?"

Unafraid to face the truth this time, Kunti replied, "He was my firstborn, and your elder brother." Explaining Durvasa's blessing, Kunti told her sons how out of childish curiosity she had used a mantra to compel Surya, the sun god, to give her a child.

Hearing their mother utter those words, the Pandavas went

> "There was a **brave** and **great archer**. ... **He** was marked with the **auspicious signs** of a **hero** and was **killed** by **Arjuna**."
>
> KUNTI TO THE PANDAVAS, STREE PARVA: THE BOOK OF WOMEN

THE REMAINS OF WAR
Dogs and vultures made a feast out of the mangled remains of warriors after the bloody war of Kurukshetra.

KUNTI'S PREDICAMENT
Kunti grieved Karna's loss and blamed herself for the long-kept secret that ultimately took his life. This performance by Kuchipudi dancer Vyjayanthi Kashi in the play *Ateet ki Parchhayian* depicts her suffering.

weak in the knees. Already struggling with the guilt of killing Bhishma who was like a father to him, and Drona who was his teacher, Arjuna was now left to deal with the realization that he had killed his own brother. "Did Karna know?" Yudhishthira asked his mother. Kunti nodded and told the Pandavas that Karna had promised her never to harm any of her sons except Arjuna. It then dawned on the Pandavas that victory had come to them stained in their brother's blood.

Last rites

Lamenting the fact that her firstborn had been sacrificed by her for a kingdom, Kunti said, "I have inadvertently caused the death of my son. This grief is consuming my limbs, like a mass of cotton in a fire." She then accompanied the women of the Kuru clan to the banks of the Ganga river to take part in the last rites of the dead. Kunti urged her sons to perform Karna's "Shraddh"—a prayer for the salvation of the dead soul. They were joined by Karna's wives, Vrushali and Supriya, who also mourned the death of their husband.

Krishna's words of wisdom

Questioning their mother's actions, the Pandavas asked, "Why did you not tell us about Karna?" Overhearing this conversation, Krishna intervened. "Kunti had to keep the secret to uphold dharma. If she had told you this, would you have fought Karna? And if you had not, the Kauravas would not have been defeated. This was necessary," Krishna reasoned. But for once, Krishna's words were unable to ease the pain and guilt of the Pandavas.

HISTORY AND CULTURE

SHRADDH

In Hindu culture, it is believed that after a person dies, a part of them still lives on. To ensure that this part enters the land of the dead, the descendants need to perform a ceremony known as "Shraddh." On completion of this ritual, the dead gain the status of "Pitru," or ancestor. If unable to cross over, they remain in the land of the living as "Preta," or ghost, haunting their descendants until the ceremony is performed.

AS PART OF THE SHRADDH CEREMONY, THE DESCENDANTS MAKE OFFERINGS OF BALLS OF RICE FLOUR, MILK, AND HONEY

> "**Kunti** kept this as a **secret** and this is also a **reason** for my **sorrow**."
>
> YUDHISHTHIRA TO SAGE NARADA, STREE PARVA: THE BOOK OF WOMEN

AFTER

The survivors from the Kaurava camp arrived in Hastinapur and tried their best to cheer the grieving parents.

COMFORTING WORDS
To console Dhritarashtra and Gandhari who were mourning the loss of their hundred sons, the three survivors from the Kaurava camp—Kripa, Kritavarma, and Ashwatthama—spoke of the Kuru warriors who had fought so bravely in the Kurukshetra War.

Speaking of Duryodhana's valor, they said, "Your son was killed while performing heroic deeds."

BEFORE

After the Kurukshetra War, an overwhelming gloom had descended on the Kuru clan.

GRIEVING FAMILIES
The families of the dead warriors mourned the loss of their loved ones and performed their last rites. Gandhari and Dhritarashtra were inconsolable over the death of their children.

The **Rage** of the **Elders**

Upon hearing that their sons had been killed in the war, Dhritarashtra and Gandhari were consumed with resentment for the Pandavas. When they saw their nephews, they could no longer contain their emotions and broke down in grief.

Soon after Gandhari and Dhritarashtra were told about the death of their children, the three survivors from the Kaurava camp, Kripa, Kritavarma, and Ashwatthama, arrived. They described the incidents of the last few days of the war to the blind king and his queen, saying that the Kauravas had battled bravely even when the odds were against them. They spoke of Duryodhana's valor, hoping to console the bereaved parents, "He fought without any fear and slew large numbers of the enemy. Your son has died after performing heroic deeds." Before leaving, they also told the king about the death of the sons of Draupadi, warning him of the Pandavas' rage.

Dhritarashtra's crushing grief

In the meantime, Krishna advised the Pandavas to set aside their own sorrow to pay their respects to Dhritarashtra and Gandhari. "Be careful of Dhritarashtra, his grief is strong," he warned Bhima. "When he comes to hug you, put an iron image of yourself before him." Heeding this advice, Bhima placed an iron image in

front of himself. Dhritarashtra, who could not bring himself to forgive Bhima for killing his sons, hugged the iron image with such force that it crumbled like soft clay in his arms. His rage spent, the king thought that he had killed his nephew and cried out, "What have I done? I have killed my nephew! I have killed one who was like a son to me!"

Krishna interposed, "O Dhritarashtra! Do not grieve. Bhima has not been killed by you. I knew that you were overcome by rage. So, I dragged Bhima away when he was in the jaws of death. Because you were tormented by sorrow over your sons, your mind had deviated from dharma."

Gandhari, who could sense Bhima's breath, was bitter. "Krishna has once again saved the Pandavas," she muttered.

Gandhari's fiery blessing

As the Pandavas approached Gandhari, Vidura, who could sense her anger, reminded her to stay calm. "Control your rage. If you curse these men, the earth will be left with no kings."

So Gandhari forced herself to be kind. But when the Pandavas touched her feet, the queen began to weep inconsolably. Gandhari's blindfold moved from her eyes, and her gaze fell on Yudhishthira's feet. That one glance was so fiery that it turned the eldest Pandava's big toe blue. At this, Gandhari's rage melted.

Having lost all her children as well, Draupadi could understand Gandhari's anguish. She went to console the queen. "What can we do but cry?" she told Gandhari, and broke down herself.

DHRITARASHTRA'S DEATH GRIP
This painting from the *Razmnama* depicts the blind Dhritarashtra, overcome with rage and grief, crushing the iron statue of Bhima, while Krishna and the Pandavas look on.

"**I do not hate** them ... Nor do I desire that they should be destroyed. But **the sorrow** on account of my sons is **powerful**."

GANDHARI TO SAGE VYASA, STREE PARVA: THE BOOK OF WOMEN

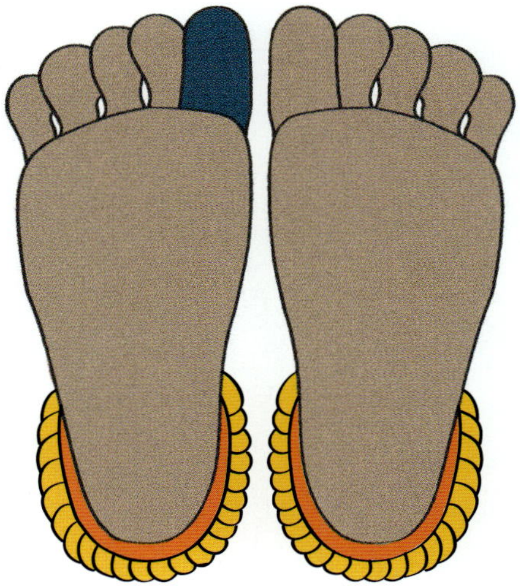

GANDHARI'S BLAZING ANGER
The austerities she had undertaken had given Gandhari many powers. Thus, when her gaze fell on Yudhishtihra's big toe, the force of her anger singed it, turning it blue.

The consequences of karma

Sensing Krishna's presence, the bereaved queen asked of him, "They're all dead. Could you not spare me even one son?"

Krishna looked at Gandhari compassionately. "It was fate, not I who killed your sons, Gandhari. Long ago, while cooking rice, you poured hot water on the ground, killing a hundred eggs that an insect had laid. The enraged insect cursed you, saying your own children would meet the same fate."

"But that was unknowingly done," Gandhari protested.

Krishna then told her about King Nriga, who gave a cow to a sage. Unknown to the king, the cow returned to his cowshed, and he gave it away to another sage. Even though he had done this unknowingly, the angry sages cursed the king, and he had to be reborn as a lizard. "Such is the law of karma," said Krishna. "Every action of ours, however innocent, has a reaction that we have to experience, if not in this life, then in the next."

KEY CONCEPT

THE BIRTH OF DEATH

The Mahabharata contains many origin myths, including one on Death. The story goes that Brahma created Mrityu, the goddess of death, when he saw that the earth was reeling under the weight of his children. But Mrityu, unwilling to bear the burden of taking lives, refused to kill. So Brahma assured her that creatures would be responsible for their own deaths based on the deeds—good and bad—they had done. "You will merely supervise the transition." So creatures die not because of external factors but because of their own karma.

AN 18TH-CENTURY PAINTING OF BRAHMA, THE CREATOR

MYTHOLOGY AND FOLKLORE

A COSTLY MISTAKE

Gandhari's sorrow at the loss of her children was acute. For those who wonder why she had to suffer so, stories of the queen's actions—and their costly consequences—offer an explanation. A story from the eastern state of Odisha describes how Gandhari sat on a rock and unknowingly crushed the eggs that a turtle had laid under it. When she saw the destroyed eggs, the mother turtle cursed Gandhari saying that she would know the same sorrow that the mother turtle had suffered.

OLIVE RIDLEY TURTLES FREQUENT THE BEACHES OF ODISHA TO LAY EGGS

AFTER

Krishna's explanation did not give Gandhari any consolation. Her sorrow and anger at fate and life began to simmer.

GANDHARI'S SORROW
The sun set on the battlefield, but Gandhari refused to return to the palace. When no amount of persuasion seemed to work, Krishna went to Gandhari and told her to go home.

"Your sorrow is great, but this too shall pass," he said. "This pain, so sharp today, will grow dimmer when you feel greater pleasure or pain."

But Gandhari laughed angrily, asking Krishna what he would know about losing children.

Gandhari's **Curse**

Krishna's efforts to comfort an inconsolable Gandhari and make her see the truth had unwelcome repercussions. It not only aggravated her grief, but also invited a curse on Krishna.

No consoling words could take away Gandhari's pain of losing her children; the desolate mother could not stop wailing. She was not ready to leave her children. "Let me comfort my sons as they lie unloved here," she said.

Krishna pleaded with a sobbing Gandhari to go back home. He explained to her, "You will forget this pain in the face of a greater pleasure or pain."

Incensed, Gandhari thought Krishna was belittling her pain. She accused him of being insensitive to her misery. "How will you understand my pain? You have not lost a hundred sons in the battlefield."

The night was filled with the howling of hungry dogs, vultures, and crows. Gandhari swung her walking stick to keep the predators away from the remains of her sons. She pitied herself for her miserable situation and was beside herself with anger and grief.

At midnight, she began to feel hungry and soon, she could think of nothing but food. Suddenly, the smell of a ripe mango assailed her senses. She made a pile of the stones that she found at her feet and climbed up to reach for the fruit. As soon as she bit into the mango, her hunger pangs abated and her senses returned. She came to the horrible realization that the stones were actually the bodies of her sons—she had made a pile of her children's corpses to pluck the fruit.

Gandhari understood that she had been deceived by Krishna into a realization of the truth. She cried, "Oh Krishna, now I know the power of maya: that something that deludes you to be unhappy can be overpowered by another delusion that causes greater unhappiness or pleasure."

Her anguish knew no bounds and she accused Krishna of using too cruel a way to show her this truth.

Burning with rage, she cursed him—that he too would experience the pain of losing his loved ones and have to stand helpless as his children and his entire clan annihilated each other, and that he would die at the hands of a hunter—the death of a beast.

"**Oh Krishna** … **Wicked** one, I **curse** you … And may you, great God, **die like a beast** at the hands of a **common hunter**."

GANDHARI TO KRISHNA, STREE PARVA: THE BOOK OF WOMEN

THE ENRAGED MOTHER
Indian dancer, choreographer, and director, Sanjukta Wagh, portrays Gandhari in the play *Rage and Beyond: Irawati's Gandhari*, in New York.

MOTHER OF THE KAURAVAS

Gandhari

"When Gandhari heard that **Dhritarashtra was blind** … she **tied up her eyes** … deciding resolutely that she would **never experience more than** what her husband could.**"**

SAGE VAISHAMPAYANA TO KING JANAMEJAYA, ADI PARVA: THE BOOK OF THE BEGINNING

Gandhari, the princess of the northwestern kingdom of Gandhara, was given in marriage to Dhritarashtra. When she learned that she was marrying a blind man, she decided to blindfold herself. By voluntarily sharing her husband's blindness, Gandhari attained the status of "sati," or the perfect wife.

A family tragedy

Soon after the wedding, Bhishma's spies found out that when Gandhari was born, astrologers had foretold that her first husband would have a short life. Her father Suvala, to subvert the prediction, decided to marry her to a goat, which was sacrificed. Technically, that made Gandhari a widow.

Bhishma was horrified that he would be a laughingstock for bringing a widow as a daughter-in-law. He imprisoned Gandhari's family and gave them so little to eat that they starved to death. Only her brother Shakuni survived, and he came to live with her in Hastinapur. Gandhari, like Ambika and Ambalika, became a captive of the Kuru household and so did Shakuni.

The mother of a hundred sons

Gandhari had conceived but mysteriously, and her pregnancy continued for two years. She decided to force the child out of her womb and asked her maids to strike her belly with an iron bar, which they did until her womb quivered and pushed out a cold ball of flesh. Sage Vyasa helped her to incubate and transform the ball of flesh into a hundred and one babies (see pp. 74–75). She named her daughter Dusshala and her hundred sons were collectively known as the Kauravas. It is said that when her eldest son was born, the palace dogs wailed, which was ominous.

Scholars have often wondered if Gandhari had only two sons, Duryodhana and Dusshasana, the only two to play a significant role in the epic. They were probably twins, the "two-year" pregnancy probably meaning a "twin" pregnancy.

Gandhari and Kunti brought up their sons amid growing tensions in the family. The two mothers advised their sons to show restraint but to no avail. Sometimes, even Gandhari and Kunti submitted to the rivalry.

A mother's blessing

Throughout the war, Gandhari and Dhritarashtra were given a blow-by-blow account of the proceedings by Sanjay. As the war progressed, Gandhari and Dhritarashtra wept as Sanjay informed them of the growing list of their dead sons killed by Bhima.

Every morning, Duryodhana would seek Gandhari's blessings and she would say, "May whoever is right, win." Knowing that Gandhari's words always came true, Duryodhana begged her to say, "May my sons win," but she refused. But after Bhima had killed ninety-nine Kauravas, motherly love got the better of her. She instructed Duryodhana to come before her totally naked.

"I will open my blindfold for the first time. My eyes are filled with the power of my piety. Every part of your body that I look at with my first glance will become immune to any harm." Krishna, however, convinced Duryodhana to cover his thighs and genitals. When Gandhari realized this she began to cry and said, "The parts that you have covered will cause your death."

The aftermath of war

Gandhari lost all her children in the war. When the Pandavas approached her for blessings, Gandhari forced herself to bless them on Vidura's insistence. Her eyes welled up with tears and as her blindfold was pushed away, she stole a glance at Yudhishthira's toe. That one glance turned his toe blue, dissipating all her rage.

After the war, Gandhari, unable to control her emotions, refused to leave her dead sons. Krishna then taught her about the nature and power of delusion. But the teaching was so cruel that she cursed Krishna so that he, too, would feel the pain of losing his entire clan. "I curse you to die like an animal at the hands of a hunter" (see pp. 360–61).

Death

After the war, Dhritarashtra and Gandhari continued to stay in Hastinapur, and Yudhishthira did his best to keep them happy. At long last, Dhritarashtra renounced worldly things and walked out of the palace with Gandhari. They wandered in the woods, meeting sages. After sometime, a fire broke out in the forest. "Run!" cried Dhritarashtra, sniffing the smoke. "Why?" asked Gandhari. "Why, indeed?" And so they sat still, allowing the wall of flames to engulf them.

THE WAILING QUEEN
A still from the dance drama *Ateet ki Parchhaiyan*, by the production company Nadroop, showing an actress enacting the role of Gandhari in the Mohiniattam dance style.

BIOGRAPHY IN BRIEF

- **Born** to King Suvala of Gandhara, and sister of Shakuni.
- **Ritually married** to a goat to fulfil the foretelling that said her first husband would die early. The goat was slaughtered later.
- **Married** the blind Dhritarashtra and blindfolded herself to share his disability.
- **Blessed** by Sage Vyasa that she would be the mother of a hundred sons.
- **Delivered** a lump of flesh after her two-year-long pregnancy.
- **Became mother** to a hundred sons and one daughter after incubating the flesh in jars of ghee according to Sage Vyasa's instructions.
- **Heard** about the events of the Kurukshetra War from Sanjay.
- **Lost ninety-nine sons** to Bhima's wrath during the Kurukshetra War.
- **Tried to make Duryodhana invincible** with her piety by removing her blindfold.
- **Lamented** the loss of all her sons after the end of the war, keeping vigil over her sons' corpses.
- **Cursed Krishna** that all his clansmen would kill each other, and that he would die at the hands of a hunter.
- **Blessed the Pandavas and Draupadi** when they sought her blessings after the war, but her rage turned Yudhishthira's toe blue.
- **Died** in a fire with Dhritarashtra and Kunti after retiring to the forest.

ART AND LITERATURE

A TAKE ON GANDHARI

Gandhari —In Search of Light is an hour-long solo performance in Hindi performed by actress Aishverya Nidhi and directed by Arvind Gaur. In the play, Shiva blesses Gandhari with a hundred sons. Because of the this, the royal family of Hastinapur wants her for a daughter-in-law, since they lack heirs. She is forced to marry the blind Kuru prince, Dhritarashtra, under the threat that his brother Pandu would attack her kingdom, Gandhara, if she did not.

Blindfolding herself is not an act of wifely devotion but one of protest. According to the director, she is objecting to both male power and the politics of dynasty. In the last six years, the play has been performed in venues like the Sydney Fringe Festival and the Hollywood Fringe Festival.

12
SHANTI PARVA: THE BOOK OF PEACE

AFTER THE WAR
In Buddhism, a lotus in full bloom represents enlightenment and self-awareness. In this parva, through Bhishma's teachings and Yudhishthira's own self-reflections, the Pandavas go through a stage of self-realization.

Shanti Parva, or the Book of Peace, is the twelfth parva of the Mahabharata. "Shanti" means peace and alludes to the lessons imparted by Bhishma to the Pandavas. This parva is the longest in the epic and recounts the events following the Kurukshetra War. It includes Yudhishthira's coronation as well as Bhishma's teachings on peace and conflict, death and immortality, and duty and desire. Bhishma's lessons help the Pandavas become able and just rulers. This parva has 3 sub-parvas, 353 chapters, and 13,006 shlokas, or couplets.

"**Yudhishthira** approached **humbly** … He grasped Bhishma's feet and honored him … Gangeya, bull among all archers [**Bhishma**], said, '**O son! Ask me** what **you wish.** O supreme among the Kuru lineage! Do not be scared.'"

SAGE VAISHAMPAYANA TO JANAMEJAYA, SHANTI PARVA: THE BOOK OF PEACE

BEFORE

Witnessing the carnage and the deaths of most of his clan in the great war, Yudhishthira lost all interest in matters of state and kingship.

END OF THE WAR

The war was over, the dead had been burned and respectfully put to rest in the Ganga river, followed by a long period of mourning. And now the time had come to set the sadness aside, raise the banners of victory, and light the kitchen fires—for the war had been won by dharma. It was time for Yudhishthira to be formally crowned the king of Hastinapur. But the son of Pandu was wracked by guilt and overcome with sorrow.

Yudhishthira's Coronation

The Pandavas had emerged victorious at Kurukshetra, but they could not shake off the feeling of melancholy that gripped their hearts. It took pragmatic reasoning and encouragement from Krishna to bring Yudhishthira to accept the Kuru throne.

The time had come for the royal coronation, but Yudhishthira could not bring himself to celebrate. Anguished by the heavy price that had been paid for him to ascend to the throne, he cried out, "How can I be fit to rule a kingdom when the blood of my family stains my hands?"

Advice from kinsmen

Seeing him so dejected, Yudhishthira's brothers tried their best to encourage him. Arjuna answered Yudhishthira, saying the point of life was to compete and excel, while Bhima urged him to forget the past and focus on a glorious future full of food and drink. Nakula advised him to create wealth and use it for the larger good of the people. Sahadeva, though wise and full of intelligent counsel, remained silent, and so did Draupadi, who was consumed with grief for her dead sons.

Vidura reminded Yudhishthira that everyone dies eventually. The important thing is to make the most of life, learn from it, enjoy it, and share it with others; so that when death approached, it would not be so terrible a fate. Still, Yudhishthira found no peace. Restlessly pacing the palace corridors, haunted by the cries of widows and orphans, he wondered if he should renounce everything and retire to the forest. It was then that Krishna stepped in.

Krishna's counsel

"That would be abandoning the rest of the world," said Krishna. "As a hermit you will get peace for yourself, but as king you can create a world where people find peace and fulfilment. Choose kingship, Yudhishthira, not out of obligation but out of empathy for humanity," he advised. Krishna then told Yudhishthira that he was best suited to be king. As someone who had gambled away his kingdom, he could understand the weakness of humanity. From his years of exile, he had learned the power of repentance and forgiveness. He had faced Duryodhana's obstinacy and experienced the power of the ego and the horrors of adharma. He had lied to his teacher, and so understood the complexities of dharma. Thus, he continued, "Only you can establish a world where there is room to listen to the head and the heart, where wisdom is valued as much as wealth, and where compassion is as important as discipline."

Finally understanding what it meant to be king, Yudhishthira decided to assume kingship. In the presence of the elders, he sat on the throne reserved for Kuru kings. As the rituals began, milk and water was poured on him. He was then given a conch-shell trumpet, a lotus flower, a mace, and a royal bow, objects that symbolized his wisdom and might as a king.

THE JUST RULER

In this Mughal miniature from the *Razmnama*, Yudhishthira takes his place on the throne as Krishna, Gandhari, Kunti, and the other Pandavas look on.

HISTORY AND CULTURE

KING'S CROWNING

An important ceremony, a king's coronation ceremony in ancient times was very similar to consecration rituals in temples by which an idol was transformed into a deity. The coronation rituals were aimed at bringing about a shift in the king's consciousness. The ceremonies were symbolic; just as a stone became divine to help devotees, an ordinary man was transformed to think like God—for the welfare of his subjects and not for his limited self and interests.

"I have **conquered** the **entire earth**. But this **great grief** is always circulating in my heart … O illustrious one! To me, this **victory** seems to be a **defeat**."

YUDHISHTHIRA TO NARADA, SHANTI PARVA: THE BOOK OF PEACE

AFTER

There was jubilation in the air, trumpets blared, and the people bowed to their new king.

QUEST FOR WISDOM

With the coronation complete, everyone was full of hope that the Pandavas would reinstate the rule of dharma, guided by their mentor Krishna. As the festivities ended, the Pandavas decided to visit their granduncle Bhishma, who lay on a bed of arrows, for advice.

THE KURU PATRIARCH

Bhishma

"I know that you are always established in the truth and that truth is your strength."

SATYAVATI TO BHISHMA, ADI PARVA: THE BOOK OF THE BEGINNING

The great Kuru patriarch Bhishma was born as Devavrata to river goddess Ganga and King Shantanu. He was the last of the Kuru bloodline.

Devavrata and Bhishma

Bhishma's father Shantanu fell in love with Ganga and married her, agreeing that he would never question her actions. Ganga had seven sons but drowned the babies. Just as she was about to drown Shantanu's eighth child, he protested. Ganga then explained that the children were the eight gods known as Vasus, cursed to be born as mortals for the crime of stealing Sage Vashishtha's cow. She had tried to keep their stay on earth brief. The eighth Vasu, Devavrata, would live, but lead a terrible life. He would neither inherit the throne nor marry, yet would be obliged to live as a householder.

Ganga had Devavrata trained by the martial sage, Parashurama, and he grew up to be a handsome prince and a great warrior.

Shantanu fell in love again, with Satyavati, a fisherwoman. Satyavati's condition for marrying him

ANALYSIS

THE RESULTS OF THE VOW

Suspended between the earth and sky, Bhishma was rejected by both in death. This was because he could not be identified as a householder or as a hermit. He did not marry, father children, or rule his father's kingdom and, in the end, died because of a woman. He also carried the burden of letting his family bloodline die. In a way, he practiced adharma. He broke the code that required men to retire when their children are old enough to take care of themselves. He refused to die, retire, or detach himself from his household.

was that only her children would be his heirs. Shantanu could not agree to her demand, as Devavrata was already the crown prince of Hastinapur. When Devavrata learned the cause of his father's misery, he renounced his claim to the throne and took a vow, saying, "I will never marry, or be with a woman, or have children."

Impressed with his vow, the Devas gave him a new name—"Bhishma"—and a blessing that allowed him to choose the time of his own death. Ironically, Bhishma, who had sworn never to have a family of his own, was entrapped by the family of his father.

HISTORY AND CULTURE

BHISHMA'S SHRINES

Although not worshipped as a deity, Bhishma is honored in some shrines. When the Pandavas came to visit a dying Bhishma, he said he was thirsty and Arjuna shot an arrow into the ground, bringing forth a gush of water. The Bhishma Kund at Naraktari, not far from the famous Brahma Sarovar in Kurukshetra, is said to mark this spot. The pond lies next to a temple dedicated to Bhishma. Another shrine stands in Allahabad, India. It was built by a lawyer in the 1960s, at the request of a devotee of the goddess Ganga, who wanted to honor her son.

BRAHMA SAROVAR AT KURUKSHETRA, HARYANA

BIOGRAPHY IN BRIEF

- **Born** to the river goddess Ganga and King Shantanu of Hastinapur as their eighth son, called Devavrata.
- **Taught** by warrior-ascetic Parashurama to become an accomplished warrior.
- **Gave up his claim to the throne** to facilitate Satyavati's condition to marry his father Shantanu.
- **Took the oath** to never marry, be with a woman, or father children.
- **Named Bhishma** by the Devas, who were impressed by his vow. They granted him the blessing to choose the hour of his death.
- **Abducted the three princesses** of Kashi for his stepbrother Vichitravirya to marry them.
- **Rejected** one of the princesses, Amba, because of his vow. Amba held him responsible for her humiliation and vowed revenge.
- **Asked to break his vow** by Satyavati, to impregnate her widowed daughters-in-law.
- **Served as a caretaker** of the Kuru princes, managed the household, as well as the kingdom.
- **Imprisoned** Gandhari's family upon realizing that she had been ritually married to a goat earlier. The family was slowly starved to death, and only Shakuni survived.
- **Could not intervene** in the gambling match as Yudhishthira played voluntarily and no law was broken.
- **Led the Kaurava army** for the first ten days of the Kurukshetra War.
- **Injured** by Arjuna's arrows, after lowering his bow against Shikhandi. Remained suspended between earth and heaven on a bed of arrows.
- **Died** peacefully after imparting all his knowledge to the Pandavas.

Bhishma's nemesis

Satyavati had two sons with Shantanu, one of whom died early. When the surviving son, Vichitravirya, grew up, his marriage had to be arranged.

The king of Kashi had organized a swayamvara for his three daughters, but did not invite Vichitravirya. Vyasa never makes it clear if the lack of an invitation was because Vichitravirya was not fit for any woman, or if the king of Kashi wanted to get back at Bhishma who overlooked the consequences of his vow of celibacy on his sister, whom he was engaged to marry.

Bhishma, however, took this as an affront to the Kuru household, abducted the three princesses, and gave them to his half-brother.

One of the princesses, Amba, who was betrothed to King Shalva, begged to go back to him. But Shalva rejected her for being with another man. She returned, but Vichitravirya refused to take her back. She then turned to Bhishma, who spurned her, too, citing his oath.

Amba then prayed until Shiva granted her the blessing that she would be the cause of Bhishma's death in her next life.

THE GREAT WARRIOR
This marble sculpture of Bhishma at Arpana Ashram in Karnal, Haryana, depicts the first Kaurava commander-in-chief on his chariot during the Kurukshetra War.

The caretaker

Satyavati's grandchildren Dhritarashtra, Pandu, and Vidura were raised by Bhishma as if they were his own sons. After Pandu abdicated, Bhishma appointed the blind Dhritarashtra as king and continued looking after the household and the kingdom. He was a father figure to the orphaned Pandavas.

The commander

Bhishma led the Kaurava army during the Kurukshetra War and proved to be an astute general. The Pandavas knew that as long as Bhishma was alive, they would not win. But they were reluctant to hurt him.

Krishna then suggested that they bring Shikhandi into the battlefield, knowing that Bhishma would lower his bow when facing a woman. Shikhandi, who was Amba in his previous birth, was born as a woman but then later acquired the body of a man.

Arjuna stood behind Shikhandi and shot hundreds of arrows at Bhishma. The arrows pierced every inch of Bhishma's flesh and kept him suspended between the sky and earth.

Death by choice

An ordinary man would have died of these injuries—but Bhishma could choose the time of his death. He decided to die after the winter solstice. After Yudhishthira's coronation, the Pandavas went to seek his blessings as he lay on the bed of arrows. He shared all he knew with the new king. At long last, eight days after the full moon that followed the end of the terrible war, Bhishma breathed his last. He was at peace, secure in the belief that all his knowledge would outlive him.

His cremation was attended by all the surviving kings and warriors of the land. He was not just an elder of the Kuru clan; he was the last representative of the old order. His death symbolized the end of an era.

The **Hawk** and the **Dove**

After Yudhishthira's coronation, the Pandavas went to their granduncle Bhishma to learn about life and wise conduct. Bhishma spoke for a long time, his teachings about a king's duty enriched by many allegories and fables, such as this one about a hawk and dove.

The coronation ceremonies had drawn to a close, and Krishna asked the Pandavas to visit Bhishma, "Go and meet your granduncle, seek his blessings. Let him share with you his knowledge before he dies."

Krishna asked the Kuru patriarch to share his wisdom. He said to Bhishma, "When you go to that world, all the knowledge you possess will be destroyed. That is the reason why the Pandavas have assembled before you, for an analysis of dharma. Though based firmly on truth, Yudhishthira's knowledge has been affected by sorrow for his kin. Tell him about the union of dharma and artha. Speak meaningful words that will alleviate his sorrow."

Even though Bhishma's life was slowly slipping away as he lay on the bed of arrows, he was eager to share all he knew with the new king. As soon as the Pandavas came near him, Bhishma asked for some water. Arjuna immediately shot an arrow into the earth; water gushed from the ground and into the mouth of the dying patriarch.

> "All the kings of the earth say that **you** have **dharma** in **your soul**. … O king! **Do not protect** it out of **avarice for dharma**."
>
> THE HAWK TO KING SIVI, VANA PARVA: THE BOOK OF THE FOREST

His thirst quenched, Bhishma told the eldest Pandava, "Listen to me, Yudhishthira, a man's life is like a river. You may struggle to change the course of a river, but the river is steadfast and will follow its own will in the end. Instead enjoy the waters of this river, don't fight it. Be refreshed by it and share it with all. In the end, do not get attached to it."

A plea

Bhishma then went on to tell a story. Once a dove, who was being pursued by a hawk, called out to King Sivi to save it. The king promptly tried to protect it. But the hawk protested against this, saying the intervention was not fair, for what would it eat? The king offered the predator any other dove to feed on. The hawk pointed out that this would not be fair to the other birds.

Seeing its point, Sivi offered his own flesh, equal to the dove's weight, to the hawk. But the hawk persisted. It wondered how much flesh could the king give. Sooner or later he would die, and eventually the dove would have to fend for itself.

"Unless one creature dies, another cannot survive, that is the natural cycle of life," said the hawk. This argument seemed irrefutable and made the king wonder if he had been wrong to save the dove. And yet, his inner voice told him he had done the right thing.

What must a king do?

The question remained with the king—what should he do? Protect doves and let hawks starve, or save hawks by letting them prey on doves? At that moment, Sivi realized how different human beings were from animals. Animals spend

HISTORY AND CULTURE

ANIMALS IN FABLES

Animals are an integral part of myths and fables in India. According to the Hindu belief in rebirth, a human being could have been an animal in a past life or be born as one in the future. The avatars of Vishnu are animal as well as human—a fish, a turtle, a boar, and a half-man-half-lion. Since in the Hindu cosmos all of creation is divine, it is believed that the Supreme is found in animals, too. In ancient stories, animals play a significant role, such as the monkey army that built a bridge for Rama or the dog that stayed with Yudhishthira until the very end. Animals are sometimes wise teachers, sometimes neutral messengers, often divine, and often all too human in disposition.

MID-FLIGHT
The Ferruginous Hawk is one of the larger raptors in the hawk family. Carnivorous birds, hawks prey on mice and smaller birds.

> "This bird is **terrified** out of fear for you and has sought shelter ... **O hawk**! do you not see that it is **supreme adharma** for me to **give up** this **dove**."

KING SIVI TO THE HAWK, VANA PARVA: THE BOOK OF THE FOREST

their entire lives focused on survival, and the survival of the fittest was the rule. But human beings have the capacity to look beyond basic issues of survival, search for meaning in life, do good to others even by sacrificing themselves, and conversely, harm others to further their own good. Humanity was blessed with the faculty of empathy as well as exploitation. Driven by these impulses, human beings have been able to leave the forest and create civilization.

MYTHOLOGY AND FOLKLORE

TALES ON A TALE

The story of Sivi is also a part of a famous Buddhist Jataka tale. Sivi (or Shibi) was a king who ruled the kingdom of Shibi and was known for his philanthropy.

In this version of the story, the hawk is actually the god Indra, while the dove is the god of fire, Agni. The whole drama had been enacted deliberately by the gods to test how far Sivi's compassion would go. In this story, the hawk agreed to accept Sivi's flesh as compensation for letting the dove go. Sivi kept cutting his flesh to make it equivalent to the dove's weight, but it mysteriously kept falling short of the mark on the weighing scale. Eventually, tired of this charade, the king put himself on the scale, offering his entire body and so, his life. Impressed by this act of selflessness, the two gods finally revealed themselves and praised Sivi for his charity.

In yet another version of this story, Indra appeared to the king as a blind man and asked him for an eye to help partly restore his vision. The king offered both his eyes to the supplicant, earning praise from the god for his generosity. A king who sacrifices his sight for another in need is called Kuai-mu Wang, or the king with happy eyes. The natural order of the relationship between the hawk and dove was essentially a test for the human character—whether to protect the weak or let the natural order of things remain, even if it meant letting the strong and the cruel rule.

Bhishma's Lessons

Surrounded by his grandnephews, Bhishma imparted all the wisdom that he felt the Pandavas would need to rule the great Kuru kingdom. Subjects such as governance, a warrior's duties, and the need for a strong army were part of this discourse.

Even as Bhishma lay on his bed of arrows, waiting for the right time to give up his mortal body, he was eager to share with his grandnephews the experiences and wisdom he had gathered over the years. He told new king Yudhishthira many tales, such as the story of the hawk and dove, to teach him about the duties of a king and the secret to peace and prosperity.

At first, Bhishma's words seemed like the ramblings of a dying man, but they all came together as valuable lessons to be learned.

On life

Bhishma spoke for many days; Yudhishthira's questions and Bhishma's answers seemed to be unending. The newly crowned king learned many things from his wise elder who had seen so much over the course of his life. The discourse included lessons from history, geography, law, polity, economics,

> **"O bull** among the **Bharata lineage! Dharma** is more **subtle** than **words** and **intelligence."**
>
> BHISHMA TO YUDHISHTHIRA, SHANTI PARVA: THE BOOK OF PEACE

ANALYSIS

A LEGACY OF KNOWLEDGE

The transmitting of knowledge and wisdom across generations, especially from one who is dying, is an important aspect of the Ramayana and the Mahabharata. In both stories, at the end of a war there is a scene of discourse before death. In the Ramayana, Rama asks Ravana, his learned opponent, to share his wisdom before he dies. In the Mahabharata, Bhishma shares his knowledge with the Pandavas before leaving his mortal body. The idea behind these episodes is that, unlike wealth or other material possessions, knowledge does not outlive death, making it imperative that it is passed on to future generations so that it does not die. Bhishma eventually dies with the satisfaction of knowing that he ha passed on his cumulative knowledge and its teachings to a worthy successor.

"It is said **one without riches** is **weak** and **one with riches** is **strong** … The **treasury** provides **dharma** and **kama,** and this world and the next.**"**

BHISHMA TO YUDHISHTHIRA, SHANTI PARVA: THE BOOK OF PEACE

and philosophy, as well as the teachings behind the tales of gods, demons, and humans.

"Life is like a river," Bhishma told Yudhishthira. "You may try your best to change its course, but eventually it will go its own way. Bathe in it, drink from it, and refresh yourself in this river of life. Learn from life, and do your utmost to enjoy it, but never get attached to it."

Duties of a king

Especially relevant for Yudhishthira was Bhishma's discourse on the duties of a king. The aged patriarch explained that it was imperative for a king to exert himself when ruling his kingdom—he must constantly look to form the right alliances, resist threats to his authority, and control the wicked. To protect the kingdom and its seven limbs—the king, the army, advisers, allies, the treasury, forts, and the territory—a king must be ready to slay even a friend, if needed. He must ensure the well-being of his subjects, help those who have no support, and protect what is right and true. He should be brave, truthful, forgiving, discreet, and learn to rise above anger. He should use his judgment to decide between right and wrong and act accordingly. He should add to the treasury, but never take from the righteous. Given how much power a king has, Bhishma cautioned, a king must keep himself under control and also choose his advisers for being virtuous and devoted to dharma. So detailed was Bhishma's guidance that he even went into the importance of keeping spies and paying attention to houses that were decaying.

Duties of a Kshatriya

Before outlining the duties of different varnas, or social groups, such as Brahmans or Kshatriyas, Bhishma laid down the nine duties that were applicable to all the social groups. These were lack of anger; truthfulness; sharing; forgiveness; procreation with one's wife; purification; non-injury; rectitude; and supporting servants.

When discussing the duties of a Kshatriya, Bhishma again underlined the precepts suitable for a king. »

A KING'S COURT
Even a king needed to confer with different groups of people to rule his kingdom well. A 16th-century miniature shows Akbar surrounded by ministers and Jesuit priests in the court advising him on matters of state.

A Kshatriya, he said, especially a king, must give to the worthy, perform sacrifices, protect his subjects, act valiantly in battle, and slay bandits. The definitive dharma of a king is to fight. But this must be done to ensure that all his subjects are happy, well protected, and established in dharma. He said that the dharma of Kshatriyas was special—if those who are unrighteous are not destroyed, no other varna would survive. There would be no Brahmans and no establishment of the order of dharma. Saving and protecting the oppressed, having compassion for all, and showing knowledge of the world were incumbent on a Kshatriya.

Tasks of a kingdom

"What is the task of a kingdom?" Yudhishthira asked Bhishma. "Consecrating a king is the first priority of a state," he replied. A kingdom without a king slips into anarchy and adharma, and everyone harms everyone else. The duty and the

> "**Tell me** accurately about **origins** of **anger**, **desire**, sorrow, confusion … **intoxication**, **jealousy**, contempt, and **pity.**"
>
> YUDHISHTHIRA TO BHISHMA, SHANTI PARVA: THE BOOK OF PEACE

MIGHT IS POWER Showcasing the fundamental importance of a strong army, this mural from the Mehrangarh Fort in Rajasthan, India, shows a ruler with a large, impressive army vital for the protection of his kingdom.

happiness of a kingdom's subjects lies in submitting to the king. If there is no ruler, property gets stolen, women can be abducted, people may be enslaved, and the stronger oppress the weaker. But when under a good king, "Men in his kingdom roam around fearlessly, like sons in the house of a father," described Bhishma.

The story of Manu

Bhishma told Yudhishthira the story of how the first king came to be. In ancient times, without a king, the people were afflicted by misery, living under the law of the jungle. Even if they reached some resolution to disputes, there was no one to enforce it. The people then asked their elders to appoint a lord who would protect them and whom they would honor. They appointed Manu, but Manu did not want the job. It seemed a difficult one, necessitating cruel deeds and dealings with wicked people. His subjects assured him this would not be the case. They promised him one-fiftieth of their cattle and gold, and one-tenth of their grain. They emphasized that their best warriors would follow him. They also promised that, since they would all follow dharma under his protection, it would mean great power for him.

Agreeing to this, Manu used his army to advance upon the wicked and made them fearful. Order was established in the kingdom, and everyone was gainfully employed. There was peace and prosperity all around. Bhishma finished his account of Manu by reminding Yudhishthira that peace and prosperity can prevail only when a king governs well and his subjects submit to him.

The unanswered question

At one point in this long and free-flowing conversation, Yudhishthira asked Bhishma, "Who gets more pleasure in life—a man or a woman?"

"The only one who could have given you a straight answer," replied Bhishma, "was perhaps a king called Bhangashvana."

Bhangashvana was cursed by Indra to turn into a woman. Only he knew what it was like to be called "mother" as well as "father"—and which call was sweeter. And only he had enjoyed the sexual pleasure experienced by men as well as women, and could choose which would be greater. Otherwise, this was a matter of pure speculation.

Freedom from karma

Finally, Bhishma told the Pandavas about the Supreme and the divine law. He explained that our merits create good fortune and bring us joy, whereas our demerits create misfortune and bring suffering. This cycle of karma binds us to the material world and compels us to take birth and die repeatedly. Taking refuge in the divine was the only way out of this cycle of bondage. We should believe in and pray to the Supreme to release us from these fetters of karma.

> "I wish to **hear** about **supreme intelligence** for a **king**, who is **confounded** because he is **surrounded** by **enemies**."
>
> YUDHISHTHIRA TO BHISHMA, SHANTI PARVA: THE BOOK OF PEACE

ART AND LITERATURE

MACHIAVELLI'S *THE PRINCE*

Bhishma's discourse on kingship can be compared to *The Prince*, a 16th-century political treatise by the Italian diplomat and political theorist Niccolò Machiavelli. *The Prince* is considered an important work in modern political philosophy. Just like Bhishma's stance that survival and the glory of the self need to be the prime objectives of princes, it postulated that the aims of a ruler or prince can justify the use of any kind of immoral means to achieve such ends. Popular understanding, however, is that Machiavelli says it is legitimate to use unethical means to achieve such ends. For instance, he advocates "criminal virtue" by which a new prince may ruthlessly kill all his enemies at one time. He also states, "A man who strives after goodness in all his acts is sure to come to ruin."

STATUE OF NICCOLÒ MACHIAVELLI IN FLORENCE, ITALY

13 ANUSHASANA PARVA: THE BOOK OF DISCIPLINE

AWAITING DEATH
A frieze from a temple in Halebid, located in the southern state of Karnataka, India, shows Bhishma lying on a bed of arrows, surrounded by well-wishers.

Anushasana Parva, or the Book of Discipline, is the thirteenth parva in the Mahabharata. "Anushasana" means discipline or instruction. This parva continues with Bhishma's lessons for Yudhishthira. As in the Shanti Parva, this section delves into themes relating to the duties and obligations of a ruler. The parva ends with the story of Bhishma's death, which signals the end of the old order. This parva has 2 sub-parvas, 154 chapters, and 6,493 shlokas, or couplets.

"You possess **wisdom, learning, good conduct,** and **behavior**. You possess all qualities and are also aged … Therefore, I am asking you about **dharma.** Does one **become a brahmana** through **austerities,** great deeds, or **learning?** Tell me that."

YUDHISHTHIRA TO BHISHMA, ANUSHASANA PARVA: THE BOOK OF DISCIPLINE

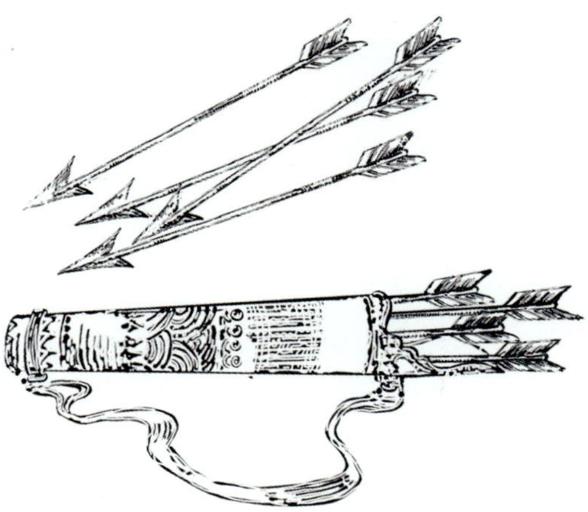

BEFORE

Bhishma had imparted all his wisdom and life lessons to Yudhishthira. Now it was time for him to die.

TO DIE AT WILL

Long ago, when Bhishma was just a young prince, his father Shantanu fell in love with a fisherwoman called Satyavati. She would marry him only if Bhishma and his future children gave up their claim to Hastinapur's throne. Aware of his father's intense love for Satyavati, Devavrata (as Bhishma was known then) took a vow that changed his life forever. He swore to never have children, nor marry, or even touch a woman. Impressed by this grand sacrifice, the gods granted Bhishma a blessing that gave him the power to choose the hour of his death, the only mortal who could die when he willed it himself.

HISTORY AND CULTURE

BHISHMA ASHTAMI

The festival of Bhishma Ashtami is observed in different parts of the country to mark the death of Bhishma. The day falls, according to the Hindu calendar, on the eighth day of the waxing moon, in the month of Magh (roughly corresponding to the months of January and February). The festival is observed in Vaishnava temples (devoted to Vishnu) with special prayers and offerings of barley or rice, sesame seeds, and flowers. Libations are also offered to the Ganga river. Since Bhishma personifies a venerated forefather, some people conduct shraddha, or death-related ceremonies, for their own ancestors on this day.

RICE AND SESAME SEEDS ARE OFFERED TO THE GANGA RIVER ON BHISHMA ASHTAMI

Bhishma's **Death**

Bhishma had watched over his dynasty through prosperity and a bloody war—and had now witnessed its downfall. The grand patriarch knew it was his time to die, and now he awaited the arrival of the auspicious moment.

The Pandavas saw that the period of Uttarayan had arrived—the sun was moving into its northerly course on the horizon. This was the time chosen by Bhishma for his death. As they waited, they arranged for ghee, garlands, fragrances, silken cloth, many jewels and garments, sandalwood, aloe, and other ingredients that were required for the funeral. The Pandavas, Draupadi, Kunti, Dhritarashtra, Gandhari, Vidura, and many kings and allies all gathered around Bhishma, awaiting his final departure.

The dying patriarch

It was eight days after the full moon that followed the end of the great war, and Bhishma still lay on his bed of arrows. With his last words, Bhishma advised Dhritarashtra not to grieve over his sons and to protect his nephews, the Pandavas. He lamented that Duryodhana had not listened to his repeated advice of making peace with the Pandavas. He then asked Krishna for permission to leave, and finally, asked all the Kurus to

"O Krishna! ... **Grant me permission**. Protect the Pandavas. They are devoted to you ... I wish to **cast aside** my breath of life. You should **grant me leave**."

BHISHMA TO KRISHNA, ANUSHASANA PARVA: THE BOOK OF DISCIPLINE

worship the wise Brahmans who had practiced austerities and were devoted to dharma.

Ready at last, Bhishma began chanting the thousand names of God, a prayer known as the Vishnu Sahasranama. It is said that his life breath shot out of the crown of his head and ascended to heaven.

Bhishma gave up the world, at peace at last. He had imparted all his knowledge to the Pandavas, who would outlive him.

Ganga's lament

When the mourners went to the banks of the Ganga river and offered her waters to the departed soul according to rituals, the river goddess herself appeared, overcome with grief for her son, Bhishma.

Ganga narrated the remarkable events of Bhishma's life and recalled his wisdom, his noble conduct, his valor, and his strength. The goddess was consumed by sadness as she stood among the throng that had come to witness the rituals. Krishna comforted Ganga, telling her that Bhishma had lived a fulfilling life and was now in heaven. He also reminded her that Bhishma was one of the eight Vasus, the gods cursed to be born on earth as a human. Bhishma had simply fulfilled the obligation this curse placed on him and returned to his true self as a Vasu.

Bhishma's cremation was attended by all the surviving kings and warriors of the land. He was not just an elder of the Kuru clan; he was the last representative of the old order. His death symbolized the end of an era. For the Pandavas, Bhishma's death was a personal tragedy; he was the only father they knew.

THE LAST HOURS
Bhishma lay on the bed of arrows, breathing his last. The scene is illustrated in this 18th-century watercolor.

AFTER

Bhishma's funeral was a procession fit for a king of a powerful empire.

BHISHMA'S CREMATION

The Pandavas and Vidura started preparing the funeral pyre. Bhishma's body was wrapped in silk, covered with garlands, and protected with an umbrella. Bhima and Arjuna fanned the body with whisks while Nakula and Sahadeva held the headdress. Women stood around and fanned the body with palm leaves. Sandalwood, scented yellow wood, aloe, and other fragrances were used in the pyre. As Bhishma's body was laid on this pyre and a fire was lit, the kings, led by Dhritarashtra, stood on the right side and performed the rites. As they surrounded the pyre with sorrow in their hearts, no one anticipated the unexpected good news that would soon come their way.

14

ASHWAMEDHIKA PARVA: THE BOOK OF CONQUEST

THE GRAND SACRIFICE
The horse sacrifice was a significant ritual, one that proclaimed the power of the ruler throughout the kingdom. The ceremony is shown in this early 19th-century painting entitled "Elopement of Horse and Bird" from Paithan, Maharashtra, India.

Ashwamedhika Parva, or the Book of Conquest, is the fourteenth parva in the Mahabharata. "Ashva" means horse and "medha" means sacrifice. The horse sacrifice announces unequivocally to the other kingdoms that the Pandavas are a force to be reckoned with. The parva tells the story of the birth of Parikshit, Arjuna's grandson, marking a new beginning for the Pandavas and the continuation of the Kuru bloodline. This parva has 1 sub-parva, 96 chapters, and 2,733 shlokas, or couplets.

"You should now **perform** many kinds of **sacrifices** … you should **follow** the **conduct** that was resorted to by your **forefathers**. There is no doubt that a kshatriya should **obtain heaven through** his **fame**."

KRISHNA TO YUDHISHTHIRA, ASHWAMEDHIKA PARVA: THE BOOK OF CONQUEST

BEFORE

Eight days after the full moon that followed the end of the terrible war, Bhishma breathed his last. In his dying moments, he was surrounded by his family, who mourned the passing of the great warrior.

A DEATH AND A BIRTH

Bhishma's death was a big blow to the Pandavas—he was like a father to all of them. But soon, the birth of Arjuna's grandson was reason for cheer, as birth always is. This birth would also signal the continuity of the Kuru empire.

The **Birth** of **Parikshit**

Despite the war and the deaths, all was not lost for the Kuru clan. Soon after Bhishma's death, Arjuna's grandson was born, signaling the beginning of the new order.

Bhishma's death was a personal tragedy for the Pandavas. But the sorrow was short-lived, as a few weeks after Bhishma passed away, Uttari, Abhimanyu's widow, went into labor.

In the meanwhile, Krishna also arrived in Hastinapur, along with Balarama, Rukmini's son Pradyumna, and his sister Subhadra. They were there to attend the horse sacrifice and also to comfort the women who had lost husbands and children in the war.

As the news spread that Uttari had gone into labor, the whole palace was abuzz with excitement. As was the tradition in those times, all the women of the palace, from Draupadi to Gandhari, rushed to the young girl's side to help her give birth.

KRISHNA'S MIRACLE

In this section on Parikshit's birth in the *Razmnama*, Parikshit is shown dead on the right, and on the left he is shown alive after Krishna restores his life.

The future king is born

As Uttari went into the last pangs of labor, the women around her waited with bated breath for the child to come into the world. When the baby was born and they saw it was a boy, loud roars of joy erupted. But this joy quickly turned to horror, as the midwife exclaimed, "The baby is not crying! He is a stillborn child."

Wails of sorrow could be heard from the women's quarters. Hearing them, Krishna rushed in.

An old vow

During the Kurukshetra War, in a bloodthirsty rage, Ashwatthama, Drona's son, had set out to avenge his father's death. He had released the dreaded weapon Brahmaastra, hoping to kill Bhima. Instead, Uttari's unborn child became its target. Enraged by this act of adharma, Krishna had vowed to bring Uttari's unborn son back to life and make sure Ashwatthama's plan to end the Kuru bloodline was foiled.

The miracle

Seeing her dead son, Uttari fainted, and all the Kuru women began to wail. Was the Kuru household cursed? Were they doomed to wither away and die? As Krishna entered the women's quarters he heard the women wailing all around. He saw many physicians and priests assembled on call, waiting for the birth of the child. Krishna noticed the big bowls of water that were set in place and the large array of medicines. He touched the water and withdrew the power of the Brahmaastra, which had taken this child's life away.

Krishna then took the newborn child's lifeless corpse in his arms and spoke to him. "Don't be afraid, child," he told the infant, "this world is not such a terrible place; you are welcome here."

As Krishna's comforting voice reached the baby, he opened his eyes and smiled. The room was once again filled with laughter and relief—this child, the son of Abhimanyu and Uttari, grandson of Arjuna, was the future prince of the Kuru dynasty.

Krishna smiled at the boy and presented him to the world. "Behold, Parikshit, the prince and the first of the next generation of Kurus."

HEALING WATER

In Hindu rituals, water is important—it signifies purity and spiritual well-being. In ancient India, water was kept near the sick as it was believed to have healing properties when coupled with the right chants.

> "**Your father** Parikshit, the **slayer** of **enemy** heroes, **was born**. He was born a **lifeless corpse** and this increased both joy and grief."
>
> SAGE VAISHAMPAYANA TO KING JANAMEJAYA, ASHWAMEDHIKA PARVA: THE BOOK OF CONQUEST

PEOPLE

PARIKSHIT

The grandson of Arjuna and Subhadra, and the son of Abhimanyu and Uttari, Parikshit was destined to take over the reins from Yudhishthira. He lived a long, peaceful life and Hastinapur prospered under him. According to the Mahabharata, Parikshit's reign lasted 24 years and he lived to the age of 60. He had two wives, Sushobhna and Madravati. Janamejaya, to whom the Mahabharata is narrated, is Parikshit's son with Madravati.

"O invincible one! Bring Abhimanyu's son **back to life**, like rain from the clouds **revives crops**."

KUNTI TO KRISHNA, ASHWAMEDHIKA PARVA: THE BOOK OF CONQUEST

AFTER

The birth of Parikshit gave the city of Hastinapur much to look forward to.

A TIME TO CELEBRATE

The war and the deaths had plunged the household in mourning. But the Pandavas were aware of the fact that it was their friend and mentor, Krishna, who had again come to their rescue.

Ashwatthama's plan would have played out and the Kurus would have died as a clan had not Krishna performed the miracle and brought back the prince to life.

Yudhishthira, too, was ecstatic at Parikshit's arrival. Dhaumya, the royal priest, proposed that the Pandavas should perform the sacrifice of the royal horse, known as the Ashwamedha yagna. The Pandavas agreed, and the preparations for the ceremony began in earnest.

POMP AND SPLENDOR
After the announcement of the birth of the heir-in-waiting, the Pandavas and the whole city of Hastinapur erupted in jubilation. This folio from the *Razmnama* captures the celebratory mood of the city.

The Horse Sacrifice

The Pandavas decided to hold a grand sacrifice—the Ashwamedha yagna. This yagna—a ritual sacrifice that involves letting a royal horse loose as it wanders through lands freely—would not only establish the Kuru might, but also strengthen Yudhishthira's claim to be king.

BEFORE

Krishna had once again saved the day for the Pandavas. They looked forward to a new beginning.

A TIME TO REJOICE

The birth of Parikshit marked an end of a dark period for the Pandavas—the war had ended and the mourning for the dead had come to an end, too. To mark the new period, Dhaumya, the family priest of the Pandavas, suggested that they should perform the Ashwamedha yagna or sacrifice of the royal horse.

Parikshit's birth restored some measure of happiness in the Kuru household. Yudhishthira was especially happy—the Pandava dynasty would survive and continue as a powerful line.

Dhaumya, the royal priest of the family, recommended an Ashwamedha yagna—the sacrifice of the royal horse. This sacrifice involved letting the royal horse loose and allowing it to roam freely for a year, followed by the army. All the lands the horse would traverse unchallenged would fall under the Pandava rule. On its return to the kingdom, the horse would be sacrificed; this would symbolize a transfer of all the power and glory to the king.

The Pandavas agreed to the proposal, and the priests divined that the most suitable horse would be one from the city of Bhadravati in the stables of King Yuvanashva. Bhima set out to fetch a horse accompanied by his grandson, Meghavarna, son of Ghatotkacha, and his nephew, Vrishadhvaja, son of Karna. Initially reluctant, Yuvanashva parted with the horse after much persuasion. The horse was brought to Hastinapur and the yagna began, after which it was let loose into the wilderness beyond the city. Arjuna led the army that followed the horse, accompanied by Nakula.

Challenge of Champakapuri

At Champakapuri, king Hamsadhvaj refused to accept Yudhishthira as the overlord and declared a war, threatening to boil in oil anyone who refused to fight. As the army gathered at the gates, the youngest son of the king, Sudhanva, was nowhere to be found. He was with his wife. The king, angry at being disobeyed, ordered that his son be boiled in oil. His wife's calls for mercy fell on deaf ears and so she turned to Krishna for help. Krishna responded and the hot oil had no effect on Sudhanva.

Meanwhile, Suratha, the eldest prince, led his father's army against Arjuna. He fought so ferociously that his body continued to fight even after his head was chopped off. So impressed were the gods that they gave Suratha's head to the deity Shiva, who wears a garland made of heads of brave warriors. Having lost his eldest son, a grieving Hamsadhvaj submitted to Arjuna and let Yudhishthira's royal horse pass through.

The enchanted grove

The horse then reached Gaurivan, a sacred grove that belonged to a goddess. Any male who entered it

> **"O Arjuna! Protect the horse ... The kings will advance against you ... You should tell them about my sacrifice ... Depart and try to have alliances with those kings."**
>
> YUDHISHTHIRA TO ARJUNA, ASHWAMEDHIKA PARVA: THE BOOK OF CONQUEST

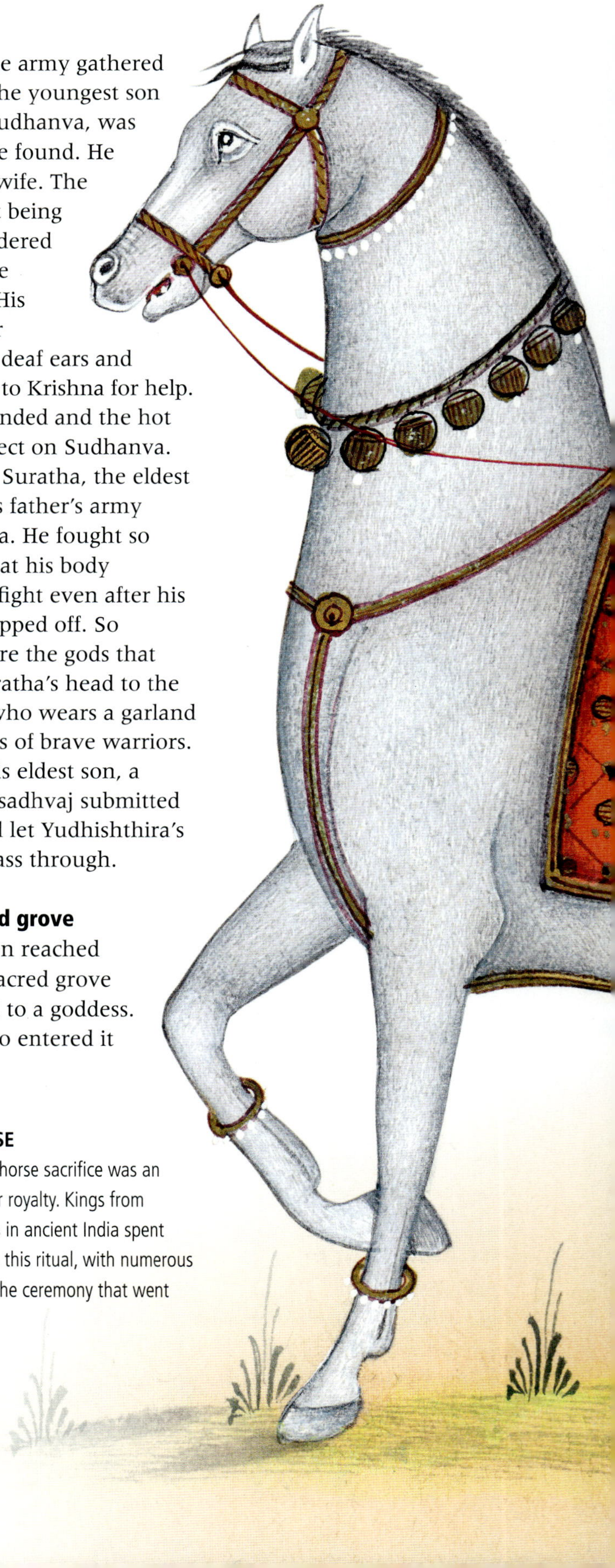

THE ROYAL HORSE

In Vedic India, the horse sacrifice was an important ritual for royalty. Kings from powerful dynasties in ancient India spent immense riches on this ritual, with numerous priests officiating the ceremony that went on for weeks.

ANALYSIS

JAIMINI'S MAHABHARATA

A scholar and philosopher in ancient India, Jaimini narrated a version of the Mahabharata that was different from that of his teacher, Vyasa. Jaimini's tale focuses more on events following the Pandavas' victory in Kurukshetra. This version dwells on events such as Yudhishthira's horse sacrifice, the Pandavas' reconciliation with the children of their enemies, and on the value of worshipping Krishna as God. Known as Jaiminiya-ashwamedha, this version has inspired many folk stories.

turned female. As soon as the horse trotted in, it turned into a mare. The army behind stopped in its tracks. The creatures of the forest advised Nakula to wait on the other side of the grove. As soon as the mare left the grove, it would become a stallion once again.

In the middle of this grove stood Naripur, the city of women. A curse prevented them from leaving the city unless they were married; but any man who wished to marry them turned into a woman as soon as he entered the grove. The trapped and frustrated queen of the city, Pramila, captured Yudhishthira's sacrificial horse, now a mare, and announced, "This mare shall pass and Yudhishthira become my overlord only if Arjuna marries me." Arjuna was at first angry at this bold demand, but later consented. He sent his new wife to Hastinapur and asked her to wait for him.

The horse went through many places, inluding Sindhu, where the Kauravas' only sister Dusshala lived, then Gandhara, where Shakuni's sons welcomed them.

The Rishi's lesson

Finally, the horse reached the sea where, because of the spiritual powers of Rishi Bakadalbhya who lived in a nearby lagoon, people could walk on water. The sage told him of his quest to find the Supreme Being, which took him from one powerful deity to another. It ended, said the sage, when he realized that Vishnu, who reclines on a serpent who lives in the ocean of milk, is the most powerful.

Arjuna returned to the shore with the horse and the journey continued. Soon the horse was captured by Mayurdhvaj, who wanted to meet Krishna, as he knew he was Vishnu's incarnation on earth. By capturing Arjuna, he knew that Krishna would come to the rescue. His plan worked, and Krishna came to rescue Arjuna. Mayurdhvaj, ecstatic to meet Krishna, let the horse proceed.

HERALDING A NEW TIME
A 19th-century opaque watercolor on paper illustrates an episode of the horse sacrifice. Krishna is shown guiding Yudhishthira through the rituals of the ceremony.

AFTER

The royal horse continued its journey across many cities, followed by the Pandava army led by Arjuna and Nakula.

ARJUNA REACHES MANIPUR
In accordance with the rules of the ceremony, the horse went through many lands. All the kingdoms paid their respects to Yudhishthira and accepted him as their lord.

Finally, Arjuna reached Manipur, where he met the ruler, Babruvahana.

"Let the **horse** be released today, so that it can progressively **roam around** the earth, as it wishes ... Following the **sacred** texts, when it roams around, let it be protected."

VYASA TO YUDHISHTHIRA, ASHWAMEDHIKA PARVA: THE BOOK OF CONQUEST

BEFORE

Passing over many lands, the sacrificial horse reached the kingdom of Manipur, where a surprise awaited Arjuna.

ARJUNA'S MANIPURI WIFE

Manipur was ruled by the warrior princess Chitrangada and her son. But the beautiful princess was not a stranger; Arjuna had married Chitrangada during his travels, having fallen in love with her warrior form. Chitrangada was in love with the legendary archer even before she saw him.

Chitrangada's father had no objection to the marriage, only a condition—that their children be brought up in Manipur. Arjuna agreed and married Chitrangada. Their son was born after his return to Indraprastha.

A **Fatal Encounter**

As the sacrificial horse reached Manipur, Arjuna met the prince of the kingdom, Babruvahana. Despite his reluctance, Babruvahana had to fight the warrior Arjuna, inadvertently fulfilling a curse by causing a death.

As the royal horse reached Manipur, it was stopped by a young man. The procession came to a halt, curious to see who this warrior was. It turned out to be Babruvahana, the young ruler of the kingdom of Manipur who was Arjuna's son by Chitrangada, the warrior princess of Manipur. Arjuna had met Chitrangada on his earlier travels when he had to leave Indraprastha for a year, as a punishment for breaking the conjugal arrangement by sharing Draupadi with his brothers.

Even though Babruvahana had never met his father, he welcomed Arjuna into the city, and was going to let the horse pass in acknowledgement of Hastinapur's might. But Arjuna thought such cooperation was unseemly for a ruler, especially his own son. He said to Babruvahana, "Challenge me! You are a warrior's son and cannot give in so easily!"

A father and son duel

Babruvahana, in deference to his father's wishes, raised his bow and to everyone's surprise, turned out to be more than a match for his father. He very easily deflected and destroyed the arrows released by his father, and everyone could see the huge effort Arjuna had to expend to destroy the arrows released by his young son. The fighting went on for a long time. Finally, after hours of fighting, the

THE DUEL
This 19th-century opaque watercolor on paper from Maharashtra, India, vividly shows the confrontation between Arjuna and his son Babruvahana.

unbelievable happened—an arrow left Babruvahana's bow and ripped through Arjuna's heart, killing him instantly.

Chitrangada, who had witnessed the fight, let out a cry. Babruvahana himself was shocked and felt shattered, for he never intended to hurt his father. He rushed to Arjuna and wailed, hugging the lifeless corpse of his father.

Ulupi saves Arjuna

Suddenly Ulupi, a Naga princess, appeared. She, too, was no stranger—Arjuna had also met her during his travels, and she had borne him a son, Iravan, who had been sacrificed on the ninth night of the war as an offering to the goddess Kali.

"Don't cry, Babruvahana," Ulupi comforted him. "It was in your father's fate to die in this way, and you were just an instrument. Your father killed Bhishma, his granduncle, who was like a father to him. Inconsolable at the death of her son, the river goddess Ganga cursed Arjuna that he would meet his death at the hands of his own son. That your arrow pierced Arjuna's heart was just the prophecy fulfilling itself. But do not fear. I have the Nagamani, a gem from the realm of serpents. It has the power to bring the dead back to life."

Revealing the gem, Ulupi placed it on Arjuna's wound and Arjuna's body healed itself.

> "**Hearing** that his **brave father** had arrived, King **Babruvahana** emerged in **humility, placing** noble brahmanas and **gifts** before him."
>
> SAGE VAISHAMPAYANA TO KING JANAMEJAYA, ASHWAMEDHIKA PARVA : THE BOOK OF CONQUEST

Arjuna is brought back to life

Arjuna started to breathe, as everyone looked on in astonishment. He opened his eyes as if waking up from a deep sleep.

Arjuna saw Ulupi, but he failed to recognize her. Many years had gone by since the night they had spent together, and he did not remember her. A heartbroken Ulupi silently turned away.

Arjuna, who had not spent much time with Chitrangada and Babruvahana, decided to stay in Manipur and get to know his family, but it was soon time for him to return to Hastinapur.

PEOPLE

BISHNUPRIYA COMMUNITY

Bishnupur was the ancient capital of Manipur. The people residing there called themselves Bishnupriya and spoke Manipuri. The people from this land later came to be identified as the Bishnupriya Manipuri community.

Many origin theories, especially an analysis of the language spoken there, seem to suggest that people moved to this part of the country from Dwaraka and Hastinapur after the Kurukshetra War. The community here traces its roots to Babruvahana himself, who they say led them to settle here.

BISHNUPRIYA DANCERS

AFTER

Heavy-hearted, Chitrangada and Babruvahana saw Arjuna leave. The sacrificial horse returned to Hastinapur.

THE ROYAL HORSE

As soon as the royal horse entered Hastinapur, it began to neigh cheerfully. The priests wondered why it was happy, since the horse knew of its impending sacrificial death. Nakula, who understood the language of animals, revealed that the horse was untroubled, as unlike other horses sacrificed in earlier yagnas, he would go to Vaikuntha, a higher heaven located above Swarga.

Curious, Yudhishthira asked, "What is this heaven located even above Swarga?" The priests replied that it was a lesser-known secret and that one day, perhaps he himself would know about it if the gods found him worthy.

BEFORE

After successfully traversing many lands, the royal horse returned to Hastinapur for the Ashwamedha rituals to commence.

THE GRAND CEREMONY BEGINS
Yudhishthira's Ashwamedha yagna was the grandest sacrificial ceremony in human memory. Kings from far and wide attended it, and no expense was spared. All the priests who conducted the yagna and chanted the mantras were given food, clothing, and cows.

Dawn of a New Era

The Ashwamedha yagna successfully concluded with Yudhishthira firmly established as a sovereign ruler. However, the ritual sacrifice was not without its share of troubles—interruptions in the ceremony signaled the arrival of a new yuga.

The Ashwamedha ceremony was magnificent. While the ceremony was still on, two farmers came to Hastinapur and asked Yudhishthira to settle a dispute. The eldest Pandava asked them to first tell him about the matter in detail, so he could help resolve it. They said that one of them had sold his land to the other. The following day, as the new owner plowed the field, he found a pot of gold buried in the ground. He went to the previous owner and said, "Even though I bought the land from you, what lies beneath it belongs to you," and he offered the pot of gold. The previous owner refused to take the pot of gold and said, "The land is yours, and with it whatever comes out of it, will be yours."

More than anything, Yudhishthira was impressed by the charitable nature of the two farmers. Not knowing how to settle the matter, he sought Krishna's advice. Krishna gave an unusual solution—he suggested that the farmers leave their pot of gold with the king and return after three months. The two farmers agreed and left.

A peculiar dispute

Confused by the proposed solution, Yudhishthira looked at Krishna quizzically and wondered what resolution would possibly present itself after three months. Krishna replied, "In three months, the situation we just saw will reverse—the same two farmers, who refused the pot of gold today, will return and squabble to be its sole owner. You will find it easier to settle the case as you will not be swayed by their kindness, but will see the greed and anger in them."

"Yudhishthira, your yagna will conclude in three months and the Kali Yuga, a new age, will dawn. Everything as we know it will change. Only a quarter

> "The **sacrifice** started … The **kings** did not **see** anything that was not made out of **gold** … There were **men** from thousands of **races**."
>
> SAGE VAISHAMPAYANA TO KING JANAMEJAYA, ASHWAMEDHIKA PARVA: THE BOOK OF CONQUEST

ANALYSIS

KALI YUGA

Kali Yuga is a concept of time. "Kali" means strife or discord, while "yuga" means an epoch or time. In Hindu belief, the world's existence is divided into four stages: Satya Yuga, Treta Yuga, Dwapara Yuga, and finally Kali Yuga. At the grand sacrifice, Krishna deliberates on this and talks to Yudhishthira about how men will live for pleasure, children will abandon responsibility, women will be like men, and men like women. He further describes how power will be respected, justice abandoned, sacrifice forgotten, and love ridiculed. The wise will argue for the law of the jungle and every victim will, given a chance, inflict harm.

ASHWAMEDHA YAGNA
Rituals that involved sacrifice have been a big part of Hindu culture. This 18th-century painting from a Marathi manuscript shows a fire ritual, or agnihotra, where milk is offered to the fire while chanting prayers.

of the values instituted by Prithu—the first consecrated king from whose name the earth got its Sanskrit name at the dawn of civilization—will survive."

Three months passed, and as Krishna had predicted, the two farmers returned angry and bitter, and fought over the pot of gold. It was now very easy for Yudhishthira to settle the dispute: he divided the gold into three equal portions. One portion was given to each farmer and the third portion was kept by the king as a fee.

The half-golden mongoose

After the royal horse was sacrificed and all the required rituals completed, the priests were about to leave when they saw a mongoose enter the sacrificial hall. The animal, half of whose body was shining like gold, jumped into the fire pit and rubbed the side that was not golden on the charred remains of the ritual. It then left the altar looking deeply disappointed.

The priests were perplexed by the mongoose and its actions. They asked the mongoose why it looked so unhappy. The animal replied,"Some time ago, when I rolled on the remains of a ritual, half my body turned into gold. When I saw this grand yagna, I had hoped the other half would turn to gold too, so I rubbed my body against the remains of this ritual. But nothing happened."

A lesser sacrifice

Everyone was now curious and wanted to know more about this earlier ritual which had turned the mongoose to gold. It said, "This happened over three months ago. A poor family starved to death. They had given up their meager supplies to feed guests who arrived at their doorstep. As I rubbed my body on the leaves on which the food was offered, I was surprised to see my skin turn to gold. But the remains of this yagna have failed to have a similar effect."

It dawned on the learned men and the priests assembled that though Yudhishthira's sacrifice was grand, it was more about power than charity; therefore, it was a lesser ritual.

AFTER

The grand horse sacrifice served its purpose, but it was also clear that the seemingly prosperous Kuru dynasty was in decline.

THE PANDAVA EMPIRE EXPANDED

Despite having all the power and might, the Kuru clan's apparent prosperity was an illusion. As a king and leader of the Pandavas, Yudhishthira could not keep the elders of the household happy, which is why they decided to leave the kingdom altogether.

Dhaumya, the priest, had divined this decline. According to him, before the Kurukshetra War all of dharma rested with the Pandavas. With the dawn of Kali Yuga, however, only Yudhishthira would continue to cling tenaciously to dharma. This dharma would sustain the world; it is only when dharma is abandoned that the world will cease to be.

"O lord of men! **This sacrifice** is **not equal** to a little bit of coarse ground meal given away by **a person** who **resided** in **Kurukshetra**."

THE MONGOOSE TO YUDHISHTHIRA, ASHWAMEDHIKA PARVA: THE BOOK OF CONQUEST

15

ASHRAMAVASIKA PARVA: THE BOOK OF HERMITAGE

RAGING INFERNO
Wildfires are fairly common in many parts of northern India. Forests often catch fire, leading to widespread destruction. When they retire to the forest, Dhritarashtra, Gandhari, Kunti, Vidura, and Sanjay die in a forest fire.

Ashramavasika Parva, or the Book of Hermitage, is the fifteenth parva in the Mahabharata. "Ashramavasika" means residents of the forest. In this section, Dhritarashtra, Gandhari, Kunti, Vidura, and Sanjay give up the comforts of the palace and make their way to the forest to live a life of austerity. Renouncing the material world, the Kuru elders prepare for the fourth stage of life, the sannyasa ashram. In the end, they all perish in a forest fire. This parva has 3 sub-parvas, 35 chapters, and 737 shlokas, or couplets.

"**We** wish to **resort** to **the forest**. With Gandhari, I will **wear tattered rags** and skins … **when** the **age is right**, one must **hand over** the **possessions** to the **son** and go to the **forest**."

DHRITARASHTRA TO YUDHISHTHIRA, ASHRAMAVASIKA PARVA: THE BOOK OF HERMITAGE

BEFORE

The Ashwamedha sacrifice had been completed, Yudhishthira had established himself as a powerful ruler, and the Kuru clan had a new scion.

PEACE AND STABILITY

With the passage of time, Hastinapur emerged as a powerful kingdom. Peace and prosperity reigned and the people were happy with their king.

Dhristarashtra, Gandhari, and Kunti made peace with their past and their wounds slowly healed.

KEY CONCEPT

FOUR PHASES OF LIFE

IN HINDU CULTURE, SANNYASA REPRESENTS RENUNCIATION – THE FINAL PHASE OF LIFE

The Sanskrit treatises called the Dharma Shastras divide life into four parts. The first part, known as brahmacharya, prepares a person for the worldly order. The second part, known as grihastha, is the time to revel in the world's pleasures and powers. The third part, vanaprastha, signals a time to step back and pass on wealth and knowledge to the next generation. The fourth and final part is sannyasa, or the time to renounce all things worldly. In the epic, all the characters, from Pratipa to Dhritarashtra, renounce the world after completing their worldly duties, leaving the young to enjoy the pleasures on earth.

The **Elders Retire**

The memories of the war had faded and there was much to look forward to in Hastinapur. All that the Kuru elders wanted was some semblance of respect and dignity, but this seemed elusive.

These were bitter-sweet times for the Kuru house. The memories of the war and deaths were fading and everyone took joy in watching young Parikshit grow into a fine young man.

Under Yudhishthira's reign, Hastinapur was peaceful and prosperous. As the years went by, Dhritarashtra and Gandhari stayed in Hastinapur, and Yudhishthira tried to ensure they were comfortable and happy.

Bhima's cruelty

Not everyone was sensitive to the plight of the father and mother of the Kauravas. Bhima, who was still as brash, was not so forgiving toward them. He never let go of any opportunity to remind them of their dead sons. Every time the family sat down to eat a meal, Bhima would crack his knuckles and slap his arms, then describe in detail how he had killed each of the Kauravas. "You should have heard the sound when I broke Duryodhana's thigh," he would say. "Oh! you should have heard Dusshasana's last gasp." He never let them forget the losses they had suffered in the bloody war.

Vidura's advice

Vidura, always gentle and wise, kept quiet for some time even though he was hurt to see his brother and sister-in-law troubled so much. One day, unable to bear the constant ill-treatment, he bristled with indignation and said to Dhritarashtra, "Brother, it pains me to see you live this life of shame. Leave Hastinapur, and live what is left of your life in peace." But Dhritarashtra only said, "Where do I go?" and resigned himself to suffer the humiliation in silence.

A tale of learning

Exasperated, Vidura knew he must do something to push his brother in the right direction, so he narrated a story. It was about a priest who once lost his way in the forest and fell into a pit. As his feet had gotten entangled in some vines, he was suspended head down. He could hear the wind howl and see the sky go dark.

THE FAREWELL

This 18th-century Mughal miniature captures the blind Dhritarashtra, a blindfolded Gandhari, and a frail Kunti leaving for the forest, as Vyasa and the Pandavas look on.

> **"**O king! When the **age is right**, one must hand over the possessions to the son and **go to the forest**. I will **reside** there.**"**

DHRITARASHTRA TO YUDHISHTHIRA, ASHRAMAVASIKA PARVA: THE BOOK OF HERMITAGE

On the edge of the pit, he saw a herd of trumpeting wild elephants. Down below, there were hissing, venomous serpents. Rats were gnawing at the roots of the vine that held him. Suddenly, he heard bees humming around a beehive. As a drop of honey fell from the hive, the priest stretched his hand out to collect the drop of honey, his fear and misery forgotten for a moment.

The realization

Dhritarashtra understood the story and realized that it was not his debilitating blindness that kept him in Hastinapur, but his attachment to the comforts of the palace and a familiar life that prevented him from seeing the truth of his pathetic situation.

He finally realized that it was time for him to leave this life behind. He mustered the courage to renounce all worldly things and walk out of the palace. He looked at his wife, Gandhari, and said, "Come, it is time for us to go." Gandhari got ready to accompany her husband, and Vidura decided to follow the two.

Seeing them, Kunti realized that it was time for her too to let go. She decided to move to the forest with the others.

ANALYSIS

ELDERS OF A FAMILY

Vyasa picked up a theme in the Mahabharata that is very relevant today—the treatment of the elderly in the modern familial structure.

Through the older generation in the epic, Vyasa portrays the plight of old men and women and the way they are treated by their sons and daughters.

Yudhishthira symbolizes the ideal behavior or conduct, while Bhima personifies the grudges the younger generation bear toward their predecessors for actions in the past that affect everyone.

AFTER

Seeing the elders, including his mother, leave, Yudhishthira broke down. He begged her to stay, but Kunti was steadfast in her resolve.

THE DEATH OF THE ELDERS

Kunti was determined to leave Hastinapur. When the eldest Pandava's pleas grew more fervent, Kunti replied, "After all this time, I am tired, son. The time has come for me to move on." For many years the elders wandered in the woods, meeting many rishis, learning from them, and understanding the true meaning of life.

Then one day, Vidura passed away as he was meditating. Gandhari had a vision of those killed in the battle clad in white, bedecked in jewels, and smiling, with no sign of sorrow or anger. These were all omens. Sometime later, a fire broke out in the forest. Smelling the smoke, Dhritarashtra turned to his wife and said, "Run!" But Gandhari, who knew their time had come, simply asked, "Why?" This is how the older generation of the Kuru clan met its end.

16
MOUSALA PARVA: THE BOOK OF THE MACE

AN UNLIKELY WEAPON
A difference of opinion turned into a civil war for the Yadavas that brought about their destruction. They attacked one another with sharp reeds imbued with the strength of iron and decimated the clan.

Mousala Parva, or the Book of the Mace, is the sixteenth parva in the Mahabharata. The word "musala" means clubs or mace. In accordance with an old prophecy, the Yadavas meet a horrific death. Krishna and his brother, Balarama, also give up their mortal existence. The parva records the humbling of a hero, when Arjuna loses his powers and realizes he is merely mortal. This section sees the end of a dynasty and the fall of a great city. This parva has 1 sub-parva, 9 chapters, and 273 shlokas, or couplets.

"When **thirty-six** years had passed, Yudhishthira saw contrary **portents** … Hearing about the **incident** with the **clubs**, they were overcome by sorrow and grief. **Distressed** and devoid of resolution, **the Pandavas** sat down."

SAGE VAISHAMPAYANA TO KING JANAMEJAYA, MOUSALA PARVA: THE BOOK OF THE MACE

BEFORE

Several years had passed since the Kurukshetra War and Yudhishthira's reign was peaceful. But all was not well in the Kuru household.

THE ELDERS LEAVE

Even though the Pandavas accepted Dhritarashtra and Gandhari in their household and took care of them, Bhima was not as sensitive to their plight.

Because of the constant reminders of their loss and a lingering sense of grief, the blind king and his wife went into the forest and decided to put an end to their life. A new age was beginning.

End of the Yadu Dynasty

While on the one hand, the old order of the Kuru clan came to an end; on the other, the Yadava dynasty faced the consequences of an old curse—one which would result in a civil war and total annihilation of the whole Yadu clan.

"**Without** the **Yadus**, I am **incapable** of looking at **this city** of the **Yadavas**. ... I will go to the forest and **practice austerities**, together with **Rama**."

KRISHNA, MOUSALA PARVA: THE BOOK OF THE MACE

Thirty-six years had passed since the battle of Kurukshetra ended. Dwaraka was a peaceful and prosperous city where the citizens led happy lives. One day, the Yadavas decided to gather on the shores of the sea at Prabhasa to make offerings to all those who had died in the war at Kurukshetra. As the ceremony was going on, an argument erupted between those who thought the Pandavas were righteous, and those who felt the Kauravas had been wronged. The Yadavas had participated in the war, and many of them had fought on the side of the Kauravas.

Who is more righteous?

Split into two opposing sides, the Yadavas who supported the Pandavas said, "The Kauravas surrounded and pounced upon

PEOPLE

SAMBA – SON OF KRISHNA

Samba is Krishna's son from the bear-princess Jambavati. Mischievous and irreverent, Samba is often portrayed as taking advantage of his father's position.

Stories abound of his pranks. In one, he dupes his father's junior wives by disguising himself as Krishna and as a punishment, is cursed with a skin disease by Krishna. His cure lay in worshipping the sun god; so Samba built many temples to the sun. All sun temples in India, from Konark in Odisha to Modhera in Gujarat to Markand in Kashmir, are attributed to him. Samba also attempted to kidnap Duryodhana's daughter. This led to major discord between the Kauravas and the Yadavas; peace was restored only when Krishna's elder brother Balarama, in a fit of fury, threatened to drag Hastinapur into the sea. Samba's nature shows that Krishna may be divine but his offspring was not. It is often speculated that Samba was a product of his father's neglect; there are many tales of Krishna guiding the Pandavas in the politics of Kurukshetra, but none of Krishna as a father.

Abhimanyu like rabid dogs." Kritavarma, another Yadava warrior who was leading the group supporting the Kauravas, retorted, "And what of Pandava honor! Drona was betrayed on the battlefield, Karna was struck when he was unarmed, and Duryodhana was hit below the waist!"

Before long, the small but passionate argument turned into a full-blown brawl, the brawl into a full-fledged battle, and the battle into a full-fledged civil war. Krishna and Balarama watched in helpless horror as in front of their eyes their brothers, friends, cousins, sons, and grandsons lunged at each other. It was then that they remembered a curse from a long time ago—a curse that would end the Yadava race.

A prank gone awry

Krishna's son Samba had always been a mischievous child who loved playing pranks. Years ago, Samba had played a prank on a group of sages. To test them, he went to the sages disguised as a pregnant woman and asked if the unborn child was male or female. The sages were not amused by this childish prank, and growled at him,"Neither male or female, but an iron bar rests in your body. Beware! It will destroy the Yadavas." Soon, an iron mace ripped itself out of Samba's thigh. Terrified, Samba pounded it to dust and threw it into the sea. The sea threw back the iron dust to the shores of Prabhasa, where it transformed into deadly reeds.

BALARAMA AND THE SERPENT-GOD NAGARAJA
A mottled red sandstone sculpture found in the northern state of Uttar Pradesh, India, depicts Balarama sheltered under a serpent.

SOMNATH TEMPLE
Located in Gujarat, India, this temple is an significant pilgrimage site. Another important site nearby is Bhalka, considered to be the spot where Krishna died.

A dire prophecy comes true

Both Krishna and Balarama knew about the scene unfolding in front of them; they had foreseen this conflict long ago. In a bid to save their clan, the two brothers hid all the weapons of the Yadava warriors. But the Yadavas were lost in a haze of fury. Unable to find a weapon, they began hitting each other with blades of the reeds that grew along the shore.

These were no ordinary reeds—they had sharp, serrated edges and pointed tips. They were made of the same iron dust that Samba had tried hard to discard into the sea. They had grown in the soil that the sea itself nourished.

Within a few hours, struck by the deadly blades of grass, the bodies of hundreds of slain Yadavas, young and old, covered the shores of Prabhasa. All the great warriors who had led the Yadu clan to victories in the past lay dead. Who sided with the Pandavas and who with the Kauravas—the argument was futile with Satyaki dead and Kritavarma too. It was like another Kurukshetra.

Krishna and Balarama stood watching and knew they could do nothing to save the Yadavas. Krishna recalled an angry Gandhari cursing him, and echoes of it came back. It had come true—he could only stand and watch as his children, and entire clan, annihilated each other. The Yadava dynasty had come to an end.

"Vasudeva's son, Samba, will **give birth** to a **terrible** and **iron club** for the **destruction** of the Vrishnis and the Andhakas. **You are** evil in conduct, **cruel** and **insolent**."

SAGES TO SAMBA, MOUSALA PARVA: THE BOOK OF THE MACE

ANALYSIS

KARMA AND FATE

Neither Krishna nor his family are able to escape Gandhari's curse. In this epic, the laws of karma affect even the divine. The Mahabharata, through the interactions between the gods and humans, shows that by making humans the masters of their own destiny and the creators of their own desires, the gods make them ultimately responsible for the life they lead and the choices they make. Again and again it is established that the gods do not interfere with fate; they simply help human beings to cope with it.

AFTER

The Yadu dynasty met a violent end, and only Krishna and Balarama were left.

DEATHS CONTINUE
Krishna and Balarama were horrified to see their brethren die in such a brutal manner. Grief-stricken, Balarama retreated to the forest where he drew his last breath. On discovering that his elder brother had passed away, Krishna realized that it was time for him, too, to give up his mortal existence.

Death of Krishna

With the Yadava dynasty wiped out and Balarama gone, Krishna, too, lost his will to live as a mortal on earth and returned to the heavens after his death.

Krishna knew that the day of death had come for both him and his elder brother Balarama. He went to meet his father Vasudeva and promised him that Arjuna would come to help the women and children of Dwaraka and take them to safety. Having ensured the safety of what remained of his clan, he went to join his brother.

On seeing the destruction of his family, the distraught Balarama lost all interest in life. He sat under a tree, practiced austerities, and waited for death to come.

As Krishna rushed back to see Balarama, he saw the life breath slip out of his brother's mortal body in the form of a giant white serpent with a thousand heads.

With Balarama gone, Krishna realized it was time to end his own mortal life. He settled under a banyan tree, cross-legged with his left foot over his right leg, and reminisced about his life. He thought about his long journey from Vrindavan through Mathura and Dwaraka to Hastinapur and, finally, the land of Kurukshetra.

As he was meditating and looking back at his life, the sole of his left foot was struck by a poisoned arrow shot by a hunter named Jara. Soon, Jara himself came running out of the bushes, eager to see the deer he thought he had struck with his arrow.

No common arrowhead, this was the only piece of the iron mace that Samba had not been able to destroy; Jara had found it in the belly of a fish. The poison soon took effect and Krishna's life slipped away from his body.

It was in this way that Krishna left the earth to return to the heaven known as Vaikuntha, located even above Swarga, and took his place as Vishnu. Balarama as the thousand-hooded serpent of time, Adi-Ananta-Sesha, was already there to receive him.

" Enveloping heaven and earth … **he rose upward** … the gods, **the best** among sages, and their followers worshipped the **lord** of **everything**."

SAGE VAISHAMPAYANA TO KING JANAMEJAYA, MOUSALA PARVA: THE BOOK OF THE MACE

DYING MOMENTS
This Bikaner-style miniature illustrates Krishna's last moments. Seeing Krishna in his divine form, Jara is overcome with guilt and bows down before him.

THE YADAVA CAPITAL

Dwaraka

> **"Krishna** ... saw that extensive region ... This place was named **Dvaravati** ... Keshava made up his mind to **construct a city** there."
>
> SAGE VAISHAMPAYANA TO JANAMEJAYA, HARIVAMSHA: THE BOOK OF KRISHNA

Dwaraka is an important pilgrimage center in the Okhamandal peninsula on the Arabian Sea, in Gujarat. It is revered as the kingdom of Krishna and his Yadava clan as well as one of the four seats of Hindu religion, established by the 8th-century Hindu teacher, Adi Shankaracharya.

The capital of the Yadavas

Dwaraka makes repeated appearances in the Mahabharata as the city of Krishna, the chief adviser and friend of the Pandavas. When the king of Magadha repeatedly attached Mathura—the capital of the Yadava clan—Jarasandha, Krishna, and Balarama gathered

DWARAKA
A city in the Indian state of Gujarat, Dwaraka is located 236 miles (380 km) from Ahmedabad, the largest city in the state.

their clansmen and retreated westward till they reached the island of Dwaraka. The city was ruled by King Revata, whose daughter Revati had become a giantess and no one was willing to marry her. It was then that Balarama accepted her as his wife. Pleased with Balarama, King Revata gave the Yadavas his island on which to settle.

Arjuna, while spending a year on pilgrimage, came to Dwaraka as a mendicant. Krishna's sister Subhadra was in love with him. She eloped with Arjuna, holding the reins of the horse pulling their chariot, so no one could accuse Arjuna of abducting her. The Pandavas also lived in Dwaraka for some time during their period of exile. When Krishna attended Yudhishthira's coronation ceremony, King Salva, a friend of the Chedi king Shishupala (see pp. 136–137), attacked so fiercely that the Yadavas were not able to defend their city. Krishna then hurried home and, using his Sharanga bow and the Kaumodaki mace, smashed Salva's missiles and beheaded the king.

The name of Dwaraka, also called Dwaravati, is interpreted as "the city of many gates" or "gateway to heaven." The Harivamsha describes Dwaraka as a city built on submerged land, with four gates and high buildings made of gold and gems. The Shrimad Bhagavata, or the Bhagavata Purana, describes the lakes and gardens of Dwaraka, suggesting that it had 900,000 palaces.

End of the Yadavas

The destruction of Dwaraka unfolded tragically. Krishna's son Samba was cursed with an iron bar emerging from his body that would end his clan. He pounded the bar and threw it into the sea, but it grew as reeds on the shore.

Years after the Kurukshetra War, the Yadava clan became dissipated and unwise. One day, an argument broke out about whether the Kauravas or Pandavas had been more unfair during the war—and this escalated into a civil war.

Krishna hid their weapons but the Yadavas plucked the deadly reeds to throw at each other and the entire clan ended up dead.

Unable to bear his grief, Balarama let go of his life. Krishna was killed by a hunter. Dwaraka became a city of mourning. As the sea rose and rain lashed the city, its walls crumbled. Arjuna came to take the women and orphans to safety, but since his powers had weakened, he was unable to save them from bandits.

Dwaraka in history

An early mention of Dwaraka was found in a copper inscription dated 574 CE. It was credited to Simhaditya, a minister of the Maitraka dynasty of Vallabhi, the capital city of the Maitrakas, also in Gujarat. There is evidence that medieval Dwaraka was an important port, and some scholars have identified it with the island of Barka mentioned in *The Periplus of the Erythrean Sea*. In the 19th century, it came under the rule of the Gaekwads of Baroda.

Dwaraka's most famous attraction, the Dwarakadhish temple dedicated to Krishna, was built by Raja Jagat Singh Rathore in the 16th century. The devout believe that it stands on the site of a 2,500-year-old temple. Recent excavations have posited that submerged settlements around the nearby island of Bet Dwaraka go back to the time of the Indus Valley Civilization.

THE DWARAKADHISH TEMPLE
This Hindu pilgrimage site in Dwaraka, Gujarat, India, is believed to have been built over an ancient Krishna temple at the same place.

BALARAMA AND REVATI
This 10th-century sculpture in copper alloy with silver inlay from Himachal Pradesh, India, shows Balarama with his wife Revati. The city of Dwaraka is said to have been gifted to him by his father-in-law King Revata.

HISTORY AND CULTURE

EXCAVATIONS AT DWARAKA

Over the decades, excavations at Dwaraka have revealed different finds. Indications of a medieval port city were found within the walls of submerged settlements, stone structures, possibly a jetty built in stone, and triangular stone anchors. In the years 2000 to 2004, the National Institute of Ocean Technology investigated the Bet Dwaraka island for artifacts. This may have been a settlement in the 17th century BCE when the Harappan culture flourished in present-day Gujarat, Sindh, and Punjab. However, it is not known whether these findings, such as pottery, indicated signs of habitation. It is a matter of speculation if the characters of the Mahabharata inhabited these cities.

Dwaraka Destroyed

Following the destruction of the Yadu clan and demise of Krishna and Balarama, a civil war broke out in Dwaraka. A grief-stricken Arjuna reached the city to salvage whatever he could; while doing so, he learned one of the most important lessons in his life.

BEFORE

The news traveled fast, and the Pandavas soon heard of the conflict among the Yadavas and how, in their rage, they had mercilessly killed each other.

Krishna's charioteer, Daruka, who had seen the destruction of the Yadavas unfold in front of him, rushed to Hastinapur. He told the Pandavas about the end of the Yadus and the death of Krishna and Balarama. Hearing of the end of their dear friend and mentor, the brothers were plunged into a deep state of grief. But it was Arjuna who was most affected with sorrow. He decided to go to Dwaraka.

Vasudeva heard of the calamity that had befallen the Yadavas. Overcome by grief, he died of a broken heart. Dwaraka was in mourning and funeral pyres lined the shores of the sea. The Yadava women wailed as they grieved over their dead. The sound of their keening reached the gods in the heavens, who joined them in their sorrow.

Grief engulfs Dwaraka

The survivors in the city now turned to Arjuna. The Pandava had rushed from Hastinapur upon hearing of the great civil war in Dwaraka—but he got there too late; there was hardly anything left of the Yadava clan to save. He had barely met Vasudeva before the Yadava patriarch died. Arjuna joined the mourners and cremated his dear friend Krishna and Krishna's elder brother Balarama, being careful to follow all the right rituals and traditions.

The women of the city, left without fathers, sons, and brothers, were distraught and helpless. Some women leapt into the funeral pyres, unable to bear the thought of life without their husbands. Many of the survivors decided to retire into the forest to live as mendicants.

Even nature seemed intent on destroying the city—the sea rose and lashed against its walls and heavy rain flooded the streets, dissolving its very foundations. Before long, the city had started to crumble.

Saving the survivors

Arjuna did his best to save as many as he could—Krishna had entrusted him with the task. He decided to take all the survivors who wanted to come back with him to Hastinapur. Panic-stricken, the widows and orphans scrambled onto rafts and boats, with Arjuna guiding them.

But misfortune followed them. On their way to safety, they were

DWARAKA SWEPT AWAY
Rainwater had flooded the streets of Dwaraka, dissolving its foundations. The Dwarakadhish temple stands on the shore in the present-day city of Dwaraka, Gujarat. It is believed that the original temple was constructed by Vajranabha, the great-grandson of Krishna, over the residence of Krishna.

attacked by barbarians who abducted many of the women and children. Arjuna raised his Gandiva to protect them, but the great Gandiva, which had destroyed hundreds of warriors with a single arrow, was now powerless. Even though the warrior tried to protect the women and children, he was greatly outnumbered. Arjuna realized that he was no longer the archer he used to be. His purpose on earth and that of the Gandiva had been served.

Arjuna's acceptance

Overpowered by this sense of helplessness and humbled by the twist in circumstances, Arjuna fell to his knees and sobbed uncontrollably.

Gradually it dawned on him that it was Gandhari's curse that had destroyed Dwaraka and its people, and that her curse had its roots in the deadly war at Kurukshetra.

Arjuna could now see clearly how he was a part of the war and how it could have been averted if only the Pandavas and the Kauravas had shown restraint, abandoned avarice, and accepted peace as the right way. He realized that, in some way, he was responsible for the fall of Dwaraka. Having come to this realization, he begged the heavens for forgiveness.

The clouds began to rumble and as a flash of lightning struck nearby, Arjuna saw a vision—a child resting on a banyan leaf, cooing happily and sucking its butter-smeared big toe. The child was cradled by the same dangerous waves that were destroying Dwaraka. In the middle of all the destruction, this child was a symbol of renewal and hope.

"He was **full** of **sorrow** and **grief** ... The **weapons** had **disappeared** ... the **valor** of his **arms** had been **destroyed.**"

SAGE VAISHAMPAYANA TO JANAMEJAYA, MOUSALA PARVA: THE BOOK OF THE MACE

MYTHOLOGY AND FOLKLORE

KRISHNA ICONOGRAPHY

BABY KRISHNA

Krishna is often visualized as a baby boy sucking his right toe while lying on a banyan leaf cradled by waves. This iconic image has been firmly assimilated into popular culture as reflected in calendar art and kitsch. While the waves symbolize the impermanent nature of life, the banyan leaf signifies the permanent presence of God, and the baby is the symbol of renewal. The left and lower halves of the body represent material delights, while the right and upper halves represent spiritual bliss. The laughing baby sucking the right toe is a message to humans to experience both material and spiritual bliss without getting overwhelmed by their impermanent nature.

AFTER

The vision, sent from the heavens, made Arjuna understand the message of God at last.

A NEW RESOLVE

Arjuna finally understood the message. He realized that life would present many sorrows and challenges, but it was up to him to respond wisely and enjoy simple pleasures, unshaken by the inevitable endless turmoil of the world.

He took the surviving Yadavas and gave them a home in Mathura. Here, Vajranabha—son of Aniruddha, grandson of Pradyumna, and great-grandson of Krishna—would rise as a great king.

17

MAHAPRASTHANIKA PARVA: THE BOOK OF RENUNCIATION

LESSONS FOR THE KING
Like any king, Parikshit had many learned men who were in charge of his education. In this miniature, Sage Shuku Deva addresses King Parikshit along with other sages.

Mahaprasthanika Parva, or the Book of Renunciation, is the seventeenth parva in the Mahabharata. "Maha" means great, and "prasthana" translates to journey or departure. The Pandavas and Draupadi leave Hastinapur for the forest, a grand journey that culminates with their departure from the material world. The section also sees the coronation of Parikshit, the grandson of Arjuna. This parva has 1 sub-parva, 3 chapters, and 106 shlokas, or couplets.

"He has **made up** his **mind** to **leave** … **Yudhisthira** took off the ornaments … and donned the bark of the trees … **Bhima, Arjuna, the twins** and the illustrious Draupadi—all of them donned garments made from the barks of trees."

SAGE VAISHAMPAYANA TO KING JANAMEJAYA, MAHAPRASTHANIKA PARVA: THE BOOK OF RENUNCIATION

Passing the Crown

As news from Dwaraka reached Hastinapur, the Pandavas were shocked at the violence that had shaken the city. The incident made Yudhishthira think that perhaps it was time to pass on the reins of Hastinapur to the new generation.

BEFORE

The death of Krishna and Balarama stunned the Pandavas. Arjuna rushed to Dwaraka to attend their cremation.

KRISHNA AND BALARAMA

ARJUNA'S VISION

While in Dwaraka, Arjuna also witnessed the complete destruction of the city. He tried his best to save what remained of the populace but could not do much. On his way back to Hastinapur, a vision of Krishna, in his child-like divine form, filled him with hope and happiness.

After hearing about the great carnage at Prabhasa and the consequent havoc wreaked on Dwaraka, Yudhishthira was consumed with grief. Even in their sorrow, the Pandavas saw that their brother was about to make a momentous decision.

Yudhishthira's decision

Though Hastinapur was peaceful and prosperous, the carnage at Prabhasa had shaken the eldest Pandava, who felt responsible for the near destruction of the Yadus. Feeling that it was time to retire to the forest, Yudhishthira spoke his mind to his brothers. Not only did Draupadi and his brothers applaud this decision, they all wanted to accompany him. Preparations for the move began.

Parikshit as king

Yudhishthira anointed Parikshit, the grandson of Arjuna and the son of Abhimanyu and Uttari, as the king of Hastinapur. Though Parikshit was old enough to take charge, he was young enough to need guidance. So Yudhishthira appointed his cousin Yuyutsu, Dhritarashtra's son by a servant, as the regent of the kingdom. As the only Kaurava to have fought from the Pandava side, Yuyutsu had become a trusted adviser and, the Pandavas felt he would be an good mentor for Parikshit.

The Pandavas were also concerned about the welfare of the Yadavas and wanted a long and peaceful reign for Mathura. So Yudhishthira told Subhadra, Parikshit's grandmother, "This son of your son will be the king of the Kurus. Vajra, the last of the Yadus, has also been made a king. Parikshit will rule in Hastinapur and the Yadava in Shakraprastha. King Vajra should be protected by you so do not let adharma enter your mind." By saying this, he had made sure that the Yadavas would remain a sovereign nation and the Kurus would not make any attempts to assimilate them in the future.

Rituals of a farewell

Relieved and happy in the knowledge that their land was in safe hands, the Pandavas and Draupadi started making arrangements for their departure. As a sign of respect, they performed proper funeral rites for Vasudeva, Krishna, and Balarama. Yudhishthira

"The **one with dharma** in his soul took the permission of **residents** of **the city**."

SAGE VAISHAMPAYANA TO KING JANAMEJAYA, MAHAPRASTHANIKA PARVA: THE BOOK OF RENUNCIATION

AN ABLE RULER

As Yudhishthira's successor, Parikshit would go on to strengthen and expand the Kuru kingdom. This 18th-century watercolor painting from the state of Rajasthan shows Parikshit on a hunting expedition.

"O immensely wise one [Arjuna]! **Time** cooks **all creatures**. **I think** all **this** has **happened because of that**. You should consider that.**"**

YUDHISHTHIRA TO ARJUNA, MAHAPRASTHANIKA PARVA: THE BOOK OF RENUNCIATION

then gave away all his material possessions—jewels, horses and chariots, garments, and villages—to the deserving among the Brahmans.

Next, he went to pay his respects to his former guru, Kripa, and asked him to be a teacher and guide to Parikshit.

Finally, Yudhishthira spoke to the citizens of Hastinapur about the Pandavas' decision. Understandably, his subjects were extremely anxious to hear that their great king would no longer be with them. But Yudhishthira was steadfast in his resolve and, together with the rest of the Pandavas, left for the forest.

ANALYSIS

RENUNCIATION

According to ancient Hindu scriptures, human life is divided into four ashramas, or stages of life, each with their own duties. These ashramas are brahmacharya, the life of a student; grihastha, the life of a householder; vanaprastha, the life of retirement, and, sannyasa, the life of renunciation. The Pandavas, by renouncing worldly life, go into the final ashrama, sannyasa.

AN ASCETIC MEDITATING NEAR A RIVER, LIVING A LIFE OF RENUNCIATION

ROYAL SYMBOLS
Crowns are symbols of power and royalty. Indian crowns bore cultural and religious motifs; this one is adorned with the deities—Vishnu (left), Ganesha (center), and Shiva (right).

AFTER

Having placed an able ruler on the throne of Hastinapur, the Pandavas had fulfilled their duties toward their subjects. It was time to leave Hastinapur.

THE PANDAVAS DEPART
The Pandavas left their kingdom with their wife Draupadi following them—the scene was reminiscent of the time they had earlier left for exile. But this time, instead of feeling shame, the brothers were calm and happy with their decision.

BEFORE

Devastated by the events at Dwaraka, Yudhishthira and his brothers made a momentous decision.

HANDING OVER HASTINAPUR
The brothers decided to give up their kingdom and hand over its reins to their grandson, Abhimanyu's son, Parikshit. As he was still young, the Pandavas asked their own guru, Kripa, accept Parikshit as a disciple and appointed Yuyutsu, Dhritarashtra's son, who had fought with them against the Kauravas, as the regent of Hastinapur.

The **Final Journey**

Deciding that it was time to move on to the next stage of their lives, the Pandavas secured the fate of the kingdom by putting Parikshit on the throne, and set off on a journey from which there was no return.

When the citizens of Hastinapur learned of the Pandavas' intention to renounce their kingdom, their cries of disbelief and dismay rang throughout the city. Yudhishthira was, however, deaf to their pleas to reconsider his decision; his mind—and that of his brothers—was made up. Convinced that they were following the path of dharma, Yudhishthira spoke to his subjects and persuaded them to accept their decision. Then the Pandavas and Draupadi began to prepare for their final journey.

The last goodbye

Exchanging their ornaments and rich clothes for those made of bark, Draupadi and her husbands left the kingdom, this time with no intention to return. Their hearts were peaceful as they completed all the prescribed rites, concluding by dousing the sacred fire of the household with water. With this symbolic renunciation of their status as householders, the six companions, having decided to follow the dharma of renunciation, immersed themselves in yoga, and set off. The citizens followed their beloved royals out of Hastinapur for the last time, overcome with grief, yet unable to give voice to their sorrow.

With Arjuna gone, Ulupi, his Naga wife, entered the waters of the Ganga and Chitrangada left for Manipur. In a show of support and to boost his spirits, Yuyutsu, Kripa, and the rest of the elders gathered around Parikshit.

After fasting, the Pandavas and Draupadi traveled toward the east and crossed many kingdoms, passing a number of rivers and mountains on their way. The party walked in single

> "There were the **five brothers**. **Krishna** [Draupadi] was **the sixth** and **a dog joined as the seventh**. … For some distance, **the citizens** … **followed** them."
>
> SAGE VAISHAMPAYANA TO KING JANAMEJAYA, MAHAPRASTHANIKA PARVA: THE BOOK OF RENUNCIATION

A LONG ROAD
After bidding farewell to their family and friends, the Pandavas and Draupadi embarked on their journey, traversing eastward to the sea and the Himalayas, never turning back.

"They departed with Draupadi as the sixth, **just as in earlier times**, they had left **after** being defeated in **the game with the dice. But** … the brothers were **cheerful**."

SAGE VAISHAMPAYANA TO KING JANAMEJAYA, MAHAPRASTHANIKA PARVA: THE BOOK OF RENUNCIATION

ATTACHMENT AND RENUNCIATION
For Arjuna, the Gandiva and its quivers had become an extension of his personality; giving them up had become inconceivable. His reluctance to part with them shows that renunciation of what one values is the hardest task of all.

file, with Yudhishthira leading the way. The rest of his brothers followed by order of birth, with Draupadi walking after them. On their way to the forest, the six were joined by a dog, which brought up the rear.

Arjuna's weapons

Eventually this company of seven reached the great, roaring Brahmaputra river, where Agni, the god of fire, barred their way. "O sons of Pandu! Listen! O brave ones! Listen! Know me to be the god of fire," he said to the brothers. "Your brother, Phalguna," he said, referring to Arjuna, born in the last month of the Hindu calendar, "can only go to the forest after casting aside the supreme weapon, the Gandiva."

Agni himself had given Arjuna the Gandiva bow, along with two quivers that never ran out of arrows, during the razing of Khandavaprastha. »

ART AND LITERATURE

JOURNEY AS A METAPHOR

The idea of a journey to attain spiritual growth is a metaphor that is seen across cultures. Over the course of the Mahabharata, the Pandavas undertake many a journey that alters their world view and helps them learn valuable lessons. In the West, this idea has been most famously depicted in John Bunyan's Christian allegory *Pilgrim's Progress*. Subtitled *From This World, to That Which is to Come*, this charts the spiritual journey of the protagonist, Christian, to salvation, overcoming many obstacles.

MYTHOLOGY AND FOLKLORE

MOUNT MANDARA

According to a Hindu creation myth, Mandara was used as a paddle to churn the ocean of milk to obtain amrita, the elixir of immortality. Mandara was so firmly lodged in the earth that it required both the gods and demons to uproot it. But dislodging it and carrying the mountain to the ocean were two different things. When Vishnu realized this, he ordered his mount, Garuda, to carry it there. When the churning began, with the celestial snake Vasuki as the rope, the mountain began to sink. Without Mandara to churn the ocean, the gods knew they would be unable to obtain amrita, so they prayed to Vishnu for help. Vishnu then took the form of a kurma, or turtle, and dived into the ocean. Supporting the mountain's weight from below, he swam toward the water's surface and restored the paddle to the gods.

"O scorcher of enemies! This princess **never committed an act of adharma**. O king! **Why has Krishna** [Draupadi] **fallen** down on the ground?"

BHIMA TO YUDHISHTHIRA, MAHAPRASTHANIKA PARVA: THE BOOK OF RENUNCIATION

» But now that the brothers no longer had any use for it, Agni wanted to return it to Varuna, the god of water, to whom it had originally belonged. Ever since he had received it, Arjuna cherished this bow, and carried it everywhere with him. In fact, the archer had almost come to blows with Yudhishthira when he had insulted it in a moment of anger during the war. So, while Draupadi and the rest of his brothers had left Hastinapur empty-handed, Arjuna had not been able to bring himself to leave the Gandiva and its quivers behind.

When they learned that Agni wanted the bow returned, his brothers urged Arjuna to give it up. As soon as Arjuna flung the Gandiva and the quivers into the river, Agni vanished, and the band of seven was able to resume the journey.

From the northern shores of the salty ocean, the Pandavas now headed in a southwestern direction, where they saw the island of Dwaraka that nature had claimed for itself. From there, the seven once again proceeded north, in an effort to circle the known world.

The ascent

Moving beyond their erstwhile kingdom, the Pandavas reached the towering Himalayas, their peaks touching Swarga, the abode of the gods. Beyond it, in an ocean of sand, they saw Mandara, the mountain that the gods had used as a rod to churn the ocean of milk. When they reached the mountain, Yudhishthira turned to his brothers and wife and suggested that they attempt to climb it. "If we have truly lived our lives in dharma, then our bodies will not die during the ascent. We will enter the realm of the gods in our mortal bodies," he told them. Everyone agreed, so the six grey-haired elders began a long and arduous journey up a sharp, narrow path to the land high above the sky, where the virtuous were in bliss.

The fall

As the group climbed up the mountain, Draupadi slipped and fell. When Bhima realized she would die, he asked his elder brother why their wife, who had never committed an act of adharma, had fallen. Yudhishthira responded that Draupadi had reaped the fruits of her actions. Though she was the wife of all five brothers, she had been partial to Arjuna, desired Karna, and manipulated Bhima, explained Yudhishthira, and walked on. Having made up his mind to give up all ties—whether to things or to people—he remained steadfast in his decision, never once pausing to look back.

Soon after, Yudhishthira heard Bhima exclaim that Sahadeva had fallen. When Bhima wanted to know the reason for his fall,

THE SEVEN TRAVELERS This depiction of Draupadi and the Pandavas' final journey in the *Razmnama*, interestingly, shows them still in their royal finery. They are duly accompanied by the dog.

"You ate too much and you **boasted about** your vigor. O Partha! You **disrespected others**. That is the reason you have fallen down on the ground."

YUDHISHTHIRA TO BHIMA, MAHAPRASTHANIKA PARVA: THE BOOK OF RENUNCIATION

Yudhishthira explained that Sahadeva had fallen because he had thought himself unparalleled in wisdom. Yudhishthira kept on walking, steady in his resolve to relinquish all bonds, so that Yama would find him worthy enough to enter Swarga in his mortal body. One by one Yudhishthira's brothers fell—Nakula, because beauty had made him insensitive; then Arjuna, who was guilty of being had been envious of all the other archers in the world; and finally Bhima, who had been a glutton, eating without bothering to serve others. But Yudhishthira refused to turn and help anyone, reminding himself at each turn that he had renounced all earthly ties. And so Yudhishthira climbed on by himself, with only the dog following behind, until t he two reached the peak of Mount Mandara.

AFTER

By the time Yudhishthira reached the peak of Mount Mandara, the company of seven had dwindled to two.

THE LONE PANDAVA

Only Yudhishthira and the dog who had joined them on the journey managed to reach the top of the mountain in their mortal bodies. Here, high up in the clouds, were the gates of Swarga, the paradise of the gods. Also known as Amravati, this was a garden of unending delights, where there was no pain or suffering, and where all dreams were fulfilled and all wishes granted. The lone Pandava saw Indra waiting to receive him at the gates.

Yudhishthira's **Final Test**

It had been a cold, grueling, and lonely journey, but Yudhishthira reached the gates of heaven at last. As he was invited into heaven by the gods and other celestial beings, it dawned on him that he had not been alone through this emotionally draining path; he'd had a companion all along.

After a long and arduous journey, Yudhishthira reached the peak of Mandara. There he found himself before the gate of Amravati, the city of Indra. Seeing Yudhishthira standing there, the Devas of Amravati beckoned him to enter. But Yudhishthira, grieving over the death of his brothers and wife, asked Indra to let them come with him, too. Indra assured him that he would meet them in heaven. The Devas called out to him again and said,"Come inside but leave that dog out."

A loyal companion

"Dog?" asked Yudhishthira, surprised. He turned around and found a dog looking up at him, wagging his tail. Confused for a moment, Yudhishthira realized this dog had followed him all the way from the streets of Hastinapur. It had been his unnoticed

THE PANTHEON
Part of a folio from an 18th-century watercolor entitled *Devimahatmya* (Glory of the Goddess) from Bundelkhand, Madhya Pradesh, India, showing the gods in heaven.

ANALYSIS

IMMORTALITY

Indra's reward for Yudhishthira's moral uprightness to allow the Pandava to enter heaven as a mortal is a gift reserved for the most noble of men. In many ways, Yudhishthira's journey is about discovering his path of dharma, and was aimed at becoming immortal.

According to Vyasa, all creatures eventually die because of merits lost and demerits earned. In this sense, one who earns no demerit cannot die. Such a person can ascend to paradise without dying, and so become immortal.

"O king! You will now obtain **immortality**, **prosperity** like mine, all kinds of great fame and the **happiness** of **heaven. Abandon** the **dog**."

INDRA TO YUDHISHTHIRA, MAHAPRASTHANIKA PARVA: THE BOOK OF RENUNCIATION

companion all the way, surviving the cold and hard journey.

"Dogs are inauspicious creatures. They wander where the dead live and they eat garbage—they are not welcome in heaven."

Yudhishthira looked down at the dog and the dog looked back at him with adoration. Yudhishthira said, "Through this long and perilous journey, this dog has stayed with me. I have had to give up everyone close to me, but this dog did not give up on me. By this virtue, he, too, has earned the right to enter paradise. You must let him in."

"No," said the Devas.

"Why should he not be allowed into paradise, while I am taken in? That is not a fair thing to do. I will not enter Swarga without this dog."

Incredulous at his insistence, the Devas exclaimed, "You refuse paradise for a dog!"

Tired from his long journey, but still indignant at this order from the Devas, Yudhishthira said firmly, "For the sake of justice, I refuse paradise."

Reward for rectitude

The Devas smiled. "Yudhishthira, once again, your integrity impresses us. The dog that followed you is Dharma, the god of righteous conduct. He followed you all the way as a loyal companion and you repaid that loyalty by not abandoning him. That earns you the right to enter heaven in your mortal body."

A mortal enters heaven

Indra, too, was full of praise. He said to the only remaining Pandava, "You possess compassion for all beings. Yudhishthira, on an earlier occasion, I had tested you in the Dwaitavana forest. Wanting to fetch some water, your valiant brothers were slain. Forgetting about your brothers Bhima and Arjuna, and showing that both your mothers were equal, you wished that Nakula could be brought back to life. Now, instead of giving up the devoted dog, you have decided to forsake the chariot of the gods. Therefore, there is no one in heaven who is your equal. O descendant of the Bharata lineage! Therefore, in your own body, you will obtain the eternal world."

After this declaration, Indra welcomed Yudhishthira into Amravati, ushering him in to the sound of conch shells. The Apsaras showered him with flowers and the Gandharvas sang songs to the glory of the Pandavas.

As Yudhishthira heard everyone in Swarga praising him, he was still troubled about the fate of his brothers and wife. He asked the Devas about them, but they advised him to abandon human sentiment and enjoy heaven instead.

DHARMARAJ
A statue showing Dharmaraj on his throne in the Dharmaraj temple of Mysore, India. Both Yama and Yudhishthira are called Dharmaraj, which literally means "king of justice."

MYTHOLOGY AND FOLKLORE

DOGS

Dogs have a peculiar status in Hindu culture. In the Rig Veda, the dog is seen as a protector, so much so that Indra sends the mother of dogs, Sarama, in search of missing cows, whenever the need arises.

But dogs are also considered ominous as they are associated with Yama, the god of death. Sarama's children, the Sarameyas, are said to be companions of Yama. They are associated not with civilization but with the wilderness, which is why they are linked to mendicants such as Dattatreya, an incarnation of the Hindu trinity of gods. Adding to their reputation for bringing misfortune, dogs are also regarded as the mount of Bhairava, the fearsome form of Shiva. Their reputation is such that they are kept away from wedding altars and holy sites, and a howling dog is a harbinger of bad luck. In fact, even the sight of a dog is considered to bring bad luck. Because of their territorial nature, dogs represent devotedness and bondage, with a need for constant attention and validation. They, therefore, become symbols of neediness, insecurity, attachment, and ego.

DOGS HAVE A MIXED REPUTATION IN HINDU CULTURE

THE PATH OF RIGHTEOUSNESS

Dharma

"Do not **doubt dharma** ... A man who doubts dharma is destined to be **born as inferior species**."

YUDHISHTHIRA TO DRAUPADI, VANA PARVA: THE BOOK OF THE FOREST

VISHNU THE PROTECTOR
When adharma threatens to overrun the earth, Vishnu is born on earth as as a mortal to reinstate dharma. Krishna was one of the nine avatars who have come and gone. The tenth is still to come.

BEYOND THE RULE OF THE JUNGLE
Small fish as prey for big fish is the natural order, but for strong humans to exploit the weak is adharma. Dharma demands that the strong protect the weak.

As a philosophical precept, the word "dharma" is very difficult to translate. It encompasses many meanings including virtue, ethics, moral duty, righteousness, justice, correct judgement, and the conquest of the self. For the layman, dharma can be explained as the path of righteousness—the right way or the right conduct through life. It is an integral concept in Hinduism, Buddhism, Jainism, and Sikhism.

PRAKRITI AND PURUSHA

Religion is effectively a way of understanding the place of humanity in the world. If the world can be understood, and if it has a definite hierarchy or structure then, by following that order, a person can live in harmony with the rest of society and with the universe as a whole. By recognizing that there is an underlying rational order to the universe and finding our place in this order, it is possible to identify dharma—the right way to live.

The recognition of rational order lifts humanity above the natural pecking order that exists in prakriti—in nature or wilderness. It is matsya nyaya or the law of the fish, the Vedic equivalent of the law of the jungle, where might becomes right and only the fittest survive. Humanity (purusha) enables us to imagine and create a civilized world where individuals look beyond themselves to include and help others less fortunate. This is dharma, the right way to live. Choosing between the right and the wrong way, dharma and adharma, is important but there are no absolutes—the context is vital. As Krishna explains to Arjuna on the battlefield, "The ego evaluates a situation against a scale of its own construction. What you consider right at the moment, Arjuna, is based on your measuring scale. What Duryodhana considers right is based on the scale he constructs. Which one of these is correct? Can either be free of bias?"

A MEANINGFUL LIFE

According to the Vedas, there are four objectives—purushartha (purusha: man + artha: meaning/ purpose)—that provide the framework to give life purpose. These are dharma (righteousness), artha (wealth), kama (desire), and moksha (spiritual liberation). Of these, dharma is the most important, as righteousness must guide every action in life. This is why dharma also translates as "law." The Dharma Shastras or law books, were meant to guide people, to help them make the right choices, and keep them from adharma as they negotiated their way through life. The Dharma Shastras laid down four stages, or ashramas, of life. Each had its own set of behavioral guidelines—duties and obligations to the family. As a child, the individual was a brahmachaari (student). He learned the skills defined by his varna that would equip him for the second stage of life. This began when the student married—he became a grihastha (householder). In this stage, it was his duty to pursue both artha (wealth) and kama (desire), though always in accordance with dharma. With the birth of his first grandchild, the grihastha moved into vanaprastha (retirement). This was the time to hand over management of the household and other duties to a son and focus on meditation and the search for a higher meaning to life. The last stage of life was that of sannyasa (renunciation), which was a distancing of the self from worldly affairs and relationships to focus on moksha. Bhishma, who is lauded as an ideal son, is also seen as one whose adharma in refusing to marry and have children eventually led to the battle of Kurukshetra.

KRISHNA SAVES DRAUPADI
Krishna's intervention in the disrobing of Draupadi serves to underline the Kaurava violation of dharma.

YAMA
The lord of death and ruler of Naraka is also the dispassionate deity of justice and dharma. It is he who balances the merits and demerits of a lifetime and directs the soul to Swarga or Naraka to await rebirth.

VARNA DHARMA

Another guiding principle that defined life's choices was the caste structure. Varna dharma implied an adherence to the rules of caste, the most basic of which was that a son must follow his father's vocation. To fight was a Kshatriya's moral duty; whereas for a Brahman, to step onto a battlefield was adharma. Drona's non-righteous acts during the war were attributed to his not being a true warrior or Kshatriya, while Karna's skills as a warrior weighed little for anyone but Duryodhana—in the eyes of the world he remained the son of a charioteer.

DHARMA AND ADHARMA

The Mahabharata is descriptive rather than prescriptive and, as such, has no ideal characters. The struggles of each individual serve as examples of the complexity of choosing between dharma and adharma—sometimes what appears to be dharma is adharma and what appears to be adharma, dharma. The most morally upright character is that of Yudhishthira, the son of Yama (or Dharmaraj the god of death and justice), but even he must lie to kill the warrior-guru Drona and win the war. Krishna, Vishnu incarnate, also resorts to adharma in many instances to preserve dharma and ensure the Pandavas' victory. Time and again, Krishna suggests a course of action that goes against ethical behavior and the code of chivalry. There are many rules of warfare that he urges the Pandavas to violate, from bringing a woman, Bhishma's nemesis Shikhandi, onto the battlefield to convincing Bhima to defeat Duryodhana by striking him below the waist.

18

SWARGAROHANA PARVA: THE BOOK OF THE ASCENT

THE DAMNED AND THE BLESSED
Yudhishthira goes to both heaven and hell. While in heaven, he meets Indra, Arjuna's father, surrounded by all the Devas and celestial beings; in hell, he meets his own father, Yama—the eighteen-armed god of dharma.

Swargarohana Parva, or the Book of the Ascent, is the eighteenth and last parva in the Mahabharata. "Swarga" means heaven, and "arohana" is ascent. In this final part of the story, Yudhishthira reaches Swarga, or heaven, only to find his cousins, the Kauravas, already there. To his immense sorrow, he finds his own family relegated to the depths of Naraka, or hell. This puts the eldest Pandava in a moral dilemma, one that changes his worldview and ultimately brings him to enlightenment. This parva has no sub-parvas, and contains 5 chapters and 194 shlokas, or couplets.

"**Your great-grandfathers**, Yudhisthira and the others, obtained **heaven, the abode of the gods**. Listen to what they did."

SAGE VAISHAMPAYANA TO KING JANAMEJAYA, SWARGAROHANA PARVA: THE BOOK OF THE ASCENT

INDRA'S SWARGA
Yudhishthira met all the Devas and celestial beings that reside in Swarga (heaven). The image shows Indra, the king of Devas, surrounded by his court.

BEFORE

Impressed by his integrity and righteousness, the Devas let Yudhishthira enter heaven as a mortal—an honor accorded to very few.

YUDHISHTHIRA ENTERS SWARGA
As his brothers and wife met their death one by one, Yudhishthira did not stop to help any of them. He stuck to his resolve of renunciation and kept telling himself that he had given up everything, even personal relationships. He made his journey only with a dog by his side. Finally, he reached the peak of the Mandara mountain and found himself before the gate of the garden of unending delights, known as Amravati.

Heaven and Hell

Yudhishthira's ascent to heaven was a journey of wonders. But the moment he realized that the passage to heaven or hell was not as simple as he had thought, his happiness changed to anger and then sadness.

As soon as Yudhishthira took a step into heaven, an unexpected sight greeted him. He saw all the Devas assembled, radiant and happy; but standing next to them were the hundred Kauravas, including Duryodhana and Dusshasana. As heaven opened itself up to welcome Dharmaraja himself, Yudhishthira saw the Kauravas, too, spread out their arms to welcome him. The eldest Pandava recoiled, and he angrily spoke to the Devas, "How can Amravati accept these warmongers?"

The gods explained, "The Kauravas were all killed as warriors on the holy land of Kurukshetra. A warrior's death on that land cleanses him of his sins and earns him the right to enter heaven. O Yudhishthira! If you thought heaven was a fit enough place for your virtuous dog, it is good enough for your cousins too."

But Yudhishthira was not satisfied. "And my brothers? And my wife? What of them? Are they here too?" he asked, his rage rising by the second.

"They are not here," the Devas replied calmly.

Yudhishthira was getting impatient with these ambiguous answers. He asked, "Then where are they?" The Devas replied, "They are not here. They are in another place."

Yudhishthira, determined to get to the bottom of all this, cried out, "Take me to them!"

"Certainly," said the Devas and led him away.

A visit to hell

The gods led Yudhishthira out of heaven, down from the sky, and along the slopes of the mountain range of Mandara. They then led him through a crevice that took them deep under the earth. At last they reached a realm that was dark and gloomy. Yudhishthira could hear cries of pain and suffering all around. This place was the opposite of Amravati in every way—Yudhishthira realized it was Naraka, the realm of misery.

An infernal encounter

Horrified, Yudhishthira asked in a strangled voice, "Are my brothers here?"

As if in response, he heard the moans of his brothers, "Yes! We are here," they called out to him.

True to his nature, Yudhishthira began wondering and analyzing how this could be, that his own brothers were in hell. Yudhishthira knew, though, that Bhima was paying for his gluttony, Arjuna for his envy, Nakula for his insensitivity, Sahadeva for his smugness, and Draupadi for her partiality. But Karna? Had his elder brother not suffered enough in his mortal life? Yudhishthira wondered what had brought his brother to hell.

> "Duryodhana was **ignorant** about **dharma**. He was wicked and **destroyed** the earth ... yet **he has** obtained the **eternal world** meant for heroes."
>
> YUDHISHTHIRA TO NARADA, SWARGAROHANA PARVA: THE BOOK OF THE ASCENT

KEY CONCEPT

MANY HEAVENS

Unlike Biblical traditions, Hindu culture believes in the existence of more than one heaven. Swarga is ruled by Indra, the king of the gods, a place where all desires are fulfilled. Indra is surrounded by wealth, beauty, and fame, but like mortals, he is insecure, fearful that someone who earns more merit in life than him will take his place.

Vaikuntha is Vishnu's abode. It is a realm where there is peace, where time stands still, and where one is free of all desires. As there is no ebb and flow of time, there are no worldly desires such as hunger or thirst; and therefore, there is no quest for their satisfaction.

> "For **those** who reside **in heaven**, all **enmity** is **destroyed**. ... **You should** follow propriety and **meet** King **Duryodhana**."
>
> SAGE NARADA TO YUDHISHTHIRA, SWARGAROHANA PARVA: THE BOOK OF THE ASCENT

AFTER

From heaven to hell, by now Yudhishthira had seen it all. But the plight of his brothers had disturbed the former Kuru king.

KARNA'S FATE
Yudhishthira asked the Devas about Karna. His disbelief at his elder brother's fate was aggravated when the Devas answered placidly, "Karna broke a promise and a friend's trust—he promised Kunti he would spare the life of four of her five sons, despite promising Duryodhana that he would kill all the Pandavas." Yudhishthira felt the weight of everyone's pain, and started to weep. He wanted to stay back in Naraka with his family.

REACHING BEYOND THE CYCLE OF REBIRTH

Moksha

> **"**One who sees the **supreme** soul, **beyond** the **human soul**, such a person is **liberated**.**"**

BUTCHER TO THE BRAHMAN, VANA PARVA: THE BOOK OF THE FOREST

GAJENDRA ATTAINS MOKSHA
Caught in a crocodile's jaws, Gajendra, the king of elephants, chanted Vishnu's name and instantly attained moksha. The story illustrates that the voice of a devotee always reaches his God.

Hindu philosophy regards moksha as the highest purpose of life, achievable through pursuing self-realization and consciousness of unity with the all-pervasive Supreme Being. It is one of those ideas that have remained central to not only all strands of Hinduism, but also the various religious beliefs that emerged from it. It reinforces the belief in an afterlife and how the consequences of righteous and unrighteous actions in one life are carried forward into another, tying the essence of an individual, the soul, in an endless cycle of rebirth. Attaining a release from this samsara, or cycle of transmigration of the soul based on karma, is moksha, the final liberation. Arriving at this state of moksha involves expanding the mind in pursuit of true knowledge of the Self and the Universe. This is possible only when an individual has given meaning to life through purushartha, which is the balanced fulfilment of social obligations (dharma), economic needs (artha), desires (kama), and spiritual needs (moksha). In the making of choices at every stage of life, the individual realizes his true, limitless Self. It is only this realization that can lead to ultimate liberation.

RECOGNIZING REALITY

Attaining moksha involves extricating the Self from the material world that comprises dharma, artha, and kama. In the Gita, Krishna uses the analogy of a banyan tree that has, in addition to the main trunk, myriad aerial roots. Over time these roots extend down to anchor themselves in the soil. They thicken and may even become indistinguishable from the main trunk. The Self is symbolized by the trunk of the banyan. Nourished by inner mental reality, it explores the world, branching out in all directions, letting down aerial roots that provide additional support and draw nourishment from external material reality. The central trunk remains calm and unmoved—the external roots, influenced by transience, suffer fear, anxiety, hunger, pain, and sorrow. Recognizing this, the wise seek to cut these external, secondary roots and validate their lives from within; to unite with the immortal, infinite Self. This search is an intensely personal journey that can have no single prescribed route, but there are three broad disciplines that many have practiced in their search for moksha.

THE BANYAN TREE
The aerial roots of the banyan frequently grow as thick as, and may even replace, the central trunk. As a result, the tree lives longer than most trees and is revered by Hindus as a symbol of immortality.

JNANA YOGA

A person who truly understands the truth of mind, matter, and material tendencies is liberated from rebirth, no matter what his lifestyle is. The single-minded pursuit of knowledge, wisdom, and direct experience of the Universal Spirit leads to moksha, but this is the most difficult. The path means renouncing both desire and action, completely freeing the mind of all attachment to cultivate spiritual insight and understanding. Jnana yoga uses the mind to explore its own nature and go beyond, breaking the bounds of self-identity and ego. The effort is to liberate the inner Self from the illusionary world of perception and preconceived ideas, and to become one with the Supreme Being.

SANNYASA YOGA
There are many paths to moksha—the renunciation of a worldly, material way of life to seek knowledge, self-realization, and direct experience of the divine, as a sannyasi is one followed by many.

KARMA YOGA

In the aftermath of the war, faced with the totality of death and destruction, Yudhishthira cried out in anguish, "My hands are soaked with the blood of my family. When I sit on a pile of corpses, how can I drink the cup of success?" He received solace from the dying Kuru patriarch, Bhishma, who advised him, saying that life is like an ever-flowing river bent on its own course. "Bathe in it, drink it, be refreshed by it, share it with everyone, but never fight it, never be swept away by its flow; never get attached to it."

Karma unfolds as life. The misguided, assuming that they are in control, act out of self-interest and, therefore, suffer pain and disillusionment. The enlightened accept that there are forces beyond their control. Their actions are guided by dharma—by what is appropriate and right—and are undertaken without any attachment to the deed or desire for results. This brings freedom from samsara.

BHAKTI YOGA

Those who make the Divine the supreme goal of all their work and act without selfish attachment, who completely devote themselves to the Divine and are free from ill will for any creature, enter into the Divine. Bhakti is a personal relationship based on loving desire rather than expectation of benefits. The devotion is in itself liberating. This union between a devotee's soul with that of the Supreme in total surrender is both the easiest and the highest path to moksha.

KEY CONCEPT

SWARGA AND VAIKUNTHA

After death, a righteous soul travels to Swarga, the domain of Indra, king of the Devas, to await rebirth. This is one of seven heavenly realms (lokas)—of which the earth (prithviloka) is one—situated on and above Mount Meru. In Swarga all desires are indulged and all dreams realized. The wish-fulfilling Kalpataru tree, one of the treasures that emerged from the ocean of milk during the manthan (churning), grows here. Vaikuntha is a higher heaven that can only be entered after attaining moksha (liberation) from samsara, the cycle of birth and death. This is Vishnu's celestial abode, peaceful and prosperous, where the deity reclines on the coils of the serpent Adi-Ananta-Shesha with his consort Lakshmi at his feet.

KALPATARU

BEFORE

Stoic and determined, Yudhishthira questioned the gods about their decision to keep his family in the depths of hell.

YUDHISHTHIRA IN HELL

Yudhishthira had seen the Kauravas in heaven but not any of his brothers or wife. When he asked about his family, the Devas took him on a journey. They walked down the sky, along the slopes of Mandara, through a crevice deep under the earth, and entered a realm that was dark and gloomy. Yudhishthira heard cries of suffering and pain all around, and he realized he had reached Naraka—hell.

The **Crossing** into the **Inferno**

Yudhishthira's odyssey to heaven took a dark turn when he realized his brothers and wife were trapped in hell. Distressed at their misfortune and brokenhearted about their destiny, he decided to stay with them in Naraka.

The Devas were getting impatient. "Shall we go back to Amravati?" they asked Yudhishthira

"No! Please don't go. Don't leave us here," Yudhishthira heard his brothers cry out.

"Well? It is time to leave," the Devas again said testily.

"Please stay," Yudhishthira heard Draupadi plead. Hearing her sound so plaintive and lost, Yudhishthira was filled with sorrow, tears welling up in his eyes. He could not bring himself to leave. How could he return to to the comforts of Swarga when his family was here?

A courageous choice

Yudhishthira decided to stay and declared to the Devas, "I cannot leave Naraka. I will stay where my wife and brothers are. I refuse to enter Amravati without them."

The Devas laughed, rising up in the air as they circled Yudhishthira, and said to him, "Were we wrong to think that you had renounced everything?"

Faced with this question, Yudhishthira became uncomfortable. "What do you mean?" he asked.

"Before entering Swarga, did you not renounce all worldly ties? Then where does this sudden wave of attachment come from? Your attachment to love and hatred reminds us of a dog who is attached to its master."

Yudhishthira had a ready argument in return, "How can Amravati accept those murderers and reject my family who have always followed the path of righteousness and dharma?"

"You accuse us of taking sides, Yudhishthira?" asked the Devas.

Seeing the misery around him and smarting under the injustice being meted out to his family, Yudhishthira snapped, "Yes!"

"You still cling on to the world and its desires. Yes, you gave up your kingdom and your clothes, but not your hatred. You defeated and killed the Kauravas in the Kurukshetra War, ruled for thirty-six long years, but still you have not forgiven them. You turned your back on your family on your way to Amravati, but remembered them the moment you saw your cousins in heaven. Listen to us, son of Dharma, this rush of love is just a reaction. You have not renounced wordly attachment—you cling to your anger, differentiate between friend and foe. How do you hope to truly attain heaven?"

The marvelous vision

Suddenly, a vision unfolded before Yudhishthira—the Virat-swarup of Krishna. This divine incarnation of Krishna spoke to him. "Behold, see within God. All that exists, everything and everyone, are within me. The Pandavas and the Kauravas, the killers and the victims, all reside within me."

MYTHOLOGY AND FOLKLORE

YAMA—GOD OF DEATH

Yama, the god of death, rules over Naraka. Yama was the first man on earth and his twin sister, Yami, the first woman. According to the Rig Veda, she approached Yama for procreation, but he refused this incestuous union. Dying childless, he was trapped forever in the land of the dead, for only an offspring left behind in the land of the living can help release the dead into the land of the living, by rotating the wheel of rebirths. Yama became the king of the dead.

YAMA AND YAMI

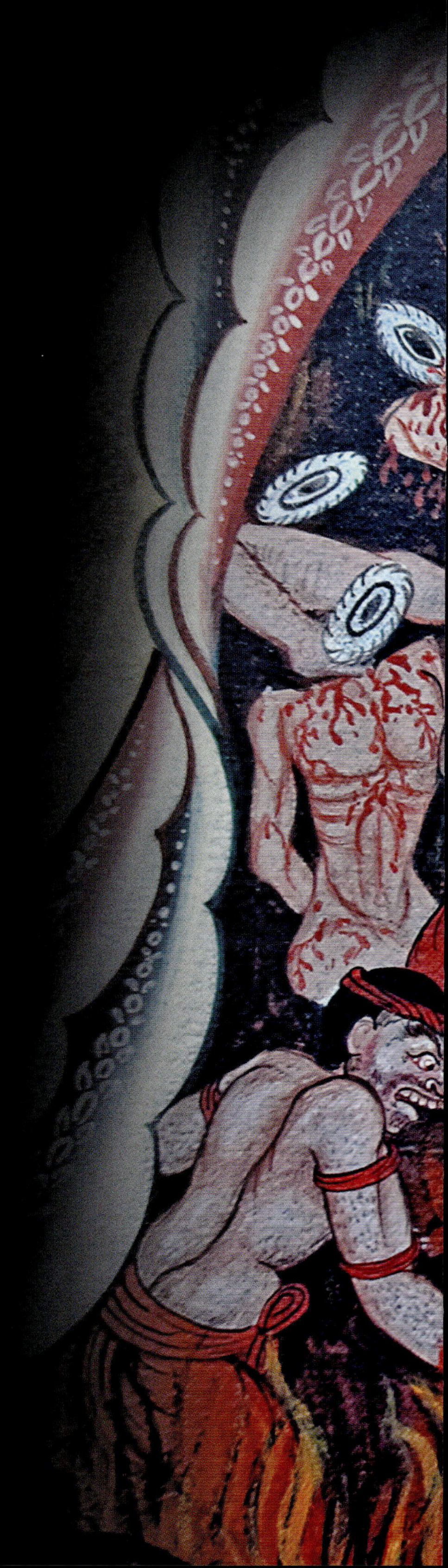

THE DAMNED

Hell is depicted in many ways across cultures. This illustration at the Buddhist temple Wat Daowadeungsaram, in Bangkok, Thailand, captures all the traditional elements of hell, such as fire, punishment, and misery.

In that instant, Yudhishthira realized he was not the great man he thought he was. He had not really overcome any of his prejudices, nor risen above petty emotions, clinging to ego and hate. Only when compassion is felt for even one's most bitter foes does one manage to conquer the ego and the self.

His illusions shattered, this new consciousness humbled Yudhishthira, and he fell to the ground and began to weep.

"O supreme gods! **Without my brothers**, what will I do in **heaven**? The place where they are is like heaven. It is my view that **this is not heaven**."

YUDHISHTHIRA TO THE GODS, SWARGAROHANA PARVA: THE BOOK OF THE ASCENT

AFTER

The omnipotent form of Krishna had created a new understanding of himself and a different world view in Yudhishthira.

A NEW "SELF"

Following the Devas, Yudhishthira then took a dip in the Ganga and arose, enlightened and purified. It dawned on him that there was no more hatred for the Kauravas in him—no more division of "them" and "us," and the good and the bad. Everyone was one. Seeing the change in Yudhishthira's state of mind, Indra shouted out, "Jaya!" Following him, the Devas and Rishis all shouted, "Jaya!" They celebrated Yudhishthira's Jaya, or victory over himself. Now the Kuru king could ascend to a heaven higher than Swarga; to Vaikuntha, the abode of Vishnu himself.

THE INEVITABILITY OF CAUSE AND EFFECT

Karma

कर्मण्येवाधिकारस्ते मा फलेषु कदाचन ।
मा कर्मफलहेतुर्भूर्मा ते सङ्गोऽस्त्वकर्मणि ॥४७॥

"You have the right to action alone. You never have the right to the fruit. Do not be motivated to act because of the fruit. But don't be motivated to not acting either."

KRISHNA TO ARJUNA, BHAGAVAD GITA, BHISHMA PARVA: THE BOOK OF BHISHMA

THE BUDDHIST ETERNAL KNOT
A symbol of the interdependence of all phenomena based on the cycle of cause and effect, this knot has no beginning and no end.

The law of karma defines one of the basic tenets of Hindu philosophy—every action is the result of a cause and every cause the result of an action. Karma is both action and reaction. Each moment of life encapsulates the effects of past actions and creates a cause for the future. This may manifest immediately or after a period of time, but what is irrefutable is that it will manifest itself. Humans classify actions as appropriate or inappropriate, good or bad, meritorious or non-meritorious, depending on the consequences. But, as not all reactions are immediate or apparent, it is not always possible to distinguish good from bad. What may appear to be a good deed could, in the long term, turn out to be bad, and vice versa. Therefore, it is best to act without anticipation or expectation of the results.

KARMA AND REBIRTH

In Hindu theory, the Self is timeless—it has no beginning, and can be identified with the single, undifferentiated reality that is the Universe. This Self takes on a physical form and is reincarnated in successive lives. The physical form it assumes in each life is determined by karma accumulated from the previous lifetimes—the sum total of actions as well as the individual's thoughts and feelings. It is past karma that determines the quality of life that it endures. The conditions, incidents, and events that occur are not random at all, but the result of past actions. Bhishma, for example, was Prabhasha Vasu, one of the deities of the elements, cursed by Sage Vasishtha to be reborn on earth as a mortal for the crime of stealing the wish-fulfilling cow, Kamadhenu.

SYMBOLISM OF LOTUS
The lotus represents spiritual enlightenment and detachment, signifying action with no concern for reward.

KARMA AND CASTE

For the Self, each birth is an opportunity. By living a virtuous life in accordance with dharma, the individual can aspire to rebirth in a higher state. The caste system reflects this hierarchy of life, starting with the Brahman at the top. In the Anusashana Parva, Bhishma says to Yudhishthira, "One is born as a Brahman only after going through innumerable orders of existence, after undergoing repeated births." The "innumerable orders of existence" come about because the choices made by an individual, the ethical and moral values followed, have little or no influence on the consequence of an action. All that can be controlled is the action; the reaction and its impact on future circumstances cannot be predicted or controlled with any accuracy at all. This seeming randomness of karma provides a balance. A Brahman in this life may well be born into a lower caste in another life, while a virtuous Shudra may accumulate good fortune to become a sage.

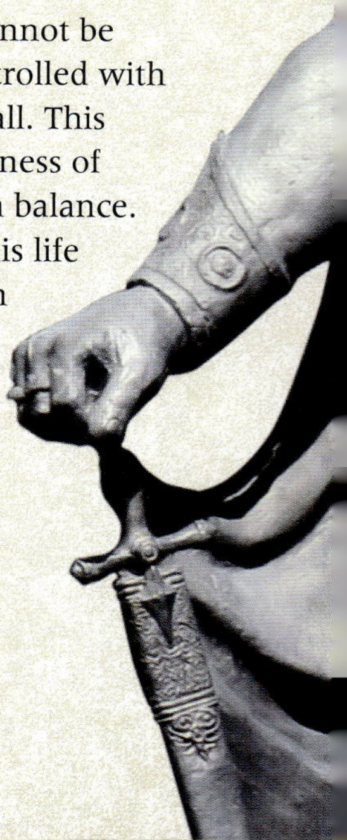

KARMA AND DHARMA

The law of karma is reiterated through the lives of all the major characters in the Mahabharata, particularly in the aftermath of the war. Duryodhana's defeat and death is seen as the direct consequence of his anger, greed, and selfishness. Each of the Pandavas has an impulsive moral flaw—Yudhishthira lied to kill Drona, Arjuna is envious of other archers, Bhima gave in to anger and gluttony, and Nakula and Sahadeva are arrogant about their looks and knowledge, respectively. Even the courageous and much-wronged Draupadi preferred Arjuna over her other husbands, desired Karna, and manipulated Bhima for revenge. Though they all set off for Swarga, only Yudhishthira is allowed to enter, as he redeems himself by refusing to abandon the dog that followed him to the gates of heaven—which turns out to be Dharma. Does never abandoning dharma result in good karma? The answer is ambiguous—life is never straightforward. Krishna, who is Vishnu incarnate, works tirelessly to re-establish dharma, only to be cursed by Gandhari to suffer a loss as great as the one she has borne. Arjuna, who does all that Krishna asks him to do, loses his sons. When Yudhishthira enters Swarga, he sees all the Kauravas there but none of his brothers; they are in Naraka. The law of karma is logical and impartial—it does not concern itself with individual perceptions and reasons. Dharma is about correct behavior and implies balanced judgement by the individual. In the battlefield, faced with an army made up of relatives, Arjuna is faced with a moral dilemma—should he fight and be responsible for the killing of family members, or not fight and fail in doing his duty as a warrior?

KARMA YOGA

In the Bhagavad Gita, Krishna explains that Arjuna must act in accordance with his Kshatriya dharma, or the duty of a warrior, without considering either his own inclinations or any thought about the results of his actions. Only by continuously acting without attachment and surrendering the ownership of action to the divine can the individual go beyond the law of karma, and free himself from the cycle of birth and rebirth to attain moksha. Passing on what he has learned and experienced to Yudhishthira from his bed of arrows, Bhishma emphasizes, "Our merits bring us joy. Our demerits create misfortune. We are thus fettered by karma. Karma binds us to the material world, compels us to be born and to die. No one can change this, except one. That one is God."

KRISHNA AND ARJUNA
On the battlefield of Kurukshetra, Krishna elaborates on the righteousness of action carried out without attachment to its consequence.

The **End** of the **Snake Sacrifice**

Curious to know who the real winners of the war were, King Janamejaya posed many probing questions at the end of Sage Vaishampayana's great tale. The sage's response had the key to understanding many mysteries of life which helped the king to overcome several of his doubts.

Sage Vaishampayana's narration came to an end. The yagna hall appeared frozen in time—the serpents remained suspended above the sacrificial fire and the priests impatiently waited to conclude the ritual. The illustrious gathering awaited Janamejaya's reaction.

The hero and the villain

At long last, the king spoke. "I am confused. Who is the hero of this great tale? And who is the villain?" he asked.

Vaishampayana asked Janamejaya in return, "Whom shall we call villain? Is it Duryodhana, the eldest Kaurava who refused to part with even the tiniest bit of land? Or is it Yudhishthira, the oldest Pandava, for gambling away his kingdom and wife?" Expecting the king to reach a conclusion on his own, the sage continued, "Is Bhishma the villain—the one who did not allow Dhritarashtra to sit on the throne, on account of his blindness? Or, Shantanu, who did not hesitate to sacrifice his son's future to satisfy his own desires? Or

NARRATION OF THE GREAT TALE
The snake sacrifice had come to a halt, with snakes suspended above the fire pit, during Sage Vaishamapayana's narration of the Mahabharata to King Janamejaya.

A CLEANSING FIRE
Vaishampayana's tale purged Janamejaya's desire for vengeance and taught him the difference between justice and dharma.

is it Gandhari, for overlooking her son's mistakes? Or, maybe Krishna, the one who had promised the earth goddess that he would rid the world of unrighteous kings? You, my king, decide who is the hero of the tale and who the villain."

Janamejaya had nothing to say. He recalled the many forces that changed the course of the tale—the many blessings and curses, and the plethora of man-made laws. It was a tale of people struggling, dealing with crises, making mistakes, and repeating them—in innocence or ignorance—while trying to make their lives worthwhile. Still confused, Janamejaya wondered why the tale was named "Jaya" when there was no real victory.

The meaning of true victory

Vaishampayana explained that there are two kinds of victory—Vijaya and Jaya. Vijaya refers to material victory, with a winner and a loser; Jaya is spiritual victory, where there are no losers. "The victory at Kurukshetra was Vijaya, and not Jaya. But when Yudhishthira let go of his anger and forgave the Kauravas unconditionally, there was Jaya," explained the sage. He called that victory the true ending to this great tale.

Swarga and Naraka

The king voiced his confusion again. "Though the unrighteous Kauravas were defeated in battle, they still ended up going to Swarga. Whereas the victors, the Pandavas, ended up in Naraka. It does not make sense."

Astika, the serpent, explained that one goes to Swarga for the merits earned in one's lives, and to Naraka for demerits. The Kauravas had been cleansed of their demerits by losing the war on sacred ground, while the Pandavas fell short because, despite the war and their victory, they had not let go of their prejudices and rage. "And thus, it was Swarga for the Kauravas and Naraka for the Pandavas," he concluded.

Still unconvinced, Janamejaya was doubtful. "It does not feel right," he said. Astika explained that the stay in Swarga or Naraka was limited, and not for eternity. "Once their merits and demerits have been exhausted, the Kauravas will fall and the Pandavas will rise. They will continue with their journey through the cycle of rebirths. They will be born again and will die again, and the cycle of earning merits and demerits will continue, until they learn what Yudhishthira learned—the purpose of existence."

"The purpose of existence is to attain wisdom, and not to accumulate merit," Astika continued. "One needs to question oneself—why do we do what we do? Once we truly accept the answer, we break free from the cycle of birth and death, to discover the realm beyond Swarga—Vaikuntha—where there is peace forever."

Unsure, Janamejaya said, "I thought the Pandavas did what they did to uphold dharma." But Astika explained that had the Pandavas followed dharma, the victory at Kurukshetra would also have led to victory over Self. The Pandavas followed Krishna's directive to do what was good for the world, but this victory did not change the Pandavas themselves—they did not gain any wisdom. And in the absence of spiritual insight, they gloated over their victory.

The sage then explained the spiritual insight that eluded his forefathers. "Conflict comes from rage, rage comes from fear, and fear comes from lack of faith. This lack of faith had to be purged from the minds of the Pandavas."

Janamejaya then remembered Krishna reciting the Bhagavad Gita to Arjuna before the war. He heard Krishna say, "If you have faith in me and the balance of merits and demerits, you will not be insecure." Enlightened by Krishna's words, Janamejaya admitted that the lack of faith made him angry with the serpents. He realized that he was deluding himself with arguments of justice and vengeance; the snake sacrifice was not dharma.

Astika and Vaishamapayana realized that Janamejaya had finally inherited the wisdom of his forefathers. An expression of peace descended upon the king. Chanting, "Shanti, Shanti, Shanti," the mantra for peace, he declared the end of the sacrifice. The king had won over his fear and gotten rid of his anger. "Shanti" did not mean peace in the external world, but was a cry for inner peace.

MYTHOLOGY AND FOLKLORE

SNAKE WORSHIP

The traditional ritual worship of snakes observed by the Hindu community, Naga Panchami is celebrated on the fifth day (the bright half) of the Hindu month of Shravan. It is believed that Astika intervened to stop the snake sacrifice organized by King Janamejaya in the month of Shravan, and the festival is observed to commemorate the day. Hindus across India and Nepal seek the blessings of snakes for the welfare of their families. Serpent deities made of silver, stone, or wood, are appeased with flowers and bathed in milk.

HINDU DEVOTEES WORSHIPPING SERPENT DEITIES DURING THE NAGA PANCHAMI FESTIVAL

"If a person **controls himself** and **reads the account** of the **Mahabharata** ... he advances toward **supreme success**."

SAGE VAISHAMPAYANA TO KING JANAMEJAYA, SWARGAROHANA PARVA: THE BOOK OF THE ASCENT

HARIVAMSHA

HARIVAMSHA:
THE BOOK OF KRISHNA

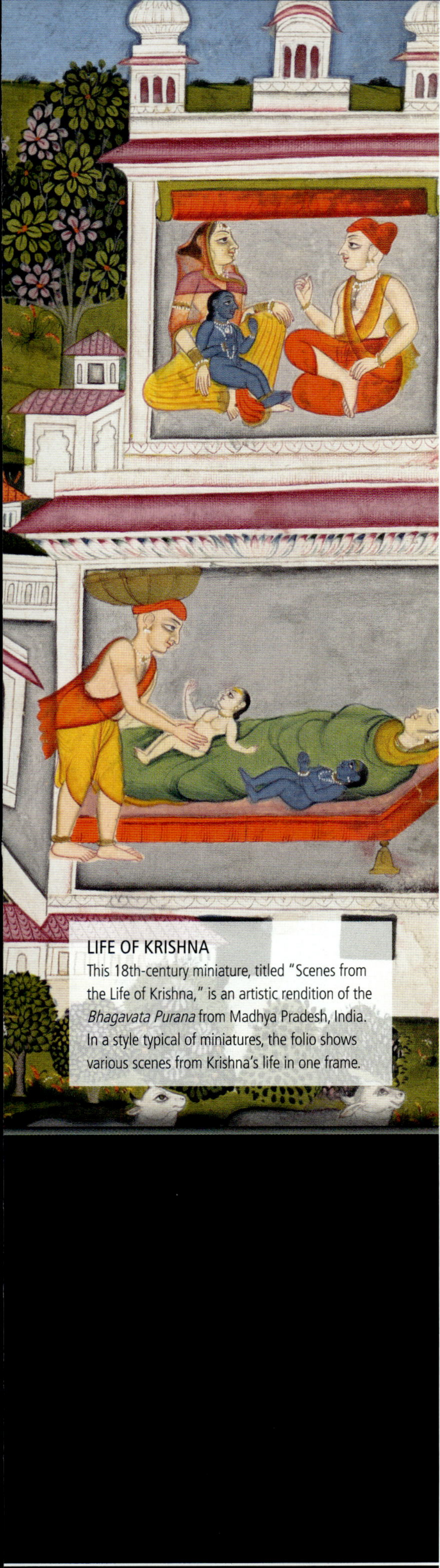

LIFE OF KRISHNA
This 18th-century miniature, titled "Scenes from the Life of Krishna," is an artistic rendition of the *Bhagavata Purana* from Madhya Pradesh, India. In a style typical of miniatures, the folio shows various scenes from Krishna's life in one frame.

Harivamsha, or the Book of Krishna, is an appendix to the Mahabharata. It recounts the tale of Krishna's birth, his childhood escapades with his elder brother, Balarama, and encounters with his arch-nemesis, Kansa. The Harivamsha is divided into three sections or sub-parvas—Harivamsha Parva, Vishnu Parva, and Bhavishya Parva. The first sub-parva describes events that precede the birth of Krishna; the second is an account of his life; and the third speaks of the Kali Yuga. Just like the Mahabharata, this epilogue, too, is narrated by Sage Vaishampayana to King Janamejaya. The Harivamsha has 3 sub-parvas, 118 chapters, and 5,965 shlokas, or couplets.

"The **two** infant **boys grew** up in **happiness**. The **elder** was named **Samkarshana** and the **younger** was named **Krishna**. Hari had entered inside **Krishna's body** and he was as **dark as a cloud**."

SAGE VAISHAMPAYANA TO KING JANAMEJAYA, HARIVAMSHA: THE BOOK OF KRISHNA

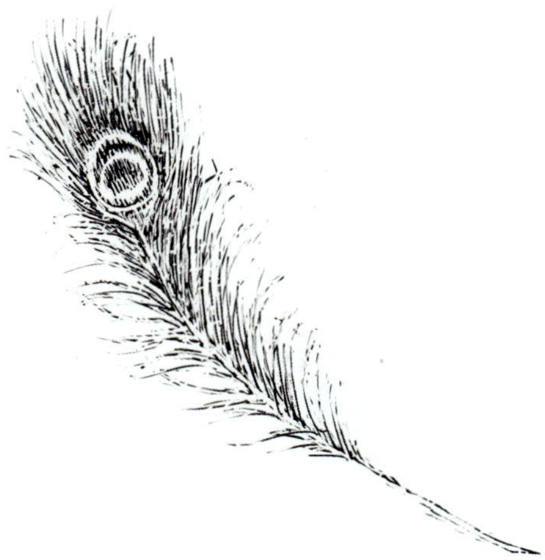

BEFORE

Devayani, the daughter of the guru of the Asuras, was married to Chandravamshi King Yayati. The king secretly also married her former best friend Sarmishtha, the daughter of the king of the Asuras.

THE CURSED KING
King Yayati led a double life until his wife Devayani caught his lie and found out about his second wife, Sarmishtha, and three children. She complained to her father Shukra, who cursed Yayati with instantaneous old age and impotence, later regretting his hastily spoken words.

"You have other sons and **you love them more than me**. O one who **knows about dharma**! **Ask this boon** of acceptance from one of the **other sons**."

YADU TO YAYATI, HARIVAMSHA: THE BOOK OF KRISHNA

THE LOST THRONE
Although deeply influential in the politics of their times, Yadu and his descendants—right down to Krishna—would never sit on a throne, in keeping with Yayati's curse. They were the king-makers, but never the kings.

The **Story** of **Yadu**

Yadu was the first-born son of King Yayati and his wife Devayani. His refusal to obey his father's command to give him his youth in exchange of old age cost him and his descendants the throne.

Shukra's anger at Yayati's duplicitous behavior led him to curse the king with immediate old age. Later, when his anger abated, Shukra realized that his hastily spoken words had given rise to circumstances that were as detrimental to his own daughter, Devayani, as they were to her husband. He amended the curse and gave Yayati the choice of exchanging his youth with one of his sons, if they agreed.

Desperate to stay youthful, Yayati turned to his eldest son Yadu, with great hope. He said to his firstborn, "My dear son, I have not yet satisfied my desires. But if you are kind to me, you can take my old age and I will take your youth so that I may enjoy life for a few years more. When that is done, I will give it back to you."

The refusal

A self-respecting man with a sound knowledge of dharma, Yadu felt that his father should respect the march of time. He refused to make the exchange, saying, "I have promised a Brahman alms, and he has not yet told me what he wants. Until that task is done, I cannot accept your old age. There are many issues associated with old age. One cannot eat and drink as one wills, O king! Therefore, I am not interested in accepting your old age."

Yayati was furious when he heard this answer. "You have slighted me," he told his son. "You or your sons will never be king." He then went on to ask his other sons Turvasu, Druhyu, and Anu, who also refused to obey his command. Desperate, Yayati then asked his youngest son Puru, if he would take on old age in exchange of his youth. Puru agreed, and grew old while his father immersed himself in the joy of worldly desires. Eventually realizing the meaninglessness of life's pursuits, Yayati reversed the exchange and in gratitude pronounced Puru heir to his throne. Puru would go on to be the patriarch of the illustrious Kuru clan; the ancestor of the Kauravas and the Pandavas.

A new lineage

An indignant Yadu left Yayati's kingdom and traveled south to Mathura, the kingdom of the Naga people. The Nagas of Mathura had no king, but were ruled by a council of elders through the system of consensus. Yadu's beauty and mannerisms impressed a Naga called Dhumravarna who made him an offer. "Marry my daughters. Be my son-in-law. Make Mathura your home," he said. Yadu agreed and realized that the Nagas' democratic rule suited him well. Cursed as he had been by his father, Yadu and his descendants could never be kings. In Mathura, they could still be rulers.

The Yadavas of Mathura

Yadu married Dhumravarna's daughters and they bore him children from whom descended various tribes such as the Andhakas, the Bhojakas, and the Vrishnis. Collectively, these descendants of Yadu were called the Yadavas. Yadu's descendant from the Vrishni lineage was Surasena, whose eldest son Vasudeva was considered to be the best and most handsome of men. As well as nine younger brothers, Vasudeva had five sisters, including Pritha who was given away for adoption to his uncle Kuntibhoja and later came to be known as Kunti. She would be the wife of Pandu, and the mother of the Pandavas.

THE NAGAS OF MATHURA
Excavations from Sonkh near Mathura, India, suggest the existence of a Naga cult there, as evidenced by this 1st-century relief carving showing a Naga man emerging from the jaws of a crocodile.

Vasudeva's eldest wife Rohini became the mother of Balarama. Vasudeva's marriage to Devaki, the daughter of Mathura's ruler Ugrasena, set forth a chain of events that would eventually take the Yadavas out of Mathura. Devaki's brother Kansa was a despotic ruler who imprisoned his father and crowned himself king of this historically democratic land. The news of his excesses reached the heavens, and the Devas joined the sages to ask Vishnu to take birth on earth and end Kansa's tyranny and reign. So it was that, on a dark and stormy night, Krishna was born to Devaki and Vasudeva.

HISTORY AND CULTURE

THE NAGAS

The story of the descendants of Yadu through Naga women comes from *Karaveer Mahatmya*, a religious scripture that narrates the local legends of Kolhapur, the temple town in Maharashtra, India. It is narrated to Krishna by a Yadava elder named Vikadru. Historians believe the ruling council of Mathura indicates the Nagas were a tribe that followed an early form of democracy. Perhaps they were descendants of or related to Indo-Greeks who settled in India following the invasion of Alexander. Yayati's marriage to the daughters of an Asura king and an Asura priest, and the marriage of Yadu to Naga women, indicate the mingling of races and tribes.

AFTER

Yadu's sprawling dynasty was firmly entrenched in Mathura, when Kansa, the son of the ruler Ugrasena, decided to crown himself king.

KANSA'S AMBITIOUS MOVE
Ugrasena's son ignored the Yadava council and became the dictator of Mathura. He was backed by the immensely powerful king of Magadha, Jarasandha, who was his father-in-law. In an attempt to preempt a prophecy that said Devaki would give birth to Kansa's nemesis, Kansa imprisoned his sister Devaki and her husband Vasudeva.

BEFORE

Yadu, the eldest son of King Yayati and his wife Devayani, refused to obey his father's command and suffer his curse of old age and impotence.

YADU'S PUNISHMENT

Yayati asked his younger son, Puru, to take on his curse, and he agreed. When it was time for Yayati to pass on his crown, he declared Puru as his successor.

Disinherited, Yadu left his father's kingdom, eventually settling in Mathura, which was governed by a council and had no king. He eventually married Naga women and became the head of the Yadava clan, into which Kansa, and later, Krishna, was born.

Kansa's **Tyranny**

Kansa, with the help of his father-in-law, Jarasandha, the powerful king of Magadha, disbanded the Yadava council that governed Mathura and declared himself as the dictator. Thus began a reign that wreaked havoc on the citizens of Mathura.

Said to be a reincarnation of Kalanemi—a demon slain by Vishnu—Kansa was the son of Ugrasena and Padmavati. He was also the nephew of Surasena, who was Kunti's birth father.

Soon after Kunti was given up for adoption to her father's cousin Kuntibhoja, Kansa overthrew the democratic council that ruled the Yadavas and declared himself the sole ruler of the kingdom. Anyone who dared to protest was either killed or imprisoned. Kansa threw his own father Ugrasena in jail, where he would remain until the end of Kansa's reign. Further, Kansa's marriage to Asti and Prapti, the two daughters of Magadha's King Jarasandha, gave him the military might few wished to face. Prone to anger and insolence, he was feared by neighboring kings and his rule was marked by cruelty and the oppression of his subjects.

Kansa's true bloodline

According to one tradition, Kansa was a child of rape; his mother, Padmavati, was seduced by a demon named Drumila who had assumed her husband's form to dupe her. Suspecting that something was amiss, the queen confronted the demon, crying out, "You are not my husband. Who are you? Why did you do this?" The demon appeared and, unrepentant, mocked her anger at being fooled. He told her that the child born out of

KANSA'S COURT
This 17th-century miniature painting from Rajasthan, India, depicts an artist's impression of Kansa's court and ministers in the city of Mathura.

their union would destroy his enemies. The queen cursed the demon. "Hear my words," she raged. "A man from my husband's lineage will kill this child you have forced upon me."

By the law established by Shvetaketu that made the Pandavas the son of Pandu, even though he was not their biological father, Kansa should have been treated as a Yadava. But he was considered illegitimate and ostracized, making him relentlessly vengeful. The deep-rooted hatred he had for the Yadavas fueled an ambition for absolute power over them. It led him to overthrow the ancient Yadava tradition of rule by consensus.

Having declared himself king, Kansa reigned with a despotic disdain for what dharma laid down as the duties of a ruler. As a result anarchy reigned, thieves walked the streets even in daylight, women were abducted, property usurped; Mathura lived in constant fear and uncertainty.

The prophecy

Kansa's younger sister Devaki had married Kunti's older brother Vasudeva. On their wedding day, oracles foretold that the eighth child born of this union would kill the Kansa. Angered by this threat, Kansa wanted to kill his sister immediately, but was persuaded to let her live on Vasudeva's assurance that as soon as the eighth child was born, he would hand him over to Kansa. Not convinced, Kansa decided to imprison Devaki and Vasudeva till the birth of the child.

When Devaki bore her first child, Kansa's apprehensions came up again. "What if the child Vasudeva presents to me is not his eighth? I must kill all of Devaki's children as soon as they are born."

Kansa stormed into his sister's prison chambers, grabbed her firstborn by the ankles and smashed the baby's head against the floor.

Beside herself with grief, Devaki did not want to bear any more children now that she had witnessed the fate that awaited them. Consoling her, Vasudeva convinced her otherwise. He reminded her of the prophecy, telling her, "We have to sacrifice seven of our children. It is the eighth child who is destined to save Mathura, and us, from Kansa's tyranny."

MYTHOLOGY AND FOLKLORE

THE CURSED CHILDREN

According to Harivamsha, the book of Krishna, Devaki's six children destined to die at Kansa's hands were, in a previous birth, the sons of Kalanemi—a demon killed by Vishnu and born on earth as Kansa himself. Instead of praying to their grandfather as was the tradition, these six demons prayed to Brahma, who granted them the blessing that would protect them from death. On hearing that they had prayed to Brahma, their grandfather Hiranyakashipu was livid. He cursed them with death at the hands of their own father, who would be reborn as Kansa.

BRAHMA, THE CREATOR OF THE UNIVERSE

> "Let Devaki be protected in her house and **guarded surreptitiously** … let her roam around freely, so that **she is not scared**."
>
> KANSA, HARIVAMSHA: THE BOOK OF KRISHNA

AFTER

Devaki and Vasudeva's seventh and eighth children survived through divine intervention.

RESCUED BY VASUDEVA
The couple's seventh child was magically transported into the womb of Vasudeva's eldest wife, Rohini. Vasudeva took the eighth-born child to Gokul to be raised by his brother-in-law Nanda and his wife, Yashoda. To suppress any suspicions Kansa might have, he brought Yashoda's newborn girl back to Mathura.

The **Birth** of **Krishna**

Six of Devaki and Vasudeva's children had been murdered by Kansa. The goddess Yogamaya transferred their seventh child into the womb of Rohini, Vasudeva's other wife. Devaki's eighth child, Kansa's foretold killer, was born on a dark and stormy night.

BEFORE

Oracles had foretold that King Kansa would be killed by his sister Devaki's eighth child.

KANSA'S DESTINY

Apprehensive that his sister and her husband Vasudeva would not hand over their eighth child to him, and that the child would survive to kill him as foretold, Kansa chose to kill all of Devaki's children. He had brutally killed six of his sister's newborn children when miraculous interventions began to validate the faith that had supported Devaki and Vasudeva through the loss of those children.

ANALYSIS

UNDERSTANDING COLOR

In Sanskrit, the word Krishna means "the dark one." Krishna and Balarama are depicted in opposite colors. While Krishna's dark blue or black complexion aligns with his world-affirming nature—he absorbs all colors—Balarama's fair or white complexion fits in with his world-renouncing nature—he reflects all colors.

The metaphorical implication of the color of the skin continues in the characters of the Hindu mythosphere—gods were generally depicted as blue or light-skinned and demons brown or dark-skinned.

THIS WATERCOLOR-AND-GOLD ON PAPER SHOWS A BLUE KRISHNA

Distraught by the killing of their newborn babies, Devaki and Vasudeva were comforted by sages who explained that the suffering brought upon them by the loss of their children was due to karmic debt. The sages said that the children had died at birth because in their past lives they had enraged sages by their misdeeds. And Vasudeva and Devaki had to watch them die because in their past they had angered some sages by stealing their cows. "All kind of suffering is due to karma. Do not fear, your seventh- and eighth-born will bring you joy. While the seventh child will be the herald of the divine, the eighth will be the divine himself," said the sages. Devaki was soon pregnant with her seventh child.

> "You are the **preceptor of everything** that moves and is still. You are the **creator**. You are the **supreme being** ... You are the **original god**."
>
> ARJUNA TO KRISHNA, VANA PARVA: THE BOOK OF THE FOREST

The seventh child

Yogamaya, the goddess of sleep, and Vishnu, the Preserver, had planned the child's escape and survival. She transferred the unborn child from Devaki's womb to that of Vasudeva's other wife Rohini. Rohini lived with her brother Nanda and his wife Yashoda across the Yamuna river in Gokul, the village of cowherds.

In Mathura, King Kansa was made to believe that fear had caused Devaki to miscarry her seventh child. This child, conceived in Devaki's womb and delivered by Rohini, came to be known as Balarama. He was also called Samkarshana, a spirit transferred between two wombs.

Balarama was as fair as the moon and as strong as a herd of elephants. He was the incarnation of Adi-Ananta-Sesha, the serpent with a thousand hoods, and in whose coils lay Vishnu, the god who sustains. Some also claim that Balarama was Vishnu himself, born of a white hair that he plucked from his own chest and placed in Devaki's womb. Vishnu also plucked a dark hair from his chest and placed it in Devaki's womb which transformed into Devaki's eighth child.

The celestial plan

Around the same time Devaki conceived her eighth child, Nanda the cowherd's wife Yashoda also became pregnant.

THE DIVINE INFANT

This 16th-century metal sculpture from Tamil Nadu, India, shows baby Krishna eating butter. Many Hindu sects pray to Balakrishna, or the child Krishna.

THE SLAYER OF KANSA
This 18th-century Pahari miniature shows Devaki and Vasudeva with their eighth child, Krishna, who was destined to kill Kansa.

The child in Yashoda's womb was the goddess Yogamaya, acting on Vishnu's instructions. According to their divine plan, the goddess would be born at the same time as Devaki's eighth child. The newborns would then be exchanged to protect the future slayer of Kansa.

Both women delivered their babies on the eighth night of the waning moon; Yashoda gave birth to a daughter while Devaki delivered a son.

Vishnu's reincarnation

Krishna—Devaki and Vasudeva's eighth child—was as dark as night. Devas, Gandharvas, Apsaras, and sages—everyone rejoiced at Krishna's birth. Flowers were showered from heaven, drums were played, and the Apsaras sang hymns to celebrate the birth that had been foretold.

The goddess Yogamaya appeared in front of Vasudeva and advised him to place the child in a basket and take it across the river to Nanda and Yashoda in Gokul. Ignoring Devaki's piteous cries, Vasudeva did as he was told. The goddess Yogamaya had put the prison guards to sleep, so he walked out with his infant son, unstopped and unquestioned, only to find that the entire city of Mathura was sound asleep under Yogamaya's spell.

Vasudeva reached the Yamuna river which was in full spate because of the heavy rainstorm. With his new son asleep in a basket held over his head, Vasudeva waded in.

MYTHOLOGY AND FOLKLORE

KRISHNA'S SISTER

Popular belief in many parts of the country maintains that the newborn girl Vasudeva carried back to Mathura, who Kansa tried to kill, was later reborn as Devaki's youngest child named Subhadra. She was the beloved younger sister of Krishna and Balarama who would grow up to marry Arjuna. In some other traditions, this girl child was reborn as Draupadi, who married the five Pandavas.

So, both Subhadra and Draupadi, who shared a special bond with Krishna, are female aspects of the divine.

A 20TH-CENTURY WATERCOLOR DEPICTING JAGANNATH, BALARAMA, AND SUBHADRA

AFTER

To make sure Krishna lived, his father smuggled him out of the prison and carried him across the Yamuna river to Gokul.

SWITCHED AT BIRTH
Vasudeva left Krishna by Yashoda's side and brought her newborn daughter back to Mathura. Kansa heard Devaki had given birth for the eighth time, and he tried to kill the little girl as he had murdered Devaki's previous six children. The baby girl, however, turned into a goddess, flew to the skies, and announced that Kansa's killer was still alive.

THIS 18TH-CENTURY WATERCOLOR SHOWS KANSA SMASHING AN INFANT AGAINST A ROCK.

JOURNEY TO SAFETY
An 18th-century miniature shows Vasudeva carrying Krishna across the Yamuna river to the village of Gokul, as Vishnu's many-headed snake shields them from the pouring rain.

Crossing the River

Vasudeva took his newborn son to Gokul where Yashoda, Nanda's wife, had given birth to a girl. He exchanged the two infants and brought Nanda's daughter back to Mathura to await Kansa's arrival.

The Yamuna river was in full turmoil and Vasudeva was anxious about the safety of the infant he held. But as soon as he stepped into the waters, the turbulence ceased. As Vasudeva lifted the baby's basket over his head and began the crossing, Vasuki, the divine ten-headed snake, emerged from the depths of the river to form a protective canopy over the basket and keep the infant Krishna safe from the torrential downpour.

Vasudeva reached Gokul to find Nanda's wife Yashoda fast asleep with her newborn daughter next to her. He quickly placed his son next to Yashoda, picked up her daughter, and carried her back to Mathura. The prison guards were still in deep sleep when he reached his wife's side and placed the baby girl beside her.

The next morning, Kansa was informed that his sister had given birth to another child. Immediately making his way to the prison cell, he was surprised to find that the eighth child, who was prophesied to kill him, was a girl. Devaki begged him to spare the life of the newborn, but he remained convinced that murdering Devaki's children was the only way to ensure his own safety.

Kansa caught the infant by her legs and raised her above his head, intent on dashing her head to the ground. But before he could swirl her around, the child slipped out of his hands and flew into the sky. Before Kansa's eyes, the infant transformed into a resplendent goddess with flowing hair and garlands around her neck.

She had a face as radiant as the moon and eight arms, each one bearing magnificent weapons. The prison filled with light, and the goddess—beautiful and terrible at the same time—laughed. She proclaimed that his slayer was alive and well, and that Kansa would die as had been ordained.

> "Though Vasudeva loved his son, he was **terrified**. He swiftly **grabbed** the **infant** and **entered** Yashoda's house."
>
> SAGE VAISHAMPAYANA TO JANAMEJAYA, HARIVAMSHA: THE BOOK OF KRISHNA

BEFORE

Vasudeva smuggled his newborn son out of Mathura and took him to Nanda and Yashoda's house in Gokul and away from Kansa.

YASHODA'S SON
Vasudeva exchanged his son for Nanda and Yashoda's newborn daughter in the middle of the night. He then presented the baby girl as his own eighth-born child to Kansa, the king who was determined to kill any child born to Devaki. Vasudeva and Devaki's son, in the meantime, was safe and sound in Gokul with his adoptive parents.

HISTORY AND CULTURE

DAHI HANDI FESTIVAL

"Dahi handi" in Hindi means an earthen pot filled with curd. The festival, celebrated one day after Krishna's birthday, involves making a human pyramid and breaking an earthen pot filled with curd tied at quite a height from the ground. This event is based on the legend of the child Krishna stealing butter.

A HUMAN PYRAMID TO BREAK THE "DAHI HANDI" IN MUMBAI, INDIA

The **Butter Thief**

Safe, secure, and adored by his adoptive parents and brother Balarama, Krishna grew up to be a beautiful but mischievous child with a legendary fondness for butter.

KRISHNA'S BUTTERBALL
According to legend, this gigantic boulder is a piece of butter stolen by Krishna. Defying gravity, it stands precariously on the edge of an incline in Mahabalipuram, Tamil Nadu, and has not shifted an inch in over 1,200 years.

Krishna and his elder brother Balarama were raised amid cattle, cowherds, milkmaids, milk, and butter. While still unborn, Balarama had been transported from Devaki's womb to Vasudeva's eldest wife Rohini's, through divine intervention. The two brothers, Balarama as fair as Krishna was dark, were inseparable.

As an infant, Krishna faced a series of murderous attacks from demons sent by Kansa. These included an attempt to poison him by a demoness posing as a wet nurse; an unexplained, runaway cartwheel that almost killed him; and a freak tornado that swept him away. He triumphed each time, but his mother, Yashoda, innocently believed that moving to a more auspicious location might save her beloved child from these seemingly unconnected mishaps.

Move to Vrindavan

So the cowherds of Gokul moved further down on the banks of the Yamuna river to settle around the base of Govardhan hill. Their new settlement was called Vrindavan. It was surrounded by forests, replete with fruit-bearing trees, sweet running water, and grass for the cattle.

The villagers settled into their new life, and soon the sounds of cows and their calves filled the settlement. Cows were milked, buttermilk was churned, and the land flowed with milk and curds. And it was here that Krishna developed a fondness for butter.

The escapades

Krishna was a mischievous prankster and nothing gave him more pleasure than raiding the dairies of milkmaids and stealing the churned butter, stored in pots hanging from the rafters. From shooting pebbles at milkmaids walking with milk jars on their heads to sneaking into homes and breaking open earthen pots of butter and buttermilk, Krishna's antics were unceasing. The exasperated milkmaids tried to stop him but he always managed to get away. Even their seemingly endless complaints to his mother did not deter the naughty Krishna.

The punishments

Tired of his pranks, Yashoda once tied him to a heavy mortar with a long rope. While she was busy, he walked away from the courtyard, pulling the mortar behind him. He walked toward the forest but the mortar got stuck between two trees. As he tugged, the trees got uprooted and he kept walking, pulling the mortar and the two trees behind him, until eventually rescued by his horrified parents.

Krishna's exploits soon became legendary. He was the adorable prankster with a butter-smeared face—the winsome butter thief for whom life overflowed with fun and games.

> "Quickly, Nandagopa **freed Krishna** from the **mortar** and swiftly placed him on his lap, as if **he** had **returned** from the **dead**."
>
> SAGE VAISHAMPAYANA TO JANAMEJAYA, HARIVAMSHA: THE BOOK OF KRISHNA

AFTER

Krishna believed it was his duty to uproot evil from the lives of his fellow villagers.

FIGHTING ENEMIES
As he grew up, Krishna's concern for the well-being of the residents of Vrindavan made him fight many demons apart from the ones set upon him by Kansa. He faced, among others, the five-hooded serpent Kaliya that had poisoned the waters of the Yamuna river. Krishna hoped to make the river water pure and sweet for the cowherds and milkmaids who showered him with their love.

CAUGHT IN THE ACT
When caught stealing butter, Krishna would escape by making up stories to prove his innocence. At other times, he would be punished. This poster shows Krishna making excuses to his mother Yashoda after spilling buttermilk as she threatens to tie him up.

Killing **Demons**

Krishna's childhood was a happy one. Kansa, mindful of the prophecy that his future killer was alive and well, recognized the child as an adversary early on. Between facing demons sent by Kansa and other dangers, young Krishna's life was full of adventure.

Krishna, meanwhile, was growing up among the cowherds and milkmaids of Gokul. Not many suspected his origins, but some did wonder how the fair Nanda and Yashoda had given birth to a dark child. Happy with his adoptive parents and his brother Balarama, Rohini's child, Krishna was a favorite of the people of Gokul.

Meanwhile, Kansa, in his search for the baby who would some day become his assassin, decided to kill all the infants born around the same time as his sister Devaki's eighth child. He knew which demons could be called upon to do his bidding as he made a plan to secure his future.

The poisoned milk

In an early attempt to eliminate his unknown future enemy, Kansa summoned the demoness Putana to kill all the newborns in his kingdom. She would pose as a wet nurse and under the pretext of feeding the babies, give them poisonous milk from her breast. Disguised as a beautiful woman, she made her way across the kingdom, ultimately reaching Gokul. Putana found an opportunity to hold Krishna in her arms and began breast-feeding the infant, but he held on to her breast and nursed until she screamed in pain. She begged to be released but the infant Krishna suckled not only the poisonous milk but also Putana's life.

Repeated attacks

When Putana failed to kill Krishna, Kansa had to acknowledge that Krishna was no ordinary child. He called another of his allies, the demon Trinavarta, who took the form of a whirlwind and tried to overturn the cradle in which Krishna slept. Krishna caught the demon by the neck and grabbed him so tight that Trinavarta gasped and choked. As the demon died, the wind turned into a gentle breeze that lulled Krishna to sleep.

In yet another attempt, the demon Shakatasura took the form of a loose cartwheel and tried to run over Krishna, but the baby kicked him with his tiny feet and smashed him to smithereens. The incidents with the wet nurse, the wind, and the cartwheel so frightened Yashoda that she insisted the entire village move from Gokul to a more favorable location.

The giant stork

Young Krishna's life in their new settlement, Vrindavan, was spent in herding cows interspersed with pranks and mischief. Kansa, in the meantime, continued with his attempts to kill Krishna and

PUTANA'S END

In this watercolor from Rajasthan, India, Krishna is suckling Putana's breast even as she lies dying, while the milkmaids from Gokul reach out to pick him up.

KRISHNA SLAYS BAKA
This sculpted panel depicts Krishna pulling apart the beak of the demon stork Baka as the stork tries to swallow him.

"He **sports like a child**. But though he assumes the form of a child, **these are not the feats of a child**."

KANSA TO THE YADAVA COUNCIL, HARIVAMSHA, THE BOOK OF KRISHNA

sent the demon Baka, who assumed the shape of a giant stork to attack Krishna with his sharp beak. He tried to swallow the young boy whole, but Krishna grabbed the two halves of the stork's beak and forced them apart, killing the bird. Kansa's plan had been foiled again.

Aghasura, the snake demon

Aghasura, the younger brother of Putana and one of Kansa's generals, was sent by Kansa to finish Krishna once and for all. The demon transformed himself into a serpent and opened his mouth against a mountain. Thinking it was a cavern, Krishna's cowherd friends entered the massive hole. Krishna, recognizing that something was amiss, went in the cave to save his friends. As he felt the snake's mouth closing around him and his friends, he began expanding his own body. Within seconds, the snake found it difficult to breathe and expanded his body as well. He could not, however, match Krishna's size and suffocated.

The wild bull

Frustrated, Kansa sent yet another demon, Aristasura, who took on the shape of a wild bull. He ran amok, terrorizing cows and humans alike as he awaited Krishna's arrival. Upon hearing people cry, Krishna came out to see the bull preparing to attack him. Observing it closely, he quickly realized that the bull was a demon in disguise. When the bull charged at Krishna, he grabbed him, squeezed his throat, and pulled out his horns. The bull fell down, fatally injured, and soon died of his wounds.

Keshi, the demonic horse

By now, Kansa's worst fears were confirmed. Krishna indeed was Devaki's eighth son. He then sent a flesh-eating demon who took on the appearance of a horse and began killing cows and cowherds in Vrindavan, eating their flesh and creating mayhem. As more and more of their cows died, the cowherds ran to Krishna begging for help.

Krishna came face-to-face with Kansa's latest demon and a bloody battle ensued. An angry Krishna struck Keshi, killing him instantly. When he heard of this killing, Kansa decided that it was time he faced his nephew and put together a plan to bring Krishna to Mathura.

FACING THE TORNADO
A 17th-century watercolor from Gujarat, India, shows Krishna caught in the tornado caused by the demon Trinavarta, as the residents of Gokul watch helplessly.

CONQUERING KALIYA
In this 18th-century painting, Krishna subdues the giant serpent Kaliya in the Yamuna river, while the residents of Vrindavan watch with concern.

Taming the Hooded **Serpent**

When a serpent made his home in a lake and poisoned its waters, young Krishna decided to take matters in his own hands and reclaim the lake for the people of Vrindavan.

One day, as Krishna wandered along the banks of the Yamuna, he came upon a lake nestled in the bend of the river. The water of the lake seemed deep and quiet, like that of an ocean. The shores were unusually empty —even predatory birds avoided drinking from the lake, and the people of Vrindavan were afraid to go near it. Krishna soon found out that along the banks of the lake were large holes full of poisonous snakes. The lake was also the home of Kaliya, a giant, five-hooded snake whose venom poisoned the waters. The area around the lake suffered, too, and nothing grew near the spot, with the exception of a solitary Kadamba tree.

"If I get rid of the serpent," thought Krishna, "it will make everyone happy." He climbed to the top of the Kadamba tree, hung from one of its branches, and jumped into the middle of the lake, creating a big splash and waking up the giant serpent. Eyes dilated with rage and tongues flickering, the five-hooded serpent emerged from the water. He shook with a fury that made the water boil and his angry breath burned down the nearby trees. Coiling his body around young Krishna, the serpent tried to crush him. The fumes from his breath overwhelmed Krishna. Terrified on seeing him faint, Krishna's cowherd friends rushed to call Nanda, Krishna's father. They stood on the banks of the lake weeping, fearing for Krishna's life.

On hearing the piteous cries of his friends and relatives, Krishna regained consciousness. He pulled apart the coils of the serpent and jumped on its hood—then he started to dance on it vigorously. Overpowered, Kaliya lowered his hood and pleaded for his life.

Krishna commanded him to leave the lake and go back to the ocean. Kaliya soon left the lake, making the people of Vrindavan happy. The water of the lake turned pure once again.

"If I again **see a snake** on this ground or in these waters, **I will slay him**, even if he is your servant or son … Let these waters be **auspicious**."

KRISHNA TO KALIYA, HARIVAMSHA: THE BOOK OF KRISHNA

BEFORE

Krishna and his brother Balarama were very close and, despite Kansa's murderous attacks on them, their life in Vrindavan was happy, if rather adventurous.

THE BROTHERS' ANTICS

Krishna and Balarama were deeply attached to each other, and together their mischief was hard to contain. Balarama recognized Krishna's abilities and divine power and was consequently not too worried about his skirmishes—neither those with Kansa's dangerous demons, nor the ones that they faced in their new home.

"Its [Dhenuka's] **gaping mouth** was like **that of Death**. ... Using **its teeth** as a weapon, **it bit him**."

SAGE VAISHAMPAYANA TO KING JANAMEJAYA, HARIVAMSHA: THE BOOK OF KRISHNA

Balarama Kills Demons

Balarama was valiant and as powerful as an elephant. As Krishna's constant companion, he had his fair share of encounters with demons—Dhenuka and Pralamba were just two of them.

The deep forests around Vrindavan were the grazing grounds for cattle, and Krishna and Balarama spent much of their time foraging the woods for fruit and fresh grass for their cows. On one such trip they came upon the forest of Talavan. It was a beautiful part of the woods with fruiting palm trees, dark earth, and green grass. Krishna suggested that they taste the fruit from the palm trees as it looked sweet and juicy. Balarama readily agreed and before long, the two brothers began shaking the branches of the trees to get at the ripe fruit.

Resident demon

Talavan was inhabited by a demon called Dhenuka who resided there in the form of a wild ass, with his herd. Such was the terror he perpetuated among humans, animals, and birds alike that the forest was no longer frequented by anyone. So, when Dhenuka heard the palm trees shake, he flew into a rage. He found the two brothers, rose on his hind legs, and grunted before resting his unblinking gaze on Balarama. His tail raised menacingly, he charged at Balarama and hit him. He then turned and struck the young lad on the chest with his hind legs.

Balarama grabbed Dhenuka by his legs and whirled him around before releasing him. Dhenuka fell hard against the nearby trees and broke his neck and back. This deeply angered his herd—they attacked Balarama, who fought back, and soon they all suffered the same fate as Dhenuka. Cleared of their evil presence, the forest became a haven for humans and animals once again.

"We ... have decided to **divide ourselves** into two ... Using **your fists** ... strike the enemy of the gods **on his head**."

KRISHNA TO BALARAMA, HARIVAMSHA: THE BOOK OF KRISHNA

Pralamba, the Asura

A demon in league with Kansa, Pralamba took on the form of a cowherd and infiltrated Krishna and Balarama's circle of friends. He decided that Krishna's divinity would make him hard to attack, and so decided to focus on Balarama.

The cowherds had begun a game of leapfrog where the loser would have to carry the winner on his back. Pralamba deliberately lost to Balarama and hoisted him on his back. He then tried to run away with Balarama on his back. Unable to bear Balarama's weight, he enlarged his body to a gigantic size even as he held on to his hostage tightly. Balarama realized he was in a tight spot and called out to his brother, asking him what he ought to do to save himself.

Krishna, who was well aware of his brother's ability to handle the situation, smiled and said, "You have adopted the features of a man and hidden the fact that you are divine. Remember who you are and act accordingly." Prodded by his brother, Balarama used his powerful fists to hit Pralamba with superhuman force and crush his skull. Bleeding, the demon fell down dead as Balarama embraced his brother.

BALARAMA KILLS DHENUKA
The scene in this 18th-century watercolor shows the series of events when Balarama comes face to face with Dhenuka, the ass-demon.

THE SLAYING OF PRALAMBA
This 17th-century miniature from Mandi, Himachal Pradesh, India, shows the demon Pralamba flying off with Balarama on his back, as Krishna and his cowherd friends look up.

MYTHOLOGY AND FOLKLORE

THE TWO BROTHERS

Much has been said about the special relationship between Balarama and Krishna. The elder brother is markedly different from his younger sibling, not just in looks but in temperament and behavior, too. Whereas Krishna is mischievous but stays calm, Balarama is somber, with a fierce temper. In the epic, Balarama is considered by some to be Shiva, the ascetic, while his younger brother, Krishna, is the avatar of the more worldly Vishnu. Some compare their relationship with Rama and Lakshmana, the main protagonists of the Ramayana. Once Lakshmana, the loyal brother of Rama, complained to his brother, "I always have to obey you because you are my elder brother." Rama responded, "In our next life, you will be the elder brother but you will still agree with me, not out of obligation or loyalty but because you will realize that all my actions are rooted in dharma." And so Lakshmana was reborn as Balarama while Rama was reborn as his younger brother, Krishna. Krishna never obeyed his elder brother but, after his initial irritation, Balarama always gave in.

AFTER

Balarama and Krishna's pastoral life carried on in Vrindavan even as the stage was being set for a face-off with King Kansa.

KRISHNA CONFRONTS INDRA
On Krishna's instruction, the cowherds of Vrindavan decided to abstain from praying to Indra and instead planned a ritual to worship their cattle and Mount Govardhan. This displeased the king of gods greatly and resulted in a clash with Krishna.

Milkmaids and Raas Leela

Every night, on the banks of the Yamuna river, Krishna would play the flute. The milkmaids, or gopis, of Vrindavan would slip out in the dark and come to the meadow to dance around him. This was their guilty pleasure, as they felt secure and loved in his company.

THE COSMIC DANCE
This detail from a mural in the Jal Mahal, a former royal pleasure garden in Jaipur, Rajasthan, depicts Krishna dancing with milkmaids in a forest grove.

Krishna's duties grew as he got older, and he was given the task of taking the cows to graze. He would go to the pastures with his brother Balarama and the other cowherds, where he would entertain them by playing his flute. The stories of his divine exploits, coupled with his dark, handsome looks and charm, soon made him irresistible to the milkmaids of Vrindavan. He would stand near the banks of the Yamuna river, in a flower-filled meadow called Madhuvan, and call to the milkmaids with his sublime flute-playing.

Neither the darkness of the night nor the creatures of the forest frightened the milkmaids as they stepped out to meet their beloved while their families slept. Fond of music and dance, he loved spending time with all of them, reveling in the Raas Leela, or divine form of dance, which gave him immense joy and pleasure. If the dancing milkmaids seemed to become possessive and demanded exclusive attention from him, he disappeared completely. Filled with great misery and longing for the absent Krishna, they soon realized that bliss is a result of love being shared with all.

Lovers' games

Krishna once stole the milkmaids' clothes when they were bathing, and then forced them to come out of the water naked. Burning with embarrassment, they stepped out of the water, but they saw no lust in his eyes, only affection and a complete appreciation of who they were; not their external forms, not their flesh, ornaments, or their looks, but their hearts.

He loved them despite their imperfections, and it showed in his eyes. It was a feeling the young maidens had never experienced before.

His feminine side

To punish him for stealing their clothes, the milkmaids would often dress up Krishna as a woman, an act generally meant as a put-down of masculinity. To their great surprise, he was not offended or ashamed of this at all —in fact, he seemed to enjoy it. He insisted upon the best clothes and jewelery and wanted the milkmaids to paint his face to make him look like a woman. What began as a punishment

EXPRESSION OF PURE LOVE
The Manipuri dance form from the northeastern state of Manipur, India, is particularly known for its elaborate Raas Leela, the divine dance performances.

turned into an act of love between the charming cowherd and his milkmaids, and they adored him for it.

End of innocence

But this idyllic life was fast coming to an end as more encounters with demons sent by Kansa followed. Once confronted with the reality of Krishna's birth, Kansa realized that it was time to meet him and ordered him to come to Mathura. Seeing Krishna leave was a moment of grief for the milkmaids of Vrindavan. They realized that this was the end of their leisurely times with him, and that the pleasures Krishna had brought them would never be repeated.

"**His face** was **beautiful**, as if the moon had descended … the **gopa women** drank in the **beauty** of his **face** with their eyes."

SAGE VAISHAMPAYANA TO JANAMEJAYA, HARIVAMSHA: THE BOOK OF KRISHNA

ANALYSIS

THE IMPORTANCE OF INTENT

The act of Krishna stealing the clothes of gopis bathing in the river can be contrasted to the disrobing of Draupadi. While in both events, women are deprived of their clothes, the intent is what makes the two drastically different. There is innocent joy and romance in Krishna's playful teasing, while Duryodhana's intention is to humiliate Draupadi. The two incidents become starkly different due to their underlying intention, despite the similarity of action.

A LATE 18TH-CENTURY MINIATURE DEPICTS KRISHNA STEALING THE MILKMAIDS' CLOTHES AS THEY BATHE IN THE YAMUNA RIVER

Krishna and Radha

The love between the cowherd of Gokul and his favorite milkmaid has been immortalized by many poets, philosophers, and painters. Yet, Radha is a figure of comparatively recent origin.

PEOPLE

MIRABAI

MIRABAI, THE MYSTIC POET

Among the most well-known "bhakti," or devotional, poets, Mira was known to be great devotee of Lord Krishna. According to popular folklore, Mira's family told her in jest that Krishna was her husband. Mira, however, took their words seriously, and from that day on considered Krishna her husband. Mira's devotion to Krishna caused her a great deal of upheaval. When she was married, her in-laws did not take kindly to her intense devotion. Mira would pray for hours before an idol of Krishna, forgetting her family obligations and duties. Soon after her husband's death, Mira left her home for Vrindavan, where she spent most of her life worshipping Krishna and composing devotional songs in his praise. While scholars acknowledge that Mira was central to the Bhakti Movement, which emphasized devotion to God, they also question the legends that are associated with her. Regardless of historical truth, Mira remains an influential figure as someone who stayed true to her beliefs in the face of social censure, but did it with a gentle grace. Her devotional songs are still sung today, while some temples are dedicated to her.

In his aspect as a lover, Krishna is frequently depicted with a flute to his lips, making music, while gopis, or milkmaids, dance around him in the forests of Vrindavan. Today, Radha is seen as chief among the gopis, but she only came into prominence around the 12th century, when the Sanskrit poet Jayadeva wrote the devotional poem, *Gita Govinda*.

Rekindling love

Gita Govinda, which translates to "song of Govinda"—Govinda being another name for Krishna—depicts him as the Supreme Being instead of an avatar of Vishnu, and describes Radha's passionate love for him. Jayadeva presents Radha's longing for Krishna as the cry of the soul for union with the divine. *Gita Govinda* took the Vaishnava (devotees of Vishnu) world by storm. With the rise of Buddhism, Kama, the god of lust, who had fired the imagination of poets and scholars such as Kalidasa and Vatsyayana, had been demonized into Mara, who had to be subjugated. With *Gita Govinda*, Jayadeva made sensuality the vehicle of devotion and spirituality. Though the love between Krishna and Radha was expressed in physical terms, they communicated a profound mystical experience. In the 14th and 15th centuries, poets such as Vidyapati and Chandidas further elaborated on the relationship between Radha and Krishna, depicting it as turbulent, oscillating between states of mind such as the pain of jealousy, separation, the joy of union, and surrender. Radha became a woman who broke social norms to be with Krishna. Some other poets of this period depicted her as a married woman; others, as his aunt; and still others as an older woman to his adolescent youth. Even in *Gita Govinda*, Radha's union with Krishna always takes place in secret. There is a constant threat of social disgrace. By portraying this relationship as illicit and clandestine, the poets heightened the emotional tension of the relationship. Theirs was a true love that transcended social custom and law. Radha became a symbol of all those who were "married" to social responsibilities, but sought liberation and union with their true love, God, who is Krishna. Others preferred to adopt a different theology where they were two halves of a whole. In this equation, Radha became the material world, he its soul; she the feminine principle, he its masculine counterpart, whose union created the universe.

These ideas gradually came to be incorporated into Puranic lore, and Radha became a goddess in her own right. Without her, Krishna was incomplete. She was the medium through which Krishna could be realized. Yet, Radha was always Krishna's beloved, never his wife. The pair represented great lovers who were destined never to unite. Perhaps that is why, except in certain religious sects, Radha is never enshrined in a temple.

THE MUSIC MAKER AND HIS MUSE
Krishna is playing his flute for Radha, his muse, in this Kalighat-style painting from West Bengal. Once he left Mathura—the city of his childhood—and Radha's company, Krishna stopped composing music.

THE DIVINE DANCE
Krishna and Radha are shown dancing in this mural painting from the south Indian state of Kerala. Many believe that Radha was not merely Krishna's favorite, but an inspiration for all the gopis who performed the Raas Leela.

THE ETERNAL LOVERS

These 17th-century brass sculptures are unusual in their depiction of Radha and Krishna. The couple is depicted without the customary finery associated with lovers, and are seen attired in simple clothes.

THE FOREMOST AMONG GOPIS

This terracotta sculpture from the Depara temple, West Bengal, depicts Krishna and the gopis taking a boat ride on the Yamuna river. As his favorite gopi, Radha is seen standing next to Krishna, leaning on him.

A PLAYFUL EXCHANGE

The couple are portrayed wearing each others' clothes in this 19th-century watercolor painting from Himachal Pradesh, illustrating a story that is part of the Radha–Krishna lore.

A LOVERS' TRYST

This Mughal-style painting of Radha and Krishna in a forest grove is full of symbolism. The couples' embrace represents the longing of the male and female to unite, while the vines on the trees recreate this yearning on a figurative level.

BEFORE

When a giant serpent polluted a lake near Gokul, Krishna decided to get rid of him.

FOR VRINDAVAN
Kaliya's poison had contaminated the lake and its surroundings. To make the area safe and the waters pure, Krishna banished him to the ocean. The cowherds and milkmaids of Vrindavan were pleased and grateful for Krishna's concern and love for them.

ANALYSIS

PRAYER RITUALS

The entry of Krishna marked a shift from the earlier ritualistic form of worship to the Vedic form. Krishna was opposed to the rituals conducted by sages, and instead preferred acts of charity and devotion.

A SACRIFICIAL FIRE AIMED AT PLEASING THE GODS IS SAID TO CLEANSE ALL SINS

KRISHNA'S FEAT
This Mughal-style painting depicts Krishna holding up Mount Govardhan on his finger. Indra, on his elephant Airavat, can be seen in the dark, lightning-filled sky.

Indra Defeated

Every year, Kansa performed a fire ceremony to appease Indra, the rain god. Krishna opposed this practice, choosing instead to worship the cattle and the mountain that gave the cowherds sustenance. This act of defiance brought Krishna into direct confrontation with Indra.

When Krishna heard of a yagna being organized, he asked the cowherds what it was for. They explained to him that Indra, the rain god, had to be appeased with a yagna as he was the lord of the clouds and only when he was pleased would he send them rain that sustained the land and made it lush green.

Krishna, however, reasoned that they were cowherds who earned their livelihood from the cows that gave them milk, the forest, and the mountain that provided them refuge. "Instead, we should worship Govardhan, the mountain that brings rain," he said. The cowherds recognized the merit of Krishna's argument and agreed to his suggestion of worshipping Mount Govardhan.

The yagna

The entire city of Vrindavan began planning for a sacrificial yagna for their cattle and the mountain. Large pots of meat and rice were prepared. Vast quantities of milk and milk products were collected. Soon the mountain Govardhan was crowded with cattle adorned with garlands and anklets. Brahmans began chanting mantras and the requisite sacrifices were made near the mountain. The cowherds and milkmaids then prayed together and circled the mountain.

The angry rain god

On finding that a yagna for him had been rejected in favor of one for another entity, Indra was livid and decided to punish the people of Vrindavan for this transgression. He ordered the clouds to burst, so that rain fell heavily on the heads of the cowherds. "Since the cows are their livelihood, let the wind and rain fall on them," he said. He then mounted his celestial elephant, Airavat, and went toward Vrindavan, which was enveloped in dark clouds rumbling with thunder and flashing with lightning. Rain poured down for seven nights. It rained so heavily that animals and birds started to flee in all directions. The cows, wet and miserable in the rain, soon became emaciated without food and shelter. On seeing people and animals suffer, Krishna was filled with rage.

Moving the mountain

With a strength borne out of his divinity, he uprooted the mountain, balanced it on his little finger, and held it aloft like a giant parasol to protect animals and humans from the torrential downpour. Indra saw this spectacle and realizing that Krishna was no ordinary being, but the divine himself, and stopped the rain. Krishna replaced the mountain, and the cowherds returned home with their cattle. Wanting to meet with Krishna, Indra came down to the earth. Deeply apologetic for his behavior, he begged forgiveness and anointed Krishna as the protector of cows on earth.

Indra then advised Krishna to destroy Kansa and the remaining demons as soon as possible. He also beseeched him to befriend Arjuna, the son of Krishna's aunt Kunti, whom Indra had fathered. Arjuna would be in dire need of a mentor and guide, Indra said. Krishna reassured Indra that he would keep Arjuna safe. Comforted, Indra, king of gods, returned to heaven.

> "I have **created** a **house** out of this mountain … bring the **herds here**, so that the cattle can **find** some **peace**."
>
> KRISHNA TO THE COWHERDS, HARIVAMSHA: THE BOOK OF KRISHNA

HISTORY AND CULTURE

WORSHIPPING MOUNT GOVARDHAN

Govardhan puja—the worship of Mount Govardhan—is also known as Annakut, a mound of grain. Its dates typically fall a few days after the festival of Diwali and involves devotees preparing many varieties of vegetarian food and offering them to the gods to show their appreciation for Krishna. Govardhan, near Vrindavan, is a major pilgrimage site for devotees of Krishna; they circle the hill and make offerings of food to it. The trek is interspersed with many shrines that devotees can visit along the way.

DEVOTEES PERFORM RITUALS DURING GOVARDHAN PUJA

AFTER

Krishna had to fight many more demons sent by Kansa before he was summoned to Mathura by his uncle.

KANSA'S DEMONS

Krishna faced Kansa's assassins many times but after he got the better of a demon posing as a wild bull, Sage Narada confirmed Kansa's suspicions about Krishna's true lineage.

RIDE TO MATHURA
Akrura, Kansa's messenger, is shown driving Krishna and Balarama to Mathura in this 17th-century watercolor from Jammu and Kashmir, India.

Kansa's **Messenger**

When Sage Narada confirmed King Kansa's suspicions that Krishna was indeed his prophesied killer, the king sent the horse-demon Keshi to eliminate the cowherd. Krishna killed the demon, showing his might yet again, but an undeterred Kansa came up with a new plan to get rid of his enemy.

The death of Aristasura the bull-demon made Kansa think of all the dangers Krishna had survived; he thenrealized that Krishna was no ordinary cowherd. A meeting with Sage Narada confirmed his worst fears. Narada explained to him, "The girl you tried to kill was Yashoda's daughter. Krishna's father, Vasudeva, exchanged the two children so that your killer could survive." Kansa then sent the horse-demon Keshi to attack. Once again, Krishna easily managed to kill the monster.

BEFORE

Krishna's defiance of Indra and his victory over the king of gods added to Kansa's distress. This made him even more determined to end Krishna's existence.

UNDERESTIMATING KRISHNA

Desperate to eliminate Krishna, Kansa made many more attempts on the cowherd's life. But when Krishna got the better of Aristasura, the demon disguised as a bull, Kansa's fears that Krishna could be his future killer grew stronger.

Kansa's council meeting

The king called all his Yadava kin, including his father Ugrasena and as his brother-in-law Vasudeva, for a meeting to discuss his fears. He accused Vasudeva of deceit as the latter had ensured his son's survival and, therefore, Kansa's death. Despite the insults Kansa hurled at him, Vasudeva kept his patience and did not uphold or refute any of Kansa's angry words. The other Yadavas assembled there were ashamed of their king's behavior.

Kansa's final plan

Kansa called one of the Yadava kin, the virtuous Akrura, and sent him to Vrindavan to bring Krishna to Mathura. Krishna was to be told that he was invited to participate in a wrestling tournament being organized in Mathura. Kansa also asked Akrura to tell Nanda, Krishna's adoptive father, to pay the annual taxes directly to him that year.

Even as Akrura set off for Vrindavan, the Yadavas protested against the king's obsession with Krishna and berated him for insulting Vasudeva. "By abusing his father," they said, "You will now have angered Krishna." Kansa, furious at being chastised by the elders, left the room.

BIDDING FAREWELL
This image from the *Bhagavata Purana (Ancient Stories of the Lord)* shows Krishna and Balarama saying goodbye to the residents of Vrindavan before leaving for Mathura.

Akrura's affection

Well aware of Krishna's divinity and valor, Akrura was eager to see him. He reached Vrindavan at dusk and saw Krishna herding cows. Akrura greeted him effusively and was gracefully received in turn. Akrura spoke of Krishna's parents, Devaki and Vasudeva, who were eager to get a glimpse of him, and their sufferings under Kansa's oppressive regime. He explained Kansa's request to Nanda, who had no choice but to let Krishna go. He did insist, however, that Krishna's elder brother Balarama go with him.

Leaving Vrindavan

All the arrangements for departure were made and Akrura, accompanied by Krishna and Balarama, set off for Mathura on his chariot. To the cowherds and lamenting milkmaids who lined the streets of Vrindavan to wish Krishna well, this seemed like a final goodbye, and they were inconsolable.

AFTER

Krishna and Balarama soon won the hearts of the residents of Mathura with their strength and beauty.

MEETING KANSA

Krishna and Kansa finally came face to face. The king was livid when he saw the brothers from Vrindavan defeating his best wrestlers in combat. His rising anger finally resulted in a confrontation between him and his nemesis, Krishna.

"You will also see **Devaki** … suffering, **bereft** of all her radiance … Because of the **separation**, **she is** tormented by **grief**."

AKRURA TO KRISHNA AND BALARAMA, HARIVAMSHA: THE BOOK OF KRISHNA

KANSA'S DEATH
This Basohli-style painting from the state of Jammu and Kashmir, India, shows Krishna still holding the tusk he had pulled from the elephant, even as he kills Kansa.

Krishna Kills Kansa

Krishna and Balarama arrived at Mathura for a wrestling match that had been organized as their death arena. But the young brothers from Vrindavan fought and killed Kansa's best fighters. Krishna then turned to face Kansa.

Fearing for their safety, Akrura, chief of the Yadavas, dissuaded Krishna and Balarama from visiting their birth parents upon their arrival in Mathura. Instead, the brothers walked around the city.

Their adventures began almost immediately, when Krishna struck a washerman who abused them and killed him instantly. The brothers then entered the king's assembly and asked to see Kansa's renowned bow. Krishna took the weapon in his hands. In trying to bend it, he broke it in half. Kansa, startled by this show of strength, grew anxious for his own life.

The king called his best wrestlers, Chanura and Mushtika, and instructed them to fight and kill the cowherds from Vrindavan in the wrestling matches scheduled to start the next day. Kansa also arranged for a mad elephant to be stationed at the entrance to the arena to attack the boys. "Krishna and Balarama will meet their end one way or the other," he thought to himself. The day of the wrestling match dawned but Kansa's plans failed spectacularly.

Krishna rebuffed an attack by the elephant by pulling out its tusks and slaying it with them. He also attacked the elephant's handler and killed him. Still holding the tusks, Krishna entered the arena. A fierce battle followed between the wrestler Chanura and Krishna. The crowd fell silent. Intent on ending the match, Krishna dealt Chanura a fatal blow that killed him instantly. Balarama took on Mushtika and slew him as well. Kansa saw his best fighters die and in his anger and fear, he called out for Nanda and Vasudeva's arrest.

Before anyone in the assembly could fathom what had happened, Krishna leaped toward Kansa and grabbed him by his hair. He then dragged the king around in the arena until he died, his crown dislodged and jewels torn away.

"Thus **grabbed** by Krishna's energy, **Kansa trembled** … As his **body** was **dragged** along, **potholes were created** there."

SAGE VAISHAMPAYANA TO KING JANAMEJAYA, HARIVAMSHA: THE BOOK OF KRISHNA

BEFORE

Krishna killed Kansa in the wrestling arena, which was supposed to be the venue of his own murder by Kansa's men.

KANSA'S DEATH

Angered by Kansa's audacious attempt to arrest Nanda and Vasudeva, Krishna's adoptive and real fathers, Krishna grabbed Kansa and dragged him around the arena until he died. The Yadavas, who had had enough of Kansa's tyranny, welcomed Krishna with open arms.

ANALYSIS

INDO-GREEK ROOTS

A STATUE OF GREEK HERO HERACLES STRANGLING A SNAKE

Following Alexander's invasion of India, the Indo-Greeks played an important role in the history of north India, from 300 BCE to 300 CE—about the same time that the Mahabharata was reaching its final form. The lore of Krishna is believed to be closely associated with many things Greek. Just like the Greek hero Heracles, Krishna escapes death as a child and comes back as a youth to avenge the wrong done to his family. Moreover, Krishna's city, Mathura, with its ruling council and aversion to monarchy, was influenced by the Greek political system. Megasthenes, the Greek ambassador in the court of Chandragupta Maurya, the founder of the great Mauryan empire in ancient India, compared Krishna with the Greek hero Heracles.

The **Destruction** of **Mathura**

Kansa's death had far-reaching consequences. His powerful father-in-law Jarasandha, the king of Magadha, was incensed at the Yadavas for abetting Kansa's murder by a cowherd. He, along with other allies, laid siege to the city of Mathura.

Having killed Kansa, Krishna was hailed as the liberator of the Yadavas. His true identity as the son of Vasudeva and Devaki was revealed. A cowherd no more, he was recognized as a Kshatriya, a descendant of Yadu. Soon, he and Balarama were sent to Sandipani, the renowned teacher, to learn the ways of a warrior. On Krishna's return, he was accepted as a member of the ruling Yadava council, which had been restored after Kansa's death. It took Krishna a while to be completely accepted as a Yadava but his marriage to Satyabhama, the daughter of Surajit, a Yadava, consolidated his position in the council.

Jarasandha's fury

King Magadha's two daughters, Asti and Prapti, were married to Kansa. When he found out about Kansa's death, he was overcome with rage. He gathered together a large army and reached the outskirts of Mathura to lay seige to the city.

Krishna and the Yadavas of Mathura saw Jarasandha's soldiers and allies at their doorstep and prepared for war, even though they were vastly outnumbered.

Jarasandha's army had a vast collection of chariots, horses, foot soldiers, and elephants, all arranged in battle formations, ready to attack.

The amassed Yadavas counter-attacked and a fierce battle ensued. Balarama and Krishna, armed with Vishnu's celestial weapons—his plow, club, bow, and mace—faced their enemies head on. Balarama smote the enemy with his plow, dragging away chariots, horses, foot-soldiers, and elephants alike. So fierce was his attack that Jarasandha was forced to reassure and soothe his allies with words of encouragement and reminders of their duty. The fighting continued with both sides suffering heavy losses. While the Yadavas took on Jarasandha and his generals with vigor, their enemy fought back no less valiantly.

"Today **this city is uneven**. The **task** before all you kings **is to level it down** to the ground."

JARASANDHA, HARIVAMSHA: THE BOOK OF KRISHNA

Divine intervention

Soon, Balarama and Jarasandha found themselves face to face in a duel. Fighting each other with clubs, the two men were well matched. Suddenly the battles around them ceased as soldiers gathered around to watch the two great warriors fight. The duel seemed unstoppable until a voice from the skies reached their ears asking the Yadavas to take heart as Jarasandha's death had been ordained for a later time—he would not meet his end in that battlefield. Taking advantage of the chaos that followed, Jarasandha retreated with his army and the allies.

The aftermath

Jarasandha's army attacked Mathura seventeen times. Each time, the Yadavas defended the city valiantly and were victorious. The eighteenth time, however, Jarasandha found an ally in Kalayavan, an invader from across the mountains. Krishna advised the Yadavas to move from Mathura to a safer land to avoid the bloodbath that was sure to follow Jarasandha's latest attack.

ANALYSIS

MATRIMONIAL ALLIANCES

The migration of the Yadavas from Mathura in the Gangetic plains to the island city of Dwaraka in the Arabian Sea following the destruction of their city, suggests a period of great turmoil. Through marriages, both Krishna and Balarama strengthened the political position of their clan and restored their glory. With Balarama's marriage to the local princess, Revati, the Yadavas gained rights over the city.

To secure the new island home of the Yadavas, Krishna married many women from surrounding kingdoms. One of them was Rukmini, princess of Vidarbha, who had appealed to Krishna to save her from the loveless marriage into which her brother was forcing her. Krishna then went on to marry many more princesses, including the princesses of Avanti, Kosala, Madra, and Kekaya.

KRISHNA'S CITY

Mathura boasts of innumerable buildings with motifs and murals associated with Krishna. One such building is the Kusum Sarovar, an 18th-century monument whose ceilings have murals that depict events from Krishna's life.

AFTER

Upon receiving the information that Jarasandha had found himself an ally who would be hard to beat, Krishna suggested that the Yadavas move from Mathura to another kingdom.

A NEW LIFE

Krishna and the Yadavas moved west, away from the river-fed plains, deserts, and mountains, toward the coast until they reached the island of Dwaraka. Through a combination of valor and marital alliances made by both Balarama and Krishna, the Yadavas were restored to their former glory.

MEETING JARASANDHA AGAIN
This 18th-century opaque watercolor-and-gold on paper shows Balarama and Jarasandha facing each other in battle after Rukmini eloped with Krishna. Until then Jarasandha believed that Krishna had been killed when he laid seige on Mathura.

The **Wives** of **Krishna**

Krishna had many wives and consorts. While he loved the gopis, or milkmaids, from his days as a cowherd, he went on to marry eight women from royal households, all of whom lived with him in Dwaraka.

As a young cowherd growing up in Mathura and Vrindavan, Krishna is known to have loved many milkmaids. Playing the flute on the banks of the Yamuna river, he reveled in the undivided attention of the gopis, who loved him unconditionally and danced with him in gay abandon, unfettered by social customs.

When Krishna moved to Dwaraka to save the Yadava clan from Jarasandha's repeated attacks, it was the end of an idyllic world. His life in Dwaraka was guided by customs and laws. He stopped playing the flute and instead picked up the conch shell of a warrior. As a Yadava who held a prestigious position, Krishna had many wives and consorts. A caring husband, Krishna, according to legend, even simultaneously manifested himself to each wife to ensure they received equal attention and felt loved. Many tales abound of Krishna's tender relationship with his wives and consorts.

Krishna had eight main queens, most of them princesses from royal households. They were Rukmini, Satyabhama, Jambavati, Kalindi, Mitravinda, Nagnajiti, Bhadra, and Lakshmana. Rukmini, an incarnation of Lakshmi, stood for the majesty and wealth of Krishna; Satyabhama, an incarnation of Bhoodevi the earth goddess, represented his kingdom; while Jambavati symbolized victory, as Krishna won her by defeating her father. After these queens, who were the most senior, came the second group, representing the nobility, and was made up of Kalindi, Nagnajiti, and Lakshmana. The junior wives were Mitravinda and Bhadra, Krishna's cousins from his father's side who represented the Yadava clan.

Other than these main wives, Krishna had 16,000 other wives, Gandharva women who were kidnapped by the demon-king Naraka. Krishna married them when they asked him to save their honor and give them his name and protection.

THE RESCUE OF RUKMINI
Rukmini, princess of Vidarbha, had always been in love with Krishna, but her brother Rukmi arranged her marriage with Shishupala, the king of Chedi. Rukmini sent a messenger to Krishna, imploring him to rescue her. Krishna and Balarama went to Vidarbha to abduct her. This 18th-century opaque watercolor-and-gold on paper from Rajasthan, India, illustrates the escape.

> "There was **no one** on **earth** who could **rival Rukmini** in **beauty**. On hearing about her, the immensely **radiant Vasudeva desired** her."
>
> SAGE VAISHAMPAYANA TO JANAMEJAYA, HARIVAMSHA: THE BOOK OF KRISHNA

MYTHOLOGY AND FOLKLORE

SYAMANTAKA – THE SUN GOD'S JEWEL

The bear-princess Jambavati's marriage to Krishna is closely associated with the story of the most famous jewel in Hindu mythology—Syamantaka. Krishna was once accused of stealing the magnificent jewel Syamantaka, much sought after for its divine powers, which originally belonged to the sun god. To clear his name, Krishna followed Prasen, a Yadava nobleman, who wore it last. The trail led him to the cave of Jambavan, the bear-king. As Krishna entered the cave, he saw a young bear cub playing with the jewel. A fierce fight ensued between Jambavan and Krishna. After 21 days, Jambavan finally realized he was fighting an incarnation of Vishnu himself. He stopped fighting and asked for Krishna's forgiveness. Not only did he give the jewel back, but also offered his only daughter Jambavati to Krishna in marriage. Jambavati became Krishna's second wife.

A WATERCOLOR FROM NEPAL SHOWS JAMBAVAN THE BEAR-KING OFFERING HIS DAUGHTER TO KRISHNA

KRISHNA'S FIRST WEDDING

A 19th-century watercolor from Himachal Pradesh depicts the splendor of Krishna's marriage to Rukmini. According to folklore, the couple first married at Madhavpur, a town by the sea in present-day Gujarat, followed by a grand wedding in his kingdom of Dwaraka.

WEDDING FESTIVITIES

Krishna's wedding to Kalindi comes alive in this 18th-century watercolor from Nepal. On a hunting expedition with Balarama, Krishna saw Kalindi, the daughter of the sun god and a river deity, walking by the river, doing penance to be able to marry Krishna. Moved by her devotion to him, Krishna accepted her as his wife.

MAIN WIVES

These copper alloy statues of Krishna and his two main wives, Rukmini and Satyabhama, date back to the 12th century.

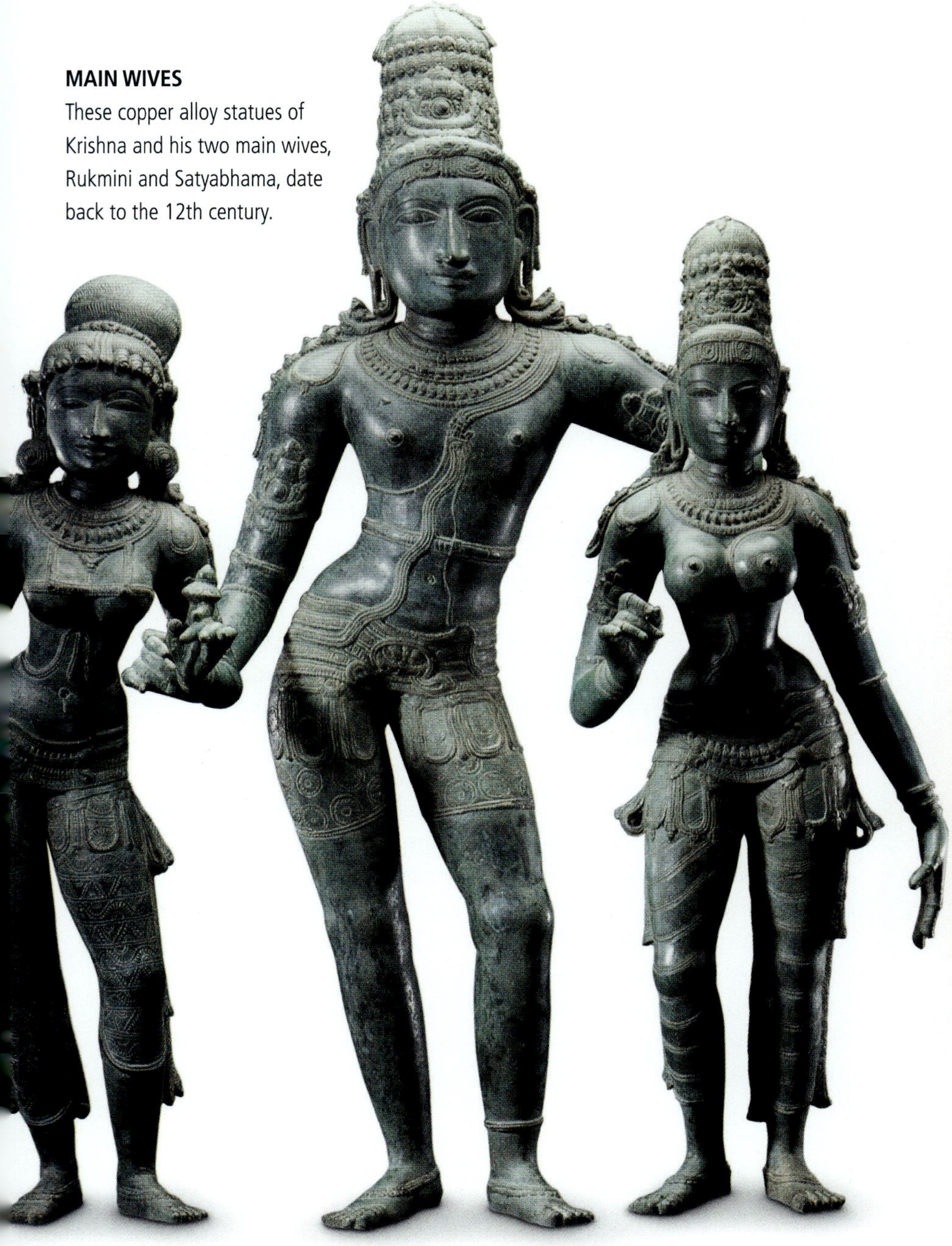

KRISHNA WITH HIS QUEEN-CONSORTS

The Tanjore school of art portrays Krishna extensively. Originating from the south Indian town of Thanjavur in Tamil Nadu, it employs simple devotional iconography and uses rich, vivid colors and gold foil.

BEFORE

Krishna, along with Balarama, and the Yadavas, had found a home in the city of Dwaraka.

LIFE IN DWARAKA

Having moved from Mathura, Krishna and the Yadavas lived peacefully in the city of Dwaraka. Krishna eloped with Rukmini, the princess of Vidarbha and, along with her and his seven other wives, created a life for himself and his clan. As Vishnu's avatar on earth, however, Krishna still had some demons to fight and kill.

Narakasura, the Demon

Indra, the king of the gods, called Krishna to rid the earth of the demon Narakasura. Born of Bhoodevi, the earth goddess, he had been granted a blessing that made him hard to kill. Krishna and his wife Satyabhama took on this task.

> "Naraka **cannot be killed** by any creature. **Having slain** that **wicked one**, you must swiftly return."
>
> INDRA TO KRISHNA, HARIVAMSHA, THE BOOK OF KRISHNA

Narakasura, the son of the earth goddess, had been granted a blessing of longevity by Brahma. But he was a troublemaker and enjoyed robbing both men and gods.

Apart from thieving, killing, and violating innocents, he once kidnapped sixteen thousand Gandharva women. Sure of longevity, he lived a life of depraved recklessness, and eventually attacked heaven itself, where he snatched the celestial earrings of Aditi, the mother of the gods. He also stole the sacred umbrella from Varuna the water deity, as well as the celestial hillock Maniparvata, from the divine Mount Meru. Indra, tired of the demon's atrocities, asked Krishna to help. Krishna was willing, and this time he was accompanied by his wife Satyabhama, who was a warrior in her own right.

> "**Naraka** ... was a **great enemy** of the **king** of the **gods** and **terrified** large numbers of **gods.**"
>
> SAGE VAISHAMPAYANA TO KING JANAMEJAYA, HARIVAMSHA, THE BOOK OF KRISHNA

The demon army

Narakasura's vast army of Rakshasas was commanded by the five-headed demon Mura. Krishna rode Garuda, the king of the birds, with Satyabhama beside him, to reach Mura and his army. Garuda swooped down on the demons and Krishna proceeded to slay them with his celestial weapons.

In a terrible bloodbath, the demons were pierced with arrows, lacerated with swords, and burned out of the skies. All Narakasura's fearsome guards— Vira, Panchajana, Hayagriva, and Nisunda—were slain. Krishna turned to confront the demon himself.

Narakasura's end

A fierce battle followed and Narakasura fought viciously until, finally, Krishna hurled his dreaded discus, the Sudarshana Chakra, at him. The chakra hit the center of the demon's head and severed Narakasura's body into two. Aditi's earrings fell to the ground. Seeing that her demon son was dead, the earth goddess picked up the jewels and presented them to Krishna, imploring him to protect Narakasura's subjects from harm.

Krishna and Satyabhama entered the demon's residence and saw his ill-gotten treasures. Along with Varuna's umbrella, there were pots of gold and silver, heaps of gems, diamonds, and pearls. The demon guards in charge of these riches brought them out for Krishna to see, and promised to take them to the Yadavas. Narakasura had also amassed a vast number of cattle, horses, and elephants. All of this was taken to Dwaraka.

The Gandharva women

Krishna then went to Maniparvata and released the Gandharva women who had been imprisoned in a cave by Narakasura. Without clan or family, they feared for their honor. Krishna married all sixteen thousand so that they would have his protection. Maniparvata was carried back to Mount Meru by Garuda and restored to its rightful place, and Aditi's earrings were returned to her. Accepting her blessing and those of the gods, Krishna and Satyabhama returned to Dwaraka.

HISTORY AND CULTURE

NARAKA CHATURDASHI

The second day of the five-day Diwali festival is commemorated as Naraka Chaturdashi. As with the rest of this festival, this day too lauds the victory of good – Krishna – over evil – Narakasura.

Rituals vary across the country, but an oil bath, or Abhyang Snan, before daybreak or an auspicious time decided by the almanac, seems to be a consistent practice. The cleansing ritual of applying a paste made of sesame oil mixed with herbs and flowers on the body, followed by a bath, is meant to facilitate a soul's easier access to heaven. In some narrations, Krishna himself took such a bath after Narakasura's death to cleanse himself of the demon's blood.

CALLED CHHOTI DIWALI, NARAKA CHATURDASHI IS ALSO CELEBRATED WITH THE LIGHTING OF LAMPS

MYTHOLOGY AND FOLKLORE

ALTERNATE VERSIONS

In another retelling of this story, Narakasura was granted a blessing of longevity and it is said that his mother, the earth goddess, was the only one who could kill him. His confidence that his mother would not do so made him fearless and tyrannical. Krishna's wife Satyabhama, said to be a reincarnation of the earth goddess, accompanied Krishna in his battle against the demon.

In a preplanned move, Krishna pretended to fall, hurt by one of Narakasura's weapons, and Satyabhama, armed with a bow and arrow, killed the demon. Her bravery was appreciated and lauded by Aditi, the mother of the gods, who granted Satyabhama a blessing that she would remain young and beautiful forever.

THE KILLING BLOW
In this 16th-century watercolor, Krishna and Satyabhama, seated on Garuda, king of birds, look on as Krishna's discus, the Sudarshana Chakra, cleaves Narakasura in two.

AFTER

Pleased with Krishna's help in eliminating Narakasura, Indra sent his best artisan to help build the city of Dwaraka.

INDRA'S HELPING HAND

The king of the gods sent for Vishvakarma, the deity of all artisans, and asked him to turn Dwaraka into a city even more beautiful than his own city of Amravati. When Krishna returned, he saw that Dwaraka had been changed into a residence fit for gods.

With its carefully laid out streets, beautiful trees, scented flowers, majestic palaces, and glorious rivers flowing by, the city was transformed beyond Krishna's expectations. He decided to settle down in Dwaraka with his wives and the rest of the Yadava clan.

Vishnu, the Preserver

Vishnu is one of the three aspects of cosmic energy that create, sustain, and destroy the universe. Each time the earth is overrun by chaos and corruption, an avatar of Vishnu is born to re-establish an order based on dharma.

VISHNU AND LAKSHMI
This miniature from the Bundi school of art from Rajasthan, India, shows Vishnu with his chief consort, Lakshmi, riding on Garuda, the king of birds.

As time progressed and cultures changed, there was general discontent with Vedic rituals, and the people felt the need for a new god. With the dawn of the Puranic age, Vishnu emerged as one of the most important deities in Hindu culture. Although there are references to Vishnu found in the Rig Veda, he appears as a minor god, pleased more by prayers than elaborate rituals.

SHREEDEVI
Another form of Lakshmi, Shreedevi is the goddess of opulence and wealth. As her consort, Vishnu becomes Shreenath, her lord.

"Vishnu **created** a **great** and **radiant being**. Know **that being** as **Manu** and manvantara is named after this"

SAGE VAISHAMPAYANA TO JANAMEJAYA, HARIVAMSHA: THE BOOK OF KRISHNA

Iconography of Vishnu

Like most gods in Hinduism, Vishnu is depicted in many ways. The most well-known depictions is of him resting on the thousand-headed serpent, Shesha, also sometimes referred to as Adi-Ananta-Shesha, which represents endless time. It is said that when the serpent uncoils, time moves forward and creation takes place; when he coils again, the universe ceases to exist. Vishnu reclining on the snake is understood to be in cosmic sleep, wherein he dreams the world into existence. Another famous depiction of Vishnu is of him standing within a lotus flower. In this form, he is shown with four hands, which represent the four directions, and indicates his absolute power over the four corners of the universe. Each hand holds an object, such as a disc, lotus, conch, and mace, which represent different aspects and elements, and come together to symbolize the absolute power Vishnu has over all existence.

Vishnu's consorts

It is said that when Lakshmi, the goddess of wealth and good fortune, rose from the great churning, she found only Vishnu worthy of her affections. As his chief consort, Lakshmi is often portrayed together with Vishnu. In every incarnation of Vishnu, Lakshmi, too, changes her form and accompanies him as his consort.

Another important consort of Vishnu is Bhoodevi, the earth goddess, who is considered to be stable, faithful, and less temperamental than Shreedevi, who is another form of Lakshmi.

The ten reincarnations

In the Hindu triad, Brahma is the Creator, Vishnu is the Preserver of the universe, and Shiva is the Destroyer. Since Vishnu preserves the cosmos, it is believed that he descends upon the earth in every yuga or era to restore order in the universe. In this way, every incarnation of Vishnu is related to a particular era, symbolizing the state of the world. Over the centuries, there have been references to Vishnu's many forms; for instance, the temple at Deogarh, Uttar Pradesh, from around the seventh-century Gupta era is called the Temple of Ten Avatars or Dashavatars. Over time, ten has become the accepted number of his incarnations, or avatars.

In many ways, the avatars of Vishnu seem to progress along a Darwinian theory of evolution. He first appears as the matsya, or the fish, that saves the first man, Manu, from the great deluge. Gradually, his form evolves into a turtle, a boar, a man-lion, a warrior-priest, a dutiful prince, a cowherd, a reformer, and finally, a messenger of doom. In each avatar he assists the destruction of the unrighteous and enables a new and righteous world to create itself. Many regard Rama, the prince, and Krishna, the cowherd, as Vishnu's most complete mortal forms, as they embody all the qualities of the god Vishnu, the Preserver, himself.

»

LIST

VISHNU'S OTHER FORMS

Though the ten incarnations of Vishnu are his primary forms, many holy texts like the *Bhagavata Purana* mention several other forms of the god.

- Balaji, the cosmic child
- Mohini, the enchantress
- Hayagriva, the horse-headed warrior
- Narada, the champion of bhakti
- Vyasa, the compiler of the Vedas
- Vishvarupa, the cosmic being
- Dhanvantari, the celestial physician
- Prithu, the domesticator of the earth
- Yagna, the embodiment of sacrifice
- Hamsa, the wise swan
- Dharma, the righteous
- Balarama, the lord of farmers
- Dattatraya, teacher of yoga and tantra

BHOODEVI
Representing the earth, Bhoodevi is Vishnu's consort; she is also the mother of Sita, Rama's wife, in the epic Ramayana.

»

SATYA YUGA: MATSYA, THE FISH

The first of Vishnu's incarnations, Matsya, is at the center of a story that lends itself to the beginning of Time, when the Great Flood swept the earth. To save the first man, Manu, Vishnu, in the form of a fish, asks him to collect all grains and animals in a boat. When the deluge hits, the great fish pulls this boat to safety, signifying the end of the old world order.

SATYA YUGA: KURMA, THE TURTLE

As the Devas and Asuras scramble to churn out the nectar of immortality from the ocean, they ask Vishnu to support the grand Mount Meru. Vishnu then takes the form of a giant turtle, his second incarnation. Meru is placed on him to enable the churning of the ocean—and a new world order is ushered in.

SATYA YUGA: VARAHA, THE BOAR

In his third avatar, Vishnu took on the form of a boar. When the demon Hiranyakashipu abducts the earth, personified as Bhoodevi, Vishnu comes to the rescue in the form of a powerful boar. He fights the demon and brings Bhoodevi up from the depths of the ocean, restoring the new world, while it was still taking shape.

SATYA YUGA: NARASIMHA, THE MAN-LION

To overpower the demon Hiranyakashipu, who received the blessing of immortality from Brahma, Vishnu in his fourth incarnation assumes the form of a creature that is half-lion, half-man. By destroying a being who sought immortality, Vishnu averts the imbalance that threatened the universe.

TRETA YUGA: VAMANA, THE DWARF

Mahabali, a benevolent Asura king, had taken over Swarga. To restore the rule of the Devas, Vishnu in his fifth avatar approaches Mahabali as a dwarf Brahman, Vamana, and asks for three pieces of land. Vamana soon transforms into a giant and walks through the heavens, the netherworld, and on the head of the Asura king himself, thus humbling Mahabali.

TRETA YUGA: PARASHURAMA, THE WARRIOR PRIEST

A warrior–priest, the sixth avatar of Vishnu stops the thousand-armed Kartaviryarjuna, an arrogant and corrupt Yadava king who is considered invincible. Parashurama is unique, for as a mortal avatar, he meets two of Vishnu's avatars, Krishna and Rama.

TRETA YUGA: RAMA, THE KING OF AYODHYA

Rama, the king of Ayodhya, is the seventh incarnation of Vishnu. He is the protagonist of the epic Ramayana, and is revered as a hero who upheld the moral values and social ideals of society. He is known as "Maryada Purushottama," or the supreme man, who is the repository of upright ideals.

DWAPARA YUGA: KRISHNA, THE COWHERD

The eighth incarnation, Krishna is the dark-skinned Yadava, who serves as the charioteer of the warrior Arjuna in the epic Mahabharata. A guide and mentor to the Pandavas, Krishna is known to be a master strategist and cunning tactician.

DWAPARA YUGA: BUDDHA, THE ASCETIC

Though the Buddhists regard Gautama Buddha as an enlightened being distinct from Vishnu, Puranic texts as well as the 12th-century poem *Gita Govinda* consider him to be the ninth incarnation. Buddha is different from Budh, the lord of Mercury.

KALI YUGA: KALKI, THE MESSENGER

The tenth incarnation, yet to descend on earth, will bring the foretold doom. A mortal man on a white horse, carrying a drawn blazing sword, will bring the doom that will erase the world and will usher in a new era—the beginning or the Satya Yuga.

REFERENCE

People in the Mahabharata

A

ABHIMANYU
The son of Arjuna and Subhadra, Abhimanyu grew up in Dwaraka with his mother's family. While still in his mother's womb, he overheard his father describe to Subhadra the deadly battle formation Chakravyuha. Unfortunately, he only heard the part about how to help others escape it and did not hear about how to get out of it himself. This incomplete knowledge proved fatal. Abhimanyu died, trapped within a Chakravyuha planned by Drona on the battlefield of Kurukshetra.

A 12TH-CENTURY SCULPTURE OF SAGE AGASTYA

AGASTYA
One of the Sapta Rishis, or seven sages, the patriarchs of Vedic Hindu religion, Agastya was the grandson of Brahma, the creator of the world. As Drona's teacher, he taught him the invocation of the Brahmaastra, one of the deadliest among divine weapons.

AGNI
The Hindu god of fire, Agni cleanses and purifies all things. When the Pandavas needed to clear the forest of Khandavaprastha to build their capital, Agni offered his services. He had lost his luster and wanted to restore it by burning something raw. Having done this by consuming the forest, the god expressed his gratitude by giving Krishna the Sudarshana Chakra and Arjuna the bow, Gandiva.

ALAMVUSHA
Also known by the name Shalakantaka, Alamvusha was a Rakshasa who fought valiantly for the Kauravas in the Kurukshetra War. He was killed by Bhima's son Ghatotkacha.

AMBA
Amba was the oldest of the three daughters of the king of Kashi. Bhishma had abducted the sisters from their swayamvara as brides for his half-brother Vichitravirya, but let Amba go when she told him of her love for Shalva. When Shalva rejected her on the grounds that she belonged to her abductor, Amba vowed vengeance on Bhishma. Through severe penance, she obtained a blessing from Shiva, the god of destruction, that she would be the cause of Bhishma's death in her next life. Amba was reborn as Shikhandi.

AMBALIKA
One of the three daughters of the king of Kashi, Ambalika was Amba's sister, taken by force by Bhishma from their swayamvara and married to his half-brother Vichitravirya, the king of Hastinapur. After Vichitravirya died childless, she became Pandu's mother, having been impregnated by Sage Vyasa.

AMBIKA
The second daughter of the king of Kashi, and Amba and Ambalika's sister, Ambika was also abducted by Bhishma from the swayamvara to be his brother Vichitravirya's bride. She gave birth to Dhritarashtra, who was born blind because Ambika had closed her eyes in fear when approached by Sage Vyasa.

ANGARAPARNA
A Gandharva, he lost a skirmish with the Pandavas when he tried to prevent them from taking water from a lake he claimed belonged to him. In gratitude for sparing his life, Angaraparna gave the Pandavas a hundred horses each.

ARAVASU
The son of Rishi Raibhya, Arvavasu was falsely accused of killing his father. Sage Lomasha narrated his story to the Pandavas to illustrate the virtue of forgiveness.

ARJUNA
Arjuna, the third of Pandu's five sons, was fathered by Indra, the king of the Devas and ruler of the sky. Trained by Drona, he became an outstanding archer and a focused warrior. However, when faced by enemy lines composed of family, teachers, and elders on the battlefield of Kurukshetra, Arjuna was overcome with doubt and ready to lay down arms. It was then that Krishna explained to him the importance of selfless action and adherence to dharma, the teachings that comprise the Bhagavad Gita.

ASHWASENA
A Naga whose family had been killed in the burning of Khandavaprastha. Determined to kill Arjuna and avenge them, Ashwasena turned himself into an arrow in Karna's quiver at Kurukshetra, but was recognized by Krishna.

ASHWATTHAMA
Though a Brahman by birth, Ashwatthama was brought up as a warrior by his father, Drona, in pursuit of his own ambition for power. He fought against the Pandavas and was made commander-in-chief of what was left of the Kaurava army by a dying Duryodhana. Unable to face defeat, he went on to kill the Pandava children while they slept and even threatened the unborn in their mother's wombs. For such total disregard for life, when it was a Brahman's dharma to protect it, Ashwatthama was cursed by Krishna to live and suffer for three thousand years.

ASTIKA
Son of the Rishi Jaratkaru and Naga Manasa, Astika called a halt to the Sarpa Sattra, or snake sacrifice, organized by Janamejaya, great grandson of Arjuna, to avenge his father Parikshit's death from snakebite. Astika asked Janamejaya to call for Vaishampayana, the storyteller sage, and listen to the story of his ancestors, which came to be known as the Mahabharata.

AYLI
One of Arjuna's many wives, Ayli was seduced by Arjuna, who slipped into her bed in the form of a serpent while she slept.

B

BABRUVAHANA
Arjuna's son with Chitrangada, princess of Manipur, Babruvahana was brought up by his maternal grandfather whom he succeeded to the throne of Manipur. After the Kurukshetra War, when Arjuna returned to Manipur, following Yudhishthira's sacrificial horse as guardian, he urged a reluctant Babruvahana to fight him. His son proved to be a worthy opponent and fatally wounded Arjuna with an arrow that ripped through his heart. Horrified by what he had done, Babruvahana could be pacified only after Arjuna was revived with the help of a Nagamani, a magical gem, by his Naga wife Ulupi.

BAKA
A Rakshasa who lived in a forest on the outskirts of a village, Baka terrorized the villagers into sending him a cartload of food every fortnight. Baka would eat not only the food, but the buffalo and the drivers of the cart as well. He was killed by Bhima.

BALARAMA
Krishna's elder brother, and the seventh child of Devaki and Vasudeva, Balarama grew up in Gokul and accompanied Krishna to Mathura to kill Kansa. Balarama taught both Bhima and Duryodhana the art of mace warfare. He did not side with either the Pandavas or Kauravas at Kurukshetra. Instead, he chose to go on a prilgrimage during that period. In Hindu mythology, Balarama is regarded as the incarnation of the thousand-hooded serpent, Adi-Ananta-Shesha, upon whose coils Vishnu, the deity who sustains the universe, rests.

BALLAVA
The disguise that Bhima assumed during the Pandavas' last year in exile, when they had to remain hidden and undetected. As Ballava, he was the talented cook who served in the kitchen of King Virata of Matsya.

BARBAREEK
Bhima's grandson and Ghatotkacha's son, Barbareek learned the art of warfare from his mother, the Naga princess Ahilawati. He always fought on the side of the loser, with only three arrows. His outstanding skill as a warrior made him invincible. He was tricked by Krishna into cutting off his own head.

BHAGADATTA
The king of Pragjyotisha, he fought on the side of the Kauravas. He was well known for his skill with his elephant and his legion of elephants was used to a great advantage by Drona.

BHANGASHVANA
An ancient king, he was cursed by Indra and turned into a woman. He was referred toas the only person who could comment on life from both a man and a woman's perspective.

BHANUMATI
Duryodhana's wife and mother of two children, Bhanumati commanded the utmost loyalty from her husband.

BHARADVAJA
An illustrious sage, he was the son of Brihaspati and priest to the Devas. Bharadvaja was the father of Drona, and one of those who taught the Kuru tutor the art of warfare and skill with weapons.

BHARATA
The son of King Dushyanta and Shakuntala, Bharata was a great king in ancient India. It was in his honor that Jambudvipa, or the rose-apple continent, came to be known as Bharatavarsha, or simply Bharata.

BHIMA
Second son of Pandu and Kunti, fathered by Vayu the god of wind, Bhima was the strongest of men and a great warrior. His preferred weapon was the gada, or mace. After the fateful gambling match and humiliation of Draupadi, Bhima had vowed to kill every single one of the Kauravas. He made a ferocious opponent as he set out to do just that on the battlefield of Kurukshetra. After killing Dusshasana, he called Draupadi to fulfil her vow, helping her tie her hair after washing it in Dusshasana's blood.

BHISHMA
The son of Shantanu, king of Hastinapur, and Ganga and granduncle to the Kauravas and Pandavas, Bhishma was the last of the true Kuru bloodline. Named Devavrata at birth, he came to be known as Bhishma after he took an inexorable vow of life-long celibacy, removing himself, and any possibility of a descendant, from any claim to the throne. The vow enabled his father to remarry. However, with no one to facilitate rebirth, it also consigned him to the land of the dead for eternity. Impressed by his sacrifice, the gods granted him a blessing that allowed him to choose the time of his death.

BHURISHRAVA
Bhurishrava was a Kuru prince, second cousin to the Pandavas and Kauravas—their paternal grandfathers were brothers. He fought for the Kauravas at Kurukshetra.

BRAHMA
In Hindu mythology, Brahma is the creator of the universe, one of the three fundamental forces or principles of all existence—creation, sustenance, and destruction. Together with Vishnu and Shiva, he makes up the supreme triad of gods. He is usually depicted with four bearded heads and four arms, seated in the lotus pose. Of all the gods, Brahma alone carries no weapon. Brahmalok, which holds within it the splendors of all worlds, is where he resides with his consort Saraswati, the goddess of learning and wisdom. His vehicle is a white swan.

BRIHANNALA
While in Amravati, Arjuna was cursed by the Apsara Urvashi to lose his manhood for a year. In the thirteenth year of exile, when the Pandavas were to remain undiscovered, Arjuna used this curse to transform himself into a eunuch. He presented himself at the Matsya king Virata's court as the dancer Brihannala, and was employed to teach the princess Uttari.

BHARATNATYAM DANCER PLAYING BRIHANNALA

BRIHASPATI
The logical, dispassionate Brihaspati, grandson of Brahma, is the lord of planet Jupiter and priest to the Devas. His wife is Tara, goddess of the stars.

BUDH
Lord of the planet Mercury, Budh was cursed to be neither male nor female. He was the child of Chandra, the moon god, and Tara, the wife of Brihaspati. Tired of her analytical husband, Tara had run away with the romantic, emotional Chandra, but because Brihaspati could not perform his priestly duties without her, the Devas ruled that she had to return to Brihaspati and that her child would belong to her husband and not his biological father. Thus, Budh was brought up by Brihaspati.

C

CHANDRA
The young, beautiful, and passionate god of the moon, he loves the goddess Tara and fathered her son, Budh.

CHITRANGADA (FEMALE)
The princess of Manipur, Chitrangada was a great warrior and one of Arjuna's many wives. Her father had agreed to the marriage on the condition that Arjuna let their son be brought up by his maternal relatives.

CHITRANGADA (MALE)
Firstborn of King Shantanu and Satyavati, Chitrangada was Vichitravirya's elder brother. He was challenged by a Gandharva king of the same name, and was killed in the duel.

D

DAMAGRANTHI
Nakula's disguise during the last year of the Pandavas' exile. As a servant called Damagranthi, the elder of the Pandava twins looked after the horses in the stables of Virata, king of Matsya.

DAMAYANTI
The princess of Vidarbha, Damayanti was considered one of the most beautiful women. She followed her husband, Nala, to exile when, like the Pandavas, he lost everything to a cousin in a game of dice.

DANTAVAKRA
King of Karusha, Dantavakra was an enemy of Vasudeva, Krishna's father, and among those who allied themselves with the Kauravas.

DEVAKI
Krishna's mother, Devaki was Kansa's sister and married to Vasudeva. A prophecy foretold that Devaki's eighth child would kill Kansa, so he imprisoned both his sister and his brother-in-law and killed any children born to them. Two children escaped death—Balarama and Krishna.

DEVAPI
Elder brother of Shantanu, Devapi was physically unfit and, therefore, could not be king. He chose the life of an ascetic when Shantanu succeeded their father.

DEVAYANI
Daughter of Shukra, priest of the Asuras, Devayani married Yayati. Her son Yadu, banished from the kingdom for failing to suffer a curse on his father's behalf, was the founder of the Yadava clan.

DHAUMYA
The royal priest and guru of the Pandavas, Dhaumya was a learned sage. He accompanied the Pandavas into exile, guiding and instructing them on how to make the best use of their time, away from their kingdom. He told them of the pilgrimages they should undertake and the significance of each, and how to live according to dharma.

DHRISHTADYUMNA
Son of Drupada, the king of Panchala and twin brother of the Pandavas' wife, Draupadi, Dhrishtadyumna was one of three children of Drupada. The king had invoked Shiva, the god of destruction, to grant him children who would avenge his humiliation by Drona and his Kuru patrons. Dhrishtadyumna was born destined to kill the warrior-priest Drona.

DHRISTAKETU
Son of Shishupala, Dhristaketu was the king of Chedi who befriended the Pandavas. He was killed by Drona during the Kurukshetra War.

DHRITARASHTRA
Father of the hundred Kaurava brothers, Dhritarashtra was the blind son of Vichitravirya, fathered by Sage Vyasa after Vichitravirya died without an heir. His lack of sight meant that he could not inherit the throne but when the king, his younger brother Pandu, sought an ascetic's life in the forest, the kingdom was left in his charge. The eldest of the Kauravas, Duryodhana believed himself to be the rightful heir to the throne, while Yudhishthira regarded Dhritarashtra as no more than a regent and claimed the throne as his. Unable to restrain his son, Dhritarashtra remained silent, allowing adharma to flourish.

DRAUPADI
The daughter of King Draupada of Panchala and sister of Dhrishtadyumna, Draupadi was the most sensuous of women and the common wife of the five Pandava brothers. Humiliated by the Kauravas, particularly Dusshasana who pulled her by her hair from the privacy of her chambers to the assembly hall, Draupadi had been staked and lost by Yudhishthira at the fateful dice game. She swore that she would not tie her hair until she had washed it in Dusshasana's blood. For the five Pandavas, through all their days in exile, her unbound hair remained a constant reminder of all they had lost.

DRONA
The son of Sage Bharadvaja, Drona was an extremely learned teacher of the Kuru princes. Although a Brahman by birth, he chose to go against varna dharma to become a warrior. He wanted to be the equal of King Drupada of Panchala after Drupada refused to give him a gift in the name of friendship but offered him alms befitting a Brahman. Drona learned advanced military skills from the great warrior-priest Parashurama but broke his promise not to share this knowledge with a Kshatriya by becoming tutor to the hundred and five Kuru princes. However, he favored his own son Ashwatthama and passed on not only his knowledge but also the ambition to be the greatest warrior in the world. Drona sided with the Kauravas, serving as commander-in-chief of the Kuru army at Kurukshetra. He was killed by King Drupada's son Dhrishtadyumna.

DRUPADA
The king of Panchala, Drupada was the father-in-law and staunch ally of the Pandavas. Drupada had once refused his childhood playmate, the Brahman Drona, a gift that he desired and offered him alms instead. The humiliated Drona took revenge by asking his students, the Kurus, to fight and capture Drupada, then demand half his kingdom to let him go. Vowing revenge not just on Drona but the Kurus as well, Drupada invoked Shiva to ask for sons who would kill the Kuru patriarch Bhishma and Drona, and for a daughter who would divide the Kuru house. Shikhandi, Dhrishtadyumna, and Draupadi were his children. Drupada was killed by Drona in the Kurukshetra War.

DURYODHANA
Eldest of the hundred sons of Gandhari and Dhritarashtra, Duryodhana was revered by his younger siblings and indulged by both his parents who found it difficult to deny him anything. Resentful and strongly competitive of the Pandavas, he refused to accept their claim to the throne, ignoring the counsel of advisers and elders, including that of Krishna and his granduncle Bhishma.

DUSSHASANA
Second of the hundred sons of Gandhari and Dhritarashtra, Dusshasana was devoted to his brother Duryodhana. It was he who dragged Draupadi out of the women's quarters into the gambling hall after she had been staked and lost by Yudhishthira. He also attempted to follow Duryodhana's instructions to strip Draupadi naked. Though he could not do so, the outraged Draupadi vowed that she would not tie her hair again until she had washed it in Dusshasana's blood—a vow she fulfilled when he was killed by Bhima at Kurukshetra.

DUSHYANTA
King of Hastinapur, Dushyanta was an ancestor of the Kuru dynasty. He married Shakuntala, who had been raised by Sage Kanva in his hermitage in the forest. Their son was Bharata, after whom the land came to be known as Bharatavarsha, or simply, Bharata.

DUSSHALA
The only daughter of King Dhritarashtra and Gandhari, Dusshala was married to Jayadratha, the king of Sindhu.

E

EKALAVYA
A Nishadha, or forest dweller, who was keen to master the skill of archery and had approached Drona to accept him as a student. Undeterred by Drona's refusal, Ekalavya put up an effigy of the master and taught himself under its guiding eye. Discovering Ekalavya's skill and wary of his outshining his star pupil Arjuna, Drona demanded that Ekalavya pay a guru dakshina—the fee paid by disciples to their gurus. Ekalavya agreed, and unhesitatingly cut off his right thumb upon Drona's request.

G

GALAVA
Son and pupil of the great sage Vishwamitra, Galava was asked for eight hundred white horses as guru dakshina, the fee paid to one's teacher, by his father. The search for such horses brought Galava to the court of Yayati, a Kuru ancestor. Galava was eventually able to put together the horses with the help of Yayati's daughter Madhavi.

GANDHARI
Married to Dhritarashtra, the blind elder son of Vichitravirya, Gandhari was the daughter of Suvala, the king of Gandhara. When she realized that her husband could not see, Gandhari blindfolded herself to share his visionless world. Mother of a hundred sons and one daughter, Gandhari saw all her sons killed in the Kurukshetra War. Grief-stricken, she cursed Krishna—that he live through the same pain before being killed.

GANESHA
The elephant-headed son of Shiva and Parvati, Ganesha is a highly popular Hindu deity revered as the god of beginnings and remover of obstacles. He is also the god of intellect and wisdom. While composing the Mahabharata, Sage Vyasa had asked Ganesha to be his scribe. Ganesha agreed on the condition that Vyasa recite the epic without a pause. To buy more time, Vyasa requested Ganesha to write only after understanding the lines being dictated.

GANGA
The personification of the pure and sacred river, Ganga in the Mahabharata is the wife of King Shantanu and the mother of the Kuru patriarch Bhishma.

GARUDA
King of birds, Garuda is the mount of Vishnu, the deity who sustains the universe. Krishna's banner carried the image of Garuda.

GAYA
Gaya was a Gandharva, who inadvertently spat on Krishna's head while flying over Dwaraka. This accident led to a direct conflict between Krishna and Arjuna, which was resolved only after Brahma's intervention.

GHATOTKACHA
Bhima's son by Rakshasa Hidimbi, Ghatotkacha had telepathic powers as well as the power of flight. During the war at Kurukshetra, he was called upon by Bhima to fight at night, a time when his powers were enhanced and made him invincible. A desperate Duryodhana asked Karna to use the infallible spear Indra had given him to kill Ghatotkacha. Mortally wounded, Ghatotkacha pulled himself to his greatest height and fell across the Kaurava army, inflicting maximum damage even in his death throes.

GIRIKA
An Apsara, she was cursed by Brahma to be a fish until she gave birth to a human. Girika

AN IDOL OF LORD GANESHA

A 19TH-CENTURY MANUSCRIPT COVER SHOWING HANUMAN, THE MONKEY GOD

eventually overcame the curse by giving birth to twins. Girika's daughter, Satyavati, married the Kuru king Shantanu.

GUNAKESHI

The daughter of Indra's charioteer, Matali, Gunakeshi was betrothed to marry Sumukha, the serpent. Their troubles were narrated to Duryodhana by the sages to illustrate the evil of arrogance.

H

HAMSADHVAJ

The king of Champakapuri, Hamsadhvaj, determined not to accept Yudhishthira as overlord, captured his sacrificial horse when it entered his territory. He fought the army led by Arjuna that accompanied the horse, submitting only after the death of his eldest son in battle.

HANUMAN

The son of Vayu, the god of wind and half-brother to Bhima, Hanuman is one of the mightiest deities and makes an appearance in the epic to teach Bhima the virtues of remaining humble even in a position of strength. Popularly revered as one who removes all obstacles and troubles, Hanuman is a great devotee of Lord Rama, another avatar of Vishnu.

HIDIMBA

Brother of Rakshasas Baka and Hidimbi, Hidimba was killed by Bhima in a duel.

HIDIMBI

Hidimba's sister, Hidimbi was greatly impressed by Bhima's valor in the battle against her brother and asked Bhima to marry her. Ghatotkachha was their son.

I

ILA

Both of male and female gender, Ila was once a prince called Sudyumna, son of Manu, the first king of humans. He was transformed into a woman when he strayed into a forest enchanted by Shiva. Unble to lift the spell, Shiva's consort Shakti changed it so that Sudyumna was a woman only for the period when the moon waned, and became a man again during its waxing. Ila found a perfect match in Budh, god of Mercury, who was neither male or female. The Mahabharata narrates the story of Ailas, the descendants of this union.

INDRA

Indra is said to be the king of the Devas. He rules over Swarga, a paradise where pain and suffering do not exist; where every desire can be indulged and every wish fulfilled. The capital of Swarga is Amravati.

IRAVAN

Also known as Aravan, Iravan was the son of Arjuna and the Naga princess Ulupi. He was sacrificed to ensure victory for the Pandavas in the Kurukshetra War as he was one of the three warriors—the other two being Arjuna and Krishna—who had the required thirty-three sacred marks on his body.

J

JAIMINI

Jaimini was a student of Sage Vyasa. Vyasa classified the ancient Vedic hymns into four and taught each to one his four chief disciples—Paila, Vaishampayana, Jaimini, and Sumantu. The Samaveda was transmitted to Sage Jaimini.

JANAMEJAYA

Great-grandson of Arjuna, Janamejaya is to whom the Mahabharata is addressed. Following the death of his father Parikshit of a snakebite, Janamejaya organized the Sarpa Sattra, or snake sacrifice. He was interrupted by Astika, nephew of Vasuki, the king of Nagas, who asked him to call the sages and listen to the story of his ancestors, the Kurus, and the great war at Kurukshetra, to try and fathom the true meaning of dharma before carrying on with the sacrifice.

JARASANDHA

The king of Magadha and a great friend of Kansa, Krishna's uncle Jarasandha swore to avenge his friend's death at Krishna's hands. He was defeated and killed in the bloody battle initiated to keep this vow.

JARATKARU

A great ascetic, he was called upon by his ancestors to save them from everlasting death by marrying and having a son to perform the required rituals. He married the sister of Vasuki, king of the Nagas. Their son was named Astika.

JATASURA

Jatasura was a Rakshasa who disguised himself as a Brahman to accompany Yudhishthira, Bhima, Sahadeva, Nakula, and Draupadi when they were traveling through the Himalayas. One day, taking advantage of Bhima's absence he made the other Pandavas and their wife captive and carried them away. He was overtaken and killed by Bhima.

JAYADRATHA

King of Sindhu, Jayadratha was married to Dusshala, the only sister of the hundred Kauravas. He was killed by Arjuna in the Kurukshetra War.

K

KANKA

Yudhishthira's disguised persona during the final year of exile, when the Pandavas were required to stay undiscovered. Kanka was a learned Brahman, an excellent adviser, and a highly skilled administrator who served in the court of King Virata, ruler of Matsya.

KANSA

Krishna's mother's brother, Kansa had declared himself the ruler of Mathura which had, until then, been ruled by a council. Terrified of a prophecy that foretold his killing by his sister's eighth child, he imprisoned both her and her husband, killing six of their children as soon as they were born. The seventh, Balarama, and the eighth, Krishna, were miraculously saved. As prophesied, Kansa was killed by the eighth child—Krishna.

KANVA

A learned sage, Kanva was the adoptive father of Shakuntala, abandoned at birth by her parents. He found her as a baby sheltered by birds in a forest.

KARNA

Kunti's son from the sun god, Surya, Karna was born before her marriage with Pandu, the Kuru king. Karna was born wearing divine golden earrings and armor on his body. Abandoned in fear by the unmarried Kunti, he was adopted by the royal charioteer of Hastinapur. He grew up to have great skill with weapons and was Arjuna's equal with the bow. He, however, was never accepted as a Kshatriya because he was raised as a charioteer. Duryodhana was the only one who stood by him and became his loyal friend. Karna fought on the Kauravas' side even after Krishna revealed to him the secret of his birth.

KAUSHIKA

A king who wanted to become an ascetic, Kaushika gave up his material possessions, took the vow of celibacy and retired to the forest to practice austerities. Distracted by an Apsara named Menaka sent by Indra for that very purpose, he forgot his vow of celibacy and surrendered to passion.

KICHAKA
Kichaka was the younger brother of Queen Sudeshna of Matsya Kingdom, where the Pandavas and Draupadi hid during the thirteenth year of exile. He could not control his infatuation with the maid Sairandhri, who was Draupadi in disguise. Unable to stand this insult to his wife, Bhima killed him.

KINDAMA
A sage, Kindama was killed while he was making love to his wife in the forest by King Pandu. As both Kindama and his wife had transformed themselves into antelopes, the Kuru king had no idea he had shot a human. The dying Kindama cursed Pandu that he would meet his end the moment he touched a woman and so would never again know the pleasure of lovemaking.

KIRMIRA
Feared by the Rishis, whom he troubled ceaselessly, Kirmira was a Rakshasa who lived in the Kamyaka forest. The Pandavas found him blocking their way when they entered the forest. Bhima struck him with a mace, pinned him to the ground, and snapped his neck.

KRIPA AND KRIPI
Children of Sage Sharadwana and an Apsara called Janpadi, Kripa and Kripi were twins found abandoned in the forest by King Shantanu who adopted them. Kripa grew up to become royal tutor to all the Kuru princes, while Kripi was given in marriage to Drona, a Brahman.

KRISHNA
Believed to be an avatar of Vishnu, the preserver of the Hindu triad, Krishna's childhood was spent in Gokul as a cowherd—the mischievous son of Nanda and Yashoda. It is in this aspect that he is worshiped by devotees all over the world. An adviser and friend to the Pandavas, he constantly directs them to the path of dharma—never more than when Arjuna, facing family and friends across the battlefield at Kurukshetra, loses the will to fight.

KUBERA
Ruler of Alakapuri, Kubera was the king of Yakshas, the guardian spirits of all things in nature.

KUNTI
Elder queen and wife of Pandu, the king of Hastinapur, Kunti was the sister of Vasudeva, Krishna's father. As a young girl she was granted a blessing that enabled her to call upon any god to father a son with her. When still an unmarried girl, she had called upon Surya, the sun god, and fearing for her reputation, abandoned the child that was born. When her husband was unable to father children, she used this blessing for herself and Madri, Pandu's second wife, to give Pandu five sons.

L

LAKSHMANI
Lakshmani was the daughter of Duryodhana, the eldest Kaurava. She was married to Samba, Krishna's son.

LOMASHA
A Brahman sage who accompanied the Pandavas on the various pilgrimages they made. He told many stories to teach them valuable lessons on life and kingship.

A 20TH-CENTURY OPAQUE WATERCOLOR ON CLOTH DEPICTING KRISHNA PLAYING HIS FLUTE

M

MADHAVI
The daughter of King Yayati, Madhavi was given to Sage Galava by her father to help him get the eight hundred white horses, with one black ear, that Galava's guru, Vishwamitra, had demanded from him.

MADRI
Princess of the Madra kingdom, Madri was the sister of King Shalya and the second wife of King Pandu of Hastinapur. She was the mother of the twins Nakula and Sahadeva, the youngest Pandavas. Madri sat in the funeral pyre of her husband and gave up her life, leaving her sons to be brought up by Pandu's senior wife, Kunti.

MANU
Manu was the son of Surya, the sun god, and the first king of humans. Manu had two sons, Sudyumna and Ikshavaku. As Ila, Sudyumna married Budh, the moon god's child, and their descendants came to be known as Chandravamshis and also as Ailas. Ikshavaku's descendants came to be known as Suryavamshis, or the solar line.

MARKANDEYA
A Rishi who, over the many years of his life, had witnessed the events that inspired the Mahabharata that Vyasa composed.

MATALI
Indra's charioteer whose daughter was betrothed to marry Sumukha. One day, Garuda, the king of the birds, arrogantly insisted on eating Sumukha, refusing to heed to Matali's pleas. Finally, Matali invoked Indra, king of the Devas, who humbled Garuda by placing a hand on his shoulder which the king of birds, try as he might, could not shake.

MAYA
After the burning of Kandavaprastha, Maya, the architect of the Asuras, came to the Pandavas. In exchange for his life, he agreed to build them a great city, which they named Indraprastha.

MAYURDHVAJ
A great devotee of Vishnu, Mayurdhvaj was the king of Ratnapur. When Yudhishthira held the horse sacrifice, Mayurdhvaj formed a plan to meet the god in person. He captured the sacrificial horse as it crossed his kingdom, knowing that when Arjuna came to its rescue, Krishna, who was Vishnu incarnate, would come with him.

MOHINI
A female form taken by Krishna to fulfil Iravan's last wish before he was sacrificed to ensure victory for the Pandavas at Kurukshetra. Iravan wanted to die a married man—one who had experienced a woman as a wife. As no woman would marry a man destined to die the next morning, Krishna transformed himself into a woman and, as Mohini, married Iravan.

N

NAHUSHA
A great king, Nahusha had earned the right to be made temporary ruler of Swarga while Indra was away. Nahusha was turned into a python when he kicked a sage in impatience. He was cursed to remain in that form until he learned the true meaning of Brahman from a descendant called Yudhishthira.

NAKULA
The older of the twins born to Pandu's second wife Madri, Nakula was the fourth Pandava. He was fathered by the Ashwin Twins, the Devas summoned by Kunti's blessing. Nakula was considered to be the most handsome man in the world. After the Kurukshetra War, Nakula and Sahadeva were made rulers of Madra, their maternal grandfather's kingdom.

NALA
The ruler of Nishada, Nala was Damayanti's husband. Much like Yudhishthira, he lost his kingdom in a game of dice and had to go into exile. Damyanti went with him.

NALAYANI
According to legend, in a previous life, Draupadi was Nalayani, the wife of a sage named Maudgalya. Her insatiable appetite for sexual pleasures caused her husband to curse her—that in another life she would be the wife of many men.

P

PANDU
Born of Ambalika with Vyasa, Pandu was the son of Vichitravirya and ascended the throne of Hastinapur. He was married to Kunti, the adoptive daughter of Kuntibhoja, and Madri, the princess of Madra. Pandu renounced his kingdom and went into the

forest to live as an ascetic after a sage named Kindama cursed him with death should he ever touch a woman. His five sons, known as the Pandavas, were fathered by different gods called by a blessing that his senior wife Kunti had been granted as a young girl.

PARASARA
A powerful sage, Parasara was the father of Krishna Dwaipayana, who later came to be known as Vyasa, the composer of the Mahabharata. His grandfather Vashishtha was one of the seven Rishis who heard the Vedas first.

PARASHURAMA
A Brahman, Parashurama held a grudge against all Kshatriyas. He had at one time decimated five great Kshatriya clans and swore to kill every Kshatriya who crossed his path. A great warrior-priest, he was highly skilled with weapons and in the art of warfare. He was one of Bhishma's teachers and also Drona's.

PARIKSHIT
Born to Uttari and Abhimanyu, Parikshit was Arjuna's grandson—the only child of the Pandavas to survive the war at Kurukshetra. He had been protected by Krishna from the weapon unleashed by Ashwatthama which could have killed him in his mother's womb. Yudhishthira crowned Parikshit as his successor when the Pandavas left Hastinapur for the Himalayas on their journey to Swarga. Janamejaya was Parikshit's son.

PARVATI
Parvati is the wife of the Hindu god Shiva—the regenerator of the universe. She is the mother of deities Ganesha and Kartikeya.

PRAMILA
The queen of the city of Naripur that stood in the middle of an enchanted grove. A curse prevented any woman from leaving the city until she was married, but any male who entered the grove became female.

PRATIPA
A Kuru ancestor and Bhishma's grandfather, Pratipa renounced the world for the forest as soon as his son, Shantanu, was old enough to rule.

PRATIVINDHYA
Yudhishthira's son and one of the five children of Draupadi, Prativindhya was killed by Ashwatthama at the end of the Kurukshetra War.

PRITHU
An ancient king, Prithu is said to be an aspect of Vishnu. Once, the earth, distressed by over-exploitation, assumed the form of a cow and went to Prithu for help and justice. In response, the king established the code of conduct, or a way of life, called dharma. To live in accordance with dharma, the strong had to look after the weak instead of exploiting them.

PURURAVA
As the son of Budh and Ila, Pururava was the first Chandravamshi. He married an Apsara, a river nymph named Urvashi. Heartbroken when she returned to Swarga, he gave up his kingdom to wander riverbanks in search of her.

PUTANA
Daughter of the Asura Bali, Putana was sent by Krishna's maternal uncle, Kansa, to kill him when he was just a baby.

R

RAMA
The son of Kaushalya and Dasharatha, Rama is the lead character of the Ramayana. His life story is narrated to Yudhishthira by Rishis when Yudhishthira bemoans his fate as an exile.

REVATA
The ruler of the island city of Dwaraka, Revata gave his kingdom to Balarama on his marriage to the princess Revati and invited the Yadavas to settle there.

RUKMINI
One of Krishna's wives, Rukmini was the princess of Vidarbha. Krishna abducted her when she appealed to him to save her from the loveless marriage that her brother had arranged for her.

A 12TH-CENTURY SCULPTURE OF RUKMINI, KRISHNA'S WIFE

S

SACHI
Considered to be an aspect of Lakshmi, the goddess of fortune, Sachi is wife of Indra, who rules over Amravati.

SAHADEVA
The youngest of the five Pandavas, Sahadeva was one of the twins born to Madri, fathered by the Ashwini twins, the lords of the morning and evening star. He is said to have complete knowledge of all events in the past and those that would occur in the future. He was instructed by Krishna not to reveal his knowledge until asked a direct question and even then, to answer with another question.

SAIRANDHRI
The name adopted by Draupadi when she disguised herself as a maid and served Queen Sudeshna, wife of King Virata, of the Matsya kingdom, during the thirteenth year of the Pandavas' exile when they were required to remain hidden.

SAMBA
Krishna's son by his wife Jambavati, Samba was married to Duryodhana's daughter Lakshmani. It was a prank he played on the maharishis that invited a curse on the Yadavas that would destroy the entire clan.

SANJAY
Charioteer to King Dhritarashtra, Sanjay had the gift of divine sight. He could see every detail of the battle at Kurukshetra and narrate it to the blind King Dhritarashtra and his blindfolded wife, Gandhari.

SARMISHTHA
Daughter of Vishaparva, king of the Asuras, she married King Yayati. Their son Puru was an ancestor of the Kauravas and the Pandavas.

SATSOMA
Bhima's son, and one of the five children of the Pandavas from Draupadi. Satsoma and his brothers were sleeping when they were killed by an angry Ashwatthama.

SATYAKI
A Yadava warrior, Satyaki was Arjuna's student and remained loyal to the Pandavas despite the fact that Krishna had promised his army to Duryodhana.

SATYAVAN
A woodcutter, Satyavan married Savitri, the daughter of King Ashwapati. A year after their marriage, Satyavan died. Unable to bear the loss, Savitri followed Yama, the god of death, until she was able to bring her husband back to life.

SATYAVATI
Known as Matsyagandha at one time because her body reeked of fish, Satyavati was the daughter of a King Uparichara but was raised by fisherfolk. She agreed to marry King Shantanu, who had fallen in love with her, on the condition that her children would inherit the throne. This request led Devavrata, Shantanu's son from his wife, Ganga, to renounce his claim to the throne, and take the vow that gave him the name "Bhishma."

SAVITRI
The only child of King Ashwapati, Savitri fell in love with a woodcutter named Satyavan and married him. Satyavan died a year later. Savitri saw Yama, the god of death, take his life away and decided to follow him, eventually succeeding in getting Satyavan back to life.

SHAKTI
The feminine personification of dynamic cosmic energy, the goddess Shakti is the consort of Shiva, god of destruction. She is Devi, the feminine creative power of the universe and the strength and power upon which Shiva.

SHAKUNI
A prince of Gandhara, Shakuni was Gandhari's brother and the uncle and chief adviser of the Kaurava princes. After the death of his father and brothers, who had been imprisoned by Bhishma, he came to live with his sister in Hastinapur. Shakuni developed a close bond with Duryodhana, who did not realize that his uncle had a vested interest in bringing about the ruin of the Kurus to avenge the deaths of his father and brothers. It was Shakuni who rolled the dice in the fateful game that ended with Draupadi's humiliation and the Pandavas exile.

SHAKUNTALA
Shakuntala was the daughter of Sage Kaushika and an Apsara named Menaka. Abandoned at birth, she was found by Sage Kanva who brought her up at his hermitage in a forest. Married to King Dushyanta, Shakuntata was the mother of the illustrious king Bharata.

SHALYA
Brother of Madri and the ruler of Madra kingdom, Shalya was an ally of the Pandavas but was tricked into fighting for the Kauravas. He was killed in the Kurukshetra battle by Yudhishthira. After his death, the kingdom of Madra was inherited by his nephews, the Pandava twins Nakula and Sahadeva.

SHANTANU
The great-grandfather of the Pandavas and Kauravas, Shantanu was Bhishma's father. It was to enable Shantanu to remarry that Bhishma took the vow of celibacy.

SHATANIKA
Draupadi's son by Nakula, Shatanika was one of the five Pandava children killed by Ashwatthama as they slept.

SHIKHANDI
Born as a daughter to King Drupada of Panchala, in answer to his prayers to Shiva for a son who would kill Bhishma, Shikhandi was Amba reborn. As Amba she had held Bhishma responsible for ruining her life by abducting her and refusing to marry her. Unable to avenge herself in her first life, Amba underwent penance until Shiva granted her the blessing to be the cause of Bhishma's death in her next life. Shikhandi was brought up as a boy by Drupada, trained in the art of warfare, and even married to a woman. As prophesied, she did become a man and joined the Pandavas at Kurukshetra to fulfil the reason for her rebirth. Refusing to accept her as a man, Bhishma lowered his weapons and was wounded by Arjuna's arrows that he shot while standing behind Shikhandi.

SHISHUPALA
The King of Chedi, Shishupala was an ally of Kansa and Jarasandha. He harbored a particular hatred against his cousin Krishna for abducting and marrying Rukmini, when she was betrothed to him. Krishna had promised Shishupala's mother that he would forgive a hundred misdemeanors and insults by her son but no more. Shishupala overstepped that mark, and Krishna lost no time in beheading him with the Sudarshana Chakra.

SHIVA
As the god of destruction, Shiva is the third aspect of cosmic energy personified in the Hindu triad that includes Brahma the creator, and Vishnu the preserver. Shiva resides on Mount Kailash with his consort, Parvati.

SHRUTASENA
One of Draupadi's five children, Shrutasena was Sahadeva's son. He and his brothers were killed by Ashwatthama, who mistook their sleeping forms to be the five Pandavas.

SITA
The wife of Rama, King of Ayodhya, Sita accompanied her exiled husband into a forest. Sage Markandeya narrated the story of Rama and Sita to the Pandavas when Yudhishthira lamented being the cause of his family's distress.

SUDESHNA
Wife of King Virata, Sudeshna was the queen of Matsya. Draupadi served as her maid during the thirteenth year of exile.

SUDHANVA
Youngest son of the king of Champakapuri, Sudhanva could not be seen on the battlefield as his father fought Arjuna to prevent the sacrificial horse from entering his kingdom. The punishment for any man not seen on the field was to be boiled in oil. Sudhanva appealed to Krishna for protection and survived unhurt.

SURATHA
The eldest son of Hamsadhvaj, king of Champakapuri, Suratha led his father's army against Arjuna in an attempt to prevent the sacrificial horse from entering the kingdom. He fought so ferociously that his body continued to fight even when his head was chopped off. This so impressed the gods that they took Suratha's head and offered it to Shiva, who wears a garland made of the heads of warriors who die valiantly on the battlefield.

AN 18TH-CENTURY PAINTING FROM BAHU, JAMMU AND KASHMIR, INDIA, SHOWING SITA IN A FOREST

SUVALA
The father of Gandhari and Shakuni, Suvala was the ruler of the kingdom of Gandhara. He and his sons were imprisoned by Bhishma over a perceived insult. Realizing that they would all die of slow starvation, Suvala chose to save one of his sons. Only the youngest, Shakuni, was allowed to eat—and live to avenge the deaths of the others. Suvala instructed Shakuni to use the bones of his fingers after he was dead to make a set of dice. The dice would roll to Shakuni's command, enabling him to win every stake. These were the dice that Shakuni used against Yudhishthira to deprive the Pandavas of all their possessions.

T

TAKSHAKA
Takshaka was the king of the Nagas. Left orphaned and homeless after the burning of the Khandava forest by the Pandavas, he had sworn to take revenge, either on Arjuna or one of his descendants. When Arjuna's grandson Parikshit was cursed to die of snakebite within seven days by a sage he insulted, it was Takshaka who delivered the fatal bite.

TANTIPALA
In the last year of their exile, when the Pandavas had to remain undiscovered, the youngest of the Pandavas, Sahadeva, disguised himself as a cattle physician named Tantipala and took care of the cows owned by King Virata of Matsya.

TARA
Goddess of the stars, Tara was the wife of Brishaspati, the god of the planet Jupiter. She fell in love with Chandra, the moon god, and had a child with him. This child was Budh, whose children became the first of Chandravamshis.

TRINAVARTA
A demon, Trinavarta took the form of a gust of wind and tried to kill baby Krishna by overturning the cradle in which he slept. Krishna caught him by the neck and choked him so tightly that the gust turned into a gentle breeze, lulling him back to sleep.

U

ULUPI
The Naga wife of Arjuna, Ulupi was the mother of Arjuna's son Iravan, who was sacrificed on the fifth day of the Kurukshetra War to ensure victory for the Pandavas. She saved Arjuna's life when he was fatally wounded by his son Babruvahana of Manipur. Ulupi healed the wound using the Nagamani—a magical gem that had the power to restore life.

UPARICHARA
King Uparichara was the father of Matsyagandha (later known as Satyavati) and grandfather of Vyasa, the biological father of Dhritarashtra, Pandu, and Vidura.

URVASHI
An Apsara, or water nymph, Urvashi married King Pururava, an ancestor of the Kurus.

UTTANAKA
The chief priest who conducted the snake sacrifice for King Janamejaya of Hastinapur.

UTTARA
Prince of Matsya kingdom, Uttara was the son of King Virata, at whose court the Pandavas spent the last year of exile in disguise. Volunteering to stay and guard the city while his father took the warriors in search of lost cows, he found himself confronting Duryodhana and the Hastinapur army at the border of Matsya. Arjuna came forward to help him, in his disguise as the eunuch Brihannala.

UTTARI
Daughter of King Virata and sister of Uttara, she learned music and dance from the eunuch Brihannala during the year the Pandavas served at the Matsya court. She was offered in marriage to Arjuna by a grateful Virata when Brihannala's disguise was revealed after his son's

victory over Duryodhana's forces at the border. Uttari eventually married Arjuna's son, Abhimanyu.

V

VAISHAMPAYANA
Called upon to narrate the tale of his ancestors at the Sarpa Sattra, or snake sacrifice, organized by King Janamejaya. A great-grandson of Arjuna, Vaishampayana was a student of Vyasa and had heard his teacher recite the original "Jaya," or the "tale of victory," which later came to be known as the Mahabharata.

VAJRANABHI
The son of Aniruddha and great-grandson of Krishna, Vajranabhi rose to become the great king of Mathura, where Arjuna settled the survivors of the Yadava clan after the death of Krishna and the destruction of Dwaraka.

VARUNA
One of the oldest Hindu deities, once revered as the supreme god, Varuna is the god of water and the sustainer of life on earth. His domain includes lakes, rivers, seas, oceans as well as clouds and rain.

VASUDEVA
Krishna's father and the Pandavas' maternal uncle, Vasudeva, along with his wife Devaki, was imprisoned by Kansa, the ruler of Mathura. His children were killed as soon as they were born because oracles had foretold that Kansa would be killed by his sister's eighth child. When the eighth child, Krishna, was born, Vasudeva was able to carry him safely to Gokul, where he grew up as the child of Nanda and Yashoda.

VASUKI
The king of Nagas, Vasuki is draped around Shiva's neck as a necklace. He was the rope the Devas and the Asuras used to churn the ocean of milk with Mount Mandara and extract the ambrosia of immortality. When the Kauravas poisoned Bhima and threw him into the river, he was rescued by the Nagas and taken to Vasuki. The king welcomed him as a relative, a descendant of Yadu who had married a Naga princess.

VATSALA
The daughter of Krishna's brother Balarama, Vatsala was to marry Duryodhana's son Lakshman, but had fallen in love with Abhimanyu, Arjuna's son. She appealed to her uncle, Krishna, who got Bhima's son Ghatotkacha to abduct her and arrange for her to marry Abhimanyu.

VAYU
The god of the winds. Pandu of Hastinapur asked his wife Kunti to call upon him to father their second child as he is believed to be the father of the mightiest of gods—Hanuman. Pandu hoped for a son with similar strength.

VEDA VYASA
The son of Parasara and grandson of Vashishtha, one of the seven Rishis to whom the hymns of the Vedas were first recited. He was named Krishna Dwaipayana and came to be known as Veda Vyasa after he grouped the Vedic hymns into four classifications—Rig, Yajura, Sama, and Atharva. He then composed *Jaya* in an effort to transcribe the abstract philosophical truths that comprise the Vedas as simple stories that could be understood by all. Over time, this original narration evolved into the epic, the Mahabharata.

VIDURA
Vidura was half-brother to the Kuru princes Dhritarashtra and Pandu. Of the three children fathered by Sage Vyasa to ensure an heir to Vichitravirya, Vidura was the most capable, renowned for his wisdom and sense of justice. However, his mother was not one of Vichitravirya's queens, but a maid. So, although he was raised by Bhishma with his half-brothers, he could not be made king. He remained the royal adviser, steadfast in following dharma and loyal to Hastinapur.

VIKARNA
The youngest son of Dhritarashtra and Gandhari, Vikarna was the only Kaurava to question his eldest brother's actions during the dice game. Although he fought on the Kaurava side in the war, when he met his death, at Bhima's hands, the Pandavas mourned him.

VIRATA
The ruler of Matsya Kingdom, where the Pandavas spent the last year of their exile disguised as his servants. His daughter Uttari married Abhimanyu, Arjuna's son, and his grandson Parikshit succeeded Yudhishthira to the throne of Hastinapur. Virata fought for the Pandavas in the Kurukshetra War during which he was killed by Drona.

VISHAPARVA
King of the Asuras, Vishaparva was the father of Sarmishtha who married Yayati, an ancestor of the Kurus.

VITATHA
The adopted son of the great king Bharata, Vitatha was fathered by Brihaspati, the god of the planet Jupiter. Vitatha grew up to be an extremely capable ruler and was crowned king by Bharata, who believed that merit was a greater claim to kingship than bloodline.

Y

YAMA
Said to be the god of death, Yama is also known as Dharma, the god of order. A dispassionate god who oversees death and destiny, Yama ensures that the law of karma is meticulously implemented on the basis of merit and demerits earned in life.

YADU
The founder of the Yadava clan and Krishna's ancestor, Yadu was the elder son of Yayati by his wife Devayani, the daughter of Shukra, priest of the Asuras. Yadu had refused his father's request to accept a curse and suffer on his behalf. Banished by his father, with the curse that neither he nor any of his descendants would ever be king, Yadu settled in Mathura, a Naga kingdom ruled by a council, after marrying a Naga woman.

YASHODA
As the one who brought up Krishna as a child in Gokul, Yashoda is given the status of being his mother. She was the wife of Nanda, whose sister Rohini was married to Vasudeva. When Krishna was born, Vasudeva carried him to Gokul and exchanged him with Yashoda's newborn girl.

YAYATI
A learned king and a great scholar of the Vedas, Yayati was a Kuru ancestor. He married Devayani, the daughter of Shukra, priest of the Asuras, but was also attracted to her maid, Sharmishtha, and married her in secret. For this duplicity, Shukra cursed him with immediate loss of his youth. Yayati would become old and impotent unless one of his sons accepted the curse in his stead, which his younger son Puru agreed to do. He gave his daughter Madhavi to Sage Galava when he was unable to give the Sage the eight hundred horses he had requested.

YUDHISHTHIRA
The eldest son of King Pandu and Kunti, Yudhishthira was fathered by Yama, the god of dharma and death. Even though his weakness for gambling cost the Pandavas their kingdom and led to thirteen years of exile, Yudhishthira is the model of dharma.

YUYUTSU
Dhritarashtra's son by the maid Sugadha, Yuyutsu did not approve of Duryodhana's actions at the dice game, and fought on the Pandavas' side in the Kurukshetra War. He was the only son of Dhritarashtra to survive, and he became the regent of Hastinapur when Yudhishthira abdicated the throne in favor of Parikshit.

A 17TH-CENTURY OPAQUE WATERCOLOR-AND-GOLD ON PAPER, SHOWING YASHODA AND KRISHNA

The **Mahabharata** in **Art**

The impact that this great epic had on the cultural milieu of the subcontinent is apparent not only in the vast quantity of literature it inspired, but also in the visual and performing arts of the region.

Over the centuries, the skill of the hands that is a vital element of cultural aesthetic has continued to evolve and reinvent itself. It has absorbed myriad influences that have inspired the potter and painter, sculptor, and weaver to perfect their craft and collectively contributing to a rich and vibrant heritage.

Within this vast heritage, the Mahabharata finds exuberant expression in all styles—classical, popular, folk and tribal. There are representations and interpretations of both events and characters; visualizations of fantastic realms and beasts; renderings of beautiful, seductive women, all inspired by the evocative words that Ganesha wrote—and this does not include the colossal repository of devotional art that is Krishna-inspired. Even today, there are contemporary artists who find inspiration in the stirring and heroic events detailed in an epic composed so long ago.

BIKANER SCHOOL
Mughal miniatures deeply influenced the schools of painting that flourished in the Rajput princely states from the 17th century onward. What differed, however, were the themes, which ranged from the mythological and devotional to the romantic. Artists in Bikaner were renowned for their delicate workmanship and lyrical portrayal of feminine beauty.

MUGHAL MINIATURES
With the Mughals came a new genre of painting that used Persian influences to create a highly individual style. Supported by imperial patronage, groups of Hindu and Muslim artists working in specific established ateliers created illustrated manuscripts, portraits, and battle scenes that are remarkable for their exquisite detail.

MEWAR SCHOOL
Early Rajput paintings grew from illustrated Jain and Hindu sacred texts. But with the impact of Mughal miniatures, each state developed its own individual style. Paintings from Udaipur in western India are notable for their grandeur and the detailed compositions rendered in brilliant colors such as lacquer red and saffron yellow.

PICHHWAI

These painted wall hangings form the backdrop for the idol of Shrinathji, an aspect of the young Krishna, the main deity of the temple town of Nathdwara in western India. The pastoral setting of many pichhwais bring to life Krishna's days as a cowherd, surrounded by dewy-eyed cows adorned with henna handprints and decorated horns.

THANJAVUR PAINTING

This highly decorative art form developed from the 18th century onward in the southern Indian kingdom of Thanjavur (Tanjore) in Tamil Nadu. In this elaborate process, layers of cloth are pasted on wooden boards; then certain features such as architecture, draperies, and jewelery are embossed and ornamented with gold leaf, colored glass, and semi-precious stones. Hindu deities, courtly scenes, and royal portraits are some of the subjects depicted.

KERALA MURALS

In the southern state of Kerala, walls of temples and palaces are covered with highly stylized figures and scenes from religious and mythological stories. Their visual impact is greater because of the use of jewel-like colors, the intricate detailing of decorative elements, and verdant green of the surrounding vegetation.

KALIGHAT PAINTINGS

Believed to be the first genuine school of modern Indian painting, this genre developed between the 19th and early 20th centuries, initially sold as mementos to pilgrims visiting the Kali temple in the eastern city of Kolkata. The paintings portrayed the Hindu pantheon, episodes from the great epics, as well as scenes from everyday life.

UDUPI
This scene from the battle at Kurushetra, at the Sri Krishna Temple in Udupi, southern India, has all the characteristic features of traditional Karnataka arts and crafts, including the headgear, which is typical of the regional Yakshagana theater performances.

TIBETAN
Buddhist deities and episodes from their lives are the focus of Thangka paintings so integral to the spiritual lives of devotees. The continuity in mythology and concepts across traditions reflect the importance of the Himalayan region to the spiritual culture of the entire subcontinent.

RAJA RAVI VARMA
The first Indian artist to paint in oil on canvas, Raja Ravi Varma was a pioneer of the Academy school of painting, a style hitherto unknown in the country. A vast body of the artist's work illustrates events from the Hindu mythology. So popular were his paintings that he set up a press to print copies (oleographs) for mass distribution.

MADHUBANI
Traditionally, women from the Mithila region, on the border of India and Nepal, decorated the walls of the kohbar ghar (nuptial chamber) with paintings celebrating life, love, and marital bliss. Divine couples and symbols of prosperity and fertility, such as the fish, feature prominently.

CHITRAKATHI PAINTINGS

Used as graphic accompaniment to storytelling by the Chitrakathi community of Maharashtra in western India, this vibrant folk art form added a dramatic visual reference to the narration of the feats of legendary heroes.

PATTACHITRA

Painted by a community of painters called Chitrakar, these religious paintings on cloth from the Puri district of Odisha in eastern India play an important role in the rituals of the Jagannath Temple. Although the most popular subject is Krishna, as Lord Jagannath, his brother Balabhadra, and their sister Subhadra, the paintings also feature stories from the epics.

PADMANABHAPURAM

The palace of the former rulers of Travancore in Kerala, in southern India, is an outstanding example of Kerala's architecture in wood. In addition to its acclaimed architectural features, there are murals and paintings of gods and goddesses executed in a flamboyant manner in the attempt to make them more divine.

GANDHARVA
Besides the main pantheon of Hindu deities, the sculptor also created a series of subsidiary divinities, including mythical beasts, dvarapalas, (gatekeepers), and Gandharvas.

BAS-RELIEF
This bas-relief from Angkor Wat in Cambodia is based on the Mahabharata. The exterior facades of temples are profusely covered with carvings that are visual interpretations of Hindu mythology glorifying the triumphs of gods and heroes.

CAVE TEMPLES
Rock-cut temples—entire hillsides chiseled to create shrines—are a tribute to the genius and dedication of the stonecutter. The Badami group of temples (6th–7th century), in southern India, are filled with carved pillars and large decorative panels on the walls as well as ceilings.

THE FEMALE FORM
Seductive and languorous maidens, whether goddesses, attendants, Apsaras, or courtesans, have been captured in stone in a range of poses, conveying different moods: at her toilette; gazing into a mirror; applying collyrium to her eyes; combing her tresses.

CONTEMPORARY ART
The Mahabharata has also inspired contemporary Indian artists such as Jitendra Sutar, whose copper statue of Karna, entitled "Vedh," portrays the tragic hero in the powerful stance of an archer, poised to release an arrow.

BRONZE CASTING

This ancient tradition is a perfect example of the lost wax technique in which a wax model is first made and then covered in a mold. The wax is then melted and replaced with a molten alloy of five metals (copper, tin, lead, silver, gold). After cooling, the mould is broken and the image finished and polished.

SANDSTONE PANEL

Sacred imagery and decorative motifs carved in relief adorn the walls and interiors of temples all over the country, transforming them into visual directories of the vast galaxy of Hindu gods and goddesses and the innumerable legends associated with them.

WOODEN STATUE

A typical example of the art that emerged in the early twentieth century. The mythological inspiration as well as influence of traditional sculpture is visible, but the deviation from classical form and the touch of calendar art is also apparent.

STONE SCULPTURES

The Chandela temples (9th–10th century) at Khajuraho, central India, are remarkable for the exuberance and density of their sculptural imagery. Divine beings, attendant deities, warriors, Apsaras, amorous couples, and mythical animals fill the walls and ceilings in a glorious visual representation of epic times.

MANIPURI DANCE
Characterized by gentle gliding movements and refined gestures, this deeply devotional, classical dance form hails from the northeastern state of Manipur, India. It is particularly well known for its expressions of the Raas Leela, Krishna's cosmic dance with the gopis of Gokul.

BHARATANATYAM
This classical dance form from southern India is traditionally performed by devadasis (temple dancers) within the sanctum sanctorum of temples of Tamil Nadu. A range of subtle eye and hand movements and poses comprises the vocabulary of communication.

KATHAKALI
This elaborate dance-drama from the southern Indian state of Kerala brings legend, mythology, and spiritual ideas to the people in public performances. Traditionally performed by an all-male cast, it is remarkable for its vivid costumes, headgear, and makeup, which can take up to four hours to apply.

WAYANG
Shadow plays from Java, Indonesia, use highly stylized handcrafted leather and wooden puppets mounted on bamboo sticks, projected on a white screen, while the dalang (master-puppeteer) narrates local adaptations of the Mahabharata.

THEYYAM DANCE

Unique to the north Malabar region of Kerala, southern India, Theyyam is performed by an all-male cast. Clad in extravagant costumes, masks, and towering, sculptural mudi (headdresses), they enthrall audiences with the virtuosity of their movements as they enact the godly deeds of the divinities they portray.

TERUKKUTTU

Stories from the Mahabharata, especially those that feature Draupadi, form the repertoire of this street theater from Tamil Nadu. Open-air performances in front of shrines are conducted by a sutradhar (narrator) who acts as the master of ceremonies, introducing the characters, joking, and commenting on current events and more. The actors sing and dance to the accompaniment of drums, cymbals, and other instruments.

CHHAU

There are three distinct forms of this martial dance form from rural eastern India—Mayaurbhanj, Purulia, and Saraikela—with the latter two using masks to represent the specific character being portrayed. These range from valiant mythological figures to animals and birds.

PANDAVANI

With a simple ektara (single-stringed instrument) in one hand, and kartal (wooden clapper) in the other, the lead singer of this folk tradition from Chhattisgarh, in central India, brings alive the exploits of the five Pandava brothers.

Glossary

ADHARMA Literally taken to mean unrighteousness, adharma is anything that goes against dharma—the correct path. It is anything that upsets the natural order of life or results in disorder in the universe.

AMARAVATI The capital city of Swarga, paradise of the gods, which is ruled by Indra, the king of the gods. This is where the souls of the meritorious await rebirth.

APSARA Water nymphs, young women of great grace and beauty, who reside in Swarga and serve in the court of Indra, the king of the gods. They are excellent dancers and are often the companions of Gandharvas, or celestial musicians.

ARDHA-NARESHWARA The composite form of the god Shiva and his consort Parvati, which symbolizes the fusion of the intrinsic duality present in all nature. The half-male and half-female figure represents the two energies of the universe, masculine (purusha/man) and feminine (prakriti/nature), that are discrete but inseparable—complete and productive only when united.

ARTHA SHASTRA The shastras are ancient Indian treatises, each on a particular subject or field of knowledge. The Artha Shastra deals with governance, economics, and military strategy.

ASHRAMA According to ancient Hindu scriptures, a man's life could be divided into four stages or ashramas—brahmachaari (student), grihastha (householder), vanaprastha (retirement), and sannyasa (renunciation). Each of these was defined by a way of life that it was his duty (dharma) to follow.

ASURAS These are beings who reside in a world under the earth. As they are hostile to humans, the Asuras are also referred to as demons. The Asuras and the Devas, or gods, are engaged in a constant struggle for power and supremacy.

ASHWAMEDHA A ritual sacrifice performed by kings in ancient India to reiterate sovereignty. It involved the selection and sanctifying of a flawless stallion, which was then let loose to wander at will. The stallion was followed by a small company of warriors. Any ruler who challenged the king's sovereignty by preventing the stallion from entering his territory was attacked. At the end of a year, if no ruler had managed to capture and kill the stallion, it was brought back and sacrificed.

ASTRA A weapon that is thrown or launched—a missile. In the Kurukshetra War, both sides used astras charged with destructive powers beyond the ordinary. In some, destructive energies were invoked through the incantation of hymns, but there were also other astras that were divine in themselves, gifted by the gods in appreciation of a service, and the practice of severe penance or austerities.

ATMAN A central concept of Hindu thought, the word atman is often translated as "soul." It refers to the eternal non-material Self that is distinct from both the mind and the body. Atman is present in all creation and is the same as the essential energy of the cosmos. Caught in the cycle of birth and death, the atman is reborn time after time; its physical form is governed by merits or demerits accumulated over past lives.

AVATAR The concept of an avatar in Hinduism refers to the reincarnation on earth of a deity. As the preserver of life in the Hindu triad, it is Vishnu who takes birth on earth whenever dharma is threatened. Nine avatars of Vishnu have come and gone, Krishna among them; a tenth is awaited.

BHAGAVAD GITA Often referred to as the Gita, the Bhagavad Gita summarizes the core concepts of Hindu philosophy in 700 verses divided over 18 chapters. Composed as a dialogue between the Pandava prince Arjuna and his charioteer Krishna, it is set in a timeless moment on the battlefield of Kurukshetra within the context of the Mahabharata. Though an essential part of that narrative, the Gita is more often read and studied on its own merit.

BHAGAVATA PURANA The ancient texts known as the Puranas—the term itself means "ancient"—supplement the Vedic scriptures with their detailed discussions on subjects that range from cosmology to music and dance. The Bhagavata Purana is one of 18 Mahapuranas. It extols absolute devotion (bhakti) to Vishnu in his Krishna avatar as the path to moksha—the ultimate liberation. The text is the source of many tales of Krishna as a mischievous child and has heavily influenced the arts and popular culture of India.

BHAIRAVA (GOD) A fierce aspect of the god Shiva, Bhairava is a guardian of a cardinal direction. In all, there are sixty-four Bhairavas, all manifestations of the one supreme Kaal Bhairava who is the keeper of time of the universe.

BRAHMACHARYA First of the four stages (ashramas) of a man's life as divided by the scriptures. During this time it was the individual's primary duty to learn the skills required for him to follow the vocation practiced by his family and ancestors. Celibacy was intrinsic to this stage, which lasted until marriage made him a householder.

BRAHMAN The focal metaphysical concept of Hindu philosophical thought, Brahman has been defined in many different ways. It is the essence of the universe; the cosmic principle within and behind all existence; the ultimate unchanging reality; the absolute consciousness.

BRAHMAN In the ancient system of social organization known as varna, the Brahman is a member of the priestly caste. Brahmans are the repositories of knowledge and the only ones who can perform yagnas and rituals to appease the gods.

CHANDRAVAMSHIS The Mahabharata narrates the story of the descendants of Chandra, lord of the moon, who were known as Chandravamshis. Influenced by the emotional, passionate nature of their ancestor, the moon, kings of this line were by nature volatile and temperamental.

CHIRANJEEVI A person who cannot die, who will be alive until the end of the current Kali Yuga, and therefore, an immortal.

DANA DHARMA The virtue of generosity, the act of giving without expecting returns, is highly esteemed in Hindu tradition and considered essential to living righteously or following dharma. It is not only the material that can be given as dana—the gift of knowledge, time, compassion, as well as food, water, clothing, all comprise dana. Following the path of dana dharma is also a valid path to ultimate liberation (moksha).

DARSHAN A glimpse or view of something auspicious or sacred. It is possible to have a darshan of a saintly person, a deity in a temple, or God. To have received darshan is to have been blessed.

DEVA Heavenly or divine beings who live in the higher worlds. Though friendly and supportive of humans, the Devas need to be regularly appeased with prayers and offerings. The feminine form of a Deva is a Devi.

DHARMA Hindu scriptures define dharma as being a way of life that follows the path of righteous conduct in thought, word, and action. The objective of dharma is the attainment of moksha or ultimate liberation. However, proper conduct can differ depending on the context—what is dharma in one situation may be adharma (unrighteous) in another. The path of dharma, therefore, is not a singular one; it cannot be prescribed but involves conscious choices to be made by individuals in daily life.

GANDHARVAS Heavenly beings of great physical beauty who play the role of musicians and singers for the Devas at Indra's court in Amravati. On earth, they prefer woodlands and forests. Gandharvas marry Apsaras.

GANDIVA Made by the Creator Brahma himself from the heavenly tree called the Gandi, the Gandiva was a bow of tremendous proportions, said to be so heavy that no ordinary mortal could wield it. It had a hundred and eight strings that rumbled like thunder when pulled and was capable of firing hundreds of arrows simultaneously over long distances. The Gandiva was given to Arjuna by Agni, the god of fire, in gratitude after he was allowed to consume the forest of Khandavaprastha.

GANGA As a goddess, Ganga is the personification of the sacred river, which is believed to have descended from the abode of Brahma, the Creator. To break the impact of the water, Shiva trapped the river in his matted hair, mitigating its flow down the Himalayas as several small streams. As a tangible aspect of cosmic energy, bringing life to all it touches, the Ganga is both pure and purifying.

GRIHASTHA The second of the four stages of life defined as ashramas. Entry to the grihastha ashrama, marked by marriage, ended brahmacharya ashrama. This was the time the individual was expected to spend immersed in worldly affairs. As a householder, it was his duty to garner wealth, have children, perform rituals, and fulfil social responsibilities.

GURU A central figure in Hindu tradition, a guru is a learned man, a teacher, or, in the simplistic meaning of the word, an expert in a particular field of knowledge. Expanded, the term refers to a spiritual guide, one who reveals the meaning and potential of life and shows the path to ultimate self-realization.

GURU DAKSHINA The traditional transaction that ended the period of learning with a guru. It was a donation made to, or demanded by, the guru which was regarded as a symbolic payment for knowledge imparted. Usually a gift of land or cows, guru dakshina could also be in the form of a particular task the guru asked to be performed.

GURU-SHISHYA The relationship between a guru and his disciple. Traditionally, a student would go and live with the guru for the entire period of his education, to both learn and perform service. This close and constant interaction was considered the best way to pass on knowledge, as it facilitated an understanding of both the spirit and substance of the knowledge being imparted.

HARIVAMSHA Also given the status of a Purana, the Harivamsha is an appendix to the Mahabharata that details Vishnu's incarnation as Krishna. The text is divided into three sections—the first, Adi Parva, deals with the creation of the cosmos and what came before the birth of Krishna; the second, Vishnu Parva, describes Krishna's life before the Mahabharata; Bhavishya Parva, the third section, gives a description of Kali Yuga, the future after Krishna.

JAMBUDVIPA The ancient name of the subcontinent. Jambudvipa can literally be translated as the land bounded by water (dvipa) where Jambu (rose-apple) trees flourish.

KAMA Generally translated as desire, kama is the pursuit of personal pleasure, not necessarily physical. It one of the four goals of human life in the Hindu tradition and an essential aspect of the second stage—a grihastha or householder.

KARMA The word karma means "action." However, an action is not an isolated occurrence. Hindu philosophy asserts that every action has a reaction; for every cause there is an effect. This is the basic law of the Universe. The reaction or effect is equal and instantaneous, though it may manifest, and be seen, much later. Thus, an individual's actions in this life forms the basis of one's birth and quality of life in the next.

KAURAVAS The collective name by which the hundred sons of Dhritarashtra and Gandhari are referred in the Mahabharata.

KSHATRIYA One of the four vocation-based divisions of the Hindu caste system. The Kshatriyas were the rulers and warriors, responsible for keeping the peace, dispensing justice, and protecting the rest of society.

MAYA An illusion, anything that seems to be that which it is not. In everyday usage, maya is magic, fraud, trickery. Taken to the level of spirituality, any existence separate from the ultimate reality, that of God, is maya. The world is itself maya, since it projects an illusion of permanence in which reality is defined by the senses of the individual and is, therefore, subjective.

MOKSHA Liberation of the soul (atman) from the cycle of birth and death, which implies a merging of the individual atman with the universal. While they may support varying methods to achieve it, most Hindu traditions agree that moksha is the ultimate goal of life.

NAGA Though the word "naga" is frequently used for any snake, a Naga is the king cobra which is revered. In Indian mythology, Nagas are serpent-like beings who are protectors of nature, particularly bodies of water such as rivers and wells. They are said to guard great treasures.

NARAKA Ruled by Yama, the god of death and dharma, Naraka is the hell to Swarga's heaven. This is where the soul is sent to expatiate the demerits accumulated during a lifetime before being reborn.

NIYOGA Ancient Hindu tradition assigned the paternity of a child to the mother's husband, not to the biological father. The law of Niyoga meant that should a man be infertile or die childless, he could still be assured an heir—more importantly, a son to perform the rites of passage — as his wife could bear him a child with another man.

PANDAVAS The collective title of the five sons of Pandu—Yudhishthira, Bhima, and Arjuna by Kunti and the twins Nakula Sahadeva—by Madri.

PENANCE A translation of the Sanskrit word "prayashchita" used by Hindus to refer to the need to atone for or expatiate sins. Charity, fasting, going a pilgrimage, and performing a prescribed ritual can all be means of penance.

PRITHVI The Sanskrit name for the earth. Prithvi is also deified as a Devi of the same name, the mother who feeds and nurtures all.

RAJASUYA An elaborate ritual performed by kings to establish sovereignty as a public announcement of independence.

RAKSHASA A category of beings who lived in the forests, most Rakshasas were hostile to humans, some even being maneaters. They were powerful warriors, with knowledge of "magic" and illusion.

REINCARNATION Rebirth of the soul of an individual in another form after the death of the physical body.

RISHI Composers of the hymns of the Rig Veda. Rishis were thinkers who devoted themselves to understanding the ultimate truth, metaphysical, spiriual, and religious.

SANNYASA The renunciation of all worldly affairs, attachment, and desires. This was the fourth and last stage of life when, according to the scriptures, the individual spent time in meditation and contemplation of the higher meaning of life.

SATI The ancient Hindu practice in which a widow sacrified herself on her husband's funeral pyre.

SHLOKA A form of verse that lends itself to the oral tradition of transmission of learning. Most classical and post-classical Sanskrit works are composed as couplets of 16 syllables.

SUDARSHANA CHAKRA Considered to be one of the most powerful weapons in Indian mythology, the Sudarshana Chakra is a spinning, disc-like weapon with serrated edges. It was made by Vishwakarma, the architect of the gods, using dust from the sun. Though said to have originally belonged to Shiva, it is primarily identified as Vishnu's weapon of choice.

SURYAVAMSHIS Descendants of Manu, the first human, who was the son of the sun god Surya. The Suryavamshis, known for their level-headed reason and logic, include a number of well-known ruling dynasties including that of Rama, king of Ayodhya, the protagonist of the epic, Ramayana.

SWARGA The celestial home of the Devas ruled over by Indra. In Swarga there is no pain or unhappiness and every desire can be indulged. It is the transitory place for righteous souls awaiting rebirth.

SWAYAMVARA An ancient Hindu practice that allowed a young woman to choose a husband from among a number of eligible suitors invited by her father.

UPANISHADS Written between 800 BCE and 500 BCE, these are a collection of texts that elaborate on the philosophy contained in the Vedas. They discuss the nature of the atman and of the Brahman and other essential philosophical truths, and can be said to be the essence of the Vedas.

VAIKUNTHA The celestial home of Vishnu, the Preserver of the Hindu triad. All who find a place here are content, without anxieties, and in complete harmony with the supreme God.

VANAPRASTHA The third of the four ashramas or stages of Hindu way of life, vanaprastha begins with the birth of the first grandchild. This event indicates the appropriate time to detach oneself from the world and prepare for retirement.

VARNA The system of social organization based on the division of labor established in ancient India. The four overarching groups were Brahmans, the priests or spiritual class; Kshatriyas, the nobility or ruling class; Vaishyas or merchants; and Shudras or servants. Varna dharma refers to the obligation of a son to follow the same vocation as his father. The first reference to the origin of varna dharma is found in the Rig Veda.

VEDAS A composite body of knowledge on a range of subjects, the Vedas are the oldest scriptures of Hinduism, composed as hymns between about 1500 BCE and 1000 BCE. Sage Vyasa is credited with classifying these hymns to create four vedas: Rig Veda, Sama Veda, Yajur Veda, and Atharva Veda.

YADAVAS A clan of Chandravamshis who trace their descent from Yadu, the older son of Yayati, an ancestor of the Kurus. Krishna belonged to the clan of the Yadavas.

YAGNA The ritual of sacrifice conducted to propitiate the gods and ensure their blessing. Essential to a yagna is the sacrificial fire to which a priest makes oblations. Vedic hymns set the context to the yagna and ensure its success.

YAKSHAS Powerful but benevolent forest-spirits who reside in all of nature. They are believed to be guardians of treasures and very fond of riddles.

YOGA A spiritual, mental, and physical discipline that leads to enlightenment and a union of the soul and the Universal Spirit. Such a balance requires consistent discipline, promotes self-awareness, and eventually leads to enlightenment.

YUGA Ancient Hindu belief holds that time is cyclic. Each cycle of time comprises four clear ages, or yugas. The first in the cycle is Satya Yuga, a golden age, the best of all the yugas. The two following yugas, Treta and Dwapara, see a gradual deterioration of humanity, the environment, and quality of life. Kali Yuga, the final age, is a time of darkness and ignorance, when the spiritual is forgotten and the relentless exploitation of both man and nature culminates in the destruction of the universe. The present era is Kali Yuga, which began around the time of Krishna's death after the Kurukshetra War.

Index

Note: Page numbers in **bold** refer to main subject entries.

A

B

C

D

L

M

N

O

P

T

U

V

W

Y

Acknowledgments

DORLING KINDERSLEY would like to thank the following people for their help in the preparation of this book.

Devdutt Pattanaik for his assistance in conceptualizing the book, and for allowing us to base the content on *Jaya: An Illustrated Retelling of the Mahabharata*.

Bibek Debroy for his guidance and for permission to use excerpts from his ten-volume translation of *The Mahabharata, Harivamsha,* and *The Bhagavad Gita*.

Kajori Aikat, Manish Gaekwad, Aruna Ghose, Juhi Saklani, and MadhuMadhavi Singh for their editorial contributions; Ashwin Raju Adimari and Deepak Negi for picture research; Divya Grace Mathew, Vineetha Mokkil, Dipali Singh, and Alka Thakur for proofreading; Priyanka Thakur for design assistance; Suresh Kumar for cartographic assistance; Umesh Singh Rawat for technical support; and Maitri Dalicha for calligraphy.

The following books and websites were used for research and reference:
Devdutt Pattanaik's *Jaya: An Illustrated Retelling of the Mahabharata, Sita: An Illustrated Retelling of the Ramayana, Shikhandi And Other Tales They Don't Tell You, Myth = Mithya: Decoding Hindu Mythology*, and *Vishnu: An Introduction*; www.devdutt.com; Bibek Debroy's *Harivamsha, The Mahabharata*, and *The Bhagavad Gita*; Wendy Doniger's *The Hindus: An Alternative History*; Romila Thapar's *Ancient Indian Social History: Some Interpretations*; Dorling Kindersley's *The Religion Book*; and Raj Kumar's *Encyclopaedia of Untouchables: Ancient, Medieval and Modern*; David Frawley's *Gods, Sages and Kings: Vedic Secrets of Ancient Civilization.*

DORLING KINDERSLEY would also like to thank Coingeit Technologies Private Limited for the index.

This book by DK is yet another retelling of the epic, striving to reach out to contemporary and international readers, and is just a drop in the ocean that is the Mahabharata.

PICTURE CREDITS
The publisher would like to thank the following for their kind permission to reproduce their photographs:

(Key: a-above; b-below/bottom; c-center; f-far; l-left; r-right; t-top)

1 PHILADELPHIA MUSEUM OF ART, PENNSYLVANIA: Purchased with the Stella Kramrisch Fund for Indian and Himalayan Art, 2012. **2-3 DREAMSTIME.COM**: Wai Chung Tang. **6 ALAMY STOCK PHOTO**: ephotocorp (bl). **DORLING KINDERSLEY**: Arun Pottirayil (br). **7 ALAMY STOCK PHOTO**: Dinodia Photos (bl). **DREAMSTIME.COM**: Amanda Lewis (br). **8 GETTY IMAGES**: Historical Picture Archive (bl). **PALLAVI NARAIN**: (br). **9 PAINTINGS OF THE RAZMNAMA BY ASOK KUMAR DAS, PUBLISHED BY MAPIN PUBLISHING, AHMEDABAD (WWW.MAPINPUB.COM), IN ASSOCIATION WITH THE BIRLA ACADEMY OF ARTS & CULTURE, KOLKATA**: (bl). **WELLCOME IMAGES HTTP://CREATIVECOMMONS.ORG/LICENSES/BY/4.0/**: Wellcome Library, London (br). **10-11 AKG-IMAGES**: Roland and Sabrina Michaud. **12-13 DREAMSTIME.COM**: Krishna Kharidehal. **14 GETTY IMAGES**: Ullstein Bild (bl). **14-15 GETTY IMAGES:** Vinod Kumar M (c). **14-487 DREAMSTIME.COM**: Peter Hermes Furian (ftl/Sun rays, tr/Sun rays). **15 GETTY IMAGES**: DEA Picture Library (cr). **LOS ANGELES COUNTY MUSEUM OF ART**: Gift of Mr. and Mrs. H. Robert Slusser (M.88.134.7) (t). **16 GETTY IMAGES**: IndiaPictures / Contributor (br); Historical Picture Archive / Contributor (bc); Dinodia Photo (clb). **LOS ANGELES COUNTY MUSEUM OF ART**: Gift of the Felix and Helen Juda Foundation (M.72.4.2) (c). **PHILADELPHIA MUSEUM OF ART, PENNSYLVANIA**: Stella Kramrisch Collection, 1994 (tr). **17 GETTY IMAGES**: Werner Forman / Contributor (br). **LOS ANGELES COUNTY MUSEUM OF ART**: From the Nasli and Alice Heeramaneck Collection, Museum Associates Purchase (M.72.53.1) (tr); Gift of the 2000 Collectors Committee (M.2000.30) (tc); Purchased with funds provided by Harry and Yvonne Lenart (M.86.126) (bl); Gift of Anna Bing Arnold (M.86.83) (tl); Gift of Mr. and Mrs. Harry Lenart (M.75.11) (c). **18-19 ALAMY STOCK PHOTO**: Imagebroker (b). **DREAMSTIME.COM**: Amnuai Butala (t). **18 LOS ANGELES COUNTY MUSEUM OF ART:** Anonymous gift (M.84.168) (bl). **19 DREAMSTIME.COM**: Cristian Mihai Vela (tc). **GETTY IMAGES**: Pascal Deloche (crb); Heritage Images / Contributor (tl); Historical Picture Archive / Contributor (tr). **PHILADELPHIA MUSEUM OF ART, PENNSYLVANIA:** Stella Kramrisch Collection, 1994 (cla). **20-21 DREAMSTIME.COM**: Jeyaprakash Maria (b); PixelParticle (Background). **21 DREAMSTIME.COM**: Ashwin Kharidehal Abhirama (tc); Jeffrey Walthall (br). **22 PHILADELPHIA MUSEUM OF ART, PENNSYLVANIA**: Stella Kramrisch Collection, 1994 (bl). **24-25 DREAMSTIME.COM**: Isabel Poulin. **26 GETTY IMAGES**: Werner Forman / Contributor (bc).

27 DREAMSTIME.COM: Mahantesh C Morabad. **28 DREAMSTIME.COM**: Farinoza (clb, cb, crb, bl). **PHILADELPHIA MUSEUM OF ART, PENNSYLVANIA**: Gift of Mr. and Mrs. Lessing J. Rosenwald, 1959 (tr). **29 GETTY IMAGES**: Mail Today / Contributor (bl). **30-31 DREAMSTIME.COM**: Krishna Kharidehal. **. 32 ALAMY STOCK PHOTO**: Ephotocorp (bc/6). **BRIDGEMAN IMAGES**: Oriental Museum, Durham University, UK (bc). **THE BROOKLYN MUSEUM, NEW YORK**: Gift of Doris and Ed Wiener (bl). **DORLING KINDERSLEY:** Sushil Soni (cr). **DREAMSTIME.COM**: Dr Ajay Kumar Singh (c/3); Aji Jayachandran (c). **AMITABHA GUPTA**: (br). **PHILADELPHIA MUSEUM OF ART, PENNSYLVANIA**: Gift of Mr. and Mrs. Lessing J. Rosenwald, 1959 (cl/1). **33 ALAMY STOCK PHOTO**: Ephotocorp (cl, c); Hakbong Kwon (bc/18). **THE BROOKLYN MUSEUM, NEW YORK**: Stella Kramrisch Collection, 1994 (tc/10). **THE CHHATRAPATI SHIVAJI MAHARAJ VASTU SANGRAHALAYA**: (tl). **GETTY IMAGES**: Historical Picture Archive (bl); Anoop Negi / Contributor (c/15); Georgy Markov (cr). **LOS ANGELES COUNTY MUSEUM OF ART**: Gift of Marilyn Walter Grounds (M.81.272.2) (bc). **THEATRE ROOTS & WINGS**: Manoj Parameswaran / 101 Lullabies, 2012 (tc)**. 34-35 PHILADELPHIA MUSEUM OF ART, PENNSYLVANIA**: Gift of Mr. and Mrs. Lessing J. Rosenwald, 1959. **36 AKG-IMAGES**: Mark De Fraeye (l). **DREAMSTIME.COM**: James Steidl (cra). **37 DREAMSTIME.COM**: Ziprashantzi (tr). **GETTY IMAGES**: Anand Purohit / Contributor (br). **38 PAINTINGS OF THE RAZMNAMA BY ASOK KUMAR DAS, PUBLISHED BY MAPIN PUBLISHING, AHMEDABAD (WWW.MAPINPUB.COM), IN ASSOCIATION WITH THE BIRLA ACADEMY OF ARTS & CULTURE, KOLKATA. 39 DREAMSTIME.COM**: Amanda Lewis (tr). **40 LOS ANGELES COUNTY MUSEUM OF ART**: Gift of Paul F. Walter (M.81.280.5) (bl). **40-41 DREAMSTIME.COM**: Dave Bredeson (Background). **LOS ANGELES COUNTY MUSEUM OF ART**: Gift of Paul F. Walter (M.83.219.2) (t). **41 ALAMY STOCK PHOTO**: World History Archive (tr, br). **42 GETTY IMAGES**: Christophe Boisvieux (c); Education Images / Contributor (bc). **43 WELLCOME IMAGES HTTP://CREATIVECOMMONS.ORG/LICENSES/BY/4.0/**: Wellcome Library, London. **44 WELLCOME IMAGES HTTP://CREATIVECOMMONS.ORG/LICENSES/BY/4.0/**: Wellcome Library, London (ca). **44-45 WELLCOME IMAGES HTTP://CREATIVECOMMONS.ORG/LICENSES/BY/4.0/**: Wellcome Library, London (b). **46 DORLING KINDERSLEY**: Mukesh Swami. Dreamstime.com: Petkov (Frame). **47 GETTY IMAGES**: Heritage Images / Contributor (br). **48-49 LOS ANGELES COUNTY MUSEUM OF ART**: Purchased with funds provided by Dorothy and Richard Sherwood (M.72.88.2). **48 WELLCOME IMAGES HTTP://CREATIVECOMMONS.ORG/LICENSES/BY/4.0/**: Wellcome Library, London (bl). **49 GETTY IMAGES**: Jeff Vanuga (br). **50-51 ALAMY STOCK PHOTO**: Classic Image. **51 DREAMSTIME.COM**: Honzahruby (bc). **LOS ANGELES COUNTY MUSEUM OF ART**: Gift of Paul F. Walter (M.86.345.6) (tr). **52-53 DREAMSTIME.COM**: Digitalfestival. **53 GETTY IMAGES**: Heritage Images / Contributor (cra). **54-55 DORLING KINDERSLEY**: Anita Kishore. **56-57 ALAMY STOCK PHOTO**: Dinodia Photos. **57 WELLCOME IMAGES HTTP://CREATIVECOMMONS.ORG/LICENSES/BY/4.0/**: Wellcome Library, London (br). **58 GETTY IMAGES**: Dinodia Photo (cl). **58-59 DORLING KINDERSLEY**: Tejas Art Gallery / Bhaskar Chitrakar (t). **59 GETTY IMAGES**: Pacific Press / Contributor (br). **60 GETTY IMAGES**: Dinodia Photo (tr); Uniquely India (cb). **60-61 DREAMSTIME.COM**: Wai Chung Tang (Background). **61 ALAMY STOCK PHOTO**: Ephotocorp (tr). **BHARATHANJALI TRUST**: (c). **62 ALAMY STOCK PHOTO**: Mahantesh C Morabad (cl). **DREAMSTIME.COM**: Ultraone (Parchments). **62-63 DORLING KINDERSLEY**: Arun Pottirayil. **64 GETTY IMAGES**: Irfan Saghir Mirza Photos (bl). **LOS ANGELES COUNTY MUSEUM OF ART**: Edgar G. Richards (M.88.66) (ca). **65 GETTY IMAGES**: Joel Sartore / National Geographic Photo Ark (cr). **LOS ANGELES COUNTY MUSEUM OF ART**: From the Nasli and Alice Heeramaneck Collection, Museum Associates Purchase (M.69.13.6). **66-67 ALAMY STOCK PHOTO**: Photos 12 (t). **67 ISTOCKPHOTO.COM**: Energyy (bc). **68-69 GETTY IMAGES**: De Agostini / G. Nimatallah. **69 GETTY IMAGES**: Print Collector / Contributor (tl). **LOS ANGELES COUNTY MUSEUM OF ART**: Gift of Mr. and Mrs. Eric Lidow in honor of the museum's twenty-fifth anniversary (M.91.90) (br). **70-71 DORLING KINDERSLEY**: Arun Pottirayil. **71 GETTY IMAGES**: Historical Picture Archive / Contributor (tl). **PHILADELPHIA MUSEUM OF ART, PENNSYLVANIA**: Stella Kramrisch Collection, 1994 (tr). **72 123RF.COM**: Pennapazza (bl). **72-73 DORLING KINDERSLEY**: Subhash Vohra. **73 ALAMY STOCK PHOTO**: Ephotocorp (tr). **74 THEATRE ROOTS & WINGS**: Manoj Parameswaran / 101 Lullabies, 2012 (bl). **74-75 ALAMY STOCK PHOTO**: Ephotocorp (t). **76-77 DREAMSTIME.COM**: Stefano

Ember. **76 LOS ANGELES COUNTY MUSEUM OF ART**: Gift of Dorothy and Richard Sherwood and Mr. and Mrs. Harry Lenart (M.77.15) (bc). **78 THE BROOKLYN MUSEUM, NEW YORK**: Gift of Terence McInerney (bl). **78-79 ISTOCKPHOTO.COM**: Landsacpe. **79 ALAMY STOCK PHOTO**: Angelo Hornak (cr). **80 ALAMY STOCK PHOTO**: Walker Art Library (tr). Dreamstime.com: Jeremy Richards (cl). **80-81 DREAMSTIME.COM**: Wai Chung Tang (Background). **81 COURTESY RAJESH SAI BABU AND RAKESH SAI BABU**: (bc). **GETTY IMAGES**: ImagesBazaar (tl). **NAAD-ROOP**: (br). **82-83 GETTY IMAGES**: Mukul Banerjee Photography (t). **82 DREAMSTIME.COM**: Ashwin Kharidehal Abhirama (b). **LOS ANGELES COUNTY MUSEUM OF ART**: Raymond and Frances Bushell Collection (AC1998.249.102) (cl). **83 DORLING KINDERSLEY**: Rujul Krishna (cr). **84 GETTY IMAGES**: Omar Havana / Stringer. **85 ALAMY STOCK PHOTO**: Age Fotostock (ca). **86 GETTY IMAGES**: Herve Bruhat / Contributor (bl). **86-87 DREAMSTIME.COM**: Kurt Kleemann (Sky). **JITENDRA SUTAR / WWW.SCULPTUREARTIST.IN. 88-89 ALAMY STOCK PHOTO**: Ephotocorp. **90-91 DREAMSTIME.COM:** Wai Chung Tang (Background). **91 ALAMY STOCK PHOTO**: Photo Researchers, Inc (cr). **92 GETTY IMAGES**: UniversalImagesGroup / Contributor (bl). **92-93 MARY EVANS PICTURE LIBRARY**: Ronald Grant Archive (b). **93 DORLING KINDERSLEY**: Board of Trustees of the Royal Armouries (c, r). **94 GETTY IMAGES**: Philip and Elizabeth De Bay / Contributor. **95 DORLING KINDERSLEY**: Alka Ranjan (cb). **WELLCOME IMAGES HTTP://CREATIVECOMMONS.ORG/LICENSES/BY/4.0/**: Wellcome Library, London (cr). **96 AKG-IMAGES**: Pictures From History (r). **DREAMSTIME.COM**: Ultraone (bl/Parchment). **97 DREAMSTIME.COM**: Saiko3p (c). **98-99 GETTY IMAGES**: Frank Pedrick (t). **98 DREAMSTIME.COM**: Amanda Lewis (cl). **99 GETTY IMAGES**: Historical Picture Archive / Contributor (tr). **PAINTINGS OF THE RAZMNAMA BY ASOK KUMAR DAS, PUBLISHED BY MAPIN PUBLISHING, AHMEDABAD (WWW.MAPINPUB.COM), IN ASSOCIATION WITH THE BIRLA ACADEMY OF ARTS & CULTURE, KOLKATA**: (bc). **100 DEPOSITPHOTOS INC**: Yogesh_More (b). **DREAMSTIME.COM**: Saiko3p (bl). **101 DREAMSTIME.COM**: Dmitry Rukhlenko (r). **102 GETTY IMAGES**: Dinodia Photo (clb). **102-103 GETTY IMAGES**: Melissa Farlow. **104 DORLING KINDERSLEY**: Mukesh Swami. **105 LOS ANGELES COUNTY MUSEUM OF ART**: From the Nasli and Alice Heeramaneck Collection, Museum Associates Purchase (M.80.6.1) (bc). **106-107 LOS ANGELES COUNTY MUSEUM OF ART**: Gift of Jane Greenough Green in memory of Edward Pelton Green (AC1999.127.37. **107 DREAMSTIME.COM**: Pathakdesigner (br). **108 DORLING KINDERSLEY**: Tejas Art Gallery / Bhaskar Chitrakar. **109 GETTY IMAGES**: Culture Club / Hulton Archive. **110-111 DREAMSTIME.COM**: Vikiclicks. **111 DREAMSTIME.COM**: Tawesit (br). **112 ALAMY STOCK PHOTO**: Dinodia Photos (cl). **112-113 BHARATHANJALI TRUST**. **113 GETTY IMAGES**: IndiaPictures / Universal Images Group (cra). **114 ALAMY STOCK PHOTO**: EPA European Pressphoto Agency B.v. (bl). **114-115 DREAMSTIME.COM**: Amanda Lewis (t). **115 GETTY IMAGES**: Kumarworks (cr). **116-117 GETTY IMAGES**: Ankur Dauneria. **117 DREAMSTIME.COM**: Aapthamithra (tc). **118 ALAMY STOCK PHOTO**: Classic Image. **119 DREAMSTIME.COM**: Adogslifephoto (br). **120 UNIVERSITY OF CALIFORNIA**: University of California Libraries (br). **WWW.ARTISANSCREST.COM**: (l). **121 PHILADELPHIA MUSEUM OF ART, PENNSYLVANIA**: Gift of Stanley F. and Margaret W. Myers (b). **122 ALAMY STOCK PHOTO**: Heritage Image Partnership Ltd. **123 DREAMSTIME.COM**: Harshvardhan (clb). **LOS ANGELES COUNTY MUSEUM OF ART:** Gift of the 2000 Collectors Committee (M.2000.30) (cra). **124 DREAMSTIME.COM**: Dwight Smith (tr). **PHILADELPHIA MUSEUM OF ART, PENNSYLVANIA**: Gift of Mr. and Mrs. Lessing J. Rosenwald, 1959 (cl). **125 DREAMSTIME.COM**: Dwight Smith. **126-127 GETTY IMAGES**: Werner Forman / Universal Images Group. **126 123RF.COM**: Orapan Jampa (bl). **128-129 DREAMSTIME.COM**: Aji Jayachandran. **130-131 GETTY IMAGES**: AFP. **130 KAMAT'S POTPOURRI / HTTP://WWW.KAMAT.COM/**: (bl). **132-133 PAINTINGS OF THE RAZMNAMA BY ASOK KUMAR DAS, PUBLISHED BY MAPIN PUBLISHING, AHMEDABAD (WWW.MAPINPUB.COM), IN ASSOCIATION WITH THE BIRLA ACADEMY OF ARTS & CULTURE, KOLKATA**. **134-135 DREAMSTIME.COM**: Antonella865. **135 ALAMY STOCK PHOTO**: PhotosIndia.com RM 5 (bc). **136 GETTY IMAGES**: Barry Kusuma (bl). **137 DORLING KINDERSLEY**: Arun Pottirayil (cr). **139 ALAMY STOCK PHOTO**: Imagebroker. **140 NAAD-ROOP**: (tr). **141 GETTY IMAGES**: Culture Club / Hulton Archive. **142-143 ALAMY STOCK PHOTO**: Dinodia Photos. **144-145 AKG-IMAGES**: Interfoto (b). **145 PAINTINGS OF THE RAZMNAMA BY ASOK KUMAR DAS, PUBLISHED BY MAPIN PUBLISHING, AHMEDABAD (WWW.MAPINPUB.COM), IN ASSOCIATION WITH THE BIRLA ACADEMY OF ARTS & CULTURE,**

KOLKATA: (br). **146-147 DREAMSTIME.COM**: Zzvet. **147 LOS ANGELES COUNTY MUSEUM OF ART**: The Madina Collection of Islamic Art, gift of Camilla Chandler Frost (M.2002.1.524) (br). **148-149 DREAMSTIME.COM**: Dr Ajay Kumar Singh. **150-151 DORLING KINDERSLEY**: Arun Pottirayil (b). **151 DREAMSTIME.COM**: Kantilal Patel (br). **GETTY IMAGES**: Pacific Press / LightRocket (tr). **152 DREAMSTIME.COM**: Lakhesis (bl); Aliaksandr Mazurkevich (tr). **152-153 DREAMSTIME.COM**: Wai Chung Tang (Background). **153 DREAMSTIME.COM**: Luceluceluce (cra). **GETTY IMAGES**: Bloomberg (crb); Hindustan Times (c). **154-155 LOS ANGELES COUNTY MUSEUM OF ART**: The Nasli M. Heeramaneck Collection of Ancient Near Eastern and Central Asian Art, gift of The Ahmanson Foundation (M.76.97.381). **154 DREAMSTIME.COM**: Viacheslav Belyaev (cl). **155 DREAMSTIME.COM**: Michael Flippo (cr). **GETTY IMAGES**: Culture Club / Hulton Archive (tc). **156-157 ALAMY STOCK PHOTO**: Mirza Ahmad Photography. **158 DORLING KINDERSLEY**: Mukesh Swami. **159 AMITABHA GUPTA**: (bc). **160-161 GETTY IMAGES**: V. Muthuraman (t). **160 GETTY IMAGES**: Dinodia Photo (bc). **162 NAAD-ROOP**: (bc). **163 TEJAS ART GALLERY**: Dhiren Sasmal. **164-165 DREAMSTIME.COM**: Wai Chung Tang (Background). **LOS ANGELES COUNTY MUSEUM OF ART**: Gift of Paul F. Walter (M.79.191.7) (b). **165 DREAMSTIME.COM**: Florian Blümm (crb). **ISTOCKPHOTO.COM**: Topten22photo (tr). **166 GETTY IMAGES**: A photograph is more than a collection of pixels (tl). **166-167 DREAMSTIME.COM**: Wai Chung Tang (Background). **GETTY IMAGES**: Fine Art / Corbis Historical. **167 GETTY IMAGES**: Angelo Hornak / Corbis Historical (tr). **168 PALLAVI NARAIN**. **169 DREAMSTIME.COM**: William Hunter (cra). **170-171 DORLING KINDERSLEY**: Tejas Art Gallery / Bhaskar Chitrakar. **171 123RF.COM**: Songsak Paname (cr). **172 LOS ANGELES COUNTY MUSEUM OF ART**: Gift of the Felix and Helen Juda Foundation (M.70.38.1). **172-173 DREAMSTIME.COM**: Wai Chung Tang (Background). **173 ALAMY STOCK PHOTO**: (tc). **174 DREAMSTIME.COM**: Antonprado (l). **174-175 DREAMSTIME.COM**: Wai Chung Tang (Background). **175 LOS ANGELES COUNTY MUSEUM OF ART**: Gift of the Michael J. Connell Foundation (M.71.49.2) (cra). **176 123RF.COM**: Saiko3p (clb). **176-177 DREAMSTIME.COM**: Wai Chung Tang (Background). **GETTY IMAGES**: Frank Bienewald / LightRocket. **178 DREAMSTIME.COM**: Zzvet (cla). **178-179 GETTY IMAGES**: Pacific Press / LightRocket. **179 GETTY IMAGES**: Prakash Mathema / AFP (cra). **180-181 DREAMSTIME.COM**: Helena Bilková. **181 ALAMY STOCK PHOTO**: Epa European Pressphoto Agency B.v. (t). **DREAMSTIME.COM**: Saiko3p (cra). **182-183 LOS ANGELES COUNTY MUSEUM OF ART**: Gift of Marilyn Walter Grounds (M.85.284.9) (b). **183 LOS ANGELES COUNTY MUSEUM OF ART**: From the Nasli and Alice Heeramaneck Collection, Museum Associates Purchase (M.72.1.27) (tc); From the Nasli and Alice Heeramaneck Collection, Museum Associates Purchase (M.73.4.7) (br). **184 ALAMY STOCK PHOTO**: Deepu Sg (cl). **185 DORLING KINDERSLEY**: Arun Pottirayil. **186 DREAMSTIME.COM**: Suraj Singh (cr). **GETTY IMAGES**: Rajesh Jantilal / Stringer (bl). **187 DORLING KINDERSLEY**: Anita Kishore. **188 ALAMY STOCK PHOTO**: The Advertising Archives (c). **DORLING KINDERSLEY**: Rajrupa Das (tr). **188-189 DREAMSTIME.COM**: Wai Chung Tang (Background). **189 DORLING KINDERSLEY**: Isha Nagar (clb). **DREAMSTIME.COM**: Bignai (cb); Vladimir Korostyshevskiy (cra). **190 GETTY IMAGES: HISTORICAL PICTURE ARCHIVE / CORBIS HISTORICAL** (clb). **PAINTINGS OF THE RAZMNAMA BY ASOK KUMAR DAS, PUBLISHED BY MAPIN PUBLISHING, AHMEDABAD (WWW.MAPINPUB.COM), IN ASSOCIATION WITH THE BIRLA ACADEMY OF ARTS & CULTURE, KOLKATA**: (b). **191 DREAMSTIME.COM**: Santia2 (t). **192 DREAMSTIME.COM**: Theeravat Boonnuang (bl). **193 123RF.COM**: Marie-Ann Daloia (cra). **GETTY IMAGES**: Culture Club / Hulton Archive (c). **194-195 ANULAL.V. 195 DREAMSTIME.COM**: Arykoswara (br). **PENGUIN AND THE PENGUIN LOGO ARE TRADEMARKS OF PENGUIN BOOKS LTD**: 9780143418368 (tc). **196 DREAMSTIME.COM**: Aniszewski (tr). **197 ALAMY STOCK PHOTO**: Classic Image. **198 ALAMY STOCK PHOTO**: Pumkinpie (c). **198-199 DREAMSTIME.COM**: Wai Chung Tang (Background). **199 LOS ANGELES COUNTY MUSEUM OF ART**: Anonymous gift (M.89.159.2) (tr). **200-201 DORLING KINDERSLEY**: Sushil Soni. **202 DREAMSTIME.COM**: Iryna Rasko (cl). **LOS ANGELES COUNTY MUSEUM OF ART**: Purchased with funds provided by Dorothy and Richard Sherwood (M.88.29.2) (bl). **202-203 BHARATHANJALI TRUST**. **203 GETTY IMAGES**: Exotica.im (cr). **204-205 SMITHIN DAS KUNDOLY**: (b). **204 CORBIS**: (bl). **206 ALAMY STOCK PHOTO**: Ajayclicks (bl). **PAINTINGS OF THE RAZMNAMA BY ASOK KUMAR DAS,**

PUBLISHED BY MAPIN PUBLISHING, AHMEDABAD (WWW.MAPINPUB.COM), IN ASSOCIATION WITH THE BIRLA ACADEMY OF ARTS & CULTURE, KOLKATA: (t). **207 DREAMSTIME.COM**: Anna Artamonova (cra). **PAINTINGS OF THE RAZMNAMA BY ASOK KUMAR DAS, PUBLISHED BY MAPIN PUBLISHING, AHMEDABAD (WWW.MAPINPUB.COM), IN ASSOCIATION WITH THE BIRLA ACADEMY OF ARTS & CULTURE, KOLKATA**: (b). **208 ALAMY STOCK PHOTO**: Ephotocorp. **209 LIBRARY OF CONGRESS, WASHINGTON, D.C.**: http://www.loc.gov/exhibits/world/heavens.html#obj92 (bc). **LOS ANGELES COUNTY MUSEUM OF ART**: Gift of Paul F. Walter (M.85.297.9) (cr). **210-211 THE BROOKLYN MUSEUM, NEW YORK**: Gift of Doris and Ed Wiener. **212 GETTY IMAGES**: Culture Club / Hulton Archive (b). **213 123RF.COM**: Natrada Kittirangsee (tr). **214 ALAMY STOCK PHOTO**: Ephotocorp. **215 GETTY IMAGES**: Herve Bruhat / Gamma-Rapho (br). **217 COURTESY RAJESH SAI BABU AND RAKESH SAI BABU**. **218-219 AKG-IMAGES**: Pictures From History. **221 DORLING KINDERSLEY**: Mukesh Swami. **222 GETTY IMAGES**: Universal History Archive (tr). **PAINTINGS OF THE RAZMNAMA BY ASOK KUMAR DAS, PUBLISHED BY MAPIN PUBLISHING, AHMEDABAD (WWW.MAPINPUB.COM), IN ASSOCIATION WITH THE BIRLA ACADEMY OF ARTS & CULTURE, KOLKATA**: (bl). **223 PAINTINGS OF THE RAZMNAMA BY ASOK KUMAR DAS, PUBLISHED BY MAPIN PUBLISHING, AHMEDABAD (WWW.MAPINPUB.COM), IN ASSOCIATION WITH THE BIRLA ACADEMY OF ARTS & CULTURE, KOLKATA**: (tr). **224 DORLING KINDERSLEY**: Tejas Art Gallery / Bhaskar Chitrakar. **225 LOS ANGELES COUNTY MUSEUM OF ART**: Gift of Jane Greenough Green in memory of Edward Pelton Green (AC1999.127.33) (cr). **PHILADELPHIA MUSEUM OF ART, PENNSYLVANIA**: Purchased with the New Members Fund, 1970 (b). **226 AMITABHA GUPTA**: (bc). **227 PHILADELPHIA MUSEUM OF ART, PENNSYLVANIA**: Gift of Stella Kramrisch, 1988. **228-229 ALAMY STOCK PHOTO**: Ephotocorp. **230-231 GETTY IMAGES**: AFP / Stringer. **230 DREAMSTIME.COM**: Kurt Kleemann (t/Sky). **232 PAINTINGS OF THE RAZMNAMA BY ASOK KUMAR DAS, PUBLISHED BY MAPIN PUBLISHING, AHMEDABAD (WWW.MAPINPUB.COM), IN ASSOCIATION WITH THE BIRLA ACADEMY OF ARTS & CULTURE, KOLKATA**. **233 GETTY IMAGES**: ImagesBazaar (cr). **234 ALAMY STOCK PHOTO**: Neil McAllister (b). **DREAMSTIME.COM**: Jorg Hackemann (cr); Saiko3p (tr). **GETTY IMAGES**: Jeremy Richards (c). **235 LOS ANGELES COUNTY MUSEUM OF ART**: Gift of Constance Harris (AC1993.187.1). **236-237 ALAMY STOCK PHOTO**: Hornbil Images. **237 GETTY IMAGES**: Philippe Lissac (cr). **238-239 ALAMY STOCK PHOTO**: Dinodia Photos. **268-269 AKG-IMAGES**: Roland and Sabrina Michaud. **288-289 123RF.COM**: Alhovik (Flags). **DREAMSTIME.COM**: Sergey Peterman. **290-291 PHILADELPHIA MUSEUM OF ART, PENNSYLVANIA**: Stella Kramrisch Collection, 1994 (b). **291 LOS ANGELES COUNTY MUSEUM OF ART**: Gift of The Michael J. Connell Foundation (M.77.111.2) (tc). **ARUN SAMADDER**: (tr). **292-293 AKG-IMAGES**: François Guénet. **293 GETTY IMAGES**: FlamingPumpkin (cr). **294-295 DREAMSTIME.COM**: Amanda Lewis. **296 GETTY IMAGES**: Culture Club / Hulton Archive (cl); Pacific Press / LightRocket (bl). **296-297 ALAMY STOCK PHOTO**: Arco Images GmbH. **298 DORLING KINDERSLEY**: Vikings of Middle England (c). **299 CORBIS**. **300 DREAMSTIME.COM**: Arykoswara (r). **301 AMITABHA GUPTA**: (t). **302-303 BRIDGEMAN IMAGES**: Oriental Museum, Durham University, UK. **304-305 PAINTINGS OF THE RAZMNAMA BY ASOK KUMAR DAS, PUBLISHED BY MAPIN PUBLISHING, AHMEDABAD (WWW.MAPINPUB.COM), IN ASSOCIATION WITH THE BIRLA ACADEMY OF ARTS & CULTURE, KOLKATA**. **305 DREAMSTIME.COM**: 1enchik (cra). **308 GETTY IMAGES**: Dinodia Photo. **309 DREAMSTIME.COM**: Emilia Ungur. **310-311 ALAMY STOCK PHOTO**: Reo Yudhono (b/Chariot). **310 DORLING KINDERSLEY**: NASA (cla). **312-313 PHILADELPHIA MUSEUM OF ART, PENNSYLVANIA**: Gift of Mr. and Mrs. Lessing J. Rosenwald, 1959 (b). **312 GETTY IMAGES**: Christopher Pillitz (bl). **313 DREAMSTIME.COM**: Dr.pramod Bansode (cra). **314-315 AMITABHA GUPTA**. **316-317 SETO HIDAYAT**. **318-319 JITENDRA SUTAR / WWW.SCULPTUREARTIST.IN**. **319 WRITERS WORKSHOP / WWW.WRITERSWORKSHOPINDIA.COM**: (bc). **320-321 PHILADELPHIA MUSEUM OF ART, PENNSYLVANIA**: Purchased with the Edith H. Bell Fund, 1975. **322-323 BRIDGEMAN IMAGES**: Restricted gift of the Joseph & Helen Regenstein Foundation (b). **DREAMSTIME.COM**: Ócsi Balázs (t). **323 LOS ANGELES COUNTY MUSEUM OF ART**: Gift of Michael Phillips (M.79.189.9) (cr). **325 DREAMSTIME.COM**: Zzvet. **326-327 THE CHHATRAPATI SHIVAJI MAHARAJ VASTU SANGRAHALAYA**. **328-329 DORLING KINDERSLEY**: Anita Kishore. **330 PAINTINGS OF THE RAZMNAMA BY ASOK KUMAR DAS, PUBLISHED BY MAPIN PUBLISHING, AHMEDABAD (WWW.

MAPINPUB.COM), IN ASSOCIATION WITH THE BIRLA ACADEMY OF ARTS & CULTURE, KOLKATA. 331 VISHNU MENON M: (bc). **332-333 ALAMY STOCK PHOTO**: Ajayclicks. **333 ARUN JOSEPH P / HTTPS://WWW.FLICKR.COM/PHOTOS/ARUNJOSEPHP**: (tc). **334-335 GETTY IMAGES**: Patrick Aventurier / Gamma-Rapho. **334 DORLING KINDERSLEY**: Board of Trustees of the Royal Armouries (tr). **GETTY IMAGES**: Dea / A. Dagli Orti (bl). **336 SHANKAR JANAKIRAMAN. 337 THEATRE ROOTS & WINGS**: Satoko Tsurudome / Urubhangam, 2009 (tr). **338 DORLING KINDERSLEY**: Board of Trustees of the Royal Armouries / © The Board of Trustees of the Armouries (clb); Vikings of Middle England (cl). **LOS ANGELES COUNTY MUSEUM OF ART**: Gift of Ramesh and Urmil Kapoor (M.86.337) (tr). **PHILADELPHIA MUSEUM OF ART, PENNSYLVANIA**: Gift of Lydia Thompson Morris, 1925 (cl/Spear, clb/Sword, bl). **338-339 DREAMSTIME.COM**: Wai Chung Tang (Background). **339 GETTY IMAGES**: Culture Club / Hulton Archive (tc); IndiaPictures / Universal Images Group (bl). **340-341 AKG-IMAGES**: Roland and Sabrina Michaud. **341 PHILADELPHIA MUSEUM OF ART, PENNSYLVANIA**: Stella Kramrisch Collection, 1994 (tr). **342-343 THE BROOKLYN MUSEUM, NEW YORK**: Stella Kramrisch Collection, 1994. **344-345 DREAMSTIME.COM**: Constantin Opris (b). **345 DREAMSTIME.COM**: Whitcomberd (tr). **346 AMITABHA GUPTA. 347 GETTY IMAGES**: DEA Picture Library (tr). **PAINTINGS OF THE RAZMNAMA BY ASOK KUMAR DAS, PUBLISHED BY MAPIN PUBLISHING, AHMEDABAD (WWW.MAPINPUB.COM), IN ASSOCIATION WITH THE BIRLA ACADEMY OF ARTS & CULTURE, KOLKATA**: (bc). **348-349 GETTY IMAGES**: Helmuth Boeger (Germany). **350 PAINTINGS OF THE RAZMNAMA BY ASOK KUMAR DAS, PUBLISHED BY MAPIN PUBLISHING, AHMEDABAD (WWW.MAPINPUB.COM), IN ASSOCIATION WITH THE BIRLA ACADEMY OF ARTS & CULTURE, KOLKATA**: (c). **351 DREAMSTIME.COM**: Alexandr Mitiuc (br). **PAINTINGS OF THE RAZMNAMA BY ASOK KUMAR DAS, PUBLISHED BY MAPIN PUBLISHING, AHMEDABAD (WWW.MAPINPUB.COM), IN ASSOCIATION WITH THE BIRLA ACADEMY OF ARTS & CULTURE, KOLKATA**: (t, bc). **352-353 ALAMY STOCK PHOTO**: Ivy Close Images. **354-355 THEATRE ROOTS & WINGS**: Manoj Parameswaran / 101 Lullabies, 2012. **356-357 ALAMY STOCK PHOTO**: Travelib Environment (b). **357 DREAMSTIME.COM**: Samrat35 (cr). **NAAD-ROOP**: (tl). **358 ALAMY STOCK PHOTO**: World History Archive. **359 GETTY IMAGES**: Ingo Arndt / Nature Picture Library (cr). **LOS ANGELES COUNTY MUSEUM OF ART**: Purchased with funds provided by Dorothy and Richard Sherwood and Indian Art Special Purpose Fund (M.80.101) (bc). **360-361 GETTY IMAGES**: Jack Vartoogian / Getty Images / Archive Photos. **362-363 NAAD-ROOP. 367 DREAMSTIME.COM**: Angelo Gilardelli (Frame). **PAINTINGS OF THE RAZMNAMA BY ASOK KUMAR DAS, PUBLISHED BY MAPIN PUBLISHING, AHMEDABAD (WWW.MAPINPUB.COM), IN ASSOCIATION WITH THE BIRLA ACADEMY OF ARTS & CULTURE, KOLKATA. 368-369 RICHARD FRIEDRICKS. 369 GETTY IMAGES**: Yvan Travert (ca). **370 DREAMSTIME.COM**: Izanbar (cb). **370-371 DREAMSTIME.COM**: Kurt Kleemann (Sky); Stephen Mcsweeny (t); Wai Chung Tang (Background). **372-373 DREAMSTIME.COM**: Wai Chung Tang (Background). **GETTY IMAGES**: DEA Picture Library. **374-375 DREAMSTIME.COM**: Wai Chung Tang (Background). **GETTY IMAGES**: Jeremy Richards. **375 DREAMSTIME.COM**: Raluca Tudor (cra). **376-377 ALAMY STOCK PHOTO**: Ephotocorp. **378-379 CORBIS**: (t). **380-381 ALAMY STOCK PHOTO**: ephotocorp. **382 DREAMSTIME.COM**: Chabkc (cra). **PAINTINGS OF THE RAZMNAMA BY ASOK KUMAR DAS, PUBLISHED BY MAPIN PUBLISHING, AHMEDABAD (WWW.MAPINPUB.COM), IN ASSOCIATION WITH THE BIRLA ACADEMY OF ARTS & CULTURE, KOLKATA**: (cl). **383 PAINTINGS OF THE RAZMNAMA BY ASOK KUMAR DAS, PUBLISHED BY MAPIN PUBLISHING, AHMEDABAD (WWW.MAPINPUB.COM), IN ASSOCIATION WITH THE BIRLA ACADEMY OF ARTS & CULTURE, KOLKATA. 384-385 ALAMY STOCK PHOTO**: Chronicle. **385 PHILADELPHIA MUSEUM OF ART, PENNSYLVANIA**: Stella Kramrisch Collection, 1994 (tr). **386-387 LOS ANGELES COUNTY MUSEUM OF ART**: (t). **387 RAMESH LALWANI**: (cr). **388-389 AKG-IMAGES**: Roland and Sabrina Michaud. **390-391 GETTY IMAGES**: Anoop Negi / Contributor (c). **392 DREAMSTIME.COM**: Shariff Che\' Lah (cl). **392-393 AKG-IMAGES**: Ms. Add. 5640 / fol. 367 v / London / British Library. **394-395 GETTY IMAGES**: Georgy Markov. **396-397 LOS ANGELES COUNTY MUSEUM OF ART**: Anonymous gift (M.91.294.3). **397 ALAMY STOCK PHOTO**: Dinodia Photos (tr). **398-399 DORLING KINDERSLEY**: Mukesh Swami. **400-401 ALAMY STOCK PHOTO**: ImageDB (bl). **401 PHILADELPHIA MUSEUM OF ART, PENNSYLVANIA**: Stella Kramrisch Collection, 1994 (tr). **402-403 123RF.COM**: Andrii Iurlov (b/Sea). **ALAMY STOCK PHOTO**: ImageDB (c). **403 PHILADELPHIA MUSEUM**

OF ART, PENNSYLVANIA: Purchased with the John T. Morris Fund, 1955 (tr). **404-405 GETTY IMAGES**: Historical Picture Archive. **406-407 LOS ANGELES COUNTY MUSEUM OF ART**: Purchased with funds provided by Sunita Mula Wadhwani, Ravi Wadhwani, and Kiran Wadhwani Samuels in memory of Mulchand Navalrai Wadhwani (AC1998.54.1) (b). **406 LOS ANGELES COUNTY MUSEUM OF ART**: From the Nasli and Alice Heeramaneck Collection, Museum Associates Purchase (M.71.1.10) (bl); Indian Art Special Purpose Fund (M.79.51) (cla). **407 GETTY IMAGES**: Martin Harvey (cr). **408-409 DREAMSTIME.COM**: Angelo Deval (b). **409 ALAMY STOCK PHOTO**: Interfoto (tr). **410-411 AKG-IMAGES**: Erich Lessing. **412 LOS ANGELES COUNTY MUSEUM OF ART**: Gift of Paul F. Walter (M.86.345.5). **412-413 DREAMSTIME.COM**: Wai Chung Tang (Background). **413 DREAMSTIME.COM**: Viacheslav Belyaev (tr); Richmond Paul Ruiz (crb). **414 ALAMY STOCK PHOTO**: Chris Wallace (clb). **LOS ANGELES COUNTY MUSEUM OF ART**: Gift of Mr. and Mrs. Harry Lenart (M.79.111) (tr). **414-415 DREAMSTIME.COM**: Wai Chung Tang (Background). **415 GETTY IMAGES**: Werner Forman / Contributor (bl). **416-417 ALAMY STOCK PHOTO**: Hakbong Kwon. **418 BRIDGEMAN IMAGES**: Indian School / Baroda Museum, Baroda, Gujarat, India / Ann & Bury Peerless Picture Library. **420 ALAMY STOCK PHOTO**: Imagebroker (tr). **420-421 123RF.COM**: Antiqueimagesdotnet (b). **421 ALAMY STOCK PHOTO**: Charles O. Cecil (crb); Ephotocorp (tr). **422-423 ALAMY STOCK PHOTO**: William Smith. **422 LOS ANGELES COUNTY MUSEUM OF ART**: Gift of Chino Franco Roncoroni (M.84.104) (bl). **424 123RF.COM**: Nikolay Kurzenko (bl); Le Do (bl/ Lotus). **DREAMSTIME.COM**: Dgmate (tr). **425 DORLING KINDERSLEY**: Shefali Upadhaya (b). **426 DREAMSTIME.COM**: Anxela (b). **PAINTINGS OF THE RAZMNAMA BY ASOK KUMAR DAS, PUBLISHED BY MAPIN PUBLISHING, AHMEDABAD (WWW.MAPINPUB.COM), IN ASSOCIATION WITH THE BIRLA ACADEMY OF ARTS & CULTURE, KOLKATA**: (tr). **427 GETTY IMAGES**: Noah Seelam / AFP (cra). **428-429 DREAMSTIME.COM**: Krishna Kharidehal. **430-431 LOS ANGELES COUNTY MUSEUM OF ART**: Gift of Marilyn Walter Grounds (M.81.272.2). **432 ISTOCKPHOTO.COM**: RonTech2000. **433 GETTY IMAGES**: (cr). **434-435 ALAMY STOCK PHOTO**: Ephotocorp. **435 WELLCOME IMAGES HTTP://CREATIVECOMMONS.ORG/LICENSES/BY/4.0/**: Wellcome Library, London (cr). **436 LOS ANGELES COUNTY MUSEUM OF ART**: Gift of the Michael J. Connell Foundation (M.71.49.7) (bl). **436-437 LOS ANGELES COUNTY MUSEUM OF ART**: From the Nasli and Alice Heeramaneck Collection, Museum Associates Purchase (M.72.1.16) (c). **437 AKG-IMAGES**: Roland and Sabrina Michaud (tc). **THE BROOKLYN MUSEUM, NEW YORK**: Gift of Emily Manheim Goldman (br). **PHILADELPHIA MUSEUM OF ART, PENNSYLVANIA**: Gift of Carl Zigrosser, 1972 (cr). **438-439 AKG-IMAGES**: Roland and Sabrina Michaud. **440 DREAMSTIME.COM**: Florian Blümm (cra). **GETTY IMAGES**: Hindustan Times (clb). **441 GETTY IMAGES**: Godong / Universal Images Group. **442 PHILADELPHIA MUSEUM OF ART, PENNSYLVANIA**: 125th Anniversary Acquisition. Alvin O. Bellak Collection, 2004 (cb). **442-443 DREAMSTIME.COM**: Wai Chung Tang (Background). **443 AMITABHA GUPTA**: (tl). **LOS ANGELES COUNTY MUSEUM OF ART**: Gift of the Michael J. Connell Foundation (M.71.49.9) (br). **444-445 ALAMY STOCK PHOTO**: Granger Historical Picture Archive. **446 THE BROOKLYN MUSEUM, NEW YORK**: Gift of the Ernest Erickson Foundation, Inc. (bl). **447 AKG-IMAGES**: Jean-Louis Nou (l). **448 GETTY IMAGES**: Amar Grover (ca). **448-449 DREAMSTIME.COM**: Wai Chung Tang (Background). **449 ALAMY STOCK PHOTO**: Dinodia Photos (b). **GETTY IMAGES**: Angelo Hornak / Corbis Historical (cra). **450 ALAMY STOCK PHOTO**: Dinodia Photos (cla). **THE BROOKLYN MUSEUM, NEW YORK**: Gift of Dr. Bertram H. Schaffner (tr). **DREAMSTIME.COM**: Kiran Pandiyath (crb). **451 GETTY IMAGES**: Historical Picture Archive / Corbis Historical (b). **AMITABHA GUPTA**: (tc). **LOS ANGELES COUNTY MUSEUM OF ART**: Gift of Myrna Smoot and Peter Smoot (M.84.228.3a-b) (tl); Gift of Corinne and Don Whitaker (M.80.232.4) (tr). **452 GETTY IMAGES**: RBB (clb). **PHILADELPHIA MUSEUM OF ART, PENNSYLVANIA**: Gift of Stella Kramrisch, 1985 (c). **453 GETTY IMAGES**: Hindustan Times (cra). **454 LOS ANGELES COUNTY MUSEUM OF ART**: Gift of the Michael J. Connell Foundation (M.71.49.1). **455 PHILADELPHIA MUSEUM OF ART, PENNSYLVANIA**: Gift of Stella Kramrisch, 1988 (cra). **456-457 AKG-IMAGES**: Jean-Louis Nou. **458-459 DREAMSTIME.COM**: Yurataranik (b). **458 GETTY IMAGES**: Heritage Images / Hulton Archive (cl). **460-461 YALE UNIVERSITY ART GALLERY**. **462 LOS ANGELES COUNTY MUSEUM OF ART**: Gift of Edwin Binney, 3rd (M.74.13) (tr). **PHILADELPHIA MUSEUM OF ART, PENNSYLVANIA**: Stella Kramrisch Collection, 1994 (bc). **463 GETTY**

IMAGES: IndiaPictures / Universal Images Group (br). **LOS ANGELES COUNTY MUSEUM OF ART**: Gift of Mr. and Mrs. Hal B. Wallis (M.70.69.1-.4) (bl); Pratapaditya Pal (AC1995.142.1) (tl). **PHILADELPHIA MUSEUM OF ART, PENNSYLVANIA**: Stella Kramrisch Collection, 1994 (tr). **464 123RF. COM**: Phive2015 (bc). **465 BRIDGEMAN IMAGES**: San Diego Museum of Art, USA / Edwin Binney 3rd Collection. **466 GETTY IMAGES**: Print Collector / Hulton Archive (c). **466-467 DREAMSTIME. COM**: Kurt Kleemann (Sky). **467 LOS ANGELES COUNTY MUSEUM OF ART**: Gift of Anna Bing Arnold (M.70.5.2) (tc); Gift of Anna Bing Arnold (M.70.5.3) (crb). **468 GETTY IMAGES**: Fine Art / Corbis Historical (bl); Historical Picture Archive / Corbis Historical (tr). **LOS ANGELES COUNTY MUSEUM OF ART**: Gift of Anna Bing Arnold (M.87.160.2) (c); Gift of Ann Rohrer (M.84.58.1) (crb). **PHILADELPHIA MUSEUM OF ART, PENNSYLVANIA**: Gift of Mr. and Mrs. Stanley F. Myers, 1995 (tl). **469 GETTY IMAGES**: Philippe Lissac (bl). **LOS ANGELES COUNTY MUSEUM OF ART**: From the Nasli and Alice Heeramaneck Collection, Museum Associates Purchase (M.69.13.5) (bc); Gift of Paul F. Walter (M.81.280.5) (tc). **WELLCOME IMAGES HTTP:// CREATIVE**commons.org/licenses/by/4.0/: Wellcome Library, London (br, tl). **470-471 DREAMSTIME. COM**: Krishna Kharidehal. **472 LOS ANGELES COUNTY MUSEUM OF ART**: Gift of the 2005 Collectors Committee (M.2005.30) (cl). **472-473 DREAMSTIME.COM**: Wai Chung Tang (Background). **473 BHARATHANJALI TRUST**: (cb). **474 DREAMSTIME.COM**: Prashant Vaidya (crb). **474-475 DREAMSTIME.COM**: Wai Chung Tang (Background). **475 PHILADELPHIA MUSEUM OF ART, PENNSYLVANIA**: Purchased with the Francis T. S. Darley Fund, 1935 (ca). **476 PHILADELPHIA MUSEUM OF ART, PENNSYLVANIA**: Gift of Carl Zigrosser, 1972 (c). **476-477 DREAMSTIME.COM**: Wai Chung Tang (Background). **477 LOS ANGELES COUNTY MUSEUM OF ART**: Gift of Mr. and Mrs. Hal B. Wallis (M.70.69.1-.4) (tc). **478 LOS ANGELES COUNTY MUSEUM OF ART**: Gift of The Walter Foundation (M.91.348.2) (bc). **478-479 DREAMSTIME.COM**: Wai Chung Tang (Background). **479 THE BROOKLYN MUSEUM, NEW YORK**: By exchange (cr). **480 DORLING KINDERSLEY**: Mukesh Swami (tr). **LOS ANGELES COUNTY MUSEUM OF ART**: Gift of Paul F. Walter (M.81.280.5) (br). **PAINTINGS OF THE RAZMNAMA BY ASOK KUMAR DAS, PUBLISHED BY MAPIN PUBLISHING, AHMEDABAD (WWW.MAPINPUB.COM), IN ASSOCIATION WITH THE BIRLA ACADEMY OF ARTS & CULTURE, KOLKATA**: (bl). **481 DORLING KINDERSLEY**: Tejas Art Gallery / Bhaskar Chitrakar (cr); Sushil Soni (t); Arun Pottirayil (bc). **GETTY IMAGES**: IndiaPictures / Universal Images Group (cl). **482 GETTY IMAGES**: Dinodia Photo (tl); DEA Picture Library (tr). **DORLING KINDERSLEY**: Anita Kishore (bl). **482-483 WELLCOME IMAGES HTTP://CREATIVECOMMONS.ORG/ LICENSES/BY/4.0/**: Wellcome Library, London (b). **483 ALAMY STOCK PHOTO**: Hornbil Images (br). **LOS ANGELES COUNTY MUSEUM OF ART**: Gift of Marilyn Walter Grounds (M.85.284.9) (tr). **PHILADELPHIA MUSEUM OF ART, PENNSYLVANIA**: Gift of Stanley F. and Margaret W. Myers (tl). **484 ALAMY STOCK PHOTO**: Dinodia Photos (crb). **GETTY IMAGES**: Heritage Images / Contributor (tl); Mukul Banerjee Photography (cl). **JITENDRA SUTAR / WWW. SCULPTUREARTIST.IN**: (bl). **484-485 CORBIS. 485 DREAMSTIME.COM**: Stefano Ember (bl). **LOS ANGELES COUNTY MUSEUM OF ART**: From the Nasli and Alice Heeramaneck Collection, Museum Associates Purchase (M.80.6.1) (tc). **PHILADELPHIA MUSEUM OF ART, PENNSYLVANIA**: Purchased with the New Members Fund, 1970 (c). **WWW.ARTISANSCREST.COM**: (r). **486 ALAMY STOCK PHOTO**: Dinodia Photos (cla). **BHARATHANJALI TRUST**: (tr). **GETTY IMAGES**: Herve Bruhat / Gamma-Rapho (bl); Barry Kusuma (br). **487 GETTY IMAGES**: Dinodia Photo (tl); Mail Today / Contributor (br); Pacific Press / LightRocket (bl). **SHANKAR JANAKIRAMAN**: (tr)

साध्याता मुनिना तेन व्याकुलत्वं जगाम ह ॥ जज्ञे चैनं
प्रांजलिस्तदा ॥ उपतस्थे मुनिवरं विश्वामित्रं सरस्व
करवाणीति प्रोवाच मुनिसत्तमं ॥१३॥ तामुवाच मु
त्वाव्यथिता नदी ॥१५॥ प्रांजलिं तु ततः कृत्वा पुंडरीक
नयारूपां तु तां दृष्ट्वा मुनिराह महानदीं ॥ अविचारं
श्कृत्वा पापं चिकीर्षितं ॥ वसिष्ठं चवभावं च जानं त्य
तू ॥ यदुक्ता सरितां श्रेष्ठा विश्वामित्रेण धीमता ॥१८

सरस्वतीनदीमूर्ति

ोर्यं महाकोपं चप्लाविनी ॥११॥ ततएनं वेपमाना विवर्णा
॥ह नवी रा यथा नारी साश्रवक्त्रु: खिन्ना भृशं ॥ ब्रूहि किं
द्धो वसिष्ठं रा घ्रमानय ॥ याव दे नं निहन्म्य द्यत
क्षणा ॥ आकंपत भृशं सीता वायुने वहता लता ॥१५
ं त्वमानय स्वादि किं मम ॥१६॥ सा न स्य वचनं ज्ञात्वा
मुवि ॥१७॥ साभिगम्य वसिष्ठं च इद मर्थ म चोदय
यो: शापयो भ्र(?) ता वेपमाना पुन: पुन: ॥ चिंतयित्वा

माहाशापं ऋषि विश्वामित्रा भृशं ॥१८॥

॥श्रीराम॥
॥५०॥